BLACK SOLDIER WHITE ARMY

The 24TH Infantry Regiment in Korea

William T. Bowers
William M. Hammond
George L. MacGarrigle

University Press of the Pacific
Honolulu, Hawaii

Black Soldier, White Army:
The 24th Infantry Regiment in Korea

by
William T. Bowers
William M. Hammond
George L. MacGarrigle

ISBN: 1-4102-2467-8

Reprinted from the 1996 edition

University Press of the Pacific
Honolulu, Hawaii
http://www.universitypressofthepacific.com

Foreword

The story of the 24th Infantry Regiment in Korea is a difficult one, both for the veterans of the unit and for the Army. In the early weeks of the Korean War, most American military units experienced problems as the U.S. Army attempted to transform understrength, ill-equipped, and inadequately trained forces into an effective combat team while at the same time holding back the fierce attacks of an aggressive and well-prepared opponent. In addition to the problems other regiments faced in Korea, the 24th Infantry also had to overcome the effects of racial prejudice. Ultimately the soldiers of the regiment, despite steadfast courage on the part of many, paid the price on the battlefield for the attitudes and misguided policies of the Army and their nation.

Several previously published histories have discussed *what* happened to the 24th Infantry. This book tells *why* it happened. In doing so, it offers important lessons for today's Army. The Army and the nation must be aware of the corrosive effects of segregation and the racial prejudices that accompanied it. The consequences of that system crippled the trust and mutual confidence so necessary among the soldiers and leaders of combat units and weakened the bonds that held the 24th together, producing profound effects on the battlefield. I urge the reader to study and reflect on the insights provided in the chapters that follow. We must ensure that the injustices and misfortunes that befell the 24th never occur again.

Six people deserve special acknowledgment for the roles they played in the production of this study. Secretary of the Army John O. Marsh first recognized the need for this work and monitored its early stages. A concerned veteran, Mr. David Carlisle, pushed continually for its completion. General Roscoe Robinson, before he passed away, read initial drafts of the early chapters and made valuable comments. Col. John Cash collected many of the documents, conducted nearly three hundred oral history interviews, walked the battlegrounds in Korea, and drafted an early account of the regiment's history. The Assistant Secretary of the Army for Manpower and Reserve Affairs, Hon. Sara E. Lister, supported our work during the past two years. The Secretary of the Army, Hon. Togo D. West, Jr., approved its publication. Special thanks is extended to each, as well as to Brig. Gen. (Ret.) Roy Flint, a combat veteran and scholar who prepared an introduction placing this study in its larger historical context. We are also gratified to report that the 1st Battalion, 24th Infantry, is once again serving proudly as part of the 1st Brigade, 25th Infantry Division, at Fort Lewis, Washington.

Washington, D.C.   JOHN W. MOUNTCASTLE
21 August 1996   Brigadier General, USA
                                    Chief of Military History

The Authors

WILLIAM T. BOWERS received his B.A. and M.A. degrees in history from Texas Christian University. Commissioned as a second lieutenant in 1969, he served in Vietnam in the 1st Cavalry Division and later as an adviser. He has commanded field artillery units in the United States and Germany and has served as a staff officer in the office of the Deputy Chief of Staff for Operations and Plans in Washington, D.C., as well as in the Joint Headquarters of the Central Army Group and the Fourth Allied Tactical Airforce (NATO) in Heidelberg, Germany. He has taught history at the U.S. Naval Academy and has been a guest lecturer at the Army War College and at the NATO School in Oberammergau, Germany. In 1992 he joined the Center of Military History as chief of the Histories Division. Having retired from the Army in 1995, he resides in Burke, Virginia, where he remains active in the field of military history.

WILLIAM M. HAMMOND graduated from the Catholic University of America, where he earned the S.T.B., M.A., and Ph.D. degrees. He currently serves as a historian with the Center of Military History, where he has authored a two-volume history of official relations with the news media during the Vietnam War, *Public Affairs: The Military and the Media*. He has also authored the Army's history of the selection and interment of the Vietnam Unknown Soldier, *The Unknown Serviceman of the Vietnam Era*; a monograph entitled *Normandy*, released in 1994 by the Army to mark the 50th anniversary of the invasion; as well as numerous shorter articles and publications. He is currently preparing a volume in the Army's Cold War series entitled "The Army and National Security: The Emergence of the Cold War, 1945–1953." Dr. Hammond has taught at Trinity College in Washington, D.C., and at the University of Maryland, Baltimore County. He currently doubles as a Lecturer in University Honors at the University of Maryland, College Park, where he teaches courses on the Vietnam War and the military and the news media in American history.

GEORGE L. MacGARRIGLE is a graduate of the United States Military Academy and has received an M.A. in history from Pennsylvania State University. Commissioned as a second lieutenant in 1952, he served with the 1st Cavalry Division in Korea as a rifle company commander and again with the 1st Cavalry Division during the Vietnam War as an infantry battalion commander. He directed the military history program while assigned to the ROTC at Pennsylvania State University. He currently serves as a civilian historian with the Center of Military History, where he has authored "The Year of the Offensive" and is working on a second volume, "The Tet Offensive," both of which tell the Army's story of combat in Vietnam.

Preface

In late September 1950, two months after the beginning of the Korean War, the commander of the 25th Infantry Division, Maj. Gen. William B. Kean, requested that the Eighth Army disband the all-black 24th Infantry Regiment because it had shown itself "untrustworthy and incapable of carrying out missions expected of an infantry regiment." Thus began a controversy that has continued to this day. Critics of the racially segregated regiment have charged that the 24th was a dismal failure in combat. The African-American veterans of the organization and others have responded that the unit did far better than its antagonists would concede and that its main problem was the racial prejudice endemic to the Army of that day. Military historians have tended to cite the lack of training and preparation afflicting all of the U.S. Army units entering combat during the early weeks of the Korean War and the inability of senior commanders to remedy deficiencies of leadership in the 24th within a reasonable period of time.

For a while, with the integration of the armed forces, the talk on all sides subsided, but when the U.S. Army's official history of the Korean War, *South to the Naktong, North to the Yalu*, authored by Roy E. Appleman, appeared in 1961, it reignited the controversy by publicizing the background of Kean's charges. During the late 1970s, as a result, a number of individuals began an effort to persuade the Army to revise its history to reflect a more balanced view of the regiment. In 1987 Secretary of the Army John O. Marsh, Jr., directed that the U.S. Army Center of Military History undertake a definitive evaluation of the 24th's role in the Korean War. If the regiment's performance was commendable, the record could be amended. But if its service was less than successful, the reasons behind its shortcomings ought to be examined for the lessons they might convey to the soldier of today.

Col. John A. Cash began the effort in 1988. Over the next several years he and several assistants conducted nearly three hundred oral history interviews, visited the battlefields in Korea, researched official records in the National Archives, and completed part of an initial draft outline for a final manuscript. Cash retired in 1992. Shortly thereafter the Center formed a team of three historians to conduct additional research and interviews and to compose a final study.

This history is the result. It analyzes the operations of the 24th Infantry during the Korean War to determine how well the unit and its associated engineers and artillery performed. In the process it asks whether deficiencies occurred, seeks their military causes, and looks at how those influences and events intersected with the racial prejudices prevalent in that day.

Starting with a brief rendition of the background of the African-American soldier in the nineteenth and early twentieth centuries, the study shows that segregated regiments and divisions performed well when called upon during the American Civil War and throughout the nineteenth century. In the same way, the men of the all-black 93d Division fought effectively under French command during World War I, as did the experienced black tank and tank destroyer battalions that often spearheaded the final Allied drive into Nazi Germany during World War II. In that light, if the 24th Infantry faltered during its first two months in Korea, the color of the majority that constituted its companies and battalions was not the reason. More obvious answers lay in the deficiencies of leadership, training, supply, and support that burdened the entire United Nations force, whether white or black, during the first months of the war in Korea. Those causes nonetheless seemed only a beginning because they exist in every war and have time and again given way to the solutions that good leadership inevitably supplies. If the 24th's problems lasted longer than a brief period, deeper reasons would thus have to be found, and they would inevitably have to reside in considerations that distinguished the 24th from all-white units, particularly the racial bias and discrimination, both open and covert, that the regiment and its people experienced throughout the unit's existence.

As authors, we faced major challenges in determining what happened. Few historical problems are more demanding than those that accompany an attempt to reconstruct the performance of a military unit in combat. Every platoon, company, battalion, regiment, and division has its own character, and each one consists of subunits that are in turn unique. All are composed of thinking human beings who act as individuals. Even so, the people who compose those units or any group will not always behave as they might on their own. A dynamic can come into play among them when unusual circumstances intrude, and the effects it produces, whether acts of extreme bravery or of mass confusion, may at times seem hardly rational. Much depends upon the bonding that exists among the group's members and the trust they place in one another and in their leaders. In addition, a group's identity can take new forms over time as circumstances and personalities change. Given those uncertainties and the many variables

involved, the attributes that produce success in combat are not always discernable. Well-experienced units with unsurpassed achievements may sometimes fail while worn units with less than perfect records may pull together at a moment of supreme terror to succeed.

Indeed, the nature of combat is such that it is difficult even for participants coherently and completely to describe the events that occurred. Danger, chaos, confusion, and stress distract attention from the main course of the fighting. Meanwhile, perspectives vary widely, depending on an individual's responsibilities and his location on the battlefield. The view and understanding of a private will hardly resemble those of a unit commander. Each will reflect the truth of what happened in his own way. On top of that, the emotional intensity of combat may deepen the natural tendency of a soldier to forget embarrassing and unpleasant events and to focus his attention on aspects of the fighting that appeal to his sense of self-worth.

As combat historian S. L. A. Marshall discovered, if time, patience, and special skills are necessary to reconstruct what happened even immediately after a battle, it is still more difficult to explain why it occurred. Marshall brought together all the survivors of an action and questioned them as a group. Each participant contributed his own view of the battle, starting at the beginning and moving step-by-step through events as they developed. At first, no one would have a complete understanding of what had occurred or why events had transpired the way they did. But after three or four days of effort, a fairly coherent picture would begin to emerge.

Nothing of the sort was possible in the case of this study. No time or opportunity existed during the early days of the Korean War for extensive combat interviews. Events were moving too fast. As a result, we had to rely upon contemporary descriptions of combat compiled by the units involved.

Those materials were often extensive. Officers at command posts in the field would keep daily journals, collect folders of operations orders and messages, and, from time to time, compose memorandums for the record. Once a month, those at battalion would draft a war diary, later called a command report, for their unit and submit it to the regimental headquarters. Using those diaries along with its own journals and reports, the regiment would then compile a report of its own for submission to the division command. The division would do the same, and so on up the line. Each report was accompanied by annexes describing particular problems that developed, lessons learned, and the personnel and supply status of the command. There were also maps, graphs, and overlays.

Despite the wealth of information that those materials presented, as the study proceeded it became clear that all of those sources, particularly the war diaries, were deficient. Unit records and human memories were sometimes incomplete or inaccurate, and those flaws might be carried over into a narrative. Compounding the problem, war diaries, although due within a few days after the end of each month, were sometimes actually written weeks after the events they described had occurred because the demands of combat had intervened. By then, daily journals and other unit records might have been destroyed or lost, some participants in the action would have fallen in battle, and the chronicle of what had happened would have had to be reconstructed from fragmentary records and scraps of memory. On occasion as well, the narratives were self-serving, presenting a more favorable view of events than the facts warranted or covering up the role that poor leadership and decision making played in some military failures. Overall, if some war diaries were thus beautifully detailed and even brutally honest while others were incomplete and less than candid, few written records of any consequence speculated on why events had occurred in the manner that they did.

Those difficulties forced the authors to make heavy use of oral history to bridge gaps and correct errors in the official records. Yet that approach had its own problems. The participants in a past action, recounting their experiences in interviews, had to struggle against their own imperfect memories. They had little access to official records, maps, and overlays and, except in rare instances, few opportunities to revisit the terrain they were attempting to describe. If they had kept a personal diary, it was often incomplete. And even where a veteran had a good recall of events, details of one combat action sometimes merged with those of others until none bore much resemblance to what had actually happened. Complicating matters, perspectives and perceptions had changed over time where race and other issues were concerned. The influence of the civil rights movement and the spread of the ideal of racial equality had worked their way so thoroughly through American society that it was often difficult to perceive where a man had stood on the issue during the war. If some of those interviewed had changed very little, others had clearly matured. Men who had earned reputations as racists among their subordinates and colleagues during the war had become remarkably more tolerant and objective over the forty years between then and now.

Some of the sources that proved most valuable to the study were the transcripts of interviews conducted by inspector general teams during the course of three official investigations into the 24th's performance in battle. Those materials must be used with great care because they are, at times, racially biased and self-serving. Nevertheless, they contain a great wealth of information about the fighting, some of it gathered within days of the events described from witnesses who would soon be killed in combat. To be sure, many whites in those interviews blamed their black subordinates or enlisted soldiers for every problem, and the blacks, on occasion, held their tongues or played blatantly to the prejudices of their interviewers to preserve or further their careers. But statements of that sort were easily balanced against one another and against those of individuals who were willing to speak their minds, whatever the consequences. In addition, some of them are virtual duplicates of stories told by other veterans long afterwards and of events detailed in radio logs and daily journals.

We employed caution in dealing with all those materials. In the case of documentary evidence, we sought to verify controversial occurrences by seeking out multiple sources for the same information. If only one source existed, we checked the reliability of previous assertions from that source and, if any doubt remained, attempted to verify the account by getting the comments of veterans who had already proved themselves forthright and knowledgeable. After that, if doubts still persisted, we did not use the information.

The same sort of approach applied to oral history interviews. We attempted in every case to corroborate stories from one source with material from others or from written records. Where that proved impossible, the credibility of the source became a concern. Was that person in a position to know? Did he have something to gain from the statement? Was the rest of the information he provided reliable and accurate as far as it was possible to tell? Had he been willing at times, to paint himself in a bad light to depict the truth? If the responses to those questions were adequate, in important cases we used the material but always with an explanation in a footnote. In the same way, we tried to label hearsay and rumor as such throughout the study, but whether or not a comment was well founded, the mere fact that a number of soldiers said substantially the same thing gave it weight as an indicator of the morale and cohesion of the regiment. In some circumstances, assertions were made in interviews that could have been proved only by an official investigation at the time. Once again, after the proper labeling, we used these comments if they seemed an adequate reflection of the thoughts of the men at the time. The race of an individual can of course play a role in how he perceives an event. Because of that, we made it a point whenever possible to label the race of officers mentioned in the body of the text. Enlisted men and noncommissioned officers are all black unless otherwise identified.

When a historian examines the history of a military unit in detail, problem areas tend to eclipse matters that went well. To achieve balance, the successes of a unit must be told along with its failures, and what went poorly must be seen in the perspective of what other military units were doing at the same time and in the same place.

We sought to do that in this study but encountered problems in making the attempt. Since the war diaries we consulted often tended to be bland or lacking in fine detail, we frequently found it difficult to identify and reconstruct episodes in which all but

the most singular achievements had occurred. In the case of Medal of Honor winner Pfc. William Thompson, for example, unit histories were completely silent until 4 January 1951, five months after the day on which the soldier earned his award by giving his life for his fellow soldiers.

As in the case of Thompson, we attempted to underscore the special deeds of units and individuals by making the best use wherever we could of our interviews and the records and depositions accompanying award citations. In that way, we were able to single out some members of the 24th who overcame the burdens not only of unpreparedness and weak leadership but also of racial prejudice by performing exemplary acts of achievement during the war.

Over the first two months of the fighting, however, the exploits of those men tended to pale in the context of what was going wrong elsewhere in the regiment. The situation changed following the breakout from Pusan, after the troops and their leaders had time to train and mend. From then on, the regiment performed more or less on a par with the rest of the Eighth Army.

Overall, we found that comparisons between the 24th and the other regiments fighting in Korea were difficult to make, not only because no two military units are precisely the same, but also because none of the other regiments experienced the particular social and psychological burdens segregation imposed. A lack of resources was also an impediment. Interviews with almost four hundred individuals, two-thirds of them African-Americans, went into the research behind the study of the 24th. An effort to do the same for other regiments serving in Korea at the time was impossible.

Within those limitations, we did attempt to provide a context for the 24th by pairing it with several similar units, the 5th, 27th, and 35th Infantry Regiments, all of which served in the same vicinity and experienced the same sort of combat. In doing so, we drew upon the official records of those units and conducted a number of interviews with their veterans to determine the quality of their leadership, the conditions their men experienced, and how well they fared in combat. Although the work was hardly as exhaustive as what was done for the 24th, we are confident that it was adequate to show how well the 24th performed by comparison.

Many people contributed to the successful completion of this book. Although we cannot mention all of them here, a number deserve special thanks. Several Chiefs of Military History, Brig. Gens. William A. Stofft, Harold W. Nelson, and John W. Mountcastle, provided continual moral and material support. The Chief Historian, Jeffrey Clarke, likewise rendered important advice and assistance. Col. John Cash, Bernard Muehlbauer, Maj. Timothy Rainey, and Young Gil Chang, who has since died, conducted the initial interviews and completed essential preliminary surveys of relevant documentation. Mary Haynes, Edward Drea, Terrence Gough, and Maj. Constance Moore, all of the Center's Research and Analysis Division, assisted with further research and interviews when the need arose. The Center's librarian, James Knight, and archivists Hannah Zeidlik and Donald Carter responded cheerfully to every request for books and documents, even the most arcane. John Wilson of the Center's Organizational History Branch was similarly helpful when confronted with urgent requests for information on obscure military organizations. Robert J. T. Joy, a professor of military medicine at the Uniformed Services University of the Health Sciences, was a constant resource for medical aspects of the study. The Eighth Army's historian, Thomas Ryan; Richard Boylan of the National Archives; David Keough of the U.S. Army Military History Institute, Carlisle Barracks, Pennsylvania; and the staff of the Army Reference Branch at the National Personnel Records Center in St. Louis also contributed heavily in locating relevant documentation on file with their respective agencies. Col. Clyde Jonas, John Elsberg, Albert Cowdrey, Graham Cosmas, Mary Gillett, and Joel Meyerson of the Center, along with the late General Roscoe Robinson, Morris MacGregor, Bernard Nalty, and Richard Ruth, read initial drafts of various portions of the book and made many valuable suggestions. The authors are also grateful to Mr. David Carlisle, who pushed for the manuscript's completion. Meanwhile, Lt. Gens. Julius Becton and Sidney Berry, Maj. Gen. Oliver Dillard, Brig. Gen. Roy Flint, Cols. John Komp and Gustav Gillert, Sgt. Maj. Richard Sanders, Stephen Ambrose, Clay Blair, Peter Braestrup, John Butler, Richard Dalfiume, Robert Goldich, Joseph Glatthaar, Phillip McGuire, David Segal, and Frank Schubert evaluated the final draft.

Gaye Patrick deserves special thanks for handling correspondence and arranging the interview summaries in a useful database form. Thanks should go as well to John Birmingham, who designed the layout for the book; Beth MacKenzie, who located many of the photographs; and Sherry Dowdy, who prepared the maps. We are also grateful to our editors, Diane Arms and Diane Donovan, who shepherded the manuscript through to final publication, as well as Susan Carroll, who compiled the index.

The members of our families merit particular mention for their patience and the constant encouragement they provided. They contributed much more than they will ever know.

Finally, the historian who finds imperfections in the written records he uses and in the memories of those he interviews must recognize that he has the same flaws in himself. Having done that, he must make a special effort to cast off his intellectual preconditioning, to step out of himself and into the moment he is trying to re-create, and to feel as his subjects felt. Only then can he begin to understand why they acted as they did. The reader of this study will have to decide whether this work succeeds in doing that. For the rest, since the historian must be true to his own instincts about his material, we, the authors, are alone responsible for all interpretations and conclusions that appear and any errors that have occurred. Our views do not reflect the official policy or position of the Departments of the Army and Defense or the U.S. government.

Washington, D.C.
21 August 1996

WILLIAM T. BOWERS
WILLIAM M. HAMMOND
GEORGE L. MacGARRIGLE

Introduction

by

Roy K. Flint

Black Soldier, White Army is a "shocking" book. So said Clay Blair after reading it. Blair was shocked by the violence of combat in Korea and by the unreadiness of the 24th Infantry Regiment and the rest of the Army to deal with that violence early in the war. Most of all he was outraged by the decision of political leaders to send an unready Army to war. This response by the author of The Forgotten War: America in Korea, 1950–1953, one who has thought long and hard about Korea, suggests that others who read this book will more clearly understand the Korean record of the 24th Infantry in the broader context of the post–World War II history of the armed forces and the Army in particular.

There has never been a decade quite as turbulent as that which followed World War II. Atomic power, military demobilization and industrial reconversion, leadership in the United Nations (UN), hostility between the Western allies and the Soviet Union, the Berlin blockade, creation of the North Atlantic Treaty Organization, and Communist Chinese ascendancy in Asia defined the American response to the Cold War. For the first five years there was little confrontation by military forces. Then the Korean conflict surprised Western policy makers and their constituents, causing the old Western alliance of World Wars I and II to form again, this time against the Soviet Union and its allies, North Korea and the People's Republic of China.

Looking back from the eve of the Korean War, it is clear that the United States had undertaken international responsibilities that became military requirements in the years that followed. To help guard against the revival of fascism and to begin the political reconstruction of its former enemies, the United States agreed to station occupation troops in Germany, Austria, Trieste, Korea, and Japan. Military leaders believed that the nation's commitment to occupy and govern the defeated territories demanded conventional military forces both in the United States and overseas. But even before the war ended, the United States began to reduce its armed strength from about twelve million to a postwar goal of about a million and a half men.

Demobilization was a political imperative in 1945. Meeting demands to bring the troops home, the Army discharged 4 million men in the first six

Brig. Gen. Roy K. Flint, United States Army (Retired), served as company commander and battalion operations officer in the 23d Infantry during the period immediately following the Korean War and as battalion commander in the 22d Infantry during the Vietnam War. He holds a doctorate in military history from Duke University. Prior to retirement in 1990, he was professor and head of the Department of History and dean of the Academic Board at the U.S. Military Academy, West Point. General Flint has been the president of the Society for Military History since 1993.

months and would release most of the remainder by the middle of 1946. The Air Force cut its strength in half, from 218 groups to 109, and the Navy reduced the fleet strength by deactivating ships, aircraft, and their crews and halting construction on those ships in the yards at the end of the war. Still, the demand for demobilization continued through 1946 and into 1947.

Dismantling the armed forces at the same time the nation increased its international obligations alarmed the military professionals. The forces in the United States were cut to a nucleus of the needed reserve, while overseas troops were thinly stretched. Moreover, as the breach between the Soviet Union and the Western European allies widened, Soviet military forces quickly replaced resurgent fascism as the main military threat to the interests of the United States. If the Soviets resorted to war, they would be able to employ overwhelming land forces almost immediately against the nations of Western Europe and the occupation forces of the United States. Moreover, the Soviets could support ground operations with powerful tactical air forces. At sea the Soviet surface navy was a negligible threat, but the Soviet submarine force was growing. The Soviet Union had abundant resources and could develop an industrial capacity far exceeding its achievement in World War II. Soviet potential, in the long term, was seen to be virtually unlimited; the essential question was: when could the Soviets effectively employ the new air-atomic weapons system?

Not surprisingly, on the eve of the Korean War the solution to the American strategic problem was to deter war by threatening air-atomic retaliation. The purpose of this deterrence was to defend Europe and the continental United States against the Soviet Union. To implement a single enemy strategy, the United States built an air force capable of air-atomic delivery that was adequate as long as the American monopoly on atomic weapons and their means of delivery existed. But by concentrating on the purchase of long-range bombing aircraft, the United States acquired atomic delivery at the expense of conventional air, land, and sea capability, a more costly and politically less attractive alter-

native. As a consequence, the Air Force was short of aircraft for the close support of ground forces; the Army was ill equipped and understrength; and the Navy, although able to employ powerful carrier task forces almost immediately, lacked the long-distance troop-lift capability upon which the Army depended. Under these circumstances, until Western European nations were rearmed and able to assume the burden of their own protection, there could be little or no conventional defense of Western Europe. Everything depended upon deterring Soviet expansion by threatening atomic retaliation. Up to the outbreak of the Korean War in June 1950, deterrence was understood to be working because, for whatever reasons, it had not yet been tested by the Soviets. In concentrating on preventing a big war, however, the nation's leaders had failed to conceive of a more conventional conflict.

Ironically, the United States was actually better prepared to fight in Korea than anywhere else in the world. Although the administration and Congress wanted to adopt air-atomic deterrence to the exclusion of more expensive conventional forces, the bureaucratic bargaining between the Joint Chiefs—who were also chiefs of the four services—and the secretary of defense prevented that solution and forced a roughly equal division of funds that ensured that a ground force was available to fight in Korea. Specifically, in or near Japan General of the Army Douglas MacArthur commanded 4 reduced-strength Army divisions of the Eighth Army; 18 fighter squadrons and a light bomber squadron of the Air Force; and 1 cruiser, 4 destroyers, and a number of amphibious vessels of the Navy. In addition, the Seventh Fleet, a powerful carrier strike force, was available if needed.

Although it may have been difficult for American leaders to understand that summer night in June 1950, the North Korean attack was to point with unmistakable clarity at the deficiencies in the combat readiness of the United States. Called upon to meet the North Korean ground attack, the Army revealed the inadequacies of a minimalist conventional military policy. For as events turned out, the North Koreans were simply undeterred by the atomic power of the United States because they had no vulnerable industrial targets upon which they relied. Moreover, they were strong in mobilized military manpower, the principal weakness of the United States, South Korea, and those countries' UN allies. In time this weakness would be remedied, but until the winter of 1950–1951 American and South Korean soldiers suffered terrible casualties holding the line against a well-trained, well-armed, and tactically effective enemy army.

So the weakness of the initial military response in Korea was a result of prewar diversions from conventional forces of men, money, and materiel to build air-atomic deterrence of the Soviet Union. As a result, MacArthur and Lt. Gen. Walton H. Walker, the Eighth Army commander, committed forces to Korea that were flawed. When Walker arrived in Japan in 1949, he had made individual training first priority in Eighth Army. After receiving reinforcements, he filled battalions sufficiently to enable realistic training. But he was still limited in his ability to maneuver offensively and defensively by regiments that had only two battalions instead of three; he could never fill his manpower or equipment shortages; and he could not create training areas adequate for Infantry-Armor-Artillery combined arms training. While individual soldiers might develop skills, combat readiness suffered from a lack of unit and combined arms preparation. In this regard, the 24th Infantry Regiment was no worse than any other unit and better off organizationally because it was the only regiment in Eighth Army with three battalions.

When MacArthur moved combat troops to Korea early in July 1950, the consequences of committing a flawed Army to battle became apparent. The first American troops to meet the enemy were virtually isolated on the battlefield and stretched by extended frontages. They were without allies, combat support, and sources of resupply. Moreover, the North Koreans attacked with a well-rehearsed and effective scheme of maneuver: they fixed the American front with a tank-infantry-artillery attack, enveloped both flanks, attacked command posts and mortars in the rear, and then formed roadblocks to cut off reinforcements and prevent escape. Once in the

rear, North Korean units disrupted the defense physically and psychologically because the defenders were ill prepared to fight surrounded. Often the primary concern of the defenders was to escape. MacArthur tried to remedy the problem by rushing troops to Korea, not only to build resistance to the North Koreans in their southward drive, but also to create a viable theater of war capable of sustaining combat forces on the battlefield. Belatedly, the tasks were accomplished, but the folly of unreadiness was made indelible by the mounting casualties.

While all units struggled to overcome organizational obstacles, the 24th Infantry Regiment experienced the especially difficult circumstances described in *Black Soldier, White Army* that led to its inactivation in October 1951. The decision to inactivate the 24th was certainly a result of dissatisfaction with its performance, but it was also the culmination of a gradual change in Army policy toward segregated units that had been under way since early 1950. In January Army regulations directed efficient employment of manpower without regard to race, and in March the Army did away with quotas that restricted the recruiting of black soldiers. As a result, enlistment of black men increased well beyond the requirements of the segregated units. Commanders therefore began assigning black soldiers wherever they were needed and expressed satisfaction with the results. Fears of hostility and tension between blacks and whites proved unfounded, and performance improved in the integrated combat units.

A segregated Army was always a bad idea, rooted in the social standards of white Americans in the twentieth century every bit as deeply as it was in the nineteenth century. Given the tensions of the Cold War and the need for economical use of manpower in the modern armed forces, it was a foolish waste. Regardless of the sentimental attachment of black veterans of the 24th Infantry and the black battalions in the 9th and 15th Infantry Regiments, segregated units had to go. Unfortunately, before Korea no one in responsible positions had the will to overcome personal prejudice or to confront political opposition to integration. Among the senior Army officers who recognized this fact and had the courage to act was General Matthew B. Ridgway, Eighth Army commander following Walker's death in December 1950 and the architect of the UN drive north of the 38th Parallel in the spring of 1951.

After replacing MacArthur as Far Eastern commander in April 1951, Ridgway proved to be the catalyst that resolved the dilemma over segregated units. His purpose was to improve combat effectiveness in all units within the Far Eastern Command, so in May, only a month after taking command, he recommended assigning black troops to all of his units in Japan and Korea. He also recommended inactivating the 24th and assigning its troops to other all-white units in the theater. The Department of the Army approved his recommendations in July and directed integration of combat units over a six-month period; service units were to integrate after the combat battalions. While inactivation of the 24th may be seen by some as an act unrelated to efficiency, it was in fact a highly visible symbol of Ridgway's dedication to a ready Army: manned, organized, trained, equipped, and supplied to go to war at a moment's notice. There would be no more Koreas.

Understandably, winding down the war in Korea sidetracked the measures needed to achieve Ridgway's goal. Nevertheless, even before the Supreme Court ruled against "separate but equal" in 1954, near the end of the decade following World War II, the Army was well on its way to creating a merit-based system that served as a model of desegregation for the civilian community. Once undertaken it was so successful that a black soldier, General Colin Powell, eventually served as chairman of the Joint Chiefs of Staff some thirty-five years later.

Black Soldier, White Army is first and foremost an important social history of black soldiers in the United States Army. It explains in vivid detail the climate of racial prejudice surrounding the regiment in Japan and Korea and then in equally harsh terms, it uncovers the legacy of that prejudice in combat. Therefore, the unfolding story is also a military history of the 24th Infantry Regiment in the first fifteen months of the Korean War. Black veterans of the 24th may be unhappy with this book as a regimental history because it has so much to say about the events leading to the inactivation of the regiment in October 1951. So too will white officers who served in the regiment and who must come to grips with the authors' carefully supported portrayal of bigotry and downright bad leadership that had so much to do with the troubles of the 24th and that make the book such an important social history. Similarly, all officers, noncommissioned officers, and soldiers who served prior to Korea must feel uneasy about the policies and practices that maintained a racially segregated Army. The attitudes about race that so damaged the morale and sense of self-worth of the men in the 24th emanated from every level of command from the battlefield to Tokyo and Washington. This is what *Black Soldier, White Army* is all about.

Contents

Illustrations

Illustrations courtesy of the following sources: pp. 21, 32, 40, 42, 44, 45, 49, 51, 61, 63, 80, 84, 85, 86, 93, 94, 97 (*left/right*), 111, 132, 136, 138, 152, 161, 166, 170, 180, 181, 184, 198, 210, 211, 225, 226 (*left/right*), 227, 234, 236, 238, 240, 242, 249, 250, 251, 252, 254, 257, 262, National Archives; and pp. 4, 9, 11, Library of Congress. All other illustrations from the files of the Department of Defense.

Black Soldier White Army

The 24TH Infantry Regiment in Korea

CHAPTER 1

Prologue: Two Centuries of Service

The soldiers of the 24th Infantry regiment who fought in Korea were heirs to a long tradition of service by blacks in America's wars. Their forebears had fought alongside the colonial militias during the nation's early years, at Lexington and Concord, and all through the American Revolution. Black seamen sailed with Commodore Oliver Hazard Perry's victorious fleet on Lake Erie and stood with General Andrew Jackson at the Battle of New Orleans in the War of 1812. Confronted by racial prejudice at a time when the North and South were beginning to drift apart over the issue of slavery, only a few African-Americans served with American ground forces during the Mexican War, but more than two hundred thousand rallied to the Union cause during the American Civil War.[1]

During the years prior to the Civil War, many northern states adopted legislation emancipating slaves, but blacks in general remained inferior to whites before the law. The ranks of the militia and the Regular Army opened to them intermittently, when a need for manpower arose in times of emergency, but they closed again as soon as peace returned. Only the Navy remained accessible. Life at sea was so harsh during those days that shipmasters, whether civilian or military, took anyone who would sign on, whatever his color.[2]

The pattern repeated itself in 1861, when the South seceded from the United States and the Civil War began. Although the Navy recruited blacks from the beginning and commanders in the field employed escaped slaves as laborers, the Army once more excluded them. President Abraham Lincoln and his advisers hoped to gain the support of such slave-holding border states as Maryland, Missouri, and Kentucky, while leaving the door open for some sort of reconciliation with the seceding states. Because the presence of armed

---

[1] A number of works detail the role of blacks in these wars. One of the most comprehensive is Bernard C. Nalty, *Strength for the Fight: A History of Black Americans in the Military* (New York: Free Press, 1986). See also John Hope Franklin, *From Slavery to Freedom: A History of Negro Americans* (New York: Vintage Books, 1969); Benjamin Quarles, *The Negro in the American Revolution* (Chapel Hill: University of North Carolina Press, 1961); Lorenzo Johnston Green, "The Negro in the War of 1812 and the Civil War," *Negro History Bulletin* (March 1951); Roland MacConnell, *Negro Troops in Antebellum Louisiana: A History of the Battalion of Free Men of Color* (Baton Rouge: Louisiana University Press, 1968).The Army dropped the regimental designation in 1917. At that time, the 24th Infantry Regiment became simply the 24th Infantry. For clarity, this book retains the old title, but it acknowledges the change by using the word *regiment* in lowercase.

[2] Nalty, *Strength for the Fight*, p. 21; Green, "The Negro in the War of 1812 and the Civil War," pp. 131f. In the Dred Scott decision, Chief Justice Roger B. Taney cited the exclusion of blacks from state militias as part of his argument that they were not citizens of the United States. See Richard M. Dalfiume, *Desegregation of the U.S. Armed Forces: Fighting on Two Fronts, 1939–1953* (Columbia: University of Missouri Press, 1969), p. 1.

Civil War soldiers

blacks among Union forces might aggravate slave holders in both areas, signifying a complete break with the South, it seemed best to all concerned for whites to do the fighting.[3]

As the war lengthened, pressure for change nevertheless began to rise. Free blacks petitioned Lincoln for the right to bear arms. Antislavery activists and politicians backed them on the grounds that the military needed men. Congress yielded in July 1862, when it authorized Lincoln to recruit blacks into the Army. In September the president issued a preliminary emancipation proclamation and set 1 January 1863 as the date for it to take effect. Although the act was designed to affect only those states that had seceded and had no bearing on those that remained loyal to the Union, it opened military service to southern blacks who were able to elude

their masters and make their way north to Union lines. From then on, field commanders took increasing advantage of escaped slaves as soldiers. Forming all-black units, they enlisted proven white officers with strong abolitionist sympathies to command runaways. By the end of the war, at least 186,000 African-Americans had served in the Army and thousands more had participated unofficially as laborers, teamsters, and cooks. Some 30,000 blacks served in the Navy.[4] Estimates vary on how many became casualties. By some accounts the mortality rate for black troops was up to 40 percent higher than for

[3] James MacPherson, *Battle Cry of Freedom* (New York: Oxford University Press, 1988), pp. 490–501. For details on the use of blacks as laborers, see General Benjamin Butler's GO 34, 1 Nov 1861, in War Department, *The War of the Rebellion, A Compilation of the Official Records of the Union and Confederate Armies*, 128 vols. (Washington, D.C.: Government Printing Office, 1880–1902), ser. II, vol. 1, pp. 774–75.

[4] Strength figures are in Nalty, *Strength for the Fight*, pp. 33–46. The number given for the Navy is an estimate because surviving records for the period are scarce. See Ltr, Secretary of the Navy John D. Long to Congressman C. E. Littlefield, 2 Apr 02, in Morris J. MacGregor, Jr., and Bernard C. Nalty, *Blacks in the United States Armed Forces: Basic Documents*, 13 vols. (Wilmington, Del.: Scholarly Resources, 1977), vol. 2, item 61. For more on blacks in the Civil War, see Dudley T. Cornish, *The Sable Arm: Negro Troops in the Union Army, 1861–1865* (New York: Longmans, Green, 1956); and Joseph T. Glatthaar, *Forged in Battle: The Civil War Alliance of Black Soldiers and White Officers* (New York: Free Press, 1990).

whites. Whether that was so or not, at least 68,000 appear to have been either killed or wounded.[5]

Black units fought well in combat, distinguishing themselves at Port Hudson, Milliken's Bend, Fort Wagner, and the Siege of Petersburg, to name just a few engagements. Many Union generals nevertheless so mistrusted blacks and their abilities that they refrained from committing them to the fighting. As a result, although African-Americans sometimes held the point in attacks because their officers believed they were the descendants of savages and therefore fierce fighters, black units on the whole tended to receive static assignments guarding bridges and securing rear areas. With little chance to move from one locale to another the way combat forces did, they stayed for long periods in one place, where many of their members fell not to the enemy but to the poor sanitary practices prevalent in armies of the day.[6]

If blacks received the right to fight, resistance to their presence in the Army remained substantial. The U.S. government considered African-Americans auxiliaries and for most of the war paid them three dollars less per month than their white counterparts, even though they shared the danger and sometimes fought in the same battles. Meanwhile, the few blacks who won commissions as officers were never allowed to command even the lowest ranking white.[7] The black soldier, for his part, was hardly insensitive to how he was treated. He could do little about the way commanders used him, but several black units protested the inequities in pay. The 54th Massachusetts even

declined to accept its wages for a year. It went into battle in Florida in 1864 singing "Three cheers for Massachusetts and seven dollars a month."[8]

Despite continuing inequities, the black soldier gained from his service in the war. Former abolitionists argued vehemently that blacks had earned a place in the nation's armed forces and succeeded over heavy opposition in pushing a bill through Congress in 1866 that gave blacks the right to serve. Under the reorganization of the military that followed, the Regular Army thus consisted of 5 artillery, 10 cavalry, and 45 infantry regiments, of which 4 regiments of infantry and 2 of cavalry were to be all black. A further reorganization in 1869 consolidated the 4 black infantry regiments into 2, the 24th and 25th Infantries, and reconfirmed the 2 regiments of black cavalry, the 9th and 10th. Racial prejudice was so prevalent that even enlightened whites gave no thought to integrating blacks into white units, but the establishment of the four black regiments was still a definite step forward.[9]

The predecessors of the 24th Infantry, the 38th and 41st Infantry regiments, formed in 1866. Some of their members were veterans of the Civil War, but others were untrained recruits. A number enlisted from the northern states, where they had lived free before the war, but many were southerners and former slaves. Life in the Army with its regular pay and free food, clothing, and shelter appealed to men who had little economic security or social acceptance on their own.[10]

The 38th and 41st were consolidated and reorganized as the 24th Infantry during September and October 1869.[11] Most of the new regiment's 35 offi-

---

[5] Franklin, *From Slavery to Freedom*, pp. 293f. Cornish puts the number of blacks killed and wounded at 68,178. See Cornish, *The Sable Arm*, p. 288.

[6] The bearing of white preconceptions on the employment of black troops is mentioned by Glatthaar in *Forged in Battle*, p. 148. See also pp. 121–68 for more on the accomplishments of African-Americans in battle. Mary C. Gillett, *The Army Medical Department, 1818–1865*, Army Historical Series (Washington, D.C.: U.S. Army Center of Military History, Government Printing Office, 1977), p. 277, speaks of sanitary conditions at the time. For more on African-Americans in the Civil War, see Benjamin Quarles, *The Negro in the Civil War* (New York: Da Capo Press, 1989).

[7] Nalty, *Strength for the Fight*, pp. 33–46.

[8] Franklin, *From Slavery to Freedom*, p. 291.

[9] Monroe Lee Billington, *New Mexico's Buffalo Soldiers, 1866–1900* (Niwot: University of Colorado Press, 1991), p. 201. See also William G. Muller, *The Twenty-Fourth Infantry Past and Present* (Fort Collins, Colo.: 1972; reprint, n.d.), pp. 2–3.

[10] Billington, *New Mexico's Buffalo Soldiers*, pp. 4–5.

[11] Theophilus F. Rodenbough and William L. Haskin, *The Army of the United States: Historical Sketches of Staff and Line With Portraits of Generals in Chief* (New York: Maynard, Merrill & Co., 1896), p. 695; GO 17, 15 Mar 1869, in L. Albert Scipio II, *Last of the Black Regulars: A History of the 24th Infantry Regiment (1869–1951)* (Silver Spring, Md.: Roman Publications, 1983), p. 123.

General MacKenzie

cers and 655 enlisted men took up station in the largely unpopulated Southwest, at Fort McKavett, Texas, 180 miles west of San Antonio. McKavett housed the main body of the 24th, the unit's headquarters and four companies, but portions of the regiment also deployed to Forts Davis, Concho, and Stockton, forming a 220-mile-long line across Texas that defined the southern edge of the Great Plains. The unit's first commander, Bvt. Brig. Gen. Ranald S. MacKenzie, was considered "the most promising young officer in the Army" by General Ulysses S. Grant, who noted that the officer had graduated from West Point during the second year of the war but had won his way to high responsibilities before its close "upon his own merit and without influence."[12]

During the next decade, units of the 24th defended frontier posts, participated with black and white cavalry units in skirmishes with bands of Indian raiders, escorted supply trains, provided security for railroad and wagon road construction teams, and often dispatched guard detachments to subposts and stagecoach stations. Although the unit participated in almost all U.S. expeditions into Mexico to pursue Indians during the period, its role was usually less than glamorous. Cavalry performed most of the combat missions while the infantry did the routine work of guarding supply lines and securing key passes and water holes.[13]

Some of the work the regiment did was still exceedingly important. Between April and December 1875, for example, Companies D and F assisted elements of the 10th Cavalry and the 25th Infantry in a survey of the Great Plains. The maps that resulted from the expedition proved indispensable for commanders planning later operations in the region. In the same way, during 1879 and 1880 soldiers from the 24th maneuvered with the 10th Cavalry during a long campaign that prevented the famous Apache warrior Victorio and his band from entering Texas from Mexico.[14]

After eleven years of duty that saw the gradual pacification of the Texas frontier, the 24th deployed to the Indian Territory in present-day Oklahoma. Its troops took up station at Forts Sill and Reno and in cantonments on the North Fork, Canadian Run, and North Canadian Rivers. Charged with performing tasks similar to those it had previously accomplished on the Texas frontier, the unit also took responsibility for thousands of Kiowa, Comanche, Cheyenne, and Arapaho Indians on reservations in the area.[15] Transferring to the Far West in 1888, the regiment once again found itself

[12] Ulysses S. Grant, *Personal Memoirs*, 2 vols. (New York: Charles L. Webster & Co., 1886), 2:541.

[13] Billington, *New Mexico's Buffalo Soldiers*, p. 5. See also Scipio, *Last of the Black Regulars*, p. 7. For classic studies of the African-American soldier on the western frontier, see William H. Leckie, *The Buffalo Soldiers* (Norman: University of Oklahoma Press, 1967); Arlen Fowler, *The Black Infantry in the West, 1869–1891* (Westport, Conn.: Greenwood Press, 1971).

[14] Scipio, *Last of the Black Regulars*, pp. 7–9.

[15] Muller, *The Twenty-Fourth Infantry Past and Present*, pp. 10–11.

serving at isolated posts—Fort Bayard in New Mexico and Forts Grant, Thomas, Bowie, and Huachuca in Arizona, among others. The unit's duties remained the same, but it also kept watch on several tribes of Apache Indians housed in such encampments as the San Carlos Indian Reservation.[16] Its commander during much of the period was Col. Zenas R. Bliss, an outstanding officer who had been cited for gallantry during the Battles of Fredericksburg and the Wilderness and had won the Medal of Honor.[17]

During this period, two soldiers from the 24th joined the twenty-three blacks who received the Medal of Honor in the post–Civil War nineteenth century. While escorting an Army paymaster traveling between Forts Grant and Thomas on 11 May 1889, Sgt. Benjamin Brown and Cpl. Isaiah Mays displayed great heroism during the course of a violent robbery. Although wounded, Mays walked and crawled two miles to a neighboring ranch to bring assistance. The paymaster, Maj. Joseph W. Wham, later reported, "I served in the infantry during the entire Civil War . . . in sixteen major battles, but I never witnessed better fighting than shown by these colored soldiers."[18]

Despite the performance of the 24th and other black units on the frontier, blacks as a group, whether inside or outside the armed services, endured increasingly difficult circumstances during the late 1870s, the 1880s, and the 1890s. Racism was growing in the United States and in many other parts of the western world. By 1900 a multitude of statutes popularly known as Jim Crow laws had been enacted in the southern United States. The Supreme Court ratified the laws in such landmark decisions as *Plessy v. Ferguson*, which became the basis for most kinds of segregation by endorsing the doctrine of "separate but equal" in travel accommodations. Jim Crow laws consigned black children to schools for blacks only, curtailed the right of African-Americans to vote in local and national elections, and imposed rigid limits on the ability of blacks to associate with whites in most public places. A favored practice in the South, segregation was less formal in the northern states but often just as real.[19] Whites on the western frontier appear to have been the most broad minded, at least toward black soldiers, who remained an important part of the U.S. Army's deterrent to Indian attack.[20]

An effort was made during those years to disband the 24th Infantry and other black military units. "The negroes are not self-sustaining," one commentator of the day argued in testimony before Congress. "They have no mechanics, no clerks, very few of them know how to read and write; . . . they lose many more equipments [*sic*] than the whites do."[21]

With blacks comprising close to 10 percent of the Army, the effort failed. Indeed, the lack of opportunity for blacks in civilian life drove some of the nation's brightest African-Americans into military ranks, where they tended to stay. Desertion rates for the Army during the post–Civil War years tell the story. They were considerably lower for blacks than for whites. Between 1880 and 1889, only 59 men deserted the 24th Infantry and only 104 the 25th. By contrast, the lowest number for an all-white regiment came to 281 men for the 2d Infantry. The highest came from the 15th Infantry, which saw 676 defections over the same period.[22]

---

[16] Scipio, *Last of the Black Regulars*, pp. 3–11.

[17] Billington, *New Mexico's Buffalo Soldiers*, p. 135; Muller, *The Twenty-Fourth Infantry Past and Present*, pp. 16–18.

[18] The number 23 includes three Seminole-Negro scouts assigned to the 24th. See U.S. Congress, Committee on Veterans Affairs, *Medal of Honor Recipients* (Washington, D.C.: Government Printing Office, 1979), pp. 273, 299. Wham's report is in U.S. War Department, *Annual Report of the Secretary of War, 1889* (Washington, D.C.: Government Printing Office, 1889), p. 185. See also Preston Amos, *Above and Beyond in the West: Negro Medal of Honor Winners, 1870–1890* (Washington, D.C.: Potomac Corral of the Westerners, 1974).

[19] For more information, see Franklin, *From Slavery to Freedom*, pp. 324–43. See also C. Vann Woodward, *The Strange Career of Jim Crow* (New York: Oxford University Press, 1966). *Plessy v. Ferguson* followed a precedent for institutionalized segregation established in the Army Reorganization Act of 1866 which established separate black regiments.

[20] Frank N. Schubert, "Black Soldiers on the White Frontier: Some Factors Influencing Race Relations," *Phylon* 32 (Winter 1971): 410–15.

[21] The testimony is quoted in Scipio, *Last of the Black Regulars*, p. 12.

[22] Billington, *New Mexico's Buffalo Soldiers*, pp. 171–73.

Although often stationed at isolated posts in the deserts of the Far West, black soldiers were hardly unconscious of the world they had left behind. Letters from home kept them informed, and some among them subscribed to the black civilian press. When a weekly published in Virginia, the *Richmond Planet*, for example, solicited funds in 1895 for the defense of two black women accused of murdering a white, men of the 24th at far away Fort Huachuca, Arizona, responded with small donations and letters to the editor on the women's behalf. In the field, the men also formed debating societies and literary clubs where they discussed issues that were important to blacks of the day—for example, the competing ideologies of Booker T. Washington, who preached a low profile for blacks attempting to survive in a white world, and William E. B. DuBois, who founded the more militant National Association for the Advancement of Colored People (NAACP).[23]

Blacks who wanted to get ahead in the Army tended to go with the system. Chaplain Allen Allensworth, for one, accepted the racial status quo in the Army. Applying for a chaplain's appointment in 1886, the well-educated former slave made it a point to note in his letter to the adjutant general that he would give no offense because of his race. "I know where the official ends and where the social line begins," he wrote, "and have guarded against social intrusion." Allensworth became a chaplain at Fort Supply in Indian Territory, where he operated a post school. Later, he established a school with a graded curriculum and a study outline at Fort Bayard in New Mexico. His reputation grew as an educator. In 1891 he was invited to Toronto, Canada, to deliver a paper at a professional conference.[24]

If some black soldiers tended to go along, however, others reacted to the growing racism around them with anger. Members of the 9th Cavalry shot up the town of Suggs, Wyoming, in 1892 to avenge a racial insult. One year later, they fired into a saloon near Fort Concho, Texas, after a group of

Texas Rangers pistol-whipped black soldiers drinking there. Shortly afterward, troopers from the 9th rescued a black veteran from a lynch mob in Crawford, Nebraska, and issued a broadside warning to residents of the town that their patience was at an end. "You shall not outrage us and our people right here under the shadow of 'Old Glory,'" the sheet's anonymous author declared, "while we have shot and shell, and if you persist we will repeat the horrors of San[to] Domingo—we will reduce your homes and firesides to ashes and send your guilty souls to hell."[25]

Although some of the men of the 9th Cavalry registered their outrage at racial prejudice by force of arms, those of the 24th took the opposite approach. In 1896, when the regiment deployed to Fort Douglas, on the outskirts of Salt Lake City, Utah, the white citizens of the area were so disturbed they sent a delegation to Washington to protest. Notwithstanding, the men of the 24th performed their duties so professionally and with such concern for the community that within a year the city's leading newspaper published an apology.[26] On 19 April 1898, when the unit departed for Tampa, Florida, to participate in the Spanish-American War, its 540 men received a heartwarming send-off. The people of Salt Lake City turned out en masse to wish them an early return.[27]

Good feelings lasted until the regiment reached Florida, where its members experienced extreme racial hostility for the first time. At Tampa, drunken whites from an Ohio volunteer regiment amused themselves by firing their weapons at a two-year-old black child. When word reached men of the 24th and 25th encamped nearby, enraged members

[23] Frank N. Schubert, "The Fort Robinson Y.M.C.A., 1902–1907," *Nebraska History* 55 (Summer 1974): 166.

[24] Billington, *New Mexico's Buffalo Soldiers*, p. 161.

[25] Quote from ibid., p. 166. See also Frank N. Schubert, "The Suggs Affray: The Black Cavalry in the Johnson County War," *Western Historical Quarterly* 4 (January 1973): 57–68.

[26] Conditions within the 9th Cavalry are described by Frank N. Schubert in "The Violent World of Emanuel Stance, Fort Robinson, 1887," *Nebraska History* 55 (Summer 1974): 203–21. See also Scipio, *Last of the Black Regulars*, p. 11; Michael J. T. Clark, "A History of the Twenty-Fourth United States Infantry Regiment in Utah, 1896–1900" (Ph.D. diss., University of Utah, 1979).

[27] Scipio, *Last of the Black Regulars*, p. 11.

The 24th Infantry marching in Cuba, 1898

of those units attacked both white soldiers and seg-regated businesses in the town. The militants with-drew only when a regiment of white volunteers from Georgia restored order, having put some thir-ty of them into the hospital.[28]

Shortly after the incident, the 24th and 25th sailed for Cuba. On 25 June they disembarked at Siboney, where they joined other units of regulars and volunteers to begin an attack on the eastern approaches to the city of Santiago.[29] Barely a week

later, on 1 July, the American commander, Maj. Gen. William R. Shafter, moved against Spanish defensive lines located to the east of the city on the San Juan Heights. During the battle that followed, the only full-scale infantry engagement of the war in Cuba, black soldiers from the 24th and the other black regiments distinguished themselves.

For most of the day, nothing went as the Americans had planned. A tenacious Spanish guard of about five hundred men at El Caney, northeast of San Juan, tied down a force of over six thousand Americans that was supposed to turn the northern flank of the main Spanish position. Meanwhile, to the east confusion reigned at the San Juan Heights, where only 900 Spanish troops were present. In the absence of clear orders, regimental and company

[28]Willard B. Gatewood, Jr., "Negro Troops in Florida, 1898," *Florida Historical Quarterly* 49 (July 1970): 4–5, 7–9. See also Nalty, *Strength for the Fight,* pp. 67f.

[29]Muller, *The Twenty-Fourth Infantry Past and Present,* p. 12; Scipio, *Last of the Black Regulars,* pp. 18–22.

officers hesitated, questioning whether to swing to the attack in the absence of the units at El Caney or to hold in place. When they decided to go ahead, their forces began to experience extreme difficulty maneuvering in the thick brush. Junior officers repeatedly had to expose themselves to enemy fire to sort through the confusion, and many lost their lives. Poor coordination and intermingling of units on the battlefield resulted. In the end, valor, numbers, and a battery of Gatling guns made the difference. Under increasing pressure, the Spaniards withdrew to a second line of defense and the 24th, mixed with portions of several other regiments, rushed forward to take a blockhouse at the top of the hill.[30]

In all, the American force suffered more than one thousand casualties during the day, losses that were hardly as grave as those suffered during some battles in the Civil War, but still heavy. Of those, nearly 9 percent—twelve killed and seventy-five wounded—were members of the 24th.[31] "The gallantry and bearing shown by the officers and soldiers of the regiment under this trying ordeal," the commander of the 2d Battalion, Capt. Henry Wygant, later noted, "was such that it [the unit] has every reason to be proud of its record. The losses of the regiment . . . show the fire they were subjected to."[32] Indeed, the 24th later incorporated the blockhouse on San Juan Hill into its regimental crest and adopted the term *Semper Paratus*, "always prepared," as its motto.[33]

Outbreaks of tropical diseases such as malaria and yellow fever followed the American victory in Cuba. According to a medical theory of the day, blacks, who were descended from natives of the tropics, were naturally more immune to those diseases than whites. As the epidemic spread and deaths occurred, commanders decided that the men of the 24th would be well suited to serve the sick and ordered the unit to assist at the hospital in Siboney. The task involved little extra risk to the soldiers who worked in the hospitals, all of whom were volunteers, because both malaria and yellow fever come as the result of mosquito bites rather than from contact with the infected. It nevertheless threw the theory of black immunity into question. Fifty percent of the 471 men who reported for duty at Siboney contracted one or the other disease.[34]

Following the war, blacks received considerable praise for their conduct in the fighting. "Being of a race which only thirty-five years ago emerged through a long and bloody war, from a condition of servitude," one commander wrote, "they . . . gave all they had . . . that the oppressed might be free, and enjoy the blessings of liberty guaranteed by a stable government."[35] Even so, when the soldiers returned home they saw little improvement in their way of life. Exposed increasingly to the effects of Jim Crow and aware that they had sacrificed much in the recent war, they became less inclined than ever to accept racial insults. As a result, armed clashes occurred between recently returned black soldiers and whites at a number of different sites. "We did our duty in Cuba," Pvt. George Washington, a member of the 24th, declared at the trial of a white who had slashed him with a razor, "and we don't think we should be insulted because we are black."[36]

[30] Reports of the 24th's role in the fighting are contained in U.S. War Department, *Annual Report of the War Department for 1898* (Washington, D.C.: Government Printing Office, 1898), pp. 434–38. See also Graham A. Cosmas, *An Army for Empire: The United States Army in the Spanish-American War,* 2d ed. (Shippensburg, Pa.: White Mane Publishing Co., 1994), pp. 209f; Nalty, *Strength for the Fight,* pp. 68–70.

[31] Ltr, Capt A. C. Markley, Actg Cdr, 24th Inf Rgt, to Adjutant General (AG), 5 Jul 1898, in *Annual Report of the War Department for 1898,* p. 434. See also Francis E. Lewis, "Negro Army Regulars in the Spanish-American War: Smoked Yankees at Santiago De Cuba" (M.A. diss., University of Texas at Austin, 1969), p. 48.

[32] Rpt, Capt Henry Wygant, Cdr, 2d Bn, 24th Inf Rgt, 5 Jul 1898, in *Annual Report of the War Department for 1898,* vol. 1, pt. 2, pp. 434–35.

[33] Scipio, *Last of the Black Regulars,* pp. 11–28.

[34] Ltr, Maj A. C. Markley to AG, 18 Sep 1898, in Muller, *The Twenty-Fourth Infantry Past and Present,* pp. 26–32. See also Nalty, *Strength for the Fight,* p. 72.

[35] HQ, 25th Inf Div, GO 19, 11 Aug 1898, reprinted in John H. Nankivell, ed., *The History of the Twenty-Fifty Regiment, United States Infantry, 1869–1926* (Fort Collins, Colo.: Old Army Press, 1972), p. 83.

[36] Quote from Michael C. Robinson and Frank N. Schubert, "David Fagen: An Afro-American Rebel in the Philippines, 1899–1901," *Pacific Historical Review* 44 (February 1975): 68.

The 24th Infantry attends sick call in Siboney.

The 24th itself returned to the West. Six companies moved back to Fort Douglas in Utah while three others went to Fort D. A. Russell in Wyoming. Over the next few months, portions of the regiment served in Washington, Montana, and Alaska. In July 1899, after the United States went to war in the Philippines to take control of Spain's former colony, the unit deployed to the islands to assist in defeating the dissident forces of guerrilla leader Emilio Aguinaldo.

The assignment was difficult for some of the men because influential segments of the black community in the United States had begun to question the justice of the war. Concerned that issues important to blacks, such as education and enfranchisement, had been shoved aside for the sake of a foreign adventure, the senior bishop of the African Methodist Episcopal Church in the United States, Henry M. Turner, for one, declared that the conflict was nothing more than "an unholy war of conquest."[37] Well aware of the questions circulating in

their community, the men of the 24th in the Philippines were quite capable of making their own opinions known. When they arrived in Manila, for example, they surprised many of the white soldiers already present. When one white called out to a debarking black, "Hello, nig. . . . What do you think you're going to do over here!" the soldier replied, with just a touch of irony, "Well, I doan know, but I ruther reckon we're . . . to take up de White Man's Burden!"[38]

Over the three years that followed, the men of the 24th fought in a number of difficult engagements against Philippine guerrillas. At San Nicolas, Company K accepted the surrender of 17 officers and 150 insurgents and recovered 101

[37]Turner is quoted by Nalty, *Strength for the Fight*, pp. 74f.

[38]Quote from Robinson and Schubert, "David Fagen," p. 70. For more on blacks in the imperial age, see Willard B. Gatewood, Jr., *Black Americans and the White Man's Burden, 1898–1903* (Urbana: University of Illinois Press, 1975), and idem, *Smoked Yankees and the Struggle for Empire: Letters From Negro Soldiers, 1898–1902* (Fayetteville: University of Arkansas Press, 1987).

rifles. The men of the 24th also aided in the organization of civil government in many towns,
supervised elections, and provided security for
the civilian population.[39]

Yet racial prejudice took its toll. Whites
looked down on all people of color, referring to
the Filipinos as "gugus," "niggers," and "black
devils," but one white general deemed the natives
of the islands "naturally more intelligent than our
[American] colored people."[40] The Filipinos
themselves attempted to capitalize on the situation by offering officer commissions to blacks who
deserted to their side. Almost all refused.
Desertion not only involved a betrayal of country
and unit, it also meant the loss of friends and cultural ties and risked execution or imprisonment
upon capture. In the end, fewer than five blacks
accepted the offer. Of those, Pvt. David Fagen of
the 24th rose to the rank of captain in the enemy's
army before apparently being killed. Doubtful
from the beginning that blacks would fight their
"Filipino cousins," the Army took Fagen's defec-
tion seriously and attempted without success to
hunt him down. It also made an example of two
captured black defectors from the 9th Cavalry,
who were executed. The point made, President
Theodore Roosevelt then commuted the death
sentences of all remaining deserters, whether
white or black.[41]

The 24th served in Montana after the defeat of
the insurrection but returned to the Philippines in
1906 to assist in suppressing outbreaks of violence
that continued to occur. It remained until 1908,
when it redeployed to Fort Ontario and Madison
Barracks in New York. It sailed once more for the
Philippines in 1911, remained on garrison duty
until 1915, then redeployed again to the United

States. Stationed temporarily at the Presidio of San
Francisco, it took up residence at Fort Russell in
February 1916.[42]

The Army moved the regiment to the
Southwest later in the year, after the Mexican ban-
dit-revolutionary Francisco "Pancho" Villa raided
Columbus, New Mexico. At first the unit guarded
lines of communication between Columbus and
other border towns. Later, it deployed across the
border to Colonia Dublan in Mexico, where it operated under the command of Brig. Gen. John J.
Pershing as part of an 18,000-man force that had
deployed into northern Mexico in a vain attempt to
capture the rebel chieftain.[43]

Although the 24th spent considerable time
outside the United States during the period
between the Spanish-American War and World
War I, it was hardly unaffected by the racism that
seemed an increasingly important feature of
American society at the time. With ships becoming more technologically complex, the Navy, for
the first time in its history, actively began to seek
a more skilled and educated all-white enlisted
force. In the process it excluded blacks from seamen's billets, relegating them to stewards' positions. Meanwhile, the National Guard in the
southern states excluded blacks from member-
ship, and the Army resisted inclusion of black
units in organizations such as the coast and field
artillery. Blacks, according to racial theories of the
day, were inferior to whites in mechanical skills
and learning abilities and served much better as
servants and menial laborers.[44]

The leaders of the nation themselves subscribed to the idea. Although Theodore Roosevelt,
for example, had at first endorsed the contributions
of black soldiers to the victory in Cuba, in later
years he attributed those accomplishments almost
completely to the leadership of whites. In the same
way, when members of the all-black 25th Infantry
allegedly raided the city of Brownsville, Texas, dur-

[39] Scipio, *Last of the Black Regulars*, pp. 32–42; Muller, *The Twenty-Fourth Infantry Past and Present*, pp. 30–43. For a first-hand account of the conflict from the viewpoint of a black noncommissioned officer in Company H, see Sanford M. Thomas, *War in the Philippines* (Privately published, 1903), MacArthur Memorial, Norfolk, Va.

[40] *Army and Navy Journal* 38 (2 February 1901): 539, quoted in Robinson and Schubert, "David Fagen," p. 72.

[41] Robinson and Schubert, "David Fagen," p. 78.

[42] Muller, *The Twenty-Fourth Infantry Past and Present*, p. 13.

[43] Scipio, *Last of the Black Regulars*, pp. 42–46.

[44] Nalty, *Strength for the Fight*, pp. 77–88.

ing 1906, causing the death of one white, Roosevelt ignored major flaws in the evidence implicating men of the unit. Presuming guilt, he used his powers as president to dismiss every soldier and noncommissioned officer on duty the night of the incident. One hundred and sixty men were driven from the Army as a result, without trial, due process, or legal procedure of any sort.[45]

Yet, when the United States declared war on Germany in 1917, blacks closed ranks with their white countrymen. If some questioned whether their participation would aid the advance of their race, many others viewed the conflict as an opportunity. Blacks had gained much through their loyalty to the nation in time of war, editor William E. B. DuBois observed in the *Crisis*, the official organ of the NAACP. Many had fought in the American Revolution, more in the War of 1812, and tens of thousands in the Civil War. In part because of their sacrifices, the slave trade had been abolished, the slaves had been freed, and the black man had won the vote. "Some ten thousand Negroes fought in the Spanish-American War," DuBois continued, "and in the twenty years ensuing since that war, despite many setbacks, we have doubled or quadrupled our accumulated wealth."[46]

If the black community tended to agree with DuBois and embraced the war enthusiastically, however, the Army had doubts. The assistant chief of staff, Maj. Gen. Tasker Bliss, believed that blacks did well in military service and that he would have little difficulty recruiting them, but he understood that any attempt to use them might involve political problems. Southern members of Congress might raise objections if they learned that armed blacks were to be stationed in their districts or trained near their homes. In the end, rather than assume any risk, the Army enlisted some 650,000 volunteers but accepted only 4,000 blacks.[47] Meanwhile, reasoning that an oppressed minority might be tempted to disloyalty by the enemy, officers within the Military Intelligence Division of the Army War College began to investigate possible black subversives and to compile dossiers on their activities.[48]

Voluntary enlistments of whites nevertheless proved inadequate to the needs of modern war. With the black community clamoring for recognition and the Selective Service system drafting increasing numbers of black men, the Army decided to establish a training school at Fort Des Moines in Iowa to prepare black junior officers for service in the all-black units it would shortly have to organize. One thousand of the men selected for the new school were to come from enlistments or mobilized National Guard units. The rest would be drawn from the corps of noncommissioned officers already serving in the Army's black regiments. Most if not all senior commanders were firmly convinced that blacks performed best under white leadership, but the need to placate the black community prevailed. They took comfort from the thought that very

[45] Franklin, *From Slavery to Freedom*, pp. 422f, 441–43; Willard B. Gatewood, Jr., "Black Americans and the Quest for Empire," *Journal of Southern History* 37 (1971): 582; Nalty, *Strength for the Fight*, pp. 90–95. An early, highly critical examination of the Brownsville affair was conducted by the Constitution League of the United States under the auspices of Republican gadfly Senator Joseph "Fire Alarm" Foraker of Ohio. The league's preliminary report, along with basic documents relating to the episode, is in U.S. Congress, Senate, *Preliminary Report of the Commission of the Constitution League of the United States on Affray at Brownsville, Texas, August 13 and 14, 1906*, 59th Cong., 2d sess., 10 December 1906, doc. 107 (Washington, D.C.: Government Printing Office, 1906). For more modern treatments, see John D. Weaver, *The Brownsville Raid* (New York: W. W. Norton, 1970); Ann J. Lane, *The Brownsville Affair* (Port Washington, N.Y.: National University, 1971).

[46] William E. B. DuBois, "The Reward," the *Crisis*, 41 (September 1918): 217, quoted in Ulysses Lee, *The Employment of Negro Troops*, United States Army in World War II (Washington, D.C.: U.S. Army Center of Military History, Government Printing Office, 1990), pp. 4f.

[47] Ltr, Maj Gen Tasker Bliss to General Robert K. Evans, 4 Apr 17, in MacGregor and Nalty, *Blacks in the United States Armed Forces*, vol. 4, item 1; Nalty, *Strength for the Fight*, p. 108.

[48] Records and correspondence relating to the program have been reproduced on microfilm by the National Archives. See M1440, Correspondence of the Military Intelligence Division Relating to "Negro Subversion," 1917–1941, National Archives and Records Administration (NARA), Washington, D.C.

few of the new officers would ever advance beyond the rank of captain.[49]

The decision to train seasoned sergeants as officers had a profound impact upon the 24th Infantry. The unit's 3d Battalion alone sent off twenty-five noncommissioned officers to participate in the program. The effects of that loss became apparent during July 1917, when the battalion transferred to Camp Logan near Houston, Texas, where it was to guard the construction of a training facility. The men of the unit became increasingly resentful of the city's Jim Crow laws, the brutality of the local police, and racial insults. An Army inspector general later summarized the attitude among local whites: "A nigger is a nigger, and . . . his status is not effected [sic] by the uniform he wears."[50]

Lacking the stabilizing influence of veteran sergeants and commanded by white officers who were few in number and either inexperienced in command or insensitive to black complaints, more than a hundred troops finally responded by taking arms and marching into the city. During a two-hour rampage, they killed sixteen whites, some in cold blood, and wounded twelve more. Four of their own number were killed by townspeople or the random firing of their comrades. A fifth—one of the ringleaders—took his own life. It was the only race riot in U.S. history in which more whites than blacks died.[51]

A similar episode involving men of the regiment's 1st Battalion took place at about the same time in Waco, Texas. In that case, however, prompt action by the unit's commanders and self-restraint on the part of the town's white civilian population kept a major confrontation from developing. Despite a brief interlude of indiscriminate firing, no casualties occurred.[52]

Over the next fourteen months, 6 soldiers from the 1st Battalion and 149 from the 3d were court-martialed in a series of four separate trials. The men involved in the incident at Waco were convicted of assault with intent to murder but received relatively light sentences, imprisonment at hard labor for five years.[53] In contrast, those charged at Houston received harsh, almost summary punishments. Of 64 charged in the first of three trials, 5 went free, 4 received lesser sentences, 42 went to prison for life, and 13 were condemned to death. The executions were carried out on 22 December, before the accused had a chance to appeal their sentences through the usual military channels and before any public announcement of the verdicts had been made. The Army took the step to minimize reactions to the executions by either angry blacks or jubilant whites. The white press in general agreed with the decision. Black newspapers were outraged: "Strict justice has been done," the New York Age declared, "but full justice has not been done."[54]

In two later trials, sixteen more soldiers were sentenced to hang, but by then the black community was in full cry. In response, President Woodrow Wilson announced a new policy committing the president himself to examine death penalty verdicts in all cases involving military law. In the end, rather than alienate blacks further or risk losing black support for the war, the War Department commuted all remaining death sentences except those for six soldiers convicted of killing specific individuals. Over the years that followed, black organizations campaigned for the

---

[49] Nalty, Strength for the Fight, pp. 109f.

[50] The inspector general is quoted in Scipio, Last of the Black Regulars, p. 135. See also HQ, Southern Dept, Office of the Department Inspector, Rpt on the Houston Riot, 13 Sep 17, file 370.61 (Riots), 11 Oct 17, Record Group (RG) 393, NARA. For more on the Army's change of attitude toward the black soldier during this period, see Marvin Fletcher, The Black Soldier and Officer in the United States Army, 1891–1917 (Columbia: University of Missouri Press, 1974).

[51] Rosalind Alexander, "Houston's Hidden History," Texas Observer, 7 Apr 89, pp. 18–20; Pamphlet, The Houston Riot and Courts-Martial of 1917, n.d., copy in U.S. Army Center of Military History (CMH), Washington, D.C., files. The best treatment of the riot and its aftermath is in Robert V. Haynes, A Night of Violence: The Houston Riot of 1917 (Baton Rouge: Louisiana State University Press, 1976).

[52] Garna L. Christian, "The Ordeal and the Prize: The 24th Infantry and Camp MacArthur," Military Affairs 50 (April 1986): 65–70.

[53] Ibid., p. 69.

[54] Quote from Franklin, From Slavery to Freedom, p. 460. The statistics are in Nalty, Strength for the Fight, p. 104.

American Negro troops in France (note the French helmet)

release of the imprisoned rioters. The Army resisted but commuted the sentences one by one. The last of the men left prison in 1938.[55]

The Waco affair and the Houston riot had far-reaching effects on the 24th Infantry and other black units. Prior to the two events, the Army had considered raising a total of sixteen regiments to accommodate the black recruits the draft was providing. After those incidents, it rejected the idea on the grounds that blacks and whites would have to train in the same encampments and that a "national calamity" might occur if either group got out of hand.[56] As a result, most of the more than 400,000 blacks who entered the Army never saw combat at all. They served in all-black utility units—as stevedores, construction crews, truck drivers, and the like. As for the 24th and 25th Infantry regiments, neither made it to France. Composed of well-trained regular soldiers who could have contributed to the fighting, the units spent the war mounting guard patrols, the 25th in the Philippines and Hawaii, the 24th at isolated outposts along the Mexican border. Both had

become objects of mistrust. As the inspector general put it in his final report on the Houston affair: "The tendency of the negro soldier, with fire arms in his possession, unless he is properly handled by officers who know his racial characteristics, is to become arrogant, overbearing, and abusive, and a menace to the community in which he happens to be stationed."[57]

With the African-American community clamoring for justice and investing heavily in war bonds, the Army was unable to keep blacks completely out of combat. In the end, it established the 92d and 93d Infantry Divisions for them and sent the units to France. As with many all-white divisions, the two went into combat with incomplete training, and many of the individual replacements who joined them later in the war possessed only rudimentary fighting skills. Compounding those problems, however, was the lack of enthusiasm that the Army displayed for black units in general. According to the commander of the 92d Division, Brig. Gen. Charles C. Ballou, the Army assigned white officers so prejudiced against the troops that the unit lacked the organizational cohesion and trust among men that it needed to succeed. As a result, despite many individual acts of bravery, the division's men showed little initia-

---

[55] Ltr, Secretary of War Newton Baker to President Wilson, 22 Aug 18, in MacGregor and Nalty, *Blacks in the United States Armed Forces*, vol. 3, item 88.

[56] Memo, Maj Gen Tasker Bliss for Secretary of War, 24 Aug 17, in MacGregor and Nalty, *Blacks in the United States Armed Forces*, vol. 4, item 5. The recommendation was the product of a study begun before the riot but approved afterward.

[57] The report is reproduced in Scipio, *Last of the Black Regulars*, p. 135.

tive in combat and sometimes straggled to the rear when surprised.[58]

If racial intolerance harmed the 92d, however, it also tended to hide the fact that there were causes for the division's lapses on the battlefield that had nothing to do with race. In its first significant combat action, for example, the division's 368th Infantry regiment, advancing across difficult, unreconnoitered terrain and lacking both effective artillery support and the tools it needed to cut through extensive wire entanglements, came up against unexpected machine guns and artillery fire directed by spotters in aircraft. Under the circumstances, close coordination was essential, yet orders were vague and liaison between companies and battalions was virtually nonexistent. Meanwhile, the front assigned to one battalion was so broad that the unit became scattered and disorganized. In the end, 58 soldiers were killed and 222 wounded. Despite those difficulties, none of which had any connection with race, and a lack of resourcefulness on the part of some white commanders, the men of the regiment and their black officers bore the brunt of the blame. In all, some thirty black lieutenants and captains were immediately relieved of their duties for general inefficiency and cowardice, and several were court-martialed for retreating in the face of the enemy.[59]

That beginning notwithstanding, the division, composed mainly of draftees, gained experience over the next several weeks. Within little more than a month, it was attacking so well that its commanding general could only commend it for a "decided improvement in offensive spirit and aggressive action." Indeed, some twenty-one members of the division earned the Distinguished Service Cross for bravery, a decoration second only to the Medal of Honor. Even so, the unit's achievements went largely unnoticed. Its failures were what officers and policymakers tended to see after the war had ended.[60]

Although faced with many of the same impediments as the 92d, the 93d did better, probably because Pershing assigned its regiments to the French, who trained, supplied, and fielded them as if they were their own, without racial prejudice. In addition, the division comprised mainly former National Guard units that had worked together for years during peacetime and possessed both cohesion and organization. Recalling a singular attack with bared bayonets in which the men of the 1st Battalion of the division's 371st Infantry regiment broke into an enemy fortification on the Hindenburg Line, the battalion's white commander, Maj. Joseph B. Pate, spoke movingly of the deep respect he held for the African-American troops who had accomplished the deed: "To have been permitted to command such a splendid body of men, from its organization to its demobilization and to share in the honor of this signal achievement, accomplished through such united courage and the supreme sacrifice of so many of our comrades, fills my heart with the greatest pride and the keenest sadness." In the end, three of the 93d's four regiments won the Croix de Guerre for valor, France's highest award for a military unit. Even so, as with the 92d, white officers tended to see only the race of the men involved. The 93d had succeeded,

---

[58] The preparation of all U.S. units in the war was questionable. For more information, see Timothy K. Nenninger, "American Military Effectiveness in the First World War," in Allan R. Millett and Williamson Murray, eds., *Military Effectiveness: The First World War* (Boston: Unwin Hyman, 1990), p. 153; Paul F. Braim, *The Test of Battle, The American Expeditionary Forces in the Meuse-Argonne Campaign* (Newark: University of Delaware Press, 1987). The performance of the 92d and many of the problems the unit faced are described in Ltr, Col C. C. Ballou to Asst Commandant, General Staff College, 14 Mar 20, in MS, Historical Section, Army War College, The Colored Soldier in the U.S. Army [May 1942], pp. 99–106, CMH files. Since Ballou was the wartime commander of the unit, his remarks might be seen as mere self-justification. They are seconded, however, by William E. B. DuBois, in "The Negro and the War Department," the *Crisis* 16 (May 1918): 7–8, quoted by Lee, *The Employment of Negro Troops*, p. 9.

[59] The story of the 92d Infantry Division is told in MS, Historical Section, Army War College, The Ninety-Second Division, 1917–1918 [1923], CMH files. See especially pp. 18–19, 33–34. See also American Battle Monuments

Commission, *92d Division, Summary of Operations in the World War* (Washington, D.C.: Government Printing Office, 1944), p. 25. For more on the handicaps under which the 92d labored, see Arthur E. Barbeau and Florette Henri, *The Unknown Soldiers: Black American Troops in World War I* (Philadelphia: Temple University Press, 1974), pp. 137–63. The 368th's attack is described on pp. 150–52.

[60] Ibid.

A kitchen and a dining room in a trench in France

they suggested in reports following the war, mainly because the French had never used the unit as a whole but had parceled its regiments out individually to separate divisions. "Colored troops will do much better," they said, "when they are associated as component parts of white organizations."[61]

With the end of World War I, the Army went through a drastic drawdown. Reduced in size to 828 men in 1922, the 24th took up residence at Fort Benning, Georgia, the home of the Infantry School, where it participated in the transformation of the post from a temporary to a permanent facility.[62] Segregated into its own special, "colored" area, the unit performed mainly housekeeping and construction chores. "After I joined the regiment in 1923," one sergeant recalled,

members of the 24th performed various labor duties for the building of several parts of the post. For example, during the day, some of us were used for road building and at night we hauled concrete by wheelbarrows, for the construction of Doughboy Stadium (the football field). Once concrete pouring began we could not stop until the sections that were being built were completed. We worked in three shifts because the work continued all night. If not otherwise needed, our band was detailed to play during our working to keep up our morale.[63]

[61] The 93d was never formally organized as a division. For a detailed if somewhat biased treatment of the unit's performance, see Chester D. Heywood, *Negro Combat Troops in the World War: The Story of the 371st Infantry* (Worcester, Mass.: Commonwealth Press, 1928). Pate tells his story in The Capture of COTE 188, attachment to Ltr, Maj J. B. Pate to Secretary, American Battle Monuments Commission, 6 Jun 27, file 719.3, no. 7, 371st Infantry Regiment, box 259, Correspondence with Former Division Officers, RG 117, Records of American Battle Monuments Commission, Washington National Records Center (WNRC), Suitland, Md. The second quote is from Memo, Col V. A. Caldwell for Asst Commandant, General Staff College, 14 Mar 20, sub: Use To Be Made of Negroes in the U.S. Military Service, in MacGregor and Nalty, *Blacks in the United States Armed Forces*,vol. 4, item 120. For brief histories of the 93d in World War I, see MS, Jehu C. Hunter and Major Clark, The Buffalo Division in World War II [copyright Jehu C. Hunter, 1985], CMH files; Barbeau and Henri, *The Unknown Soldiers*, pp. 111–36.

[62] See L. Albert Scipio II, *The 24th Infantry at Fort Benning* (Silver Spring, Md.: Roman Publications, 1986).

[63] Scipio, *Last of the Black Regulars*, p. 58. Quote from Interv, John A. Cash with Randall Reuben, 10 Sep 88, CMH files. All interviews hereafter cited by John A. Cash, Bernard L. Muehlbauer, Timothy Rainey, William T. Bowers, Richard O. Perry, and George L. MacGarrigle are in CMH files.

Other soldiers from the 24th worked at a logging camp on post, maintained the base's stables (a prestige assignment because of the high level of skill involved in training horses), delivered coal to officers' quarters during the winter, policed the post for cleanliness, gardened, and performed general maintenance on the physical plant.[64]

The soldiers were carried on the Army's books as riflemen, machine gunners, and so forth, but, in fact, for years most continued to be little more than heavy laborers, gardeners, or cooks. Very little combat training occurred, especially during the first decade of the unit's stay at Benning, except for exercises in marksmanship, close-order drill, and military courtesy. The men made a snappy appearance, were noted for their saluting, and were well disciplined, rarely getting into trouble with the police of Columbus, Georgia. As M. Sgt. Joe Black explained, although Benning and the town of Columbus were segregated, "we didn't mind it; we soldiered through it and went by the rules and tried to stay out of trouble." As for the regiment's officers, most were detailed to special duty at the base's signal office, post exchange, and the various academic departments of the Infantry School.[65]

Some attempts were made in 1934 to improve the unit's ability to perform military missions, but for a time the old role still appears to have prevailed. During large-scale maneuvers conducted in May 1935, under the direction of the headquarters of the IV Corps Area, for example, the unit was assigned to participate but could provide no more than 11 officers and 227 enlisted men out of an authorized strength of 717. The rest were already committed to "special duties" and could not be spared.[66]

The maneuvers in 1936 went better. The 24th took to the field as a two-battalion regiment and was commended by the commanding general for the role it played in the exercise. Even so, that same year, when Benjamin O. Davis, Jr., reported for duty as a new second lieutenant fresh from West Point, he learned that the white 29th Infantry performed all of the "high visibility" tasks on post and that the 24th served mainly as a labor pool. Assigned as a platoon leader in Company F, Davis recalled that he went into the field for uncomplicated maneuvers only twice during the entire year he held the job.[67]

Although treated for the most part as manual laborers, many of the men in the 24th entered the Army and remained because garrison life, even if segregated, held many more attractions for them than the lack of opportunity on the outside. The Army paid great attention to physical fitness and sports, and the men of the 24th excelled in those areas. They won recognition and championships in competitions against whites, especially in boxing and swimming. In addition, the Army provided a boost for men who would otherwise have lived seriously disadvantaged lives.

The experience of M. Sgt. Harry Woods of the 24th was typical. Woods entered the service in 1936, during the final years of the Great Depression. He possessed at best a grade-school education and no vocation. The Army changed that. He finished high school, rose to the rank of master sergeant, obtained the respect that came from the exercise of authority, and earned a good enough living to send two children through college. In an interview fifty years later, he said, "The Army did a lot for me."[68]

As World War II loomed and the Army prepared for the possibility that it might shortly face combat, blacks became concerned that the conflict

[64] Intervs, Cash with Harry Woods, 8 Aug 88; Eugene Pleas, 22 Oct 88; Eddie H. Lucky, 20 Oct 88; Tommie J. Baugh, 9 Sep 88; Willie Fortson, 25 Feb 89; Bennie Livingston, 25 Feb 89; Hiram Davis, 10 Sep 88; Isham W. Alexander, 7 Sep 88; Lewis Portis, 21 Oct 88; Reuben, 10 Sep 88; Bernard L. Muehlbauer with Sam Malone, 4 Dec 89. The emphasis on fatigue details instead of training continued into 1940.

[65] Scipio, The 24th Infantry at Fort Benning, p. 121. Quote from Interv, Cash with Joe Black, 10 Sep 88. See also Interv, Cash with John E. Cole, 8 Oct 88.

[66] Scipio, The 24th Infantry at Fort Benning, pp. 121–23.

[67] Interv, Cash with Lt Gen Benjamin O. Davis, Jr., United States Air Force (USAF) (Ret.), 13 Jun 90. See also Benjamin O. Davis, Jr., An Autobiography, Benjamin O. Davis, Jr., American (Washington, D.C.: Smithsonian Institution Press, 1991), pp. 58f; Intervs, Cash with Alexander, 7 Sep 88; Fortson, 25 Feb 89.

[68] Interv, Cash with Woods, 8 Aug 88.

would only provide their domestic critics with another excuse to try to prove the inferiority of their race. Following World War I, DuBois had charged that, rather than allow a black regiment officered by blacks to succeed, "Negro haters entrenched in the Army" had conducted "a concerted campaign [of slander]." Something of the sort might happen in the war to come. Increasingly powerful as a voting bloc during the 1930s, blacks began to agitate for their rightful place in American society and for concessions by the military.[69]

In particular, black leaders voiced their determination to resist any attempt on the part of the Army to restrict their people to labor battalions in the coming war. President Franklin D. Roosevelt's political opponents seized on the issue as the election of 1940 approached, pointing out in full-page advertisements in black newspapers the disparities African-Americans suffered in the armed forces in comparison with whites. An advertisement in the influential *Baltimore Afro-American*, for example, made the point that 100 white colonels had been promoted over Col. Benjamin O. Davis, the highest ranking black in the U.S. Army.[70]

On 25 October 1940, shortly before the November election, President Roosevelt responded by appointing Davis as the Army's first black general. On the same day, he announced that the first black federal judge, William H. Hastie, would become civilian aide on Negro affairs to the secretary of war. If those appointments gained wide approval in the black community, however, they were offset by the prejudices of white military planners who continued to view blacks as inferiors.[71] Unwilling to experiment and convinced that African-Americans could perform in combat only after intense training and under the

leadership of superior white commanders, those officers concluded that wartime conditions would preclude the sort of effort required and that blacks would once more have to spend the war in labor units.[72]

White planners set a limit of 10.6 percent on African-American enlistments and inductions into the Army. In that way, the service would be able to organize itself efficiently for segregation by budgeting only the units and accommodations it needed to maintain racial separation. As World War II unfolded, however, the Army failed to fill that quota. At the beginning of the war it held back on inducting black draftees, failing to request even one black from the Selective Service draft call that followed the Japanese attack on Pearl Harbor. Later, it reduced enlistment quotas for blacks and postponed the induction of those already notified, citing the need to build segregated facilities and to transfer veterans from existing black units to train the new recruits. The poor health and illiteracy of many blacks also figured in. Selective Service rejection rates for blacks on those grounds ran at over 50 percent between 1943 and 1945, as compared with 30 percent for whites. Nevertheless, a proportionally larger number of blacks than whites volunteered for military service. Since many more whites than blacks held skilled jobs in civilian life and were often deferred, proportionally more blacks were also drafted.[73]

The Army's reluctance to bend sometimes approached the absurd. When the all-black National Medical Association, for example, began to press the government to employ black doctors and nurses in military hospitals, the service complied by establishing an all-black hospital at Fort Huachuca, an isolated, largely black post located deep in the Arizona desert. The new facility was near an all-white hospital that, while staffed largely by whites, had always served both races. The base commander at Fort Huachuca attempted to reduce the resulting tensions by importing black entertainers and establishing a

---

[69] "Opinion of W. E. B. DuBois: Bullard," the *Crisis* 30 (September 1925): 218–29, quoted by Lee, *The Employment of Negro Troops*, p. 15.

[70] Dalfiume, *Desegregation of the U.S. Armed Forces*, pp. 26–41. The advertisement is noted on p. 40.

[71] Lee, *The Employment of Negro Troops*, pp. 78–80. Judge Hastie's role in World War II is described in Phillip McGuire, *He, Too, Spoke for Democracy: Judge Hastie, World War II, and the Black Soldier* (New York: Greenwood Press, 1988).

---

[72] Lee, *The Employment of Negro Troops*, pp. 17–19.

[73] Dalfiume, *Desegregation of the U.S. Armed Forces*, pp. 50–51, 91.

variety of off-duty educational programs. Blacks assigned to the post, however, had little choice but to conclude that they were nothing more than inferiors in the eyes of the Army.[74]

Black officers also suffered indignities. Although the service went to great lengths to keep them separate as well, it soon found it had little choice but to integrate at least their training. The education of blacks was so inferior in the United States that only an elite few qualified for officer candidate school, too few to justify a separate program. Even then, more blacks obtained commissions than the Army could comfortably accommodate because the War Department persisted in assigning whites to officer black units. In the end, many young black lieutenants found themselves occupying undesirable billets in service elements while sometimes less qualified whites went to combat organizations. Serving in designated units and grades and unable to command even the lowest ranking white officer, black officers were never allowed to think that they were anything but unwanted.[75]

The system bred racial tension, especially in the South, where violent outbreaks sometimes occurred. In Fayetteville, North Carolina, for example, white military policemen boarded a bus of unruly blacks returning from leave and with little apparent provocation attempted to discipline the men with nightsticks. In the melee that followed, a black stole a policeman's pistol. Within moments, one black and one white lay dead and three more blacks and two whites were wounded.[76] At Fort Benning, a black soldier was found hanging from a tree with his hands tied securely behind his back. Although the facts of the case were never determined, blacks had little doubt that the dead man had been lynched. There were black military police on base, black Sgt. John McClary recalled, but they could do little to curb the activities of white civilians, who on one occasion even attempted to kill a black policeman.[77]

The assistant secretary of war, John L. McCloy, attributed much of the violence to the black press, which he accused of overemphasizing alleged instances of mistreatment. More to the point were the observations of Benjamin Davis. Surveying the situation for the Army, the general concluded that much of the problem could be traced to the prejudiced attitudes of white soldiers and to poor leadership on the part of white officers commanding black units.[78]

In the end, although many whites steadfastly contended that blacks accepted the separation of the races, rigid segregation proved so controversial and unworkable that the Army felt compelled to abolish some of the constraints it had imposed upon blacks. As a result, from 1944 onward theaters, post exchanges, and recreational facilities, although they might still be reserved for the use of particular units, could not be restricted on the basis of race. The innovation made little practical difference because blacks by then usually occupied self-contained areas and had little need to share facilities, but it did improve the morale of the black soldier. As for the attempt to establish segregated hospitals, it failed almost completely. Throughout the war, black and white patients in military hospitals found themselves occupying adjacent beds.[79]

To blacks, however, one of the most annoying features of segregation was the Army's practice of employing them, whatever their education and background, almost exclusively in service units. The men resented the duty because it confined them to manual labor and excluded them almost completely from combat. As rifleman Leon Hiers of the 24th Infantry recalled, all concerned believed they had trained for "something better."[80]

---

[74] Lee, *The Employment of Negro Troops*, p. 315.

[75] Nalty, *Strength for the Fight*, p. 163; Dalfiume, *Desegregation of the U.S. Armed Forces*, p. 92.

[76] Memo, John McCloy for Chief of Staff, 3 Jul 43, sub: Negro Troops, in MacGregor and Nalty, *Blacks in the United States Armed Forces*, vol. 5, item 73.

[77] Nalty, *Strength for the Fight*, p. 164; Interv, Cash with John McClary, 9 Sep 88.

[78] Dalfiume, *Desegregation of the U.S. Armed Forces*, pp. 75–76. McCloy is quoted on p. 87.

[79] War Department Pamphlet 20–6, *Command of Negro Troops* (Washington, D.C.: Government Printing Office, 1944), in MacGregor and Nalty, *Blacks in the United States Armed Forces*, vol. 5, item 83. See also Nalty, *Strength for the Fight*, p. 165.

[80] Interv, Cash with Leon C. Hiers, 24 Mar 89. Other veterans of the period agreed. See Intervs, Timothy Rainey with

The 24th Infantry receives last-minute instructions before going out to patrol the Bougainville jungle.

What happened to the 24th fit the pattern. The unit departed Fort Benning for the West Coast on 2 April 1942. Its preparations for combat were incomplete because many of its NCOs and experienced soldiers, as was common practice throughout the Army at the time in both white and black units, had been siphoned off to become cadre for newly forming black organizations. Morale was nevertheless high. The men expected to do their part. Upon arriving in San Francisco, the unit spent several days training at the city's horse arena, the Cow Palace, then sailed for the South Pacific. "We sailed approximately three days before instructions were released concerning our whereabouts or what to expect when we debarked," one sergeant recalled. "Every day aboard ship was devoted to calisthenics and lectures on tropical diseases and jungle warfare." Arriving on the island of Efate in the New Hebrides on 4 May 1942, the men found to their chagrin that they were destined not for combat but to serve as a garrison force for a logistical

base. They occupied the island for five months without ever seeing an enemy soldier.[81]

The 24th moved to Guadalcanal early in 1943, after the fighting there had also ended. Its battalions again filled a support role, loading and unloading ships, building roads, maintaining wire communications, draining marshy areas to control mosquitos, and guarding air bases. The 1st Battalion even reorganized some of its men into a provisional truck company.[82] By the end of the year, only the unit's 3d Battalion had experienced anything close to contact with the enemy. Stationed in the New Georgia island group, the battalion was far enough forward to come under heavy air bombardment. Because of that, it received battle credit for participating in the Northern Solomons Campaign.[83]

By the beginning of 1944, the Army's racial policies were under heavy attack in the United States. The black press was indignant and organizations such as the NAACP were contending angrily that blacks had been excluded unfairly from the Army's combat arms. Seeing an opening, President Franklin Roosevelt's political opponents in Congress took up the cry. A veteran of the 93d Division in World War I, Republican Congressman Hamilton Fish of New York, declared that, in a war undertaken to advance freedom, the sons of 14 million black Americans should have "the same right as any other American to train, to serve, and to fight . . . in defense of the United States." Hastie's successor as civilian aide on Negro affairs to the secretary of war, Truman Gibson, underscored Fish's message by noting that the Republicans clearly intended to make black participation in combat an issue in the coming presidential campaign.[84]

Malone, 4 Dec 89; Cash with McClary, 9 Sep 88; Walter Scott, 10 Sep 88; Booker T. Washington, 6 Jan 90. See also Scipio, *Last of the Black Regulars*, pp. 74f; Nalty, *Strength for the Fight*, p. 167.

[81] M. Sgt. Claude Breitenbach is quoted in Scipio, *Last of the Black Regulars*, p. 71. See also Intervs, Rainey with Malone, 4 Dec 89; Cash with McClary, 9 Sep 88; Scott, 10 Sep 88; Washington, 6 Jan 90.

[82] Interv, Rainey with Malone, 4 Dec 89; Scipio, *Last of the Black Regulars*, pp. 70–78.

[83] Ibid.

[84] Quote from U.S. Congress, House, "Colored Troops in Combat," *Congressional Record*, 78th Cong., 2d sess., 23 February 1944, pp. 2007–08. See also Nalty, *Strength for the Fight*, p. 168.

The failure to make full use of black troops had critics within the Army as well. They noted that the practice wasted valuable manpower and exposed the service to unnecessary criticism. Repeated studies of black units meanwhile brought forward not only the usual criticisms levied against black troops but also praise from some frontline commanders. Those officers made the point that members of all-black units in dangerous forward areas had won medals. One air base security battalion at the Faid Pass in North Africa had held its ground even when a white organization had panicked and fled to the rear, abandoning most of its equipment in the process.[85]

The pressure had its effect. Under instructions from the War Department, commanders in the Pacific relieved the 1st Battalion of the 24th of its duties as a service element and attached it to the 37th Infantry Division fighting on the island of Bougainville. On 11 March 1944, the battalion transferred to the operational control of the 148th Infantry regiment, which immediately moved Company B forward to reinforce units in contact with the Japanese. Coming under enemy attack that very evening, the company held its ground, but at the cost of two men killed. Those soldiers, Pfc. Leonard Brooks and Pvt. Annias Jolly, appear to have been the first black infantrymen and the first members of the 24th to be killed by enemy grenade and rifle fire in World War II. Despite the fumbling that usually occurs when inexperienced units of any race first enter combat, the battalion continued to hold its own in the fighting that followed, sending out patrols and suffering more casualties.[86]

The 24th took up station on the islands of Saipan and Tinian during December 1944, supposedly to perform routine garrison duty. The islands, however, concealed many Japanese holdouts. Entering combat, the unit became so adept at the often bloody process of cleaning out pockets of enemy resistance that a visiting inspector general team commended it for its diligence to the deputy chief of staff of the Army. "The conduct of the 24th Infantry as observed on Saipan

was so meritorious as to be deemed worthy of special mention," the team reported in April 1945.

Upon arrival at Saipan, the 24th Infantry regiment was given the task of clearing the island of all Japanese not previously subjugated. Since then, this regiment is credited with having killed or captured an impressive number of the enemy, and even today is engaged in continuous patrolling and jungle fighting. The morale of this regiment is high, its discipline is excellent and it has definitely demonstrated what can be accomplished with negro soldiers under the leadership of competent officers and noncommissioned officers.[87]

The team made it a point to note that the regimental commander, Col. Julian G. Hearne, Jr., had been with the regiment for four years and had advanced from battalion to regimental command during that time. In addition, a dozen or more noncommissioned officers had been with the regiment since before the war and had taken pains to maintain the unit's customs and traditions.[88] Following the lead of the inspector general's team, the commander of U.S. Army Forces, Pacific Ocean Areas, Lt. Gen. Robert C. Richardson, commended the men of the 24th for their "military proficiency" and their "unwavering devotion to duty" during the fighting on Saipan.[89]

With Saipan and Tinian in U.S. hands by July 1945, the 24th proceeded to the island of Okinawa for another clearing operation. The war ended one month later. Although relegated to routine tasks for much of World War II, the men of the 24th had managed nonetheless to show their mettle by succeeding in the difficult job of eliminating, one by one, die-hard enemy resisters determined to perish to the last man.

If the 24th gained a measure of distinction in the war, other black units were embroiled in controversy almost from the moment they entered combat.

[85] Lee, *The Employment of Negro Troops*, pp. 456–58, 468–72.

[86] Scipio, *Last of the Black Regulars*, p. 75.

[87] Memo, Maj Gen Virgil L. Peterson, Actg Inspector General (IG), for Deputy Chief of Staff, 14 May 45, sub: Exemplary Conduct of the 24th Infantry at Saipan, in MacGregor and Nalty, *Blacks in the United States Armed Forces*, vol. 5, item 95.

[88] Lee, *The Employment of Negro Troops*, pp. 533–35.

[89] Commendation, Commanding General, U.S. Army Forces, Pacific Ocean Areas, n.d. [1945], reprinted in Scipio, *Last of the Black Regulars*, p. 128.

Serving as part of the 93d Division, the 25th Infantry, for one, fought well on Bougainville, but portions of one of its companies, untried in combat, became overly alarmed during an early engagement. In the wild firing that followed, a black lieutenant and nine enlisted men were killed and twenty enlisted men wounded, mostly by friendly fire.[90]

The event was the sort of thing that might have happened to green troops of any race freshly committed to combat in the jungle, but it took on racial overtones when a rumor spread throughout the Pacific theater that the 93d Division itself had broken under fire. General of the Army Douglas MacArthur told *New York Post* correspondent Walter White that the report was "false and ridiculous." He added that he knew "from experience with the 25th Infantry and the Filipino Army . . . that race and color have nothing whatever to do with fighting ability."[91] The slander nevertheless endured. Four years later, the wartime chief of staff, General George C. Marshall, repeated it, erroneously asserting in an interview that the men of the 93d on Bougainville "wouldn't fight—couldn't get them out of the caves to fight."[92]

The all-black 92d Infantry Division in Italy also became the subject of contention. Fighting along the Gothic Line, a series of German fortifications that stretched across the Italian boot from La Spezia north of Florence to Pesaro on the Adriatic, the unit lost momentum and bogged down.[93] Failures to communicate, badly organized attacks, and missing officers were often the reason. The men of the unit fought at times with extreme courage; one group held off eight German counterattacks before using up its ammunition and finally withdrawing. Still, whole platoons occasionally refused to advance out of confusion, on account of conflicting orders, or due to lack of motivation.[94]

The division's commander and his staff tended to impute the problems the unit experienced to supposed characteristics of the black race. "During my period of observation," a regimental executive officer for six months, Lt. Col. John J. Phelan, declared, "I heard of just as many acts of individual heroism among Negro troops as among white. . . . On the other hand, the tendency to mass hysteria or panic is much more prevalent among colored troops."[95] The blacks, meanwhile, blamed their white officers, asserting that their commander, Maj. Gen. Edward M. Almond, was so prejudiced against them that he wanted them to fail to discredit their race.[96]

In fact, as Truman Gibson noted after an inspection of the unit in 1945, the system imposed by segregation was itself a major cause of what had happened. The 92d possessed two commands, Gibson said, one black and junior, the other white and senior. The blacks seethed at promotion policies that excluded them from higher rank. The whites, meanwhile, avoided close association with the blacks whenever they could. The lack of mutual confidence between the two groups made little difference while the 92d was in training and transit, but it became apparent under the strains of combat. White commanders could hardly hide their lack of reliance on the abilities of their subordinates. Black soldiers who perceived that attitude came to place more emphasis upon personal survival than success in battle.[97]

Toward the end of the war, social scientists from the Research Branch of the Army's

---

[90]Lee, *The Employment of Negro Troops*, pp. 506–12.

[91]White paraphrases MacArthur. His article appeared in the *New York Post* during the week of 26 March 1945 and was widely reprinted in the black press. It is quoted by Lee, *The Employment of Negro Troops*, p. 531.

[92]The Marshall interview occurred on 25 July 1949. It is quoted by Lee, *The Employment of Negro Troops*, fn. 35, p. 512.

[93]For combat operations of the division, see Thomas St. John Arnold, *Buffalo Soldiers: The 92nd Infantry Division and Reinforcements in World War II, 1942–1945* (Manhattan, Kans.: Sunflower University Press, 1990), and MS, Hunter and Clark, The Buffalo Division in World War II.

[94]Lee, *The Employment of Negro Troops*, pp. 548–51.

[95]Phelan is quoted in Lee, *The Employment of Negro Troops*, p. 549.

[96]Ibid., p. 577.

[97]Memo, Truman K. Gibson, Jr., Civilian Aide to the Secretary of War, for John J. McCloy, Asst Secretary of War, 20 Dec 44, in MacGregor and Nalty, *Blacks in the United States Armed Forces*, vol. 5, item 94; Lee, *The Employment of Negro Troops*, pp. 576f. The role of the 92d's leadership in the unit's problems is examined in Dale E. Wilson, "Recipe for Failure: Major General Edward N. Almond and Preparation of the U.S. 92d Infantry Division for Combat in World War II," *Journal of Military History* 56 (July 1992): 487.

Information and Education Division did a survey of the attitudes and motivation of black soldiers that added further dimensions to Gibson's perception. They found that although blacks shared the patriotic attitudes of whites when the United States entered the conflict, those concerns and aspirations were offset at least partially by bitterness about the treatment they received at the hands of their countrymen and by resentment toward the Army's racial policies. Given their mixed feelings, they came to be less likely than whites to express a desire for action in combat. Although convinced that they were making a valuable contribution to the war and proud of the units they served, 71 percent of those interviewed thus preferred to do their duty in a stateside unit, versus 54 percent of a carefully matched sampling of whites. Overall, the researchers asserted in their final report, black soldiers tended to perceive the world in racial terms, as members of an oppressed minority. In that sense, if some were eager to fight because they believed their sacrifices would benefit their race, many more were concerned about the black community's lack of progress at home.[98]

Having little status to lose in black society for a failure to conform to white norms, they doubted that they would acquire much of benefit for themselves or for their race if they performed well in combat. The United States had always been a white man's country, so the reasoning went, and it would remain one after the war had ended. By conforming to white expectations, blacks would do little more than maintain the status quo. "It seems to me," a black lieutenant in the 92d's 365th Infantry regiment, Wade McCree, Jr., observed, "you cannot treat people as second-class citizens or second-class soldiers and expect them to behave in a first-class fashion, partic-ularly when they are ambivalent about the mission they are called upon to perform and can't relate it to the success of the larger enterprise."[99]

Many members of the 92d fought well, but that very fact also told against the unit. Outstanding black officers and NCOs became casualties quickly while less effective men who took fewer chances tended to survive and rise to positions of authority. Commanders of white units had the ability to move outside of their own organizations to find suitable replacements. The 92d had to look mainly to itself, especially for the experienced black officers who could inspire the troops, because there were none to be had in nearby units. The Army's limited ability to supply black enlisted replacements added a further dimension to the problem. Already hampered by the poor education that inferior "separate but equal" schools in the United States had dealt the black soldier, the division often had to settle for men who were psychologically unfit for combat, had gone AWOL from the Army's East Coast Processing Center, or were former inmates of disciplinary facilities. Those individuals did not do well in combat.[100]

Reasoning that the press already knew of the 92d's failure but had little inkling of why it had happened, Gibson held a press conference in Rome to put the division's experience into context. His candid remarks were replayed throughout the United States, where the press laid heavy emphasis on comments he had made about low literacy rates

---

[98] See Samuel A. Stouffer et al., *The American Soldier: Adjustment During Army Life* (Princeton: Princeton University Press, 1949), pp. 507, 521, 526–27, 587; MS, Bell Wiley, The Training of Negro Troops, Study 36 [Washington, D.C.: U.S. Army, Historical Section, Army Ground Forces, 1946], p. 12. For a more complete treatment of the issue, see Joyce Thomas, "The 'Double V' Was for Victory: Black Soldiers, the Black Protest, and World War II" (Ph.D. diss., Ohio State University, 1993), pp. 22–26.

[99] Ibid. For the views of African-Americans serving in the armed forces, see Phillip McGuire, *Taps for a Jim Crow Army: Letters From Black Soldiers in World War II* (Lexington: University of Kentucky Press, 1993). McCree, who later graduated from Harvard Law School and became a circuit court judge, is quoted in Mary Penick Motley, *The Invisible Soldier: The Experience of the Black Soldier, World War II* (Detroit: Wayne State University Press, 1975), p. 304.

[100] Lee, *The Employment of Negro Troops*, p. 552. In a detailed study of the 92d Division during World War II, Jehu Hunter and Major Clark point out that the unit achieved more than might have been expected, given the Army's attitude and the personnel policies it followed. See MS, Hunter and Clark, The Buffalo Division in World War II, pp. 2, 95–97. Mary Penick Motley uses a series of telling interviews with veterans of the division to make many of the same points. Motley, *The Invisible Soldier*, pp. 258–347.

among black soldiers and a supposed assertion that some units had "melted away" in combat.[101]

Gibson later denied he had ever said that units of the 92d had "melted away." Instead, he said he had merely confirmed that individuals in some units had retreated in a panicky fashion, a fact well known to all newspapermen in the theater, including those who worked for the African-American press. He continued that some of the information he had supplied to reporters as background had never made it into print. He had pointed out, for example, both in his press conference and later at the War Department, that segregation as a policy would "inevitably produce militarily unsound results." He had then contrasted the educational level of the men of the 92d with that of white divisions, adding that the Army applied one standard to white units and quite another to black units. "I further pointed out that military authorities repeatedly stated that no units could efficiently operate which consisted of more than 10 percent class 5 men. The 92nd Division included more than 80 percent class 5 troops. The investigation further revealed and I therefore stated that because only Negro replacements could be furnished to the 92nd Division, untrained service troops had been rushed into combat while trained infantry replacements were made available to white units." Collins George, a black war correspondent for the *Pittsburgh Courier* who was present at the news conference, later confirmed Gibson's story. He blamed the episode on an inept substitute reporter who attended the session in place of the regular correspondent for *Stars and Stripes*.[102]

Gibson's remarks were well founded, but since no other division in the entire European theater had been singled out for such criticism, the black press took umbrage and began to call for the counselor's resignation. "If the 92nd is made of . . . illiterates and near-illiterates, whose fault is it?" the *Crisis* asked.

Certainly not the Negroes. . . . Why would the War Department, if it really wanted to give a fair test, send a division into the front lines with 92 out of every 100 men in the two lowest classifications? The 92d was licked before it started.

It must be remembered that these men [during their training] were beaten up by bus drivers, shot up by military and civilian police, insulted by their white officers, denied transportation to and from the post, restricted to certain post exchanges, and jim crowed in post theaters.[103]

Gibson had defenders, especially among black journals that employed correspondents in the field who had long known of the 92d's problems, but he was still stunned by the reaction. Returning to Washington, he remarked in an interview, "It is hard for me to see how some people can, on the one hand, argue that segregation is wrong, and on the other hand, blindly defend the product of that segregation."[104]

If many white military men found support in the performance of all-black units for their contention that African-Americans were best suited only for service in labor battalions, evidence backing a different set of conclusions emerged in the winter of 1944–1945, after the Battle of the Bulge. At that time, the Army experienced a severe shortage of infantry replacements. In order to fill the gap, suggestions arose that U.S. commanders integrate black volunteers into any unit that needed them, without regard to race. The U.S. commander in the European theater, General Dwight D. Eisenhower, resisted the suggestion on the grounds that it was contrary to War Department policy. He agreed, however, to form black volunteers into platoons that could be attached to white units.[105]

---

[101]See "A Behavior Pattern," *Newsweek*, 26 Mar 45, p. 37.

[102]Gibson is quoted in Lee Nichols, *Breakthrough on the Color Front* (New York: Random House, 1954), pp. 12–13. The interview with Collins George is in Motley, *The Invisible Soldier*, pp. 345–46.

[103]The *Crisis* 52 (April 1945): 97, quoted by A. Russell Buchanan, *Black Americans in World War II* (Santa Barbara, Calif.: Clio Books, 1979), p. 97.

[104]The newspapers and Gibson are quoted in Lee, *The Employment of Negro Troops*, pp. 579–80.

[105]Lee, *The Employment of Negro Troops*, pp. 689–95; Dalfiume, *Desegregation of the U.S. Armed Forces*, pp. 99–101. See also Russell F. Weigley, *Eisenhower's Lieutenants* (Bloomington: Indiana University Press, 1981), pp. 229–31, 960–63.

The experiment succeeded beyond the most optimistic expectations. In surveys completed shortly after the war ended, a majority of whites who had fought alongside the blacks approved of the platoons' performance in combat, with the highest ratings coming from officers in companies where blacks had seen the hardest fighting. Some whites argued that the men were volunteers and therefore more willing to fight than the normal black soldier, but others contended that "an average of Negroes would probably do as well as the average of white soldiers." Both officers and enlisted men reported that blacks and whites got along well together, and 77 percent of whites reported that their feelings had become more favorable as a result of the experience. Many whites observed that relationships among the men were better in combat than in garrison, but they could cite few if any instances of overt friction. Overall, blacks and whites got along so well in the mixed units that 96 percent of the officers interviewed pronounced themselves agreeably surprised.[106]

General Davis and others within the Army who advocated an end to segregation sought to have the results of the survey released to the public to show that the integration of whites and blacks could succeed. Nonetheless, the Army held back, apparently in the belief that publication would threaten support for a peacetime draft on the part of southerners in Congress. As soon as the war ended the platoons were disbanded, with their men transferring to service battalions or returning home for discharge.[107]

So had it been over all the years of American history. Time and again, the black soldier had demonstrated that he could fight well when given a fair chance, but after every war racial prejudice had intervened to erase the gains he and his race should have received. The experience of the 24th Infantry was a case in point. The unit accomplished as much as any white regiment fighting under similar circumstances on the American frontier, during the Spanish-American War, and in World War II. Yet few white officers paid any attention. Official surveys and analyses set aside the accomplishments of the black soldier in those wars to concentrate on the failures of black units and the supposed infirmities of the African race. No one admitted to the injustices at the root of the problem or to the fact that people denied even routine opportunities for education and advancement had little incentive to give their lives for the system that had failed them. It would take another war for that to occur, and even then the advance would come reluctantly, after racial prejudice had once more taken a heavy toll.

106 Stouffer et al., *The American Soldier: Adjustment During Army Life*, pp. 587–90.

107 Ibid., p. 593; Dalfiume, *Desegregation of the U.S. Armed Forces*, p. 100.

CHAPTER 2

Turbulence and Reappraisal, 1945–1950

At the end of World War II, the U.S. Army consisted of 8,268,000 men organized into 89 divisions. Of that number, 694,333 were black. They constituted 8.5 percent of the Army's ground force strength and 9.5 percent of its enlisted ranks. Most worked in combat service support units as stevedores, truck drivers, wiremen, cooks, and mess men.[1]

Over the years that followed, as the American public clamored for budget cuts and the United States readjusted its priorities to fit a peacetime economy, military strength and readiness fell. The Army shrank to 1,891,000 men in 1946; to 991,999 in 1947, when Congress permitted the draft law to expire; and to 554,000 in 1948. The total climbed to 660,000 in 1949, when a peacetime conscription law temporarily spurred enlistments. But on 30 June 1950, at the brink of the Korean War, Army commanders could count only 591,000 men in uniform. Of those, 1,317 officers and 56,446 enlisted men were black—9.8 percent of ground force strength and 10.9 percent of all enlisted ranks. Most still served in support units.[2]

The combat readiness of the troops during the period of heaviest drawdown, between 1946 and 1947, was marginal at best. In those years, the Army's regiments and divisions became for all practical purposes demobilization centers whose strength fluctuated wildly from month to month as veterans of the war and recent draftees arrived, took up temporary residence, and then either departed for home or to some new station. The 24th Infantry provides a case in point. Numbering 152 officers and 3,053 enlisted men at the height of World War II in 1944, its strength declined to just 82 officers and 384 enlisted men by April 1946. The numbers then began to increase as the Army prepared the unit for service as part of the U.S. occupation force in Japan. By 31 January 1947, it totaled 104 officers and 3,271 enlisted men. During the months that followed, many of the men were transferred to higher priority service units in Japan and others completed their terms of enlistment. By 31 December the unit once more comprised fewer than one thousand enlisted men.[3] (*Table 1*) So precipitous was the nation's demobilization, President Harry S. Truman would later

---

[1] Office of the Adjutant General of the Army, STM–30, Strength of the Army (hereafter cited as STM–30), 30 Jun 50, CMH files.

[2] STM–30, 30 Jun 50. See also Eliot A. Cohen, *Citizens and Soldiers* (Ithaca, N.Y., and London: Cornell University Press, 1985), pp. 154–55. This chapter is deeply indebted to the work of Morris J. MacGregor, Jr., in *The Integration of the*

Armed Forces, 1940–1965, Defense Studies series (Washington, D.C.: U.S. Army Center of Military History, Government Printing Office, 1989).

[3] HQ, 24th Inf Rgt, Annual Histories of the 24th Infantry Regiment for 1946, 1947 (hereafter cited as Annual Hist of the 24th Inf Rgt), 2 Mar 48, copy in CMH files.

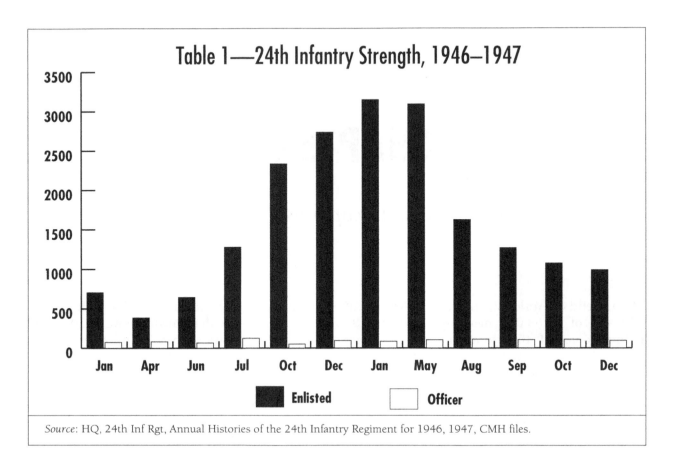

Table 1—24th Infantry Strength, 1946–1947

Legend: ■ Enlisted   □ Officer

Source: HQ, 24th Inf Rgt, Annual Histories of the 24th Infantry Regiment for 1946, 1947, CMH files.

remark, that it hardly seemed a demobilization at all. "It was disintegration."[4]

As reductions continued, the Army ransacked its forces around the world not only to provide troops for the occupation of Germany and Japan but also to build up a reserve in the United States. As a result, by 1948 all but a few of the regiments stationed in Japan and other theaters of occupation fielded two rather than the usual three battalions. Similarly, artillery battalions had two firing batteries rather than three, and active infantry battalions carried two rather than three line companies. Despite those economies, the number of men available was so uncertain that the units designated to enter combat first if an emergency occurred, in theory the most battle-ready forces within the Army,

could conduct company or battalion-size field exercises only by drawing all of their regimental personnel into a single unit.[5]

[4] Truman is quoted by David McCullough, *Truman* (New York: Simon & Schuster, 1992), p. 474.

[5] *Annual Report of the Secretary of the Army, 1947* (Washington, D.C.: Government Printing Office, 1948), p. 35. All secretary of the Army annual reports are hereafter cited as *Annual Report of the Secretary of the Army* with the pertinent year. See also Lt Col Joseph Rockis, Reorganization of the Army Ground Forces During the Demobilization Period, Army Ground Forces Study 3 [1948], pp. 36–52, CMH files; Working Paper, William W. Epley, Demobilization and Rebuilding of the Army, 1945–1950 [U.S. Army Center of Military History, 1992], pp. 1–3, CMH files; Russell F. Weigley, *History of the U.S. Army* (New York: MacMillan, 1967), p. 503; Maurice Matloff, general editor, *American Military History* (Washington, D.C.: U.S. Army Center of Military History, Government Printing Office, 1989), pp. 528–42; James F. Schnabel, *Policy and Direction: The First Year*, United States Army in the Korean War (Washington, D.C.: U.S. Army Center of Military History, 1972), pp. 42–46.

Hard put to supply replacements for the many units requiring them, the Army slashed basic training for new recruits from the seventeen weeks it had observed during World War II to just eight in 1946. It increased the term to fourteen weeks in March 1949, when pressures decreased, but in the interim soldiers arrived at their duty stations around the world with only the barest knowledge of military life and little practical feel for the duties they were about to undertake. By 1950 cutbacks were again having an effect. Officers commissioned that year, even those who graduated from the U.S. Military Academy at West Point, went to their duty assignments without spending an interval at the schools for their designated specialties, as had been the custom in earlier years.[6]

With policymakers convinced that the atomic bomb was America's main defense and that little chance remained within the foreseeable future for a major war involving the Army, budget cutters also reduced military funding for personnel and equipment. The development of new conventional weapons thus lagged, and projects only remotely connected with traditional military concerns gained prominence. During 1948 and 1949, as a result, units in the field made do with materiel left over from World War II, much of it in increasing disrepair because of replacement part shortages and a lack of trained maintenance specialists. Meanwhile, the Army diverted major portions of its procurement budget to Marshall Plan programs designed to stabilize postwar Europe.[7]

As the armed forces demobilized, blacks tended to remain in uniform. Many had less combat time than whites and therefore lower eligibility for discharge. Others feared reentry into a hostile society and preferred the security that even segregated military life provided. A number, poorly educated by white standards, lacked the ability to compete for the opportunities postwar America offered. While younger, better-educated blacks often left the Army to take a place in that new world, those less skilled tended to reenlist.[8]

If the Army seemed a refuge for some, life in its segregated system still irritated many. Racial incidents proliferated during the years following the war, both in the United States and overseas. Indeed, the Eighth Army reported in 1946 that "racial agitation" was one of the primary causes of assaults, the most frequent violent crimes among American troops in Japan.[9]

The turbulence brought on by the rapid decrease in the Army's size, along with the freedom and expanded leisure time soldiers experienced with the coming of peace, created additional stresses. According to official statistics, black soldiers were court-martialed and punished out of all proportion to their percentage in the Army's population. In 1945, for example, when blacks were 8.5 percent of the Army's average strength, 17.3 percent of the soldiers entering rehabilitation centers, disciplinary barracks, and federal penal institutions were black. In 1946, with 9.35 percent of the Army composed of blacks, 25.9 percent of the soldiers confined in military stockades were black. They committed 49.6 percent of reported offenses against senior officers, 17.4 percent of desertions, 13.4 percent of rapes, 33.1 percent of robberies, 46.3 percent of acts of manslaughter, 29 percent of burglaries, and 59 percent of assaults. In Europe, blacks had a court-martial rate of 3.48 per thousand compared to 1.14 for whites. In the Far East, black service units suffered a court-martial rate nearly double that of the Eighth Army as a whole.[10]

Although those statistics seem straightforward, their meaning is open to question. On one hand, during the early postwar period most black soldiers were assigned to service units which, because of their locations, the nature of their duties, and

[6] Weigley, *History of the U.S. Army*, p. 504; Epley, Demobilization and Rebuilding of the Army, pp. 2, 10; Schnabel, *Policy and Direction*, p. 45.

[7] Weigley, *History of the U.S. Army*, pp. 502f; Epley, Demobilization and Rebuilding of the Army, p. 9. Diversions of Army funds to the Marshall Plan are mentioned in *Annual Report of the Secretary of the Army, 1949*, p. 155.

[8] MacGregor, *Integration of the Armed Forces*, p. 154.

[9] U.S. Eighth Army, Occupational Monograph of the Eighth Army in Japan, January–August 1946, vol. 2, p. 176, CMH files.

[10] The statistics are cited in MacGregor, *Integration of the Armed Forces*, pp. 206–09.

relaxed discipline, provided more of an opportunity for troublemaking and wrongdoing than other units. On the other, commanders defined the offenses, and they possessed great latitude in the framing of charges. In that sense, the heavy weighting of crime statistics toward black offenders might have been the result of racial prejudice. Where one commander could have viewed the facts of a case narrowly and might have accused a black of aggravated assault, another, dealing with an identical set of circumstances, might have charged a white lawbreaker with a lesser offense.[11]

A review of statistics contrasting civilian with military crime rates on the basis of race might provide some insight, especially since 1946 was the worst year in the decade between 1941 and 1950 for crime in the United States. Comparisons are nonetheless difficult to make. Except for federal statutes, which apply primarily to offenses committed on government property, no single body of criminal law or procedure covers the United States as a whole. As for state and local laws, their definitions of what constitutes a particular crime may vary between jurisdictions and may sometimes differ from those that apply to military offenses.[12]

The problems blacks faced become evident, however, in an analysis of the high incidence of venereal disease (VD) that occurred among U.S. troops serving in Europe and Japan at the end of the war. As was the case with crime, the statistics for blacks far exceeded those for whites.[13] In that light, it was easy for some commanders to conclude that blacks as a group were less sexually inhibited than whites. In fact, as a study done by the Army's Preventive Medicine Section in 1945 demonstrated, the situation was far more complicated.[14] The study's author, Samuel Stouffer, observed that since men with the lowest educational levels experienced the highest percentage of cases, a lack of education among blacks was probably involved. He did not give that consideration heavy weight, however, because the Army had taken pains to indoctrinate blacks on the danger of VD, and tests indicated that they were as aware as whites of the prophylactic measures necessary to avoid infection. More important appeared to be the locations of black units and the sort of women available to black soldiers. Many African-Americans were assigned to port facilities located in areas populated by large numbers of prostitutes. Others served in transportation companies, where they frequently performed their duties without close supervision. In both cases, sexual inhibitions were not what mattered. Blacks simply had more opportunities for sexual contact and were thus more likely to contract the disease than whites, who were based more often in desirable areas and in touch with a higher class of women.[15]

---

[11] Ibid., pp. 206f.

[12] During 1946, 745,282 major crimes—including murder, nonnegligent manslaughter, rape, aggravated assault, and burglary—were known to have occurred in the 353 U.S. cities inhabited by 25,000 persons or more. Over that year, federal statistics show that some 645,000 people were arrested, of whom 478,000 were white and 159,000 were black. Although the numbers seem impressive, the two indices have only a tenuous relationship to one another because the arrest figures involve detentions not only for major offenses but also for minor infractions such as drunkenness and vagrancy. In addition, although the arrest statistics provide a useful index to racial involvement in crime, they are burdened by detentions for crimes such as disorderly conduct that are easy to solve. They also fail to equal the number of individuals actually taken into custody. Instead they note each separate occasion in which a person was detained, notified, or cited without accounting for the fact that an individual may be arrested several times during the course of a year on different charges. See U.S. Department of Commerce, Bureau of the Census, *Historical Statistics of the United States, Colonial Times to 1970* (Washington, D.C.: U.S. Department of Commerce, 1975), pt. 1, ch. H, Crime and Correction (ser. H 952–1170), pp. 407–09.

The figures are from ibid., Table, Urban Crime by Type of Major Offense: 1937 to 1957, p. 413. See also ibid., Table, Persons Arrested by Race, Sex, and Age: 1932 to 1970, p. 415.

[13] HQ, U.S. Eighth Army, Japan, Occupational Monograph of the Eighth U.S. Army in Japan, September 1946–December 1947, vol. 3, p. 171, CMH files. The figures for Europe are in MacGregor, *Integration of the Armed Forces*, p. 209.

[14] HQ, U.S. Eighth Army, Japan, Occupational Monograph of the Eighth U.S. Army in Japan, September 1946–December 1947, vol. 3, pp. 172–73.

[15] For a more extended treatment, see Stouffer et al., *The American Soldier: Adjustment During Army Life*, pp. 545–49. Testimony to the general validity of the study appears in the fact that when the incidence of VD reported by the men in the sample for themselves was projected against that of the

A delegation of black newspaper publishers toured U.S. military installations in Europe during 1946. Its conclusions also show that the behavior problems black units experienced had more to do with the circumstances in which African-Americans found themselves and the corrosive effects of racial prejudice than with the race of the men. If discipline lagged in all-black military organizations, the editors told the secretary of war in their final report, they could readily attribute the problem to poor camp locations, inadequate recreation facilities, hostile military policemen, the lack of education of many black soldiers, inexperienced noncommissioned officers, the Army's failure to commission enough black officers, and the fact that new recruits often arrived in Europe without basic training. The discriminatory practices the Army condoned only added to the problem, the publishers said, by promoting racial prejudice among whites and corresponding disaffection among blacks. The system's effects were readily apparent in the resentment and poor morale of black regulars. Although proud of their service in combat, those soldiers believed they had gained little for their sacrifices during the war. As soon as the conflict had ended, they had been relegated once more to the menial tasks that had seemed the lot of their race. The publishers concluded that the Army would experience difficulties with its black soldiers until racial discrimination ended.[16]

Army leaders themselves had long been concerned about how best to employ blacks in the postwar years. Two weeks after the war ended in Europe, the War Department issued questionnaires to determine how commanders had employed their black troops and to ascertain their recommendations for the future. The responses that returned were largely unfavorable. The officers conceded that small black units had fought well during the last months of the war, when platoons of black volunteers had seen action in combination with larger, all-white forces. But most characterized the black soldier, officer or enlisted, as unreliable, ineffective, and difficult to train. They understood that racial discrimination contributed to poor morale among black troops, but they viewed segregation as a given and were concerned mainly that turbulence might result if the Army stepped too far ahead of American society as a whole. For the sake of efficiency, they said, the Army might reduce the size of its all-black units and fill them with better qualified men. Even so, it should retain the practice of appointing whites to positions of command.[17]

There were dissents. Col. Noel Parrish, the former commander of the Army Air Field at Tuskegee, Alabama, where the all-black 99th Fighter Squadron had trained, pointed out in August 1945 that if the Army dealt with blacks as a group they would come to think and react as a group. Over time, group feeling and spirit would prevail, even when it was contrary to national feeling and spirit. In that case, criticism of one soldier would tend to become criticism of all. Such fierce resentment might result that "even the boldest commander will not dare criticize his troops or their performance if they happen to be colored." The best policy, Parrish said, was one that looked forward to the end of segregation and that took measured but definite steps toward treatment of blacks as individuals.[18]

Lost in the chorus of complaints about black soldiers, Parrish's comments had no effect. Of greater impact was a discovery by the Army later in the year that the percentage of nonwhites within its ranks was increasing and might well reach 15 percent by 1947. Given the lack of education of many blacks and the resulting possibility that a large proportion of the Army's future enlisted strength might be unskilled and difficult to train, Chief of Staff of the Army General George C. Marshall, at the direc-

---

Mediterranean theater as a whole it matched known rates among whites and blacks almost exactly. See also Lee, *The Employment of Negro Troops*, pp. 278f.

[16] Frank L. Stanley, Report of the Negro Newspaper Publishers Association to the Honorable Secretary of War on Troops and Conditions in Europe, 18 Jul 46, CMH files; MacGregor, *Integration of the Armed Forces*, pp. 209–11.

[17] MacGregor, *Integration of the Armed Forces*, pp. 130–43.

[18] Ltr, Col Noel Parrish to Brig Gen William E. Hall, Deputy Asst Chief of Air Staff, Personnel, United States Army Air Force (USAAF), 5 Aug 45, in MacGregor and Nalty, *Blacks in the United States Armed Forces*, vol. 7, item 19.

tion of Secretary of War Robert P. Patterson, appointed a board of inquiry to study what should be done. Convened during October 1945 under the direction of Lt. Gen. Alvan C. Gillem, Jr., a Tennessean who had risen through the ranks to command a corps in Europe during the war, the panel was to prepare a policy to achieve the best possible use of black manpower if some national emergency occurred.[19]

The board's members recognized that racial discrimination harmed the morale of the black soldier and avowed that the Army should "eliminate at the earliest practicable moment, any special consideration based on race." Even so, the system they proposed left the Army's practice of segregation largely undisturbed. In their draft recommendation to the chief of staff, they proposed that black soldiers should work side by side with whites, perform the same kind of duties in the same units, and compete with whites on an equal basis. But blacks should still live and eat in separate barracks and messes. In the same way, the Army should abolish all-black division-size units in the postwar period but retain smaller segregated units of up to regimental size that could be grouped with larger white organizations.[20]

The board's other recommendations were similarly pragmatic. Warning that the Army should refrain from experimenting in areas that threatened "the disruption of civilian racial relationships," the panel indicated that blacks should have the opportunity to enter a broader selection of military occupations than in the past. Nevertheless, the Army should adopt a quota system to ensure that the ratio of black to white manpower in the civilian population became the accepted proportion of blacks to whites in its own ranks. Although all officers, regardless of race, should meet the same standards and enjoy equal opportunity for advancement and black officers should command black

Truman Gibson

units, the board made no mention of the custom of restricting black officers to service in black units, a practice that sorely inhibited their ability to compete with whites.[21]

The civilian aide on Negro affairs to the secretary of war, Truman Gibson, and the assistant secretary of war, John McCloy, both considered the report an advance but also saw flaws. Gibson believed that the Army had begun a process that would weaken racism and lead inevitably to the end of segregation. If he was willing to settle for less than total integration as an interim measure, however, he asserted that the report was too vague and that it needed a clear statement on the basic issue of segregation.[22]

[19] MacGregor, *Integration of the Armed Forces*, p. 153.

[20] Memo, General Gillem for Chief of Staff, 17 Nov 45, sub: Report of Board of General Officers on the Utilization of Negro Manpower in the Post-War Army, Chief of Staff of the Army, 291.2, War Department Records, National Archives and Records Administration (NARA), Washington, D.C.

[21] Ibid. For a full description and analysis of the board's recommendations, see MacGregor, *Integration of the Armed Forces*, pp. 152–205.

[22] MacGregor, *Integration of the Armed Forces*, pp. 159–60. See also Nalty, *Strength for the Fight*, pp. 215–16.

TURBULENCE AND REAPPRAISAL, 1945–1950

McCloy agreed—experience had shown that it was impossible to enforce policies that allowed for any measure of misinterpretation. If the board wanted black officers to command whites or if it believed the Army should try mixed units, it should say so. McCloy continued that the panel clearly wanted the Army to take advantage of recent advances in black education by suggesting that the service deny reenlistment to blacks who failed to meet minimum educational criteria. What it gave with one hand, however, it took away with the other by imposing the quota. Since poorly educated and skilled careerists would inevitably occupy many positions approved for blacks under the system, a large number of highly qualified young blacks would never have a chance to enlist.[23]

If McCloy and Gibson criticized the board's report for its imprecision, others approved of it for that very reason. It committed them to little and left existing institutions largely intact. The assistant chief of staff for organization and training, Maj. Gen. Idwal H. Edwards, thus concurred with the report's recommendations but immediately began to backpedal by warning that the Army, in attempting to use black manpower, had to pay due attention to the "ineptitude and limited capacity of the Negro soldier." The chief of the General Staff's Operations Division, Lt. Gen. John E. Hull, warned that even if black and white officers should be subjected to the same standards, no black should have command of white troops. The deputy commander of the Army Air Forces, Lt. Gen. Ira C. Eaker, agreed with the board that the Army should never become "a testing ground for problems in race relationships." The headquarters of the Army Ground Forces approved the report but suggested that the Army should not act alone. Instead, the War Department should frame a policy applicable to the entire military establishment. The acting commanding general of Army Service Forces, Maj. Gen. Daniel Noce, meanwhile reported that his organization had already successfully employed a larger percentage of blacks than the board contemplated. Nevertheless, he said, the War Department should

refrain from dictating how commanders used their men since that would infringe upon the legitimate right of officers in the field to select and assign personnel as the demands of war might require.[24]

In the end, the Gillem Board stood by its report but added a number of clarifications that did little more than compromise the message it had hoped to send. While asserting that the Army's ultimate objective should be the effective use of all available manpower "without regard to antecedents or race," it refused to set a timetable or any intermediate goal "beyond the utilization of the proportionate ratio" it had set. In the same way, if black units eventually ought to fall under the command of black officers, the Army did not need to assign black commanders to white units. As for the quota, it was necessary for planning purposes and suitable for the moment but could always be altered in the future.[25]

The War Department accepted the Gillem Board's recommendations in April 1946, but only superficial changes resulted. Black enlisted men began to enter many military occupational fields; black infantry and artillery battalions were incorporated into formerly all-white regiments and divisions; and the Army began an attempt to recruit more black officers while replacing white officers in all-black units. Even so, racial prejudice remained a compelling feature of military life. Although the Army was going to put black battalions in white divisions, the commanding general of Army Ground Forces, General Jacob L. Devers, told his staff, when notified in 1946 to begin incorporating black units into all-white contingents, the move was "purely business." Segregation on all other levels would continue. There would be no mixing on what Devers called "the social side."[26]

---

[23] Ibid.

[24] The reactions are summarized in MacGregor, *Integration of the Armed Forces*, pp. 158–61.

[25] Quote from Supplemental Report of War Department Special Board on Negro Manpower, 26 Jan 46, CMH files. The Army promulgated the Gillem Board's findings in War Department Cir 124, Utilization of Negro Manpower in Postwar Army Policy, 27 Apr 46, in MacGregor and Nalty, *Blacks in the United States Armed Forces*, vol. 7, item 28.

[26] Devers is quoted by MacGregor, *Integration of the Armed Forces*, p. 165.

True to Devers' word, over the years that followed, the small black units that the Gillem Board had sought to distribute equitably throughout major commands were grouped with white units as far as work was concerned but remained segregated otherwise. Meanwhile, since the number and nature of black units determined the assignments and training their members could receive, 198 of 490 military occupational specialties and more than half of the Army's schools remained closed. There were simply too few technical specialty positions in the segregated units that remained in the Army's force structure. On top of that, even when blacks were eligible to receive specialized training, racial prejudice limited their opportunities. For example, although the Ordnance Department declared itself ready to train the representatives of all races, the 440 openings at the department's school in Atlanta were still inaccessible to blacks more than a year after the Army accepted the Gillem Board's recommendations.[27]

The diminishing size of the Army made matters worse. Many of the blacks who managed to receive training found their new knowledge of limited use simply because the Army had less need than before for all kinds of specialists, whatever their race. The graduates of the Army's Medical and Signal Corps schools provide a case in point. A number received certification in those specialties only to learn upon arrival at their duty stations that no openings existed in their fields. Entering some less skilled occupation, they had to content themselves with jobs as riflemen, wiremen, or clerical assistants.[28]

The inadequate preparation of many blacks joining the service further complicated matters. One hundred and eleven of the Army's 124 school courses required a test score above 90, the bottom of Category III, for admission. Because of the deficient education many blacks received and the low rankings they achieved on general qualifications tests, most failed to qualify. Indeed, 62 percent of new black recruits in 1949 fell into the Army's two lowest classifications for educational accomplishment and aptitude, Categories IV and V, compared with only 33 percent of the whites.[29] (*Table 2*)

Those low scorers became a continual drag on the efficiency of all-black Army units because they often lacked the ability to read technical manuals and were less adaptable and more difficult to train than better-educated soldiers. The Army might have solved the problem quickly by discharging all men in the lowest categories, but the number of whites in those classes equaled or exceeded the number of blacks. Since the service could parcel those men out, a few at a time, to a broad range of units, it barely felt the effect of their presence and saw no reason to exclude them. Under segregation, however, the blacks had to be concentrated in a relatively small number of all-black units. Their effect upon efficiency was sometimes pronounced.[30]

Declining the simple solution, the Army thus attempted time and again to restrict the number of black low scorers by reducing draft calls and rejecting unqualified volunteers. Yet recruiters were under great pressure to boost enlistments because of manpower shortages and often subverted the system by accepting enlistees without concern for what seemed to them mere paper requirements. The quota imposed by the Gillem Board, as McCloy had predicted, only made matters worse. Limiting the proportion of blacks in the Army to 10 percent, it ensured that there was often no space left for highly accomplished enlistees because the slots they might have occupied were already filled by poorly skilled careerists unlikely ever to depart. The Army attempted to limit reenlistment to men who had scored higher than 70 on its general classification test but even then had to make exceptions—especially for sol-

---

[27] MacGregor, *Integration of the Armed Forces*, pp. 197–99; Nalty, *Strength for the Fight*, pp. 251–52.

[28] Nalty, *Strength for the Fight*, p. 227.

---

[29] The table is drawn from Operations Research Organization, Johns Hopkins University, *Utilization of Negro Manpower in the Army: A 1951 Study* (Washington, D.C.: Research Analysis Corporation, 1951), p. 4, CMH files. See also MacGregor, *Integration of the Armed Forces*, pp. 138, 198–99. Category I required a test score of 130 or better; II, 110–129; III, 90–109; IV, 60–89. Category V included all scores below 59.

[30] MacGregor, *Integration of the Armed Forces*, p. 204.

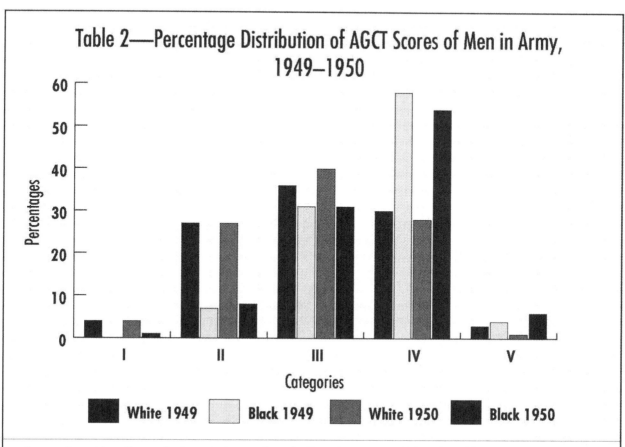

Table 2—Percentage Distribution of AGCT Scores of Men in Army, 1949–1950

Source: Operations Research Organization, Johns Hopkins University, *Utilization of Negro Manpower in the Army: A 1951 Study* (Washington, D.C.: Research Analysis Corporation, 1951), p. 4, CMH files.

diers decorated for valor and for those with marginal test scores who had nonetheless received recommendations from commanders.[31]

In the end, the service achieved a measure of relief only by opening special schools in each command for men with less than a fifth-grade education. It also invoked Army Regulation 615–369, which allowed commanders to terminate soldiers incapable of meeting military standards. Included were those who were mentally unfit, required continual special instruction,

exhibited habitual drunkenness, or repeatedly contracted venereal disease. The total number of soldiers discharged under the regulation is unknown, but the 24th Infantry alone processed 301 cases during 1946.[32]

The effects of education and command attention can be seen in a decline in VD rates for black servicemen in the Eighth Army during 1946 and 1947. When commanders took steps to remedy the problem by promoting proper prophylaxis, disci-

[31] Ibid., p. 183.

[32] HQ, 24th Inf Rgt, Annual Hist of the 24th Inf Rgt for 1946, 2 Mar 48.

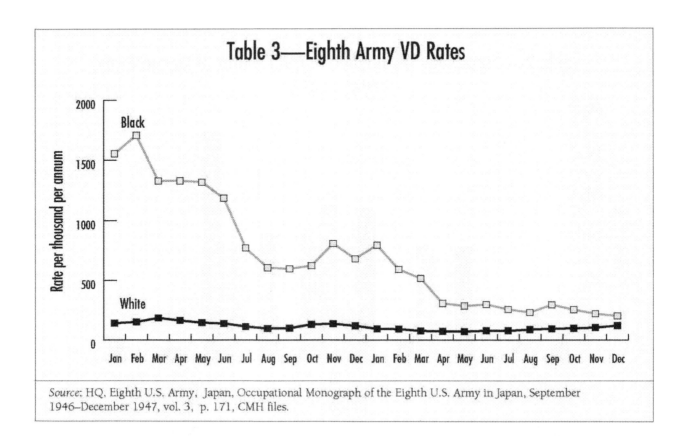

Table 3—Eighth Army VD Rates

Source: HQ, Eighth U.S. Army, Japan, Occupational Monograph of the Eighth U.S. Army in Japan, September 1946–December 1947, vol. 3, p. 171, CMH files.

plining those who contracted VD, and eliminating repeat offenders from the service, incidence of the disease fell drastically from 1,186 per thousand in June 1946 to 202 per thousand in 1947.[33] (*Table 3*)

In general, if the Army's leaders made do with half measures, insisting that their response to the Gillem Board's recommendations had been reasonable and adequate, enough changes were occurring within American society at large to render the stance untenable.[34] As soon as the war had ended, for example, the NAACP had redoubled its effort to achieve racial equality for African-Americans.

Reacting to Nazi atrocities against Jews and other minorities during the war, civic associations, religious denominations, and labor organizations had taken up the call. So had the federal courts, which found increasingly in favor of blacks seeking redress for racial injustices. As for blacks themselves, starting in World War I and continuing through World War II, they had conducted a massive migration north in search of opportunity. Once established, they registered to vote in such numbers in some northern cities that they frequently held the balance in close elections.[35]

President Truman himself was stricken in conscience. "My very stomach turned," he told a friend shortly after the war, "when I learned that Negro soldiers just back from overseas were being dumped out of Army trucks in Mississippi and beaten." Referring to an incident in which a return-

---

[33] HQ, U.S. Eighth Army, Japan, Occupational Monograph of the Eighth U.S. Army in Japan, September 1946–December 1947, vol. 3, p. 171.

[34] See, for example, the statement of Secretary of the Army Kenneth C. Royall in Transcript, National Defense Conference on Negro Affairs, 26 Apr 48, pp. 49–51, 58–59, in MacGregor and Nalty, *Blacks in the United States Armed Forces*, vol. 8, item 153.

[35] Franklin, *From Slavery to Freedom*, pp. 608–14.

ing soldier, Isaac Woodward, had lost his sight, Truman continued: "When a mayor and a city marshal can take a Negro sergeant off a bus in South Carolina, beat him up and put out one of his eyes, and nothing is done by the state authorities, something is radically wrong with the system."[36]

Truman appointed an interracial committee in 1946 to investigate the status of civil rights in America. The committee's final report denounced Jim Crow and issued a ringing call for the elimination of segregation. A second interracial panel commissioned that same year highlighted inequities in higher education between black and white schools and called upon the government to abandon all forms of discrimination in higher education. Neither report had much influence on the Army, which still viewed integration only as an option for the far future.[37]

The increasing power of the black electorate took on new significance in 1948 when the approaching presidential election found Truman facing apparent defeat in his bid to retain the White House. His Republican opponent, Thomas A. Dewey, sought to capitalize on the disaffection of blacks by promising to put an end to segregation in the armed forces. The Democratic Party meanwhile seemed increasingly divided, with northern liberals seeking to expand civil rights through the enlargement of federal authority, while southern conservatives stood fast for states' rights and segregation. The liberals gained the upper hand at the party's national convention, winning approval for a platform that committed the candidate to voting rights for blacks, equal opportunity for all, and an end to segregation in the armed forces. Southern delegations then walked out to form a new party that selected Governor Strom Thurmond of South Carolina to run for president as States Rights candidate. The far left wing of the party also broke away to promote the presidential candidacy of Vice President Henry Wallace, who favored accommo-

dation with an increasingly hostile Soviet Union.[38]

All seemed lost for the president, but he rebounded quickly. Seeking to build a new political coalition that included the increasingly influential black electorate, he issued Executive Order 9981 on 26 July 1948. This measure stipulated equal treatment and opportunity for all within the armed services without regard to race. The directive allowed the military enough time to make the change without damaging efficiency or morale, but Truman left no doubt about its ultimate intent. Questioned at a news conference on whether the order meant an eventual end to segregation, he replied with an unequivocal yes. The rejoinder had the desired effect. Although Truman received a cool reception when he appeared before Congress on the day after issuing the order, black leaders who had earlier planned a program of civil disobedience against the draft called off the effort and rallied to his side. In the end, aided by blacks and other groups that had also received concessions, Truman won the election by a narrow margin.[39]

Even with the president on record as supporting an end to segregation, the Army continued to delay. The policies established by the Gillem Board, Secretary of the Army Kenneth C. Royall declared, were "sound in the light of actual experience" and already largely in accord with the president's wishes. When a committee Truman had established to monitor compliance with the order suggested that the Army break up its all-black units and replace the quota system with one based principally on test scores rather than race, the service rejected the proposal.[40] In doing so, Secretary of the Army Gordon

---

[36] Woodward lost the sight in both of his eyes. Truman is quoted by Margaret Truman, *Harry S. Truman* (New York: William Morrow, 1972), p. 429. See also McCullough, *Truman*, pp. 588–89.

[37] Franklin, *From Slavery to Freedom*, pp. 608–11.

[38] McCullough, *Truman*, pp. 639–40. See also Joseph Goulden, *The Best Years, 1945–1950* (New York: Athenaeum, 1976), pp. 215–33; Nalty, *Strength for the Fight*, pp. 238–42.

[39] EO 9981, 26 Jul 48, and The President's News Conference of 26 July 1948, in MacGregor and Nalty, *Blacks in the United States Armed Forces*, vol. 8, items 164 and 165, respectively.

[40] Memo, President's Committee on Equality of Treatment and Opportunity in the Armed Services for Secretary of the Army, 8 Sep 49, sub: Substitution of a GCT Quota for a Racial Quota, in MacGregor and Nalty, *Blacks in the United States Armed Forces*, vol. 11, item 22.

Gray, who succeeded Royall in June 1949, declared that the quota remained the best means for ensuring that the Army received only the highest quality black recruits.[41]

In the end, the committee's chairman, Charles Fahy, took the matter to Truman himself and won the president's support. Shortly afterward, the Army agreed to a compromise and on 15 January 1950 announced the enactment of Special Regulation 600–629–1, requiring that "Negro manpower . . . be utilized in accordance with [its] skills and qualifications." In pursuit of that goal the service would assign soldiers where needed, without regard to race.[42] A further concession came two months later, when Army administrators agreed to replace the quota with a system that relied upon nonracial physical, mental, and psychological standards. Even then, however, Secretary Gray could bring himself to bend only to a degree. The Army would give the new system a fair trial, he told the president, but reserved the right to return to procedures based on race if the experiment failed.[43] Truman responded with a quiet emphasis that left little doubt that there would be no turning back. "I

am sure," he told Gray politely but pointedly, "that everything will work out as it should."[44]

The end of the quota in April 1950 marked the beginning of racial integration in the Army. Although the service was inclined to hold back, the Korean War started a mere two months later. When recruits began to arrive in Army training centers, planners found it impossible to predict how many would be black or white. Lacking firm numbers, they could not provide for separate facilities to accommodate each race. They proposed the integration of training units as a solution. In the same way, with casualties running high in the field and commanders hard pressed to find replacements, soldiers were shoved into the line where needed, without regard to race. When the performance of blacks in the integrated units matched that of whites, no excuses were left. The Army moved to put an end to segregation.[45]

The indecision and half measures that had distinguished the Army's journey to that point in the years following World War II nevertheless had their effect, especially on the 24th Infantry. As the great debate over segregation proceeded in Washington, the regiment had taken up station in the Far East, where it occupied a world in which the old standards still prevailed and in which forward movement on matters of race seemed almost imperceptible. The problems that resulted were manageable as long as peace endured, but once war began and the unit entered combat, their consequences were profound.

[41] Memo, Secretary of the Army for Secretary of Defense, 30 Sep 49, sub: Equality of Treatment and Opportunity in the Armed Services, in MacGregor and Nalty, *Blacks in the United States Armed Forces*, vol. 11, item 25. See also Nalty, *Strength for the Fight*, p. 253.

[42] DOD Press Release 64, 16 Jan 50, Army Revises Policy Governing Utilization of Negro Manpower, in MacGregor and Nalty, *Blacks in the United States Armed Forces*, vol. 11, item 29. See also Dalfiume, *Desegregation of the U.S. Armed Forces*, p. 196.

[43] Ltr, Gordon Gray to the President, 1 Mar 50, in MacGregor and Nalty, *Blacks in the United States Armed Forces*, vol. 11, item 33.

[44] Memo, Harry S. Truman for Secretary of the Army, 27 Mar 50, in MacGregor and Nalty, *Blacks in the United States Armed Forces*, vol. 11, item 36.

[45] Dalfiume, *Desegregation of the U.S. Armed Forces*, p. 203.

CHAPTER 3

Gifu: "Our Own Little World"

As the end of World War II approached in early August 1945, the 24th Infantry transferred from Saipan and Tinian to the Ryukyu Islands to assist in mopping-up operations on the Kerama Islands, some fifteen miles to the west of the southern tip of Okinawa. The regiment reached perhaps its highest point for the war on 22 August, when its commander, Col. Julian G. Hearne, Jr., accepted the surrender of Aka Island, the first formal capitulation of a Japanese Army garrison.[1] Shortly thereafter, the regiment joined occupation forces on Okinawa, an area that had been ravaged by some of the war's worst fighting. The troops were greeted, according to Sgt. Maxie Fields, by "empty tents, nothing more." It was the beginning of a long letdown.[2]

Okinawa and Japan

The unit had hardly arrived when two typhoons, three weeks apart in September, destroyed 95 percent of the island's tentage and severely damaged the few permanent structures that had survived the fighting. Conditions improved during January 1946, when the regiment occupied buildings that had formerly housed the 9th General Hospital. From then on, with that facility as a base of operations, the unit carried out a range of missions—from guard duty at the Yontan-Kadena ammunition depot to patrolling for fugitive Japanese soldiers. To assist the 186th Port Battalion in moving perishable food from dock to destination as quickly as possible, Company M became a provisional trucking unit with 5 officers and 100 enlisted men. Meanwhile, the rest of the regiment took instruction in such subjects as military courtesy, first aid, sanitation, Army organization, and the history of the 24th Infantry. In addition, an ad hoc school staffed by some of the unit's better-educated soldiers taught reading, writing, and simple arithmetic to those men whose formal education in the United States had been more limited.[3]

With some stability, life might have become very pleasant for the men of the 24th. They had few major tasks, according to former enlisted man Edward Pratt. During abundant free time, they played cards with the Japanese prisoners in their charge and gambled with white officers who would stop by their barracks on payday. On the many days when there were no details or training, they would get up in the morning and go to the beach. For a time they even had a zoo with pet monkeys, parrots, and dogs.[4]

---

[1] Lee, *The Employment of Negro Troops*, p. 535.

[2] Interv, Bernard L. Muehlbauer with Maxie Fields, 2 Nov 88, CMH files. All interviews hereafter cited by John A. Cash, Bernard L. Muehlbauer, Timothy Rainey, William T. Bowers, Richard O. Perry, and George L. MacGarrigle are in CMH files.

[3] HQ, 24th Inf Rgt, Annual History of the 24th Infantry Regiment (hereafter cited as Annual Hist of the 24th Inf Rgt) for 1946, 2 Mar 48, pp. 1–2, copy in CMH files.

[4] Ibid. See also Interv, John A. Cash with Edward Pratt, 16 Jun 89.

Aerial view of the 24th Infantry regiment area, Gifu, Japan

All that changed, however, as 1946 progressed. With the Army pursuing its postwar drawdown, the regiment became little more than a holding detachment. Officers and enlisted men arrived continually, remained just long enough to qualify for rotation home, and then departed. The constant turnover in personnel left the unit scarcely able to fulfill even a limited mission. On 1 January 1946, for example, out of an authorized strength of 135 officers and 2,861 enlisted men, the regiment totaled 75 officers and 706 enlisted men. By April, 82 officers but only 384 enlisted men were present. In June the number of officers decreased to 73 while that of the enlisted men rose to 1,321. Of the officers assigned in June, at most 50 were on hand for duty. The rest had received temporary duty assignments elsewhere on Okinawa with units as badly short of officers as the 24th. The number present held steady at 51 during July, but 36 of those officers were eligible to rotate home as soon as a ship arrived to take them.[5]

The turbulence had a serious effect on readiness. With few soldiers to fill the 24th's rifle and weapons companies, the regiment soon had to inactivate some of its battalions to provide minimal staffing for those that remained. By June the regiment had no choice but to organize its companies by their assigned missions. The headquarters company of the 1st Battalion, for example, contained all of the men employed as guards for Japanese prisoners of war and the staff required to administer that activity. Company A provided construction workers, Company B utilities personnel, and Company C cooks and mess crews. Company D and the headquarters company for the 3d Battalion contained administrative personnel. At the direction of the commanding general of the services command on Okinawa, Company F became a provisional trucking unit similar to Company M.[6]

Shortages of drivers, mechanics, and heavy equipment operators also began to occur, threatening the ability of motor pools and truck companies to operate safely. Since few maintenance men remained for long, crews had to be trained continually to operate plumbing, water pumps, electrical generators, and communications equipment. In the end, the movement of men in and out of the regiment became so rapid that formal training ceased and on-the-job instruction became the rule. Meanwhile, by July so many men began to arrive from branches of the Army other than the infantry that the unit had to conduct continual on-the-spot training just to familiarize its personnel with such rudimentary tasks as guard duty and patrolling. The regiment's commander, Col. Michael E. Halloran, who had seen some of the heaviest fighting on Okinawa as commander of the 96th Infantry Division's 381st Infantry regiment, departed on 15 February after little more than a month with the unit. A temporary commander took his place until 10 July, when the former commander of the 96th's 382d Infantry, Col. Macey L. Dill, took charge.[7]

With so many officers and enlisted men arriving on Okinawa and departing, discipline declined among all the troops, both white and black. Bored, resentful because of the primitive conditions they sometimes endured, and lacking consistent supervision, many American soldiers sought relief among the prostitutes who flourished in the island's villages. Taking temporary,

[5] Strengths are from Annual Hist of the 24th Inf Rgt for 1946, 2 Mar 48, pp. 1–7. The authorized strength figure is taken from Adjutant General (AG) Form 016, 24th Inf Rgt, copy in CMH files.

[6] Annual Hist of the 24th Inf Rgt for 1946, 2 Mar 48, p. 6.
[7] Ibid.

"French" leave—no one could truly desert on the island—some inevitably contributed to a rising crime rate that characterized the initial stages of the American occupation. Numerous cases of rape, kidnapping, and assault occurred along with a number of murders. Although blacks were sometimes blamed, there is no indication in official records that the men of Dill's command were involved to any great extent. If, as Sgt. Michael Pierre recalled years later, the soldiers of the 24th had as little to do as everyone else and were often just as bored, crime reports that survive from the period mention individuals assigned to various truck and port units but say nothing about any of the men of the regiment.[8] Indeed, by that time the unit was undergoing intensive training to prepare for occupation duties in Japan. Its officers made it a point to note in their reports that their platoons and companies were in better condition than they had seen in many months.[9]

On 18 September 1946, the 24th departed for the island of Ie Shima, some three miles west of Okinawa. The site of a small airfield, military depots, and a cemetery, it had seen heavy fighting during the war, when it had gained notoriety as the site of war correspondent Ernie Pyle's death. The regiment would stay on the island only long enough to incorporate enough men to reach its authorized strength and to train the newcomers to infantry standards. Then it would relocate to Japan, where it would join the occupation as part of the 25th Infantry Division. After the 24th arrived on Ie Shima, Dill sent nine

officers and seventy-six enlisted men from Company C to Japan to prepare for the arrival of the entire regiment.[10]

However temporary, the 24th's sojourn on Ie Shima, Japanese for *Ash Island*, represented a low point in the regiment's history. According to enlisted man Fred Thomas, there were still skeletons in the island's caves, and live ammunition left over from the war was scattered about. Amenities were few. A quonset hut with two Ping-Pong tables served for an enlisted men's club, and the only other forms of entertainment were cards and dice. The food was wretched. The men varied their diets with wild sugarcane and sweet potatoes they harvested themselves from abandoned fields. There was even a shortage of cigarettes. Red Cross personnel, all black according to Thomas, were hoarding them, possibly for later sale on the black market. Although a black special service hostess, according to Edward Pratt, visited white officers, there were few if any other women nearby. The cook's tent became the "red light district," Fred Thomas observed, with the unit's homosexuals—termed "sissies" or "field WACs" by the men—serving as hosts.[11] Overall, the men considered themselves prisoners in exile.[12]

Despite privations and short rations, commanders labeled September a "Gold Star" month. The regiment, in preparation for the move to Japan, at long last received much-needed officer replacements: a lieutenant colonel, 10 captains, 11 first lieutenants, and 2 chief warrant officers. October was perhaps even better. Nine hundred and twenty-six more enlisted men arrived along with another complement of officers: 5 captains and 7 first lieutenants. All of the officers in the second group were black, an indication that the Army was putting the Gillem

[8] Interv, Cash with Michael Pierre, 29 Nov 89. For concerns about black involvement in crime, see Memo, Director of General Affairs, Lt Cdr James T. Watkins IV, for Deputy Cdr for Military Government, 6 Apr 46, sub: Negro Troops—Withdrawal From Okinawa, HQ, U.S. Naval Military Government, Watkins file, Record Group (RG) 200, National Archives and Records Administration (NARA), Washington, D.C.; Memo, Public Safety Department, Military Government, Ryukyu, for Deputy Cdr for Military Government, 3 Sep 46, sub: Report of Public Safety Department for Month of August 1946, copy in CMH files; Memorandum for the Record (MFR), Public Safety Department, Military Government, Ryukyu, 31 Oct 46, sub: Report of Public Safety Department for the Month of October 1946, copy in CMH files.

[9] Annual Hist of the 24th Inf Rgt for 1946, 2 Mar 48, p. 8.

[10] Ibid., pp. 8–9; Interv, Cash with Alexander Shearin, 17 Aug 88. See also Scipio, *Last of the Black Regulars*, p. 79.

[11] Intervs, Cash with Pratt, 16 Jun 89; Fred Thomas, 24 Aug 89. Thomas is the only one to mention homosexuals on Ie Shima, but there is little reason to doubt his story. The presence and activities of homosexuals in the 24th in Japan and throughout the Army are well documented.

[12] See Ltr, Waymon R. Ransom to John A. Cash, 22 Oct 88, CMH files; Interv, Cash with Pratt, 16 Jun 89.

Board's recommendations into effect. Another 667 enlisted men arrived during November. Of those, 161 had test scores in the very useful ranges above 70 (Category IV). A number were also either qualified for skilled jobs or showed enough potential to warrant special training.[13]

Many of the new men were draftees or enlistees with at best eight weeks of basic training. In addition, 800 of the 926 men who had arrived during September had transferred into the unit from branches of the service other than the infantry. Some were former airmen. In order to build esprit de corps among the new men, the regiment set aside a special day during October to commemorate the 80th anniversary of its founding and to honor Sgt. Edward J. Nickens, who had spent twenty-six of his twenty-eight years in the Army as a member of the 24th.[14]

The unit also began heavy training in basics such as military courtesy, drill, and weapons familiarization. The island's lava ate great holes in the men's shoes and ripped field jackets and trousers to shreds, but the effort had its effect. By the end of November, although the men's shoes were sometimes stuffed with old newspapers, commanders could note with satisfaction that 984 members of the regiment had qualified on the M1 rifle and 990 had fired submachine guns and M1 carbines for familiarization.[15] A board of officers convened at that time under the provisions of AR 615–369 to rate soldiers who had been referred for separation because of low test scores or discipline problems. By 23 December 1946, it had processed a total of 301 cases. As the year ended, regimental strength stood at 93 officers and 2,463 enlisted men.[16]

The 24th completed its thirteenth and final week of training on 4 January 1947. According to unit reports, its soldiers were solidly grounded in infantry basics with 98.5 percent of them qualified on their weapons. A number had also

Enlisted men of the 24th Infantry ride through the shallow Kiso River.

received specialized training as medics and personnel administrators.[17]

During the first week in January, the regiment moved to Japan. Arriving at the port of Kobe on the island of Honshu, 270 miles southwest of Tokyo, it rode a train to Gifu, midway between Kobe and Tokyo, and then marched to Kagamigahara Airfield, a former Japanese kamikaze base located some ten miles east of the town. (*See Map 1.*) The post had recently housed a sister regiment in the 25th Division, the all-white 27th Infantry regiment. "I recall the Japanese kids licking their fingers and then running up to us and rubbing it [*sic*] on our skin to see if it would come off," Fred Thomas recalled. "They called us 'chocoleta' soldiers and called the 27th 'ice cream' soldiers. The 27th had been there before us and was leaving. They said, 'soldiers why you no washa washa.'"[18] Camp Gifu, as it came to be called, would be the unit's home until the beginning of the Korean War three years later. The other regiments of the 25th Division, the 35th

---

[13] Annual Hist of the 24th Inf Rgt for 1946, 2 Mar 48, p. 9.
[14] Ibid.
[15] Interv, Cash with Thomas, 24 Aug 89.
[16] Annual Hist of the 24th Inf Rgt for 1946, 2 Mar 48, p. 9. See also Interv, Muehlbauer with Fields, 2 Nov 88.

[17] Annual Hist of the 24th Inf Rgt for 1947, 2 Mar 48, p. 1. See also Intervs, Cash with Edward Dixon, 20 Jan 89; Shearin, 17 Aug 88.
[18] Interv, Cash with Thomas, 24 Aug 89. Leonard H. Kushner mentions the 27th's stay at Gifu. See Interv, Cash with Leonard H. Kushner (Mrs. Kushner participated in her husband's interview), 16 Jun 89.

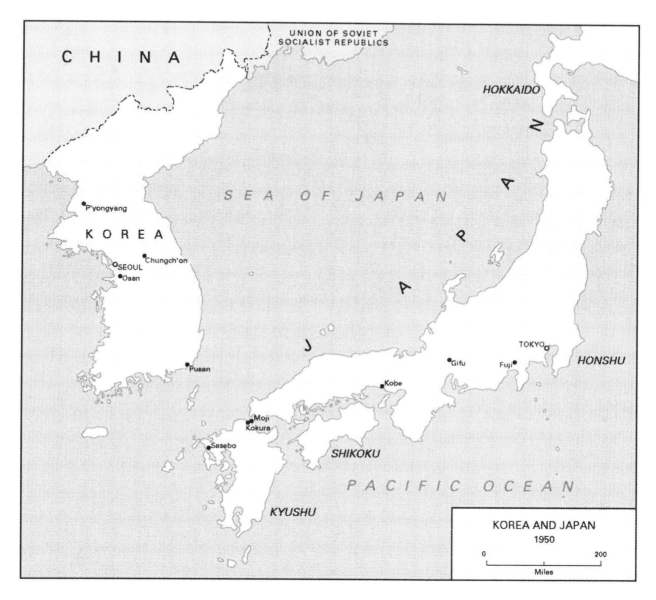

Map 1

and 27th Infantry regiments, were stationed in similar facilities nearby.[19]

Despite the efforts of the 27th, which had done some ground work, and the 85-man team that had preceded the unit, the accommodations at Gifu were rudimentary at first. Officers' quarters were dirty and had holes in them. There were few indoor latrines.

The facility's runway was littered with wrecked and cannibalized aircraft.[20] To make matters worse, the Army's supply system would take several months to catch up with the unit. During that time, mops were

[19] Annual Hist of the 24th Inf Rgt for 1947, 2 Mar 48, p. 1.

[20] Intervs, Cash with Kushner, 16 Jun 89; Shearin, 17 Aug 88; Thomas, 24 Aug 89; Muehlbauer with Norman Taylor, 16 Sep 88; Charles A. Smith, 27 Sep 88; Clifford Allen, 18 Oct 88; Bill W. Gunter, 28 Feb 89.

Camp Majestic, near Gifu, Japan, home of the 24th Infantry, 12 June 1947

unavailable, stocks of soap were insufficient, the camp's dry cleaning and laundry facilities often lacked solvents and detergent, and the men had to continue to wear clothing and shoes torn to shreds by Ie Shima's lava.[21] According to Edward Pratt, the supply problem came to the attention of the U.S. Eighth Army's commander, Lt. Gen. Robert L. Eichelberger, during an inspection shortly after the regiment arrived in Japan, when the general's wife was moved almost to tears by the men's lack of shoes. A few days later, a train arrived with combat boots.[22]

Those problems notwithstanding, by 15 March enough repairs had been made at Gifu for the 24th to begin to feel at home. The regiment experienced a setback on 29 March, when the enlisted quarters for Companies E, F, and G were destroyed in a fire that blazed for six hours, killing one enlisted man and injuring two others. By the end of the month, however, forty-five units of family housing had been built and fifty-eight more were slated to be done by the end of April to accommodate the fam-

ilies that would arrive over the months to come. A new regimental aid station was in place, and completion of a new steam plant was well in sight.[23]

When the men of the 24th began their stay at Gifu, their mission was to complete their training as an infantry regiment in order to assume their share of the duties assigned to the four-division force occupying Japan. To that end, although hampered by a lack of training areas near Gifu because the camp was surrounded by rice paddies, they spent most of 1947 honing their skills as infantrymen by undergoing tactical and technical instruction. Officers took courses in military law and the fundamentals of command; noncommissioned officers attended classes in leadership, administration, and methods of instruction; the regimental motor officer conducted a driver's school; and infantrymen continued their training on squad- and platoon-level tactics.[24]

As was the case with many all-black units, a few college and high school graduates were

---

[21] Annual Hist of the 24th Inf Rgt for 1947, 2 Mar 48, pp. 1–2. See also Interv, Cash with Thomas, 24 Aug 89.

[22] Interv, Cash with Pratt, 16 Jun 89.

[23] Annual Hist of the 24th Inf Rgt for 1947, 2 Mar 48, pp. 1–2; Interv, Cash with Richard Haynesworth, 6 Sep 88.

[24] Ibid. See also Ltr, John S. Komp to George L. MacGarrigle, 14 May 95, CMH files.

among the troops, but a large number of the enlisted men possessed below a fifth-grade education. Some of the veterans were completely unschooled. According to Richard W. Saxton, who served in the personnel section during 1947, the problem was so acute that only four enlisted men in the regimental headquarters company possessed a high school education. Saxton added that one of his platoon sergeants could neither read nor write. "I had to read the rosters for him."[25] The regimental historian, for his part, could only note that the lack of education of many of the men within the regiment ranked high among the impediments to progress within the unit. "Despite our gains," he observed in his conclusion for March 1947, "we have not attained the desired degree of proficiency which we are striving for. This is due largely to the fact that the regiment is not adequately equipped and has not received sufficient numbers of the desired calibre of personnel."[26]

In an attempt to find a solution, following the policies of the Eighth Army command, the 24th gave self-improvement and education great emphasis. Within two months of arriving in Japan, 220 of its members were involved in academic, trade, or business courses sponsored by the Army Education Program. In addition, the unit's literacy school was in full swing, with 125 soldiers attending either morning or evening classes. The literacy effort in particular achieved some benefit according to Sgt. Edward L. Horne, who worked in the program during 1947. The men were eager to learn, and 85 percent made good progress, especially those under thirty years of age.[27] Over the years that followed, remedial instruction continued to receive special emphasis from both the regimental commander,

White stucco building at Camp Majestic, occupied by Company D, 24th Infantry

who kept close tabs on the effort, and the sergeants, who advised their men to seek an education if they wanted to succeed in the world.[28]

Colonel Halloran returned to take command of the regiment in April 1947. Known as "Screaming Mike" because of his booming voice—the result of a hearing impairment—he took immediate action to remedy the supply deficiencies afflicting his unit. A troop commander with the all-black 92d Infantry Division during the early days of World War II, when the unit was still training in the United States, Halloran also understood the value of education to a black unit and made it a priority within the regiment.[29]

Most of the enlisted men admired the colonel because he seemed forthright in manner and honest in his dealings with them.[30] "Screaming Mike" was "something else . . . a character," rifleman Norman Taylor asserted, but he "loved us; wouldn't let anything happen to us." First Sgt. Richard

[25] Intervs, Cash with Richard W. Saxton, 3 Dec 88; Shearin, 17 Aug 88; Albert Griffin, Jr., 5 Oct 88; William A. Bobo (Mrs. Bobo participated in her husband's interview), 27 Jan 90; Rollie Evans, 13 Oct 88; Robert Taylor, 15 Sep 88; Harold Rogue, Jr., 14 Oct 88; Muehlbauer with William M. Factory, 2 Nov 88; Houston McMurray, Jun 88.

[26] Quote from Annual Hist of the 24th Inf Rgt for 1947, 2 Mar 48, p. 3. See also Intervs, Cash with Leroy Williams, 6 Oct 88; William T. Bowers with Richard Sanders, 5 May 95.

[27] Interv, Muehlbauer with Rev. Edward L. Horne, 3 Nov 88. See also MacGregor, *Integration of the Armed Forces*, p. 216.

[28] Ibid. See also Annual Hist of the 24th Inf Rgt for 1947, 2 Mar 48, p. 4; Intervs, Muehlbauer with Harry A. Davis, 26 Sep 88; Richard Sanders, 16 Dec 88; Cash with Griffin, 5 Oct 88; Walter Smith, 25 Sep 88; Saxton, 3 Dec 88; Theodore R. Eldridge, Jr., 26 Aug 88.

[29] Interv, Muehlbauer with Horne, 3 Nov 88.

[30] See, for example, ibid.; Intervs, Cash with James Perkins, 28 Jul 89; Robert Taylor, 25 Sep 88; Muehlbauer with Beverly Scott, n.d.

Haynesworth and others considered him "a soldier's soldier," who was open to his troops and available to them twenty-four hours a day. He was a fantastic person, medic James Perkins avowed, an officer who loved the regiment and did many things for the men.[31]

The enlisted men's attitude was built upon their perception that Halloran was on their side. He attempted to make sure they were well supplied, supported their interest in sports, fostered their advancement through education, and at times took their part when other officers of the regiment seemed unfair. Halloran did not play favorites, MP Sgt. Clarence Ferguson asserted. If something was wrong, it was wrong. As a result, Ferguson said, when several clearly prejudiced white officers joined the regiment, Halloran had them reassigned. Halloran never drove to work, Joel T. Ward observed. Instead he would walk across the training area. If it was cold outside, he would tell the men to go indoors. He visited them everywhere, Fred Thomas added—in the barracks, in training, at play. "Considering those days, I would give him an AA rating as a white officer."[32]

Affectionate stories about Halloran, some bordering on myth, were repeated continually among the men. On one occasion, it was said, the Eighth Army failed to invite the 24th's honor guard and band to participate in an annual Fourth of July parade in Tokyo. The colonel sent them along anyway, with instructions to report directly to the U.S. commander in the Far East, General Douglas MacArthur. As a result, the band received a place in the parade. Soldiers also told of how Halloran, on at least one occasion during an inspection, supposedly came upon a private whose boots were so ragged they were almost unwearable. Receiving unsatisfactory explanations from the man's commanding officer and supply sergeant, he instructed the individual responsible to exchange his own footwear with the soldier in full view of a company formation. The men also told the story of an unannounced inspection in which Halloran stood up to a general. When that officer arrived at Gifu to begin the review, the colonel was said to have met him at the gate and to have informed him, "You didn't say you were coming. We aren't ready, and you aren't inspecting."[33]

The regiment's officers dealt with Halloran on a different level and had of necessity a different perspective. Among the most negative was black 1st Lt. Richard L. Fields, who asserted that Halloran had reprimanded him in front of the regimental sergeant major because he had won too many acquittals for soldiers tried by court-martial. Young lieutenants were afraid of Halloran, Fields said. He screamed, ranted, and cursed. Overall, if he was paternalistic toward the enlisted men, he was prejudiced against blacks as a group and looked down on them. "I did not respect him," Fields said, "as a man, commander, officer, or whatever."[34]

Senior black Capt. William A. Bobo conceded that Halloran had his faults. He expected more than could be produced, the officer said, and ended a few careers, black and white. Nevertheless, Bobo continued, Halloran was as fair as most people, and he had become so identified with the 24th that some said he could have been born black. In the same way, a black second lieutenant at Gifu, Albert Brooks, who had served with Halloran in an earlier assignment, asserted that the colonel was known for raising hell and had never pleased everyone. Even so, he was "totally colorblind."[35] Screaming

---

Cash with Thomas, 24 Aug 89; Girard Sammons, 27 Aug 88; Vernie Scott, 7 Sep 88; Hollis Reese, 24 Sep 88; Taylor Moore, 19 Aug 88; Walter Smith, 25 Sep 88; Joel T. Ward, 21 Jul 88.

[33] Intervs, Muehlbauer with Ferguson, 2 Sep 88; Cash with John W. Anderson, 2 Sep 89; John French, 21 Jul 89; Leo Roberts, 10 Nov 88. Quote from Interv, Cash with Albert Brooks, 6 Aug 88.

[34] Interv, Cash with Richard L. Fields, 18 Aug 88.

[35] Intervs, Cash with Bobo, 27 Jan 90, and quote from Cash with Albert Brooks, 6 Aug 88. See also Interv, Timothy Rainey with Harold Montgomery, 26 Mar 90. Montgomery had served under Halloran both during World War II and at Gifu. Although he made no specific comments about the colonel, it was obvious that there was a mutual respect between the two officers.

---

[31] Intervs, Cash with Haynesworth, 6 Sep 88; James Perkins, 28 Jul 89; Muehlbauer with Norman Taylor, 16 Sep 88; Factory, 2 Nov 88. Over a hundred veterans spoke of Halloran positively. Only a handful had anything negative to say.

[32] Intervs, Muehlbauer with Clarence Ferguson, 2 Sep 88;

Mike was an intense and demanding officer, white platoon leader Charles E. Green observed, constantly out checking on his units and screaming when things were not done as he expected. He liked doing what the Army paid him to do, and he did it with a vengeance.[36]

Halloran had yet to arrive when the turbulence affecting the rest of the Army once more began to tell upon the 24th. During March the unit absorbed 25 officers and 515 enlisted men from its sister regiment, the all-black 25th Infantry, which was moving to Fort Benning prior to inactivation. That put it at 137 regularly assigned officers and 3,174 enlisted men. From then on the totals fluctuated. During April the unit was under its authorized strength of 3,055 by some 190 men, but by the beginning of May it had grown to 153 officers and 3,215 enlisted men. The numbers dropped after that. At the end of the month, they stood at 126 and 2,951 respectively. June was worse—by the last day of the month commanders could count only 121 officers and 2,348 enlisted men. At the end of July, at best 119 officers and 2,272 enlisted men were present.[37]

Training continued at first despite the turbulence. During July the 3d Battalion and elements of the 2d traveled to the Fujino-Susono Maneuver Area (called Fuji for short), on the slopes of historic Mount Fujiyama, to participate in weapons practice and combat simulations. Toward the end of the month, the 1st Battalion and the remaining portions of the 2d took to the field to undergo the same program. By the beginning of September, however, only 105 officers and 1,616 enlisted men remained, forcing the regiment to curtail training and to place the 2d Battalion in an inoperative status.[38]

Further reductions in the months that followed prompted more realignments. The unit managed to conduct a three-day, two-night field test exercise and bivouac with the 3d Battalion during October, but by November that battalion, one platoon of the antitank company, one platoon of the cannon company, and the intelligence and reconnaissance (I&R) platoon were the only combat components of the regiment still operational. By the end of December, the 24th numbered only 94 officers and 988 enlisted men. As on Okinawa, unit-level instruction ended and commanders had no choice but to conduct on-the-job training to sustain basic services at Gifu. For their own part, the soldiers who remained could do little more than preserve their basic individual skills.[39]

During the first months of 1948, as replacements began to arrive from the phase-out of all-black units in the United States, the 24th gradually regained its strength, growing to 126 officers and 2,446 enlisted men by the end of May. As the last black regiment in the U.S. Army serving overseas, it was in effect a segregated holding unit for the many black soldiers who arrived in the Far East.[40]

By contrast, because of the cutbacks and stringencies plaguing the Army at the time, white regiments operated with far fewer soldiers. During May, for example, the 27th Infantry contained only a fraction of the men the 24th could count, 59 officers and 391 enlisted men. The 35th Infantry meanwhile numbered 49 and 355 respectively. Whole battalions in those units were all but inoperative, retaining a first sergeant, a supply sergeant, and little else.[41]

If the 24th had reached relative equilibrium by mid-1948, personnel turbulence continued in other forms. Approximately 80 percent of the officers in the regiment, both white and black, were reservists subject to reduction-in-force programs affecting the officer corps.[42] In order to gain career

---

[36] Interv, George L. MacGarrigle with Charles E. Green, 16 Jun 94.

[37] Annual Hist of the 24th Inf Rgt for 1947, 2 Mar 48, p. 3.

[38] Ibid.

[39] Ibid., pp. 3, 9; Ltr, Ransom to Cash, 22 Oct 88.

[40] Schnabel, *Policy and Direction*, p. 52; 25th Inf Div, History of the Occupation of Japan, May 48, p. 3, CMH files. See also Matloff, *American Military History*, pp. 528–42; Intervs, Cash with Steve G. Davis, 2 Sep 88; Shearin, 17 Aug 88; Ltr, Ransom to Cash, 22 Oct 88.

[41] The figures for the 27th and 35th are in HQ, 25th Inf Div, History of the Occupation of Japan, May 48, pp. 4–5.

[42] See "Reserve Officer Morale," *Infantry Journal* (May 1950). For more on reductions in the 24th, see Intervs, MacGarrigle with Sam J. Adams, Jr., 15 Jun 94; Sidney B. Berry, 11 Aug 93; Bowers with Charles L. Gray, 2 and 3 May 94; Rainey with Leopold Hall, 2 Jun 90; Cash with Shearin, 17 Aug 88; Richard L. Fields, 18 Aug 88. In 1947 only 8 percent

stability, many decided to participate in what the Army called the Competitive Tour program.[43] Serving in a series of command and staff positions for three months at a time, they moved from assignment to assignment within the regiment. In the end, if an individual achieved high enough ratings in each job and met certain predetermined standards, he received an appointment to the Regular Army. That opened up career and educational opportunities denied to less permanent members of the armed forces and spared him from the uncertainties that remained a feature of Army life for reserve officers on active duty. The continual switching of officers from job to job nonetheless took a toll on the men of the regiment. They would hardly become accustomed to a commander before another would arrive to take his place.[44]

Life at Gifu, 1946–1948

Overall, life at Gifu had many attractions. Although some Japanese showed disdain for black Americans, racial friction itself appears to have been rare. The local people needed the money and commodities the soldiers could provide and were eager to work. As a result, both noncommissioned and commissioned officers, whether accompanied by families or not, had servants. Enlisted soldiers meanwhile enjoyed the ministrations of Japanese laborers who made beds, performed kitchen duties, and might for a small fee even clean personal weapons after stints on the firing range. That left the men with time to tour the country, study Japanese, and enroll in martial arts classes. Although a nonfraternization policy was in effect, some soldiers and a few officers dated Japanese women and lived with their female friends off post. When the policy changed just before the 24th went to Korea in 1950, despite official discouragement a few marriages occurred.[45]

Many officers brought their wives and children to Gifu. In August 1947 the base housing area contained 108 families. By May 1948, 148 families totaling 254 dependents lived there. The addition of so many civilians created problems for the regiment. Food and tempers sometimes grew short. Colonel Halloran responded by advising one and all to stay home, stay out of trouble, and avoid becoming involved in military affairs. The chaplains meanwhile spent considerable time in marriage counseling. Despite the challenges, the presence of so many young families was beneficial. It added a sense of permanency and stability to the installation that would have been absent otherwise.[46]

Many of the facilities at Gifu were integrated, but social segregation still marked life at the base. Although black and white officers sometimes mingled at the officers' club, the two groups largely kept apart at the facility, occupying separate seating and

---

of the officers at Gifu were West Point graduates or members of the Regular Army. They were mostly in the ranks above major and almost all were white because black regular officers were rare. The number of regulars increased to 19 percent in 1948, bringing the 24th into line with its sister regiment, the 35th Infantry, where, by the end of 1949, 22 percent of the officers were regulars. See Unit Rosters, 24th Inf Rgt, 6 Jun 47, 1 Nov 48, 1 Mar 49, and 35th Inf Rgt, 1 Nov 49, all in CMH files.

[43] See Col. Henry C. Newton, "The Officer Problem," *Infantry Journal* (December 1948), p. 19.

[44] The Competitive Tour is described in "General Staff: Personnel & Administration, Competitive Tours," *Infantry Journal* (June 1948). See also Intervs, Cash with Gorham L. Black, Jr., 18 Dec 88; Don Eunice, 3 Nov 89; Joseph Hilyer, 17 Aug 88; Jasper Johnson, 5 Oct 88; Kushner, 16 Jun 89; John B. Zanin, n.d.; Muehlbauer with Wilbur T. Felkey, 3 Sep 88.

[45] Komp mentions that some Japanese refused to welcome black Americans. See Ltr, Komp to MacGarrigle, 14 Apr 95. The overall attitude of Japanese toward blacks is mentioned in General Headquarters (GHQ), Far East Command (FEC), Operations of the Civil Intelligence Section, vol. 9, Intelligence Series, Documentary Appendices (II), n.d., p. 10, CMH files. See also Intervs, Cash with Eugene Edmonds, 6 Jan 90; Bobo, 27 Jan 90; Albert Brooks, 6 Aug 88; Bradley Biggs, 15 Aug 88; Ward, 21 Jul 88; Walter Bufford, 13 Mar 89; Muehlbauer with Clinton Moorman, 5 Sep 88. Bufford married a woman from Gifu. Other units besides the 24th experienced the good life. The 24th Division at Camp Kokura employed 1,352 Japanese laborers by the month and 842 by the day in 1947. See Occupational Monograph of the 24th Division in Japan, Jun 47, p. 7, CMH files.

[46] Annual Hist of the 24th Inf Rgt for 1947, 2 Mar 48, p. 10; HQ, 25th Inf Div, History of the Occupation of Japan, May 48, p. 13. Intervs, Cash with Shearin, 17 Aug 88, and quote from Cash with Bobo, 27 Jan 90. Although senior NCOs were sometimes accompanied by their families, junior enlisted men were not.

Members of the 24th Infantry Band march during an inspection and review of the troops.

table areas even at official functions. In the same way, chapel services tended to be predominantly black with only a few whites attending.[47] As far as living arrangements were concerned, some enclaves were apparent. West Point graduates had their own special canton, but the Bachelor Officer Quarters and dependent housing were integrated. Field-grade officers, at least one of whom was black, all lived in a special area known as "the Circle" if their families had joined them in Japan.[48]

The dependent school at Gifu likewise served all, but there an unwritten code existed. Black and white children played and studied together from kindergarten through junior high school but went their separate ways when high school and puberty approached. A black female, the wife of an infantry officer, served for a time as principal of the school

and headed an integrated teaching staff. She became the social arbiter for the black civilian women on base because no formal Officer's Wives Club existed, only a euphemistically named bridge club for whites only.[49]

Since blacks and whites were not expected to fraternize socially, most in-quarters social events were confined to single-race affairs. Nevertheless, some mingling did occur, especially among the families of the younger white officers and their black counterparts.[50] Even where people stayed apart, most got along, and many whites had at least a few black friends.[51]

Racial prejudice was so ingrained in the society of the day, however, that the men of the 24th faced

[47] Interv, Cash with Richard L. Fields, 18 Aug 88.

[48] Gorham Black says housing was basically segregated. See Interv, Cash with Gorham L. Black, Jr., 12 Mar 89. Bradley Biggs, William Bobo, and Albert Brooks, however, say that all facilities were integrated even though a segregated social climate prevailed. Bobo mentioned "the Circle." See Intervs, Cash with Biggs, 15 Aug 88; Bobo, 27 Jan 90; Albert Brooks, 28 Sep 88; Rainey with Hall, 2 Jun 90.

[49] Intervs, Cash with Kushner, 16 Jun 89; Bobo, 27 Jan 90; Albert Brooks, 6 Aug 88; Richard L. Fields, 18 Aug 88.

[50] Intervs, Cash with Bobo, 27 Jan 90; Kushner, 16 Jun 89. See also Ltr, Bobo to Cash, 28 Jan 90, CMH files.

[51] Intervs, Cash with Bobo, 27 Jan 90; Kushner, 16 Jun 89; Biggs, 15 Aug 88; John W. Anderson, 28 Aug 88; Ellis Dean, 7 Aug 88; French, 21 Jul 89; Haynesworth, 6 Sep 88; Hilyer, 17 Aug 88; Sammons, 27 Aug 88; Saxton, 3 Dec 88; Edward Simmons, 18 Mar 89; Muehlbauer with Ira Simon, 2 Sep 89; Rainey with Frank Kelly, 23 Oct 89.

special difficulties whenever they left Gifu or came in contact with the other regiments of the 25th Division. The annual Fourth of July parade in Tokyo marked a particular low for some. They felt degraded and insulted by cat calls, racial slurs, and comments from the sidelines about "blackbirds," "boys," and "niggers." They also complained because their band received the position behind the tanks, at the very end of the line of march, where it seemed certain to go unnoticed by reviewers. The day often degenerated into arguments and brawls.[52]

The bad feelings that resulted from occasions of that sort obscured reality in the memories of some of the men. The fights, for example, according to platoon sergeant Walter Bufford, often resulted less from racial antipathies than from intense competition between the men of the 25th Division and those of the 1st Cavalry, which was stationed in Tokyo. There were also fights in Yokohama with men from the 11th Airborne Division because some of the soldiers of the 24th liked to wear jump boots. As for the band, the unit's flag bearer, Harold Rogue, recalled that even if it did come last, it was so good and the men marched with such rhythm and spirit that all of the spectators on the main reviewing stand cheered wildly when it stepped around the corner into view. At some of the parades, Colonel Halloran stood proudly next to MacArthur as his men passed. Their step—a "jive turkey type of march" according to Lieutenant Hilyer—was so distinctive and so popular that on at least one occasion the men were asked to reassemble for an encore.[53]

A few members of the regiment suggest that the Army considered them so inferior that higher headquarters all but ignored them. General MacArthur, some avowed, never once paid a visit to the base at Gifu. In fact, whatever the prejudices of the high command, the 24th received its full share of inspectors and official visitors. MacArthur himself arrived during 1949. Although few details survive, black 1st Lt. Gorham Black recalled that he served as public affairs officer for the occasion, and Mrs. William A. Bobo recalled that Mrs. MacArthur visited the 24th's school at least once.[54]

Despite segregation and the humiliations it involved, the camp at Gifu itself became an enclave where black soldiers could pursue their own interests without undue stress from the outside world. They had their own newspaper. Those who wished to do so could swim at the regimental pool. They also had access to an American Red Cross club on post that was so popular it counted 10,000 patron visits during the month of July 1947 alone. One of the most attractive places in the camp, the club contained a lounge, a photographic laboratory, a library, a craft shop, a canteen, writing and game rooms, a patio, and a "Little Theater"—all for the use of enlisted personnel. Eventually, the camp would also include a commissary, a post exchange, a school for dependent children, and a combination stage and movie house equal to those found in many large cities. The men of the 24th also had the exclusive use of Camp Patterson, a former Japanese hotel and recreation facility located near Gifu on the picturesque Kiso River. Overall, life with the regiment was so pleasant that it exceeded anything many of the soldiers had ever known. It was so agreeable, indeed, that some of the men preferred the assignment to Gifu to service elsewhere and were reluctant to leave when their tours of duty in Japan ended. The base at Gifu was, as Norman Taylor put it, "our own little world."[55]

Unit pride was high within the 24th. James Perkins recalled that commanders wanted the regi-

[52] Intervs, Cash with Albert Kimber, 11 Mar 89; Earline Richardson, 6 Aug 88; Ward, 21 Jul 88; Willard D. Carter, 24 Sep 88.

[53] Intervs, Cash with Rogue, 14 Oct 88; Bufford, 13 Mar 89; Perkins, 28 Jul 89; Hilyer, 17 Aug 88; Ward, 21 Jul 88; Thomas, 24 Aug 89. A veteran of the 35th Infantry, Lt. Gen. Sidney Berry, agreed with Bufford. Men of his unit also fought with members of the 1st Cavalry. See Ltr, Sidney Berry to Jeffrey J. Clarke, 14 Mar 95, CMH files.

[54] Intervs, Cash with Biggs, 15 Aug 88; Richard L. Fields, 18 Aug 88; Gorham Black, 12 Mar 89; Bobo, 27 Jan 90.

[55] Annual Hist of the 24th Inf Rgt for 1947, 2 Mar 48, pp. 4–8; Intervs, Cash with Eldridge, 26 Aug 88; Raymond C. Hagins, 28 Aug 88; Jerry Johnson, 23 Sep 88; Moore, 19 Aug 88; Rogue, 14 Oct 88; Ward, 21 Jul 88; Bowers with Genous S. Hodges, 13 Apr 94; Muehlbauer with Norman Taylor, 16 Sep 88; Harry A. Davis, 26 Sep 88. Camp Patterson is described in Interv, Cash with Bufford, 13 Mar 89.

Colonel Halloran with Pfc. Buffalo Simmons, a 24th Infantry boxing team member

ment's men to dress well and ensured that they looked smart when they left the base on leave. He recalled that on one occasion he was turned back at the gate three times until he got his uniform in order. Some of the men, Perkins noted, would carry the habit to Korea, going into combat with their uniforms looking as though they were ready for a parade.[56]

The 24th's band added to the men's self-esteem by winning renown throughout the Far East Command, where it was on constant call to perform at special functions. Due in part to the large pool of black soldiers available, the regiment also fielded many of the best athletic teams in the Eighth Army. Its members dominated sports such as baseball, football, basketball, and boxing and often filled the ranks of teams from higher headquarters. During 1949 a heavyweight boxer from the 1st Battalion, M. Sgt. Howard "Big Boy" Williams, won the All Japan, Far East Command, Inter-Command, and All Army Boxing titles. In December of that year, the unit's football and basketball teams also won divisional championships. The coach of the successful football team, 2d Lt.

Joseph W. DeMarco, received a special letter of commendation.[57]

The unit's athletic prowess was a source of particular pride for Colonel Halloran, who could always be found at sporting events, especially those that pitted his soldiers against teams from the 27th and 35th regiments. Following the custom of the Army in that day, Halloran made practice and conditioning the principal occupations of soldiers with exceptional athletic ability while banishing those who failed in interunit competitions to the status of riflemen.[58]

Most soldiers at Gifu presented their officers with few serious disciplinary problems beyond those common to any military unit. Although some of the replacements who arrived during early 1948 were street toughs who had chosen to enter the Army rather than go to jail, commanders gradually eliminated those who failed to listen to reason, either reassigning them at the first opportunity to port units or invoking AR 615–369, a regulation designed to remove enlisted personnel from the service for ineptitude or unsuitability. Meanwhile, the 24th's military police detachment, the 512th MP Company, whose members were selected for their size and intimidating appearance, kept behavior problems on and near the base to a minimum. Those that did occur usually involved black-market trading, curfew violations, unauthorized absences, public intoxication, or fistfights.[59]

---

[56] Intervs, Cash with Perkins, 28 Jul 89; Rainey with William Cobb, 4 Dec 89; Kelly, 23 Oct 89.

[57] See Annual Hist of the 24th Inf Rgt for 1949, 21 Jan 50, p. 3, CMH files. The Annual History of the 24th Infantry Regiment for 1948 is missing. See also Intervs, Cash with Saxton, 3 Dec 88; Bufford, 13 Mar 89; Colon Britt, 18 Aug 88; HQ, 24th Inf Rgt, Letter of Commendation to 2d Lt Joseph W. DeMarco, 31 Jan 50, CMH files.

[58] 24th Inf Rgt Newsletter, May 49, CMH files; Annual Hist of the 24th Inf Rgt for 1949, 21 Jan 50, p. 7. Ellis Dean talks about Halloran's approach to failed athletes. See Interv, Cash with Dean, 7 Aug 88. See also Intervs, Cash with Haynesworth, 6 Sep 88; Muehlbauer with Allen, 18 Oct 88; Harry A. Davis, 26 Sep 88; Ferguson, 2 Sep 88; Bowers with Donald E. LaBlanc, 28 Feb 94. An officer in the 27th Infantry, Uzal W. Ent, notes that similar practices prevailed in that unit. See Interv, MacGarrigle and Bowers with Uzal W. Ent, 20 Oct 93.

[59] Intervs, Cash with Biggs, 15 Aug 88; Bufford, 13 Mar 89; Edmonds, 6 Jan 90; Ward, 21 Jul 88; Muehlbauer with

As with Army units around the world, venereal disease was a constant concern. It caused more lost duty time in the Eighth Army than any other illness, including the common cold.[60] Commanders and regimental medics labored continually to remedy the problem, yet they were never truly certain they had it in hand. Some units, both white and black, saved face by failing to report VD cases or by labeling them "non-specific urethritis." In addition, at least a few of the soldiers who became infected consulted civilian doctors rather than face damage to their military careers.[61]

The Japanese police were of little assistance because local law had no provisions banning prostitution. They took hundreds of girls into custody for physical examination but could do little else to keep them off the street. Those found to be infected were sent to hospitals for treatment with medications supplied by U.S. forces, but since the drugs involved had to be outdated before the Army could release them to civilians, the procedure was rarely effective. Indeed, it appears to have made matters worse. After the women were released they were regarded as preferred risks by their customers. As a result, so many volunteered for treatment, medical officers concluded that the entire process encouraged rather than inhibited spread of the disease.[62]

Contacts with prostitutes posed little problem for the 24th while it was on Ie Shima, but difficulties began as soon as the regiment arrived at Gifu. Unable to stop the disease at its source, by inspecting local prostitutes and providing effective treatment for them, the unit concentrated on its own people. Regimental chaplains continually lectured on the subject, and medical officers conducted VD prevention classes, distributed prophylactic kits, maintained treatment stations for each battalion, and operated a rehabilitation center (some called it "a VD company") to handle the cases that came to light. Before the troops left post to go downtown, they received a "penicillin cocktail." As they went through the camp's gates, they were also exposed to large, cartoon-style posters showing the effects of the disease. When they returned, they had to certify in writing whether they had performed a sex act.[63]

The 24th conducted unannounced monthly inspections to determine whether individual soldiers had broken out with symptoms of the disease. Those who had were called to Halloran's office with their commanding officers, where all concerned were chastised. First-time offenders received thirty days of medical attention and underwent a punishing regime of physical conditioning. In an attempt to incorporate unit pride into the treatment process and to ensure that officers understood they would be held responsible for failures within their units, Colonel Halloran also saw to it that the company with the most venereal disease cases in a month carried a guidon during regimental parades marked with a prominent VD.[64]

The regiment's efforts had their effect, but parts of the program proved counterproductive over the long run. Continual doses of penicillin, for example, brought out allergies in some of the men or built up immunities to the drug. Meanwhile, peer pressure had a more powerful influence over the

Allen, 18 Oct 88; Eddie Capers, 2 Nov 88; Ferguson, 2 Sep 88; MacGarrigle with Green, 16 Jun 94. The gang members were mentioned both by Waymon R. Ransom and William A. Hash. See Interv, Bowers with William A. Hash, 17 Mar 94; Ltr, Ransom to Cash, 22 Oct 88.

[60] HQ, Eighth U.S. Army, Japan, Occupational Monograph of the Eighth U.S. Army in Japan, January–December 1948, vol. 4, pt. 1, pp. 107–08, CMH files.

[61] HQ, I Corps, Eighth Army, Annual Command and Unit Historical Reports, 1949, p. 17, AG 314.7–D, box P–473, RG 338, WNRC. Quote from Interv, Cash with Perkins, 28 Jul 89.

[62] HQ, Eighth U.S. Army, Japan, Occupational Monograph of the Eighth U.S. Army in Japan, September 1946–December 1947, vol. 3, p. 171, CMH files. See also Interv, Rainey with Cobb, 4 Dec 89.

[63] For a description of the Eighth Army's VD programs, see HQ, Eighth U.S. Army, Japan, Occupational Monograph of the Eighth U.S. Army in Japan, September 1946–December 1947, p. 172. See also Intervs, Rainey with Cobb, 4 Dec 89; William Hough, 16 Nov 89; Cash with Edmonds, 6 Jan 90; William E. Gott, 2 Sep 89; Waymon R. Ransom, 5 Aug 88; Saxton, 3 Dec 88; Thomas, 24 Aug 89; Williams, 8 Oct 88; Muehlbauer with Houston McMurray, Jun 88; MacGarrigle with John S. Komp, 1 Jun 94.

[64] Ibid. The story of the guidon is mentioned in Interv, Cash with Biggs, 15 Aug 88.

conduct of soldiers than strictures laid down by officers. Indeed, most took it as a matter of honor to have sex while on leave, and any who denied that they had opened themselves to the laughter of their fellows. As for attempts to badger offenders and their officers, they were so demoralizing, according to the commander of Company L, Capt. Bradley Biggs, that at least one commander ceased reporting the full extent of VD infection within his unit. Others probably did the same. Some enlisted men attempted to hide the disease by treating themselves with black-market penicillin or by resorting to quack doctors in Gifu whose remedies only made matters worse.[65]

One procedure Colonel Halloran began worked very well. Halloran warned his troops that he would send a letter to the parents or wives of those who contracted the disease more than once to explain the problem and the course of therapy. The threat alone was usually enough to keep relapses from occurring. If a man came down with VD three times, he was discharged as a recalcitrant.[66] By December 1947 the regiment's efforts had paid off. The command could boast that it had discovered only five cases of venereal disease during the month. At that time the Eighth Army as a whole was experiencing a rate of 202 per thousand among blacks in general and 121 per thousand among whites.[67]

By the start of 1948 the 24th had completed its training and was prepared to take up its occupation duties. As with the other American units serving in Japan, it began searching the countryside for abandoned Japanese weapons and munitions, conducting police patrols in the area around Gifu, and furnishing security assistance to the military government. During April, when civil disturbances broke out among angry Korean immigrants at Kobe, some of the unit's men assist-ed in restoring order. After an earthquake struck at Fukui during June, the regiment provided a medical team to aid in relief efforts.[68]

According to Sgt. Waymon Ransom, if 1947 "saw the peak of the 24th," 1948 was "the beginning of the end." Since the regiment had more members than any other in Japan, the Eighth Army assigned it to provide security for Kobe Base, an important dock, ordnance depot, and storage area located west of Osaka. Beginning in January 1948 the battalions of the regiment alternated in the task, standing guard on a ninety-day rotation schedule.[69]

At that time, Kobe was a major transshipment point for reparations materiel going abroad in accord with the terms of Japan's surrender. An international city, it was a magnet for vices of every sort, a hub of prostitution, and an important point of entry into the country for hard drugs. Duty there was dangerous—several members of the 24th were killed by Japanese, Korean, or American thieves attempting to steal valuable equipment from the warehouses—but it was also attractive to the men of the 24th because life at the port was much more interesting than at Gifu. Commanders attempted to keep their troops out of trouble, going so far as to post guards between housing for the regiment and that of a problem-ridden U.S. quartermaster company stationed permanently nearby, but the duty was a losing proposition from the start. Although some of the men did their jobs so well they were commended for their initiative and attention to duty, many more caused problems. By March venereal disease had begun once more to rise within the unit, black-market activities were increasing, and drugs, for the first time, were becoming a concern.[70]

---

[65] Intervs, Cash with Biggs, 15 Aug 88; Muehlbauer with McMurray, Jun 88; MacGarrigle with Komp, 1 Jun 94; Ltr, Komp to MacGarrigle, 14 Apr 95.

[66] Interv, Cash with Thomas, 24 Aug 89.

[67] Annual Hist of the 24th Inf Rgt for 1947, 2 Mar 48, p. 17; HQ, Eighth U.S. Army, Japan, Occupational Monograph of the Eighth U.S. Army in Japan, September 1946–December 1947, vol. 3, p. 171.

[68] Annual Hist of the 24th Inf Rgt for 1947, 2 Mar 48, p. 17. The earthquake duty is covered in HQ, Eighth U.S. Army, Japan, Occupational Monograph of the Eighth U.S. Army in Japan, January–December 1948, vol. 4, pt. 2, G–3 Annex C, Incl 6, CMH files. The 24th's role in deterring civil disturbances is mentioned in ibid., Judge Advocate General's section, vol. 4, pt. 2, app. M–1.

[69] Ltr, Ransom to Cash, 22 Oct 88; Annual Hist of the 24th Inf Rgt for 1947, 2 Mar 48, p. 17.

[70] HQ, I Corps, Eighth Army, Annual Command and Unit Historical Reports, 1949, p. 17; Kobe Base Historical files, boxes P–266, P–268, RG 338, WNRC. See also Intervs, MacGarrigle

Where the men were housed at Kobe was part of the problem. The commander of Company B, Capt. William A. Hash, recalled that his unit was stationed in an old Japanese hospital that had been damaged during the war. No longer used for its original purpose, the building contained long hallways and many rooms into which the men could disappear when off duty. Another Japanese hospital across the street still functioned as a medical facility, treating female patients who had contracted venereal disease. The street between the two was populated with drug peddlers and other unsavory characters.[71] The combination of those circumstances came close to tearing a battalion apart. It would take three months, platoon leader 1st Lt. Leonard Kushner avowed, to reconstitute a unit after it had returned from Kobe. Then it would be time to go back again.[72]

The problem with VD declined later in the year when commanders renewed their efforts to stem the spread of the disease, but drug abuse grew, not only at Kobe but also at Gifu. Prostitutes at the port and others nearby would lure the men into buying heroin by offering their favors free to users. The men would then carry their addictions back to Gifu, where they would at times sell their gear, down to the sheets off their beds, to service their habits. At one point, just prior to the 24th's deployment to Korea, the problem became so serious at Gifu that 3d Battalion platoon leader 2d Lt. Alfred Tittel found syringes and needles scattered everywhere in one of the unit's latrines. A few drug users overdosed and died. Others managed to hide their dependencies. Some became addicted for life and even carried their habits into combat in Korea, where they continued to indulge.

The full extent of the problem itself is difficult to determine. Few officers were familiar with drug abuse and its consequences at the time, and doctors sometimes misdiagnosed overdoses as heart attacks or as alcohol poisoning.[73]

As commanders became more familiar with the problem, they took what steps they could to suppress it. One of their favorite tactics was the so-called shakedown. They conducted night raids, searched the men's lockers, separated suspects from the rest of the troops, and then held the men for up to seventy-two hours in their underwear to see which would develop withdrawal symptoms. During 1949 and 1950, criminal investigation teams made a special effort to entrap and apprehend drug pushers at Gifu. Urinalysis tests were also conducted when they became available. Early in 1950, one of the few black field-grade officers in the Army, Lt. Col. Forest Lofton, took charge of drug eradication efforts at the camp. He seemed stern and harsh to Pvt. William Cobb. When he caught an offender, Cobb said, he would throw the man in jail and begin the process of removing him from the Army.[74]

Raids and searches notwithstanding, as the commander of the 3d Battalion's Company K, 1st Lt. Jasper Johnson, avowed, the regiment never managed to determine who the dealers were because of a seemingly unbreakable code of silence among the men. Captain Hash agreed— although he was able to apprehend drug users from time to time, he never caught a dealer until one of his best soldiers was killed in Korea. Opening a small Bible retrieved from the man's body, he found the records of the soldier's clients and their transactions and suddenly realized that

with Adams, 15 and 17 Jun 94; Lloyd V. Ott, 19 Jul 94; Cash with Willie Brooks, 14 Oct 88; Kushner, 16 Jun 89; Gorham Black, 12 Mar 89; Muehlbauer with Marion Boyd, 13 Feb 89.

[71] Interv, MacGarrigle with Hash, 9 Jun 94. Regimental personnel officer Sam Adams notes that drug abuse became a particular problem for the 24th because of the requirement for the regiment to station a battalion at Kobe. See Intervs, MacGarrigle with Adams, 15 and 17 Jun 94.

[72] Interv, Cash with Kushner, 16 Jun 89. See also Intervs, MacGarrigle with Adams, 15 and 17 Jun 94; Ott, 19 Jul 94. Only two battalions were available for duty at Kobe. The 2d Battalion remained inactive because of personnel shortages.

[73] Ltr, Ransom to Cash, 22 Oct 88; Annual Hist of the 24th Inf Rgt for 1947, 2 Mar 48, p. 17. See also Intervs, Cash with Gorham Black, 12 Mar 89; Nathaniel Reed, 6 Jan 90; Jasper Johnson, 5 Oct 88; Rainey with Cobb, 4 Dec 89; Muehlbauer with Harry Davis, 26 Sep 88; Bowers with Alfred F. Tittel, 15 Apr 94; MacGarrigle with William A. Hash, 9 Jun 94; Ltr, Komp to MacGarrigle, 14 Apr 95.

[74] Intervs, Rainey with Cobb, 4 Dec 89; Cash with Jasper Johnson, 5 Oct 88; Reed, 6 Jan 90; MacGarrigle with Komp, 1 Jun 94.

some of his troops were still using drugs even as combat raged around them.[75]

Overall estimates of the size of the problem vary. Although a few veterans of the regiment remain unconvinced that much of a problem existed, Jasper Johnson asserted that he had thirteen soldiers in the stockade on drug charges when his unit embarked for Korea and that most of them rejoined the force for the trip. Cobb observed that perhaps ten out of a hundred men were involved in one way or another. Sergeant Ransom claimed that by the spring of 1950, up to one-third of the regiment's assigned strength was either using drugs or dealing in them.[76]

The extent of the problem in other units is difficult to determine, but it must have been substantial, at least in those serving near ports and large cities. Eighth Army provost marshal summaries for the first half of 1950 indicate that criminal violations involving narcotics constituted the largest single category of crimes committed within the command, running at an average of 25 percent of all offenses in any given month between January and May.[77]

Although venereal disease and drug abuse were serious within the regiment, they paled in comparison with a further affliction that ate continually at the 24th. For if, as the Gillem Board had stipulated, the 25th Division dealt evenhandedly with the regiment where training and occupation duties were concerned, racial prejudice was still woven into the very fabric of military life as blacks knew it. The black members of the unit, whether officers or enlisted, who did their jobs well, avoided prostitutes, and never touched drugs understood that their good conduct and performance meant little because the Army considered them second rate and put whites first.

The regiment's black officers experienced the problem most acutely, beginning with the assignment process that brought them to Gifu. When a black officer arrived in Japan, the U.S. Eighth Army interviewed him as though it had positions matching his training and ability and sent him around the country to speak with various commanders who supposedly also had openings. All concerned nevertheless understood that the procedure was a charade. Except for one public affairs officer, some military policemen, and a few civilian federal employees, the Eighth Army employed no blacks at its headquarters in Tokyo. Meanwhile, the segregated 24th Infantry and the 77th Engineer Combat Company, both located at Gifu, and the affiliated artillery unit, the 159th Field Artillery Battalion, located somewhat to the south of Gifu at Nara, were the only combat commands in Japan where blacks were welcome. As the commander of the 24th's Company I, black 1st Lt. Gorham Black, Jr., observed, black officers, whatever their skills and backgrounds, always ended up at Gifu, at Nara, or with a service unit.[78]

Racial discrimination continued once a black officer joined his unit. Following the dictates of a 1944 War Department pamphlet, *The Command of*

[75] Ltr, Ransom to Cash, 22 Oct 88; Intervs, Rainey with Cobb, 4 Dec 89; Cash with Hagins, 28 Aug 88; Jasper Johnson, 5 Oct 88; MacGarrigle with Hash, 9 Jun 94. For other comments about drugs in Korea, see Intervs, Cash with William Shepard, 27 Oct 88; Edward Simmons, 18 Mar 89; Bowers with Hodges, 13 Apr 94; Clifton F. Vincent, 20 Apr 94; Tittel, 15 Apr 94.

[76] Ltr, Ransom to Cash, 22 Oct 88; Intervs, Rainey with Cobb, 4 Dec 89; Cash with Jasper Johnson, 5 Oct 88.

[77] The Provost Marshal Reports are in Eighth U.S. Army, Korea, Monthly Historical Summaries, Jan–May 50, box P–480, RG 338, WNRC. The extent of drug abuse in Japan appears never to have come close to what the Army experienced during the Vietnam War. In 1971, 45 percent of a random sampling of soldiers leaving Vietnam who were interviewed under promises of immunity from prosecution admitted that they had used unauthorized narcotics, barbiturates, or amphetamines at least once during their tours of duty. Twenty-nine percent said they had used them regularly (more than ten times and more than weekly), and 20 percent reported that they had been addicted. See Lee N. Robbins, Executive Office of the President, Special Action Office for Drug Abuse Prevention, *The Vietnam Drug User Returns* (Washington, D.C.: Government Printing Office, 1973), pp. vii–ix, 29–44.

[78] Interv, Cash with Gorham Black, 12 Mar 89. For experiences of other black officers, see Intervs, Bowers with Clifton F. Vincent, 19 and 20 Apr 94; Cash with John "Tommy" Martin, 12 Jan 90; Roger Walden, 18 Mar 89. See also MS, Bradley Biggs, Were Black Scapegoats for Our Failures in Korea? n.d., p. 1, CMH files.

Negro Troops, the Eighth Army allowed black lieutenants and captains to lead only at the platoon and company levels and assigned field-grade positions at the rank of major and above almost entirely to whites. Indeed, the few black majors and lieutenant colonels at Gifu were either chaplains or filled administrative positions within the regiment's headquarters. Even in those cases, blacks were convinced that discrimination occurred.[79] The regimental chaplain in the 24th was a black lieutenant colonel, John Deveaux. In all-white regiments, Chaplain Gray Johnson observed, majors usually served as chaplains at the regimental level while lieutenant colonels became the chaplains of divisions. Deveaux was the exception. He failed to receive a job appropriate to his standing because of his race.[80] In the same way, Leo Hall observed, two black majors who had served in combat with the 92d Division, Maj. Augustus Hamilton and Maj. James A. Porter, failed to receive positions appropriate to their rank. Hamilton became the regimental support services officer and Porter the camp utilities officer.[81]

Although the number of black officers in the 24th was substantial—ranging from 52 percent in June 1947 to 40 percent in March 1949—those individuals almost never supervised or commanded white officers, even in cases where their dates of rank gave them precedence.[82] The regimental command

would even reassign officers wholesale within a battalion or in the regiment rather than allow a black to lead anyone but other blacks.[83] Indeed, each time the race of a commander changed in one of the regiment's twelve companies, a turnover in officers from white to black or black to white occurred. Between 6 June 1947 and 1 November 1948, as a result, Companies B, C, E, and K exchanged black officers for white while Companies G and L went from white to black.[84] In the same way, although most of the black officers in the 24th did well and were respected by both their men and their white counterparts, whites obtained most of the career-enhancing positions and sometimes moved rapidly ahead while blacks stayed in place, rarely advancing to ranks above captain.[85] One of the few exceptions was Capt. Richard W. Williams, a superlative leader who earned the admiration of his black officer colleagues and the awed reverence of his enlisted subordinates. As operations officer for the 1st Battalion in Japan, Williams was in a position where upward movement was possible.[86]

---

[79] War Department Pamphlet 20–6, *The Command of Negro Troops,* in MacGregor and Nalty, *Blacks in the United States Armed Forces,* vol. 5, item 83; Intervs, Cash with Gorham Black, 12 Mar 89; Albert Brooks, 6 Aug 88; Oliver Dillard, 26 Oct 88; Charles Bussey, 6 and 14 Jan 89; Biggs, 15 Aug 88.

[80] Interv, Cash with Gray Johnson, 23 Mar 89.

[81] Interv, Rainey with Hall, 2 Jun 90. See also Interv, Cash with Richard L. Fields, 18 Aug 88. For the positions of Majors Hamilton and Porter, see Officer Rosters, 24th Inf Rgt, 1 Nov 48 and 1 Mar 49, CMH files.

[82] The percentages were taken from unit rosters on file in CMH. See Officer Rosters, 24th Inf Rgt, 6 Jun 47, 1 Nov 48, 1 Mar 49, 18 Sep 50, CMH files. Some blacks did supervise whites at the battalion and regimental levels. Capt. Richard W. Williams, for example, was a battalion operations officer for a time in Japan. Although rumors exist that other blacks occasionally commanded whites, unit rosters give no indication that anything of the sort occurred in Japan. See Interv, Bowers with Leonard H. Kushner, 29 Jun 94. A few blacks did com-

mand whites in Korea, where, for example, the black commander of Company A, Capt. William J. Jackson, commanded at least one white, 1st Lt. Clair L. Rishel.

[83] Interv, Cash with Biggs, 15 Aug 88. The commander of Company D, John Komp, described such a change of command. See Interv, MacGarrigle with Komp, 1 Jun 94. Harold Montgomery recalls that all of the white officers were transferred out of his company just before he took command. See Interv, Rainey with Montgomery, 26 Mar 90.

[84] The changes become visible when the various rosters for the 24th Infantry are compared.

[85] For judgments on the quality of black officers, see Intervs, Cash with Kushner, 16 Jun 89; Haynesworth, 6 Sep 88; Perkins, 28 Jul 89; Pratt, 16 Jun 89; Reed, 6 Jan 90; Rogue, 14 Oct 88; Simmons, 18 Mar 89; Robert Taylor, 25 Sep 88; John S. Williams, 5 Aug 88; Bowers with Hash, 17 Mar 94. The Information and Education Branch survey of African-American soldiers in World War II noted that black soldiers overwhelmingly preferred black to white officers. See Stouffer et al., *The American Soldier: Adjustment During Army Life,* p. 580. For information on the relative promotability of blacks and whites, see Intervs, Cash with Biggs, 15 Aug 88; Richard L. Fields, 18 Aug 88; James Perkins, 10 Aug 88; Walden, 18 Mar 89; Rainey with Hall, 2 Jun 90; Muehlbauer with Moorman, 5 Sep 88.

[86] "Black Daddy" Williams was mentioned in more than forty interviews, almost always in a positive vein. See, for example, Intervs, Cash with Albert Brooks, 6 Aug 88; Richard

Unlike the regiment's black officers, the unit's noncommissioned officers were able to move ahead in their careers because they were competing only among themselves and not with whites. Many among both their subordinates and their superiors considered them exemplary soldiers. Some had been officers during World War II and a number had combat experience. If their test scores were often low, they still knew their weaponry, understood their soldierly duties, and were of enormous assistance to newly assigned lieutenants just beginning to feel their way.[87]

Opinions of that sort, however, were hardly universal. In the estimation of some enlisted men, the senior NCOs in particular were sometimes harsh, illiterate time servers and compromisers who had long since sold their souls to the white power structure and stayed in the Army because they had nowhere else to go. Wireman Raymond Hagins contended that his NCOs, in order to gain and keep their jobs, had learned to keep quiet and to stay in their place.[88] Mortarman Robert Taylor labeled many of his NCOs illiterate "Uncle Toms" who ruled by fear. "My 1st sergeant . . . was killed in Korea and I was so glad to see it. He was so mean and evil."[89]

As for the officers, their opinions varied. If many loyally stood behind their NCOs, others were critical. While most could name senior NCOs they considered exceptional, some considered the overall quality of the group less than desirable. Many senior NCOs were outstanding,

Company K's white commander, Lieutenant Johnson, thus observed, but few of the younger men coming up behind them had much to offer. Some were very sharp but most had been promoted too fast and lacked the qualifications and experience to do the job properly.[90] The white commander of Company B, Captain Hash, agreed. Although he would have willingly followed some of his senior sergeants anywhere, he said, he had to remove twelve to fourteen of his corporals after he took command because they lacked the skills to be good NCOs.[91] Company D's white commander, 1st Lt. John S. Komp, remarked that if his first sergeant, Sgt. James Geiger, was an excellent soldier who got things done, the abilities of the rest of his NCOs ran a gamut from good to bad. One, Komp noted, was decidedly substandard, but he was smart enough to find a bright young junior NCO to tend to the day-to-day business of his operations.[92]

The white officers serving with the 24th often had little choice as to their assignment, but some were volunteers who had taken up station at Gifu because the facilities were better and family housing was more plentiful than in other units.[93] A number of northerners were present, but many of the regiment's officers appear to have been from the South. If Army studies after World War II had established that black soldiers preferred to serve under black officers or failing that, under whites from the North, the word had been slow to move through the chain of command.[94] As a result, Army personnel officers still continued to believe that African-Americans performed best under white southerners. When shortages of officers occurred, they assigned whoever was qualified to the 24th, but if enough officers were present or too many

L. Fields, 18 Aug 88; Griffin, 5 Oct 88; Leroy Williams, 8 Oct 88. Williams retired a full colonel but gained the assignments necessary to do so in the years following the war, when the Army adopted a policy of equal opportunity for all. His chances for higher promotion may have been affected by his alcoholism, which was well known both at Gifu and in Korea.

[87] Intervs, Cash with Kushner, 16 Jun 89; Shearin, 17 Aug 88; Gorham Black, 12 Mar 89; Biggs, 15 Aug 88; Richard L. Fields, 18 Aug 88; Rainey with Montgomery, 26 Mar 90; Bowers with Hash, 17 Mar 94.

[88] Interv, Cash with Hagins, 28 Aug 88.

[89] Interv, Cash with Robert Taylor, 25 Sep 88. Leonard Kushner gives an example of the harsh discipline that black sergeants sometimes dealt to their men. See Interv, Bowers with Leonard H. Kushner, 29 Jun 94.

[90] Intervs, Bowers with Hodges, 13 Apr 94; Jasper Johnson, 18 Apr 94. Captain Hash was also critical of the regiment's junior NCOs. See Interv, Bowers with Hash, 17 Mar 94.

[91] Interv, Bowers with Hash, 17 Mar 94.

[92] Intervs, MacGarrigle with Komp, 5 May and 1 Jun 94.

[93] Intervs, Cash with Gray Johnson, 23 Mar 89; MacGarrigle with Berry, 11 Aug 93.

[94] Stouffer et al., *The American Soldier: Adjustment During Army Life*, p. 580.

arrived in theater at one time, the southerners tended to be the first chosen.[95]

According to both black and white veterans of the unit, while a number of the whites did well as commanders and dealt equitably both with their troops and their black counterparts, others complained bitterly, blaming everything that went wrong on the troops they commanded.[96] "What do they expect us to do?" white Lieutenant Hilyer recalled one asking. "Look at the troops we got."[97] A few, as enlisted ambulance driver James T. Burke perceived, so detested blacks that they made hardly any attempt to hide their feelings. Burke described his own immediate superior, a surgeon, as "very prejudiced. Very prejudiced."[98] Kushner agreed. His own battalion commander, he said, frequently disparaged the black officers under him, sometimes in their presence. He also excluded them from officer calls, preferring to present them with a condescending, five-minute briefing after the whites had departed.[99]

Exposed to such treatment, many black officers lost confidence in their white superiors. Becoming frustrated and resentful, some concluded that the Army expected so little of them that it had turned the 24th into a dumping ground for white officers no other unit would have. The 24th was a "penal" regiment for white officers who had "screwed up," black 2d Lt. Albert Brooks thus believed. It was their last chance to redeem their careers. The officers kept the feeling mostly to themselves, but once in a while it broke into public. On one occasion during a training exercise, Lieutenant Johnson recalled, a frustrated young black officer lashed back at an abusive white by saying, "The only reason you are here is because you are no damned good."[100]

The unit's enlisted men were often of the same opinion. The more charitable among them dismissed problems with their white officers as a product of the cultural gap between blacks and whites. It was difficult for the average white officer to command black troops, Walter Bufford said, because they had little understanding of their men.[101] Others concluded that their white commanders hated them and were not above retaliating, when they could, against those they perceived to be the most against them.[102]

A case in point occurred when the 1st Battalion of the 24th Infantry, commanded by the officer Kushner referred to as a bigot, was selected to participate in a special parade at Osaka honoring Secretary of the Army Royall. The men practiced diligently and looked good at Gifu, but they traveled to Osaka overnight by train. Arriving tired and in wrinkled uniforms, they were unfairly reprimanded for their appearance by their commander, who was probably under considerable stress himself but should have known better.[103]

They got back at him during the parade that followed. When the unit received the order "eyes right," up to 20 percent of its members fell apart on

---

[95] The commander of Company K, 1st Lt. Jasper Johnson, would later assert that twenty-one of the twenty-three officers that he and his wife could recall from their service in Japan were northerners. See Interv, Cash with Jasper Johnson, 5 Oct 88. Others dispute the observation. See, for example, Intervs, Cash with Hilyer, 17 Aug 88; Richard L. Fields, 18 Aug 88. Houston McMurray notes that he and four other southerners were assigned to the 24th on the same day because there was an oversupply of officers when they arrived in Japan. See Interv, Muehlbauer with McMurray, Jun 88. Since the Stouffer study makes a point of the Army's predilection for appointing white southern officers to all-black units and many members of the 24th commented on the practice, we have sided with Hilyer, McMurray, and the others. See Stouffer et al., *The American Soldier: Adjustment During Army Life*, pp. 580–84.

[96] Intervs, Cash with Jasper Johnson, 5 Oct 88; Adolf Voight, 21 Sep 88; Biggs, 15 Aug 88; Albert Brooks, 6 Aug 88; Jerry Johnson, 23 Sep 88; Reed, 6 Jan 90; Rainey with Montgomery, 26 Mar 90; Muehlbauer with Ferguson, 2 Sep 88.

[97] Interv, Cash with Hilyer, 17 Aug 88.

[98] Interv, Muehlbauer with James T. Burke, 23 Jan 89.

[99] Interv, Cash with Kushner, 16 Jun 89.

[100] Intervs, Bowers with Jasper Johnson, 18 Apr 94; Cash with Albert Brooks, 6 Aug 88. Some white officers agreed. One told 1st Lt. Leonard Kushner that he had fouled up in an earlier assignment and had been sent to the 24th as punishment. See Interv, Bowers with Kushner, 29 Jun 94.

[101] Interv, Cash with Bufford, 13 Mar 89.

[102] Intervs, Cash with Albert Brooks, 6 Aug 88; Reed, 6 Jan 90; Robert Taylor, 15 Sep 88.

[103] Intervs, Cash with Kushner, 16 Jun 89; Bowers with Kushner, 29 Jun 94.

cue, slouching, scratching themselves, and losing step. Then, when the command "ready front" was given, they all returned to the march and performed flawlessly. All the while, the battalion's commander marched smartly in the lead, oblivious to what was happening, while General MacArthur and the other officials on the reviewing stand looked on in chagrin. In the end, none of the soldiers were punished because none of the culprits could be identified, but their commander was roundly rebuked for his poor leadership by the 25th Division's commanding general, Maj. Gen. William B. Kean.[104]

Although Colonel Halloran was admired by many within the 24th for his lack of racial bias, an attitude of condescension appears to have prevailed within the unit, even among whites who were well disposed. It mirrored the low expectations the Army as a whole held toward blacks. "This corps has the only colored regimental combat team in this theater and the largest group of colored combat units within Eighth Army," the annual history of the I Corps command, which contained the 24th Infantry, reported at the end of 1949. "The command and training of such units has always presented certain problems. By assignment of the better officers to these units and increasing the time allotted for completion of training phases, it is possible for colored units to reach the same standard of training as other similar type units."[105]

A comparable attitude was plain to see in the 24th Infantry. A recruiting officer in Japan who visited all the units, Capt. Martin A. Peters, for example, told the Eighth Army inspector general that the 24th's officers "would more or less bend" in the direction of their black subordinates to "keep them happy and avoid any rumors of discrimination." He added that he did so himself. "My remarks are guarded; I never say anything in their presence or indirectly that might indicate discrimination. I wouldn't want to injure their feelings. I have seen that with a lot of other people."[106]

Lieutenant Hilyer agreed. Commanders at Gifu rarely came down hard on their men, he said. Instead, there was "a lot of pussy footin' around." A white West Point graduate, 1st Lt. Houston McMurray, added that when black NCOs complained that he was prejudiced because he had required them to salute and to follow regulations, the company commander called him in and told him, "You have come over here for a 30-month tour in the Far East. You're assigned to this outfit. What you're going to have to do is lower your standards and go with the way things are and not the way you'd like them to be."[107] Colonel Halloran may not have been responsible for the many problems at Gifu—high rates of drug abuse, low literacy levels, the VD problem—the 1st Battalion's white intelligence officer, Capt. Gustav J. Gillert, Jr., observed, but under him "a climate of cover-up, benign neglect, acceptance of inadequate performance, and often resignation" prospered.[108]

The idea that more could be tolerated in the 24th than in a white unit appears to have extended, to some degree, to the unit's homosexuals. Most were very capable and kept to themselves, but the regiment apparently had enough difficulties to prompt comments from a number of knowledgeable soldiers.[109] The problem was "terrible," enlisted man James Perkins remarked. "It scared me half to death."[110] It extended from minor episodes of sexual harassment—cat calls while units were drilling and comments in passing, such as "ain't he cute," that women have long had to endure—to incidents of brazen indiscretion.[111] Some of the

---

[104] Ibid.

[105] HQ, I Corps, Eighth Army, Annual Command and Unit Historical Reports, 1949, p. 18.

[106] Interv, Inspector General (IG) with Capt Martin A. Peters, 7 Feb 51, exhibit B–91, in General Headquarters, Far

East Command, Report of Investigation Regarding Alleged Irregularities in the Administration of Military Justice in the 25th Infantry Division, 27 Mar 51, boxes 1013–1014 (hereafter cited as Far East Command Inspector General Investigation), RG 159, WNRC.

[107] Intervs, Cash with Hilyer, 17 Aug 88; Muehlbauer with McMurray, Jun 88.

[108] Interv, MacGarrigle with Gustav J. Gillert, 4 May 94.

[109] See Intervs, Cash with Gorham Black, 12 Mar 89; Perkins, 28 Jul 89; Rogue, 14 Oct 88; Ransom, 5 Aug 88; Saxton, 3 Dec 88; William Shepard, 27 Oct 88.

[110] Interv, Cash with Perkins, 28 Jul 89.

[111] Ibid.

unit's officers were alleged to have been homosexual, and Halloran's orderly himself is said to have thrown wild homosexual parties in his quarters at times when the colonel was absent.[112] There were also instances of outright corruption. Since homosexuals were heavily concentrated in the regiment's personnel section, I&R platoon member Harold Rogue observed, they were in a position not only to take care of their own but also to provide many of the same services to heterosexuals in return for bribes. On one occasion, Rogue said, he gave "the man" in the recreation office $100 and received three weeks instead of one at Camp Patterson.[113]

As in the case of the mess tent on Ie Shima, commanders at Gifu looked the other way, even though the Army itself was in the process of tightening its policies on homosexuals and beginning in 1947 had tripled its discharge rate per thousand for men and women of that persuasion.[114] They may have been naive, as Gorham Black observed, speaking of himself, or they may have been lax to the point of ineptitude, as Capt. Charles Bussey commented in the case of a failure by the 25th Division and the Eighth Army to permit the discharge of a flagrant homosexual who had set up a veritable love nest in the 77th Engineer Combat Company's barracks at Gifu.[115] Nonetheless, a suspicion lingers that they declined to take action in at least some cases, as Waymon Ransom alleged, because they expected little from blacks, and the unit's homosexuals were among the regiment's most intelligent and efficient members.[116] When one soldier complained about the homosexu-

als in his unit, squad leader Roscoe Jones recalled, Halloran laughed the issue away by declaring at a troop formation, tongue-in-cheek, that if every member of the regiment were homosexual the unit would have no VD problem.[117]

A Time of Change, 1949

If 1947 was a peak for the 24th and 1948 seemed a year in which problems predominated, 1949 was a time of change. During the spring, the United States eased its occupation policies toward Japan in preparation for that country's return to full independence. At that time, the Eighth Army dropped many of the policing and administrative functions that had occupied its men. Meanwhile, tensions were increasing between the Soviet Union and the United States. Much of Eastern Europe had fallen into the Communist orbit, and the pro-American government of Nationalist China had given way to the Communist forces of Mao Tse-tung. Since threats to the United States were on the rise around the world and the men of the Eighth Army had less and less to do, the commander in chief of the Far East Command, General MacArthur, decided to put an end to the easy life that was sapping his forces in Japan and to begin a course of intensive training that would energize them into the hard, competent, combat-ready team they were supposed to be.[118]

To that end, the Eighth Army's commander, Lt. Gen. Walton H. Walker, instructed all Eighth Army combat units in Japan to complete their training at the rifle company level by December 1949. Battalion-level conditioning was to be finished by May 1950 and regimental exercises by July. Between July and December full divisions would train as complete units. Meanwhile, logisticians, signalmen, and other specialists were to refine their skills. Once all concerned had reached maximum

---

[112] Interv, Cash with Ransom, 5 Aug 88.

[113] Interv, Cash with Rogue, 14 Oct 88. A platoon leader in the 14th Infantry, Edward King, also noted that homosexuals tended to congregate in the personnel, mess, and administrative sections of Army units. See Interv, Cash with Edward L. King, 27 Jun 89.

[114] Allan Berube, *Coming Out Under Fire: The History of Gay Men and Women in World War Two* (New York: Free Press, 1990), p. 262. See also Colin J. Williams and Martin S. Weinberg, *Homosexuals and the Military* (New York: Harper & Row, 1971), pp. 26–29, 45–49.

[115] Interv, Cash with Gorham Black, 12 Mar 89; Charles M. Bussey, *Firefight at Yechon: Courage and Racism in the Korean War* (Washington, D.C.: Brassey's [U.S.], 1991), pp. 65–69.

[116] Ibid. See also Interv, Cash with Ransom, 5 Aug 88.

[117] Intervs, Cash with Roscoe Jones, 16 Jun 89; Ransom, 5 Aug 88.

[118] For more on the period, see Schnabel, *Policy and Direction*, pp. 41–60; Steven L. Reardon, *History of the Office of the Secretary of Defense, The Formative Years, 1947–1950* (Washington, D.C.: Historical Office, Office of the Secretary of Defense, 1984), pp. 209–308.

Troops of the 25th Infantry Division unload trucks and equipment at Sasebo Railway Station, Japan.

efficiency, the Eighth Army's combat units were to begin joint training exercises with U.S. Air Force units stationed in Japan.[119]

For a number of reasons, as with the other regiments in Japan the 24th Infantry achieved only mixed results from its training. Personnel turbulence, for example, remained heavy, with the unit sometimes experiencing annual turnover rates exceeding 50 percent. Understrength by about 100 men at the beginning of 1949, it was 600 men over its assigned enlisted complement of 3,400 in March but fell short of that number by more than 400 on 31 December. At that time, it numbered 150 officers, 8 warrant officers, and 2,993 enlisted men. The churning created such turmoil that training inevitably lagged and routine duties themselves seemed difficult to fulfill.[120]

Complicating matters further, the Army reduced basic training in the United States from thirteen weeks to eight or less during 1948, forcing the regiment to complete the familiarization and individual instruction of newly arrived recruits before proceeding with unit training. As a result, when 526 inadequately prepared replacements arrived at Gifu during March 1949, commanders had no choice but to turn the newly reactivated 2d Battalion into a basic training unit. At that point, with one battalion still in residence at Kobe, only one battalion remained available to carry on with the regiment's routine duties.[121]

Heavy training appears to have begun in earnest during June, when the new men had completed their basic courses. At that time, the regiment conducted a three-day road march and field exercise, the first overnight bivouac many of the unit's soldiers had ever experienced. Work continued during July and August 1949, when the 24th—minus its 2d Battalion, on duty at Kobe—participated in exercises at the Mount Fuji training area. Companies and battalions ran individual and crew-served weapons instruction sessions and practiced attacking, patrolling, scouting, and outposting. While better than nothing, whether the effort had much effect on the unit's readiness for war is difficult to tell. As in the rest of the Eighth Army, equipment in the 24th was often outdated and in poor condition, training areas were few and small in size, and experienced officers and NCOs were lacking. In addition, the poor education of many of the 24th's men, more than 70 percent of whom continued to occupy the two lowest rungs on the Army's aptitude scale, meant that large numbers of the unit's soldiers lacked the necessary background and qualifications to absorb complex instruction in the time allotted. The situation improved slightly during 1950 with 62 percent of the unit's men in categories IV and V, but the 24th was still at a disadvantage in comparison with the all-white units of the 25th Division.[122] (*Table 4*)

[119] HQ, I Corps, Eighth Army, Training Directive 2, 15 May 49, box P–473, RG 338, WNRC. See also Schnabel, *Policy and Direction*, p. 55.

[120] The Eighth Army had a turnover rate of 43 percent between 1946 and 1948. Rpt, First Office of the Chief of Army Field Forces Observer Team to Far East Command, 16 Aug 50, pp. 4–9, box 171, RG 337, WNRC. See also Schnabel, *Policy and Direction*, p. 54.

[121] Schnabel, *Policy and Direction*, p. 45; Annual Hist of the 24th Inf Rgt for 1949, 21 Jan 50, pp. 2–4. The basic training cycle increased to fourteen weeks in March 1949.

[122] Annual Hist of the 24th Inf Rgt for 1949, 21 Jan 50, p. 3. See also HQ, I Corps, Eighth Army, Annual Command and

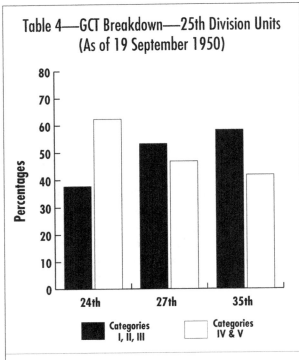

Table 4—GCT Breakdown—25th Division Units (As of 19 September 1950)

Source: Memo for AG, 19 Sep 50, sub: GCT Breakdown, exhibit D–2, in Eighth U.S. Army, Korea (EUSAK),Report of Investigation Concerning 24th Infantry Regimentand Negro Soldiers in Combat, 15 Mar 51, boxes 1013–1014, RG 159, WNRC.

the ploy probably had little effect on the readiness of the unit. Personnel turnover within the regiment was so great that only 27 percent of the men who had supposedly passed the tests remained with the unit at the end of the year.[124]

During August Colonel Halloran's assignment with the 24th came to an end. If a few of his officers were happy to see him go because they had been offended by his intimidating ways and his practice of rebuking commanders in front of their subordinates, most enlisted men regretted his departure.[125] Halloran had been "a forgiving father" to them, Lieutenant Kushner noted, and whatever his faults he had instilled a sense of pride within the unit. Some of the men wept when they learned that he was leaving.[126]

Halloran's successor, Col. Horton V. White, had served with the all-black 25th Infantry during the 1920s and early 1930s. An intelligence specialist, he had won the Army's Distinguished Service Medal in May 1945 for planning and coordinating the liberation of 500 Americans from the notorious Japanese prisoner-of-war camp at Cabanatuan in the Philippines. Some saw his assignment to the 24th as a possible reward for that effort and as an opportunity which the Army provided for White to put in the time he needed with a combat unit to qualify for a brigadier general's star.[127]

At the end of August the 25th Division's companies tested the skills of their squads and platoons. Those of the 24th all passed, possibly because the highly trained men of the regiment's I&R platoon moved quietly from unit to unit to take the lead in performing technical exercises, such as map reading, that poorly lettered sergeants were sometimes incapable of completing. When the instructors finally discovered what was going on, according to Sergeant Ransom, a member of the platoon, their sense of the importance of the exercise and perhaps of the regiment itself was so small that they disregarded the cheating.[123] In the end,

Unit Historical Reports, 1949, p. 15. Problems with training continued into 1950. See Rpt, First Office of the Chief of Army Field Forces Observer Team to Far East Command, 16 Aug 50, pp. 4–9.

[123] Interv, Cash with Ransom, 5 Aug 88. William Hash describes the way the tests were run in Interv, MacGarrigle with William A. Hash, 5 Jul 94.

[124] Annual Hist of the 24th Inf Rgt for 1949, 21 Jan 50, p. 1; Rpt, First Office of the Chief of Army Field Forces Observer Team to Far East Command, 16 Aug 50, pp. 4–9.

[125] See, for example, Intervs, Cash with Richard L. Fields, 18 Aug 88; Eldridge, 26 Aug 88; MacGarrigle with Komp, 5 May and 1 Jun 94; Gillert, 4 May 94; Green, 16 Jun 94.

[126] Intervs, Bowers with Kushner, 29 Jun 94; Muehlbauer with Norman Taylor, 16 Sep 88; Horne, 3 Nov 88; Cash with French, 21 Jul 89; Willie Griffith, 10 Nov 88; Haynesworth, 6 Sep 88; Moore, 19 Aug 88; Perkins, 28 Jul 89; Sammons, 27 Aug 88.

[127] *Register of Graduates and Former Graduates of the United States Military Academy*, Horton V. White, no. 7145 (West Point, N.Y.: Association of Graduates, USMA, 1986); Interv, Cash with Biggs, 15 Aug 88. See also Clay Blair, *The Forgotten War: America in Korea, 1950–1953* (New York: Times Books, 1987), pp. 147, 150–52.

Whatever White's accomplishments, the colonel made less of an impression on his subordinates, whether white or black, than Halloran had. If the white operations officer of the 3d Battalion, Capt. John Zanin, considered him an excellent officer and white Captain Gillert believed him to be intelligent, hardworking, low key, and direct, the regiment's white personnel officer, Capt. Sam J. Adams, considered him aloof and uncomfortable when dealing with the men. Meanwhile, black 1st Lt. Gorham Black saw only a nice enough man who rarely if ever "raised hell." Black Capt. Bradley Biggs asserted that White rarely left his desk to visit the regiment's companies, and black Chaplain Gray Johnson was simply unimpressed. Rifleman Clarence Ferguson added an ominous note, asserting that the number of racial incidents in the unit increased under White because the commander failed to follow the strong example his predecessor had set. Whatever the validity of those observations, as white Lieutenant Hilyer observed, Halloran had presented a difficult act for White to follow: "You could still hear his footprints."[128]

Conditions changed at Gifu just as the new commander was taking charge. During August the Eighth Army installed bright lights and began to employ war dogs and civilian Japanese guards at Kobe and other seaports to free its regiments for training. As a result, while Company F remained on duty at Kobe, the rest of the 2d Battalion returned to Gifu.[129] The arrival was a mixed blessing. Although some of the morale problems that accompanied duty at the port diminished and almost the entire regiment was in one place for the first time in almost two years, simplifying command and control, an extreme housing shortage resulted. Making do with tents at first, the regiment had no choice when winter approached but to squeeze the men into whatever buildings were available. With the

Colonel White

battalion's elements scattered across the post, the unit became extremely difficult to supervise.[130]

Intensive training continued during the final months of 1949 and into 1950. Over that time, the 24th established a technical instruction school at Gifu where each specialist could further his education in his field. Officers either taught a subject or attended classes themselves. During December all battalions conducted a review of squad, platoon, and company tactics at the Fuji training area, with the final four days of the ten-day program devoted to battalion-level maneuvers. The commander of the 25th Division, Maj. Gen. William B. Kean, was present for part of the exercise.[131]

During April 1950, despite many deficiencies noted by General Kean, both the 1st and 2d Battalions of the 24th passed field forces tests administered by the Eighth Army. The 3d Battalion proved deficient on its first attempt—as did the 2d Battalion of the 27th Infantry, and an entire regiment, the 31st Infantry, stationed in northern

---

128 Intervs, Cash with Zanin, n.d.; Gorham Black, 12 Mar 89; Biggs, 15 Aug 88; Hilyer, 17 Aug 88; Muehlbauer with Ferguson, 8 Sep 88; MacGarrigle with Adams, 15 and 17 Jun 94.

129 The regiment continued to rotate one company to Kobe until March 1950, when the commitment ceased. See U.S. Eighth Army, Korea, Monthly Historical Summary, Mar 50. box 480. RG 338. WNRC.

130 Annual Hist of the 24th Inf Rgt for 1949, 21 Jan 50, p. 4. See also HQ, I Corps, Eighth Army, Annual Command and Unit Historical Reports, 1949, p. 17.

131 Ibid.

Japan—but the unit succeeded with difficulty after a second try during May.[132] Shortly after the testing ended, the 1st and 2d Battalions participated in regimental maneuvers at Fuji with their supporting units, the 159th Field Artillery Battalion, the 77th Engineer Combat Company, and Company A of the 79th Heavy Tank Battalion. It was the first time since World War II that major segments of the regiment had exercised in proportions near those of a full combat team.[133]

How well prepared was the regiment for the test to come? A firm judgment is difficult to reach. The 24th Infantry was hardly homogeneous. It had 3 battalions, 9 rifle companies, 3 weapons companies, a heavy mortar company, and 4 headquarters companies, to name just its major components. Each was an entity unto itself with its own officers and NCOs, all of whom possessed different attitudes, standards, and capabilities. Some of those commanders placed heavy emphasis on spit and polish but were less than diligent about other aspects of discipline, perhaps because higher commanders placed it in low priority or because they wanted to avoid charges that they were racially prejudiced.[134]

Other commanders kept better watch over their soldiers and enforced better discipline. The troops sometimes accused them of racial bias because their policies were so stringent in comparison with those of other units, but the commander of Company B, Capt. William A. Hash, had an effective response. Confronted by the allegation at a company formation, he responded that yes, he was prejudiced, but not against people of color. He was prejudiced against soldiers who failed to clean their rifles or stole overcoats and sheets and took them to town to trade for drugs and prostitutes.[135]

Under the circumstances, a strong, sensitive hand capable of instilling trust was needed to set standards and bring the unit together. Colonel Halloran came close, winning the support of the regiment's enlisted men and most of its officers. His policies nevertheless centered mainly upon building pride and esprit de corps by concentrating on sharp dress, expert marching, and success in sports. Because of the occupation-oriented duties of the regiment, its problems with VD and drugs, and the personnel turbulence afflicting the entire Eighth Army, he had no choice but to concentrate his main attention on issues that had little bearing on readiness for combat. His regime, as a result, sometimes gave the appearance of tolerating poor performance and fostering benign neglect.[136] As for Colonel White, he appears to have been intelligent and hardworking, but he lacked the force of personality that Halloran had projected. Since he was inclined to stay in his office, aloof from the men, his arrival left a void.

In some ways, the 24th as a whole was better off than the all-white portions of the Eighth Army. In others, it was as poorly prepared as they. In a few, because of its segregated nature, it was at a definite disadvantage. On the positive side, the regiment was up to strength with a full complement of men, a condition characteristic of few other American units in Japan. In addition, all of its battalions had passed their tests. Two had even participated in rudimentary regiment-level exercises at Gifu with portions of their supporting engineering, artillery, and tank elements.

More negatively, the 24th still suffered from the problems confronting the occupation forces guard-

[132] U.S. Eighth Army, Japan, G–3 Rpt, Reinforced Infantry Combat Firing Tests, April–May 1950, box 480, RG 338, WNRC; U.S. Eighth Army, Japan, G–2 Rpt, Battalion Tests, April–May 1950, box P–602, RG 338, WNRC. For comments about the 3d Battalion test failure, see Intervs, Muehlbauer with Amos Turner, 26 Sep 88; Bowers with Roscoe E. Dann, Jr., 23 Mar 94; MacGarrigle with Roscoe E. Dann, Jr., 28 Mar 94; Adams, 15 and 17 Jun 94. Kean's displeasure is noted in Interv, MacGarrigle with Hash, 5 Jul 94.

[133] For the state of training in general in the 24th, see Intervs, Cash with Willie Brooks, 14 Oct 88; Carter, 24 Sep 88; Jerry Johnson, 23 Sep 88; Richard L. Fields, 18 Aug 88; Gray Johnson, 23 Mar 89; Biggs, 15 Aug 88; Muehlbauer with Charles Piedra, 3 Nov 88.

[134] Lack of diligence on the part of some commanders is apparent in a number of interviews. See, for example, Intervs, Cash with Hilyer, 17 Aug 88; Ransom, 5 Aug 88; Muehlbauer with McMurray, Jun 88; MacGarrigle with Gillert, 4 May 94. See also Interv, MacGarrigle with Green, 16 Jun 94.

[135] Hash's comment is in Interv, Bowers with Hash, 17 Mar 94.

[136] Gustav Gillert makes this charge. See Interv, MacGarrigle with Gillert, 4 May 94.

ing Japan: drugs, venereal disease, black-market trading, and all the institutional debilities brought on by the post–World War II drawdown of the Army. As with the rest of the force in Japan, because of wear and tear and a lack of spare parts, the unit's equipment was substandard and often in disrepair. In the same way, its training limped. Although most of the units in the Eighth Army ultimately passed squad, platoon, company, and battalion tests, many experienced little sense of urgency in doing so. According to the reports of official observers from the headquarters of the Army Field Forces, mastery of such basic combat techniques as scouting, patrolling, night operations, and the selection and preparation of firing positions for weapons left much to be desired in all units across the board.[137]

If the 24th was one with the rest of the Eighth Army in many of the difficulties it experienced, its segregated nature nonetheless compounded every problem. Over the years, some of the white officers assigned to the unit had come to view themselves as outcasts. Their black counterparts meanwhile had no doubt that the Army considered them second-class soldiers and that the military system they served was designed to prevent them from moving ahead. The blacks stayed on because life at Gifu and in the Army appeared a cut above what was available to them in the civilian world, and they clearly made every attempt on that account to keep up appearances. Beneath the surface, however, neither group associated much with the other, and mutual respect and trust were often in short supply.

Ironically, lacking any point of comparison and equating spit and polish, the ability to march well, and good sports teams with combat capability, the men of the 24th tended to believe that they were ready for war. With the conditions prevalent in the Eighth Army in the spring of 1950 they may have been as well prepared as was possible. Nevertheless, given the corrosive influence of segregation and the

mistrust it instilled, they were sorely handicapped in comparison with their white counterparts. For what matters the most in battle is the loyalty that bonds one man to the next and to his officers and his unit—the instinctive, trusting, mutual dependence that welds the whole into the sort of force that can withstand the worst hardships and tribulations and still keep fighting. On that score, even if a few units within the regiment may have measured up, a suspicion lingers that many others did not.[138]

The discontents that festered beneath the surface of the regiment were difficult to see at Gifu, while the relaxed conditions of garrison life prevailed and everyone had room to get along. But when the 24th entered combat in Korea and bloodletting began, the men had to confront the possibility that some of them might die. When they did, their commitment to one another, to their unit, and to the larger society which they represented came under consideration. A question arose upon whose answer the fates of many would hang, not only within the 24th but also within the other units that would fight nearby. As a black communications officer in the 1st Battalion, 1st Lt. Beverly Scott, put it, why should black Americans give up their lives for the independence of South Korea when they themselves still lacked full rights at home?[139]

[137] Schnabel, *Policy and Direction*, pp. 55–61; Rpt, First Office of the Chief of Army Field Forces Observer Team to Far East Command, 16 Aug 50, pp. 4–9. See also Intervs, Muehlbauer with Harry A. Davis, 26 Sep 88; MacGarrigle with Hash, 9 Jun 94; Cash with Gustav J. Gillert, n.d.; Gorham Black, 12 Mar 89.

[138] For views that the 24th was well trained, see Intervs, Cash with Albert Brooks, 6 Aug 88; Dixon, 20 Jan 89; Olin Dorsey, 6 Oct 88; Richard L. Fields, 18 Aug 88; Hagins, 28 Aug 88; Jerry Johnson, 23 Sep 88; Charlie Lee Jones, 6 Sep 89; Roscoe Jones, 16 Jun 89; Kimber, 11 Mar 89; Wilfred Matthews, 23 Sep 88; Reed, 6 Jan 90; Eugene Rumpf, 15 Aug 88; Saxton, 3 Sep 88; Walter Smith, 25 Sep 88; James Thompson, 6 Aug 88; Rainey with William Hough, 16 Nov 89; Montgomery, 26 Mar 90; Muehlbauer with Gunter, 28 Feb 89; Norman Taylor, 16 Sep 88; Roscoe Van Buren, 3 Nov 88; Bowers with Henry D. Doiron, 22 Apr 94. See also William Darryl Henderson, *Cohesion: The Human Element in Combat* (Washington, D.C.: National Defense University Press, 1985), pp. 161–66; Nora Kinzer Stewart, *South Atlantic Conflict of 1982: A Case Study in Military Cohesion* (Alexandria, Va.: U.S. Army Research Institute for the Behavioral and Social Sciences, 1988), pp. 11–26.

[139] Interv, Muehlbauer with Beverly Scott, n.d. Other soldiers brought up the same question. See Intervs, Cash with Charles Bussey, 6 Jan 89; Charlie Lee Jones, 6 Sep 89.

CHAPTER 4

Korea

When the North Korean Army invaded South Korea on Sunday morning, 25 June 1950, the United States was poorly prepared to take action. During the years leading up to the attack, American policymakers and strategic planners had considered Korea of minor importance to American ends in the Far East and had acceded to a de facto partition that split the country along the 38th Parallel between Communist and non-Communist factions. Official Washington appears to have viewed the arrangement as temporary and to have been prepared to concede that the Communist side would eventually gain control over the entire peninsula. Since North Korea bordered in part on the Soviet Union, so the reasoning went, the Communists would have all the natural advantages in any great power competition over the region. If an emergency occurred in the Far East, it seemed far better to defend the Japanese islands and to concentrate the main body of U.S. Army forces on Okinawa, the Marianas, and Honshu.[1] (*See Map 1.*)

Those intentions notwithstanding, the United States found it difficult to back away from North Korea's challenge when that country, urged on by the Soviet Union and the People's Republic of China, invaded the South. It was one thing to allow South Korea to slide almost imperceptibly into the Soviet camp, but quite another to permit it to fall to an act of outright aggression. When the United Nations Security Council, in the absence of the Soviet Union, issued a declaration that the invasion constituted a breach of world peace and called upon all member nations "to render every assistance" to South Korea, President Truman used the opening to authorize his Far East commander, General Douglas MacArthur, to dispatch ammunition and equipment to South Korea and to evacuate American dependents.[2] As appropriate, MacArthur was to employ his air and naval forces to ensure that both operations proceeded unmolested. The next day, in response to continuing bad news from the field and frantic appeals from South Korean President Syngman Rhee, Truman broadened MacArthur's mandate to permit air and naval attacks against North Korean forces operating below the 38th Parallel. He took the action on his own, but the Security Council ratified it on 27 June with a second resolution calling emphatically for member nations to "furnish such assistance to the Republic of Korea as may be necessary to repel the armed attack and to restore international peace and security in the area."[3]

---

[1] Schnabel, *Policy and Direction*, pp. 49–52.

[2] The Soviet Union was boycotting the meetings to protest the selection of the Republic of China (Nationalist) over the People's Republic of China (Communist) as the legitimate representative of the Chinese people in the United Nations.

[3] The United Nations resolutions are quoted in Schnabel, *Policy and Direction*, pp. 66–74. See also Roy E. Appleman, *South to the Naktong, North to the Yalu (June–November 1950)*,

Despite intelligence indicating that war might be imminent, the assault on South Korea had come as a surprise. As a result, although four of South Korea's nine divisions, a total of twelve regiments, supposedly guarded the border, no more than one-third of the force, four regiments, was in position on the day of the attack. The rest of those units had stood down for the weekend or were scattered in reserve positions well to the rear.[4]

Even if South Korean forces had been present in full strength, it is doubtful that they could have done much more than delay the enemy onslaught. Although they numbered 154,000 men at the start of the war and had the benefit of 482 American military advisers, most of their members were trained only to the company level. They possessed U.S. Army motor vehicles and 105-mm. howitzers, but ammunition for all their weapons was in short supply and they lacked heavy mortars, recoilless rifles, and antitank weapons capable of stopping the latest Soviet tanks. They had no tanks of their own because their U.S. advisers had judged the land, roadways, and maintenance capabilities of South Korea poorly suited to the efficient use of armor. Fifteen percent of their weapons and 35 percent of their vehicles were unserviceable because of a lack of spare parts.[5]

By contrast, the North Korean Army was well prepared for its task. Many of the soldiers in the 135,000-man force, especially those at the spearhead of the attack, were battle-hardened veterans who had fought on the side of the Communists in the Chinese civil war. Well equipped, they could rely for support on 150 late-model Soviet T34 tanks and 180 mostly propeller-driven aircraft.[6]

At first there seemed some hope that the air and naval operations Truman had authorized might alone suffice and that the South Koreans would be able to hold their own on the ground. On 27 June American fighter bombers flew 163 sorties and claimed a total of seven North Korean aircraft. Meanwhile, the 6th South Korean Division, firmly entrenched at Ch'unch'on, a religiously significant town located atop Peacock Mountain to the northeast of Seoul, shattered the *6th North Korean Regiment* and held off most of the *2d North Korean Division* for three days. The air operations nevertheless gained little long-term effect, and ground resistance, even when determined, proved futile against the heavy weight of the enemy onslaught. When Seoul itself fell on 29 June Truman felt he had no choice but to take further action. The next day, he authorized MacArthur to commit American ground forces to the battle and to begin a naval blockade of North Korea's coastline.[7]

MacArthur's Eighth Army was ill prepared for the task. All of its regiments but the 24th were understrength, and their equipment was old and heavily worn. Although some of the officers and NCOs had seen intense combat in World War II, others had little idea of what war was like.[8] In most units, training at the regimental level was incomplete because of insufficient time and a shortage of adequately sized exercise areas. Interest in night operations and the maintenance of defensive positions, the problems that would preoccupy American forces during their first months in Korea, had also been scant. As for the men, it would be unfair to say that they were in poor physical condition—training at company and battalion levels dur-

United States Army in the Korean War (Washington, D.C.: U.S. Army Center of Military History, Government Printing Office, 1961), pp. 37–40.

[4] Ibid., pp. 61–62; Robert K. Sawyer, *Military Advisors in Korea: KMAG in Peace and War* (Washington, D.C.: U.S. Army Center of Military History, Government Printing Office, 1962), p. 114.

[5] Appleman, *South to the Naktong, North to the Yalu*, pp. 13–17. For a more detailed discussion of the South Korean Army prior to the war, see Sawyer, *Military Advisors in Korea*, pp. 27–113.

[6] Appleman, *South to the Naktong, North to the Yalu*, pp. 10–12. For more detailed information, see Far East Command,

Allied Translator and Interpreter Section (ATIS), Interrogation Rpts, 1951, Intelligence Research Collection, U.S. Army Military History Institute (MHI), Carlisle Barracks, Pa.

[7] Appleman, *South to the Naktong, North to the Yalu*, pp. 26–27, 37–40, 46–47, 59; Schnabel, *Policy and Direction*, pp. 76–80. For the fighting at Peacock Mountain, see Sawyer, *Military Advisors in Korea*, p. 116.

[8] The commander of the 24th Infantry Division, Maj. Gen. William F. Dean, noted that no more than 15 percent of his men were combat veterans. See Maj. Gen. William F. Dean, *General Dean's Story* (New York: Viking Press, 1954), pp. 13–14.

ing 1949 and early 1950 had been intense and hard—but their mental condition was a different matter. Many had joined the Army to learn a skill or to escape hardship at home. Inured to occupation routines that left considerable time for personal pursuits, even those who were unaffected by easily available prostitutes, drugs, and alcohol were unprepared for the sacrifices that war entailed.[9]

The unit MacArthur chose to lead the move to Korea, the 24th Infantry Division, commanded by Maj. Gen. William F. Dean, was among the least prepared in Japan. It had the smallest number of men (12,197) and the lowest effectiveness rating (65 percent) in the command. Since it shared many of its defects with the other divisions in the Eighth Army and because it was stationed in southern Japan at a location readily accessible to ports near Korea, MacArthur decided time was what mattered. Augmenting the division with nearly four thousand men from other divisions, he sent it off in hopes that it would delay the enemy long enough for more units to arrive.[10]

Task Force Smith, composed of two reinforced companies, preceded the division to its destination on 2 July. Arriving at Pusan, a major port on South Korea's southern coast, the unit moved north hoping either to deter or to slow the enemy advance. Little better prepared for the enemy's armor than the South Koreans and hopelessly outnumbered, the task force was crushed on 5 July, just to the south of Seoul near the town of Osan. Learning of the disaster, Dean rushed the rest of his division north to block the enemy advance, only to see his regiments outflanked and overrun in turn. Within the week the division's strength declined from 15,965 to 11,440 men. Fifteen hundred were missing in action.[11]

The 24th Infantry Prepares for War

Following an initial alert at the time of the North Korean invasion, most portions of the Eighth Army prepared for the possibility that they would soon move to Korea, but the 24th Infantry at first experienced only minor disruptions. Although commanders canceled a track meet at Tokyo and the members of the 24th's baseball team returned home abruptly on 25 June after finishing an out-of-town game, the all-black regiment contributed none of its men to the effort to reinforce the 24th Division. Instead, its 3d Battalion continued training at Fuji and various individuals departed Gifu to participate in official activities in other parts of Japan. Capt. Bradley Biggs, for example, traveled to a naval base south of Tokyo to observe a Marine amphibious exercise.[12]

Overall, the men of the regiment appear to have remained largely unconcerned about the possibility that they would go to war. "A lot of people felt that we weren't going to go," 1st Lt. Houston McMurray recalled. The regiment had served as a port unit during much of World War II, he said. The men "were aware of that, and they were operating [in Japan] more as a port unit than . . . as combat troops." According to a squad leader in

---

[9] This paragraph is based upon a broad range of interviews with the men of the 24th Infantry. See also Schnabel, *Policy and Direction*, pp. 52–57; William Glenn Robertson, *Counterattack on the Naktong, 1950*, Leavenworth Papers 13 (Fort Leavenworth, Kans.: Combat Studies Institute, 1985), p. 4; Roy K. Flint, "Task Force Smith and the 24th Division," in Charles E. Heller and William A. Stofft, eds., *America's First Battles, 1776–1965* (Lawrence: University of Kansas Press, 1986), pp. 272–74. Most histories assert that the men of the Eighth Army were in poor physical condition. The history of the 24th Infantry and of the other regiments covered in this study fails to support that. Although there were exceptions, the men were in generally good physical shape. If they tired in combat in Korea, it may have been because of the climate and terrain, which were more extreme than those of Japan; or the living conditions, especially poor rations and the lack of sleep over long periods; or the psychological burdens they carried, particularly the change in personal expectations the advent of war entailed.

[10] The story of the 24th Division is summarized in Robertson, *Counterattack on the Naktong, 1950*, pp. 6–11. See also Appleman, *South to the Naktong, North to the Yalu*, pp. 59–100. That General Dean had served earlier in Korea may have been a consideration in the selection of the 24th Division to go first. See Dean, *General Dean's Story*, pp. 11–12.

[11] Ibid. Dean's story is told in Appleman, *South to the Naktong, North to the Yalu*, p. 177.

[12] Intervs, John A. Cash with Bradley Biggs, 15 Aug 88; Walter Bufford, 13 Mar 89; Ellis Dean, 7 Aug 88; Bernard L. Muehlbauer with Charles B. Gregg, 8 Sep 88. All interviews hereafter cited by John A. Cash, Bernard L. Muehlbauer, Timothy Rainey, William T. Bowers, Richard O. Perry, and George L. MacGarrigle are in CMH files.

General Kean commanded the 25th Infantry Division from
August 1948–February 1951.

Company M, Sgt. Richard Sanders, one of the officers in the unit, 2d Lt. Joseph DeMarco, told his
men outright that the regiment's chances of going
to Korea were "about zero" because few if any
blacks had fought in World War II.[13]

The 1st Battalion's intelligence officer, Capt.
Gustav Gillert, avowed that there was some discussion, for a time, over whether the Army would disband the regiment, integrate it, use it to guard
newly vacated U.S. installations in Japan, or send it
off to Korea as it was.[14] The talk appears to have
been groundless. According to the 25th Division's
operations officer, Lt. Col. Wayne Hardman, no one
in a position to know ever addressed the possibility of leaving the 24th Infantry behind. At least one
officer, the regimental adjutant, Capt. Sam J.
Adams, Jr., protested at a meeting that the 24th was

poorly trained and psychologically unprepared to
enter combat immediately. Hardman insisted, however, that it was most unlikely that the commander
of the 25th Division, Maj. Gen. William B. Kean,
would have broached an idea of that sort to the
Eighth Army command. Adams himself observed
that his word apparently carried little weight.
Shortly after he returned from the meeting, on 6
July, he said, the regiment received notice that it
was going to Korea.[15]

As the 24th prepared for war, three all-black
units, the 159th Field Artillery Battalion, the 77th
Engineer Combat Company, and the 512th Military
Police Company, were assigned to accompany it.
With their addition, the 24th Infantry became a
regimental combat team. Armor and other combat
and combat service support elements would join
the unit in due course, as soon as they could assemble. In Korea the 512th would be detached from
the 24th and would operate solely in rear areas.

At first few leaders had much idea of what was
happening. Although the commander of the 3d
Battalion, Lt. Col. Samuel Pierce, Jr., kept his officers
informed as well as he could, the news, heavily salt-
ed with rumors and guesses, appears to have trick-
led down mainly by word of mouth. Black 2d Lt.
Albert Brooks of the headquarters company learned
that he was going to Korea from a bartender in Gifu.
The commander of Company D, black Capt. Charles
Piedra, thought the unit was undertaking a thirty- to
sixty-day temporary assignment and that it would
then return to Japan.[16]

Soldiers within the enlisted ranks were even
more confused. Since President Truman had
described the conflict as a "police action," some concluded that they would be serving on riot-control
duty or standing guard on the docks in Korea, much
as they had done earlier at Kobe. Others believed

[13] Intervs, Muehlbauer with Richard Sanders, 16 Dec 88;
Houston McMurray, Jun 88; William T. Bowers with Genous S.
Hodges, 13 Apr 94.

[14] Interv, Cash with Gustav J. Gillert, 20 Aug 90.

[15] Intervs, George L. MacGarrigle with Wayne Hardman,
6 Jul 94; Sam J. Adams, Jr., 15 and 17 Jun 94.

[16] Intervs, Muehlbauer with William M. Factory, 2 Nov
88; Sanders, 16 Dec 88; Amos Turner, 22 Dec 88; Roscoe Van
Buren, 3 Nov 88; Cash with Biggs, 15 Aug 88; Rollie Evans, 13
Oct 88; Jerry Johnson, 23 Sep 88; Harold Rogue, Jr., 14 Oct
88; Eugene Rumpf, 15 Aug 88; William Shepard, 27 Oct 88;
Bowers with Roscoe E. Dann, Jr., 23 Mar 94.

that they would be gone for only a few days or that they would travel only as far as the Japanese port of Sasebo, where the regiment would fill in until the regularly assigned unit, the 24th Division, had completed its duties in Korea and returned.[17]

Col. Horton V. White did little to dispel the confusion. He met with his officers at the post theater to brief them and to take questions, but the information he relayed was apparently little better than theirs. Commenting that he believed the unit would be in Korea for only "a short time," he indicated in particular that officers should pack their "pinks and greens" because the semidress uniforms would be needed for "a big parade."[18]

The official newspaper for the U.S. armed forces in the region, *Pacific Stars and Stripes*, added little to the discussion. Throughout the period the journal's headlines spoke mostly of success. On 30 June, even as Seoul fell, the paper stated: "NORTH KOREANS HIT BY AIR, SOUTH KOREANS HOLDING." It had no choice on 1 July but to confirm that the South Korean line had cracked, yet by 4 July it was again optimistic: "U.S. TROOPS REPEL ATTACK." The theme held through 7 July—"CRACK RED UNIT HELD OFF BY OUT-NUMBERED YANKS"; on 8 July—"U.S. LINES IN KOREA STABLE, OUTLOOK BETTER"; and on 9 July—"SOUTH KOREANS HALT INVADERS." All the while the enemy was advancing relentlessly, mauling one after another of the American units in his way. Reality only began to penetrate on 10 July, when a brief notice appeared to the effect that all dependent travel in the Pacific theater had been suspended, a sure sign to knowledgeable soldiers that a major emergency was in progress. On 12 July the newspaper revealed that the North Koreans were killing American prisoners of war and that all members of the Far East Command had been retained on station until further notice.[19]

With that, any remaining illusions began to disappear. Although many of the men still believed that it would be a short war or that the 24th would mainly fill a service role, a number became anxious. The stories about soldiers being executed by the enemy bothered some. Others realized that the easy life was ending. Those who had brought families with them worried about the well-being of their loved ones. With time, all those concerns diminished. As rifleman James Little put it, there were no alternatives. "Everyone had gotten used to the idea of going."[20]

When the possibility emerged that the 24th might face combat, the commander of the 25th Division, General Kean, and Colonel White began a major effort to strengthen the quality of leadership within the regiment. In some cases, combat veterans replaced officers with only peacetime experience. In others, the physical fitness of the officer in charge may have been a concern.[21] Whatever the reason, the changes seemed to come "out of the blue" for some of the men, and instability, with all the uncertainties it brought, appeared the rule.[22]

The process of change had actually begun during the weeks just prior to the outset of the crisis in Korea, when Colonel White had made a number of officer reassignments. With the advent of war, he left virtually all of those in place and retained recent substitutions in Company D that had altered that unit's command from all white to all black. He did, however, replace six out of twelve company commanders—three in the 1st Battalion, one in the 2d, and two in the 3d—exchanging captains, where he could, for first lieutenants. At that time the 1st Battalion received a new commander, Lt. Col. Paul F. Roberts, and a new executive officer, a former military policeman, Maj. Eugene J. Carson. The 2d Battalion acquired a new executive officer, Maj. Horace E. Donaho. A number of shifts also occurred among the regiment's lieutenants. Adding

[17] Intervs, Muehlbauer with Charles Piedra, 3 Nov 88; Cash with Albert Brooks, 6 Aug 88.

[18] Interv, MacGarrigle with Lloyd V. Ott, 19 Jul 94. A first lieutenant with Company H, Ott is the only officer to recall the briefing, but he is quite specific.

[19] Copies of pertinent issues of *Stars and Stripes* are on file at the U.S. Army Military History Institute.

[20] Intervs, Cash with Biggs, 15 Aug 88; Muehlbauer with James Little, 27 Aug 88.

[21] Intervs, Bowers with Henry D. Doiron, 22 Apr 94; Hodges, 13 Apr 94.

[22] Intervs, MacGarrigle with Adams, 15 and 17 Jun 94.

Table 5—Racial Distribution of Officers When the 24th Infantry Deployed to Korea					
Unit	Race	Comment	Capt	1st Lt	2d Lt
1st Bn, A . . . . Black			1	4	2
B . . . .White			1	3	2
C . . . .White			1	5	1
D . . . . Black		Weapons Co.	1	1	3
2d Bn, E . . . .Mixed		(1 Black 2d Lt)	1	3	3
F . . . . Black			0	2	5
G . . . .White			1	2	2
H . . . .Mixed		Weapons Co. (1 Black 1st Lt)	1	2	2
3d Bn, I . . . . . Black			1	1	4
K . . . .White			0	2	3
L . . . . Black			1	4	2
M . . . .White		Weapons Co.	0	5	1
Totals . . . . . . .5 White 5 Black 2 Mixed			9	34	30

Source: Officer Rosters, 24th Inf Rgt, CMH files.

to the turbulence, the Army's Competitive Tour assignment program stayed in effect throughout the period. Within a week of deploying to Korea, indeed, the regiment had to reassign a seventh company commander to comply with the system's requirements.[23]

Through it all, segregation remained the norm. Although the regiment appears to have been preparing to comply with the Gillem Board's recommendations and had in fact appointed a senior

black, Lt. Col. Forest Lofton, as commander of the 1st Battalion just prior to the outbreak of war, the officer remained in charge for only a few days. Why his tenure was so short remains unclear, but when the 24th moved out for Korea, a white, Roberts, was again in command of the battalion.[24] At that time, except for black Captain Piedra, who briefly supervised a white warrant officer serving in Company D, no blacks commanded whites. Instead, the 1st and 3d Battalions each had two companies officered entirely by whites and two by blacks. As for the 2d Battalion, Company F had a black commander and Company G a white. Companies E and H had both blacks and whites in

[23] A black officer, Oliver Dillard, describes some of the problems that resulted from the change of officers, particularly from the men's tendency to test their new commanders. See Interv, Cash with Oliver Dillard, 26 Oct 88, p. 24. For the experiences of a white officer and the resentment some faced, see Interv, MacGarrigle with Alfred F. Tittel, 20 Apr 94. Some of the changes are described in Ltr, John S. Komp to George L. MacGarrigle, 14 May 94, CMH files.

[24] Intervs, MacGarrigle with Adams, 15 and 17 Jun 94; William A. Hash, 9 Jun 94; Gillert, 4 May 94; Bowers with Charles L. Gray, 2 and 3 May 94.

positions of command, but the black officers in each were junior in rank.[25] (*Table 5*)

Other units in the Eighth Army also made changes. The 7th Infantry Division was virtually demolished to provide replacements for understrength units departing for Korea. Nevertheless, few regiments experienced the large-scale shifts among commanders that occurred in the 24th. Although the 27th Infantry regiment received a new regimental commander, Lt. Col. John H. Michaelis, and one new battalion commander, a platoon leader at the time in the unit who later became a brigadier general, Uzal W. Ent, could recall hardly any other changes prior to the regiment's departure for Korea. A platoon leader in the 35th Infantry regiment who later became a lieutenant general, Sidney B. Berry, recalled that a number of NCOs from his regiment became replacements for the 24th Division prior to its departure for Korea, stripping the unit of first-line NCO leadership and necessitating the promotion of inexperienced men to key positions. Even so, he could recall few changes among the officers. The regimental commander, Col. Henry G. Fisher, he said, made some shifts to adapt his force for combat but ordered no wholesale reassignments.[26]

Colonel Fisher had wanted White's new 1st Battalion commander, Roberts, for his regiment, but General Kean decided that the officer would be more useful in the 24th Infantry. Although assigned as the 25th Division's personnel officer at the time, Roberts had led a battalion in Europe during World War II and had also served as a regimental executive officer. Well seasoned in combat, he would be especially valuable to the 24th because the unit's other two battalion commanders had much less experience but were impossible to replace on short notice and from the pool of personnel available at the time. In denying Fisher's request, Kean signaled his concern. "Don't mention this again," he told the colonel. "Do you want me to completely destroy the 24th?"[27]

A survey of the backgrounds of the regiment's other two battalion commanders shows why Kean was concerned. The 2d Battalion's commander, Lt. Col. William M. Cohoon, was successful and well liked at Gifu but had virtually no experience in war. A commander of a National Guard battalion activated during World War II, he had supervised the training of his unit but had never left the United States except for a brief tour of duty in Alaska after all the fighting there had ended. An unknown quantity on that account and nearly forty-three years of age, he seemed too old for combat to some of his men, or not tough enough.[28]

The commander of the 3d Battalion, Lt. Col. Samuel Pierce, Jr., had even less experience. An ROTC instructor in the United States during World War II, he had completed a tour of duty with the Army Service Forces at the Pentagon before accepting a commission in the Regular Army and joining the 24th at Gifu in 1949. The assignment was his first with troops. The commander of Company K, white 1st Lt. Jasper Johnson, considered him well intentioned but green, the sort of officer who had no choice in combat but to place inordinate reliance on more knowledgeable subordinates. In that regard, Johnson said, the 3d Battalion's operations officer, Capt. John B. Zanin, held particular importance. The regimental adjutant, white Capt. Samuel J. Adams, agreed with Johnson's estimate, asserting that Zanin was indeed "the glue" that held

[25] Changes in Company D are described in Ltr, Komp to MacGarrigle, 14 May 94. The various changes were determined by analyzing regimental rosters. Companies A, C, D, F, G, I, and K received new commanders.

[26] Intervs, MacGarrigle and Bowers with Uzal W. Ent, 20 Oct 93; MacGarrigle with Sidney B. Berry, 11 Aug 93. See also War Diary (WD), 2d Bn, 35th Inf Rgt, 13–14 Jul 50. Unless otherwise indicated, records for June and July 1950 relating to the 25th Infantry Division, its three regiments, and the supporting units, including war diaries, historical summaries, command and staff reports, and staff journals, are contained in boxes 3746–3747, Record Group (RG) 407, Washington National Records Center (WNRC), Suitland, Md.

[27] Ltr, Henry G. Fisher to Roy E. Appleman, 22 Jul 53, attached comments on Appleman manuscript, copy in CMH files. See also Ltr, Bernice A. (Mrs. Paul F.) Roberts to David Carlisle, 27 Jan 90, copy in CMH files.

[28] DA (Department of the Army) Form 66, Personnel Record for William M. Cohoon, CMH files; Intervs, Cash with Colon Britt, 18 Aug 88; Joseph Hilyer, 17 Aug 88; Bowers with Bradley Biggs, 23 Mar 94.

Pierce's battalion together. According to Company L's commander, black Captain Biggs, the colonel showed little interest in the troops and appeared to have reservations about serving with blacks. He visited Company L only once in seven months, Biggs said, and had been overheard to say that he would have preferred to serve in Europe rather than with "these people." The acting personnel officer of the battalion, white 2d Lt. Roscoe E. Dann, Jr., also believed that Pierce would have liked to have been elsewhere. Whatever the colonel's attitude, Pierce's battalion was the one that failed its tests at Fuji and that missed the 24th's important regimental field exercise in May because of a retest.[29]

Colonel White's experience, for that matter, also left much to be desired. A West Point graduate, class of 1923, the 24th's commander had served with the all-black 25th Infantry between 1923 and 1926 and again from 1929 to 1931, but had never again commanded troops until joining the 24th. Instead, he had followed a successful career in intelligence that had included service as the chief of intelligence for the Sixth Army during World War II. After the war, he had continued in that occupation, serving with the Korean Military Advisory Group and later at the Intelligence School at Fort Leavenworth. His assignment to the 24th may have been a reward for long service well done.[30]

White appears to have been a capable administrator, but a number of his officers considered him aloof and inexperienced as an infantry commander. He seemed uncomfortable leading troops, whether black or white, Captain Adams observed. "He didn't fit into foxholes." The tendency might have mattered little if the unit's battalion commanders had been strong, knowledgeable leaders, but two out of three were still learning their jobs. In that case, as White's predecessor, Halloran, had done, it was incumbent upon the regimental commander to fill in the gap by closely monitoring the training of his troops and by supervising the work of his battalion commanders with their companies. White, however, appears to have been too reserved for that. He supported the chain of command and attempted to tighten discipline at Gifu, an assistant regimental operations officer, 1st Lt. John S. Komp, observed, but he spent most of his time in his office rather than out with his men.[31]

By contrast, White's counterparts in the 27th and 35th Infantry regiments, Colonels Michaelis and Fisher, had enormous combat experience and knew how to prepare men for battle. The commander of an airborne regiment in Normandy during World War II, Michaelis had received a battlefield promotion from lieutenant colonel to colonel and had served as the chief of staff of the 101st Airborne Division at Bastogne during the Battle of the Bulge. Reduced to the rank of lieutenant colonel in the drawdown that followed the war, he was still one of the Army's brightest stars. Indeed, his regiment had earned a Distinguished Unit Citation during World War II and an equivalent honor from the government of Holland. Intensely

---

[29] DA Form 66, Personnel Record for Samuel Pierce, Jr., CMH files; Intervs, Cash with Jasper Johnson, n.d.; John B. Zanin, n.d.; MacGarrigle with Zanin, 22 Oct 93; Adams, 15 and 17 Jun 94. The Biggs quote is from Interv, Cash with Biggs, 15 Aug 88. See also Interv, Bowers with Dann, 23 Mar 94. Zanin declined to say anything about Pierce's abilities. Regarding matters of race, he considered the colonel the sort of realist who accepted conditions as they were but never spoke or acted as a bigot. See Interv, MacGarrigle with Zanin, 27 Oct 93.

[30] Interv, Cash with Biggs, 15 Aug 88. See also Interv, MacGarrigle and Bowers with Ent, 20 Oct 93. A detailed military record for Colonel White is in George W. Cullum, *Biographical Register of the Officers and Graduates of the United States Military Academy* (Chicago: R. R. Donnelley & Sons, 1950), vol. IX, item 7145. In an interview with Clay Blair, General John H. Michaelis remarked that many of the regiments that went to Korea were commanded initially by officers with noncombat backgrounds. Enjoying servants, staff cars, and well-appointed quarters, they went to war as ordered but

were miserable until replaced. See Interv, Clay Blair with General John H. Michaelis, n.d., U.S. Army Military History Institute Senior Officer Oral History Program, Combat Leadership in Korea series, p. 38, MHI.

[31] Intervs, MacGarrigle with Adams, 15 and 17 Jun 94; Komp, 5 May and 1 Jun 94; Zanin, 22 Oct 93; Cash with Biggs, 15 Aug 88; Gray Johnson, 23 Mar 89; Bowers with Gray, 2 and 3 May 94. Adams was the regimental personnel officer at Gifu. Later he became the operations officer. Biggs and Komp were company commanders. Johnson was a chaplain. Gray was a platoon leader in Company F and an evaluator of the 24th's final tests at Fuji during April and May 1950.

interested in the infantry and infantrymen, the colonel was a hands-on commander similar to Halloran. If White seemed to keep a low profile, rifleman Nathaniel Pipkins thus observed, "when Michaelis was around, everyone knew it."[32]

Fisher was perhaps even more accomplished. Commander of the 317th Infantry regiment of the 80th Infantry Division in Europe during World War II, he had come ashore following the Normandy invasion and had led his unit through ten months of the war's most vicious fighting, including the relief of Bastogne. Highly decorated for his service, he held the Silver Star, two Bronze Stars, and the French Croix de Guerre. Unlike Michaelis, he retained his rank when the war ended. Although less demonstrative than his more colorful counterpart, he was a man of strong opinions, the sort of complete professional who left nothing to chance where his troops were concerned.[33]

Although White clearly intended to improve the efficiency of his regiment, the effect of the changes he made among his officers on the morale and effectiveness of the 24th is difficult to discern. For officers such as black 1st Lt. Roger Walden, White's efforts appear to have become a source of resentment. "I commanded A Company just until we went to Korea," Walden protested angrily in an interview years later. "I had trained the unit for six months but had to turn it over to a captain." Even so, some of the men who came in were well respected. The captain who took Walden's place in Company A, William J. Jackson, for example, was one of the most senior of the regiment's black officers and a former commander of the unit's headquarters company at Gifu. Walden himself ultimately received command of Company F when the former commander, black 1st Lt. Charles Ellis, became the regimental ammunition officer. "Since I had just given up A Company," Walden said, "I was a prime candidate." Nevertheless,

some of the other replacements had little infantry experience. The new commander of Company C had been the regimental signal officer, a position that provided hardly any preparation for combat command in an infantry unit. The company's new executive officer, who might have compensated for some of his commander's inexperience, had spent much of his time as a military policeman. One of Company C's new platoon leaders had been the regimental athletics officer at Gifu.[34]

Overall, in combination with the persistent turmoil fostered by the Army's Competitive Tour program and the desire to maintain racial segregation among company officers, the abrupt imposition of so many unfamiliar officers and the adaptations soldiers had to make to the standards and styles of the new commander intensified problems of leadership and discipline already present within the regiment. The effect can be seen in the contrast between Company B—considered one of the most reliable units in the regiment during the first months of the war—and other companies in the 24th Infantry. In combat, Company B experienced the lowest casualty rate in the regiment among its officers. The figures for the rest of the regiment were much higher.[35]

---

[32] Michaelis retired as a four-star general. See General Officer Biographical file, John H. Michaelis, CMH files. Michaelis served on the Eighth Army staff in Japan and took command of the 27th as it was deploying to Korea. See Interv, Muehlbauer with Nathaniel Pipkins, 23 Aug 88.

[33] Obituary, Henry Granville Fisher, U.S. Military Academy, *Assembly*, Mar 85, p. 126.

[34] Interv, Cash with Roger Walden, 18 Mar 89. Officer assignments were drawn from Officer Roster, 24th Inf Rgt (officers present with unit upon arrival in Korea, 12 July 1950), 18 Sep 50, exhibit D–12, Eighth Army Inspector General Investigation. See also Bussey, *Firefight at Yechon*, p. 123; Intervs, Cash with Alvin Bryant, 7 Oct 88; Bowers with Gray, 2 and 3 May 94; Donald E. LaBlanc, 28 Feb 94; Laurence M. Corcoran, 1 Mar 94; MacGarrigle with LaBlanc, 1 Mar 94.

[35] 24th Inf Rgt Casualty Statistics, Officer and NCO, Jul–Sep 51, in 24th Inf Rgt Command Rpt, Sep 51, box 3848, RG 407, WNRC. Company B experienced 26 casualties among its officers and NCOs between July and September. Company C had 80. Most of the regiment's companies suffered between 44 and 60. When the 25th Division investigated the 24th later in the year, the inspector general remarked on the divergence. See Interv, Inspector General (IG) with Capt William A. Hash, 14 Feb 51, exhibit B–142, in General Headquarters, Far East Command, Report of Investigation Regarding Alleged Irregularities in the Administration of Military Justice in the 25th Infantry Division, 27 Mar 51, boxes 1013–1014 (hereafter cited as Far East Command Inspector General Investigation), RG 159, WNRC.

Although the unit was often used as a backup and may have been somewhat less exposed to enemy fire on that account, special circumstances within the company clearly contributed to the effect. Its commander, white Capt. William A. Hash, had never participated in the Competitive Tour program. As a result, he not only remained with the company for a year before the war but also took it to Korea. A "cautious, methodical" commander, according to the 1st Battalion's intelligence officer, white Capt. Gustav Gillert, Hash used the time to earn the respect of his troops.[36] Gifted with a strong sense of detail, he kept the unit on course, enforcing regulations, developing a consistent program of training and morale building, and refusing to condescend to his men just because they were black. When he discovered by chance, for example, that his first sergeant was a homosexual, he declined to overlook the matter and had the man removed.[37] When Company B departed for Korea, the battalion headquarters recognized that it was one of the most stable in the unit. The company thus spent much of its time during its first weeks in combat responding to emergencies, conducting counterattacks, and plugging gaps in the line.[38]

If personnel turbulence kept the 24th's roster of officers in turmoil, the regiment's enlisted ranks were in better shape than those of the other units in Japan. While the Eighth Army levied its all-white regiments to fill out the 24th Division, withdrawing 20 percent of the enlisted strength and 39 percent of the NCOs from just one company of the 35th Infantry, it left the 24th alone to maintain segregation.[39]

A number of new men arrived just as the regiment was preparing to depart for Korea. Some were replacements fresh from the United States or from support units stationed in Japan, but others appear to have been members of the regiment who had been detached for special duties such as sports or housekeeping. Ellis Dean, for one, had functioned as a high jumper for the regiment and held the Eighth Army record in that event. With the beginning of the war, he was assigned to the antitank and mines platoon in the regiment's headquarters company. When he joined the unit, he said, he had no knowledge of infantry tactics other than what he had learned during eight weeks of basic training almost three years before.[40]

Dean, at least, was physically fit. According to the regimental supply officer, black Lieutenant Brooks, many of the other new arrivals were what he considered the "servants" of the Army—mess men, cooks, quartermasters, teamsters, and clerks of various sorts. Brooks emptied the regiment's clothing store in an attempt to bring the men's gear up to par.[41] Augmenting the influx were a number of soldiers from the Eighth Army's stockade. Company K, for one, had thirteen soldiers in confinement on charges of heroin abuse or distribution. Most, Jasper Johnson observed, went to Korea with the unit. The same was true in other units of the regiment.[42] Although poorly prepared replacements such as the ones Brooks encountered were common throughout the Army and remained a drag on the regiment during much of the war, the "punks" from the brig, as Company D's commander, black Captain Piedra, and a platoon leader in Company E, 2d Lt. Joseph Hilyer, observed, sometimes "fought like Hell."[43]

[36] Interv, MacGarrigle with Gillert, 4 May 94.

[37] Interv, MacGarrigle with Charles E. Green, 16 Jun 94. Green was a platoon leader in Company B.

[38] Ibid. See also Interv, IG with Hash, 14 Feb 51, exhibit B–142, Far East Command Inspector General Investigation.

[39] Intervs, MacGarrigle and Bowers with Ent, 20 Oct 93; MacGarrigle with Berry, 11 Aug 93. See also WD, 2d Bn, 35th Inf Rgt, 13–14 Jul 50; Appleman, *South to the Naktong, North to the Yalu*, p. 59.

[40] Interv, Cash with Dean, 7 Aug 88.

[41] Interv, Cash with Albert Brooks, 6 Aug 88.

[42] Interv, Cash with Jasper Johnson, 5 Oct 88. For similar instances in other companies, see Intervs, Bowers with Hash, 17 Mar 94; Cash with Hilyer, 17 Aug 88; Muehlbauer with Piedra, 3 Nov 88; Bussey, *Firefight at Yechon*, p. 81.

[43] Quote from Interv, Muehlbauer with Piedra, 3 Nov 88. See also Intervs, Cash with Hilyer, 17 Aug 88; MacGarrigle with Ott, 19 Jul 94. For testimony on the poor quality of replacements and their effect on the regiment, see Interv, IG with M Sgt David Robinson, Co E, 15 Sep 50, exhibit B–6, in Eighth U.S. Army Korea, Report of Investigation Concerning 24th Infantry Regiment and Negro Soldiers in Combat, 15 Mar 51, boxes 1013–1014 (hereafter cited as Eighth Army Inspector General Investigation), RG 159, WNRC.

As the day of departure approached, the poor condition of the regiment's equipment became a matter of increasing concern. The 3d Battalion was on maneuvers at Fuji when the call to war arrived. It returned immediately to Gifu, but its equipment remained loaded on flatcars for the move to Korea. Everything went straight to the combat zone without cleaning or maintenance.[44] Meanwhile, heavy training at Fuji over the previous year had taken its toll. Numbers of trucks were deadlined, in need of maintenance, overhaul, or repair. Eighty percent of the radios on hand in the regiment were nonoperational because of poor upkeep and heavy usage in the field, and the unit's basic load of communications wire was in bad condition with many breaks.[45] Many of the World War II–vintage M1 rifles in the hands of the troops were heavily worn and unreliable. A few even lacked firing pins.[46]

Physical shortages of weapons and supply parts also dogged the regiment. Browning automatic rifles (BARs), 4.2-inch mortars, light machine guns, rocket launchers, and the supplies to maintain them were rare or nonexistent in some units. Companies B, E, F, and G lacked radios at the platoon level, and even in portions of the regiment that had them, batteries were in short supply. In the end, commanders had no choice but to scrounge. Company L, for example, had few light machine guns and BARs. But the company commander still managed to equip himself with a .50-caliber machine gun, which he mounted on his jeep just before departing for Korea. Company M meanwhile had to cannibalize several weapons to render just one 75-mm. recoilless rifle operative.[47] Concerned that the regiment

would be unable to repair weapons that broke during combat and to replace those that were lost or destroyed, supply officers dispatched a second lieutenant, Albert Brooks, to Tokyo to gather what parts and weapons he could.[48]

Given the personnel turbulence, the uncertainties caused by the regiment's poor equipment, and the historic mistrust of black soldiers in the U.S. Army, doubts festered among some officers of the regiment, both black and white. Uncertainty circulated in particular around the highest ranking black in the regiment, Lt. Col. Forest Lofton, who had commanded a black battalion at Fort Dix and had just taken charge of the 1st Battalion. According to the battalion's intelligence officer, Captain Gillert, Lofton personally declined to accompany the regiment to Korea. Gillert said that he was in Lofton's office when Colonel White called to inform the officer that the 24th would be committed to combat. Lofton responded, Gillert said, that the regiment was neither trained nor prepared for war and that the event would be a disaster. He "wanted no part of that" and requested reassignment. White took him at his word and made him the commander of the detachment in charge of maintaining the base at Gifu until the regiment returned.[49]

Lofton, for his part, never communicated any personal doubts when informing his commanders of the change. According to Captain Hash, he simply said that he was being replaced and would not be allowed to command the battalion in combat. That being the case, blacks within the regiment came to their own conclusions. Learning that Lofton would stay behind, they viewed the change in command as one more indication of white prej-

[44] Interv, Cash with Gorham L. Black, Jr., 12 Mar 89.

[45] WD, 24th Inf Rgt, 6–31 Jul 50, p. 5. See also Interv, Cash with Waymon R. Ransom, 5 Aug 88.

[46] Interv, Muehlbauer with Calvin Bryant, 1 Mar 89.

[47] WD, 24th Inf Rgt, Jul 50; Intervs, Muehlbauer with Bryant, 1 Mar 89; Bowers with Corcoran, 1 Mar 94; Doiron, 22 Apr 94; Gray, 2 and 3 May 94; Hash, 17 Mar 94; Sanders, 5 May 95; MacGarrigle with Komp, 5 May and 1 Jun 94; Cash with Gorham Black, 12 Mar 89; George Bussey, 13 Nov 88; Albert Griffin, Jr., 5 Oct 88; Jerry Johnson, 23 Sep 88; Biggs, 15 Aug 88; Walden, 18 Mar 89. See also John G. Westover, *Combat Support in Korea*, U.S. Army in Action series

(Washington, D.C.: U.S. Army Center of Military History, Government Printing Office, 1987), p. 238.

[48] Intervs, Cash with Biggs, 15 Aug 88; Albert Brooks, 6 Aug 88; George Bussey, 13 Nov 88; Roscoe Jones, 16 Jun 89; Walden, 18 Mar 89.

[49] Quote from Interv, MacGarrigle with Gillert, 4 May 94. See also Interv, Cash with Gillert, 25 Mar 89. Lofton's role at Gifu is described in Interv, Muehlbauer with Norman Taylor, 16 Sep 88; Ltr, Waymon R. Ransom to John A. Cash, 22 Oct 88, CMH files.

udice. Since Lofton was a lieutenant colonel and a battalion commander, so the reasoning went, he would have had to command white officers in combat. Rather than see that happen, the regiment had contrived an excuse to leave him behind.[50]

White officers, especially those recently assigned to the unit, also had concerns. According to 1st Sgt. Peter Paulfrey, who would later be court-martialed for abandoning his company, they seemed nervous and upset and showed signs of fear. They "began to question the NCO's pertaining to the men. They were completely afraid. They heard rumors or had been taught that the Negroes were cowards and they would question us as to whether the men would seek revenge on the battle-front."[51] Condemned to prison at the time he made the statement, Paulfrey may well have blamed his own poor performance on the bad faith and leadership of his officers. Since some of those individuals were newcomers with little practical knowledge of the regiment or its men, their questions may in fact have been nothing more than an awkward attempt to gain a feel for problems within their units and for what they would need to do once they reached Korea.

Even so, a suspicion lingers that Paulfrey had touched a nerve. A story was circulating at the time among white officers to the effect that a black chaplain had observed in a sermon to enlisted personnel that he felt it was inappropriate for black Americans to fight an enemy of "color."[52] The exact content of what was said, if anything of the sort even occurred, has been impossible to determine. The existence of the rumor, however, is in itself telling—an indication that profound mistrust festered beneath the surface of the regiment. Indeed, it appears that Colonel White himself had misgivings. Questioned several months after being relieved of command on the combat effectiveness of the regiment when it had gone to war and any changes that had occurred, he had difficulty suppressing his disgust. "I had no great amount of confidence because of their past history," he responded, "but my estimate gradually deteriorated."[53]

White 1st Lt. Houston McMurray was even more to the point. Although some men in his unit were the sort of soldiers with whom he would have been happy to go to war, he said, "By and large, I had a lot that I was disappointed with, and it became a case that you didn't really . . . develop any esprit de corps. You didn't really feel like this is my outfit. . . . Under these conditions it was hard to feel like, well, you were pulling together and everybody was in this all the way through. . . . Some way, you have to feel like somebody's covering my left rear, my right rear, and so on. If I'm there and I trust them explicitly and I don't have to worry about them, I just have to take care of what I have here." McMurray added that with the advent of war, personnel turbulence only made matters worse. "Once you started turning over officers over there, you really didn't know anything about the people you were with. . . . If you don't know the people, how much real trust do you have?"[54]

The conduct of some of the men on one of the evenings just prior to the unit's departure from Gifu did nothing to allay white concern. Aware that the troops were keyed up and that discipline might slide in the confusion that preparations for a major move always entailed, Colonel White canceled leaves and restricted his soldiers to post. Lower-ranking officers questioned the decision, considering the move an invitation to disorder because many of the men had formed close attachments to women in nearby towns and would want some final time with them. "A bunch of us," black 2d Lt. Clinton Moorman recalled, "said if these guys can't get off post here, we're in deep trouble. We don't

---

[50] Intervs, MacGarrigle with Hash, 9 Jun 94; Muehlbauer with Emmett Allen, 23 Aug 88; Cash with Nathaniel Reed, 6 Jan 90. Lofton would have been a prime candidate for an interview, but the Army has no address for him, an indication that he is probably deceased.

[51] Interv, IG with Sgt Peter J. Paulfrey, 29 Dec 50, exhibit B–31, Far East Command Inspector General Investigation.

[52] Interv, Cash with Gillert, 20 Aug 90.

[53] Interv, IG with Col Horton V. White, 27 Sep 50, exhibit B–21, Eighth Army Inspector General Investigation.

[54] Interv, Muehlbauer with McMurray, Jun 88. The punctuation of the quote has been changed for the sake of clarity. One of the regiment's new officers, 2d Lt. Alfred F. Tittel, felt the same way. See Interv, Bowers with Tittel, 15 Apr 94.

even need to take them into Korea if they can't get off of this post."[55]

Those apprehensions were soon borne out. When some of the men went AWOL to see their girlfriends and the military police attempted to round them up, at least fifty joined in confrontations that became, in the words of rifleman James T. Burke, "Real heavy. Real heavy."[56] Refusing to obey orders, some gave cat calls and threw rocks. Others were armed, according to the new regimental adjutant, white Maj. John Wooldridge, and fired weapons. The 24th Infantry investigated the incidents but dismissed them because no one had been hurt and no desertions had occurred.[57] The next night, however, a change of policy appears to have gone into effect. A number of prostitutes and girlfriends, according to Burke, were allowed unofficially to come on post.[58]

The Journey to Korea and First Assignments

The 24th's band, which would stay behind at Gifu, played at the railroad station on 11 and 12 July, when the regiment departed Gifu on the first leg of its journey to Korea. The mood among the men was upbeat, bandsman Walter Bufford recalled. It seemed like a football game. The soldiers even called out as they passed, "Be ready to play us back at Thanksgiving!"[59]

Although few of the men could recall any problems, disturbances did apparently occur. Many Japanese girls were present. Some climbed aboard one of the trains, slowing its departure by what seemed to mortarman William Hough several hours. Soldiers were pulling them through the windows, Hough said, and the police had problems getting them off. In another case, according to rifleman William Gregg, a black GI attempted to kiss his Japanese girlfriend goodbye on the loading platform at Camp Gifu. When a military policeman intervened, a scuffle occurred in which a number of nearby men participated. In the end, those incidents were minor. Much more menacing was a little-noticed pattern of activity witnessed by a white platoon leader in Company K who had just arrived from the 7th Infantry Division, 2d Lt. Alfred Tittel. As the trains pulled out, Tittel said, girls ran alongside, passing packages through the windows to their boyfriends within. Some of the bundles, according to Tittel, were later found to contain drugs.[60]

During the trip that followed, due to unexpected congestion at the ports, the Eighth Army diverted the 24th from its original destination at Sasebo to Camp Juno near the port of Moji, 100 miles to the northeast. It did the same to the all-white 27th and 35th Infantries, portions of which also used Moji. Since no plans had been prepared to load the 24th at the port, an advance party of four officers had to improvise everything. Within a scant sixteen hours they set up a holding facility at Moji and a loading area at Kokura; located a small collection of fishing boats, fertilizer haulers, coal carriers, and tankers to transport the regiment to Korea; and made what arrangements they could to accommodate the unit's men before the convoy departed. A lack of time and proper facilities kept the officers from preparing personnel-loading rosters. They also found it impossible to draw up plans to connect and move the regiment's various parts with their equipment. Instead, equipment and personnel went on board the ships in the approximate order of their arrival.[61]

The confusion that reigned when the men of the 24th began pouring into the port provided an opportunity for lawless elements within the regi-

[55] Interv, Muehlbauer with Clinton Moorman, 5 Sep 88.

[56] Interv, Muehlbauer with James T. Burke, 23 Jan 89. See also Interv, Muehlbauer with Benjamin Headden, 24 Aug 88.

[57] Interv, IG with Maj John Wooldridge, 23 Aug 50, exhibit 1 attached to Ltr, Maj Gen W. B. Kean, 25th Inf Div, to Commanding General, Eighth U.S. Army (Korea), 9 Sep 50, sub: Combat Effectiveness of the 24th Infantry Regiment. Kean's letter and its attachments are contained in Far East Command Inspector General Investigation, sec. BX, boxes 1013–1014, RG 159, WNRC. Statements attached to General Kean's letter each have an exhibit number and are hereafter cited as in the Kean Letter file. See also Interv, Muehlbauer with Burke, 23 Jan 89.

[58] Interv, Muehlbauer with Burke, 23 Jan 89.

[59] Interv, Cash with Walter Bufford, 13 Mar 89.

[60] Intervs, Muehlbauer with Gregg, 8 Sep 88; Timothy Rainey with William Hough, 16 Nov 89; Bowers with Tittel, 15 Apr 94.

[61] WD, 24th Inf Rgt, 6–31 Jul 50, pp. 2–3.

General Wilson (*front left*) confers with officers.

ment to step out of line. While officers struggled to feed the troops and organize loading details, a number of individuals from Pierce's 3d Battalion decided to slip away for one last evening in town. Shortly thereafter the regimental adjutant, Major Wooldridge, received a call from the 25th Division's assistant commander, Brig. Gen. Vennard Wilson, who stated that enlisted men from the 24th were "all over town causing disorders, such as being drunk, fighting, beating up civilians, and attempting rape."[62] The assistant operations officer of the 3d Battalion, white 2d Lt. Roscoe Dann, recalled walking down the middle of a street with Wilson and ordering men to "fall in." He did not recall any great problem. A cook with the 3d Battalion, Joseph Davis, however, remembered vividly that some of the men had weapons and that "they shot the town up. It was very bad." A platoon leader in Company I, black 2d Lt. Reginald J. Sapenter, also

recalled shooting. He was alerted in the middle of the night, he said, to go into town and round up the troops. He met General Wilson in a jeep in the middle of a road and warned him to take cover because the men had weapons and ammunition and were taking pot shots. Wilson responded that Sapenter and his men had weapons as well, the clear implication being that they should respond as the situation dictated. In the end, return fire was unnecessary. Over the next three hours, according to Wooldridge, battalion officers organized squads to comb the town, detaining about seventy-five enlisted men and marching them down to the docks where they were needed to load ships. A number more escaped.[63]

Since all concerned rejoined their units and everyone embarked on time for Korea, neither the regiment nor the Eighth Army was much inclined to pursue the matter. When the Japanese police lodged a formal complaint, however, alleging that approximately one hundred black deserters from an unknown unit had killed a Japanese citizen, seriously injured another, and committed acts of rape, U.S. military authorities in Japan had no choice but to investigate. Unable to contact Wooldridge or other eyewitnesses within the 24th who could have confirmed, as enlisted man Joseph Davis put it, that the 24th had "shot up" Moji, the investigators were quick to dismiss the report as a gross exaggeration. Only ten soldiers had been implicated, they asserted, and no one had been killed or injured. They did concede, however, that the troops involved had responded with gunfire

---

[62] Interv, IG with Wooldridge, 23 Aug 50, exhibit 1, Kean Letter file. See also Interv, Muehlbauer with Burke, 23 Jan 89.

[63] Intervs, IG with Wooldridge, 23 Aug 50, exhibit 1, Kean Letter file; Cash with Joseph C. Davis, 21 Jan 89; MacGarrigle with Dann, 28 Mar 94; Bowers with Reginald J. Sapenter, 10 Mar 94. Several other officers and enlisted men confirmed the incident. See Intervs, Cash with Charlie Lee Jones, 6 Sep 89; Muehlbauer with Ray Koenig, 20 Mar 89; Ltr, Komp to MacGarrigle, 14 May 94. Japanese journalist Seiichi Matsumoto wrote a book on the episode, *Kuroji no E* [*Picture on a Black Background*]. On 9 May 1993, the Japanese television station Kyushu TV–Asahi aired a documentary on Matsumoto's life that gave extensive coverage to what it called "the Kokura incident." See Ltr, Betsy Cooke, Masaoka & Associates, Inc., to Richard Boylan, Archivist, National Archives, 23 Sep 93, with attached fact sheet, copy in CMH files.

when the military police had arrived and that no one had been punished.[64]

Although only a small minority of the more than three thousand members of the 24th were involved in those incidents and the majority of the unit's men went off to war without demur, the wholesale change of officers preceding and even during the move, the rumors and lack of communication attending it, and the episodes of undiscipline at Gifu and Moji raise many questions. Were the regiment's leaders at all levels, especially the new officers in the companies, capable of overcoming the problems that were clearly widespread within the regiment while at the same time dealing with the special circumstances of war? Would the lack of trust within the unit between whites and blacks, both officer and enlisted, have a bearing on how the regiment performed in battle? Was discipline, itself a function of trust, sufficient to give the men the tenacity and determination they would need to survive in combat?

Whatever the answers, the problems that accompanied the 24th's move to Korea appear not to have occurred in all-white regiments making the same journey. Because of that, the disorders tended to confirm the prejudiced stereotypes of whites who were already disposed to question the decision to commit an all-black regiment to the war. "[Despite] the background of WW II in which like organizations functioned, the training background of the 24th in Japan and the inherent characteristic [sic] of the negro soldier," the 35th Infantry's commander, Colonel Fisher, thus avowed, "the decision was to move the organization to Korea. The undisciplinary conduct on the part of this organization while it was awaiting sea transportation in Kokura, Japan, was a final demonstration indicative of the type of conduct which could be expected against an enemy."[65]

The trip from Moji, on Japan's west coast, to Pusan, on the southeastern tip of the Korean peninsula, occurred on 11 and 12 July, took more than twelve hours, and covered 150 miles. With conditions Spartan in port and aboard ship, it was anything but refreshing for the officers or the men of the 24th. The equipment and personnel of the regiment were loaded on an assortment of old Japanese and American ships, many of them used for hauling fish and fertilizer. "After much confusion," the 3d Battalion's war diary noted:

the battalion was alerted to board ship at 1200 hours and movement to the docks began. . . . Three companies . . . were returned to the staging area by direction of Brigadier General Wilson . . . with orders to wait there until all material, equipment, etc., had been loaded. At 2013 hours the units were again ordered aboard ship and . . . loaded on a Japanese vessel, *Hari-Mura* [sic], during the remainder of the night . . . The Battalion Commander and the Executive Officer were fortunate in being billeted in a 6'X 15' cabin. There was no fresh water, cooking facilities, nor toilets aboard ship. All the rest of the battalion sat or slept on the filthy deck.[66]

Years afterward, the commander of the battalion's Company L, Captain Biggs, recalled that the ship assigned to his unit still had fish in its hold. Alluding to the pungent smell that hung over much of Korea because the farmers of the country used human waste as fertilizer, he commented that "we stunk of fish and the smell of Pusan before we even saw it."[67]

If the crossing to Korea proceeded without problems for most of the 24th, disorders continued here and there aboard ship. According to Lieutenant Komp, some stealing of rations, equipment, and even rifles occurred among the men on

[64] Interv, Cash with Joseph C. Davis, 21 Jan 89; Far East Command (FEC) Provost Marshal Weekly Summary, 15 Jul 50, box 9894, RG 331, WNRC.

[65] Ltr, Col Henry G. Fisher to Col S. W. Foote, Chief, Histories Division, Office of the Chief of Military History, 19 Nov 57, CMH files. Fisher knew what had happened because his unit had arrived at Moji just after the 24th Infantry had departed. Although a search was made for similar episodes in

other American units, none remotely comparable have come to light. Since the Eighth Army attempted to play down what had happened in the 24th, similar, more successful cover -ups may have occurred in the case of other units. It stands to reason, however, that if evidence of misconduct by all-white units existed, Japanese commentators would have brought it to light when they dealt with the 24th. To date, they have not done so.

[66] WD, 3d Bn, 24th Inf Rgt, 8–31 Jul 50.

[67] Ltr, Bradley Biggs to Clay Blair, 20 Oct 86, Clay and Joan Blair Collection, Forgotten War, 24th Division, MHI.

his ship. It was a sign, he said, that at least a few had little trust in their fellows and viewed the coming test of battle as every man for himself. Others, rifleman James Burke observed, had loaded a truck with "booze." As a result, he said, "When we got to Korea, most of us were feeling pretty good."[68]

In fact, if some seemed to be out for themselves, morale among the majority of the regiment's members was high. Taking Colonel White at his word and packing their "pinks and greens" for a victory parade, few of the officers expected the war to last long. As for the enlisted men, some, according to rifleman Jerry Johnson, seemed eager to get to the front because the war would be an adventure, and it provided an opportunity to earn the coveted Combat Infantryman's Badge. Others, according to rifleman Nathaniel Pipkins, were just "tired of running up and down [the training area at] Fuji. This would be different."[69]

All elements of the regiment had reached Pusan by 1400 on 13 July. When they arrived, they encountered a number of problems brought on by the haste in which the United States had gone to war. A lack of cranes and other equipment for unloading the ships at the port of Pusan was complicated by a sitdown strike by local stevedores either sympathetic to the Communists or hoping to sell their services at the highest possible profit. In the end, some units enlisted help in unloading their ships at gunpoint while others did the work themselves.[70]

The haphazard loading of some of the vessels snarled matters further. Since some of the materiel and supplies the men would need almost immediately in the field had been stowed deep within the holds of the ships and would take over a day to unload, the regiment's battalions moved out of the port toward the combat zone without all of the vehicles and supplies they had packed. Compounding those problems, many of the men had brought excess baggage—winter uniforms, athletic equipment, and the sort of creature comforts that they had been allowed to carry when they had traveled to Fuji for exercises. All of that gear had to be stored, much of it never to be seen by its owners again.[71]

When the regiment arrived at Pusan on 12 and 13 July South Korea seemed on the verge of collapse. On the west General Dean's 24th Division was pulling back under heavy pressure to the Kum River, and there was no assurance that the force would be able to hold the line for long. Meanwhile, to the east, in South Korea's central region and along the far coast, some five enemy divisions were advancing south, putting the important east coast port of P'ohang-dong at risk and threatening to cut off the entire American force from its base at Pusan. The combat effectiveness of the enemy force varied. The *1st North Korean Division* was highly aggressive, but U.S. intelligence ranked the effectiveness of two others as low. Even so, the five understrength South Korean divisions contesting the enemy advance were poorly armed, supplied, and trained. As with Dean's force, no one knew how long they would last or when they might break. Surveying the situation, Eighth Army commanders decided to use the 25th Division to back up the South Koreans in the central and eastern highlands but to put it in a position where, if necessary, it could also slide west in support of Dean.[72] (*Map 2*)

The regimental headquarters and the 2d Battalion were the first segments of the 24th Infantry to reach port, arriving in midmorning on 12 July. On instructions from Eighth Army headquarters, they immediately moved north to P'ohang-dong, a 110-mile trip by rail. Both were on station by evening, but the 2d Battalion was short Company H, which had stayed behind in Pusan to finish unloading the unit's equipment and vehicles. The move was so hasty and supplies so lacking that the men had no rations of any sort. Many resorted to eating the local fruit and came down with diarrhea.[73]

[68] Intervs, MacGarrigle with Komp, 5 May and 1 Jun 94; Muehlbauer with Burke, 23 Jan 89.

[69] Intervs, Muehlbauer with Allen, 23 Aug 88; Eddie Capers, 2 Nov 88; Pipkins, 23 Aug 88; Cash with Biggs, 15 Aug 88; Jerry Johnson, 23 Sep 88; Walden, 18 Mar 89.

[70] WD, 24th Inf Rgt, 6–31 Jul 50. See also Intervs, Cash with Albert Brooks, 6 Aug 88; Gorham Black, 12 Mar 89.

[71] Ibid.

[72] WD, 25th Inf Div, Jul 50.

[73] WD, 24th Inf Rgt, 6–31 Jul 50; WD, 2d Bn, 24th Inf

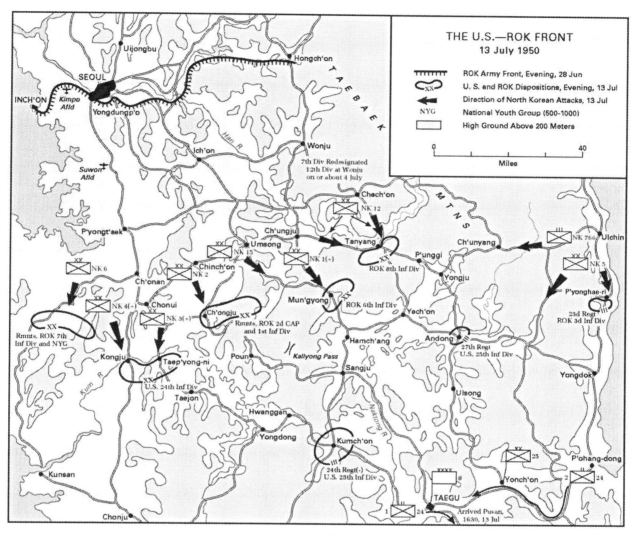

Map 2

The next day, responding to further reverses on Dean's front, the Eighth Army repositioned the 24th to the west of the Naktong River at the town of Kumch'on, 85 miles west of P'ohang-dong by road and 100 miles from Pusan by train. The 2d Battalion immediately began to load for the trip but the move took until midnight on 13 July to finish. By then the 3d Battalion had already arrived, hav-ing departed Pusan by train directly for Kumch'on at 0500. The 1st Battalion arrived in port that evening and also began the trip north. By the next day the entire regiment, minus work details that had remained behind at Pusan, was present at Kumch'on, where it was in position either to move north some thirty miles to protect an important road junction at Hamch'ang, or to swing west some forty miles to support Dean at Taejon.[74]

Rgt, 13–31 Jul 50. See also Interv, Cash with Britt, 18 Aug 88. For food shortages in other units, see Intervs, Cash with Biggs, 15 Aug 88; Jasper Johnson, 5 Oct 88.

[74] WD, 24th Inf Rgt, 6–31 Jul 50; WD, 2d Bn, 24th Inf Rgt, 13–31 Jul 50.

When the unit arrived in Pusan and began its move north into position, the enthusiasm of some of the men began to fade, a characteristic common of soldiers approaching combat for the first time.[75] The sight at Pusan of jeeps and trucks filled with stretchers and wounded soldiers caused stress and uncertainty. "I felt bad," enlisted man Raymond Hagins recalled. "Who's goin' to help us. . . . They got whipped." At that point, according to rifleman Eugene Rumpf, a junior NCO went mad and had to be taken away in a straitjacket.[76] Apprehension increased during the ride north. The floors of some cars on the trains were covered with bloody straw; seats in the coaches were also bloody, and many windows had been shot out. The trip itself was often arduous, adding to the effect. "I recall vividly," Company C's commander, Capt. Laurence Corcoran, said, "that we had to get off the train and help push it up . . . [a] hill."[77]

As the anxiety of the men increased, rumors spread, especially one to the effect that the regiment's white executive officer, Lt. Col. James B. Bennett, who had been evacuated for medical reasons, had faked a heart attack along the way rather than face the rigors ahead.[78] When the unit arrived at Kumch'on and its various portions settled into night positions, some of the men were so anxious they began to fire indiscriminately at anything. As Sgt. Richard Sanders of the 3d Battalion's Company M recalled, they "killed a lot of trees." One enlisted

The 24th Infantry waits to move out from Pusan, 14 July 1950.

man was wounded by an accidental weapons discharge. Much the same thing happened in other units. When the 27th Infantry spent its first night in the field at Andong, Uzal Ent recalled, the troops became nervous and fired freely from their positions in the hills around the town.[79]

Yech'on

Late on the night of 13 July the 1st and 2d Battalions of the 24th went into Eighth Army reserve, prepared to move either to the Hamch'ang or Taejon areas, as circumstances required. The 3d Battalion, augmented by an artillery battery, was directed to proceed to Yech'on, a small town seventeen miles northeast of Hamch'ang by road.[80]

The continuing enemy advance had dictated the order. Reports had arrived that enemy forces were threatening to push the 8th South Korean Division out of the town of Tanyang in the Han River valley and south through the mountains

[75] Richard Holmes, *Acts of War: The Behavior of Men in Battle* (New York: Free Press, 1985), p. 138.

[76] Intervs, Cash with Raymond C. Hagins, 28 Aug 88; Rumpf, 15 Aug 88. See also Interv, Muehlbauer with Burke, 23 Jan 89.

[77] Intervs, Cash with Britt, 18 Aug 88; Hagins, 28 Aug 88. Quote from Interv, Cash with Corcoran, 28 Jul 89.

[78] Intervs, Cash with Walden, 18 Mar 89. See also Interv, Cash with Ransom, 5 Aug 88; Bussey, *Firefight at Yechon*, pp. 84, 86. Whether Bennett's physical problem was a heart attack is unknown. In support of the heart attack, see Interv, MacGarrigle with Gillert, 4 May 94. Captain Hash says Bennett commented openly that he would never go into combat with a black unit. See Interv, MacGarrigle with Hash, 18 and 22 Mar 94. Some evidence exists of a nervous breakdown. See Intervs, Cash with Leonard H. Kushner, 16 Jun 89; Bowers with LaBlanc, 28 Feb 94.

[79] Interv, Muehlbauer with Sanders, 16 Dec 88; Memorandum for the Record (MFR), MacGarrigle and Bowers, 26 Oct 93, CMH files. For details on the first death in the unit resulting from an accidental weapons discharge, see Interv, Rainey with Hough, 16 Nov 89. See also Interv, MacGarrigle with Sapenter, 21 Mar 94. Sapenter of Company I describes indiscriminate weapons firing that killed a cow in the dark a few days later near Yech'on.

[80] WD, 25th Inf Div, 13–14 Jul 50.

Soldiers on a flatcar ready to move out from Pusan

toward Andong, an important crossroad on the Naktong River, twenty miles east of Yech'on. Kean sent the 27th Infantry to backstop the South Korean defense by securing the high ground north of Andong. The 3d Battalion of the 24th was meanwhile to do the same at Yech'on, which stood at a critical position on the enemy's line of advance because it commanded roads running east to Andong and southwest to Hamch'ang. If the North Koreans took it, they would be in position to move either east or west.[81]

With the other two battalions of the 24th still en route to Kumch'on, only the 3d Battalion was available for the mission. It had just arrived itself, after a four-day trip from Gifu that had included 20 hours on a train in Japan, 17 hours aboard ship, and 12 hours on the train that carried it to its final destination. There had been little time for unbroken sleep and little food or water on the way. Indeed, the first regular meal the men ate came only at 2300 on 13 July, close to seven hours after they arrived in Kumch'on and a scant five hours before they were alerted to begin preparing for the move to Yech'on—another seven-hour ride by truck. Two officers and twenty-five enlisted men from the battalion still remained behind in Pusan to find lost equipment—including the unit's kitchen

trucks—and to complete the unloading and shipment of materiel.[82]

Because of time constraints, the unit's officers had difficulty finding enough train coaches and boxcars to move the battalion by rail. Trucks themselves were hard to find. In the end, after an exhausting search, the unit had to await the arrival of trains from Pusan bearing some of its trucks. When those proved too few, it borrowed the remainder of what it needed from the 90th Field Artillery Battalion, which was supplying a battery to support the operation. Since there was little room for nonessentials, the troops themselves carried only combat packs—a change of socks and underwear, indispensable personal items, and no more than a day's supply of C-rations. The remainder of their gear was stored under guard in a school building at Kumch'on.

The battalion arrived at Yech'on at 1600 on 14 July and had its command post in place within thirty minutes. By 1745 the troops themselves were digging into defensive positions on high ground and preparing to patrol the roads leading into the town. Battery A of the 90th Field Artillery Battalion positioned its 155-mm. guns to support the infantry, placing two in forward positions where they could serve as antitank weapons. Later in the evening, the 3d Platoon of the 77th Engineer Combat Company arrived.[83] Since the 3d Battalion was to cooperate with South Korean soldiers and policemen already in the area, an intelligence specialist from the South Korean II Corps joined the unit. Contact with higher headquarters was difficult to maintain because of the shortage of radios and the continuing lack of spare parts.

The problem with communications diminished the next morning, when the commander of the 27th Infantry, Colonel Michaelis, arranged for the 25th Division to provide the battalion with a powerful SCR–193 radio so he could stay in touch with the unit protecting his flank.[84] Shortly there-

81 WD, 25th Inf Div, 14 Jul 50.

82 WD, 3d Bn, 24th Inf Rgt, 8–31 Jul 50.

83 WD, 65th Engineer (Engr) Bn, 14 Jul 50, p. 8.

84 G–1 Journal, 25th Inf Div, 15 Jul 50, in WD, 25th Inf Div, Jul 50.

Troops of Company G, 24th Infantry, ready to move to the firing lines, 18 July 1950

after the assistant division commander, General Wilson, arrived. Wanting the division to do well in its first engagements with the enemy, he had spent the day before with the 27th Infantry. He would remain at Yech'on all that day and spend the night, inspecting the 3d Battalion's positions and conferring with its officers.

Despite all the attention from higher-ups, the battalion's first contact with the enemy was less than auspicious. On 15 July a platoon from Company I on a long-range reconnaissance patrol encountered scattered mortar fire and moved back to the company position, abandoning some equipment in the process. The platoon leader, black 2d Lt. William D. Ware, along with his sergeant, after being reprimanded by the company commander, walked two miles to the battalion command post to report that

he was unable to hold his position in the face of enemy fire. Ordered to return his men to their original position, he did so. As with the firing at Kumch'on during the regiment's first night in the field, the episode was an indication of the uncertainty, indecision, and anxiety that inexperienced troops and leaders sometimes feel when facing combat for the first time. Less than two weeks later, on 26 July, Ware would earn the Army's second highest medal for valor, the Distinguished Service Cross, while giving his life for his men.[85]

---

[85] Interv, IG with Maj Theodore J. Cook, Exec Ofcr, 3d Bn, 24th Inf Rgt, 23 Aug 50, exhibit 10, Kean Letter file. Ware's citation is in Eighth U.S. Army, Korea (EUSAK), GO 54, 6 Sep 50. Unless otherwise indicated, general orders for this volume are on file in the Army's Awards Branch of the Personnel Service Support Division of the Adjutant General Directorate

Wilson departed on the morning of 16 July but his superior, the commander of the 25th Division, General Kean, arrived to inspect the front line. Kean also spent the night. The 3d Battalion continued to depend on its regimental headquarters for supplies and ammunition, but it came under the operational control of Michaelis' 27th Infantry shortly after the general arrived.[86]

Throughout 16 and 17 July the American commitment in the area increased. Company A of the 79th Heavy Tank Battalion (less one platoon) arrived from the 27th Infantry. Later, Company B of the 65th Engineer Battalion also took up station to finish a partially constructed landing strip in a nearby riverbed. Both were white units. During the afternoon Company I fired on an unidentified aircraft. The plane returned fire, making two strafing runs over the battalion command post before withdrawing to the south. The weather was hot and humid with scattered showers.[87]

While Kean was visiting, the unit's members complained about the condition of their automatic weapons. Inventory checks had meanwhile confirmed that fully one-third of the equipment that had supposedly accompanied the unit from Gifu had never arrived from Pusan. With combat possible at any time, Kean arranged to provide enough additional equipment from division stocks to bring the force up to strength.[88]

The general had much to consider. To the north, one of North Korea's most dangerous units, the *1st Division*, was fighting a bitter battle with the 6th South Korean Division over a pass at

Mun'gyong that commanded a critical communications corridor running due south 90 miles from Wonju to Kumch'on through the rugged mountain range that separated the watersheds of the Han and Naktong Rivers. If the pass fell, Hamch'ang, 10 miles to the south, would follow and the road to Kumch'on, the Naktong River valley, and Pusan would beckon. Meanwhile, east of the Mun'gyong Pass and north of Yech'on, the troubled but still powerful *12th North Korean Division* had captured the Han River town of Tanyang on 14 July and was pushing the 8th South Korean Division south, back across the mountains toward Andong, 35 miles to the southeast. Advancing down the Tanyang-Andong road, the enemy appeared to have split his force, with the main body continuing on toward Andong while the *31st Infantry Regiment* veered south in the direction of Yech'on.[89] To make matters worse, to the east, the *5th North Korean Division* was advancing southward along the coastal highway. It had taken the town of P'yonghae-ri, 50 miles above P'ohang-dong, on 13 July and had then sent the *766th Independent Infantry Unit* inland across the coastal mountains with instructions to cut communications between Pusan and the Eighth Army's headquarters at Taegu.[90]

With the 21st Regiment of the 8th South Korean Division opposing the *31st Regiment's* advance toward Yech'on and reports arriving that the enemy was threatening Hamch'ang, General Kean decided to organize Task Force ABLE under General Wilson to secure the Hamch'ang-Kumch'on road. Receiving permission to detach the 2d Battalion of the 24th from Eighth Army reserve, on the evening of 17 July he moved it

---

of the U.S. Total Army Personnel Command (PERSCOM), Alexandria, Va. Ware's citation stations him with Company L rather than I, but Ware was clearly part of Company I. See Officer Roster, 24th Inf Rgt, 18 Sep 50. The S–3 of the 3d Battalion, Zanin, confirmed Cook's story, as did a fellow platoon leader in Company I. See Intervs, MacGarrigle with Zanin, 22 Oct 93; Bowers with Sapenter, 10 Mar 94. All the lost equipment was apparently recovered, but it is not clear how that was done.

[86] 25th Inf Div Opns Rpt 6, 16 Jul 50. See also WD, 25th Inf Div, 16 Jul 50.

[87] WD, 25th Inf Div, 16 Jul 50. See also Interv, Bowers with Sapenter, 10 Mar 94.

[88] WD, 25th Inf Div, 16 Jul 50.

[89] ATIS, Research Supplement, Interrogation Rpt, issue 99, 24 Apr 51, *7th NK Infantry Division*, pp. 44–45, Intelligence Research Collection, MHI.

[90] Appleman, *South to the Naktong, North to the Yalu*, pp. 101–08. See also 25th Inf Div Periodic Info Rpt 7, 19 to 20 Jul 50, in WD, 25th Inf Div, Jul 50; FEC, Military Intelligence Section, Order of Battle Information, North Korean Army, 15 Oct 50, MHI, hereafter cited as North Korean Order of Battle; ATIS, Research Supplement, Interrogation Rpt, issue 9, no. 1468, 29 Sep 50, Interrogation of Senior Col Lee Hak Ku, former Chief of Staff, *13th North Korean Division*, pp. 158–74, Appleman Papers, MHI.

north from Kumch'on to hold roads coming through the mountains near Sangju, a town some ten miles south of Hamch'ang. Wilson took operational control of that battalion, the 3d Battalion of the 24th, and Company A of the 79th Tank Battalion shortly thereafter. He planned to use the 3d Battalion to block the roads around Hamch'ang. Employing the vehicles of Company B of the 65th Engineer Battalion to assist in transporting the unit to Hamch'ang, he left the engineers at Yech'on temporarily to serve as a rear guard.[91]

The 3d Battalion hastily redeployed south to the Hamch'ang area at 0900 on 18 July, at a time when the unit's men were already unsettled. As a result, the force began to experience problems almost as soon as it reached its destination. About noon a vehicle arrived from the division reconnaissance company with word that five or six enemy tanks were on the approach, a scant five miles away. The battalion's commander, Colonel Pierce, sounded the alarm, whereupon a heavy mortar platoon attached to the battalion turned its vehicles around, drove at high speed to the rear, and ended up plowing eight of its trucks into rice paddies that lined the road. Other men were caught up in the confusion and began to mount their own vehicles, but officers quickly asserted their authority and managed to regain control.[92] Nothing came of the supposed enemy attack, but on the same day, when South Korean units some seven hundred yards to Company I's front became involved in a firefight, that company likewise started to withdraw. It went back into position upon order, however, abandoning none of its equipment.[93]

Shortly after arriving at Hamch'ang, General Wilson learned that the situation there was far less threatening than intelligence analysts had supposed. South Korean troops still held the town and its approaches and remained in possession of the Mun'gyong Pass to the north. With circumstances on that front in hand for the time being, Wilson decided to return the 3d Battalion to Yech'on the next morning. But he modified his decision late that afternoon, when a patrol from the 27th Infantry reported that enemy activity was increasing near the town.[94] Concerned about the engineers he had left in place there, Wilson immediately instructed Colonel Pierce to form a task force under the 3d Battalion's operations officer, Capt. John B. Zanin, and to send it back to Yech'on immediately. Composed of a platoon of tanks from Company A of the 79th Tank Battalion, a 75-mm. recoilless rifle section, and a section of heavy machine guns, the force departed at 1800.[95]

Zanin's force had hardly reached Yech'on at 2000 when advance elements of the enemy's *31st Regiment* arrived and the engineers began to receive mortar fire and to register small-arms fire from their front, right, and left rear. Zanin immediately brought his tanks into position to support the defenders but, under increasing enemy pressure, within the hour decided he was poorly positioned to withstand any kind of a ground attack and withdrew his force to Hamch'ang. As the move began, the retreating column encountered a truck blocking the road, a sign that the enemy was about to spring an ambush. The vehicle wheeled and sped off when the force neared, but machine guns then opened fire from both sides of the road.

---

[91] WD, 25th Inf Div, 17 Jul 50. See also WDs, 24th Inf Rgt; 2d Bn, 24th Inf Rgt; and 3d Bn, 24th Inf Rgt. All for Jul 50, in WD, 24th Inf Rgt, Jul 50. WD, 65th Engr Bn, Jul 50, in WD, 25th Inf Div, Jul 50. For the operations of the 21st South Korean Regiment, see FEC Communique 87, 170100–171430 Jul 50, CMH files; Interv, MacGarrigle with Rennie M. Cory, 10 Jun 94.

[92] WD, 3d Bn, 24th Inf Rgt, Jul 50, p. 6; Interv, IG with 1st Lt Christopher M. Gooch, 26 Aug 50, exhibit 25, Kean Letter file. Gooch was the intelligence officer (S–2) of the 3d Battalion.

[93] Interv, IG with Cook, 23 Aug 50, exhibit 10, Kean Letter file. Cook was the executive officer of the 3d Battalion. A forward observer from Battery A of the 90th Field Artillery

Battalion recalled being abandoned in the field at Hamch'ang by a company of the 24th Infantry. See Interv, MacGarrigle with Cory, 10 Jun 94.

[94] WD, 25th Inf Div, 18 Jul 50. The whereabouts are unknown of the 21st South Korean Regiment that had earlier opposed the enemy's advance down the Tanyang-Yech'on road.

[95] The 25th Division's war diary says Wilson told Pierce to appoint a staff officer. See ibid. Zanin says he was appointed directly by Wilson. See Interv, MacGarrigle with Zanin, 22 Oct 93.

Zanin's tanks, in a brief but sharp engagement, eliminated the problem. His force continued on its way, reaching Hamch'ang at 0310 on 19 July. Zanin reported that he had fought his way out of Yech'on against heavy opposition and that nine enlisted men from the engineer company were missing. In all, he said, the force had lost a 2 ½-ton truck and four ¼-ton trailers. Two casualties were evacuated. Zanin and Pfc. Jesse J. Willingham of Company M both received Silver Stars for their roles in the action.[96]

Rather than dash back to Yech'on, General Wilson reacted with caution. Although assigning Company K to patrol the roads in the direction of the town and moving Company I to a position five miles east of Hamch'ang, he postponed the return of the 3d Battalion to Yech'on that he had earlier ordered. He may have been waiting for Battery B of the 159th Field Artillery Battalion to arrive or for an instruction team from the 24th Infantry that was slated to brief men from the unit on the use of the Army's new 3.5-inch rocket launcher, a weapon lethal to North Korea's tanks. He may also have been concerned about the events that day in Hamch'ang and may have sought to provide time for Pierce's men to settle down.[97]

For a time, Wilson was of a mind to leave the 3d Battalion at Hamch'ang and to shift the 2d Battalion from Sangju to Yech'on. At 1720 on 19 July he issued orders to that effect, and the unit's commander, Colonel Cohoon, set the process in motion.[98] At the last moment, General Kean stepped in. He may have been aware that it would be difficult for the 2d Battalion to move and regroup with the sort of dispatch that circumstances required. He may also have concluded that the job at Hamch'ang was best suited for a

regimental commander and that Wilson, his assistant division commander, would be of more use elsewhere. Whatever the reason, late that night he gave the 35th's commander, Colonel Fisher, charge of the entire Yech'on-Hamch'ang-Sangju area. Establishing a headquarters at Hamch'ang, Fisher was to return the 2d Battalion of the 24th to Sangju, bring his own 2d Battalion forward to Hamch'ang, and move the 3d Battalion of the 24th back to Yech'on. With those deployments in place, he would be able to support the South Korean forces fighting north of Hamch'ang while both assisting Cohoon's battalion at Sangju and backing up Pierce's move against Yech'on. Although the 3d Battalion would make the initial attack on Yech'on, plugging the gap that appeared to have developed in the allied line, the plan was for the 18th Regiment of the South Korean Capital Division to fill in for the unit as soon as possible.[99]

Pierce's task force departed for Yech'on the next morning, 20 July, after being relieved by the 2d Battalion, 35th Infantry, in its positions around Hamch'ang. It was supported by the 3d Platoon of the 77th Engineer Combat Company, Battery B of the 159th Field Artillery Battalion, and a detachment from the 25th Division's signal company. Preceded by scouts from the battalion's intelligence section and protected from surprise attack on the northern flank by a screening force from the 35th Infantry's intelligence and reconnaissance platoon, leading elements of Pierce's column arrived at a position about one mile from Yech'on at midmorning. (*Map 3*) The weather was cloudy and cool.[100]

The men of Company L, under Captain Biggs, left the trucks that had brought them from Hamch'ang and moved up the main road toward

[96] Zanin's report is in WD, 3d Bn, 24th Inf Rgt, Jul 50, p. 6. The war diary for the 65th Engineer Battalion reported 1 killed, 2 missing, and 2 wounded. See WD, 65th Engr Bn, Jul 50. Zanin described the action in Interv, MacGarrigle with Zanin, 22 Oct 93. See also 25th Inf Div GO 107, 4 Sep 50, and GO 123, 8 Sep 50.

[97] WD, 3d Bn, 24th Inf Rgt, Jul 50.

[98] WDs, 2d Bn, 24th Inf Rgt, Jun 50; 3d Bn, 24th Inf Rgt, Jun 50.

[99] WDs, 2d Bn, 24th Inf Rgt, Jun 50; 3d Bn, 24th Inf Rgt, Jun 50; 2d Bn, 35th Inf Rgt, Jun 50; S–2/S–3 Journal, 35th Inf Rgt, 19 Jul 50; Historical Rpt, 25th Inf Div, 8–31 Jul 50.

[100] WDs, 25th Inf Div, 20 Jul 50; 3d Bn, 24th Inf Rgt, 20 Jul 50; Unit Journal, 2d Bn, 35th Inf Rgt, 20 Jul 50; Morning Rpt, HQ, 3d Bn, Co L, 24th Inf Rgt, 20 Jul 50, CMH files; Comments by Col Henry G. Fisher on Appleman MS, 27 Oct 51, Appleman Papers, MHI.

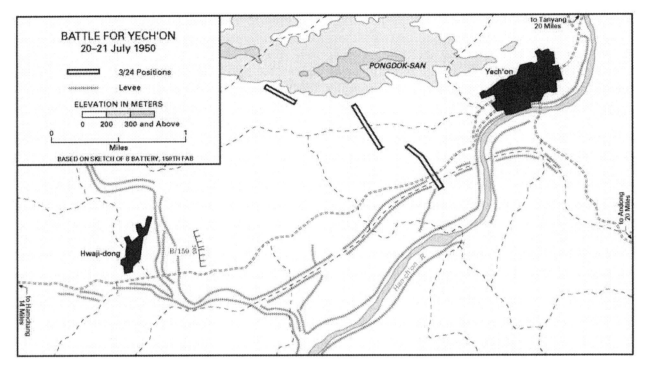

BATTLE FOR YECH'ON
20–21 July 1950

▭▭▭▭   3/24 Positions
·········   Levee

ELEVATION IN METERS

0   200   300 and Above

0   1
Miles

BASED ON SKETCH OF B BATTERY, 159TH FAB

Map 3

Yech'on on foot. After a short distance, they shifted to the left of the road to avoid clusters of houses and small villages scattered along the way that might provide cover for an ambush. As they neared a group of houses located to the side of a small irrigation ditch about one-half mile from Yech'on, their leading elements came under rifle and mortar fire. About that time, enemy mortar fire from the hills north of Yech'on began to hit the road, separating Biggs' unit from the remainder of the task force, which was beginning to assemble near the point where Company L had dismounted and moved off.[101]

Pierce replied by ordering his own mortars and artillery to silence the enemy's weapons. The mortarmen of Company M and the platoon from the heavy mortar company responded almost at once, but the artillery had difficulty moving into position because the road was jammed with the infantry's vehicles. In the end, the artillery commander cleared the way only by instructing his men to push many of the vehicles into surrounding rice paddies. Once the artillery was in position in a dry, sandy riverbed about three thousand yards behind Biggs and prepared to fire, Pierce added to the confusion by questioning the commands the unit's officers were issuing. When the artillery battalion commander responded by explaining the artillery's grid system for targets, Pierce relented and apologized, but the episode set poorly nonetheless. The artillery fired its first rounds at 1545.[102]

---

[101] WD, 3d Bn, 24th Inf Rgt, 20 Jul 50; Morning Rpts, HQ, 3d Bn, Co L, Co M, 24th Inf Rgt, 20 Jul 50, CMH files; MS, Bradley Biggs, Were Black Scapegoats for Our Failures in Korea? n.d., CMH files; Intervs, Bowers with Walter W. Redd, 18 Feb and 24 Mar 94; Clifton F. Vincent, 19 and 20 Apr 94; Muehlbauer with Turner, 22 Dec 88. There is conflicting evidence on the route Company L took. This version is based on the account of the company commander which is supported by WD, 159th Field Artillery (FA) Bn, Jul 50, sketch 4.

[102] WD, 159th FA Bn, Jul 50, pp. 3–4; Morning Rpt, Battery B, 159th FA Bn, 20 Jul 50, CMH files.

Company I, commanded by black Capt. Thurston Jamison, and Company K, under 1st Lt. Jasper Johnson, arrived in midafternoon. Pierce ordered Jamison to move his unit toward high ground to the northeast to cover Company L's flank while Johnson moved against Yech'on along the main road. As Company K advanced, checking the huts in the small villages along the way, an enemy force opened fire and wounded one of the unit's platoon leaders. Even so, part of Johnson's force moved on ahead and managed to enter Yech'on.[103]

After Jamison's and Johnson's companies began to move out, the 77th Engineer Combat Company commander, black 1st Lt. Charles Bussey, arrived in the area where the battalion's trucks were parked. He had mail for his men. Observing that the 3d Battalion's units were under mortar and machine-gun fire from enemy forces on the high ground, he maneuvered a squad equipped with two machine guns to commanding terrain and attempted to provide relief. When friendly mortars registered on the enemy position and some of the enemy soldiers began to break and run, Bussey was in position and brought many of them down. He won a Silver Star for his role in the episode.[104]

With the coming of darkness, enemy fire died down. Johnson, however, decided his position was too exposed with the enemy retaining the high ground and requested permission to pull back.[105] Shortly thereafter, Pierce broke off the assault and drew his battalion into defensive positions to await the dawn. The artillery fired throughout the remainder of the night, expending more than seven hundred and fifty rounds and setting Yech'on ablaze. Its officers later claimed that the battery destroyed several enemy mortar positions at the cost of one forward observer.[106]

As the battle progressed, higher headquarters had at best a confused impression of what was happening. Colonel Fisher in Hamch'ang had received word at noon on 20 July that Company K had killed two of the enemy and captured one at Yech'on.[107] That evening the 25th Division reported: "K Co inside city limits, opposition negative. Encountered 120mm mortar and mortar fire comp[arable] to our 60mm at 201710 July 50, estimated YECHON will be secure by our forces by 201800 Jul 50."[108]

Whatever sense of success those reports may have indicated was short lived. When Pierce reported at 2155 that his force was still pushing the assault and that it had been held up outside of Yech'on, Fisher grew concerned and requested more information.[109] General Kean also became anxious and began to monitor the situation closely. At 0013 on 21 July, aware that a South Korean regiment was preparing to relieve the 3d Battalion, he instructed Fisher to take Yech'on before turning it over to the arriving force. At 0018 he called to ask, "Has your mission been accomplished?" At 0035 he requested information on the disposition of the units attached to the 3d Battalion, including the battery from the

103 WDs, 3d Bn, 24th Inf Rgt, 20 Jul 50; 159th FA Bn, Jul 50, sketch 4; Morning Rpts, Co I, Co K, 24th Inf Rgt, 20 Jul 50, CMH files; Intervs, Cash with Jasper Johnson, 5 Oct 88; Bowers with Jasper Johnson, 18 Apr 94; Roy Appleman with Jasper Johnson, 11 Jul 52, cited in Appleman, *South to the Naktong, North to the Yalu*, p. 190; Bowers with Tittel, 15 Apr 94; MacGarrigle with Tittel, 20 Apr 94; Bowers with Dann, 23 Mar 94; MacGarrigle with Dann, 28 Mar 94. Two of Johnson's platoon leaders state that they did not get into Yech'on, but the company commander is certain that at least part of his force did. Portions of Company L may also have entered the town. See Interv, Bowers with Redd, 24 Mar 94.

104 Although the war diary for the 3d Battalion, 24th Infantry, describes the fight at Yech'on, it makes no mention of Bussey's encounter. The war diary of the 65th Engineer Battalion contains only a very general description of Bussey's actions. The account given here is based on the war diary of the 65th Engineer Battalion, Bussey's award citation for the Silver Star, and an interview. See WD, 65th Engr Bn, Jul 50, dtd 24 Oct 50, p. 13; 25th Inf Div GO 324, dtd 12 Nov 50, Award of the Silver Star for Capt Charles M. Bussey. See also Sworn Statement, LaVaughn E. Fields, 25 Jun 84, CMH files; Interv, Cash with LaVaughn E. Fields, 5 Feb 89. Bussey's own account of the episode is in Bussey, *Firefight at Yechon*, pp. 100–106.

105 Intervs, Cash with Jasper Johnson, 5 Oct 88 and n.d.; Roy Appleman with Jasper Johnson, 11 Jul 52, cited in Appleman, *South to the Naktong, North to the Yalu*, p. 190.

106 WD, 159th FA Bn, 20 Jul 50; S–2/S–3 Journal, 35th Inf Rgt, 19 Jul 50.

107 S–2/S–3 Journal, 35th Inf Rgt, 20 Jul 50.

108 25th Inf Div Periodic Opns Rpt 19, 20 Jul 50, in WD, 25th Inf Div, Jul 50.

109 S–2/S–3 Journal, 35th Inf Rgt, 20 Jul 50.

159th. He repeated the request at 0250 and five minutes later radioed again urgently, "Has . . . mission been accomplished?"[110]

Determined to complete the operation, Pierce assembled his commanders and staff and turned the meeting over to Captain Zanin, his operations officer. Zanin laid out the attack order for the following day. The operation would begin at 0500, 21 July, with Biggs' Company L driving "straight through the center of Yech'on" to seize foothills north of the town. Jamison's Company I in echelon to the west would take high ground to the left while Johnson's Company K would stand in reserve.[111] Although Pierce and Zanin could not have known it at the time, evidence exists that the *31st Regiment* had been ordered to rejoin its parent unit in the attack on Andong. Advance elements of the force slated to continue the attack at Yech'on, the *8th North Korean Division*, may have been moving up, but the main body would not arrive until four days later, on 24 July. The 3d Battalion's assault would fall into the gap.[112]

As planned, Biggs' unit moved to the attack at first light on 21 July. The lead platoon, under 1st Lt. Oliver Dillard, followed by the other platoons, approached the town directly with the intention of running straight through it.[113] Biggs recalled years later that those units came under sporadic machine-gun and sniper fire. Silencing the enemy's weapons, he said, "we moved out on the double, down the main street, firing at anything that fired at us. . . . We did not bother to do any search of huts or go up any of the side streets. Our objective was to get to the end of the city and occupy our previous positions."[114]

The attack was over within an hour but Colonel Pierce appears to have had little idea of what was going on. More than two miles to the rear, unable to see clearly because of smoke from fires in the town, lacking good communications with his frontline units, and hearing heavy firing in the distance, he concluded that Biggs was in trouble. At 0825, after the attack on Yech'on had actually ended, Pierce radioed the 35th Infantry to report that he was unable to go any farther because of heavy enemy fire and requested reinforcement by either a tank or a quad-50 half-track. He cited casualties from the previous day—in all, two had been killed and twelve wounded—to support his request. The regiment sent several tanks, but they did not arrive until much later in the day.[115]

About the time Pierce made his request Colonel Fisher arrived to see for himself what was happening. Locating Pierce far to the rear, where the officer was attempting to follow the action with binoculars, Fisher at first learned little. Unaware that Biggs had already captured the heights around the town, he decided to drive forward to investigate. Encountering no resistance upon entering Yech'on, he concluded that Pierce had been overly cautious and ordered him to move his troops to their objectives. Shortly thereafter, Pierce reported that he had possession of Yech'on and that he was preparing to defend it. Fisher himself then turned cautious. He waited two hours before reporting the development to 25th Division headquarters. In all, the 3d Battalion counted two dead and twelve wounded for the entire two-day operation, almost all from Companies K and M. Vehicle, weapons, and equipment losses may have been substantial but the record remains unclear. Enemy casualties were unknown.[116]

[110] S–2/S–3 Journal, 35th Inf Rgt, 19 Jul 50 and 21 Jul 50.

[111] WD, 3d Bn, 24th Inf Rgt, Jul 50; Interv, Cash with Biggs, 15 Aug 88; Ltr, John B. Zanin to MacGarrigle, 21 Apr 95, CMH files.

[112] ATIS, Research Supplement, Interrogation Rpts, issue 99, 24 Apr 51, *7th NK Infantry Division*, pp. 44–45, and issue 4, p. 22, Intelligence Research Collection, MHI.

[113] Interv, Cash with Dillard, 26 Oct 88.

[114] MS, Bradley Biggs, The Attack Into Yechon, n.d., p. 5, CMH files. See also WD, 3d Bn, 24th Inf Rgt, 21 Jul 50. For the account of another soldier in the assault, see Interv,

Muehlbauer with Sanders, 16 Dec 88. Cpl. Reginald Washington of Company M received a Silver Star for his role in the action. See 25th Inf Div GO 62, 17 Aug 50.

[115] S–2/S–3 Journal, 35th Inf Rgt, 21 Jul 50; WD, Co A, 79th Hvy Tank Bn, Jul 50. See also Interv, Cash with Jasper Johnson, n.d.

[116] Ltr, Fisher to Col S. W. Foote, 27 Oct 57, CMH files. Weapons losses are mentioned in the journal but the account is garbled. It reads, "Lost 3 lot [sic] of vehicles and weapons,

A South Korean town (Yech'on) burns after being shelled by American artillery on 21 July 1950.

Yech'on was enough of a victory to cause elation at Eighth Army headquarters, but the Far East Command in Japan paid little attention.[117] On 20 July the enemy had overrun the 24th Infantry Division's forces in Taejon and the division's commander, Maj. Gen. William F. Dean, had disappeared, ultimately to become a prisoner of war. In that light, Yech'on seemed insignificant. General MacArthur and his officers afforded it scant notice, crediting the achievement to the South Koreans in official communiques.[118]

During the weeks that followed, nevertheless, the victory received wide acclaim in the United States. Drawing upon an account by Associated Press reporter Tom Lambert, who had been present

at Yech'on, black periodicals such as the *Pittsburgh Courier* and the *Washington Afro-American* made much of the story. So did such prominent white newspapers as the *New York Times*.[119] Congress itself took notice. Thomas J. Lane of Massachusetts praised the victory on the floor of the House of Representatives, specifically mentioning that black soldiers had been responsible.[120] So did Walter H. Judd of Minnesota, who added that the men of the 24th, by fighting gallantly and willingly for free institutions and the rule of law, had contradicted Communist assertions that the American effort in Korea was merely an attack by whites on the colored people of Asia.[121]

Although journalists and politicians sought to play up Yech'on for reasons of their own, the battle told little about what would happen to the 24th Infantry during the weeks to come, when combat would begin in earnest. Far more revealing were events and circumstances that had long preceded

and equipment. Need supplies." See S–2/S–3 Journal, 35th Inf Rgt, 21 Jul 50. For the views of Fisher's S–3, who accompanied the colonel to Yech'on, see Intervs, MacGarrigle with Carleton S. Johnson, 12 and 19 May 94. Dead and wounded statistics are taken from HQ, 25th Inf Div, Reported Casualties of the 24th Infantry Regiment, n.d. [Jul 50–Sep 51], box 3848, RG 407, WNRC.

[117] Interv, Cash with John "Tommy" Martin, 12 Jan 90. Martin was a black public affairs officer assigned to Eighth Army headquarters at the time.

[118] FEC Communique 113, 21 Jul 50, CMH files. See also "SK Unit Holding Invader," *Stars and Stripes*, 22 Jul 50; Map inset with accompanying text, "Communist Columns," *Stars and Stripes*, 23 Jul 50; "Build-Up Gains in Fourth Week," *Stars and Stripes*, 23 Jul 50, all in MHI files. All cites are from the Pacific edition of *Stars and Stripes*.

[119] See Tom Lambert, "Negro Troops Score Victory; Few Losses," *Los Angeles Examiner*, 22 Jul 50; Lindesay Parrott, "Yongdok Regained," *New York Times*, 22 Jul 50; "Oldest Negro Regiment," *New York Times*, 23 Jul 50; "Negro Troops Take Yechon," *New York Times*, 23 Jul 50; "Negro GI's First Heroes, 24th Takes City in Bloody Battle," *Pittsburgh Courier*, 29 Jul 50. There is some doubt as to when Lambert arrived at Yech'on and how much of the fighting he witnessed. Although Bradley Biggs, a company commander in the 3d Battalion, said that Lambert accompanied his unit from Hamch'ang, Lambert himself stated in an interview 37 years later that he flew into Yech'on and that the engagement could hardly have been much of a battle if he had done so. Although Lambert's article was written as an eyewitness account, the officer that he claimed was next to him during the fighting was Fisher's S–3, Carleton Johnson, who arrived at Yech'on only on the morning of 21 July, after the fighting had ended. Johnson believes that a reporter accompanied him and Fisher to Yech'on. So did Fisher. But both Fisher and Johnson saw little resemblance in Lambert's article to what they had seen. See Intervs, Richard O. Perry with Tom Lambert, 5 Nov 87; MacGarrigle with Carleton Johnson, 12 and 19 May 94; Ltr, Fisher to Foote, 27 Oct 57.

[120] U.S. Congress, House, "First United States Victory in Korea Won by Negro GI's," *Congressional Record*, 81st Cong., 2d sess., vol. 96, pt. 8, 24 July 1950, p. 10866.

[121] U.S. Congress, House, "Negro Troops Fighting Valiantly in Korea Give Lie to Soviet Propaganda," *Appendix to the Congressional Record*, 81st Cong., 2d sess., vol. 96, pt. 8, 31 July 1950, p. A5531.

Yech'on from top of a hill after U.S. troops moved in on 21 July 1950

the engagement. At Gifu wholesale changes in command, designed to improve leadership but calculated as well to ensure that segregation persisted on the field of battle, may have improved the quality of leadership in some units, but they fostered resentment in others, and they left intact the racial prejudice that would fester beneath the surface of the regiment in the weeks to come. At Moji the rioting and looting brought on by a lack of discipline in part of one battalion augured poorly for the regiment as a whole. For if some companies seemed reasonably well trained and led, others clearly lacked the sort of discipline and leadership they would need during the trials to come.

Meanwhile, from the moment the unit had received notice that it would go to war, rumors had circulated that chaplains had given sermons questioning the propriety of black men fighting brown, that white officers were either afraid of their troops or unwilling to lead blacks in battle, that a black lieutenant colonel had been pushed aside so that white officers could continue to be rated and ranked by whites, and that the unit's executive officer had faked a heart attack rather than go into combat. Whether those stories were true or not, the widespread, uncritical certainty with which they were received by both whites and blacks was a sure sign that deep-seated divisions existed within the regiment and that the basic requisites for survival and success in war, mutual trust and unity of purpose among men, were sorely lacking. By themselves, none of those impediments was fatal. But when combined with the inexperience of the officers and men of the 24th, the understandable fears of soldiers new to battle, the prevalence of worn and outdated arms and equipment, and the presence of a well-armed and motivated enemy, they made a powerful combination.

CHAPTER 5

Sangju

When the 3d Battalion moved to Yech'on on 14 July 1950, the rest of the 24th Infantry remained at Kumch'on to guard against an enemy threat that seemed to increase by the day. To the north, the *1st* and *12th North Korean Divisions* pushed southward through the Mun'gyong and Tanyang Passes toward Hamch'ang and Andong against the battered remnants of the 6th and 8th South Korean Divisions. To the west, on the Kum River above Taejon, the *3d* and *4th North Korean Divisions* continued their attack against Dean's hard-pressed 24th Infantry Division. Meanwhile, between the two forces, a third drive was developing at Chongju and Koesan as the *2d* and *15th North Korean Divisions* began to attack south toward Poun and the important rail and agricultural center at Sangju, twenty-two miles above Kumch'on. The remnants of the South Korean 1st, Capital, and 2d Divisions stood in their way, along with the inexperienced 1st and 2d Battalions of the 24th Infantry regiment. The men of the 24th had the mission of patrolling in force to the rear, preparing to counterattack in any direction where the need arose.[1] (*See Map 2.*)

The 24th Moves South

On 17 July the commander of the 25th Infantry Division, General Kean, visited Colonel White at Kumch'on to discuss the situation. The 27th Infantry and White's 3d Battalion were already supporting the South Koreans on the approaches to Andong. It seemed time to send additional units north to cover other areas. To that end, Kean decided to keep Fisher's 35th Infantry at the east coast port of P'ohang-dong, where the U.S. 1st Cavalry Division was slated to land shortly. Meanwhile, to fill the gap between Hamch'ang and Kumch'on, White was to dispatch the 24th Infantry's 2d Battalion to Sangju to participate in General Wilson's Task Force Able. The 1st Battalion and the regimental headquarters would remain in reserve at Kumch'on.[2]

Although White kept tabs on his 2d and 3d Battalions, they were out of his control. His attention was thus of necessity directed toward his 1st Battalion, where minor organizational problems had developed. On 18 July, the day the unit assumed its

---

[1] For the enemy situation, see Appleman, *South to the Naktong, North to the Yalu,* pp. 101–05. The mission of the 24th is in War Diary (WD), 24th Inf Rgt, Jul 50, p. 6. Unless otherwise indicated, records for July 1950 relating to the 25th Infantry Division, its three regiments, and the supporting units,

including war diaries, historical summaries, command and staff reports, and staff journals, are contained in boxes 3746–3747, RG 407, WNRC, Suitland, Md. See also 25th Inf Div Periodic Intelligence Rpt 1, 13–14 Jul 50, in WD, 25th Inf Div, Jul 50.

[2] WD, 25th Inf Div, Jul 50. The missions of the 1st and 2d Battalions are described in WD, 1st Bn, 24th Inf Rgt, Jul 50, p. 1, and WD, 2d Bn, 24th Inf Rgt, Jul 50, pp. 2–3, both in WD, 24th Inf Rgt, Jul 50.

mission as reserve, its leader, the only combat-expe-rienced battalion commander White had at his dis-posal, Lt. Col. Paul F. Roberts, had moved to regi-mental headquarters to assume the duties of the executive officer, who had been evacuated as a non-battle casualty. With no other officer replacements immediately available, Roberts' executive officer at the battalion, Maj. Eugene J. Carson, took temporary charge. An infantry platoon leader at the end of World War II who had gone on to become a military policeman, Carson was a "no-nonsense" officer who had both a measure of experience and good instincts. Because of the heat, for example, he ordered the men to carry only essentials into com-bat—food, water, entrenching tools, weapons, and ammunition. He was nonetheless an unknown who had been with the unit for less than two weeks. He would have to earn the men's trust and respect.[3]

On 19 and 20 July, while the 1st Battalion con-ducted patrols and prepared for contingencies, the situation to the west continued to deteriorate. On those dates, in heavy fighting around Taejon, part of Dean's 24th Division was overrun and Dean himself was reported missing in action. In response, the Eighth Army ordered the arriving 1st Cavalry Division forward to the area below Taejon, where it would replace the remnants of Dean's command. As for the 25th Division, Fisher's 35th Infantry would take charge at Hamch'ang; Michaelis' 27th would reposition itself to the area northwest of Kumch'on and tie in with the 1st Cavalry Division on its left; and White's 24th would relocate with the division headquarters to Sangju, where it would cover the gap between Kumch'on and Hamch'ang and prepare to assist in the relief of the South Korean Capital, 1st, and 2d Divisions fighting west of Sangju.[4]

White moved his headquarters and the 1st Battalion to Sangju on 21 July in a driving rain caused by Typhoon Grace.[5] The regiment entered an exceedingly rugged area with mountains that sometimes rose to more than two thousand feet above sea level. Two dirt roads crossed it. One, a northwest-southeast route between Koesan and Kumch'on, traversed the Kallyong Pass, twenty miles to the northwest of Sangju. The other ran between Sangju and Poun, some thirty miles to the west. White directed the 1st Battalion to move west and block the Poun road. The 2d would rejoin the 24th and link up with the well-experienced 17th South Korean Regiment, operating south of the Kallyong Pass, on 22 July. The 3d Battalion would remain under the operational control of the 35th Infantry for the time being. When it arrived from Yech'on, it would initially become White's reserve.[6]

The 2d Battalion had operated in the Sangju area since 17 July, patrolling, maintaining contact with the 17th Regiment, skirmishing with the enemy's forward elements, and suffering its first casualties. For a time, General Wilson had slated it to spearhead the assault on Yech'on. On 19 July, indeed, he had ordered it to withdraw from its positions near Sangju and to proceed to Hamch'ang, where it would gather for the attack. Company F and the headquarters had held for the time being at Sangju, but Companies G and H had immediately begun the first leg of the journey, moving to Hamch'ang by truck. Company E had followed on foot. Later that night, when General Kean had reversed Wilson's decision, assigning Yech'on to the 3d Battalion, Companies G and H had experienced little difficulty making the return trip to Sangju in their trucks. Company E, howev-er, lacked transportation. Holding in place overnight on the road to Hamch'ang, it had no

[3] The change in command is mentioned in WD, 1st Bn, 24th Inf Rgt, Jul 50, p. 1. Carson's methods are described in Intervs, John A. Cash with Gray Johnson, 23 Mar 89, and George L. MacGarrigle with William A. Hash, 18 and 22 Mar 94, all in CMH files. All interviews hereafter cited by John A. Cash, Bernard L. Muehlbauer, Timothy Rainey, William T. Bowers, Richard O. Perry, and George L. MacGarrigle are in CMH files. Quote from Interv, MacGarrigle with Gustav J. Gillert, 4 May 94. Carson was the 25th Infantry Division's provost marshal when the war began.

[4] WD, 25th Inf Div, Jul 50, Narrative Summary, p. 4.

[5] WD, 24th Inf Rgt, Jul 50, p. 18. For the weather, see WD, 25th Inf Div, Jul 50, Narrative Summary, p. 5.

[6] For a description of the terrain, see Map, Korea, 1:250,000, series L551, 3d edition, Army Map Service (AMS) 1950, sheets J 52 U and J 52 T, and Map, Korea, 1:50,000, series L751, 4th edition, AMS 1950, Sheets 6723 II and 6823 III, both in National Archives and Records Administration (NARA), College Park, Md. For details on unit missions, see

A patrol from Company F, 24th Infantry, moves up a hill to observe Communist-led North Korean action near Sangju, Korea; (right) North Korean–held territory, fifteen miles west of Sangju.

choice the next morning but to make a wearisome, eight-mile trek on foot back to its former position. When it arrived, the troops had no time to rest. Since enemy activity was increasing to the west, the battalion commander, Colonel Cohoon, ordered it to send out patrols. Having made contact with the enemy, those units returned in the evening with two prisoners.[7]

Incidents Near Idang

On 21 July, after several more successful skirmishes, the 2d Battalion received instructions to conduct a joint operation with the 17th South Korean Regiment. Word had arrived that portions of a North Korean regiment had entered the area. The attack would strike its forward elements and throw them off balance. In preparation, the 2d Battalion moved to Idang, a small village about thirteen miles by air to the west of Sangju on the road to Poun. Artillery batteries went into position nearby. After arriving, the command post and

other units of the 2d Battalion and Battery A of the 159th Field Artillery Battalion came under enemy artillery fire. That evening, the battalion commander and his staff traveled forward to the Korean headquarters to evaluate the latest intelligence and to coordinate final plans for the attack.[8] (*Map 4*)

The enemy unit moving toward Sangju, the *15th North Korean Division*, was one of North Korea's least capable. Although it possessed a core of combat-experienced commissioned and non-commissioned officers, it had received most of its soldiers from youth training camps in late June, after the attack on South Korea had begun. As a result, the bulk of its fighting strength comprised relatively new conscripts whose training varied from four months to just a few days, depending upon the induction date of the individual. Its forward element, the *48th Regiment*, had possessed

WD, 24th Inf Rgt, Jul 50, pp. 18–21; WD, 1st Bn, 24th Inf Rgt, Jul 50, p. 1.

[7] WD, 24th Inf Rgt, Jul 50, p. 13; WD, 2d Bn, 24th Inf Rgt, Jul 50, pp. 4–5; 25th Inf Div Periodic Intelligence Rpt 7, 19–20 Jul 50, in WD, 25th Inf Div, Jul 50.

[8] WD, 24th Inf Rgt, Jul 50, p. 19; WD, 2d Bn, 24th Inf Rgt, Jul 50, pp. 5–6. See also 25th Inf Div Periodic Intelligence Rpt 8, 20–21 Jul 50, in WD, 25th Inf Div, Jul 50; WD, 159th Field Artillery (FA) Bn, Jul 50, p. 3; Intervs, William T. Bowers with Joel T. Ward, 13 and 15 Jul 94. The order to the 24th Infantry for this operation on 20 July 1950 is recorded in WD, 35th Inf Rgt, Operation Orders and Instructions, Jul 50.

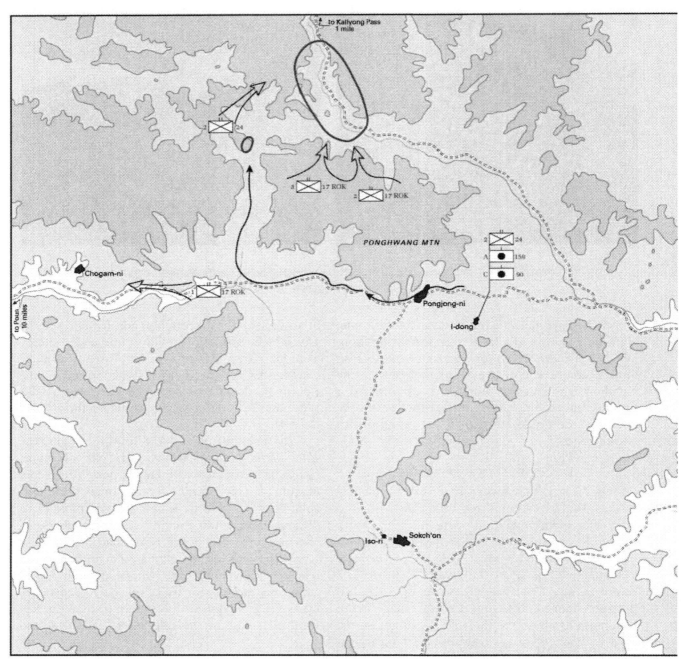

to Kallyong Pass
1 mile

24

4 ⊠ 17 ROK   2 ⊠ 17 ROK

PONGHWANG MTN

2 ⊠ 24
A ● 159
C ● 90

Chogam-ni

1 ⊠ 17 ROK

Pongjong-ni

I-dong

to Poun
10 miles

Iso-ri   Sokch'on

Map 4

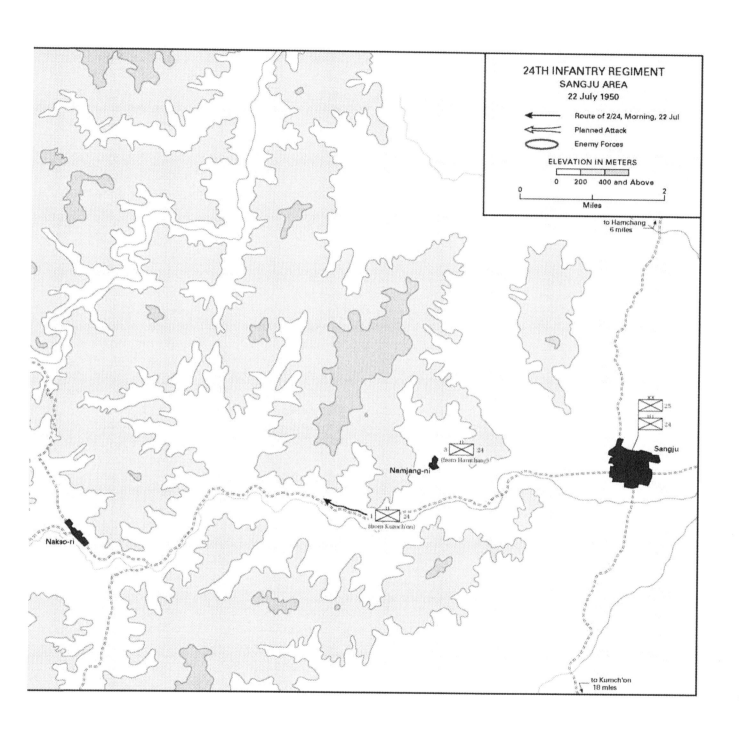

to Hamchang
6 miles

Sangju

Namjang-ni

(from Hamchang)

(from Kumch'on)

Nakso-ri

to Kumch'on
18 miles

more veteran troops than its sister regiments at the beginning of the war, but the South Koreans had inflicted such a heavy toll on the unit that it had taken in 500 replacements during mid-July. Most of those men were raw recruits inducted by force from captured South Korean towns. Meanwhile, ammunition stocks were beginning to decline because of the continual pounding of U.S. air attacks, and morale was deteriorating because of high casualties, poor medical care, and harsh discipline.[9]

Cohoon had planned a relatively simple assault. The 2d Battalion would work its way into the hills northwest of Idang to attack from the west positions supposedly held by portions of the *48th North Korean Regiment*. The 17th South Korean Regiment would position two of its battalions south of the enemy to support the American effort. A third would go farther west to shield Cohoon's exposed flank. The 2d Battalion would take responsibility for the assault itself, but the more experienced Koreans would stand by to provide assistance if necessary.[10]

To reach the point of departure for the attack, slated to begin at 1000 on 22 July, the troops would have to march more than five miles from their bivouac. The final leg of the maneuver followed a trail to the north through a two-mile-long defile dominated at its far end by a 500-foot-high hill overlooking the last segment of the line of approach. The walls of the gorge were daunting. Those to the west towered more than one thousand feet in height. On the east, they were lower and slightly more sloping but still loomed nearly eight hundred feet above the trail. A stream flowed to the right of the trail down the entire length of the draw. It was swollen by rain on the day of the attack, which began overcast with intermittent showers but lightened during the afternoon.[11]

Although planning seemed detailed, poor tactics, communication failures, and inept leadership marred the operation from the beginning. On the morning of the attack, the 2d Battalion moved up the gorge two men abreast in a column of platoons with Company E in the lead, followed by Company F and then Company G. Although the companies initially had radio communications with the headquarters of the 2d Battalion, platoons within the companies relied on runners because of a lack of operable radios. As the operation developed, the forward companies lost radio contact. Instead of moving forward with his men, Cohoon sent his operations officer, Capt. James O. Gardner, forward with the column while he remained in his command post at Idang, more than five miles to the rear of the battalion's destination. He may have believed that the operation involved little threat because of the presence of the veteran 17th Regiment, or he may have been waiting for the battalion to get into position for the attack before moving forward himself by vehicle. Whatever the reason, he was in the wrong place to learn immediately about what was happening or to respond to circumstances as they developed.[12]

[9] Far East Command (FEC), Military Intelligence Section, Order of Battle Information, North Korean Army, 15 Oct 50, U.S. Army Military History Institute (MHI), Carlisle Barracks, Pa., hereafter cited as North Korean Order of Battle; FEC, History of the North Korean Army, 31 Jul 52, CMH files; Annex to 25th Inf Div Periodic Intelligence Rpt 17, 29–30 Jul 50, in WD, 25th Inf Div, Jul 50. Details on the composition and history of the *15th North Korean Division* vary somewhat between intelligence reports, but all agree on the poor quality of the unit. See Annex to 25th Inf Div Periodic Intelligence Rpt 1, 13–14 Jul 50, and Annex to Opns Directive, 31 Jul 50, both in WD, 25th Inf Div, Jul 50.

[10] WD, 24th Inf Rgt, Jul 50, Map Overlay 3; WD, 2d Bn, 24th Inf Rgt, Jul 50, pp. 2–5. The plan of attack is also described in Interv, Inspector General (IG) with M Sgt David Robinson, Co E, 15 Sep 50, exhibit B–6, in Eighth U.S. Army Korea, Report of Investigation Concerning 24th Infantry Regiment and Negro Soldiers in Combat, 15 Mar 51, boxes 1013–1014 (hereafter cited as Eighth Army Inspector General Investigation), RG 159, WNRC. According to South Korean police patrols, there were no more than sixty to a hundred men on the objective. See 25th Inf Div Periodic Intelligence Rpts 8, 21 Jul 50, and 9, 22 Jul 50, in WD, 25th Inf Div, Jul 50.

[11] The ground is described in WD, 24th Inf Rgt, Jul 50, p. 19. More exact details may be gleaned from Map, Korea, 1:50,000, series L751, 4th edition, AMS 1950, sheet 6723 II. See also Intervs, Bowers with Ward, 13 and 15 Jul 94.

[12] WD, 24th Inf Rgt, Jul 50, pp. 19–20; WD, 2d Bn, 24th Inf Rgt, Jul 50, p. 6. The position of Cohoon's command post is shown on Situation Overlay 3 and Attack Plan, for 2d Bn, 24th Inf Rgt, and 17th Republic of Korea (ROK) Inf Rgt, 22 Jul 50, in WD, 24th Inf Rgt, Jul 50. The position of the operations

When Company E's lead platoon reached the upper end of the gorge, it came under fire from an enemy force of undetermined size stationed on the hill to its front. At that time a platoon leader, 1st Lt. Leonard Preston, was seriously wounded. "We were supposed to make contact with the 17th regiment of the ROK and make a coordinated attack," recalled the battalion intelligence officer, 2d Lt. Colon R. Britt, who was near the head of the column. "We never did make contact. While going up the draw the leading elements were hit with what I believed to be three machine guns, and small arms fire and mortar fire."[13] Advised by Korean officer guides to push to either side of the hill to envelop the enemy force and relieve the pressure on the front, the company commander, Capt. Frank O. Knoeller, failed to take any action and allowed the forward platoons, now under 2d Lt. Joseph Hilyer, to fight alone for more than an hour.[14] During that time, Lieutenant Britt moved to the rear to report to Captain Gardner.[15] Gardner informed Cohoon, who appears initially to have issued instructions to "hold if possible, withdraw if necessary," but later called for a withdrawal. Complying with the second order, Gardner followed standard procedure in specifying a phased pullback. Company F was to provide a shield as Company E withdrew. In turn, Company G would cover for F.[16]

Britt moved back toward the head of the column with Gardner's instructions in hand. As he did, he noticed men drifting to the rear. "There would be one man who had been wounded," he said, "and four or five others [rendering assistance]." Directed by Gardner to coordinate covering fire in order to ease the withdrawal, he could get none of the men to stop. "They just continued on with no regards for orders."[17]

Shortly after receiving the order to withdraw, Captain Knoeller informed Lieutenant Hilyer. Hilyer assumed that following customary practice his unit would fall back first under the covering fire of his own parent company. Knoeller declined to make any commitment of the sort. Citing the authority of the battalion commander, he said he had been told to break contact and leave. The leading elements of Company E, in other words, would have to fend for themselves.[18]

"I had some wounded in action," Hilyer told an interviewer years later. "I stayed up there and got them all out. We floated them down the creek. The current carried them out." He added that one of his gunners, employing a Browning automatic rifle, had done especially effective work. Recently released from the Eighth Army stockade in Japan, the soldier had leapfrogged down the creek, time and again providing the critical covering fire the

officer is mentioned in Interv, IG with 2d Lt Colon R. Britt, S–2 of 2d Bn, 24th Inf Rgt, 21 Aug 50, exhibit 12, attached to Ltr, Maj Gen W. B. Kean, 25th Inf Div, to Commanding General, Eighth U.S. Army (Korea), 9 Sep 50, sub: Combat Effectiveness of the 24th Infantry Regiment. Kean's letter and its attachments are contained in Far East Command Inspector General Investigation, sec. BX, boxes 1013–1014, RG 159, WNRC. Statements attached to General Kean's letter each have an exhibit number and are hereafter cited as in the Kean Letter file. See also Ltr, Waymon Ransom to John A. Cash, 22 Oct 88, CMH files; Interv, Cash with Ransom, 5 Aug 88; Interv, IG with Col Horton V. White, 5 Sep 50, exhibit 28, Kean Letter file; Interv, IG with Maj Owen H. Carter, 25 Aug 50, exhibit 14, Kean Letter file. Deficiencies in communications are covered in Intervs, William T. Bowers with Ward, 13 and 15 Jul 94; Charles L. Gray, 2 and 3 May 94; Henry D. Doiron, 22 Apr 94; Cash with Edward Simmons, 18 Mar 89.

[13] Interv, IG with Britt, 21 Aug 50, exhibit 12, Kean Letter file.

[14] Interv, IG with Carter, 25 Aug 50, exhibit 14, Kean Letter file.

[15] Interv, IG with Britt, 21 Aug 50, exhibit 12, Kean Letter file.

[16] Most sources indicate that Gardner gave the order, but Cohoon was clearly in radio contact with Gardner even if communications at lower levels had given out. The 25th Division Assistant Chief of Staff, G–3, Lt. Col. Charles R. Herrmann, mentions the "hold if possible" order. He asserts emphatically that the order came from neither the division nor the regiment. See Statement of Lt Col Charles R. Herrmann, 17 Sep 50, exhibit D–20, Eighth Army Inspector General Investigation. The regimental war diary states that the order was issued by the battalion commander. See WD, 24th Inf Rgt, Jul 50, p. 19. See also Interv, IG with Capt James O. Gardner, 24 Aug 50, exhibit 24, Kean Letter file.

[17] Interv, IG with Britt, 21 Aug 50, exhibit 12, Kean Letter file.

[18] Intervs, Cash with Joseph Hilyer, 17 Aug 88; Bowers with Ward, 13 and 15 Jul 94.

unit needed to make its escape. Hilyer, a white, stressed that his platoon had acted honorably, whatever the performance of the rest of Company E. "We left under orders from the Battalion Commander," he said. "We did not pull out on our own or break and run. I did not approve of what we did, but then, I was only a second lieutenant."[19]

At Sangju, Colonel White began to hear rumors and to receive unconfirmed reports that the 2d Battalion was in trouble.[20] Since radio contact with the battalion had ceased, he decided to go forward to see for himself. Collecting his operations officer, Maj. Owen Carter, and his intelligence officer, Capt. Walter Simonovich, and enlisting the assistance of the intelligence and reconnaissance (I&R) platoon to provide security, he drove up the road toward Cohoon's headquarters at Idang. Three miles west of the village, he observed a jeep careening down the road toward him at excessive speed. It was overloaded with unarmed, frightened men. White stopped the vehicle and questioned its occupants. They said that at least one company of the 2d Battalion had been wiped out and that the battalion itself was surrounded on at least three sides. During the conversation, ten more vehicles arrived, all similarly overloaded with men and piled with odds and ends of equipment. Cohoon was in the group along with three white officers of his headquarters company.[21] He told White that he was withdrawing his command post to a more secure location because the enemy had cut him off from

his battalion and the old position had become a target of enemy artillery fire.

While the conversation continued, Captain Simonovich climbed a nearby hill. He could see that if Cohoon's headquarters had abandoned Idang, it had left the artillery behind. At least one battery was still in position and firing. Simonovich informed White, who turned on Cohoon and ordered him to go back and find his people. By that time a traffic jam more than a mile long had developed. Several vehicles had slid off the road, blocking the shoulders and further contributing to the chaos. Cohoon moved up the road a short distance, sat down on a rock, and, according to Sgt. Waymon Ransom of the intelligence and reconnaissance platoon, began to cry.[22]

In the end, White determined that none of the men he encountered except those from the command post had been ordered to withdraw. Instead, rear-area personnel had based their decision to move on the displacement of Cohoon's command post and rumors that the units fighting closer to the front had been either surrounded or destroyed.[23] The battalion aid station had remained in place, but the withdrawal affected the artillery. When White arrived at Idang he found that the battery from the 90th Field Artillery Battalion had withdrawn from its position, bringing its guns with it, and that the battery from the 159th had attempted to depart but had held up when one gun had slipped into a ditch. Waymon Ransom described the scene: "We went back up there and the 159th had started to withdraw but . . . the battery commander, he ain't leaving that tube. So here's an artillery battery with five pieces standing there bangin' away . . . just bangin' away in general. And here's a battalion headquarters sittin' there empty and no troops."[24]

White and his officers began the process of rounding up the men but were only partially suc-

[19] Ibid. See also 25th Inf Div GO 63, 18 Aug 50, which awarded the Bronze Star to Hilyer, and 25th Inf Div GO 352, 18 Nov 50, which awarded the Silver Star to M. Sgt. David Robinson. Unless otherwise indicated, general orders for this volume are on file in the Army's Awards Branch of the Personnel Service Support Division of the Adjutant General Directorate of the U.S. Total Army Personnel Command (PER-SCOM), Alexandria, Va.

[20] Unless otherwise indicated, this description is based on Interv, IG with Carter, 25 Aug 50, exhibit 14, Kean Letter file. See also Interv, IG with White, 5 Sep 50, exhibit 28, Kean Letter file.

[21] The officers are mentioned by name by M. Sgt. Dean Russell, the 24th Infantry's sergeant major, who accompanied White forward. See Interv, IG with M Sgt Dean Russell, 23 Aug 50, exhibit 17, Kean Letter file.

[22] Interv, Cash with Ransom, 5 Aug 88.

[23] Statement of Herrmann, 17 Sep 50, exhibit D–20, Eighth Army Inspector General Investigation.

[24] Interv, Cash with Ransom, 5 Aug 88; WD, 159th FA Bn, Jul 50, p. 3. For the aid station, see 25th Inf Div GOs 341, 15 Nov 50, and 352, 18 Nov 50, which awarded the Bronze Star to eight medics.

cessful. Some of the retreating soldiers reached the position of the lead elements of the arriving 3d Battalion at Namjang-ni, just outside of Sangju. Piling into the parked vehicles of the unit—which had lined up its machine guns to defend itself in case of an enemy breakthrough—they drove on into the town at breakneck speed. The 3d Battalion's officers attempted to stop them, but their efforts were in vain. It took several hours to retrieve the vehicles and to return them to their units.[25]

The 1st Battalion had also just arrived. Moving up the road toward Idang on the way to Poun, where it was slated to relieve the 1st South Korean Division, it ran headlong into the "disturbingly tangled" 2d Battalion.[26] Arriving on the scene shortly thereafter, Colonel White instructed the commander of the 1st Battalion, Major Carson, to position his unit on nearby high ground to shield the retreating men. Upon consideration, Carson elected to station his men 1,000 yards farther to the rear, where the ground seemed better suited to defensive action. The battalion spent the night in the area but encountered no enemy.[27]

As for the units in direct contact with the enemy, the withdrawal was initially disorderly. Company G held in place, but the other companies immediately began to experience difficulties. "The unit leaders in all positions could not control their men," the battalion's operations officer, Captain Gardner, noted. "The personnel from F Company and some from E Company were hurrying to the rear, and in many cases went as far back as the rear train area, some using organic transportation." With time, officers reestablished control. One commander even assembled his men and marched them to the rear. By the end of the day, as a result, all three units had reestablished

themselves to the east of Idang and were sending out patrols.[28]

The next morning, 23 July, the South Koreans seized the hill at the end of the gorge where the episode had begun, capturing two light machine guns, one mortar, and thirty enemy soldiers. Most of the soldiers they took appeared to have been operating as guerrillas. In all, twenty members of the 2d Battalion went down as casualties, but none were killed.[29]

Although the losses incurred by the 2d Battalion were relatively small, the damage to the unit's morale and discipline was serious and required immediate attention. The men needed encouragement, rest, and refitting, and a number of officers merited removal and reassignment. Cohoon in particular seemed vulnerable. His decision to position himself far to the rear while his troops had been moving to the attack was questionable. More important, his attempt to relocate his command post even farther to the rear at the very moment when he should have been moving forward to assert his authority cast serious doubt upon both his fortitude and his ability as a combat leader. In the face of a strong enemy attack rather than an ambush by a small force of guerrillas, his poor judgment might have spelled disaster not only for his battalion but for the entire regiment.

---

[25] Interv, IG with 1st Lt Christopher M. Gooch, 26 Aug 50, exhibit 25, Kean Letter file. See also Intervs, MacGarrigle with Lloyd V. Ott, 19 Jul 94; John B. Zanin, 27 Oct 93. Zanin, the 3d Battalion's operations officer, recalls working that evening with General Wilson to untangle vehicles.

[26] WD, 1st Bn, 24th Inf Rgt, Jul 50, p. 2.

[27] Ibid. For other recollections from the 1st Battalion, see Intervs, MacGarrigle with Gillert, 4 May 94; Lyle Rishell, 10 Aug 93.

[28] Interv, IG with Carter, 25 Aug 50, exhibit 14, Kean Letter file; Statement of Herrmann, 17 Sep 50, exhibit D–20, Eighth Army Inspector General Investigation; Interv, IG with Gardner, 24 Aug 50, exhibit 24, Kean Letter file. For the withdrawal of the line companies, see, in addition to the Gardner interview, WD, 2d Bn, 24th Inf Rgt, Jul 50, p. 6; Intervs, Bowers with Gray, 2 and 3 May 94; Ltr, Charles L. Gray to William T. Bowers, 9 May 94, CMH files. See also Intervs, Bernard L. Muehlbauer with Nathaniel Pipkins, 23 Aug 88; Cash with Joshua Storrs, 8 Sep 89; Roger Walden taped comments to David Carlisle, 25 Feb 87, CMH files. The commander of Company F, Roger Walden, disputes Gardner's assertion that officers in all positions failed to control their men. He says his unit came out in good order. See Walden Reply to MacGarrigle interview on 28 and 29 June 1995, 7 Sep 95, CMH files.

[29] The casualties are taken from HQ, 25th Inf Div, Reported Casualties of the 24th Infantry Regiment, n.d. [Jul 50–Sep 51], box 3848, RG 407, WNRC. The breakdown of casualties is the following: Headquarters, 2d Battalion, 1; Company F, 3; Company G, 1; and Company E, 15, including the commander, 2 platoon leaders, and 3 NCOs.

Colonel White, however, took no action beyond replacing the 2d Battalion's lost equipment. Stating for the record with less than total honesty that "as the fighting troops were still in position no harm was done," he failed to re-form the unit or to rest its men.[30] Instead, at 0300 on 24 July he ordered the battalion to move east to the outskirts of Sangju, eight miles to the rear. The trip took five hours by foot. Then, shortly after Cohoon's men arrived at their destination, they received instructions to retrace their steps and to position themselves astride the road to the Kallyong Pass at a point some fifteen miles to the northwest of where they were starting. "Troops departed the assembly area at 1030 hours by foot and motor," the author of the unit's war diary noted, "without receiving any rest from the previous day's activities." The battalion arrived at its new position in the hills above the road at 1600 and immediately began preparing defensive positions for the night. The men were exhausted.[31]

As for the officers, White again did nothing. Even Cohoon received a second chance. The colonel may have believed he had no choice because the next in line for command, Cohoon's executive officer, Maj. Horace E. Donaho, was a recent arrival and an unknown. Then again, White and other officers may have presumed that failures of leadership and the possible cowardice of white commanders were less to blame for what had happened than the blackness of the soldiers themselves. "Have you ever seen the pictures of 'Step-and-Fetchit' where [the actor's] eyes were sticking out?" white 1st Lt. Donald F. Pidgeon of the 2d Battalion asked the inspector general, referring to the antics of a popular black actor during the 1940s who played to white prejudices. "That is what they reminded me of."[32]

An example of how White should have reacted occurred within the 24th's sister regiment, the 35th Infantry, on almost the same date as the breakdown at Idang. On 21 and 22 July, twenty miles north of Sangju, Company F of that regiment's 2d Battalion also encountered a baptism by fire and experienced extreme difficulties. Becoming heavily engaged with a North Korean battalion, a force three times its size, the unit fought well during the first day, inflicting heavy casualties on the enemy. It nevertheless ran into trouble on the second, when a rain-swollen river to its rear overflowed, cutting all lines of support and reinforcement. During midafternoon on 22 July, assisted by intense artillery and mortar fire and accompanied by five tanks, the North Koreans attacked again. When the South Korean battalion supposedly guarding the company's right flank disappeared and engineers found it impossible to float rafts across the river because of continuing enemy fire, some of the unit's men panicked and drowned while attempting to swim the gap. Others straggled down the embankment for four miles before coming upon a bridge that allowed them to cross. A number abandoned their weapons.[33]

Although stung by the mishap, the regimental commander, Colonel Fisher, set to work immediately. Seeing to it that the company's members received a warm meal and new equipment, he brought in new leaders from other units within the battalion and replaced the wounded company commander. Those men who had distinguished themselves in the fighting—the unit first sergeant had stayed behind with the wounded until he could bring most to safety—were written up for medals and quickly received their awards. For two days Fisher intentionally kept the unit in the rear near his command post, where he instituted a rigorous retraining program designed to restore the men's confidence in themselves. No one was pam-

---

[30] Quote from Interv, IG with White, 5 Sep 50, exhibit 28, Kean Letter file.

[31] Quote from WD, 2d Bn, 24th Inf Rgt, Jul 50, p. 7. See also WD, 24th Inf Rgt, Jul 50, p. 20, and app. VI, item 9. The reason for the move remains unclear. There was considerable confusion in the orders issued by the regimental and division command posts.

[32] Interv, IG with 1st Lt Donald F. Pidgeon, S–4, 2d Bn, 24th Inf Rgt, 25 Aug 50, exhibit 26, Kean Letter file.

[33] This paragraph is based on WD, 35th Inf Rgt, 12–31 Jul 50; 35th Inf Rgt Narrative Rpt, Jul 50; S–2/S–3 Journal, 35th Inf Rgt, Jul 50. See also Intervs, MacGarrigle with Carleton S. Johnson, 12 and 19 May 94; Rennie M. Cory, 10 Jun 94. Johnson was the operations officer for the 35th Infantry. Cory was an artillery observer supporting the 2d Battalion, 35th Infantry.

pered, but all learned that their commanders cared for their well-being and that survival in battle depended upon training and each individual soldier's loyalty to the group. The company then went back on line. Over the weeks that followed, it held up well in combat.[34]

In contrast, by 24 July Cohoon's 2d Battalion had not recovered, and straggling was becoming a serious problem in some portions of the 24th. Shortly after the 2d Battalion moved into position on that date, for example, the unit began to receive heavy artillery fire. A number of the troops moved to the rear, leaving positions so poorly defended that at one point Company E had only four men defending an entire hill on the battalion perimeter.[35] The regimental adjutant later stated that about two hundred men drifted to the rear, many using kitchen trucks and other vehicles from Company H to make their way. Sometimes as many as ten men occupied a single jeep.[36]

In the end, Cohoon succeeded in loading the stragglers on trucks and returned them to the front, but by then other problems were occurring in the line. Six miles to the west on the road to Poun, in an action reminiscent of the 3d Battalion's nervousness prior to their first combat at Yech'on, a black lieutenant in Company A of the 1st Battalion, 2d Lt. Theodore R. Joyner, led his platoon to the rear after receiving a scant few rounds of enemy fire. He was intercepted by the battalion executive officer, black Capt. Richard W. Williams, Jr., and relieved of command on the spot. The lieutenant later returned to his unit. He was killed in action on 20 August.[37]

General Wilson became involved early on the morning of 25 July, when he received word that some of the troops were deserting their positions above Sangju. Traveling to the scene to investigate, he encountered five men from Company I of the 3d Battalion coming down a trail in single file. "They had thrown away their weapons," he later told the inspector general,

and when questioned reported that the enemy was in their position and that the entire platoon had left. The company commander was not aware of the situation. He investigated after having been informed by me. . . . He found very little of his platoon left, so immediately he sent his reserve platoon into the positions that had been deserted. This was done without difficulty as there was no enemy in the positions. There was mass hysteria in the platoon that deserted its positions. I found 5 more of these men at the aid station for minor injuries, obviously they were more scared than hurt.[38]

As time passed, it became clear that the loss of weapons and other equipment was also becoming a problem. On 25 July the 2d Battalion's supply officer, Lieutenant Pidgeon, observed a machinegun section from his unit's heavy weapons platoon moving to the rear under orders. The group had both of its machine guns when it started out, but by the time it reached its destination the weapons were gone. Since there had been no enemy firing at the time, Pidgeon could only conclude that the men had abandoned both guns rather than endure the inconvenience and discomfort of having to carry them over a distance. During the next month, he told interviewers, the battalion lost all seventeen of its assigned heavy and light .30-caliber machine guns. Half of its assigned complement of eight .50-caliber machine guns also disappeared. Despite those losses, the unit was able to produce only one damaged weapon to show that any had been hit or destroyed by enemy fire. Inadvertently confirming the wisdom of the 1st Battalion's commander,

[34] Ibid. See also Unit Journal, 2d Bn, 35th Inf Rgt, entries for 26 and 30 Jul 50, in WD, 35th Inf Rgt, Jul 50. Two members of Company F were recommended for the Distinguished Service Cross, four for the Silver Star, and three for the Bronze Star.

[35] WD, 24th Inf Rgt, 24 Jul 50, p. 23; WD, 2d Bn, 24th Inf Rgt, Jul 50, p. 7.

[36] Interv, IG with Maj John R. Wooldridge, 23 Aug 50, exhibit 1, Kean Letter file.

[37] Interv, IG with Carter, 25 Aug 50, exhibit 14, Kean Letter file; Interv, IG with Maj Richard W. Williams, Jr., 10 Feb 51, General Headquarters, Far East Command, exhibit B–109, in Report of Investigation Regarding Alleged Irregularities in the Administration of Military Justice in the 25th Infantry

Division, 27 Mar 51, boxes 1013–1014 (hereafter cited as Far East Command Inspector General Investigation), RG 159, WNRC. See also Interv, MacGarrigle with Rishell, 10 Aug 93.

[38] Interv, IG with Brig Gen Vennard Wilson, 5 Sep 50, exhibit 29, Kean Letter file.

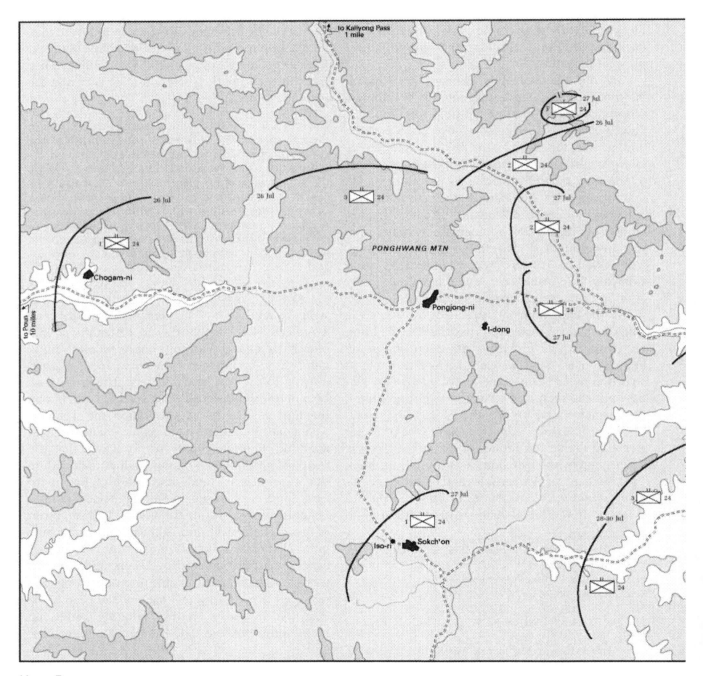

Map 5

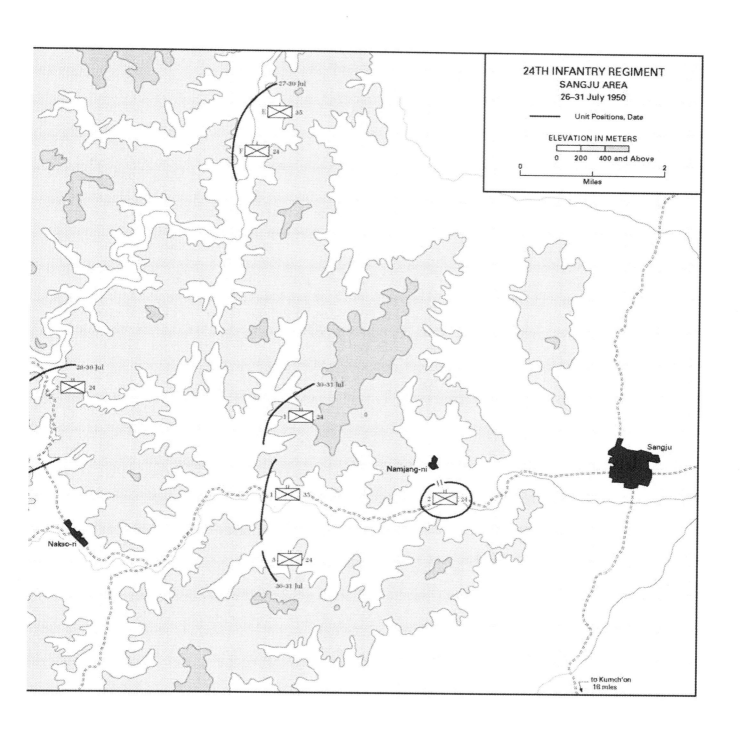

24TH INFANTRY REGIMENT
SANGJU AREA
26–31 July 1950

Unit Positions, Date

ELEVATION IN METERS

0   200   400 and Above

0   2

Miles

27-30 Jul

28-30 Jul

30-31 Jul

Namjang-ni

Sangju

Nakso-ri

30-31 Jul

to Kumch'on
16 miles

Major Carson, who had stripped his men to the essentials upon entering combat, Pidgeon added that within one week of making first contact with the enemy the individual soldier in the battalion's line companies had abandoned all of his equipment except for his personal weapon and the clothing on his back.[39]

By 25 July all three battalions of the 24th Infantry occupied a line that intersected both the Kallyong and the Poun roads through very rough terrain. (*See Map 5.*) The frontage they manned totaled more than seventeen thousand yards, an area at least twice the width prescribed by military manuals for a regiment involved in a defensive action.[40] The 1st Battalion held the western flank in the hills above Chogam-ni, some nineteen miles west of Sangju, and blocked the road to Poun. The 3d, taking over positions from the 17th South Korean Regiment, occupied the middle ground on Ponghwang-san mountain (Hill 741), which peaked at 741 meters above sea level and whose slopes paralleled the Kallyong road at a point where it bent to the east toward Sangju. The 2d Battalion was on the right, manning positions on either side of the Kallyong road but extending to the east, well into the hills.[41] Conditions were Spartan. The position of the 1st Battalion's Company C was so remote, it took up to eight

hours to resupply the unit on foot from the farthest point attainable by vehicle. Backed by a narrow road, the 3d Battalion was more accessible, but even there a five-hour round trip was necessary to supply the unit. As a result, few of the men in either battalion received hot meals, and even C-rations were in short supply.[42]

Those difficulties notwithstanding, the 24th Infantry's position presented problems much more serious than mere supply. Even with a third battalion, which other regiments deploying from Japan lacked, Colonel White had nowhere near the troops he needed to defend his assigned sector. As a result, his thinly manned, overextended line was unconnected to those of other allied units and presented the enemy with an easy opportunity for a flanking attack. On top of that, because of the rough terrain, it was impossible to plug holes in the line. Enemy infiltration thus became an ever-present possibility, and a danger existed that the entire position would fall prey to an enemy attack concentrated on one of its weak points.

Ordinarily, reserve units stationed to the rear would have stood ready to counter any threat that developed, but White had only one platoon from Company A and the regiment's I&R platoon under his immediate control for that purpose. Each battalion did what it could to compensate. The 1st and 2d on the regiment's flanks each held a company off of the line, while each line company of the 3d Battalion in the center held a platoon in reserve, but those arrangements were stopgaps at best. Although better than nothing, they left White with little ability to effectively commit his reserves if a major enemy attack occurred at one point or another in his line. In addition to the problems with unity and self-confidence that had begun to develop in some of the regiment's companies and platoons over the previous few days, the situation did not bode well for the future.[43]

[39] Interv, IG with Pidgeon, 25 Aug 50, exhibit 26, Kean Letter file. The numbers of weapons in a battalion are tallied in Department of the Army, Table of Organization and Equipment (T/O&E) 7–15N, 16 Apr 48, CMH files.

[40] See Robert J. Best, *Analysis of Personnel Casualties in the 25th Infantry Division, 26–31 July 1950*, Technical Memorandum ORO–T–22 (FEC) (Chevy Chase, Md.: Operations Research Office, 1952), p. 12, copy in CMH files; Department of the Army (DA) Field Manual (FM) 7–40, *The Infantry Regiment*, 11 Jan 50, pp. 234–37.

[41] WD, 24th Inf Rgt, Jul 50, Overlay 5, Disposition of 24th RCT on 26 Jul 50, to Map, Korea, 1:50,000, series L751, 4th edition, AMS 1950, sheets 6723 II and 6823 III. There is some confusion in the war diaries. They state that the 3d Battalion relieved the 19th South Korean Regiment. The 19th, however, was part of the South Korean Capital Division. The 3d Battalion in fact relieved the 17th South Korean Regiment, a part of the 1st South Korean Division. See WD, 24th Inf Rgt, Jul 50, pp. 18, 21, 25; Paik Sun Yup, *From Pusan to Panmunjon* (Washington, D.C.: Brassey's [U.S.], 1992), p. 27.

[42] WD, 24th Inf Rgt, 24 Jul 50, p. 24.

[43] WD, 24th Inf Rgt, Jul 50, p. 25, and Overlay 5; WD, 1st Bn, 24th Inf Rgt, Jul 50, p. 2; Eighth U.S. Army, Korea (EUSAK), Combat Lesson 1, attachment to Periodic Intelligence Rpt 7, 19–20 Jul 50, and Interrogation Rpt, North Korean Methods of Operation, attachment to Periodic Intelligence Rpt

As the day progressed, North Korean combat patrols began to probe the front and flanks of the American position, and reports arrived that the enemy was bringing up reinforcements. During the afternoon, according to Sgt. Waymon Ransom, the I&R platoon observed the approach and deployment of "a very large North Korean force" to the front of the 3d Battalion. The platoon's members kept watch and repeatedly passed word of developments along to higher headquarters.[44] American artillery fire dispersed some enemy forces, on one occasion reportedly aborting an attack by catching 250 North Korean troops in the open.[45] The North Koreans nevertheless also scored, inflicting casualties in Company I with an early morning mortar attack. An enemy mine planted by infiltrators also blew up a ¾-ton truck, wounding a warrant officer and three enlisted men. The 24th faced the growing threat alone. At 0800 that morning, after conducting an early attack to disrupt the enemy advance, the 17th South Korean Regiment departed for a new assignment. The weather on 25 July was hot and humid.[46]

Combat, 26–31 July 1950

The enemy chose the 3d Battalion's sector as his target. In that area, Company K held the left. Company I in the center had dug in on Hill 741, which rose several hundred feet higher than the surrounding terrain. Company L was to the right. The North Koreans began their assault under cover of darkness at 0004 on 26 July, when several mortar rounds landed in the vicinity of the 3d Battalion's command post. A number of rounds were also directed at Company K but fell short. Scattered small-arms and mortar fire followed, killing at least one American. As day broke, at 0625, enemy attackers struck Company K's right flank in earnest. Within minutes, the entire battalion was engaged all along the line.[47]

Heavy fighting ensued, with the main enemy attack, supported by heavy mortar and automatic weapons fire, falling on Company I and the right flank of Company K. Early morning fog and North Korean smoke rounds obscured the men's vision and reduced the effectiveness of the American defensive fire. Shortly before 0800, an enemy force rushing out of the haze hit the platoon on the right flank of Company I on Hill 741. After a brief struggle in which the unit's leader, 2d Lt. William D. Ware, was killed, the troops fell back. When survivors reached the base of the hill, Company I's executive officer, 1st Lt. Vernon Dailey, ordered the reserve platoon under 2d Lt. Reginald J. Sapenter to counterattack. Sapenter's men moved forward until stopped by intense fire about two hundred yards from the crest. With the enemy maneuvering to cut off his platoon, Sapenter ordered a withdrawal. About the same time, the other platoon of Company I on the west end of Hill 741 recognized that it was in danger of being cut off and also fell back. At 1030 the remnants of the company began taking up blocking positions at the base of the hill.[48]

With the collapse of Company I's position on Hill 741, Company K's defenses to the left became unhinged. The company commander, white 1st Lt. Jasper Johnson, recalled that up to that time North Korean attacks had "bounced off" the unit. If enemy fire was heavy, a platoon leader, 2d Lt. Alfred F. Tittel, added, the attackers themselves seemed to be "young kids." When Company I

13, 24–25 Jul 50, both in WD, 25th Inf Div, Jul 50. See also Ltr, Oliver Dillard to David Carlisle, 26 Oct 88, CMH files; Interv, Bowers with Reginald J. Sapenter, 10 Mar 94.

[44] Ltr, Ransom to Cash, 22 Oct 88. See also WD, 24th Inf Rgt, Jul 50, pp. 24–25.

[45] WD, 159th FA Bn, 7–31 Jul 50, p. 4. See also WD, 24th Inf Rgt, Jul 50, pp. 24–25.

[46] WD, 24th Inf Rgt, Jul 50, p. 25; Paik, *From Pusan to Panmunjon*, p. 27.

[47] WD, 24th Inf Rgt, Jul 50, pp. 27–30; WD, 3d Bn, 24th Inf Rgt, Jul 50, pp. 10–11; WD, 2d Bn, 24th Inf Rgt, Jul 50, pp. 7–8; WD, 1st Bn, 24th Inf Rgt, Jul 50, p. 3; WD, 159th FA Bn, Jul 50.

[48] Intervs, Bowers with Sapenter, 10 Mar 94; Cash with Charlie Lee Jones, 6 Sep 89; 25th Inf Div GO 82, 25 Aug 50, awarding the Silver Star to Pfc. Jesse Hooks of Company I, and G–1 Journal, 25th Inf Div, 26 Jul 50, in WD, 25th Inf Div, Jul 50. There are some discrepancies on the details of Lieutenant Ware's death. See the interviews mentioned above with Sapenter and Jones and citation in EUSAK GO 54, 6 Sep 50, which awarded the Distinguished Service Cross to Lieutenant Ware.

moved back, however, the enemy moved swiftly to fill the gap left in the line by its absence and soon reached Company K's rear. At 1105 the unit reported receiving enemy attacks in waves and heavy mortar fire. When ammunition ran low, the troops withdrew by sliding down a steep slope to the west into a canyon-like valley. When the men reached the company command post, Lieutenant Johnson ordered them back up the hill, but only a few responded. Advancing up the first ridge, they were soon driven back by enemy fire.[49]

Since loss of the high ground in the center also threatened Company L, the unit's acting commander, black 1st Lt. Oliver W. Dillard, who had been in place for only a day and had been with the company less than a month, notified Colonel Pierce that he was launching a counterattack with his reserve platoon. The effort failed. Not only was the enemy firmly in possession of the hill, but also,

of the 20 men in my small attack group, only a handful, eight or nine, actually aggressively fired their weapons and moved with me when I gave the signal to open fire and advance up the slope. . . . [Meanwhile] the light machine gun I had placed to form my base of fire failed after a few bursts of sustained fire, and with this failure the machine gunner froze in fear and frustration.[50]

Dillard had no choice but to pull his troops back to their starting point. There, he learned that his right flank platoon was withdrawing under heavy enemy pressure. "I could find only a handful of men from this platoon," he said, "who I put in position near the crest of the mountain." There, he and his men held on, completely surrounded and in need of ammunition resupply.

As the day lengthened, they made a good account of themselves. With black 2d Lt. Edward Greer from Battery B of the 159th Field Artillery Battalion spotting for that unit's 105-mm. howitzers and Dillard himself calling in fire from regimental and battalion mortars, Company L circled its position with a heavy ring of artillery and mortar fire. Dillard noted that some of those barrages had a "telling effect" on the North Koreans attempting to bypass the unit through the Company I position. Meanwhile, to the enemy's rear, air strikes sought out North Korean mortar and artillery positions and enemy vehicles attempting to move down the Kallyong Pass.[51]

By late morning, with the failure of the local company counterattacks, the 3d Battalion's commander, Colonel Pierce, scraped together a force from his headquarters personnel and Company M, the heavy weapons company. At 1215 that group attacked up the hill in an attempt to open a route to Company L. After advancing for fifteen minutes to a point just 300 yards from the beleaguered unit, they came under heavy fire and stopped. A platoon from Company A of the 1st Battalion arrived from regimental reserve and entered the fray. Advancing through Company I at the base of the hill, it also came under enemy fire and bogged down.

By that time, General Wilson had taken charge at the scene. Pulling Captain Hash's Company B out of the 1st Battalion's position to the west, he ordered the unit to restore Company I's position and to relieve the pressure on Company L. The operations officer of the 3d Battalion, Captain Zanin, met Hash at the base of the hill to fill him in on what had happened. As Hash recalled, the situation was confused. Zanin told him that part of Company I, which had several men missing, was still on top of the hill and that his unit was to advance only to the first ridge and then to wait for instructions.[52]

The delay may have been meant to clarify what was happening to Company I or to attempt

[49] Intervs, Bowers with Jasper Johnson, 18 Apr 94; Alfred F. Tittel, 15 Apr 94; MacGarrigle with Tittel, 23 May 94. See also 25th Inf Div GO 62, 17 Aug 50, which awarded the Silver Star to Sfc. Joseph Simmons who took over as a platoon leader in Company K.

[50] Ltr, Oliver Dillard to David Carlisle, 20 May 87, copy in CMH files. Dillard retired from the Army as a major general.

[51] Ibid. See also Intervs, Cash with Dillard, 26 Oct 88; Edward Greer, 9 Nov 88; Bowers with Clifton F. Vincent, 19 and 20 Apr 94; Walter W. Redd, 24 Mar 94. Greer retired from the Army as a major general. For the air strikes, see the interview with Vincent and WD, HQ Btry, 159th FA Bn, 26 Jul 50, in WD, 25th Inf Div, Jul 50.

[52] Intervs, MacGarrigle with Hash, 18 and 22 Mar 94; Charles E. Green, 16 Jun 94; Zanin, 27 Oct 93.

Members of Company M, 24th Infantry, prepare to move out of a riverbed in the Sangju area.

to arrange a coordinated attack by Company B and Company G of the 2d Battalion to the east of Company L's position. Whatever the reason, the attack of Company B got under way in the late afternoon. As it advanced, it came across four or five groups of 2 or 3 men from Company I withdrawing from the hill. Each indicated that Company I had been wiped out. Just at dark, Hash's men reached the first ridge, with 3 killed and 4 wounded in the process. As he was consolidating the position and preparing to continue the attack, Hash received orders to pull back because of darkness and to cover the withdrawal of the 3d Battalion.[53]

Meanwhile, Company L continued to fight on. Although in constant contact through artillery and mortar radio channels, Dillard remained unaware

that counterattacks were attempting to break through to his position or that higher headquarters considered the situation grave. Liaison planes dropped ammunition and medical supplies in the afternoon. About 2000, enemy fire from Company I's former position on Hill 741 became intense and several soldiers were wounded. As Dillard recalled, it was at that point that

suddenly and surprisingly the voice of the company executive officer could be heard calling to us. He had crawled up the rear slope of our position to within calling distance. He indicated that we were surrounded. He also stated that a company had been trying to get through to us all afternoon without success and that we had better "come out of there." With this call all but a few men of the company began to crawl out of their holes and off the mountain dragging what they could but leaving behind some weapons, ammunition, and rations. I signaled the remaining few to go.

A short while later, after leading his men off the hill, Dillard and three volunteers returned in the dark with a stretcher to retrieve a seriously wounded soldier they had been forced to leave behind. Carrying their comrade to the rear, they came within a few feet of enemy soldiers cooking their evening meal.[54]

[53] Ibid. See also Interv, IG with Maj Eugene Carson, 6 Sep 50, exhibit 21, Kean Letter file; 25th Inf Div GO 146, 14 Sep 50, awarding the Silver Star to 2d Lt. Lionel Dubuque of Company B. The regimental war diary states that Companies A and B attacked together. See WD, 24th Inf Rgt, 26 Jul 50. But the 1st Battalion war diary and Hash state that only Company B attacked. This indicates that the Company A attack mentioned in the regimental war diary was by the reserve platoon and occurred earlier in the afternoon. Green, a Company B platoon leader, states that some of the casualties were from friendly fire. See Intervs, MacGarrigle with Hash, 18 and 22 Mar 94; Green, 16 Jun 94; WD, 3d Bn, 24th Inf Rgt, Jul 50, pp. 10–11.

[54] Quote from Ltr, Dillard to Carlisle, 20 May 87. Intervs, Bowers with Vincent, 19 and 20 Apr 94. For aerial resupply,

Several soldiers in the 3d Battalion later received awards for gallantry in the action, but questions remained about the unit and its performance that day.[55] Large quantities of equipment had been left behind: eighty-three M1 rifles, nineteen M1 carbines, twelve .30-caliber machine guns, three .50-caliber machine guns, eight 60-mm. mortars, three 81-mm. mortars, four 3.5-inch rocket launchers, nine SCR–300 radios, and sixteen EE8 telephones.[56] Conversely, casualties were relatively light. The total for the entire 24th Infantry amounted to 45, but of that number only 27 came from the 748 officers and men on hand in the 3d Battalion. Two lightly wounded and 2 missing in action came from Company L, and 2 seriously wounded and 2 missing came from Company K. Company I incurred the most casualties: 4 lightly wounded, 2 seriously wounded, and 13 missing in action.[57]

The scene at the bottom of the hill added to doubts about the performance of the 3d Battalion. Exhausted and confused soldiers, arriving in disorder after traversing very rugged terrain, created an unfavorable impression on those without first-hand knowledge of what had happened at the top. The acting commander of the 1st Battalion, Major

Carson, ventured an opinion in interviews that the 3d Battalion was so well situated on its hill that it should have held against all but overwhelmingly superior odds. The enemy could hardly have been present in great numbers, he added, because North Korean forces failed to follow through on their victory by cutting all too vulnerable American supply lines that ran to the rear of the battalion. Indeed, he said Company B encountered only light resistance in its counterattack. General Wilson was of the same mind. He told interviewers from the Eighth Army without qualification that "the positions could have been held as evidenced by the successful defense conducted by L Company. The enemy forces which had penetrated the positions were not too strong as evidenced by the successful counter-attack of Company B."[58]

Testimony of that sort to the contrary, there were other explanations for what had happened. Patrols had observed the buildup of a large North Korean force the day before, and reports from all three companies told of strong assaults or a large volume of fire directed at their positions. Company B's counterattack, which both Carson and Wilson cited as evidence of the enemy's weakness, moved only part way up the hill before encountering enemy fire that inflicted several casualties. The attack then ceased because of darkness, and the company withdrew, hardly convincing evidence of weak opposition.

General Wilson's contention that Company L's successful defense also exemplified enemy weakness was similarly open to question. Initially the focus of only a secondary effort by the enemy, whose main attacks were directed against the companies to the west, the unit most probably survived when the enemy finally turned on it with full force only because artillery and mortar fire kept it from being overrun.

---

see 25th Inf Div Periodic Opns Rpt 37, 26 Jul 50, and 25th Inf Div G–3 Activities Rpt for 26 Jul 50, both in WD, 25th Inf Div, Jul 50.

[55] In addition to the awards already noted, Lieutenant Greer received a Silver Star as did 1st Lt. Walter W. Redd, a Company L platoon leader; Lieutenant Dillard received a Bronze Star. See 25th Inf Div GOs 51, dtd 11 Aug 50; 333, dtd 13 Nov 50; and 513, dtd 26 Dec 50.

[56] The losses listed are for the 3d Battalion. See Interv, IG with WOJG Clyde C. Duncan, Asst S–4, 24th Inf Rgt, 23 Aug 50, exhibit 13, Kean Letter file. See also Interv, IG with Maj Theodore J. Cook, Exec Ofcr, 3d Bn, 24th Inf Rgt, 23 Aug 50, exhibit 10, Kean Letter file.

[57] Regimental reports of the time do not agree on the number of casualties. The totals cited are taken from the closest thing to a final tally that could be found. It is a roster of all casualties, listing killed, missing, lightly and heavily wounded, all by date and unit, for the entire war up until the end of September 1951. See HQ, 25th Inf Div, Reported Casualties of the 24th Infantry Regiment, n.d. [Jul 50–Sep 51]. The assigned strength for 26 July 1950 is taken from G–1 Daily Summary 14, 25th Inf Div, in WD, 25th Inf Div, Jul 50.

---

[58] Interv, IG with Maj Eugene Carson, 14 Sep 50, exhibit B–2, Eighth Army Inspector General Investigation. Quote from Interv, IG with Wilson, 5 Sep 50, exhibit 29, Kean Letter file. For Wilson's actions and locations during the battle, see Statement of Lt Charles A. Munford, in Award file of Brig Gen Vennard Wilson, box 154, RG 338, WNRC.

Even the assertion that the enemy failed to follow through at the end of the day is open to question. According to U.S. intelligence, the *15th North Korean Division* had already been weakened in earlier fighting with the South Koreans. In addition, food was short within the unit and ammunition resupply was intermittent at best. Those conditions, along with the continual pounding of American air and ground fire and counterattacks by the companies of the 24th, may have made North Korean commanders cautious enough to decide that they would do well to consolidate their gains before pressing on into the valley where their men would become even better targets for American air and artillery.

The relatively small number of American casualties is at least partially due to the fact that the 3d Battalion had occupied the prepared positions of the 17th South Korean Regiment and had spent a day on its own improving them. Dillard, for example, remarked how his men had hugged their foxholes and observed that "miraculously our casualties were light although the small arms fire was intense at times."[59]

Yet another influence on the low casualty rate was that many troops failed either to stay in position and fight when outflanked and attacked from the rear or to counterattack and close with the enemy when required. A platoon leader assigned to Company K two weeks earlier, white Lieutenant Tittel, described how his unit's defense fell apart when the North Koreans moved around his flank and to his rear. Dillard, who had assumed command of Company L only the day before, likewise confirmed that some of his own men drifted to the rear or were otherwise unresponsive to orders. Dillard, Tittel, and a platoon leader in Company I, black Lieutenant Sapenter, all commented on how their counterattacks either collapsed or degenerated into long-range exchanges of fire.

Dillard suggested that inexperience and the limited training of all the American troops involved in Korea at that time were mainly to blame for what

happened, but unseasoned leadership also appears to have contributed. In addition to Dillard in Company L, for example, Companies I and K had new commanders, and several of Company K's officers were likewise recent arrivals. As Dillard later noted, after officers demonstrated their worth to the men and imposed solid discipline, the troops tended to settle down. Soldiers whom he had personally seen running during the early days of the war later charged bravely into the face of almost certain death.[60]

Although conditions were not the same, something similar happened to the 27th Infantry regiment when it first faced the enemy. In that case, however, despite green troops and junior leaders, the imagination and combat experience of the regimental commander, Colonel Michaelis, and his battalion commanders made a major difference.

The incident occurred on 23 July. Ordered into the line south of the 24th Infantry near the town of Hwanggan to keep the *2d North Korean Division* from advancing along the road from Poun to Kumch'on, Michaelis deployed his two battalions in depth on a very narrow front. To his mind, the strong front would allow units in the lead to hold position while those to the rear dealt with inevitable enemy flanking movements. He made plans for the liberal use of artillery, mortars, and air attacks, and he let the commanders of his forward units know that they were not expected to fight to the finish but only until the pressure became too great. At that point, they were to fall back to the positions of the units to the rear.[61]

The initial brush with the enemy occurred on the night of 23–24 July, when a reinforced platoon went forward to locate the enemy. After a brief exchange of fire, the unit returned with fourteen men missing, nine of whom found their way back to American lines the next day. After that beginning, the 1st Battalion of the 27th waited for the enemy to attack. At 0400 on 24 July heavy North Korean artillery and mortar fire began falling on the

[59] Ltr, Dillard to Carlisle, 20 May 87. The positions taken over from the South Koreans are described in Interv, Cash with Dillard, 26 Oct 88.

[60] Interv, Cash with Dillard, 26 Oct 88.

[61] Historical Rpt, 27th Inf Rgt, Jul 50, p. 2. See also an interview with Colonel Michaelis in Harold H. Martin, "The Colonel Saved the Day," *Saturday Evening Post*, 9 Sep 50, p. 187.

unit. Two hours later, enemy ground forces attacked, approaching through the fog just as they had in the case of the 24th. Supported by heavy artillery, mortar fire, and air strikes, the battalion as a whole held even though parts of it were at times overrun. At one point, it repelled a North Korean tank assault. By noon, hundreds of North Korean dead littered the ground. Finally, after dark, the battalion withdrew a short distance to regroup. The enemy repeated the same sequence time and again over the next several days, always to much the same effect.[62]

In this case, Michaelis and his regiment had not stopped the enemy, but they had delayed and punished him with heavy casualties while remaining intact themselves to fight other battles. All the while they were learning and gaining confidence. As Michaelis noted, "The point [was] . . . that the kids won the first couple of battles and won them big. From that time on, they were intolerable. You couldn't stand them, they were so cocky. . . . I don't think we were the most popular organization around."[63]

If the 27th Infantry's successful delaying action and the competence of its commanders showed forth for all to see, the plodding of the 24th, despite the examples of heroism and the fortitude shown in the fighting on the twenty-sixth, seemed equally clear. To many high-ranking officers in the regiment and at division, the reasons for the failure of the 3d Battalion to hold position and the loss of so many weapons were likewise obvious. Whatever the extenuating circumstances, many commanders believed that race was at the root of what had happened. "I think that when [the men of the 24th] . . . become scared they react with an animal instinct,

which is to run," Major Carson thus told Eighth Army investigators, echoing comments to the same effect by Wilson and others. "I am not saying that all the men are like that. Five or ten percent are not, but I am saying that there is about 85 or 90 percent that do react this way. . . . These people are different in instincts."[64]

As the 24th Infantry withdrew to the east on the night of 26–27 July, General Kean took steps to help Colonel White. That very night a platoon of military policemen was assigned to the 24th to assist in the control of stragglers. To provide a backstop, elements of the 35th Infantry rushed from the Hamch'ang area to a blocking position six miles west of Sangju, arriving at 2230. Farther south, Company A of the 79th Heavy Tank Battalion, which had been fighting with the 27th Infantry, was likewise ordered to move as quickly as possible to Sangju. Arriving at 0220 on 27 July, it came under control of Fisher's 35th Infantry. That day, the 25th Reconnaissance Company began to patrol to the south of the 24th while a company from the 35th Infantry reinforced by a platoon of tanks moved to the northeast.[65]

While those forces were moving into place, in an attempt to form the regiment in a stronger, more compact configuration, Colonel White pulled the 3d Battalion 1.5 miles to the rear to a position just to the south of the 2d Battalion near where the Kallyong road joined the road to Poun. To cover the open right flank of the regiment, but apparently without making any prior ground reconnaissance, commanders had already moved the 2d Battalion's Company F, commanded by Capt. Roger Walden, well to the north and east of the rest of the battalion to a position beyond the supporting range of

---

[62] Historical Rpt, 27th Inf Rgt, Jul 50; 1st Bn, 27th Inf Rgt, Opns Rpt, Jul 50; 2d Bn, 27th Inf Rgt, Summary of Activities, Jul 50. See also Ltr, Gilbert Check to Maj Gen R. W. Stephens, 25 Nov 57, CMH files; Interv, MacGarrigle and Bowers with Uzal W. Ent, 20 Oct 93. The account contained in Brig Gen G. B. Barth's Tropic Lightning and Taro Leaf in Korea, n.d., pp. 8–10, in CMH files, provides details not found in most other printed accounts.

[63] Interv, Clay Blair with General John H. Michaelis, n.d., U.S. Army Military History Institute Senior Officer Oral History Program, Combat Leadership in Korea series, p. 20, MHI.

[64] Quotes from Interv, IG with Carson, 14 Sep 50, exhibit B–2, Eighth Army Inspector General Investigation. The comments of twenty-four officers and NCOs concerning the "Negro characteristics" of the 24th's soldiers are summarized in exhibit D–27, Eighth Army Inspector General Investigation.

[65] WD, 2d Bn, 35th Inf Rgt, 26 Jul 50, in WD, 35th Inf Rgt, Jul 50; WD, Co A, 79th Hvy Tank Bn, Jul 50, p. 3. See also 25th Inf Div Periodic Opns Rpt 37, 26 Jul 50; 25th Inf Div G–3 Activities Rpt for 27 Jul 50; and G–1 Journal, 25th Inf Div, 26 Jul 50, entry 740 (2400), all in WD, 25th Inf Div, Jul 50.

the unit's sister elements. Walden's men were to break down into squads, spread over a large area, and patrol to the east to make contact with the 35th Infantry. The 1st Battalion meanwhile occupied positions at Iso-ri, 2.5 miles southwest of the 3d Battalion and 12 miles west of Sangju. Its mission was to block a spur of the Poun road that circled southward and then turned east toward Sangju.[66]

At 0630 on 27 July, the enemy attacked and drove back Company F's outpost line. Portions of the company, mainly members of the platoon stationed farthest to the left and nearest the Kallyong road, drifted to the rear. But the unit's attached 81-mm. mortar section reportedly did good work, inflicting heavy casualties on the attackers. Receiving word of the engagement, the artillery fired on the enemy but was ineffective. Outflanked and in danger of being cut off, Walden followed instructions received the previous night, broke contact with the enemy, and withdrew the remainder of his company with its section of mortarmen to the east, away from his own regiment and toward the shelter offered by the 35th Infantry. In so doing, he abandoned his mortar tubes and lost communication with his superiors. Upon learning of his action, the division headquarters directed that Walden's men remain with the company of the 35th Infantry already working the area to form a task force to cover the open flank. Word of the decision, however, failed to trickle down to the 2d Battalion. Uncertain of Company F's location, Cohoon used the stragglers from Walden's unit to secure his battalion command post while he continued attempts to locate the rest of the company.[67]

During the morning, in a confused sequence of events that occurred while Company F was coming

under fire, the 2d Battalion's Companies E and G withdrew toward Sangju. Later that day, they were nevertheless instructed to return to their former position, apparently because an attached heavy mortar platoon had never received word of their withdrawal and had suffered heavy casualties as a result. During the operation that followed, Cohoon was injured in a fall and had to be replaced by his executive officer, Major Donaho. In the end, the two companies never reached their objective, which had already fallen into enemy hands and was firmly defended. Donaho withdrew his force, moving his companies back toward Sangju.[68]

As the day progressed and overnight, straggling within the 2d Battalion reached epidemic proportions. At least one hundred and fifty men deserted their positions, according to the unit's black adjutant, 1st Lt. Gorham L. Black, Jr., more than ever before or after on a single occasion. The situation became so bad that the 24th Infantry set up a straggler control point on the main road, 1.5 miles west of Sangju. The next day the military police platoon arrived to assist. According to the regiment's white personnel officer, Maj. John R. Wooldridge, they apprehended an average of 75 men per day. The 2d Battalion's supply officer noted that on 27 July alone, "I returned one group of 27 men (stragglers) from the kitchen to the front. I then picked up 15 stragglers at the regimental CP and returned them to the front. I then returned 12 more from the kitchen." On the same day, he added, "the battalion was placed in a precarious position because the battalion ammunition trucks drove off when a shell hit near them. One truck was gone for 18 hours."[69]

Major Carson's 1st Battalion also began to experience difficulties. When Company A and portions of Company D near Iso-ri attempted to move to

---

[66] WD, 24th Inf Rgt, Jul 50, pp. 30–31, and Overlay 6, Regimental Situation 270400 July 50; WDs, 1st, 2d, and 3d Bns, 24th Inf Rgt, Jul 50.

[67] WD, 2d Bn, 24th Inf Rgt, Jul 50, pp. 8–9. The regimental war diary gives a different, less candid version of events that fails to mention any straggling. See also WD, 24th Inf Rgt, Jul 50, pp. 33–34. For the arrival of Company F in the 35th Infantry, see S–2/S–3 Journal, 35th Inf Rgt, 27 Jul 50, entries for 1207 and 1233. See also Intervs, Bowers with Gray, 2, 3, and 11 May 94; Oscar L. Pusey, 29 Apr 94. For the formation of the task force, see G–3 Activities Rpt for 27 Jul 50.

[68] WD, 2d Bn, 24th Inf Rgt, Jul 50, pp. 8–9; WD, 24th Inf Rgt, Jul 50, p. 31. The regimental war diary says that the 2d Battalion was ordered to retake Company F's old position.

[69] Interv, IG with 1st Lt Gorham L. Black, Jr., 21 Aug 50, exhibit 7, Kean Letter file; Interv, IG with Wooldridge, 23 Aug 50, exhibit 1, Kean Letter file. Quote from Interv, IG with Pidgeon, 25 Aug 50, exhibit 26, Kean Letter file. See also Provost Marshal Activities Rpt for 28 Jul 50, in WD, 25th Inf Div, Jul 50.

higher ground, the enemy mounted an attack in response. Carson broke it up with mortar fire, but a large number of the men fled. Pfc. Robert J. Jones from Company D was helping his section dig a 75-mm. recoilless rifle into Company A's defensive line when the North Koreans struck. "They came through," he said, "and the whole countryside was covered with them." According to Jones, the rifle company left its position without orders, taking the vehicles of Company D to move to the rear. Jones' section fired at its own vehicle to get it to stop so that it could haul the recoilless rifle out of the area.[70]

Carson was furious when he heard what had happened: "I went back on this position that had previously been occupied by 'A' Company, with 3 soldiers, and recovered two 81-mm. mortars, one [SCR] 300 radio, an undetermined amount of ammunition, several packs, a 50 caliber machine gun, with mount, a 3.5 rocket launcher, and other items that had been left on position by this company."[71]

During the afternoon of 27 July Lt. Col. Gerald G. Miller assumed command of the battalion. Forty-four years old, Miller had served as an enlisted man for eleven years before entering Officer Candidate School in 1941. An infantry troop commander for six months after graduating, he had served in various transportation and port units until 1943, when he had transferred to the 25th Division in the Pacific. He had functioned as a headquarters commandant for the rest of World War II and then had commanded training battalions at Forts Bragg, McClellan, and Dix in the United States. He soon showed himself personally brave and was often with his troops in forward positions, but his experience in combat with infantry was nil. Several veterans noted in interviews years later that at times he seemed uncertain about what to do.[72]

Miller faced his first test shortly after he arrived. At dusk on the evening of 27 July, the motor park for his battalion came under heavy mortar fire. The drivers stampeded toward Sangju in their vehicles, leaving him and the rest of the unit with no transportation. Officers at regiment stopped the vehicles and sent them back. After that disappointing beginning Miller went on with his work, spending much of the rest of the night resupplying his units and preparing to defend the road against what seemed a mounting enemy threat.[73]

About noon the next day, 28 July, in a hastily conceived and poorly coordinated operation, the battalion was ordered to move back up the road to the west to reoccupy the high ground it had relinquished the previous afternoon and to recover abandoned equipment. Companies A and C took the lead, proceeding abreast and astride the road. Company B was in reserve to the rear. Advancing rapidly for 800 yards, they ran into automatic weapons fire and stopped short near the village of Sokchon, located just east of Iso-ri. Miller called for tanks, but they were unable to move forward because American engineers had earlier mined the road. Soldiers attempted to clear a path through the mines, but after a short lag up to three companies of enemy troops using artillery, mortars, and small arms counterattacked. They inflicted nearly 60 casualties within an hour, 30 of them in Company D. One of those killed was black 2d Lt. William M. Benefield, Jr., a platoon leader in the 77th Engineer Combat Company. Apparently concerned that enemy fire was too intense and that many of his men would be killed in the effort to clear the mines, he assumed the task himself but was cut down within 200 yards of enemy positions before he could complete it. He received a posthumous Distinguished Service Cross for his sacrifice.[74]

[70] Interv, IG with Carson, 14 Sep 50, exhibit B–2, Eighth Army Inspector General Investigation. See also Interv, Cash with Robert J. Jones, 25 Aug 89.

[71] Interv, IG with Carson, 14 Sep 50, exhibit B–2, Eighth Army Inspector General Investigation. Carson said he returned to the position the next morning, but the records indicate it was in the afternoon.

[72] DA Form 66, Personnel Record for Col Gerald G.

Miller, CMH files; Intervs, MacGarrigle with Stuart Force, 8 Aug 94; Gillert, 4 May 94; Hash, 18 and 22 Mar 94; Joseph Baranowski, 24 Aug 94.

[73] WD, 1st Bn, 24th Inf Rgt, Jul 50, p. 4. See also Interv, MacGarrigle with Gillert, 4 May 94.

[74] WD, 1st Bn, 24th Inf Rgt, Jul 50, p. 4; WD, 24th Inf Rgt, Jul 50, p. 34. The casualties are tallied in Best, *Analysis of Personnel Casualties in the 25th Infantry Division, 26–31 July*

Despite the attack and heavy casualties, the battalion held. When a platoon led by white 1st Lt. Leonard H. Kushner was surrounded and Kushner himself was severely wounded, a number of men moved to rescue them. It took four hours, but they prevailed. The popular lieutenant, who had successfully defended a number of soldiers in court-martial proceedings at Gifu, left the battlefield strapped to the back of a tank.[75]

Circumstances began to deteriorate toward evening, when Miller attempted to withdraw his unit into a defensive position for the night. With Company B and the 25th Reconnaissance Company covering, the movement began well but soon disintegrated into a wholesale retreat toward Sangju. Panic does not appear to have been a consideration, at least at first. Once begun, the move to the rear continued and gained momentum because Miller, when given permission to withdraw, had not been told where to halt. Assuming that the battalion was participating in a general pullback, the retreating column rolled past a battery from the 159th Field Artillery Battalion in a firing position. There it encountered Colonel White. Thoroughly astounded to see that the artillery would soon be in the front lines, White and a few of his staff members went out onto the road to stop the retreating men. By that time, however, the head of the column had reached the Kallyong-Sangju road.[76]

With many casualties among platoon leaders and noncommissioned officers from the fighting

earlier in the day, restoring order required some effort. According to Capt. Alfred Thompson, a liaison officer from the 159th, it was 0200 the next morning before the 1st Battalion pulled into position, and there were so many stragglers that only part of the unit could be reassembled. A witness to the whole affair, the 1st Battalion's intelligence officer, Capt. Gustav Gillert, said that White was furious and that he complained that the 1st Battalion had gone to the rear without orders, leaving the artillery and the regimental command post undefended. Miller stood his ground, informing White that his last orders had been to move to the rear. White's only recorded rejoinder came much later in an interview with a division investigator. Describing the episode, he noted sourly that "I had no help from the battalion officer [Miller]."[77]

The confusion and uncertainty at higher levels in the regiment and Colonel White's seeming inability to control the deteriorating situation were by then becoming apparent. The new operations officer, who joined the regiment on 22 July, Major Carter, found his commander "to be an extremely nervous, shaky officer, who seemed to be at a loss as to what to do. Most of the time he remained at the CP [command post]."[78]

Aware of the problem, General Kean seems to have insisted that all operational orders for the regiment go first to Carter before they went to White. The move, however, was at best partially successful because Kean's assistant division commander, General Wilson, appears to have been as dissatisfied as Kean, not only with White but also with the operation of the whole regiment. Interposing himself between the regimental headquarters and units in the field whenever he felt the need, he issued orders directly to battalion commanders and their

1950. Benefield's actions are described in EUSAK GO 54, 6 Sep 50. See also Statement of Lt Charles A. Munford, in Award file for Brig Gen Vennard Wilson; Intervs, MacGarrigle with Gillert, 4 May 94; Rishell, 10 Aug 93.

[75] Intervs, Cash with Leonard H. Kushner, 16 Jun 89; Albert Griffin, Jr., 5 Oct 88; Bowers with Lawrence M. Corcoran, 1 Mar 94.

[76] Intervs, IG with White, 5 Sep 50, exhibit 28, Kean Letter file, and 27 Sep 50, exhibit B–21, Eighth Army Inspector General Investigation. See also Intervs, IG with Capt Alfred F. Thompson, 24 Aug 50, exhibit 11, Kean Letter file; MacGarrigle with Gillert, 4 May 94; John S. Komp, 5 May and 1 Jun 94; Rishell, 10 Aug 93; Green, 16 Jun 94; Hash, 18 and 22 Mar 94; Force, 8 Aug 94; Gustav H. Franke, 14 Jul 94; Ltr, Komp to MacGarrigle, 14 May 94, CMH files. The incident is mentioned in neither regimental nor battalion war diaries.

[77] Intervs, IG with Capt Alfred F. Thompson, 24 Aug 50, exhibit 11, Kean letter file; MacGarrigle with Gillert, 4 May 94. Quote from Interv, IG with White, 5 Sep 50, exhibit 28, Kean Letter file. Interv, IG with White, 27 Sep 50, exhibit B–21, Eighth Army Inspector General Investigation.

[78] Intervs, MacGarrigle with Owen H. Carter, 21 and 24 Jun 94; Sam J. Adams, Jr., 15 and 17 Jun 94. Adams had been the operations officer until replaced by Carter. Adams then became the regimental communications officer.

staff officers without informing the regimental headquarters. As a result, the regimental staff sometimes had only the faintest idea of what was going on in the field.[79]

Several others noticed that something was badly wrong. First Lt. Sandro A. Barone, reporting to the regimental command post with some other officer replacements in late July, remarked that, "Covered bodies lined a walkway to a schoolhouse where the headquarters was. Colonel White looked extremely old, haggard, and had little to tell the new men. Mortar and automatic weapons fire could be heard in the vicinity." Major Carter was also concerned. Toward the end of the month, he observed, "When White would light his cigarette, the match in his hand was embarrassingly shaking. He was on the verge of a nervous breakdown."[80]

In the days that followed the incident with Miller's 1st Battalion, the enemy continued to press the 24th Infantry. By the morning of 29 July, the regiment was located eight miles to the west of Sangju, where it held a front over ten thousand yards wide. Donaho's 2d Battalion, minus Company F, which was operating to the northeast with a company of the 35th Infantry, held the Kallyong-Sangju road and faced north. To the south came Pierce's 3d Battalion. With its right flank anchored on the road, the unit extended far to the southwest, where it tied in with Miller's 1st Battalion. That unit was facing west in order to cover the Iso-ri road. Two battalions of 105-mm. artillery and a battery of 155-mm. artillery provided support along with a platoon of tanks. Despite the increased artillery, Colonel White's position was still too extensive for the force he had at hand, and, more important, a one-mile gap separated the understrength 2d Battalion from the 3d.[81]

That day observers with Company C discovered a large enemy force to their north massing for an attack against the 3d Battalion's left flank. Raking the North Koreans with mortar and automatic weapons fire, they broke up the attack and caused many casualties.[82] In the afternoon, the regiment received orders from the 25th Infantry Division to withdraw during the night to a defensive line four miles to the rear.[83] At dusk, however, before the movement could begin, the enemy attacked and quickly penetrated between the 2d and 3d Battalions. The main attack fell on the 2d Battalion's Company G astride the Kallyong road. After several hours of fighting, the company commander, Capt. Herman W. Roesch, repelled the assault by calling in artillery fire close to his own position. At other locations on the battlefield, tanks drove back an enemy force that was threatening the 2d Battalion's command post. The 1st and 3d Battalions also came under attack but were able to hold their ground.[84]

After midnight on the morning of 30 July, elements of the regiment began withdrawing to a new position to the east, but around dawn heavy attacks struck the 2d and 3d Battalions, both of which had yet to begin the move. In the 2d Battalion's zone,

[79] Ibid. For other views of White's and Wilson's dealings with battalions, see Intervs, MacGarrigle with Zanin, 27 Oct 93; Gillert, 4 May 94; Komp, 5 May and 1 Jun 94.

[80] Interv, MacGarrigle with Sandro A. Barone, 14 Apr 94. Quote from Intervs, MacGarrigle with Carter, 21 and 24 Jun 94.

[81] WD, 24th Inf Rgt, Jul 50, Overlays 7, Situation 24th Infantry 280700 July 50, and 8, Situation of 24th RCT as of 291800 July 50; WD, 159th FA Bn, Jul 50, sketch 6. The 64th (2 batteries) and 159th (3 batteries) Field Artillery Battalions were present along with Battery C, 90th Field Artillery Battalion. The tank platoon was from Company A, 79th Heavy Tank Battalion. The defensive doctrine of the day called for frontages of 2,400 yards for broken terrain and 4,800 in flat, open terrain. The defense of a front of up to 10,000 yards was to be undertaken only if key terrain features were organized in strength and the remainder of the main line of resistance was lightly held. See Army FM 7–40, *The Infantry Regiment*, 11 Jan 50, pp. 234–37.

[82] WD, 24th Inf Rgt, Jul 50, pp. 36–37; WD, 1st Bn, 24th Inf Rgt, Jul 50, p. 5.

[83] 25th Inf Div G–3 Activities Rpt for 29 Jul 50, dtd 30 Jul 50, in WD, 25th Inf Div, Jul 50. The order had originated from Eighth Army.

[84] WD, 24th Inf Rgt, Jul 50, pp. 35–36; WD, 1st Bn, 24th Inf Rgt, Jul 50, p. 5; WD, 2d Bn, 24th Inf Rgt, Jul 50, pp. 9–10; WD, 3d Bn, 24th Inf Rgt, Jul 50, pp. 12–13. See also Intervs, IG with Horace E. Donaho, 22 Aug 50, exhibit 19, Kean Letter file; Bowers with Doiron, 22 Apr 94; Genous S. Hodges, 13 Apr 94.

Company G managed to destroy a North Korean tank on the road but was eventually overrun along with part of the battalion command post. As enemy pressure increased, Company E tried to cover G's withdrawal, but the plan immediately went awry. As the men from Company G rose to execute the move, so did those from E.[85] The two units withdrew together in disorder, so precipitously that a 75-mm. recoilless rifle platoon was left in position. The platoon held off two enemy tanks before at last retreating.[86]

In the 3d Battalion's area, enemy attacks began before 0500. By 0930 Company K was holding but Company I's position was beginning to give way. Shortly before 1100, Company L entered the fighting from reserve. Thirty minutes later, the battalion's headquarters company itself came forward in an attempt to stop the enemy. Pierce's command post came under artillery fire at 1210. On the left flank of the regiment, Company A of the 1st Battalion also experienced heavy fighting, and the 1st Battalion's command post had to displace because of enemy mortar fire. With casualties and large numbers of stragglers streaming to the rear and the regiment's defensive line collapsing, Colonel White ordered the units to break contact with the enemy as best they could and to fall back to the rear.[87]

Straggling undoubtedly contributed to the final collapse, despite the attempts of many capable and heroic officers and soldiers to stand and fight.[88] The straggler control point operated by the military police west of Sangju had continued to apprehend about seventy-five soldiers a day during the fighting. Other points operated by the regiment and

battalions in forward areas also collected a large number. At that time as at others, shirkers congregated in mess areas and around artillery positions. Battalion aid stations were a favored destination, with observers remarking that five or six soldiers would sometimes accompany one of the walking wounded to the rear.[89]

Most of the men were compliant when confronted by straggler control parties, but after they returned to their units they would often straggle again, as soon as an enemy assault occurred. In some cases, the mere word that an attack was imminent was enough to set them off. Most carried their weapons to the rear, but up to 25 percent, by some estimates, left them behind. The names of stragglers were rarely recorded at that time and few if any were punished. White Capt. Johnny L. Bearden, who served at a straggler control point about two miles from the front lines, said that there were so many it was impossible to keep track of them. The regimental adjutant, white Maj. John R. Wooldridge, who coordinated all of the straggler pick-up points, was more emphatic. "The regiment was . . . sorely pressed by the enemy and every man was needed at the front."[90]

Although a number of the stragglers were obviously malingerers and shirkers who deliberately sought to avoid combat, individuals of that sort were a problem in any military unit, white or black.

[85] Interv, IG with Robinson, 15 Sep 50, exhibit B–6, Eighth Army Inspector General Investigation.

[86] WD, 2d Bn, 24th Inf Rgt, Jul 50, pp. 10–11.

[87] WD, 24th Inf Rgt, Jul 50, pp. 38–40; WD, 2d Bn, 24th Inf Rgt, Jul 50, pp. 10–11; WD, 3d Bn, 24th Inf Rgt, Jul 50, p. 13. See also 25th Inf Div Opns Directive, 30 Jul 50, with Overlay dtd 301250 Jul 50, in WD, 25th Inf Div, Jul 50.

[88] For acts of individual heroism, see awards for the Bronze Star in 25th Inf Div GOs 330, 13 Nov 50; 420, 25 Nov 50; 430, 26 Nov 50; 473, 11 Dec 50; and 475, 12 Dec 50; and awards of the Silver Star in 25th Inf Div GOs 84, 27 Aug 50; 175, 22 Sep 50; 178, 23 Sep 50; and 359, 19 Nov 50.

[89] WD, 24th Inf Rgt, Jul 50, p. 40. See also Intervs, IG with Johnny L. Bearden, 21 Aug 50, exhibit 5, Kean Letter file; Wooldridge, 23 Aug 50, exhibit 1, Kean Letter file; Donaho, 22 Aug 50, exhibit 19, Kean Letter file; Ernest M. Brolley [Bralley], Jr., 24 Aug 50, exhibit 6, Kean Letter file; Pidgeon, 25 Aug 50, exhibit 26, Kean Letter file; Gorham Black, 21 Aug 50, exhibit 7, Kean Letter file; Bowers with Marshall R. Hurley, 13 Apr 94.

[90] Intervs, IG with Wooldridge, 13 Feb 51, exhibit B–132, Far East Command Inspector General Investigation; Bearden, 21 Aug 50, exhibit 5, Kean Letter file. The official count of stragglers for July 1950 was 29 for the 24th Infantry, 7 for the 27th Infantry, and 2 for the 35th Infantry. See Certificate, Office of the Provost Marshal, 25th Inf Div, 13 Feb 51, exhibit K, Far East Command Inspector General Investigation. For an example of numbers apprehended but not officially charged, see Provost Marshal Activities Rpt for 28 Jul 50, in WD, 25th Inf Div, Jul 50.

Many more, however, clearly were soldiers who had been caught up in confusion and disorganization at the front, where unseasoned and often ineffectual officers and noncommissioned officers were unable or unwilling to assert their authority. In that sense, the failure to take action to stop the straggling was bound up with the straggling itself. If weak leadership in the companies had allowed the problem, weak leadership at regiment and the battalions had permitted it to continue.[91]

If failures of leadership, complicated by a mounting casualty toll among officers and sergeants and their inexperienced replacements, undoubtedly contributed to what was happening, circumstances peculiar to the 24th were nonetheless also involved. A white platoon leader in Company G, 1st Lt. Genous S. Hodges, remarked, "There was a lot of withdrawing. Often [soldiers] . . . would be pushed off of a position with mortar and sniper fire. This should not have been enough to force them off of a position."[92]

A white platoon leader in Company K, 2d Lt. Roscoe E. Dann, explained what was happening. "When the 24th Infantry deployed to Korea . . . some of its junior officers had a poor attitude; these officers had not wanted to be in the unit from the start. They had little faith in their men, who in turn probably had little in them." The condition led to straggling on both sides. "When the situation became tense," he said, "and direction from higher headquarters was unclear, some platoon leaders as well as their men had a tendency to leave their position without orders."[93]

The problem of manning a defensive position or of conducting an orderly withdrawal was compounded by the fatigue of the soldiers, who were deprived of adequate sleep for days at a time and were often physically exhausted. It was thus hardly unusual for units of all races hurriedly withdrawing through rugged terrain to lose individuals or small groups who would drop back because they could not keep the pace. Later, the survivors would appear in rear areas with perfectly honest stories of being separated from their units. That shirkers would use the same excuse was of course to be expected.[94]

Whatever its cause, straggling increased the difficulty of holding a line. Attuned to constant and unexpected withdrawals, a soldier who saw his buddies leaving was hardly disposed to remain behind to question whether they were falling back on orders. "The unit would set up in position and fire at the enemy until they got return fire," Pvt. William Cobb of Company C remarked. "The unit would then 'bugout'—or pull back to the next designated position. . . . If you didn't leave when you got the word to 'bugout,' you would get left behind."[95]

The excessive straggling and failure to hold positions, despite the best efforts of many, endangered the entire regiment as it fell back in disorder on the afternoon of 30 July. Only the presence of a battalion of the 35th Infantry in blocking positions on ridges four miles to the east appears to have saved the day. Miller assembled what he could of his 1st Battalion to the north of that unit while Pierce's 3d Battalion took station to the south. The 2d Battalion moved to the rear.[96]

In the chaos, rumors arose among angry white officers that a wounded lieutenant had been abandoned and allowed to die when his stretcher bearers, alarmed by nearby mortar fire, dropped his lit-

[91] Only three offenders were charged for straggling during the fighting at Sangju in July. All involved incidents that occurred in Company E on 29 July. See exhibits C, D–1, D–2, Far East Command Inspector General Investigation.

[92] Interv, Bowers with Hodges, 13 Apr 94.

[93] Intervs, MacGarrigle with Roscoe E. Dann, Jr., 24 Mar 94; Bowers with Doiron, 22 Apr 94.

[94] WD, 24th Inf Rgt, Jul 50, p. 39. For excuses given by stragglers, see Intervs, IG with Bearden, 21 Aug 50, exhibit 5, Kean Letter file; Gorham Black, 21 Aug 50, exhibit 7, Kean Letter file; Charles Heard, 23 Aug 50, exhibit 9, Kean Letter file.

[95] Interv, Timothy Rainey with William Cobb, 4 Dec 89. See also Intervs, Bowers with Tittel, 15 Apr 94; MacGarrigle with Tittel, 20 Apr 94.

[96] WD, 24th Inf Rgt, Jul 50, p. 40; WD, 35th Inf Rgt, Jul 50, p. 7; WD, 1st Bn, 35th Inf Rgt, 11–31 Jul 50. Fisher's 2d Battalion, which had been west of Sangju, moved south and was replaced by the 1st Battalion, which had been fighting with Michaelis' 27th Infantry. See 25th Inf Div Opns Directive, 30 Jul 50, with Overlay dtd 301250 Jul 50. See also Interv, MacGarrigle with Sidney B. Berry, 11 Aug 93.

ter and fled. Whether anything of that sort actually occurred is difficult to say. What is known is that on the next day the acting commander of the 1st Battalion's Company A, black 1st Lt. Leon A. Gilbert, refused a direct order from the acting commander of the 2d Battalion, Major Donaho, to return to the front with a group of his men. According to the regimental commander's driver, black enlisted man Sylvester Davis, who was present, the regiment's executive officer, Colonel Roberts, pleaded with Gilbert to go back with his men: "Don't you know what they'll do to you?" Gilbert responded, "No, I'll get killed." After a later interview with Colonel White, who also gave Gilbert every opportunity to change his mind, the officer was arrested and charged with desertion in the face of the enemy, a capital crime. At the end of the session, according to white 1st Lt. John Komp, who witnessed what happened, Colonel White swore in anger and threw his helmet across the room. The only black officer serving at the Eighth Army's headquarters at the time, Maj. John "Tommy" Martin, a public affairs officer, related years later that the Gilbert case became "a major black eye" for the 24th Infantry.[97]

Over the night of 31 July–1 August, on orders from the Eighth Army, which had decided to begin pulling American forces behind the protection of the Naktong River, the entire regiment retreated to the east of Sangju. With the town indefensible and word circulating that enemy forces were attempting to cut roads to the rear, it seemed a moment of great danger. "Sangju was reached before midnight," the author of the 1st Battalion's war diary remarked, "then our trail was turned south through a valley several miles east of the enemy. . . . The foot troops had no crew served weapons within reach. A calculated risk was made to send all these heavy weapons on carriers over another route, thus relieving the load on the foot troops. . . . The rate of march was slowed to approximately one mile per hour by the exceedingly large number of refugees who clogged the roads for miles on end."[98]

Despite the rumors, the enemy failed to press the retreating units, and the regiment took up a new defensive line between Sangju and the Naktong River without incident. On the night of 1 August, covered by the 25th Division's reconnaissance company, the 77th Engineer Combat Company, commanded by 1st Lt. Charles Bussey, destroyed Sangju's factories, warehouses, and electrical and communications systems and damaged key installations in the railroad yard. With that, the 24th's activities in the area came to an end. On 2 August the regiment received orders to move south along with the rest of the 25th Division to deal with a new threat developing west of Pusan.[99]

Since its arrival in Korea, the 24th Infantry had suffered about a 15 percent loss: 34 killed in action, 275 wounded, and 99 missing along with another 53 nonbattle casualties.[100] The corps of officers had

---

[97] The command to Gilbert is mentioned in Interv, IG with Donaho, 22 Aug 50, exhibit 19, Kean Letter file. The wounded officer is mentioned both by Donaho and by Capt. James O. Gardner. See Interv, IG with Gardner, 24 Aug 50, exhibit 24, Kean Letter file. The Gilbert affair is also dealt with in Intervs, MacGarrigle with Gillert, 4 May 94; Komp, 5 May and 1 Jun 94; Cash with Sylvester Davis, 19 Sep 89; John "Tommy" Martin, 12 Jan 90; Ltr, Komp to MacGarrigle, 14 May 94.

[98] WD, 1st Bn, 24th Inf Rgt, Jul 50, p. 5. See also Memo, Provost Marshal, 25th Inf Div, for Chief of Staff, 31 Jul 50, in WD, 25th Inf Div, Jul 50. It was estimated on 31 July 1950 that 85,000 refugees had passed through Sangju and that 55,000 remained in the area.

[99] WD, 24th Inf Rgt, Aug 50, pp. 1–3, and Overlay 1, box 3750, RG 407, WNRC. For the destruction at Sangju, see, in addition to the war diary, Silver Star Recommendation, 1st Lt Charles M. Bussey, signed by Maj Milledge Beckwith, 31 Aug 50, in CMH files.

[100] G–1 Daily Summary, 25th Inf Div, 14 and 31 Jul 50, in WD, 25th Inf Div, Jul 50. The percentage of losses for the 24th Infantry was derived by comparing the 14 July strength of 3,157 with total battle and nonbattle casualties of 461. These are not the final numbers since many of those considered missing in action (MIA) were eventually accounted for. In October, when the 24th Infantry's war diary for July was compiled, there were only 3 MIA for the month. The 27th Infantry had about an 18 percent loss (435 battle and nonbattle casualties out of a strength of 2,370 on 14 July). The major difference between the 24th and 27th was in officer casualties. In the 27th Infantry, the six line companies only lost 5 officers. The 35th Infantry suffered 6 percent casualties for July (122 casualties out of 1,979 assigned on 14 July). See Best, *Analysis of Personnel Casualties in the 25th Infantry Division, 26–31 July 1950;* Officer Rosters, 24th Inf Rgt, 27th Inf Rgt, 29th Inf Rgt,

been especially hard hit. Twenty-eight percent, 7 out of 25, had been killed or evacuated as nonbattle casualties or for wounds in the 1st Battalion; 58.3 percent, 14 out of 24, in the 2d; and 43.5 percent, 10 out of 23, in the 3d. Companies E, F, and L had each lost 4 of 7 officers, and Company K had lost 3 of 5. In addition, of 4 lieutenants who had joined the regiment as replacements, 2 had been killed in action and 1 wounded by the end of the month.[101] Although no comparable statistics exist for sergeants, the toll among them was also heavy. By 2 August Company C had lost 11 leaders of the rank of corporal or above in combat, D had lost 12, E 15, G 14, and I 16.[102] As General Vennard Wilson and others observed, many of those losses had come about because unit leaders had been forced to expose themselves to an undue extent while attempting to control their men.[103]

By the beginning of August, the 24th bore little resemblance to the unit that had traveled to Kumch'on and had fought at Yech'on just two weeks before. Not only had it lost the equivalent in men of over half of any one of the battalions that had fought in the hills west of Sangju, much of its equipment was missing. Although most soldiers might have been in good physical condition when they deployed, they were not prepared for the rigors of combat in the mountains of Korea. Lieutenant Dann recalled constantly moving from one position to another in the rear. "The weather was hot, humid, and I was terribly tired. On one occasion, I must have gone to sleep while walking

because when I woke up, I was stumbling into a rice paddy."[104]

Physical exhaustion, combined with confusion, defeats, constant withdrawals, and an enemy who rarely gave quarter and seemed ever present, produced a powerful effect on the unit's morale, discipline, and combat effectiveness.[105] Some soldiers reacted with anger and an increased effort to try to turn things around. For many others, their spirit seemed broken. "As far as I am concerned," a black master sergeant from Company E, David Robinson, told an interviewer with disdain, "we actually have men who are afraid."[106]

Fear, however, hardly explains the full dimensions of what was happening. As a team of high-ranking officers from the United States noted after visiting all of the American divisions and regiments in Korea in late July and early August, the entire Eighth Army was experiencing difficulties similar to those of the 24th at that time. "The troops were fighting under severe disadvantages," the authors of the group's final report noted,

having been . . . commited [sic] more or less piecemeal, after incomplete training, and at reduced strength, with much of their equipment of marginal serviceability. . . . Our troops were opposed by an enemy who vastly outnumbered them, and who was well trained, well equipped, skillfully led and inspired by a fanatical determination to attack. . . . The frontages were enormous and precluded a continuous line of defense. This facilitated outflanking and penetrating operations by the enemy and forced a continuous withdrawal.[107]

and 35th Inf Rgt, exhibits D–12 thru D–19, Eighth Army Inspector General Investigation.

[101] HQ, 25th Inf Div, Reported Casualties of the 24th Infantry Regiment, n.d. [Jul 50–Sep 51]. See also Officer Roster, 24th Inf Rgt (officers present with unit upon arrival in Korea, 12 July 1950), 18 Sep 50, exhibit D–12, Eighth Army Inspector General Investigation.

[102] HQ, 25th Inf Div, Reported Casualties of the 24th Infantry Regiment, n.d. [Jul 50–Sep 51].

[103] This is the consensus of virtually all the officers queried on the subject during the inspector general investigation of the 24th Infantry during 1950. See Intervs, IG with Wilson, 5 Sep 50, exhibit 29, Kean Letter file; Gooch, 26 Aug 50, exhibit 25, Kean Letter file; Gardner, 24 Aug 50, exhibit 24, Kean Letter file.

[104] Intervs, MacGarrigle with Dann, 24 and 28 Mar 94.

[105] For an example of discipline problems, see Msg from Chief of Sangju Police Station, translation, 30 Jul 50, in WD, 25th Inf Div, Jul 50.

[106] Interv, IG with Robinson, 15 Sep 50, exhibit B–6, Eighth Army Inspector General Investigation.

[107] Rpt, First Office of the Chief of Army Field Forces Observer Team to the Far East Command, 16 Aug 50, pp. 1–3 and app. B, box 171, RG 337, WNRC. The team was in Korea from 24 July to 3 August 1950. They visited the 24th Infantry on 29 July talking with White, Miller, Donaho, and Pierce and visiting Companies E and G. For a description of the problems afflicting other units at the time, see Roy K. Flint, "Task Force Smith and the 24th Division," in Heller and Stofft, America's First Battles, 1776–1965, pp. 272–74.

The team went on to observe that the Americans on line were less mature and of lower intelligence than enlisted personnel in World War II. On top of that, personnel policies had led to the assignment of inexperienced and inadequately prepared officers and noncommissioned officers to combat units. "This had often resulted in poor leadership, especially at the regimental and lower levels."[108]

More disturbing, the group continued, was a "noticeable absence" of combat aggressiveness in many infantry units.

The absolute discipline and automatic obedience to command that is vital for control in combat is lacking. All troops were deficient in measures for cover and concealment, and in maintaining signal communications. The troops were disinclined to leave the roads, and were unskilled in use of mines and in night operations. Like all green troops, they magnified the strength of the enemy, and tended to become panicky and stampede when small hostile groups got in their rear. . . . Infantry troops were specifically deficient in . . . aggressiveness in counter-attack, steadiness under fire, [and] confidence in their own weapons. . . . Lack of leadership in regimental and subordinate echelons was often evident, in both field and company grades, and among the noncommissioned officers.[109]

Recognizing that there was little that could be done in the United States to provide immediate solutions to most of the problems, the report's authors concentrated on recommendations for improving equipment, the system of supply, and personnel and training policies. For the rest, no short-term remedies were possible. The units in Korea were left to find their own solutions for their problems.[110]

While the 24th Infantry shared the tactical defects found in all the other units, the observers still considered it a special case. After talking to the white leadership of the regiment and of the 25th Infantry Division and after visiting only two companies for part of one day, they reported that the "effectiveness of colored troops . . . was about 80%

of white troops."[111] In reaching that conclusion, they shared the prejudices of other whites who were at that time evaluating the effectiveness of the regiment. Those individuals tended to blame the 24th's failures upon the racial characteristics of the soldiers who composed the unit without considering the inexperience of the men, the effects of substandard equipment, the problems that necessarily accompanied a withdrawal under attack for even the most veteran troops, their own failures as commanders, or the contribution that segregation had made to the climate of mistrust that prevailed within the regiment and that had damaged the unit's ability to function as a dependable whole. Even if the observers and the leaders of the regiment themselves had recognized the true nature of what was wrong, however, it is doubtful if they could have made meaningful changes. The war was moving so fast at that moment that the commanders of most units were hard put to stay even, much less to make the sort of wholesale changes in personnel and procedure that might have made a difference in the 24th.

General Kean, with his command post located at Sangju and his assistant, General Wilson, directly involved in the fighting, was nevertheless well aware that something had to be done. Shortly after the 24th pulled back behind the Naktong, he attempted to replace Colonel White. By then, however, the regiment was so tainted with failure and so beset by white racial prejudices that few colonels were eager to take the job. When the commander of the Eighth Army, Lt. Gen. Walton Walker, took up the issue, he met with the same problem. "When I reported to Walker in Korea," one colonel remarked years later, "he wanted me to take over the all black 24th regiment. Nobody, including me, wanted command of the 24th."[112] In that light and under the circumstances, it was thus perhaps inevitable that the problems the unit had encountered at Sangju would repeat themselves at Masan, a town some thirty miles by road west of Pusan, where the regiment would fight during the coming month.

[108]Rpt, First Office of the Chief of Army Field Forces Observer Team to the Far East Command, 16 Aug 50, p. 4.
[109]Ibid., pp. 8–9.
[110]Ibid., pp. 12–16.
[111]Ibid., p. 4.
[112]Interv, Clay Blair with Ned D. Moore, in Blair, The Forgotten War, p. 164.

CHAPTER 6

The Pusan Perimeter

While other North Korean Army units pushed down South Korea's eastern coastline and poured across the country's central mountain passes toward Kumch'on and Sangju, the *6th North Korean Division* turned off the main Seoul-Pusan highway to begin a sweep down South Korea's western coastline. In the days that followed, the division encountered only minor resistance from scattered South Korean military units before capturing Kunsan, a port town at the mouth of the Kum River. Moving inland at that point, it secured the town of Kwangju on 22 July 1950 and took only three more days to reach Sunch'on, where it paused briefly to regroup before pushing toward the crossroads town of Chinju, a mere fifty-five miles by air to the west of Pusan. Halfway to Chinju, at Hadong, it met and almost destroyed a newly arrived battalion from the U.S. 29th Infantry.[1] (*Map 6*)

Composed of the *13th, 14th,* and *15th Regiments*, the *6th North Korean Division* possessed a hard core of highly trained and motivated leaders, many of whom had seen duty in the Chinese civil war. Although it outran its supply system during its drive to the south, it made good many of its logistical difficulties by appropriating local resources and by using captured South Korean and American weapons, including at one point six U.S. tanks. The morale of the unit's personnel was high—the troops had met with little opposition on their way south and were flushed with victory.[2]

The Eighth Army Withdraws

Chinju itself fell on 31 July, but from that point on the division began to meet increasing opposition as the U.S. 19th and 27th Infantry regiments moved to obstruct its path. Even if those forces inflicted heavy casualties, however, General Walker recognized that the enemy's deep drive into his western flank still had a good chance of cutting his main supply line out of Pusan. To eliminate that possibility, shorten his defensive lines, and take advantage of the additional protection that natural

---

[1] Far East Command (FEC), Allied Translator and Interpreter Section (ATIS), Research Supplement, Interrogation Rpt, issue 100, *6th NK Infantry Division*, 30 Apr 51, pp. 34–37, Intelligence Research Collection, U.S. Army Military History Institute (MHI), Carlisle Barracks, Pa.; FEC, Military Intelligence Section, Order of Battle Information, North Korean Army, 15 Oct 50, MHI, hereafter cited as North Korean Order of Battle; FEC, History of the North Korean Army, 31 Jul 52, pp. 62–64, CMH files. For the 29th Infantry combat, see Appleman, *South to the Naktong, North to the Yalu,* pp. 214–21 and 4th Historical Detachment, Action at Chinju, 31 Jul 50, n.d., CMH files. The 29th Infantry was a separate unit unconnected with a division.

[2] ATIS, Research Supplement, Interrogation Rpt, issue 100, 30 Apr 51, *6th NK Infantry Division,* pp. 28–30, 35; North Korean Order of Battle; FEC, History of the North Korean Army, 31 Jul 52, pp. 62–63. The *6th North Korean Infantry Division* had been the *166th Division, 56th Chinese Communist Army,* until 25 July 1949, when it moved to North Korea.

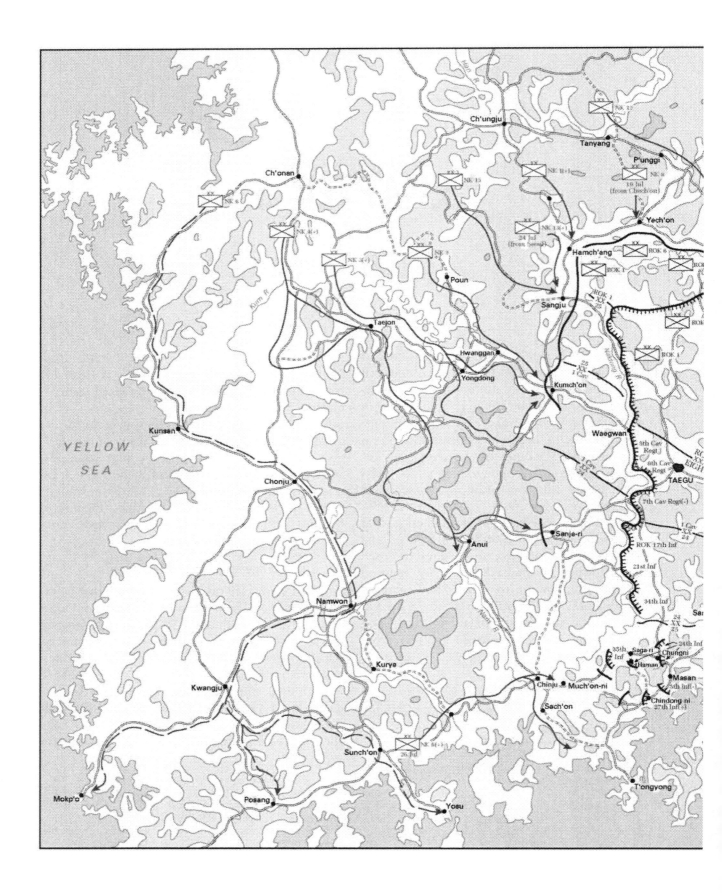

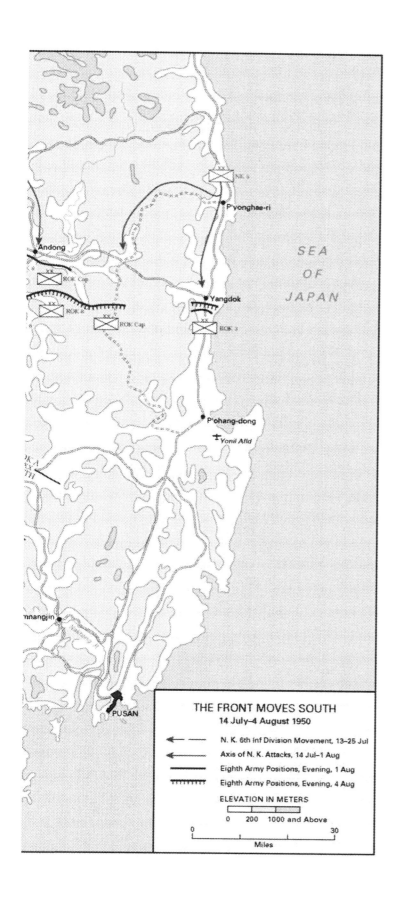

SEA

OF

JAPAN

Andong

ROK Cap

ROK 8

ROK Cap

P'yonghae-ri

Yangdok

ROK 3

P'ohang-dong

✛ Yonil Afld

nnangjin

PUSAN

THE FRONT MOVES SOUTH
14 July–4 August 1950

N. K. 6th Inf Division Movement, 13–25 Jul

Axis of N. K. Attacks, 14 Jul–1 Aug

Eighth Army Positions, Evening, 1 Aug

Eighth Army Positions, Evening, 4 Aug

ELEVATION IN METERS

| 0 | 200 | 1000 and Above |

0   30

Miles

Map 6

barriers could provide, he had already decided to abandon South Korea's central region and to pull his forces behind the Naktong and Nam Rivers. To that end, on the morning of 1 August he instructed General Kean to begin moving the 25th Division south to Samnangjin, a town some thirty-five miles northwest of Pusan by air and just to the east of the point where the Nam and Naktong joined. The next day, at a conference with Kean, he had second thoughts and changed the division's destination to Masan, a port located thirty miles west of Pusan on the enemy's probable line of attack.[3] (*See Map 6.*)

The move south was dogged by difficulties. In the case of the 24th Infantry, the troops departed the Sangju area by motor and on foot on 2 August, using the Kumch'on-Waegwan road, the only route leading from the Sangju region to the lower Naktong. When they arrived at Waegwan, where they were to cross the Naktong, they found a horde of refugees clamoring to board trains that had been assigned to take the troops south. Adding to the confusion, the 17th South Korean Regiment simultaneously arrived in the town, on its way west to reinforce the exhausted 24th Division. Many delays followed, but individual units shoved through the chaos, cleared the refugees from the trains, and loaded their men and equipment aboard.[4]

Even as they did, however, more problems were developing. When the regiment's trucks, after returning to Sangju to pick up the rear guard, began the journey back to Waegwan, they encountered the 1st Cavalry Division crossing their path at right angles. If the enemy had chosen that moment to launch a strong attack, all might have been lost. Instead, officers at the scene served as traffic police-

men and managed to maintain order. Although the meeting broke the convoy's line of march, the trucks reached Waegwan before the trains departed. In the end, confusion and delays notwithstanding, it took the 25th Division a scant thirty-six hours to reach its final destination at Masan, 100 miles to the south. The division received a Republic of Korea Presidential Unit Citation for the achievement.[5]

Although General Walker believed that the Eighth Army had begun to lose its aggressive spirit, he had few options. He pushed the 25th Division into the path of the oncoming *6th Division*, giving it charge of the region between Chinju and Masan that stretched south of the Nam and Naktong Rivers to the sea.[6] Within that sector, the division assumed command of all United Nations forces. They included a sprinkling of South Korean battalions known as Task Force Min, the just-arriving U.S. 5th Regimental Combat Team (RCT), the battered 1st and 3d Battalions of the 29th Infantry regiment, the 89th Medium Tank Battalion, and the 1st Provisional Marine Brigade. At that time, the 27th Infantry returned briefly to division control, but it would go back into Eighth Army reserve as soon as the 5th RCT was in place.[7]

Overall, allied forces were too few to establish anything like a continuous line of defense. Instead the 35th Infantry regiment, which replaced the 19th Infantry regiment when that unit moved north to rejoin the 24th Division, guarded the northern portion of the division's area of responsi-

---

[3] Robertson, *Counterattack on the Naktong, 1950*, pp. 1–11; Schnabel, *Policy and Direction*, pp. 113–14, 125–27; Blair, *The Forgotten War*, pp. 166–72; WD, 25th Inf Div, 1–2 Aug 50, box 3748, RG 407, WNRC, Suitland, Md.

[4] Appleman, *South to the Naktong, North to the Yalu*, pp. 248–49; WD, 1st Bn, 24th Inf Rgt, Aug 50, pp. 3–4, box 3750, RG 407, WNRC. See Department of the Army (DA) GO 35, 4 Jun 51. Unless otherwise indicated, general orders for this volume are on file in the Army's Awards Branch of the Personnel Service Support Division of the Adjutant General Directorate of the U.S. Total Army Personnel Command (PERSCOM), Alexandria, Va.

[5] Ibid. For a description of the confusion within the 24th Infantry during the move south, see Intervs, George L. MacGarrigle with William A. Hash, 18 and 22 Mar 94. All interviews hereafter cited by John A. Cash, Bernard L. Muehlbauer, Timothy Rainey, William T. Bowers, Richard O. Perry, and George L. MacGarrigle are in CMH files.

[6] Robertson, *Counterattack on the Naktong, 1950*, p. 10. See also Appleman, *South to the Naktong, North to the Yalu*, p. 253.

[7] WD, 24th Inf Rgt, Aug 50, p. 5, box 3750, RG 407, WNRC; WD, 25th Inf Div, 3 Aug 50, box 3748, RG 407, WNRC. The 89th Medium Tank Battalion was originally denominated the 8072d. The unit was redesignated the 89th by the Eighth Army on 7 August 1950. See WD, 8072d Medium Tank Bn, 1–31 Aug 50, p. 3, box 3751, RG 407, WNRC. In early August the battalions of the 29th Infantry were incorporated into the 27th and 35th Infantry regiments to bring them up to three battalions.

bility, a zone that extended from the confluence of the Nam and Naktong Rivers south toward the coastal town of Chindong-ni, six miles southwest of Masan. The 27th and later the 5th took charge to the south, an area that straddled the road running between Chindong-ni and Chinju to the west. The 24th Infantry was responsible for the region between Masan and Haman, a town nine miles to the west, with the mission of suppressing enemy guerrillas and infiltrators in the 25th Division's rear areas.[8]

North of the 25th Division, the worn U.S. 24th Division guarded a twenty-mile stretch of the Naktong above the river's confluence with the Nam. The U.S. 1st Cavalry Division went into the line above that for about the same distance. South Korean divisions held the remainder of the perimeter, from Waegwan in the west to Naktong-ni in the north and then eastward some fifty miles toward Yongdok and the coast. About one hundred and forty miles in circumference, the "Pusan Perimeter," as it was dubbed by journalists, was two to three times longer than it should have been for the number of troops that held it. Even so, it blocked all the roads into the region, gave Walker's forces the flexibility of interior lines of communication, and provided a margin of security for the port at Pusan, through which reinforcements were already beginning to arrive.[9]

The 24th Infantry arrived at Masan on 3 and 4 August. The 1st Battalion assumed positions some five miles northwest of the city, while the 2d moved three miles farther north. The 3d Battalion went to Haman, nine miles west of Masan, where it occupied positions on the high ground commanding the roads into Masan from the west. Each battalion had been reinforced with a South Korean company. Upon arrival, all units began housekeeping chores, laying

emphasis on physical musters of their personnel, weapons checks, vehicle maintenance, and personal hygiene. Beginning on 4 August, patrols began to suppress guerrilla activity and infiltration into the Masan area. No contact with the enemy occurred.[10]

Combat, 5–15 August 1950

It rained heavily the next day, 5 August. All battalions began to patrol their areas while holding reaction forces in reserve to counter any enemy threat that developed. Units of the 1st Battalion apprehended six South Korean deserters but made no contact with the enemy. The 2d Battalion also sent out patrols that failed to result in action, but it suffered one casualty in a strafing attack by an unidentified aircraft during the early morning hours. The 3d Battalion launched its patrols toward Sobuk-san, a large hill five miles to the south of Haman, where one took a prisoner. The man revealed that approximately 200 enemy soldiers were in the vicinity. At 1500, with rain continuing, the 3d Battalion's commander, Colonel Pierce, moved out to engage the force. He was accompanied by his intelligence and operations officers, an artillery liaison party headed by Capt. Alfred F. Thompson, Company L reinforced with a portion of Company I and elements from Company M, and the battalion's attached company of South Koreans. In all, he had the better part of a battalion at his disposal.[11]

The force rode part of the way toward Sobuk-san on vehicles loaned by the 159th Field Artillery Battalion. During the trip out, the battalion operations officer, Capt. John B. Zanin, broke off with a patrol of five men to reconnoiter the area. Discovering after dark that he was separated from Pierce's main force by an enemy unit of unknown

[8] WD, 24th Inf Rgt, Aug 50, p. 5; WD, 25th Inf Div, 3 Aug 50; WD, 24th Inf Rgt, 1–31 Aug 50, Overlay 3, box 3750, RG 407, WNRC. See also Appleman, *South to the Naktong, North to the Yalu*, p. 253.

[9] Appleman, *South to the Naktong, North to the Yalu*, p. 255. See DA Field Manual (FM) 7–40, *The Infantry Regiment*, 11 Jan 50, pp. 234–37. A regiment in defense was normally assigned a frontage of 2,400 to 4,800 yards depending on the type of terrain. In the Pusan Perimeter, regimental frontages averaged about 10,000 yards. At that time, several regiments still had only two understrength battalions.

[10] WDs, 1st, 2d, and 3d Bns, 24th Inf Rgt, Aug 50; WD, 24th Inf Rgt, Aug 50, p. 5; and 24th Inf Rgt Periodic Opns Rpt 42, 4 Aug 50. All in box 3750, RG 407, WNRC. See also Intervs, MacGarrigle with Hash, 18 and 22 Mar 94.

[11] WD, 24th Inf Rgt, 5 Aug 50, p. 6; Letter of Instruction, 24th Inf Rgt, 5 Aug 50; and WD, 3d Bn, 24th Inf Rgt, 5 Aug 50. All in box 3750, RG 407, WNRC. WD, 159th Field Artillery (FA) Bn, 1–31 Aug 50, p. 2, box 3751, RG 407, WNRC. For details of the terrain, see Map, Korea, 1:50,000, series L751, Army Map Service (AMS) 1950, sheets 6819 I, 6819 II, 6819 III, 6819 IV, 6919 III, and 6919 IV, all in NARA, College Park, Md.

size, Zanin took evasive action until dawn and then led his men back to friendly lines on his own.[12]

Moving forward, elements of the rest of the battalion task force encountered and dispersed a small enemy party. At dusk Pierce dispatched a platoon from Company L to determine whether a nearby village contained more North Korean troops. The platoon leader, white 1st Lt. Sandro A. Barone, a newly arrived combat veteran of World War II, noted that his troops "were noisy and seemed untrained in night patrolling." A short while later, determining that no enemy were in the village, the platoon returned to Pierce's position.[13]

Meanwhile, the rest of the battalion had halted on the approaches to a small plateau south of the village. The battalion staff, company command elements, and many of the officers gathered in a hollow to await the return of the patrols and to discuss what to do next. Inertia grew. No one laid out defensive positions, and Pierce himself went to sleep. "They were all just sort of sitting around," black 1st Lt. Oliver Dillard recalled. "No one seemed in command, and the troops, of course, had been told to stop, and when troops are told to stop, as they do in the Army today, they just stop where they are and go to sleep, resting on their packs."[14]

After dark, just as Barone's platoon was rejoining the battalion, a small group of North Koreans estimated to number fewer than thirty men pushed quietly to within small-arms range of the unit and opened fire with automatic weapons. Whether the South Koreans or the men of Company L broke first is unclear. What is known is that after a brief fight both groups fled down the hill, overturning two jeeps in the process and abandoning a radio, a number of M1 rifles and carbines, and most of their heavy weapons. Pierce was shot in both legs. Company L's recently arrived commander, black Capt. Rothwell W. Burke, was killed along with two enlisted men. Eleven American soldiers were wounded and two were listed as missing and never recovered. Losses among the South Koreans are unknown.[15]

White officers would later use the incident as one indication that the men of the 24th Infantry had lost their nerve. In fact, if Company L and its attached units were routed, the officers were as much to blame as those who had run. Pierce had allowed his troops to wait for several hours in the dark without insisting that they establish defensive positions or guard against surprise attack. It was a surefire formula for disaster, especially when troops who were already tired and skittish faced an enemy who had turned the tactics of the unexpected into a fine art.[16]

---

[12] WD, 159th FA Bn, 1–31 Aug 50, p. 2; Interv, MacGarrigle with John B. Zanin, 27 Oct 93.

[13] Intervs, MacGarrigle with Sandro A. Barone, 14 Apr 94; Interv, Inspector General (IG) with Christopher M. Gooch, 26 Aug 50, exhibit 25, attached to Ltr, Maj Gen W. B. Kean, 25th Inf Div, to Commanding General, Eighth U.S. Army (Korea), 9 Sep 50, sub: Combat Effectiveness of the 24th Infantry Regiment. Kean's letter and its attachments are contained in Far East Command Inspector General Investigation, sec. BX, boxes 1013–1014, RG 159, WNRC. Statements attached to General Kean's letter each have an exhibit number and are hereafter cited as in the Kean Letter file. See also WD, 159th FA Bn, Aug 50, p. 2; WD, 3d Bn, 24th Inf Rgt, Aug 50, p. 2; Statement by Eddie S. Lowery, 5 Nov 50, in William Thompson Award file, box 172, RG 338, WNRC; Interv, MacGarrigle with Gustav H. Franke, 14 Jul 94. The village was Habyol, about four miles south of Haman on a trail leading to Sobuk-san. See Sketch Map, in Thompson Award file cited previously. Gooch, who accompanied Barone's men, stated that the platoon started for the rear when they heard a prearranged signal of three shots and had to be stopped "with force." Neither Barone nor any others in the vicinity mention this incident.

[14] Quote from Interv, John A. Cash with Oliver Dillard, 3 Jun 89. The location is well described in Ltr, Oliver Dillard to

David Carlisle, 20 May 87, copy in CMH files. Other comments on the lack of security and carefree attitude of Pierce are in Interv, MacGarrigle with Franke, 14 Jul 94.

[15] Intervs, Cash with Dillard, 3 Jun 89, and MacGarrigle with Barone, 14 Apr 94. Lost equipment is detailed in Interv, IG with Walter Simonovich, 24 Aug 50, exhibit 16, Kean Letter file. The number of wounded is mentioned in Interv, IG with Alfred F. Thompson, the artillery liaison officer who accompanied Pierce, 24 Aug 50, exhibit 11, Kean Letter file. A more precise count can be gleaned from HQ, 25th Inf Div, Reported Casualties of the 24th Infantry Regiment, n.d. [Jul 50–Sep 51], box 3848, RG 407, WNRC. See also Interv, IG with Christopher M. Gooch, 26 Aug 50, exhibit 25, Kean Letter file; Interv, Cash with George Bussey, 13 Nov 88; WD, 3d Bn, 24th Inf Rgt, 1–31 Aug 50, p. 2, box 3750, RG 407, WNRC. Some details of the fighting are in statements in the Thompson Award file previously cited. Gooch said the enemy numbered thirty; Barone put them at fifteen.

[16] Interv, IG with Gooch, 26 Aug 50, exhibit 25, Kean Letter file. Oliver Dillard remarked later that Gooch had ruined

Pfc. William Thompson, posthumous Medal of Honor winner

Whatever the condition of the unit as a whole, some of its men were clearly willing to stand their ground. Pfc. William Thompson of Company M, for one, covered the retreating force with his machine gun. Hit repeatedly by enemy grenade fragments and small-arms fire, he refused the entreaties of comrades to withdraw and continued to lay down covering fire until his company was clear of the area and he was mortally wounded. But for him, casualties that day might have been far worse. In the same way, rifleman George Bussey and others saw to it that the wounded Pierce reached safety. Thompson received a posthumous Medal of Honor for his valor and two other men received Silver Stars, but the action was, in many respects, a dismal and embarrassing defeat.[17]

By 0230 on 6 August the men of Pierce's force were beginning to congregate at Haman, five miles to the rear. They would continue to straggle in throughout the morning. At 0915 Company I, reinforced with one platoon from the 77th Engineer Combat Company, attempted to return to the area of the attack to collect lost weapons and to search for the missing. Encountering the enemy in strength before reaching that goal, the force was pinned down by intense small-arms and mortar fire. In the ensuing engagement, Company I became separated from the engineers. Many of its men headed south to Chindong-ni where they joined up with other American units.[18]

Trailing Company I, the engineer platoon, under black 2d Lt. Chester Lenon, was also pinned down. Lenon sought to eliminate the enemy's machine guns with grenades but fell wounded in the attempt. Staying behind to cover his platoon's withdrawal, he hid for five days along with six wounded enlisted men. A seventh, Pfc. Edward Sanders, sometimes crawling, sometimes walking, eluded enemy patrols to make his way eight miles to the rear to seek help. Bitten by a poisonous snake during the journey and terribly swollen as a result, the man was found by an American patrol on 11 August, five days after he and his comrades had been written off as dead. When informed, the commander of the unit, 1st Lt. Charles Bussey, set out immediately with two platoons to rescue the lost men. When he arrived, he found that two had died. Burying them temporarily on the spot, he delivered the others to the regimental clearing station.[19]

---

the reputation of the regiment with the story by telling it without mentioning the leadership failures that had accompanied the incident. See Intervs, William T. Bowers with Dillard, 8 and 9 Mar 95.

[17] The recommendation for the Medal of Honor was not submitted until 4 January 1951, apparently only after an

exhaustive and vigorous investigation by the 3d Battalion's commander at the time, Lt. Col. Melvin Blair. See Thompson Award file; Interv, MacGarrigle with Melvin Blair, 15 Feb 95. For other awards for the action, 25th Inf Div GOs 345, 6 Nov 50, Silver Star Award Citation for Capt Rothwell Burke, and 319, 11 Nov 50, Silver Star Citation for Sfc Laurence Lane.

[18] WD, 24th Inf Rgt, Aug 50, pp. 7–8. The war diary states that Company I became disorganized and dispersed. A platoon leader of Company I disputes this and says there was no straggling. See Intervs, MacGarrigle with Reginald J. Sapenter, 14 and 21 Mar 94. The battalion war diary is silent on the matter. See WD, 3d Bn, 24th Inf Rgt, Aug 50, p. 2.

[19] WD, 24th Inf Rgt, 1–31 Aug 50, pp. 7, 8; WD, 65th Engr Bn, Aug 50, pp. 7–11, box 3751, RG 407, WNRC. See also Statements of Sgt Joseph Knight, Sfc Bennie R. Cox, and

Colonel Champeny

On 5 August, while Company L was suffering its ordeal, General Kean had relieved Colonel White as commander of the 24th Infantry and had appointed Col. Arthur J. Champeny to take his place. Present at the regimental command post when White had received the word, the operations officer of the 159th Field Artillery Battalion, Maj.

Cloyd V. Taylor, remarked that Kean's move clearly had come as no surprise to White and that the officer seemed glad to hear the news. His exertions had been too much for him, Taylor said. He had lost a great deal of weight and seemed almost gaunt.[20]

At fifty-seven years of age, Champeny was four years older than Kean himself, but he was an experienced combat commander. He had won a Distinguished Service Cross and the French Croix de Guerre during World War I and had commanded the 351st Infantry regiment of the 88th Infantry Division for thirty-two months during World War II. While leading the unit in Italy during the Cassino campaign of 1944, he had received a second Distinguished Service Cross. Following the end of the war, he had served as deputy commander of the U.S. Military Government in Korea, a position that had required him to wear the star of a brigadier general even though he had not at that time been promoted to the rank. When the Korean War broke out, he was serving at the Boston Army Base. Identified as a proven regimental commander because of his experience in the two world wars, he was immediately assigned to Korea. A man of "amazing energy and courage," according to the 25th Division artillery commander, Brig. Gen. George B. Barth, he was also "peppery and brutally frank."[21]

Champeny's combat experience notwithstanding, he got off to a bad start with the 24th. At noon on the day after taking command, becoming aware of the misfortune that had befallen Pierce's unit near Sobuk-san, he called together those portions

Cpl John G. Van Ness, attachments to Eighth U.S. Army, Korea (EUSAK), GO 54, 6 Sep 50, Distinguished Service Cross Citation for Chester J. Lenon. See also Interv, Cash with Chester J. Lenon, 7 Dec 88. Lenon received the Distinguished Service Cross for his actions in rallying his men on the day of the attack. Sanders was recommended for a Medal of Honor but never received it. Since many unit award files from the Korean War period are missing, it is unclear whether he received some alternate decoration. See Intervs, Cash with David Carlisle, 24 Aug 89; John French, 21 Jul 89. Details of the fighting can be found in award citations in 25th Inf Div GOs 189, 25 Sep 50, awarding a Bronze Star to Sgt LaVaughn Fields; 227, 10 Oct 50, Silver Star for Sgt Joseph Knight; 478, 12 Dec 50, Bronze Star for Cpl Thomas; and 21, 4 Jan 51, Silver Star for Sgt Jerome Barnwell.

[20] Intervs, MacGarrigle with Cloyd V. Taylor, 23 Aug 93; Owen H. Carter, 21 and 24 Jun 94; WD, 24th Inf Rgt, 1–31 Aug 50, p. 7.
[21] U.S. Department of Defense, Office of Public Affairs, Biography of Brig Gen Arthur Seymour Champeny, USA, 19 Jun 52, CMH files; Sawyer, Military Advisors in Korea, pp. 13, 172. Quote from Brig Gen G. B. Barth, Tropic Lightning and Taro Leaf in Korea, n.d., p. 16, CMH files. After receiving a third Distinguished Service Cross for his Korean War service, Champeny was promoted to brigadier general in 1951 and returned to Korea as an adviser to the South Korean armed forces. He was later named commandant of the Republic of Korea (ROK) Leadership School. His service was controversial. See Memorandum for the Record (MFR), 5 Jun 53, sub: IG 201.61 O'Hearn, Wm. Joseph Wall, with attachments, CMH Champeny file.

of the 3d Battalion that were present at Haman and delivered an angry dressing down. Correspondent James L. Hicks of the *Baltimore Afro-American* was nearby and later told investigators what he had heard. "He got up and told them . . . that he had been in the 88th [Division] in Italy, and at that time he had an element of the [all-black] 92d [Infantry] Division attached to him, and he said that this was the outfit that had a reputation for running, and they ran all over Italy, and he said that his observations had proved that colored people did not make good combat soldiers, and that his job down there was to change the frightened 24th into the fighting 24th." Hicks continued that a number of the men present had been in the 92d and had not run and that they had left the meeting insulted and angry. "I went to Champeny," Hicks said, "and asked him why he made the statement such as he did, and he said 'I said it . . . Isn't it the truth?' Those were his very words. It almost knocked me out. . . . He said that he did not intend to insult my race. He was only trying to make those men so mad that they would really get mad enough to fight."[22]

Champeny's hard-boiled approach, if that is what it was, appears to have split the men of the regiment into two groups. On one hand, many knowledgeable blacks and even some whites resented the colonel's methods. Years later, the white intelligence officer of the 1st Battalion, Capt. Gustav Gillert, observed that Champeny's remarks demonstrated the colonel's "misunderstanding of the combat situation and the poor tactical condition of the regiment." They "appalled me and others," he continued, "who had put our anatomies on line over the previous two months and were working hard at motivation and personal leadership." Sgt. Daemon Stewart of the intelligence and reconnaissance platoon recalled that Champeny was one

of the worst officers he encountered during his military career. Rifleman Charlie Lee Jones, who was present for Champeny's speech, observed that many of the men believed the colonel was bluffing and from then on declined to place any trust in him. "If you don't trust officers," he added, "you won't fight for them."[23] On the other hand, the regiment's awards and decorations officer, black 2d Lt. Clinton Moorman, recalled that Champeny was fairly well respected; Zanin considered him a top-notch commander; and Hicks himself remarked that he considered the officer the victim of an ill-advised impulse. "Col. Champeny is a brave and a hard working man," he said. "I had to get out there at 5:30 a.m. to catch him, and he would stay out until 9:00 o'clock [P.M.], but it takes time to take these unfortunate things down."[24]

The 1st Battalion operations officer at the time, black Capt. Richard W. Williams, Jr., was hardly as generous. Implying in sworn testimony before an Eighth Army inspector general that the colonel was a bigot, he gave an example of what he meant. "One time, when I was commanding 'Charlie' Company, I had a position organized and had white and colored NCO's and Negro and ROK troops. Col. Champeny told me to build a wire enclosure around the hill with a six-foot opening, so the colored troops wouldn't run, and if they did run, they would hurt themselves. He also stated in front of many of those people that he would not have a Negro NCO in charge of ROK troops and white troops." Champeny later confirmed in an interview that on 6 September he had indeed ordered double-apron wire fences constructed around the 1st

22 Interv, IG with James L. Hicks, 8 Sep 50, exhibit B–23, in Eighth U.S. Army Korea, Report of Investigation Concerning 24th Infantry Regiment and Negro Soldiers in Combat, 15 Mar 51, boxes 1013–1014 (hereafter cited as Eighth Army Inspector General Investigation), RG 159, WNRC. See also Intervs, MacGarrigle with Barone, 14 Apr 94; Stuart Force, 8 Aug 94; Ltr, John S. Komp to George L. MacGarrigle, 14 May 94, CMH files.

23 Intervs, Bernard L. Muehlbauer with Daemon Stewart, 2 Nov 88; Cash with Gustav J. Gillert, 25 Mar 89; Charlie Lee Jones, 6 Sep 89. The quote from Gillert is in Ltr, Gillert to MacGarrigle, 22 May 95, CMH files. For other negative reactions to Champeny, see Intervs, Muehlbauer with William M. Factory, 2 Nov 88; Charles B. Gregg, 8 Sep 88; MacGarrigle with Roscoe E. Dann, Jr., 24 Mar 94.

24 Intervs, Muehlbauer with Clinton Moorman, 5 Sep 88; MacGarrigle with Zanin, 27 Oct 93; IG with Hicks, 8 Sep 50, exhibit B–23, Eighth Army Inspector General Investigation. For generally favorable opinions of Champeny, see Intervs, MacGarrigle with Sam J. Adams, Jr., 15 and 17 Jun 94; Charles E. Green, 16 Jun 94; Owen Carter, 21 and 24 Jun 94; Komp, 5 May and 1 Jun 94.

Battalion to "impress upon the men . . . that if they would remain in their fox holes, they would not get hurt."[25]

Whatever Champeny's intentions, his approach did nothing to restrain those among the unit's white officers who were inclined to racial prejudice. According to Williams, several instances occurred during the weeks that followed, while intense combat raged, in which those individuals ridiculed the men of the regiment instead of encouraging them. "This caused the troops to lose confidence in themselves," Williams said. "Then they lost all hope."[26]

During the days following Champeny's arrival, General Walker concentrated his attention on the region between Chinju and Masan and the enemy's *6th Division*. Since U.S. forces were stronger in that area than anywhere else on the Pusan Perimeter, he decided to counterattack and gave the task to the 25th Division. Designated Task Force Kean, the effort would disrupt the enemy's advance, relieve pressure on U.S. and South Korean positions in the area, and buy time for American forces to regroup and continue their buildup.[27] (*Map 7*)

There were three roads that connected Chinju with Masan. The main route, about twenty-five miles long, ran in a southeasterly direction from Chinju through the town of Muchon-ni to the coast. There it turned eastward to pass through the town of Chindong-ni before entering Masan. The second route, making a wide sweep to the south, stretched 6 miles from Chinju to the town of Sach'on. Turning southeast at that point and running 16 miles to the town of Kosong, it then swung northeast toward Chindong-ni and Masan, covering a distance of some fifteen miles more. A third route followed the main road from Chinju to Much'on-ni, but after that it veered to the north some six miles through a long, narrow pass to the town of Saga-ri. Turning east, it then covered a final 4 miles into Masan.[28]

Low hills interspersed with rice paddies typified the entire area, but there were two significant mountain barriers. One, traversed by a low pass, was located 7 miles to the east of Chinju on the road to Masan through Saga-ri. The other, a larger and more mountainous obstacle, 2,400-foot-high Sobuk-san, stood 12 miles east of Chinju above the heavily traveled road that ran through Much'on-ni and Chindong-ni to Masan. The land farther to the south along the coastal road through Sach'on was lower but remained rugged. The weather at that time of year was troublesome. By 7 August, when Task Force Kean began, the rain in the area had ceased but scorching heat had become the rule. The temperature often rose to 105° during the day, and on some occasions it reached 120° in midafternoon.[29]

The plan for Task Force Kean envisioned a three-pronged attack. Fisher's 35th Infantry would follow the northern route through Saga-ri to Chinju while the 5th RCT took the route through Chindong-ni to Much'on-ni. At a point where the roads the two regiments were following converged, near Much'on-ni, the 5th and 35th would join and push together through a pass that overlooked Chinju. The 5th U.S. Marine regiment would meanwhile advance from the south along the road through Kosong and Sach'on. The 24th Infantry was to operate in the rear of the attack, especially in the region around Sobuk-san, clearing enemy units and infiltrators who managed to elude the main assault. The regiment was also to secure a six-mile-long, north-south road that ran to the west of Masan from Chindong-ni through Haman to Saga-ri. A battalion of South Korean marines and a second battalion of South Korean army troops were

25 Interv, IG with Maj Richard W. Williams, Jr., 10 Feb 51, exhibit B–109, in General Headquarters, Far East Command, Report of Investigation Regarding Alleged Irregularities in the Administration of Military Justice in the 25th Infantry Division, 27 Mar 51, boxes 1013–1014 (hereafter cited as Far East Command Inspector General Investigation), RG 159, WNRC. Williams commanded Company C briefly in late August and early September after Captain Corcoran left the unit. Champeny's comment is in Interv, IG with Col Arthur S. Champeny, 28 Sep 50, exhibit B–22, Eighth Army Inspector General Investigation.

26 Ibid.

27 Barth, Tropic Lightning and Taro Leaf in Korea, n.d., p. 15. See also Appleman, *South to the Naktong, North to the Yalu*, pp. 266–67.

28 Appleman, *South to the Naktong, North to the Yalu*, p. 268.

29 Ibid., p. 269. See Map, Korea, 1:50,000, series L751, AMS 1950, sheets 6819 I, 6819 II, 6819 III, 6819 IV.

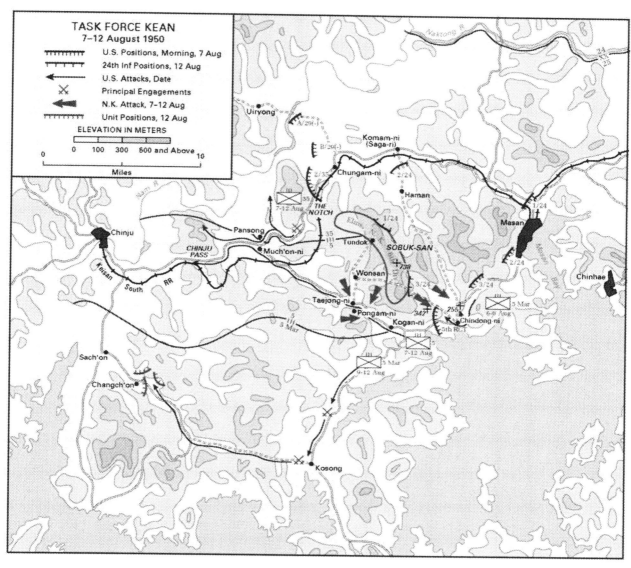

Map 7

attached to the 24th for a time, but they were withdrawn after only a few days.[30]

The operation began on 7 August with elements of the 35th Infantry striking west toward Chinju. They immediately encountered an estimated five hundred enemy troops but, after a hard fight lasting more than five hours, destroyed much of that force. On the following day, the regiment advanced to the high ground above Much'on-ni and dug in to await the arrival of the 5th. "The morale of the men was high," General Barth, who arrived at the scene shortly after the battle, later commented, "and they seemed eager to press on."[31]

---

[30] 25th Inf Div Opns Order 8, 6 Aug 50, and WD, 25th Inf Div, 6 Aug 50, pp. 6–7, both in box 3748, RG 407, WNRC; WD, 24th Inf Rgt, 1–31 Aug 50, p. 9.

[31] WD, 25th Inf Div, 7–8 Aug 50, box 3748, RG 407, WNRC; Barth, Tropic Lightning and Taro Leaf in Korea, n.d.,

The 5th Infantry was less fortunate. When Task Force Kean began, the enemy's *6th Division* was continuing its advance to the east and had begun to filter troops onto the ridge lines dominating the road the regiment would use in its westward thrust toward Chinju. As a result, when the operation commenced on the morning of 7 August, the unit's 1st Battalion at first encountered little opposition when it moved out along the road. The 2d, echeloned to the right along enemy-occupied high ground, came under attack. In the intense fighting that followed over the next two days, the enemy attempted to cut the 25th Division's supply line out of Chindong-ni while the 5th, assisted by the 5th Marines, sought to take control of rocky outcroppings to the northeast of the town that dominated the terrain in that entire area. The enemy yielded those positions only on 9 August, after two days of heavy pounding by American artillery, tanks, air strikes, and mortars. During one 36-hour period, Batteries B and C of the 159th Field Artillery Battalion fired 1,600 rounds in support of the operation.[32]

The 24th Infantry for its part took charge of a territory that included virtually everything of any importance between the 35th Infantry's line of attack along the Saga-ri–Chinju road and the route which the 5th Infantry was supposed to follow between Chindong-ni and Chinju. In the process, the 1st Battalion moved to Pup'yong-ni, a village two and one-half miles north of Chindong-ni. Meanwhile, the 2d Battalion moved south to relieve a Marine unit fighting on the Masan–Chindong-ni road, and the 3d Battalion, which had earlier relocated from Haman to a position in the hills just north of Chindong-ni, was ordered back to Haman. Unable to assume its new role because the marines were in heavy contact

The men of Battery A, 159th Field Artillery Battalion, fire a 105-mm. howitzer.

with the enemy, the 2d Battalion held up overnight with the 3d Battalion.[33]

The next morning, 8 August, the 2d and 3d Battalions were in the process of moving out when the enemy launched an attack from the ridge and hillside that the 3d Battalion had just vacated. Recognizing that the enemy's new position threatened communications between Haman and Chindong-ni, General Kean at that time canceled the 3d Battalion's move north and ordered the unit to drive the enemy from the hill. That done, the unit was to screen the 25th Division's supply lines in that area from further enemy attack.[34]

Under the temporary command of the regimental executive officer, Lt. Col. Paul F. Roberts, because Pierce had been evacuated for his wounds,

---

p. 16. See also WDs, 35th Inf Rgt, 7–8 Aug 50, and 2d Bn, 35th Inf Rgt, 7–8 Aug 50, both in box 3750, RG 407, WNRC.

[32] WD, 25th Inf Div, 7–9 Aug 50, box 3748, RG 407, WNRC; WD, 159th FA Bn, 1–31 Aug 50, pp. 2–3; WD, 25th Recon Co, 25th Inf Div, Jul 50, p. 1, box 3751, RG 407, WNRC. See also Lynn Montross and Nicholas A. Canzona, *The Pusan Perimeter* (Washington, D.C.: HQ, U.S. Marine Corps, 1954), pp. 103–22.

[33] The regimental war diary puts the 1st Battalion north of Chung-ni. See WD, 24th Inf Rgt, 1–31 Aug 50, p. 8. The battalion's war diary says the unit was to patrol in the vicinity of Pup'yong-ni, where the 2d and 3d Battalions were also located. See WD, 1st Bn, 24th Inf Rgt, 1–31 Aug 50, p. 5, box 3750, RG 407, WNRC. The battalion's version is followed here. WD, 159th FA Bn, 1–31 Aug 50, p. 3; WD, 3d Bn, 24th Inf Rgt, 1–31 Aug 50, pp. 2–3.

[34] Ibid.

the battalion launched the attack during the after-noon but made little headway. Instead, old patterns reasserted themselves. The men moved forward reluctantly, the battalion's white executive officer, Maj. Theodore J. Cook recalled, and some began to straggle. Those who remained "would go for a few yards and get behind cover, and then it was next to impossible to get them to go forward again." When the battalion came within 100 yards of the top of the hill, misdirected fire from friendly planes added to the unit's agony, scattering many of the men who had thus far stood their ground and fought.[35]

At dark, the hill was still in enemy hands, and the 3d Battalion had no choice but to withdraw. That day and overnight, regimental and battalion officers scoured rear areas for stragglers, apprehending well over a hundred. They sent some forward with sup-plies for the men who had remained at their posts, but by the time those groups arrived at their desti-nations, many of their members had once more dis-appeared. Colonel Champeny spoke to some of the stragglers, perhaps in another attempt to instill fight-ing spirit. His words went unrecorded.[36]

At the time, the white regimental operations officer, Maj. Owen Carter, remarked that officers within the regiment were forced to expose them-selves so regularly to enemy fire to keep their men moving that it had become possible on some occa-sions to predict who the next casualty would be. Something of the sort happened on the hill. Observing a nearly exhausted second lieutenant from Company K moving his men along, General Kean remarked to the 3d Battalion's operations offi-cer, Captain Zanin, that the officer would probably never make it. Kean was right. After the air strike, the officer, white 2d Lt. William H. Hall, collected six of his men and led them in a savage charge that almost succeeded in gaining the top of the hill

before an enemy counterattack threw it back. Observing that his battalion was withdrawing, Hall then laid down covering fire until he was killed.[37]

The battalion continued its attack the next morning, but encountered little opposition. Attaining its objective by 1100, it began to police the position and to dig in for the night. During the patrolling that followed, Company I captured six enemy prisoners and counted ten enemy dead from the day before. The weather was so hot that more American casualties resulted from the heat that day than from combat.[38]

While the 3d Battalion was fighting for the hill near Chindong-ni, the 1st and 2d Battalions were starting their own operations. On the morning of 10 August, after patrolling for two days without making any contact with the enemy, the 1st Battalion received orders to move by foot along the ridge lines leading to Haman to engage North Korean units believed to be operating in the area. It sighted the enemy but made no contact. At 1500 it came under long-range enemy small-arms fire and halted. Meanwhile, the 2d Battalion relieved the marines operating near Chindong-ni. As the 5th Infantry again began to move west along the road to Much'on-ni to link up with the 35th, the 2d Battalion patrolled to the rear, seeking out pockets of enemy bypassed in the advance. On that day, Lt. Col. George R. Cole took command of the battal-ion, allowing Major Donaho to return to his posi-tion as the unit's executive officer. A West Pointer, Cole had earned a Silver Star during World War II and had served in combat as a battalion comman-der during the final three months of the conflict.[39]

The 1st Battalion's move north faltered on 11 August when the unit came up against an enemy force of unknown size near Haman. Since those troops appeared to be withdrawing to the west,

[35] WD, 3d Bn, 24th Inf Rgt, 1–31 Aug 50, pp. 2–3. Quote from Interv, IG with Maj Theodore J. Cook, Exec Ofcr, 3d Bn, 24th Inf Rgt, 23 Aug 50, exhibit 10, Kean Letter file. Intervs, IG with Maj Owen H. Carter, 25 Aug 50, exhibit 14, Kean Letter file; MacGarrigle with Zanin, 27 Oct 93; Tittel, 23 May 94. See also EUSAK GO 54, 6 Feb 51, Distinguished Service Cross Citation for 2d Lt William H. Hall; William Hall Award file, box 161, RG 338, WNRC.
[36] Ibid.
[37] Ibid.
[38] WD, 3d Bn, 24th Inf Rgt, 1–31 Aug 50, p. 3.
[39] WD, 1st Bn, 24th Inf Rgt, 1–31 Aug 50, pp. 5–6; WD, 2d Bn, 24th Inf Rgt, 1–31 Aug 50, pp. 4–5, box 3750, RG 407, WNRC. Cole's career is described in U.S. Military Academy, Assembly, Winter 71, p. 129. See also Cullum, Biographical Register of the Officers and Graduates of the United States Military Academy, vol. IX, item 934.

Communist-led North Koreans hid in this old gold mine in Tundok, which was subsequently captured by the 24th Infantry.

Colonel Miller received orders to concentrate on clearing Tundok, a mining village on the western slopes of P'il-bong Mountain, about four miles to the southwest of Haman. As part of that operation, Company C, assisted by radio vehicles and drivers provided by the artillery liaison officer for the battalion, received instructions to flank the enemy by road from the north. The convoy was to proceed north through Haman to Saga-ri, turn west along the road the 35th Infantry had taken in its drive toward Much'on-ni, and then swing back at Chungam-ni on a byway that wound into the mountains toward Tundok. Unknown to the Americans until later, the enemy was turning the area into a major entrepot. Honeycombed with

mine shafts virtually immune to American artillery and air strikes, it provided excellent concealment for his storehouse and command facilities. He had no intention of giving it up.[40]

During the course of the afternoon Colonel Miller's men succeeded in occupying two ridges between Mount P'il-bong and Tundok, but by nightfall, despite air strikes that leveled Tundok and produced a large secondary explosion, the 1st

---

[40] WD, 1st Bn, 24th Inf Rgt, 1–31 Aug 50, p. 6; WD, 24th Inf Rgt, 1–31 Aug 50, p. 10; WD, 159th FA Bn, Aug 50, p. 5. The dates in the war diary for the 159th are wrong, but there is no doubt that the action the chronicle describes corresponds to the one mentioned in the battalion and regimental diaries. See also Interv, Bowers with Edward H. Skiffington, 14 Apr 94.

Battalion failed to gain the top of a third ridge immediately overlooking the town.[41] Meanwhile, accompanied by two tanks, Company C, under Capt. Laurence Corcoran, worked its way down the road from Chungam-ni. About 1700, rifleman Albert Griffin recalled, "A recon jeep with a Lt. White [actually 1st Lt. Donald LaBlanc] asked for volunteers to go ahead into the mountains. Several soldiers went with the jeep including Jesse Hatter. . . . who went because he could ride. After the jeep left they heard gunfire. Sergeant Williams [an acting platoon leader] persuaded [Captain] Corcoran to see what had happened. The company got ambushed trying to get the recon people out."[42] One tank was in the front while the second held up at the rear, Cpl. William Cobb remembered. The bulk of the company was in the middle. "They moved forward until the tank came to a bridge that wouldn't bear its weight. The enemy attacked and knocked out the rear tank. . . . The enemy must have watched them move forward all day."[43]

Caught in the initial ambush, LaBlanc had been severely wounded and was playing dead. When an opportunity arose, he managed to escape and attempted to warn the approaching company, but to no avail. In the confusion that followed, some of the men threw down their weapons and ran. A number of officers and sergeants attempted to rally the troops, and, when that failed, covered their men's withdrawal with fire. One of them, white 1st Lt. Ralph S. Gustin, was killed in the process. White Captain Gillert described the scene: "An enemy force of about a platoon ambushed Company C. Many of the troops panicked. What had been a company when the firing started had all but 'evaporated.' All sorts of weapons and equipment were left behind." Gillert believed that "this action had a devastating effect on Corcoran, who must have realized what he thought to be the 'good' unit had suddenly collapsed and fled."[44] In the

end, Company C came out of the engagement badly shaken and had to be "re-equipped and reorganized" when it rejoined its battalion. The incident further confirmed Champeny's already low opinion of the regiment.[45]

The next morning, 12 August, with the enemy still holding out against the 1st Battalion, Champeny brought up the 2d Battalion to strengthen the attacking force. Moving along the ridge lines overlooking the road that Company C had followed the day before, the battalion attacked southward toward the area where the unit had come to grief.[46]

Fighting began in earnest on the morning of the thirteenth, when Company G of the 2d Battalion encountered a well-entrenched and -camouflaged enemy force and began to receive heavy fire. Company F also began to take fire, but the unit held in place because its commander, black Capt. Roger Walden, determined that it would not be able to move forward until Company G had secured the high ground from which the enemy was firing. By that time, casualties were beginning to flow to the rear from Company G's position along with a large number of stragglers, many of whom asserted that they were merely accompanying the wounded. There were moments of heroism. A medic, the All-Army Heavyweight Boxing Champion for 1949, Cpl. Levi Jackson, for one, lost his life while using his own body to shield two of the wounded from enemy fire.[47]

[41] WD, 1st Bn, 24th Inf Rgt, 1–31 Aug 50, pp. 6–7; WD, 159th FA Bn, 1–31 Aug 50, pp. 5–6.

[42] Interv, Cash with Albert Griffin, Jr., 5 Oct 88.

[43] Interv, Timothy Rainey with William Cobb, 4 Dec 89.

[44] Quote from Interv, MacGarrigle with Gillert, 4 May 94. Distinguished Service Cross Award file for 1st Lt Ralph S.

Gustin, box 153, RG 338, WNRC; Silver Star Award file for 2d Lt Donald E. LaBlanc, box 154, RG 338, WNRC; 25th Inf Div GO 177, 22 Sep 50, Award of Silver Star to M Sgt Howard Williams; 25th Inf Div GO 203, 27 Sep 50, Award of Bronze Star to 1st Lt William Blackburn. See also Intervs, MacGarrigle with Komp, 5 May and 1 Jun 94; Donald E. LaBlanc, 1 Mar 94; Bowers with LaBlanc, 28 Feb 94.

[45] WD, 1st Bn, 24th Inf Rgt, Aug 50, p. 7; Interv, IG with Champeny, 28 Sep 50, exhibit B–22, Eighth Army Inspector General Investigation. See also Intervs, MacGarrigle with Komp, 5 May and 1 Jun 94. Members of the 24th wounded in the action appeared at the aid station of the 1st Battalion, 29th Infantry. See S–2/S–3 Journal, 1st Bn, 29th Inf Rgt, 11 Aug 50, item 3, box 3750, RG 407, WNRC.

[46] WD, 1st Bn, 24th Inf Rgt, 1–31 Aug 50, pp. 6–7; WD, 24th Inf Rgt, 1–31 Aug 50, p. 11.

[47] WD, 2d Bn, 24th Inf Rgt, 1–31 Aug 50, p. 6. Jackson received the Distinguished Service Cross. See EUSAK GO 77,

By the end of the day, according to Eighth Army investigators, fewer than seventeen men from Company G remained in position. The artillery liaison officer for the 2d Battalion, white Capt. William M. Kennedy, would later allege, however, that none held. "I talked to [1st] Lt. [Joseph] O'Neil, G Company commander, and he told me that the men ran off and left him on the hill alone. He said he pleaded with them to stay, but they left him. He apparently was the last man off the hill as he was coming from that direction when I saw him."[48] Fighting continued for another day, but the battalion's efforts were hampered by rain and poor visibility. On 15 August Champeny ordered the two battalions to break contact with the enemy and to form a defensive line north of Sobuk-san.[49]

According to the black commander of the 77th Engineer Combat Company, Capt. Charles Bussey, who often accompanied units of the 24th Infantry into combat, some of those who straggled did so because they were fed up with their circumstances. The troops "were very bitter," he said. "They felt they were stupid to risk their lives unduly because when they got home they didn't have the rewards citizenship should have provided . . . such as voting. This was another thing we [officers] had to deal with."[50]

Other soldiers, Bussey continued, had been intimidated. The enemy had made it a point to terrify his opponents, and word flowed through the ranks about how the North Koreans tortured and

killed captured Americans. A number of soldiers had personal experiences to tell. According to Cpl. Joel T. Ward, one young rifleman had been tied between a truck and a tree and then torn in two when the vehicle drove off. On another occasion, according to Pvt. Jerry Johnson, both white and black American captives were burned alive in a bonfire within full view of American patrols. Both times, the heart-rending screams of the victims were audible to their comrades, who inevitably resolved not to be captured themselves.[51] In response, many Americans in frontline units established their own, unofficial policy of no quarter and brought back captives only when ordered to do so. Others allowed their fears to predominate and ran to the rear whenever combat was imminent and they could find an opening.[52]

Whatever the men's concerns, General Kean decided that straggling had been tolerated for so long within the 24th that it had become almost routine. Resolving to take action, he distributed a letter on 9 August to all units within the division directing commanders to take action to punish men guilty of misconduct before the enemy. Where White had disciplined only a few soldiers for straggling on the grounds that the fast-moving situation precluded the proper gathering of evidence, Champeny had instructions to prosecute all who left their positions without permission.[53]

One week after Kean issued the letter, on 15 August, he appointed an infantry officer, Capt. Merwin J. Camp, to begin an investigation of the 24th to determine the names of men worthy of punitive action. Because of the episode at Tundok, Company G became Camp's initial target. The effort to gather evidence was difficult, in part because officers in the field had never bothered to record the names of those who had strayed or received warnings. In addition, according to Camp, a code of silence prevailed, with those men who had stood their ground fearing retaliation if they gave testi-

---

23 Sep 50. See also 25th Inf Div GOs 172, 21 Sep 50, and 276, 1 Nov 50, for other examples of heroism in Company G on 13 August.

[48] The investigators' findings are in Statement of Capt Merwin J. Camp, 9 Sep 50, Reference 24th Infantry Regiment, exhibit D–21, Eighth Army Inspector General Investigation. But see Interv, IG with Capt William M. Kennedy, 25 Aug 50, exhibit 15, Kean Letter file. O'Neil is identified as Company G's commander. Unit rosters for July and September 1950 place him in Company H. See Officer Roster, 24th Inf Rgt, 18 Sep 50, exhibit D–13, Eighth Army Inspector General Investigation.

[49] WD, 2d Bn, 24th Inf Rgt, 1–31 Aug 50, p. 6. See also Interv, IG with Capt James O. Gardner, 24 Aug 50, exhibit 24, Kean Letter file. Gardner alleges Company E also collapsed with many stragglers, but the war diary is silent on the issue. Gardner was possibly describing the Company G action.

[50] Interv, Cash with Charles Bussey, 6 Jan 89.

[51] Ibid. See also Intervs, Cash with Joel T. Ward, 21 Jul 88; Jerry Johnson, 23 Sep 88; Theodore R. Eldridge, Jr., 26 Aug 88.

[52] Intervs, Cash with Hollis Reese, 24 Sep 88; Floyd B. Williams, 6 Aug 88; Robert H. Yancy, 21 Jan 89.

[53] The letter is summarized in WD, 24th Inf Rgt, 8 Aug 50, box 3750, RG 407, WNRC.

mony against those who had run. By 9 September, as a result, only a relative few had been charged.[54] Court-martial was a last resort, Kean would later assert, against men who were well aware of the consequences of their deeds but had flagrantly chosen to ignore their responsibilities. The situation confronting the 25th Division was grave, he added. The effectiveness of the 24th Infantry as a fighting force was at stake.[55]

While the 1st and 2d Battalions were moving to Tundok and beginning their attempt to take the town, changes were occurring within the 3d Battalion. On 9 August the unit had received word that it had a new commander, Lt. Col. John T. Corley, a West Point graduate who had commanded battalions in North Africa and Europe during World War II. A self-assured Irishman who spoke "Brooklynese" out of the side of his mouth, he had risen from first lieutenant to lieutenant colonel in just three years during World War II and numbered among his decorations for valor not only five awards of the Silver Star, but also the Distinguished Service Cross. Although Corley joined the battalion on 9 August, he apparently took formal command on the twelfth. During the interim, he exercised authority indirectly, with Colonel Roberts retaining nominal full control.[56]

Over the months that followed, Corley became very popular with his men. Although there were indications that he had his prejudices—black Capt. Charles Bussey would later assert that the officer had told him he had downgraded an award to a Silver Star because he did not want smart black officers to do well—almost all of the officers and enlisted men who observed Corley closely liked him. As black 2d Lt. Albert Brooks observed, he seemed "a man of culture and human feeling." His driver, enlisted man Sylvester Davis, who was with him often and in a position to know, considered him unprejudiced. Black 1st Lt. Gorham Black described him as even tempered and unbiased. Pfc. Floyd B. Williams asserted that men in combat looked at him and drew strength. Sgt. Calvin Bryant had even seen the officer give a cold enlisted man his field jacket.[57]

Corley received his first mission at 0130 on the tenth. Champeny instructed him to move his battalion northwest from Pup'yong-ni to the town of Wonsan, some three miles to the south of Tundok on the same road where Company C would shortly come to grief. During the advance that followed, the main body of the battalion traversed another rough mountain road that ran directly to Wonsan from Chindong-ni. Because vehicles found the rugged terrain impassable, Corley took his command post along the more-traveled southerly route that the 5th Infantry was following in its attack toward Chinju, the Chindong-ni–Much'on-ni road. Arriving about one mile south of Wonsan, at 1730 that evening, he decided the position was too exposed for his command post and backtracked

[54] Statement of Camp, 9 Sep 50, Reference 24th Infantry Regiment, exhibit D–21, Eighth Army Inspector General Investigation. Black newspaperman Frank Whisonant later labeled Camp a racist. See Frank Whisonant, untitled newspaper clipping, *Pittsburgh Courier*, 25 Nov 50.

[55] Interv, IG with Maj Gen William B. Kean, 14 Feb 51, exhibit B–135, Far East Command Inspector General Investigation.

[56] DA Form 66, Personnel Record for John T. Corley, CMH files. See also Obituary, Brig Gen John T. Corley, U.S. Military Academy, *Assembly*, Sep 84, p. 143. Joseph Baranowski mentioned Corley's manner and distinctive accent. See Interv, MacGarrigle with Baranowski, 24 Aug 94. Corley mentioned the lag between his assignment and his formal assumption of command in an interview with a 25th Division inspector general. He asserted in the interview that Roberts remained in charge for twenty-four hours after his arrival. The battalion's war diary, however, asserts that Roberts relinquished command. Since some overlap is common during changes of command in military units, the account that follows places both Roberts and Corley in the area if not always at the scene of the fighting. See Interv, IG with Lt Col John T. Corley, 26 Aug 50, exhibit 2, Kean Letter file; WD, 3d Bn, 24th Inf Rgt, 1–31 Aug 50, p. 3.

[57] Intervs, Cash with Charles Bussey, 6 Jan 89; Albert Brooks, 1 Nov 89; Sylvester Davis, 19 Sep 89; Gorham L. Black, Jr., 12 Mar 89; Floyd B. Williams, 6 Aug 88; Muehlbauer with Calvin Bryant, 1 Mar 89. Black Chaplain Gray Johnson, who was in a position to know, also asserted that Corley was not a racist. See Interv, Cash with Gray Johnson, 23 Mar 89. An Air Force officer who worked closely with Corley as a forward observer, Edwin W. Robertson, asserted that Bussey's story was entirely out of character for Corley. See Interv, Cash with Edwin W. Robertson, 29 Mar 89. White 2d Lt. Ray Koenig complained just as vehemently as Bussey that white officers in the 24th had problems with decorations because of "reverse discrimination." See Interv, Muehlbauer with Ray Koenig, 20 Mar 89. See Chapter 7, p. 174, for another episode that calls Corley's racial objectivity into question.

about a mile to Yongch'on-ni, where he set up for the night with Battery B of the 159th Field Artillery Battalion and the 3d Platoon of the 24th Infantry's heavy mortar company.[58]

At 0300 on 11 August an unknown number of enemy armed with automatic weapons and antitank guns attacked the position. Three vehicles loaded with ammunition and a fourth laden with gasoline went up in flames almost immediately. Other vehicles also caught fire, including two radio trucks used to control air strikes, causing a conflagration that lit up the surrounding area. The Americans responded quickly. Four drivers courageously drove their vehicles, some of them loaded with ammunition, away from the explosions, burning gasoline, and small-arms fire, and 1st Lt. Paul F. Mauricio, a Filipino, was killed silencing a machine gun. At dawn the enemy could be seen on the adjacent hills, and howitzers began shelling the North Korean positions with point-blank fire. It took seven hours, but by 1030 the defenders had beaten off the attack. Shortly thereafter, Corley's command post group redeployed to Taep'yong-ni, one and one-half miles northwest of Chindong-ni, near where the rest of the battalion was going into action.[59]

While Corley and his command post were still under attack, the main body of the 3d Battalion had been attempting to reach its objective at Wonsan. That morning, about two and one-half miles from the town, the unit came under fire and halted. The battalion's white operations officer, Captain Zanin, coordinated its response. Zanin recalled later that he immediately attempted to keep the companies moving forward to gain the crest of a nearby ridge. From there he would be able to direct heavy fire upon the enemy's positions. Over the next three hours, however, in the face of an estimated two companies of enemy but suffering only six rounds

of mortar fire and at most ten casualties, Companies K and L dwindled from a fighting strength of over a hundred men each to about fifty. Company I retained most of its strength because it was occupying a flanking position and remained relatively uninvolved in the attack. At noon on the next day, according to Corley, Company L would number at best twenty effectives and Company K thirty-five. Once again, many of the stragglers left their positions on the excuse that they were accompanying wounded men to the rear.[60]

Unable to take its objective, the battalion was ordered to hold in place overnight and to resume the attack the next day, 12 August. Zanin followed instructions, but the unit again made little progress. With snipers all around, the troops kept low and declined to move. In the end, Zanin was cut down attempting to get the troops to advance. Turning his radio and map over to a lieutenant who he said seemed virtually immobilized, the captain stumbled to the rear alone. Roberts found him and saw to it that he reached the battalion aid station. He later received the Distinguished Service Cross for his actions and fortitude.[61]

---

[58] WD, 3d Bn, 24th Inf Rgt, 1–31 Aug 50, p. 3; WD, 159th FA Bn, Aug 50, p. 4. The spelling of Wonsan differs between sources; the one used here is from Map, Korea, 1:50,000, series L751, AMS 1950, sheet 6819 II.

[59] WD, 3d Bn, 24th Inf Rgt, 1–31 Aug 50, pp. 3–4, box 3750, RG 407, WNRC; WD, 159th FA Bn, Aug 50, pp. 3–4. For awards, see 25th Inf Div GOs 169, 19 Sep 50; 205, 27 Sep 50; 264, 30 Oct 50; and 319, 11 Nov 50.

[60] Since the battalion war diary is less than candid on the subject, this treatment is based upon Intervs, MacGarrigle with Zanin, 27 Oct 93; IG with Corley, 26 Aug 50, exhibit 2, Kean Letter file. Some details can also be gleaned from the recommendation for the Distinguished Service Cross that Zanin later received. See in particular the Statements of 2d Lt Reginald J. Sapenter, 2d Lt Roscoe E. Dann, Jr., and 1st Lt Vernon C. Dailey, all for 4 Nov 50, attachments to Decorations and Awards Action Sheet, John B. Zanin, 27 Dec 50, Awards Branch, PERSCOM. In his interview, Corley speaks as if he was present during the action, using such phrases as "my attack." Zanin, however, does not mention him, and Corley was clearly occupied for at least part of the time with the problems that accompanied the enemy's attack on his command post. Where he was and what he was doing for the rest of the time remains unclear. Roberts' role in the action is also vague but he appears to have been nearby, perhaps in a command post somewhat to the rear.

[61] Intervs, MacGarrigle with Zanin, 27 Oct 93; Dann, 24 Mar 94; Tittel, 20 Apr 94; IG with Corley, 26 Aug 50, exhibit 2, Kean Letter file. See also WD, 24th Inf Rgt, 1–31 Aug 50, p. 11. First Lieutenant Vernon Dailey, commander of Company I, asserts that his unit in fact progressed for 800 yards before bogging down, and one of his platoon leaders supports him. Company I, however, was making a flanking maneuver. This account follows Zanin's recollection, which states that the bulk of the battalion made no progress. Statements of Company K platoon leaders support his assertion. See Statements of 1st Lt

The episode was a sorry revelation for Corley, who told investigators two weeks after the event that during the action a powerful force of 550 men had dribbled away to 260, a number that included the members of Company I, which saw little combat, and rear-area support troops. Although the men who stayed in position had done "all that could be expected of any soldier," Corley continued, leadership in the battalion's squads and platoons was almost nonexistent. "In the main, . . . Company C.O.'s had to control their units by working directly with platoon leaders, [and] the chain of command stopped at company level." As a remedy, Corley could only suggest that the 25th Division double the number of officers in the battalion. "One officer must lead," he said, "and the other must drive."[62]

While Corley's unit was suffering its ordeal, the 5th Infantry to the southwest was also experiencing serious difficulties. Over the preceding week, the unit had worked its way west toward its rendezvous with the 35th Infantry at Much'on-ni. By 11 August its lead battalion had reached that goal, and the other two had advanced to a point just beyond Taejong-ni, where the road to Wonsan and Tundok connected with the main route the regiment was following. Shortly before midnight that evening, after failing in an attack the night before that had included the assault on Corley's command post at Yongch'on-ni, an estimated two enemy battalions launched a fierce assault against the rearmost elements of the 5th Infantry. In the fight that ensued, the unit's 1st Battalion suffered heavy losses but the two artillery battalions supporting the operation were virtually annihilated, losing all of their guns and over 50 percent of their people. The regiment's supply train, strung out in a long column that extended through Taejong-ni to a pass above it, also came under heavy fire, and many of its vehicles were destroyed. By 0800 the next day, the enemy was in firm possession of Taejong-ni and its surroundings and had cut off the 5th from Chindong-ni.[63]

Appalled at the disaster, General Kean would wait three days until the regiment had reassembled but would then relieve its commander. In the meantime, while the smoke was still rising at Taejong-ni and the remnants of the 5th were continuing their move to the west, the commander of the 25th Division's artillery, General Barth, received instructions to retrieve as many of the 5th's lost guns and missing soldiers as he could. To that end, Barth gained control of two battalions of marines and Corley's 3d Battalion. The 2d Battalion of the 24th also received instructions to move south, but at that time it was still heavily engaged near Tundok.[64]

For a time it seemed as though Corley's force might make the difference in Barth's counterattack. It was already fighting in the mountains above Taejong-ni and seemed well positioned to strike the enemy from the flank and rear. That, however, was not to be. By late afternoon on 12 August, Barth noted in a postwar memoir, "time was running out and it was . . . apparent from . . . reports [by air observers] that the guns were in enemy hands and only a handful of survivors remained. . . . The one hope was for a successful attack by the 3d Battalion of the 24th, but Corley reported to me about four o'clock that his battalion had been driven back and was badly scattered." Barth's marines began their attack at first light the next morning, after abandoning what had been a successful assault along the far south road through Kosong. They reached the hills above Taejong-ni that afternoon but withdrew when they received orders to move immediately to another sector of the Pusan Perimeter. At that time, they reported that the town was in enemy

Vernon C. Dailey, 4 Nov 50, attachments to Decorations and Awards Action Sheet, John B. Zanin, 27 Dec 50; Interv, MacGarrigle with Sapenter, 14 Mar 94.

[62] Interv, IG with Corley, 26 Aug 50, exhibit 2, Kean Letter file.

[63] Barth, Tropic Lightning and Taro Leaf in Korea, n.d., p. 20. See also WD, 24th Inf Rgt, 12 Aug 50, box 3750, RG 407, WNRC; WD, 90th FA Bn, Aug 50, box 3751, RG 407, WNRC; Intervs, MacGarrigle with D. Randall Beirne, 19 Aug 93; Cash with Rennie M. Cory, 29 Aug 89. Only fragments of the records for the 5th Infantry regiment for this period have survived.

[64] Ibid. The 2d Battalion's orders are mentioned in WD, 24th Inf Rgt, 12 Aug 50.

hands and that none of the American missing could be seen.[65]

A final footnote to the story came one month later, when American forces recaptured Taejong-ni, or "Bloody Gulch" as it later came to be called. Entering the town, they discovered that many of the artillerymen had gone out fighting. There were shell casings everywhere along with many bodies, and the tubes of the artillery pieces had rounds lodged in them, rendering them inoperable. In the end, some of the men had surrendered. The searchers found the decaying remains of fifty-five Americans in a house and on a nearby hill, all executed with their hands tied securely behind their backs.[66]

The 25th Division began to pull back Task Force Kean shortly after the debacle at Bloody Gulch. General Kean's force, primarily through the efforts of the marines and the 35th Infantry, had thrown the enemy at least briefly onto the defensive and had exacted a heavy toll on the *6th North Korean Division*.[67] The marines had displayed consistent aggressiveness and unit cohesion, an indication of the soundness of the prewar training they had received. Colonel Fisher's 35th Infantry demonstrated that it likewise had become a reliable, combat-experienced unit. The defeat of Company F at Hamch'ang was in the past. The confidence-building successes of the companies that had fought with Michaelis' 27th Infantry and that had formed the line to cover the retreat at Sangju were what the men remembered.

The same could not be said for Kean's other two regiments. In its initial combat the 5th Infantry had showed many of the same weaknesses as the other regiments from Japan in their first battles.

Deploying from Hawaii with three battalions composed of a few noninfantry fillers but many combat veterans, the unit failed primarily because of its senior leaders, whom a platoon leader, 1st Lt. D. Randall Beirne, described as "armchair officers." Morale was affected by the lack of success, and it was obvious to Beirne that some company commanders and field grade officers had to be replaced. General Kean agreed, beginning the process by relieving the regimental commander.[68]

The 24th Infantry, for its part, was unique. Although hardly a green, inexperienced unit facing its first combat, it continued on the whole to perform as one. With minor exceptions, it experienced no successes, only a string of failures. Some of its problems could be attributed to poor and careless leadership, but in other cases the heroic actions of commissioned and noncommissioned officers failed to move the troops forward. Even though a number of officers resorted to forcing soldiers to advance at gunpoint, the straggling that had begun at Sangju continued unabated.[69]

The wastage among leaders continued to mount. On 13 August, when Company G fell apart on the ridges above Tundok, there were only two officers in the company, both lieutenants. One had been with the unit for two days, the other for five. In Corley's battalion, Company L had lost all of the officers who had deployed with the unit and had gone through five company commanders by 11 August, when it dwindled to almost nothing.[70] Officer replacements continued to arrive, several with combat experience and solid reputations for tactical expertise. But a number, such as the new regimental commander, brought preconceived notions about blacks and a bluntness that did little to settle the men. Overall, as the units of Task Force Kean began to withdraw, the 24th Infantry was regarded with suspicion and dissatisfaction by white leaders in both the division and the regiment.

[65] Quote from Barth, Tropic Lightning and Taro Leaf in Korea, n.d., p. 20. See also WD, 24th Inf Rgt, 12 Aug 50; Montross and Canzona, *The Pusan Perimeter*, pp. 147–52.

[66] Interv, Muehlbauer with James T. Burke, 23 Jan 89. Burke was with the party that entered the town. His story is confirmed by General Barth. See Barth, Tropic Lightning and Taro Leaf in Korea, n.d., p. 20.

[67] ATIS, Research Supplement, Interrogation Rpt, issue 100, 30 Apr 51, *6th NK Infantry Division*, pp. 37–38. Because of casualties from Task Force Kean and earlier combat, which were about 50 percent, the division was ordered to go on the defensive to await replacements.

[68] Interv, MacGarrigle with Beirne, 19 Aug 93.

[69] Intervs, Bowers with Genous S. Hodges, 13 Apr 94; MacGarrigle with Sapenter, 14 Mar 94; Barone, 14 Apr 94.

[70] Officer Roster, 24th Inf Rgt (who deployed and were replacements), 18 Sep 50, exhibits D–12 and D–13, Eighth Army Inspector General Investigation.

Battle Mountain

On 15 August all units of the 25th Division pulled behind a line that stretched southward from the Nam River through Saga-ri and then followed the ridge lines toward Chindong-ni and the Yellow Sea. The 35th Infantry held the division's northern limits from the Nam River to a point about a mile north of Haman. The 5th took charge of an area that stretched from Sobuk-san south to the Yellow Sea. The 24th stood in between with responsibility for a rugged stretch of ridges and crags dominated by 743-meter-high Mount P'il-bong.[71] (*Map 8*)

Within the 24th's sector, Colonel Cole's 2d Battalion went to the north, taking charge of a region that extended from the regiment's boundary with the 35th to a position southwest of Haman, about one mile northwest of P'il-bong. Colonel Miller's 1st Battalion went into the important high ground around P'il-bong itself and extending southeast to Sobuk-san. Corley's 3d Battalion stood in reserve to the rear in the lowlands. Badly battered during Task Force Kean, the battalion would serve as a reaction force if the other two came under threat but would spend the first few days undergoing retraining, especially in patrolling, all-around defense, care and cleaning of weapons, fire and maneuver tactics, and ambush prevention.[72]

At six miles in length, the regiment's area of responsibility was considerably wider than normal, but the situation still had some advantages. For the first time since the Sangju campaign, the 24th would occupy a defined regimental front against the North Koreans with other regiments on its flanks. As a result, enemy envelopments were no longer a major concern, and supporting artillery would be able to mass its fires in greater volume than in the past. Meanwhile, the regimental commander would know where his forces were at any moment and have the ability to coordinate their efforts efficiently.

The North Koreans, for their part, were determined to drive the 25th Division back and to seize Masan. To the north, at the end of August, the *7th North Korean Division*, which had followed the *6th* to Chinju, would take up station at Uiryong, a town on the west side of the Nam River eleven miles to the northwest of Haman. Opposing Fisher's 35th Infantry, the unit would remain in the area until well into September. Just to the south, the *6th Division* continued to oppose the 24th Infantry. It had been badly bloodied by Task Force Kean but was still in the fight. Although newly captured prisoners of war reported that the unit had suffered over four thousand casualties out of an initial strength of 10,000 and that it had lost 20 percent of its artillery, 30 percent of its trucks, and 40 percent of its rifles, it had received a contingent of 3,100 South Korean replacements during August and was making repairs. The new men had no basic training and received weapons only when they entered combat, but they advanced on command. According to North Korean prisoners of war, special guards followed the frontline troops into battle and killed anyone who straggled or attempted to desert. Throughout the rest of August, the *6th Division* would hold in place to the west of Haman, probing the 24th Infantry's lines and those of the 35th and 5th, sometimes in company strength.[73]

Anticipating enemy pressure, the 24th's planners took stock of the formidable terrain in the regiment's sector, especially around Hill 665, one-half mile to the northwest of P'il-bong, which would shortly become known as "Old Baldy," "Bloody Peak," or "Battle Mountain." They found that whoever occupied the summit of either that hill or Mount P'il-bong could observe his opponent's rear area. That would allow him to receive early warning of attacks and to direct artillery and mortar fire against any target that appeared. Since the hills were easy to approach from the enemy side but steep and treacherous from American lines, and since the North

---

[71] WD, 24th Inf Rgt, Aug 50, Overlay 6A, Planned Defense, 15 Aug 50, box 3750, RG 407, WNRC. See also Barth, Tropic Lightning and Taro Leaf in Korea, n.d., p. 20.

[72] WD, 24th Inf Rgt, 1–31 Aug 50, pp. 13–15, and Overlay 6B, box 3750, RG 407, WNRC; Interv, IG with Corley, 26 Aug 50, exhibit 2, Kean Letter file. See also Intervs, MacGarrigle with Sapenter, 14 Mar 94; Randall P. Stephens, 18 and 27 Jul 94.

---

[73] North Korean Order of Battle; ATIS, Research Supplement, Interrogation Rpt, issue 100, 30 Apr 51, *6th NK Infantry Division*. See also ATIS, Research Supplement, Interrogation Rpt, issue 99, 24 Apr 51, *7th NK Infantry Division*, Intelligence Research Collection, MHI.

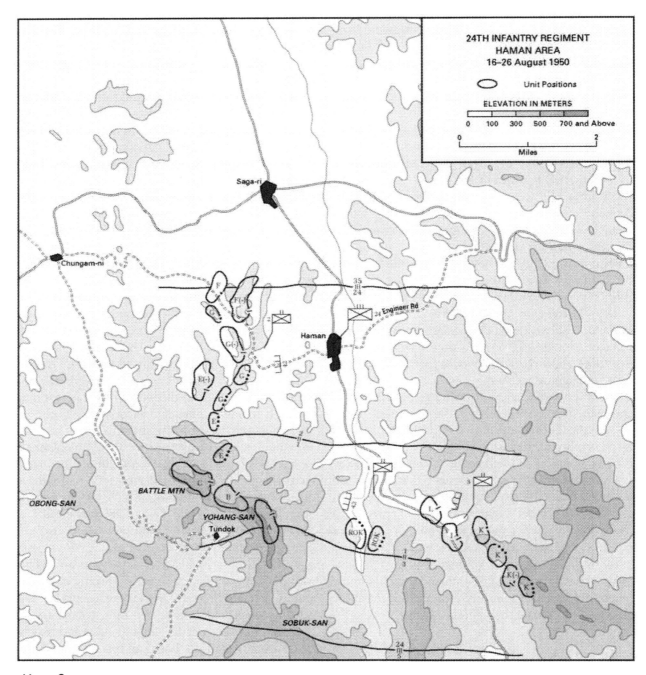

Map 8

Korean sector contained a number of abandoned mines that afforded excellent cover, Colonel Champeny understood that the area would pose major challenges to the 24th. Rapid resupply and reinforcement for his units would be a problem, and evacuation of the wounded would be difficult. In addition, if pushed back the defenders would have trouble reorganizing quickly for counterattacks.

Following the lines of the land, the colonel laid out a simple plan. Stationing Companies F, G, and E of the 2d Battalion, in that order, north to south, on a series of small ridge lines that lay to the north of Battle Mountain, he placed Companies C, B, and A of the 1st Battalion, in that order, again north to south, on the mountain itself. The 3d Battalion went into the lowlands behind the 1st Battalion to serve as a reserve and to guard the road stretching south from Haman to Chindong-ni. Wherever necessary, Champeny laid mines, built obstacles, and strung wire barriers in order to impede enemy movement into the 24th's zone.[74]

The 25th Division did what it could to bolster the 24th. When it became apparent that a 4,000-yard gap existed between Champeny's unit and the 5th Infantry, General Kean assigned a 400-man South Korean National Police force to plug the hole. In the same way, with an estimated twenty-five hundred enemy operating in the division's immediate area, General Kean approved work to shorten and protect the 24th's critical supply line by expanding a trail that ran from the Masan–Saga-ri road directly to Haman. Bussey's 77th Engineer Combat Company built the southern portions of the new route while other companies of the 65th Engineer Combat Battalion worked on those to the north. Later to gain fame as "Engineer Road," the bypass would avoid Saga-ri and a section of road that crossed the enemy's most likely avenue of approach. Cutting the time it took supplies to reach Haman from Masan, it would provide an emergency backup if an attack severed the regiment's vulnerable main supply line.[75]

While those efforts continued, General Barth prepared defensive fire plans for his batteries. He very carefully avoided locating his guns directly to the rear of the 24th Infantry and instead positioned most of them to its side, behind the regiments on its flanks. The arrangement complicated artillery support for the 24th by increasing the distance the batteries had to fire and by causing occasional communications problems, but Barth had already suffered the annihilation of the better part of two of his battalions and had no intention of suffering further disasters. During the previous weeks, he noted in explanation, portions of the 24th Infantry had withdrawn without warning, leaving his batteries unprotected from mass infantry attacks. "It is expected in this type of warfare," he said, "that any battery may be attacked by infiltration and must defend itself. However, a battery of artillery is not heavily enough armed to hold out against large scale attacks." Colonel Champeny objected to the arrangement and insisted that at least one battery remain near Haman. When Champeny hastened completion of Engineer Road to enhance resupply and reduce the threat to the town, Barth complied with his wishes. Even so, the battery in question stood just across the line between the 24th and the 35th, in the 35th's area of responsibility.[76]

Although Barth blamed the unreliability of the 24th for his decision on the location of his batteries, an examination of the terrain leads to a suspicion that he would have done the same thing, whatever the units on P'il-bong and Sobuk-san. The roads in the area ran across the enemy's front from north to south rather than away from it to the

[74] WD, 24th Inf Rgt, 16, 17, 18 Aug 50, box 3750, RG 407, WNRC.

[75] Ibid.; WD, 65th Engr Bn, Aug 50, pp. 13–21; Interv, Cash with Charles Bussey, 6 Jan 89. See also Bussey, *Firefight at Yechon*, pp. 157–59. According to Bussey, Champeny opposed building the road.

[76] Barth makes the point about the positioning of his batteries in Memo, Brig Gen George B. Barth for Col William O. Perry, IG, EUSAK, 8 Sep 50, sub: Statement of Brigadier General George B. Barth Concerning Performance of 159th Field Artillery, exhibit D–1, Eighth Army Inspector General Investigation. The war diary of the 159th Field Artillery Battalion shows the positioning of that unit's batteries, all of which were located outside of the 24th Infantry's sector despite the fact that the 159th was in direct support of the regiment. See WD, 159th FA Bn, Aug 50, p. 8, and attached Sketch 6. The dispositions of the 90th Field Artillery Battalion were similar. See WD, 90th FA Bn, Aug 50.

east. In case of a North Korean breakthrough, the artillery batteries would have found it difficult to withdraw and might have had to be abandoned. The Engineer Road into Haman remedied part of the problem, but nothing similar existed to the south, directly behind the 24th. By contrast, the Masan–Saga-ri road fed from east to west into the 35th Infantry's sector, making a location in that area much safer. The same was true in the 5th Infantry's sector, where artillerymen had the support of the Masan–Chindong-ni road.

As the 25th Division readied its defenses, the North Koreans continued to probe. During the predawn hours of 17 August, they launched the first of a series of attacks against the 35th Infantry's positions on Sibidang Mountain, four miles northwest of Haman. In the five days of fighting that followed, units of the regiment's 1st Battalion were forced off of their positions several times but on each occasion regained them in counterattacks. On the morning of 20 August, while visiting a forward observation post, the regimental commander, Colonel Fisher, discovered a large enemy force advancing to renew the attack. Calling in air strikes and artillery, he caused an estimated three hundred and fifty North Korean casualties. Undeterred, the enemy renewed the attack at the same point during the early morning hours of 22 August, driving Company A of the 1st Battalion from its position. Counterattacking, the company regained the ground it had lost by the end of the day. The next morning the enemy withdrew.[77]

Throughout the period, if some members of the 35th Infantry ran to the rear, their number was unremarkable and easily managed. The 25th Division's provost marshal compiled a list by unit of stragglers apprehended in the division rear area. The numbers were small for all units. Even so, keeping in mind that the 24th had a larger population than most all-white units, the statistics provide a small-scale representation of straggling within the various regiments of the division. During August the provost marshal collected 116 men from the 24th Infantry, 15 from the 27th, and 12 from the 35th. Among artillery units, the all-black 159th Field Artillery Battalion had 32, while the all-white 90th had 5, the 8th 6, and the 64th 3.[78]

While enemy units probed the 35th to the north, the *6th North Korean Division* tested the lines of the 24th Infantry. The attacks began early on the morning of 18 August, when one of the division's units overran a platoon of the 1st Battalion's Company C on Battle Mountain. Company C's commander, Capt. Laurence Corcoran, adjusted his defenses and managed to hold in place.[79]

While that was happening, the enemy also sent probes north to attack the 2d Battalion. In the fighting that followed, portions of Company E were overrun, and the company commander, 1st Lt. Gabriel C. Anselmo, was killed. With that, some of the unit's platoons began to buckle, but as they did a platoon leader in the battalion's weapons company, white 1st Lt. Ernest M. Williams, assisted in maintaining order by rallying his men just as they were beginning to withdraw. Killing three of the enemy with his carbine, he manned a machine gun until seriously wounded. In so doing, he brought some stability to the company's line by gaining the time his men needed to regroup and return to their positions.[80]

Even with that assistance, Company E proved unable to retake the ground it had lost. Turning to a fresh unit, the battalion commander, Colonel Cole, instructed Company G to attack and called in an air strike to assist. In the confusion that followed, poor communication and improper marking of the target brought the strike down on friendly forces, leaving them no choice but to

---

[77] WD, 25th Inf Div, 20–23 Aug 50, box 3748; WD, 35th Inf Rgt, 15–31 Aug 50, box 3750; WD, 1st Bn, 35th Inf Rgt, 20–23 Aug 50, box 3750. All in RG 407, WNRC.

---

[78] Certificate, Office of the Provost Marshal, 25th Inf Div, 13 Feb 51, exhibit K, Far East Command Inspector General Investigation. Regimental strengths as of 31 August 1950 were 3,024 for the 24th Infantry, 2,577 for the 27th, and 2,910 for the 35th. See G–1 Daily Summary 50, 25th Inf Div, 31 Aug 50, in WD, 25th Inf Div, Aug 50, box 3748, RG 407, WNRC.

[79] WD, 1st Bn, 24th Inf Rgt, 1–31 Aug 50, pp. 9–10. See also Intervs, IG with Capt Laurence M. Corcoran, 1 Sep 50, exhibit 3, Kean Letter file; Cash with Griffin, 5 Oct 88.

[80] WD, 2d Bn, 24th Inf Rgt, 18 Aug 50, p. 8, box 3750, RG 407, WNRC; 25th Inf Div GO 255, 28 Oct 50, Silver Star Citation for 1st Lt Ernest M. Williams.

withdraw. Seeking a more experienced hand, Champeny immediately replaced Cole with Roberts. Under the new commander's direction, Company G counterattacked and reclaimed all of the lost ground.[81]

Although forced in the end to withdraw, the enemy was only testing American strength and foraging for food and weapons. In the days that followed, his goals became clearer and his purposes hardened. On 20 August North Korean forces all across South Korea received final instructions to begin preparations for an all-out push against Pusan. The *6th North Korean Division* was to anchor the southernmost flank of the effort, advancing through Haman and Masan to the western outskirts of Pusan.[82]

Ten days were to elapse before the start of the offensive, but the *6th Division's* commander apparently considered American possession of Sobuksan, P'il-bong, and Battle Mountain a threat. Rather than continue probing for weak points while building up for the assault, he therefore spent considerable time and effort throughout the period attempting to take control of at least the mountain crests. In that way, he would gain the high ground before the final attack, hide the movements of his own troops from prying American eyes, and receive an unobstructed view of the 25th Division's dispositions in the valleys beyond.

Beginning on the morning of 20 August the North Koreans intensified their attacks against the 24th Infantry, making Battle Mountain and the ridge lines to its north and south their targets. Companies B and G held their own in the assaults that followed, but one platoon of Company E buckled. Avowing later that only eight of his men had stood and fought, the platoon leader, black Sfc. Willis Blakley, became so angry that he gave sworn depositions against fifteen who had run. Although Blakley was killed in action a few days later, his story was confirmed by three others,

including Colonel Cole. As a result, charges were preferred against the men.[83]

Company C on Battle Mountain bore the brunt of the attack and likewise began to waver almost immediately. "At 0630," the unit's commander, Captain Corcoran, told investigators, "I received a call from Lieutenant Blackburn. He was being attacked in force. I went over to the observation post of the 2d Platoon, and while I was there the Sergeant and another soldier came running to me and told me that the enemy had broken through our front. . . . At 0800, I found that I and 25 men were the only ones left on the high ground."[84] Corcoran pulled his men back to a supply point on the reverse side of the mountain. Cut off from the rest of the regiment, the company continued to resist, even though many of the men who remained were demoralized and only a few put up much of a fight. During a lull in combat, a North Korean officer came forward under a flag of truce to offer surrender terms. Corcoran declined the invitation, and one of his soldiers, without instructions, apparently shot the messenger in the back as he tried to return to his lines.[85]

The fight became more desperate. Corcoran ordered 1st Sgt. Peter J. Paulfrey to attempt a breakthrough to the rear to inform the battalion commander, Colonel Miller, that he would hold his position for as long as he could but that he needed reinforcements.[86] "Sgt. Paulfrey came off the

[81] WD, 2d Bn, 24th Inf Rgt, 1–31 Aug 50, pp. 8–9; WD, 24th Inf Rgt, 18 Aug 50.

[82] FEC, History of the North Korean Army, 31 Jul 52, p. 63; ATIS, Research Supplement, Interrogation Rpt, issue 100, 30 Apr 51, *6th NK Infantry Division*, pp. 39–40.

[83] WD, 1st Bn, 24th Inf Rgt, 1–31 Aug 50, pp. 10–11; WD, 2d Bn, 24th Inf Rgt, 1–31 Aug 50, p. 9; Statement of Camp, 9 Sep 50, Reference 24th Infantry Regiment, exhibit D–21, Eighth Army Inspector General Investigation. Cole was in the Battle Mountain area commanding a task force.

[84] WD, 1st Bn, 24th Inf Rgt, 1–31 Aug 50, pp. 9–10; Interv, IG with Corcoran, 1 Sep 50, exhibit 3, Kean Letter file. Corcoran's dating is off and the number of men that he says remained differs from the number in other accounts, but the combat he describes clearly occurred on 20 August.

[85] Interv, Cash with Griffin, 5 Oct 88. Griffin tells the same story in a letter to the secretary of the Army, but fails to mention that the North Korean was killed. See Ltr, Albert Griffin, Jr., to Secretary of the Army, 22 May 88, CMH files.

[86] Interv, Cash with Corcoran, 28 Jul 89. Another officer, 1st Lt. Louis Anthis, was also ordered to break through for help. He arrived at the 1st Battalion headquarters after Paulfrey. See 25th Inf Div GO 176, 22 Sep 50, Silver Star Citation; Interv, Cash with Griffin, 5 Oct 88.

hill . . . with a few men," the battalion's executive officer, Major Carson, later recalled, "and reported that the company had been overrun and that there was no one left on the hill. As a result of [Paulfrey's] report, the hill was strafed and napalmed . . ., and his company commander and twenty men of his company were still in position on the hill."[87]

The air strikes ended the battle. After a prolonged resistance, Corcoran and his men pulled back. "I don't know what [Paulfrey's] motivation was at the time," the officer observed years later. "Maybe it was the stress of the moment or maybe he wanted to do me in, I don't really know. I had never had a problem with him. He was considered one of the top sergeants in the 24th." Later in the fighting, on 23 August, after apparently lingering in the rear for over a day, Paulfrey would be arrested for refusing to obey a direct order from Carson to rejoin his unit. He was convicted of disobedience to a superior officer and sentenced to twenty years in prison.[88]

"At the close of this day's operation," the 1st Battalion's historian later remarked in the unit's war diary, "it was apparent that the North Korean forces had struck a mortal blow to the regiment's defensive positions. Company C was disorganized, [white 1st] Lt. [Louis] Anthis was able to round up only 40 men to return to its position. Also significant was the fact that a gap of 1,400 yards existed between Companies B and E. The said gap was being occupied by North Korean forces of unknown strength."[89] Late in the day Champeny ordered the

regimental reserve, Companies I and L of the 3d Battalion, to restore Company C's position. The two units worked their way to a point below the crest of the mountain, but then pulled in for the night.[90]

Corcoran received the Silver Star for his role in the battle, as did Anthis, who led a patrol to the rear to bring help but arrived too late at the battalion command post to stop the air strike. Second Lt. Alexander Hunt, who went forward in the face of enemy fire to direct air strikes against the enemy with hand signals, also received a Silver Star. Corcoran saw to it that virtually every one of the thirty-five riflemen and medics who had stayed with him on the hill received the Bronze Star for valor.[91]

Fighting continued on the next morning, 21 August, when the enemy launched a probing attack against Company G. All of the men in the unit except for a small group around the company commander abandoned their positions. The battalion's operations officer, Capt. James Gardner, told investigators later that week that "I personally heard the company commander pleading with the men to stay on the hill."[92] Company E was not attacked, but, according to the battalion's executive officer, Maj. Horace E. Donaho, some of its men left their positions as well. "We had a strong point set up," the officer recalled. "I was informed that their machine gun position had been overrun. They left the tripod and all their ammo. Upon checking, I found that neither enemy or friendly shots had been fired, that friendly troops withdrawing through 'E' Company positions had reported the enemy was right behind them." The company's officers later collected the stragglers and sent them back into their old positions on the hill. They met with no enemy resistance.[93]

---

[87] Carson said that Corcoran was on the hill for twenty hours and that the air attacks came the next morning, but the 24th Infantry war diary says the air and artillery attacks began in the early afternoon on 20 August. We have followed the war diary's version. See Interv, IG with Lt Col Eugene Carson, 9 Feb 51, exhibit B–114, Far East Command Inspector General Investigation; WD, 24th Inf Rgt, 1–31 Aug 50, p. 18. Corcoran also tells the Paulfrey story. See Interv, Cash with Corcoran, 28 Jul 89.

[88] Interv, Cash with Corcoran, 28 Jul 89. Carson describes the Paulfrey incident in Interv, IG with Carson, 6 Sep 50, exhibit 21, Kean Letter file. The particulars of Paulfrey's court case are in Court-Martial Data Sheet, M Sgt Peter J. Paulfrey, Jr., n.d., exhibit D–1, Far East Command Inspector General Investigation. For more on the air strike, see Interv, Muehlbauer with Arthur Thompson, 14 Sep 88.

[89] A rare statement in a battalion war diary. See WD, 2d Bn, 24th Inf Rgt, 1–31 Aug 50, p. 11.

[90] WD, 24th Inf Rgt, 1–31 Aug 50, pp. 18–19.

[91] See 25th Inf Div GOs 176, 22 Sep 50; 178, 23 Sep 50; 215, 2 Oct 50; 217, 3 Oct 50; 218, 3 Oct 50; 219, 3 Oct 50; 220, 3 Oct 50; 221, 3 Oct 50; and 222, 4 Oct 50.

[92] Interv, IG with Gardner, 24 Aug 50, exhibit 24, Kean Letter file.

[93] Interv, IG with Horace E. Donaho, 22 Aug 50, exhibit 19, Kean Letter file. A period has been added between *overrun* and *they* in Donaho's statement for the sake of clarity. The battalion war diary is silent on these incidents, only noting that

While those incidents were occurring, the 3d Battalion was continuing its effort to retake Company C's former position. Colonel Corley kept his command post close to the action and described what happened. The attack, he said, went brilliantly, with the troops showing courage and initiative. In the face of heavy enemy resistance, the commander of Company L, black 1st Lt. Randall P. Stephens, led his unit up the steep mountain slope without the benefit of cover or concealment or the assistance of mortar and artillery fire. Making use of all the advantages that fire and maneuver could bring to bear, the officer and his men took three hours and suffered seventeen casualties but achieved their objective.[94]

What happened next was less encouraging. Three hours later, when the enemy launched a counterattack and began to converge on Company L's flank, the unit wavered and withdrew down the hill. Although Stephens again played a prominent role, rallying the men into strong defensive positions which allowed them to repel two subsequent attacks, the development stunned Corley. A few days later, reflecting on what had happened, he could only conclude in an interview with the inspector general that the incident should never have occurred and that the officers' inexperience was to blame. Suggesting that the unit's commanders had somehow failed either to dig in properly or to take other precautions that might have thwarted the assault, he attributed "this unexplained withdrawal after such a brilliant attack to the complete lack of security of the men of Company L." A strong force of approximately eighty-five men, he added, was in position on the hill when the attack occurred.[95]

Corley reorganized the company and on the morning of 22 August sent it back up the hill, but the unit, its men badly shaken, continued to wobble. A platoon leader, white 2d Lt. Gerald Alexander, who had arrived less than two weeks before, described what happened:

It took me over one hour to get the men to move 200 yards and we were not receiving a round of fire. They would not move with hand signals. I had to plead with them, give them a direct order, and I had to curse them and by the way, the latter proved to be most effective. I continually had to move from man to man to get each individual to move. I led, I went to the rear and pushed. It took an hour to move a distance that would normally take ten minutes. Finally when we reached our objective, three grenades were thrown by the enemy that slightly injured six men, including myself. The entire attacking force took off down the hill. . . . I got them stopped after they had run a hundred yards, and we made the attack again. I had them all throw their grenades and then I ordered them to assault the knoll, but no one would go. Finally, myself and a B.A.R. man went up and found no one alive on the hill. The men finally came up on the knoll with me, but to get them down on the other side it took me another thirty minutes.[96]

While the attack proceeded, Colonel Corley monitored the action from a position less than two hundred yards to the rear, coordinating artillery support and often personally directing the fire of individual riflemen and machine gunners. When the attack faltered and Company L came back off the hill, he committed Company I to the action and joined the assault himself. His presence appears to have bolstered the morale of both the men and their officers. The battalion retook the hill and, with Company C following behind as a reserve, consolidated the position.[97]

The enemy launched six counterattacks on 23 August, two of company size. During one, accord-

---

the unit received small-arms fire and encountered small groups of enemy infiltrators. See WD, 2d Bn, 24th Inf Rgt, 21 Aug 50, p. 9, box 3750, RG 407, WNRC.

[94] Corley told the story only three days after the event. See Interv, IG with Corley, 26 Aug 50, exhibit 2, Kean Letter file. See also Intervs, MacGarrigle with Stephens, 18 and 27 Jul 94; Sapenter, 14 and 21 Mar 94.

[95] Quote from Interv, IG with Corley, 26 Aug 50, exhibit 2, Kean Letter file. Stephens received the Silver Star. His role is described in 25th Inf Div GO 214, 2 Oct 50. See also Intervs, MacGarrigle with Stephens, 18 and 27 Jul 94; Sapenter, 14 and 21 Mar 94.

[96] Interv, IG with 2d Lt Gerald N. Alexander, 2 Sep 50, exhibit 20, Kean Letter file.

[97] Interv, IG with Corley, 26 Aug 50, exhibit 2, Kean Letter file. See also EUSAK GO 141, 27 Oct 50, Distinguished Service Cross Citation for Lt Col John T. Corley, with attached Statements by Sgt Levy V. Hollis and Sgt George Wilkerson, both 12 Oct 50.

A chaplain conducts Sunday morning services along the Pusan Perimeter.

ing to Corcoran, the North Koreans used percussion grenades which "made a lot of noise and started a panic; there were two or three officers there with myself and we rallied the men into a counterattack and we took the position; and we had one heck of a time accounting for the personnel . . . that we had originally, before the counter-attack." In the end, despite the straggling, all of the enemy's attacks failed.[98]

Even so, the defense was chaotic at best. Company C was so crippled by casualties and straggling that it could place fewer than sixty men on the hill. Meanwhile, American units were so thinly spread across the broad front they had to defend that enemy infiltrators succeeded in penetrating to the rear, where snipers became a continual threat. Complicating matters, firing discipline was weak. "Men on the extreme left flank of the positions," Corley noted, "would indiscriminately open fire

when a probing attack would hit the right flank. The men had no . . . idea of how to conduct an organized company defense. The position was held by mortar and artillery fire and by the officers taking groups of men regardless of platoons' assignment and coordinat[ing] their fire." Although the assault companies received fewer than a dozen incoming mortar rounds and no enemy artillery or air action occurred, "this engagement . . . was as rough as the toughest action I have had in a campaign in World War II in Europe. I never felt secure about the position. Prior to relief, . . . L Company reported a fox hole strength of 17 and I Company 46, yet half way down the mountain L Company's strength had jumped to 48 and I Company to 75. The next morning, both units had over 100 men in them." Overall, the two units suffered the loss of 6 officers and 114 enlisted men in the engagement.[99]

---

[98] Interv, IG with Corcoran, 13 Feb 51, exhibit B–125, Far East Command Inspector General Investigation.

[99] The 1st Battalion's war diary delineates many of the problems confronting the hill's defenders. The 3d Battalion's war diary is less communicative. See WD, 3d Bn, 24th Inf Rgt, 1–31 Aug 50, pp. 5–6; WD, 1st Bn, 24th Inf Rgt, 1–31 Aug 50,

On 24 August Companies I and L withdrew from the crest, leaving it in the hands of Company C and a company of South Korean police. Although the South Korean commander was killed and communication proved a problem between the two groups, they repelled four enemy assaults over the next two days, on one occasion employing flamethrowers to good effect. Throughout the period they tried to link up with units to the north and south, but the 24th Infantry's front remained so extended and enemy resistance was so strong that the effort proved impossible. When the 1st Battalion called in heavy air strikes, enemy forces pulled off their positions, only to return and counterattack when the aircraft departed.[100]

Over the days that followed, the North Koreans continued to probe the 24th all along the line to determine the unit's weakest links. After midnight on the morning of 25 August, following a series of small attacks, they launched a heavy assault against Company F, located well to the north on the seam between the 24th and 35th Infantry regiments. One platoon of the company gave way, allowing enemy troops to occupy its position, but artillery fire soon beat them back. The acting battalion commander, Colonel Roberts, later observed that the episode "had no detrimental effect on the overall plan."[101]

If that was so, the incident still told a great deal about the readiness of the unit. According to General Wilson, who arrived at the scene shortly after American forces recaptured the position, some of those who lost their lives in the attack did so because of poor training and discipline. "On 25 August," he said, "I inspected a position of 'F' Company which had been vacated the night before, and there were dead on the ground, all of whom were outside of their fox holes. The Company C.O. [a black, Capt.

Roger Walden] informed me that he had done his best to keep them in their holes at the approach of the enemy. They threw their grenades too soon and stood up in their fox holes, fired one clip from their rifles, and ran." Wilson remarked that the company commander had told him he thought the men were "superstitious about staying in holes."[102]

On 25 August, to improve coordination in the area between the 1st and 2d Battalions, especially on Battle Mountain, Colonel Champeny established Task Force Baker, comprising Company C, a platoon from Company E, and a unit of South Korean police. Commanded by Colonel Cole, the force held off the enemy for the next two days, coordinating air strikes and beating back continuing enemy attacks. At one point during the action, fighter-bombers caught a 100-man enemy force in the open on a hillside and obliterated it with a hail of bombs, cannon fire, and napalm.[103]

On 28 August Companies I and L of the 3d Battalion relieved the 1st Battalion on Battle Mountain and the adjacent ridges. Companies A and B went into reserve, but Company C, heavily worn from the fighting, remained in place on the crest under the operational control of Cole's Task Force Baker.

Intense fighting began early on the morning of 29 August, with the command posts for both Task Force Baker and Company C receiving heavy mortar and tank fire. At that time, some of the men from Company C left their stations, but the company's commander, Captain Corcoran, and one remaining officer, black 1st Lt. John M. Jenkins, reorganized enough of the troops to beat the enemy back and regain the position. The contest ran all that day and into the night, with Company C virtually surrounded and at times fighting hand to hand. Air and artillery fire kept enemy forces from massing for a final attack during the day, but after dark the North Koreans infiltrated a force behind Company C and succeeded for a time in penetrating the unit's command post. A platoon from

pp. 12–13. Quotes from Interv, IG with Corley, 26 Aug 50, exhibit 2, Kean Letter file.

[100] WD, 1st Bn, 24th Inf Rgt, 1–31 Aug 50, p. 13. See also WD, 25th Inf Div, 1–31 Aug 50, p. 27, box 3748, RG 407, WNRC. See Interv, MacGarrigle with Tittel, 15 and 20 Apr 94, for the connection with the 5th Infantry on the southern flank.

[101] WD, 2d Bn, 24th Inf Rgt, 1–31 Aug 50, p. 11; Interv, IG with Lt Col Paul F. Roberts, 13 Sep 50, exhibit B–1, Eighth Army Inspector General Investigation.

[102] Intervs, IG with Brig Gen Vennard Wilson, 5 Sep 50, exhibit 29, Kean Letter file; MacGarrigle with Walden, 5 Jul 95.

[103] WD, 1st Bn, 24th Inf Rgt, 1–31 Aug 50, pp. 13–14; Interv, Cash with Corcoran, 28 Jul 89.

Company E was also surrounded along with the command post for Task Force Baker.[104]

Company I received orders to counterattack but before it could, at 2300, the enemy launched a sharp assault on the left flank of Company C. Corcoran described what happened next. "Some unidentified soldier ran across our position yelling, 'Withdraw. Withdraw. We are being attacked.' The rest of the men immediately pulled out and left."[105] Out of an original strength of between eighty-five and ninety-five men, Corcoran could count only seventeen who remained: three artillery men, several wounded, and the command-post group. Notifying his superiors of the situation, he requested and received permission to abandon the position.[106] As for Company C, the 1st Battalion's historian could only say that the unit had become "completely disorganized," that its men were "extremely fatigued," and that its combat efficiency was "questionable."[107]

During the hours that followed, the main body of the enemy vacated the mountaintop and grouped in a wooded area some five hundred yards to the west. Champeny called in artillery and then ordered Company B of the regimental reserve to counterattack. The unit met light resistance. At 1300 the company's commander, Capt. William A. Hash, reported Battle Mountain secure.[108] Taking Company C's place on the mountain, Hash's company began to repair the position's defenses. According to the 1st Battalion's war diary, the area had assumed by that time "all the appearances of a World War I No-man's Land."[109]

The scene was an indication of the difficulty the soldiers of the 24th had in defending Battle Mountain and the other isolated hilltop positions around P'il-bong. It was a major ordeal to reach the units to provide basic necessities such as food, water, and ammunition. A number of Korean porters were hired to assist in the resupply effort, but some of them were found to be porters by day and North Korean soldiers by night. When enemy troops were close, the porters faded away, and airdrops by light liaison aircraft were sometimes required in emergencies. As one platoon leader of Company K remarked, "This is when I gave up wanting to be a millionaire, because if I had all the money in the world, I believe that I'd [have] bought a drink of water and ammunition."[110]

Because of the supply problems, concertina wire was not available in most positions, and the only available protection was from foxholes. Because of the rocky ground, they tended to be shallow and provided little safety. A newly arrived platoon leader in Company C, white 2d Lt. Wilbur T. Felkey, described the defensive positions as "shallow graves."[111] Bodies could not be buried, and the injured and wounded had to be hauled down the mountain in a painful and time-consuming journey which not all survived.[112]

The defenders were under constant stress from the threat of attack from any direction, the lack of sleep and need for constant vigilance, and the miserable living conditions. As if to make sport of the Americans' discomfort, North Korean propagandists chose the night that Company B replaced Company C on Battle Mountain to broadcast a loudspeaker message in which they

[104] WD, 24th Inf Rgt, 1–31 Aug 50, pp. 27–28.

[105] Quote from Interv, IG with Corcoran, 1 Sep 50, exhibit 3, Kean Letter file. Corcoran attributes some of his information to Jenkins. Since his comments were typed as delivered, in a stream of consciousness, punctuation has been added for clarity. The regimental war diary tells the same story. See WD, 24th Inf Rgt, 1–31 Aug 50, pp. 27–28.

[106] Ibid. Corcoran tallied the men who remained in Interv, IG with Corcoran, 13 Feb 51, exhibit B–125, Far East Command Inspector General Investigation. See also Intervs, MacGarrigle with Komp, 5 May and 1 Jun 94.

[107] WD, 1st Bn, 24th Inf Rgt, 1–31 Aug 50, p. 16. For more on Company C's condition, see Intervs, MacGarrigle with Gillert, 4 May 94; Green, 16 Jun 94.

[108] Ibid.

[109] WD, 1st Bn, 24th Inf Rgt, Aug 50, p. 16.

[110] Quote is from Interv, Muehlbauer with James C. Yadon, 22 May 89. Poor living conditions within the 24th were mentioned by many veterans. Problems with rations, water, heat, and fatigue were widespread at times within the Eighth Army as a whole. For comments on the problems of supply, see Intervs, MacGarrigle with Gillert, 4 May 94; Muehlbauer with Wilbur T. Felkey, 8 Sep 88; Isaac Smith, 27 Sep 88; Cash with Edward Dixon, 20 Jan 89; Raymond C. Hagins, 28 Aug 88.

[111] Interv, Muehlbauer with Felkey, 8 Sep 88. See also Interv, MacGarrigle with Green, 16 Jun 94.

[112] Interv, Cash with Dixon, 20 Jan 89; Muehlbauer with Felkey, 8 Sep 88; Isaac Smith, 27 Sep 88.

asserted in good English that "Americans should not fight North Korean soldiers. We have nothing against you."[113]

General Kean had much to consider as August ended. His division had done about as well as could be expected during Task Force Kean. The fight on the Pusan Perimeter had been equally difficult but no less successful. Battle Mountain had changed hands many times, but, along with Sobuk-san and P'il-bong, it remained under American control. Meanwhile, the enemy's continual forays had cost him dearly. During lulls in the battle, American forces had collected hundreds of enemy dead, many the products of U.S. air strikes and artillery.[114]

Nevertheless, much remained to be done. On 28 August prisoner-of-war interrogations had revealed that the enemy was planning a major attack.[115] Kean was confident that most of his regiments would stand up to the assault, but he distrusted the 24th. The unit had paid a heavy price during July and August, suffering a large number of casualties, particularly among noncommissioned and junior officers. When properly led, portions of it did well, and examples abounded of men who stood by their officers to the end, whatever the cost.

Even so, as a whole the regiment was unreliable. Some of its companies seemed badly demor-

alized, and the stresses it had experienced had begun to affect the performance of other units in the division. The division artillery commander, General Barth, in particular, insisted that the strain of working with the 24th was causing severe anxiety among his liaison officers. Expected to serve with a unit over long periods of time, those individuals had been abandoned to the enemy so regularly by members of the 24th who had run that an undue proportion of them had become casualties. The rest had to be rotated in and out of the unit much more frequently than in other regiments to avoid mental breakdowns.[116] Kean could do little over the short term because of the enemy's threatening offensive, but he knew that action of some sort was imperative. He had instructed his inspectors earlier in the month to investigate allegations that were beginning to circulate about the regiment and its performance. They were already hard at work. He would make up his mind on what to do as soon as he had a report.[117]

---

[113] WD, 1st Bn, 24th Inf Rgt, Aug 50, p. 16.

[114] WD, 1st Bn, 24th Inf Rgt, 1–31 Aug 50, p. 14; WD, 24th Inf Rgt, 1–31 Aug 50, p. 24.

[115] WD, 2d Bn, 24th Inf Rgt, 1–31 Aug 50, p. 12.

[116] Memo, Barth for Perry, 8 Sep 50, sub: Statement of Brigadier General George B. Barth Concerning Performance of 159th Field Artillery, exhibit D–1, Eighth Army Inspector General Investigation. Other interviews support Barth. See, for example, Intervs, Bowers with Skiffington, 14 Apr 94; MacGarrigle with Franke, 14 and 28 Jul 94; IG with Kennedy, 25 Aug 50, exhibit 15, Kean Letter file; Alfred F. Thompson, 24 Aug 50, exhibit 11, Kean Letter file.

[117] Statement of Camp, 9 Sep 50, Reference 24th Infantry Regiment, exhibit D–21, Eighth Army Inspector General Investigation.

CHAPTER 7

The Great Offensive

As August gave way to September, the 24th Infantry regiment remained in place at the center of the 25th Infantry Division's line, covering a frontage of some thirteen thousand yards. To the north the 35th Infantry regiment manned a 22,000-yard line, and to the south the 5th Infantry regiment defended 12,000 yards. All were augmented by South Korean marine, army, and police units. The combat west of Masan had been hard, but it was only a prelude for the three regiments. Understanding that Pusan was the source of American strength, the enemy resolved to eliminate the threat. On the night of 31 August 1950, he set out to do so, attacking the entire Pusan Perimeter. Some of the most intense fighting occurred in the sector occupied by the 25th Division.[1] (*Map 9*)

The *6th North Korean Division* would comprise the backbone of the enemy effort, striking not only the 5th and the 24th Infantry regiments but also the southern portions of the 35th. Although American intelligence analysts considered the 10,000 original members of the unit resourceful, tenacious, experienced fighters, by mid-August their number had shrunk to fewer than six thousand. Thirty-one hundred replacements had arrived shortly thereafter, but more casualties had occurred over the subsequent two weeks, leaving the unit with an estimated strength of 6,380 men on the eve of the offensive. A hard core of several thousand veterans remained, but many of the rest were untrained recruits dragooned into service from South Korea's cities and villages. They were hard to hold in place during attacks. Overall, the division was unable to provide its members with proper nourishment and medical assistance. It lacked heavy artillery and air support and had lost most of its armor to American artillery and air assaults.[2]

To the north of the *6th*, staging out of Uiryong, the *7th North Korean Division* would cross the Nam River to strike the northernmost portions of the 35th Infantry. Formed in early July 1950, the unit had incurred heavy casualties during earlier engagements and had likewise received a large number of untrained replacements. At most 30

---

[1] War Diary (WD), 25th Inf Div, 1 Sep 50, box 3752, Record Group (RG) 407, Washington National Records Center (WNRC), Suitland, Md. For problems of South Korean Army troops serving with U.S. forces, see Eighth U.S. Army, Korea (EUSAK), Special Problems in the Korean Conflict, 5 Feb 52, pp. 15–23, CMH files.

[2] Far East Command (FEC), Military Intelligence Section, Order of Battle Information, North Korean Army, 15 Oct 50, U.S. Army Military History Institute (MHI), Carlisle Barracks, Pa., hereafter cited as North Korean Order of Battle; 25th Inf Div Narrative Rpt, 25th Infantry Division in Korea, September 1950, n.d., pp. 21–22, attachment to WD, 25th Inf Div, Sep 50, boxes 3752–3754, RG 407, WNRC, hereafter cited as Narrative Rpt, 25th Inf Div in Korea, Sep 50. See also FEC, Allied Translator and Interpreter Section (ATIS), Research Supplement, Interrogation Rpt, issue 100, 30 Apr 50, *6th NK Infantry Division*, Intelligence Research Collection, MHI.

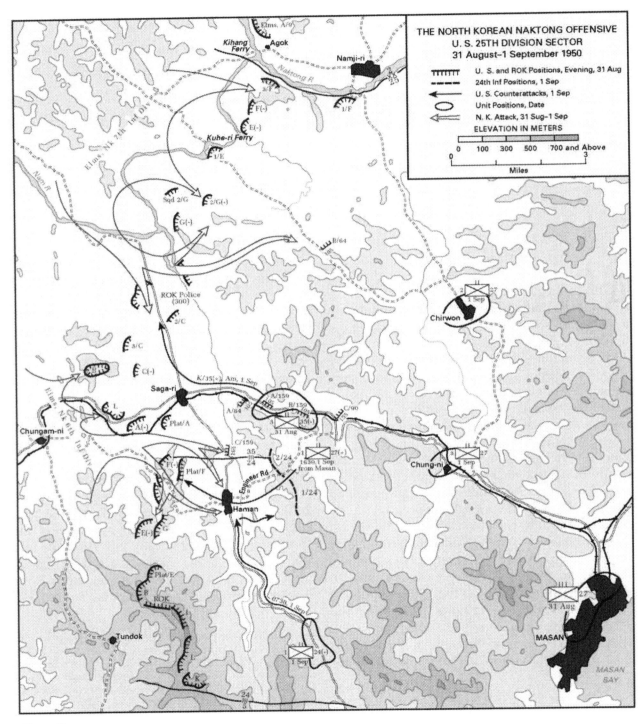

THE NORTH KOREAN NAKTONG OFFENSIVE
U. S. 25TH DIVISION SECTOR
31 August–1 September 1950

ꚙꚙꚙꚙ	U. S. and ROK Positions, Evening, 31 Aug
— ·· — ·· —	24th Inf Positions, 1 Sep
◀—	U. S. Counterattacks, 1 Sep
⬭	Unit Positions, Date
⇐	N. K. Attack, 31 Sug–1 Sep

ELEVATION IN METERS

| 0 | 100 | 300 | 500 | 700 and Above |

0   Miles   3

Map 9

Table 6—25th Division Losses by 31 August

Unit	Strength on Arrival in Korea	Battle Casualties	Nonbattle Casualties	Percent Loss	Strength on 31 August	Authorized Strength	Weeks in Combat
24th Infantry 3157		883	352	39.1	3024	3793	6
27th Infantry 2370		535	255	39.0*	2557*	3793	6
3d Battalion, 29th Infantry (attached to 27th on 7 Aug 51) 922		437	58				
35th Infantry 1979		318	350	37.4*	2810*	3793	6
1st Battalion, 29th Infantry (attached to 35th on 6 Aug 50) 922		284	133				
5th RCT 3497		724	403	32.2	3221	4653	4

*Includes totals for attached battalions

Source: G–1 Daily Summaries, 25th Inf Div, 14 Jul and 31 Aug 50, in War Diaries, 25th Inf Div, Jul 50, boxes 3746–3747, and Aug 50, box 3748, both in RG 407, WNRC; 5th Inf Rgt Unit Rpt 1, 031800–041800 Aug 50, and 5th Inf Rgt Regimental History, n.d., both in box 1, RG 338, WNRC.

percent of its soldiers were experienced fighting men. Of the rest, as was the case in the *6th*, many of the men would respond to orders and advance because they either believed in their cause or feared what would happen if they failed to obey. Even so, a high percentage was of doubtful reliability in extended combat.[3]

The 25th Division at the End of August

The regiments of the U.S. 25th Division had also suffered greatly. By the beginning of September each had incurred a loss approaching 40 percent of its men as battle and nonbattle casualties. Although some replacements had arrived and the 27th and 35th had each gained third battalions, they all

remained far below authorized strength. Meanwhile, the 5th Regimental Combat Team, which had been attached to the division, had seen less combat but had taken over one thousand casualties.[4] (*Table 6*)

While officers arrived throughout the period, the availability of enlisted men as replacements was limited until August. During July, as a result, the 24th Infantry received 24 officers but only 94 enlisted men to compensate for 408 casualties. At the end of August, although the officer shortage had ended, there was still a shortage of enlisted men, but 53 more officers, 3 warrant officers, and 841 enlisted men then joined the unit. For a time, there were

[3] Ibid.; ATIS, Research Supplement, Interrogation Rpt, issue 99, 24 Apr 51, *7th NK Infantry Division*, Intelligence Research Collection, MHI.

[4] Percentages were obtained by comparing the strength of the units upon arrival in Korea with total casualties as of 31 August. See G–1 Daily Summaries, 25th Inf Div, for 14 Jul and 31 Aug 50, in WDs, 25th Inf Div, Jul 50, boxes 3746–3747, and Aug 50, box 3748, both in RG 407, WNRC.

more black than white replacements available. That led to the assignment of newly arriving black soldiers to all-white segments of the 25th Division as well as to the 2d and 24th Infantry Divisions.[5]

If the new men were welcome, many of them turned out to be cooks, truck drivers, clerks, automotive mechanics, and various other categories of soldier rather than the trained infantrymen the unit needed. The old members of the regiment were better fighters, but a significant number of them had fallen in battle, the acting commander of Company E, black 1st Lt. Charles Ellis, could only lament. Some of the new arrivals were incapable of even breaking down a rifle.[6]

Seasoned sergeants and corporals might have offset some of the inadequacies by conducting intensive training, but out of a total of 426 noncommissioned officers (NCOs) who joined the regiment between 1 August and 18 September 1950, only 107 were in infantry-related specialties. The rest had spent their time in the Army as construction foremen, supply sergeants, communications supervisors, or performing other administrative or housekeeping tasks.[7] With heavy combat continuing, the trained men went into the line immediately. The rest filled in where they could but were often a burden.

"I have a[n] SFC that cannot do a job a corporal in a squad can do," Ellis told interviewers. "I have 29 SFC's, about 20 of whom are noncombat men from service units, and they are jumpy."[8]

The 25th Division stationed a number of white NCOs with the regiment at about that time to help remedy the problem. All were volunteers who had been promised promotion to officer status if they succeeded in their duties. Assigned to Company A under a black captain, they were so few in number that the development—signaling the breakdown of segregation under the pressures of combat in Korea—appears at first to have gone unnoticed by everyone except the regiment's higher-ranking enlisted men and NCOs, some of whom became incensed. As one enlisted man in the 3d Battalion, Charlie Lee Jones observed, the whites received battlefield commissions to second lieutenant, taking places that might have gone to blacks under other circumstances.[9]

Because adequate numbers of American infantry replacements were unavailable to reconstitute depleted regiments, the U.S. Army inaugurated the Korean Army Troops, United States Army (KATUSA), program to integrate South Korean soldiers into American units. It was not long before difficulties arose. With little more than ten days of training and a significant language barrier, the KATUSAs, as they came to be called, were often considered more of a hindrance than a help. In the 25th Division, commanders either employed them

---

5 WDs, 24th Inf Rgt, Jul and Aug 50, Strength and Replacement Statistics, boxes 3746–3747 and box 3750, respectively, RG 407, WNRC. For integration in the 2d Division, see Memo, Col C. C. Sloane, Jr., for General Craig, 29 Oct 50, exhibit D–6, in Eighth U.S. Army Korea, Report of Investigation Concerning 24th Infantry Regiment and Negro Soldiers in Combat, 15 Mar 51, boxes 1013–1014 (hereafter cited as Eighth Army Inspector General Investigation), RG 159, WNRC. For integration in the 24th Infantry Division, see Interv, Inspector General (IG) with Maj Gen John H. Church, 15 Nov 50, exhibit B–31, Eighth Army Inspector General Investigation. For integration of the 25th Infantry Division, see Memo for Adjutant General (AG), 19 Sep 50, sub: GCT Breakdown, exhibit D–2, Eighth Army Inspector General Investigation.

6 Interv, IG with Capt Charles Ellis, 15 Sep 50, exhibit B–5, Eighth Army Inspector General Investigation. See also Interv, Bernard L. Muehlbauer with James C. Yadon, 22 May 89. All interviews hereafter cited by John A. Cash, Bernard L. Muehlbauer, Timothy Rainey, William T. Bowers, Richard O. Perry, and George L. MacGarrigle are in CMH files.

7 Ibid. See also HQ, 25th Inf Div, Replacements Received First Four Grades in 24th Inf Rgt Between 1 August 1950 and 18 September 1950, 20 Sep 50, exhibit D–8, Eighth Army Inspector General Investigation.

8 Ibid. Quote from Interv, IG with Ellis, 15 Sep 50, exhibit B–5, Eighth Army Inspector General Investigation. Ellis' first sergeant told much the same story. See Interv, IG with M Sgt David Robinson, Co E, 15 Sep 50, exhibit B–6, Eighth Army Inspector General Investigation.

9 See Interv, IG with Capt William J. Jackson, 16 Sep 50, exhibit B–16, Eighth Army Inspector General Investigation. See also Interv, Clay Blair with John H. Michaelis, n.d., U.S. Army Military History Institute Senior Officer Oral History Program, Combat Leadership in Korea series, pp. 24, 34–36, MHI; Ltr, John S. Komp to George L. MacGarrigle, 14 Apr 95, CMH files. The assignment of whites to the 24th is described in Frank Whisonant, "White GI's Join All-Negro Unit," *Pittsburgh Courier*, 9 Sep 50. Whisonant says the men were greeted with open arms. The resentment of the white sergeants by the regiment's NCOs and enlisted men is mentioned in Intervs, John A. Cash with Charlie Lee Jones, 6 Sep 89; Floyd B. Williams, 6 Aug 88.

The enemy side of rocky crags on Battle Mountain

in separate squads or platoons or paired each Korean with an American "buddy." Either way, they were unreliable and difficult to control in battle.[10]

On 31 August the 25th Division itself was stretched from the Naktong River to the Yellow Sea. To the north, Colonel Fisher's 35th Infantry had responsibility for an area extending from the junction of the Nam and Naktong Rivers to a point about halfway between Haman and Saga. The regiment's 2d Battalion held the northern flank along the river. Its 1st Battalion, augmented with Company L of the 3d, straddled the Masan–Chungam-ni road to the south. A battalion of South Korean National Police filled the space between the two, while Companies I and K of the 3d Battalion held back in reserve.[11] Next in line came the 24th Infantry, with Colonel Roberts' 2d Battalion blocking the western approaches to Haman, while Corley's 3d Battalion, augmented by Company B of the 1st, held the ridge line between Battle Mountain and Sobuk-san.

Companies A and C of the unit's 1st Battalion stood to the rear in reserve. Several platoons of raw South Korean troops filled gaps here and there in the line.[12] Farthest to the south came the 5th Infantry regiment, now under the command of Lt. Col. John L. Throckmorton. The regiment's three battalions stood in line, the 1st holding the southern approaches to Sobuk-san, the 2d blocking the Chinju–Chindong-ni road, and the 3d guarding the region between the road and the sea.[13] (*See Map 9.*)

Adding to American strength, Lt. Col. John H. Michaelis' solid 27th Infantry regiment had just returned to the 25th Division after serving as the Eighth Army's reserve. It was holding at Masan on the night of 31 August, enjoying a brief respite before moving forward to replace the 5th Infantry on line south of the 24th Infantry. The unit's presence in the area gave General Kean a temporary

[10]EUSAK, Special Problems in the Korean Conflict, 5 Feb 52, pp. 15–23.

[11]WD, 35th Inf Rgt, 1–30 Sep 50, box 3755, RG 407, WNRC.

[12]WD, 24th Inf Rgt, 1–30 Sep 50, box 3755, RG 407, WNRC. See also Intervs, MacGarrigle with Stuart Force, 8 Aug 94, with Force's accompanying notes; Roscoe E. Dann, Jr., 24 and 28 Mar 94.

[13]WD, 5th Inf Rgt, 1–30 Sep 50, boxes 1–2, RG 338, WNRC.

advantage. In effect, until the exchange of regiments was completed, the 25th Division would consist of four full infantry regiments rather than three. "We knew that something big was in the wind," the division's artillery commander would later write, "but never before had there been plentiful uncommitted reserves behind our precarious lines. If the Reds had written us a letter and asked when we would like to have them attack, the answer would have been 'on September 1st.'"[14]

The North Koreans Attack

On the afternoon of 31 August forward observers within the 24th Infantry's 2d Battalion noticed enemy activity increasing 2,000 yards to their front and called for air strikes and artillery. From that moment on, all units within the regiment were on alert.[15] North Korean mortars and artillery opened up at 2330, laying fire along the entire American front with one of the heaviest bombardments they had ever imposed. The gunners paid particular attention to regimental and battalion command posts and to the roads leading into Haman.[16]

Enemy ground forces moved in under the barrage shortly after midnight on the morning of 1 September, mounting attacks from one end of the American line to the other. To the south, in the 5th Infantry's sector, enemy troops entered the position of one company of the 1st Battalion, but the unit held its ground and drove them back after an intense exchange of fire. About 0150 the regiment's 3d Battalion came under attack. Overrunning an outpost line and driving on the battalion's command post, the North Koreans managed to penetrate the positions of all three of the battalion's rifle companies as well as that of a company from the 2d Battalion. In the end, however, they were again driven back with heavy losses. In all, Throckmorton later reported that the 5th Infantry lost 8 killed, 23 wounded, and 5 missing in the action.[17]

A much more serious attack occurred on the 25th Division's northern flank, where the *7th North Korean Division* along with elements from the *4th* and *6th Divisions*—between eight and ten thousand men—fell upon Fisher's 35th Infantry. At the beginning of the attack, shortly after midnight on 1 September, a force estimated at four companies thrust down the Masan road toward the regiment's 1st Battalion, striking an attached company from the north while attempting to slip around the unit's southern flank. Meanwhile, on Sibidang Mountain, four miles to the northwest of Haman, another company came under attack, as did the South Korean police companies manning the gap between the 1st and 2d Battalions. Well dug in and surrounded by several layers of concertina wire and barbed-wire fencing, most of the Americans held, but the South Koreans gave way in a matter of minutes. Discovering the gap shortly after it occurred, a reserve company assisted by tanks counterattacked and reclaimed partial control of the area. By that time, however, up to a regiment of enemy had passed through. The force began to operate to Fisher's rear, causing trouble as far away as Chung-ni, some six miles to the east of Saga.[18]

Over the day that followed, 2 September, Fisher's beleaguered force held firm, calling air strikes and artillery down upon enemy troops attempting to cross the Nam River from Uiryong and obstructing enemy efforts to resupply the units that had penetrated to the rear of the American position. Setbacks occurred. Widely dispersed and therefore vulnerable, the 2d Battalion suffered a number of enemy breakthroughs. One of its companies, fighting both to the front and the rear, was

[14] Brig Gen G. B. Barth, Tropic Lightning and Taro Leaf in Korea, n.d., p. 28, CMH files; WD, 25th Inf Div, Sep 50, p. 2, boxes 3752–3754, RG 407, WNRC.

[15] Interv, IG with 1st Lt John L. Herren, 16 Sep 50, exhibit B–8, Eighth Army Inspector General Investigation; WD, 24th Inf Rgt, Aug 50, pp. 31–32. See also Interv, Cash with Colon Britt, 18 Aug 88.

[16] WD, 24th Inf Rgt, 1–30 Sep 50; Interv, IG with Lt Col Paul F. Roberts, 13 Sep 50, exhibit B–1, Eighth Army Inspector General Investigation.

[17] WD, 5th Inf Rgt, 1 Sep 50, boxes 1–2, RG 338, WNRC. See also Interv, MacGarrigle with D. Randall Beirne, 19 Aug 93.

[18] WD, 35th Inf Rgt, 1 Sep 50, box 3755, RG 407, WNRC. Although elements of the *4th North Korean Division* were positioned in front of the 35th, it is unclear whether they participated in the attack on the regiment or devoted their full attention to the U.S. 2d Infantry Division to the north.

completely cut off for a time and incurred heavy casualties. A platoon from another company was driven from its position by a large enemy force. Even so, air drops of ammunition and medical supplies allowed surrounded units to survive, and troops driven from their positions by overwhelming force time and again rallied to regain lost ground.[19]

In the end, augmented by clerks and other administrative personnel from headquarters units, engineers fighting as infantry, and a battalion from the 27th Infantry that arrived in time to provide critical assistance, the 35th prevailed. Although the enemy force to the regiment's rear remained active, the main force to Fisher's front withdrew to draw breath. Never before, General Kean would later observe, had a unit under such heavy assault closed the gaps in its front line while fighting a full-scale battle to its rear. He nominated the 35th for a Presidential Unit Citation.[20]

On 1 September, at the time when the enemy struck the 5th and 35th Infantry regiments, the 24th Infantry also came under attack. While North Korean patrols probed Corley's 3d Battalion on Battle Mountain, disrupting the unit's communications but otherwise doing little damage, the main enemy force, an estimated one to two thousand men, swept into the 2d Battalion's position on the Haman–Chungam-ni road, four miles to the north. "Fighting was heard until 0530 hours in the sectors occupied by the 2d [Battalion]," Corley's officers later reported from their vantage point on the mountain, "also in Haman, to our rear, and north and northeast of that town. The entire town of Haman appeared to be in flames."[21]

As the attack developed, Capt. Roger Walden's Company F astride the road and 1st Lt. Gorham Black's Company G to the south received particular attention. A platoon of South Korean troops to the north of Company F's position disintegrated almost immediately, as did a second platoon of South Koreans to the south, on the northern flank of Company G's position. A third, on the north flank of Company E, also began to give way.[22]

When the commanders of the American units involved saw what was happening, they attempted to mend the developing wound. Informed that the South Koreans were retreating, a sergeant in Company G, for one, stopped some of the fleeing men to determine what had happened. They indicated that they were out of ammunition but a search of several revealed that they had sufficient quantities to remain on line. Nevertheless, the men kept retreating. The acting commander of Company E, Lieutenant Ellis, also tried to stop them. "I went down to the Korean captain who was in charge," he recalled later, "and asked him why he was pulling out of position. He said: 'Enemy was coming.' I said you cannot fight them if you run." The officer tried to pull his men back into position, Ellis said, but they killed him and continued to run.[23]

It took little time for the advancing enemy to find the gaps the departing Koreans had left. Although American artillery had been targeted in advance on the road into Haman and a 50-caliber machine gun and a 75-mm. recoilless rifle supposedly barred the way, they could do little but slow the onslaught without the assistance the Koreans could have provided. The artillery con-

[19] WD, 25th Inf Div, 1 Sep 50; Narrative Rpt, 25th Inf Div in Korea, Sep 50; WD, 2d Bn, 35th Inf Rgt, 1 Sep 50, box 3755, RG 407, WNRC.
[20] Narrative Rpt, 25th Inf Div in Korea, Sep 50; WD, 25th Inf Div, 1 Sep 50.
[21] Different estimates are provided for the size of the enemy force which struck the 2d Battalion. Based on prisoner interrogations, the regimental war diary estimated the enemy to be in regimental strength. The war diary further stated that was about three thousand men, but the strength of the *6th North Korean Division* at this time was about sixty-three hundred, making a regiment about two thousand strong. The regimental operations officer, Maj. Owen H. Carter, estimated the enemy force to be about one thousand. The 3d Battalion,

observing the fighting soon after daylight, estimated six to eight hundred enemy near Haman. See WD, 24th Inf Rgt, Sep 50, p. 3. Quote from WD, 3d Bn, 24th Inf Rgt, Sep 50, p. 1. Both in box 3755, RG 407, WNRC. Intervs, MacGarrigle with Owen H. Carter, 21 and 24 Jun 94.
[22] Ltr, Richard F. Archer to David Carlisle, 6 Jul 89, CMH files; Intervs, IG with Herren, 16 Sep 50, exhibit B–8, Eighth Army Inspector General Investigation; Ellis, 15 Sep 50, exhibit B–5, Eighth Army Inspector General Investigation.
[23] Intervs, IG with Herren, 16 Sep 50, exhibit B–8, Eighth Army Inspector General Investigation; Ellis, 15 Sep 50, exhibit B–5, Eighth Army Inspector General Investigation.

tinued to fire for a time, but the two direct-fire guns quickly and inexplicably fell silent.[24]

As the breakthrough continued, the platoon from Company F closest to the road was enveloped and badly mauled. It disintegrated.[25] That put the rest of the company at risk. Although the unit's men had dug in, they lacked many of the defenses the 35th Infantry had constructed to the north. They had never, for example, been organized around strongpoints and were very spread out.[26] As a result, the company's center platoon was also overrun and an 81-mm. mortar position somewhat to the unit's rear near the road likewise went down.[27]

Walden had stationed himself in a forward observation post located toward the northern end of his company's line. As the attack developed, he called in fire support so close to his own position that battery commanders questioned the map coordinates he was giving them.[28] In the end, however, courage was not enough. Communications with battalion headquarters broke down. In addition, although a number of Walden's men held firm, some had lost heart and fled.[29] As for the rest, they

seemed in danger of annihilation, either by the enemy or by friendly artillery and mortar fire.[30]

Deciding after daylight on 1 September that he could not hold out, Walden pulled his men to the rear in hopes of relocating them on a hill he had earlier plotted as a fall-back position. Arriving toward noon, he found that the enemy already occupied the site and concluded that he had no choice but to continue north toward the 35th Infantry. Circling east toward the Haman-Saga road, he would then be able to make his way back to the 24th.[31] Eighty-five men took part in the trek that followed, out of a total of 185 who had been present at the beginning of the attack.[32] When they arrived in the 35th's area and informed commanders that there was nothing left on their southern flank, those officers were, as Walden put it, "somewhat aghast." The group made it back to the 24th's lines at 1800 that evening. Champeny assigned it to provide security for the regimental command post until he could reassemble the 2d Battalion.[33]

While the remnant of Walden's unit was holding on the hill, the rest of the 2d Battalion came under pressure and began to crumble. For a time, the northernmost portions of Company G held firm, but many of the men were so skittish, according to white 1st Lt. Houston McMurray, that most expended their ammunition and grenades on false targets and imaginary noises before the enemy attacked in earnest. When the final assault came, they had little left and began to fall back as small groups straggled to the rear. In the end, McMurray avowed, "Out of the 21 ROK's and the 48 men in my platoon, there were only between 12 and 15 [left] . . ., and a little over half were my men." Bypassed, the group pulled into a close circle and held out until dawn. Then the enemy discovered its position and forced a retreat.[34]

---

[24] American artillery had been zeroed in on the enemy's probable avenue of approach days before the attack. See Interv, MacGarrigle with Preston A. Davis, 18 Apr 94. See also Interv, IG with 1st Lt Arthur Jackson, 16 Sep 50, exhibit B–17, Eighth Army Inspector General Investigation.

[25] Interv, Cash with Roger Walden, 25 Feb 87.

[26] The defenses of the unit are mentioned in Interv, MacGarrigle with Preston Davis, 18 Apr 94. Davis was a forward observer assigned to Company F by Battery B of the 159th Field Artillery (FA) Battalion. See also Interv, IG with 1st Lt Arthur Jackson, 16 Sep 50, exhibit B–17, Eighth Army Inspector General Investigation. Jackson was a lieutenant in Company F.

[27] WDs, 24th Inf Rgt, 1 Sep 50, and 2d Bn, 24th Inf Rgt, 1–30 Sep 50, p. 1, both in box 3755, RG 407, WNRC.

[28] See Interv, MacGarrigle with Preston Davis, 18 Apr 94. See also 25th Inf Div GO 306, 6 Nov 50, Silver Star Award Citation for Capt Roger Walden. Unless otherwise indicated, general orders for this volume are on file in the Army's Awards Branch of the Personnel Service Support Division of the Adjutant General Directorate of the U.S. Total Army Personnel Command (PERSCOM), Alexandria, Va. See also Interv, Cash with Edward Simmons, 18 Mar 89. Simmons was Walden's radio operator.

[29] Lieutenant Jackson observed that little straggling occurred until after the breakthrough. See Interv, IG with 1st Lt Arthur Jackson, 16 Sep 50, exhibit B–17, Eighth Army Inspector General Investigation.

[30] Interv, Cash with Walden, 25 Feb 87.

[31] Ibid. See also Hand-drawn Map of Haman area, prepared by Roger Walden, Jul 93, CMH files.

[32] Interv, IG with Roger Walden, 14 Sep 50, exhibit B–3, Eighth Army Inspector General Investigation.

[33] Roger Walden comments to David Carlisle, 25 Feb 87, CMH files.

[34] Interv, IG with 1st Lt Houston M. McMurray, 5 Sep 50, exhibit 4, attached to Ltr, Maj Gen W. B. Kean, 25th Inf Div, to

Farther south, Company E also broke down. At the first sign of the enemy attack, the leader of the 3d Platoon, a lieutenant with no previous combat experience, began to move his men to the rear. The acting commander of Company E, Ellis, intercepted him. "I asked him where was he going," Ellis told interviewers. "He said the enemy was attacking them in force. I knew it was a damn lie because no small arms [were] fired. I threatened to kill him if he did not get back in position. I fired a shot between his feet just to scare him. He went back into position."[35]

Pinned down by enemy fire shortly thereafter, Ellis could give no orders and watched helplessly as the lieutenant and his men once more panicked and ran. Some were cut down by enemy machine-gun fire. Others fell into their own minefields. "The men were just running anywhere," an acting platoon leader in Ellis' company, M. Sgt. David Robinson, remembered. "Many who were killed would have survived if they had stayed in their foxholes and fought."[36] A squad leader in Company E, Cpl. Joel Ward, later related that he had shot a replacement for running.[37] Seeing the slaughter, other soldiers also stayed in place. They endured for two days against seven attacks, much of the time without food or water, before a relieving force arrived. Except for one man who fell to artillery fire, every one of those men survived.[38]

The remnants of Companies E and G continued to fight on, but to no avail. In the hours before dawn on 1 September, according to the battalion commander, Colonel Roberts, between one-third and one-half of the men in his unit straggled, with many withdrawing to the battalion command post, collocated with the command post for the battalion's weapons unit, Company H, some nine hundred yards to the rear of Company F's position. The men were placed in security details until they could return to their units, but their presence made little difference. About 0300 the enemy arrived. Using the American 75-mm. recoilless rifle that had earlier blocked the road to the rear of Company F, he destroyed a tank barring his way and breached the position's outer defenses. With that, the stragglers who had congregated at the site began to move out. Their panic spread to other troops who also broke and ran, opening the way for the enemy to enter the command post itself.[39]

The men who remained fought hard. "We manned our defensive positions to defend the battalion CP which was on the edge of a village," Company H radioman Nathaniel Pipkins recalled. "We received small arms fire from the vicinity of the village which was about 100 yards away. We returned the fire. . . . The battalion S–2 [white 1st Lt. Colon Britt] organized a counterattack force and pushed the enemy to the other side of the village. . . . The enemy counterattacked and hit us on all sides. I could see the flash of weapons all around. We lost the Company commander . . . and the S–2. . . . There was a fierce firefight. Grenades were being thrown. I was blown over and stunned."[40] Other soldiers continued the fight. Cpl. Columbus Samuels, for one, later received the Silver Star for manning the artillery liaison switchboard throughout the attack, despite enemy small-arms, machine-gun, and mortar fire and the presence of enemy soldiers who at times came within twenty feet of his position. The officers and men of the battalion aid station, located nearby, also stayed on line, treating some ninety wounded soldiers at

Commanding General, Eighth U.S. Army (Korea), 9 Sep 90, sub: Combat Effectiveness of the 24th Infantry Regiment. Kean's letter and its attachments are contained in Far East Command Inspector General Investigation, sec. BX, boxes 1013–1014, RG 159, WNRC. Statements attached to General Kean's letter each have an exhibit number and are hereafter cited as in the Kean Letter file. See also Interv, IG with Herren, 16 Sep 50, exhibit B–8, Eighth Army Inspector General Investigation.

[35] Interv, IG with Ellis, 15 Sep 50, exhibit B–5, Eighth Army Inspector General Investigation. Sfc. Edward Marshall tells the same story, observing that there was no enemy on the hill. See Interv, IG with Sfc Edward Marshall, 15 Sep 50, exhibit B–7, Eighth Army Inspector General Investigation.

[36] Interv, IG with Robinson, 15 Sep 50, exhibit B–6, Eighth Army Inspector General Investigation.

[37] Interv, Cash with Joel T. Ward, 21 Jul 88.

[38] Interv, IG with Ellis, 15 Sep 50, exhibit B–5, Eighth Army Inspector General Investigation.

[39] WD, 24th Inf Rgt, 1 Sep 50; Interv, IG with Roberts, 13 Sep 50, exhibit B–1, Eighth Army Inspector General Investigation. See also Intervs, MacGarrigle with Lloyd V. Ott, 19 Jul 94; Cash with Joshua Storrs, 8 Sep 89.

[40] Interv, Muehlbauer with Nathaniel Pipkins, 23 Aug 88.

great risk to their own lives. Many were cited for their heroism.[41]

Colonel Champeny sent a platoon from Company A of the 1st Battalion along with two tanks from Company A of the 79th Heavy Tank Battalion to provide relief and to rescue Roberts. Slowed by enemy sniper and artillery fire, the platoon penetrated only as far as a heavy mortar position one-half mile to the rear of the 2d Battalion's command post. The tanks continued, reaching their goal shortly before 0400. By then, however, all communication between the 2d Battalion headquarters and the regimental command post in Haman had ceased.[42] The tanks assisted in the evacuation of Roberts and a number of vehicles, but could do little more. Most of the men who had defended the position were gone, and key officers in the battalion's command—the executive, operations, and intelligence officers along with the commander of Company H—were all either dead or seriously wounded. The break of dawn shortly thereafter revealed a scene of incredible carnage and destruction.[43]

At 0730, with the remnants of Companies E and G holding on doggedly, Roberts and the officers who remained attempted to collect enough of their men to assist an effort by portions of the 1st Battalion to restore their unit's old position. Only forty men could be found to make the attempt. The assault proceeded as scheduled but soon bogged down and collapsed. Hit by a counterblow, the men retreated to positions two miles to the rear on the high ground east of Haman. By then, the regimen-

General MacArthur presents Colonel Roberts with Oak Leaf Clusters to the Silver and Bronze Stars.

tal command post in Haman itself had come under threat. Champeny responded by relocating it to a valley east of the town near Engineer Road. When that location came under fire, he moved it again even farther to the rear.[44] Battery C of the 159th Field Artillery Battalion, located just to the north of Haman, also came under attack. After fighting at close quarters to preserve its guns, it made a hair's breadth escape down the Haman road and out the

---

[41] Ibid.; Interv, Cash with Britt, 18 Aug 88. For Samuels, see 25th Inf Div GO 176, 22 Sep 50. For the medics, see 25th Inf Div GOs 310, 7 Nov 50; 339, 15 Nov 50; and 346, 16 Nov 50. In all seven medics received the Bronze Star.

[42] WD, 24th Inf Rgt, 1 Sep 50.

[43] Intervs, IG with Roberts, 6 Sep 50, exhibit 30, Kean Letter file; Roberts, 13 Sep 50, exhibit B–1, Eighth Army Inspector General Investigation; Col Arthur S. Champeny, 28 Sep 50, exhibit B–22, Eighth Army Inspector General Investigation. The Company H withdrawal is described in Interv, Cash with Storrs, 8 Sep 89. See also 25th Inf Div GO 235, 20 Oct 50, Award Citation for Cpl Wyatt. For a description of the carnage at the command post, see Lyle Rishell, *With a Black Platoon in Combat: A Year in Korea* (College Station: Texas A&M University Press, 1993), pp. 73–74.

[44] WD, 24th Inf Rgt, 1–30 Sep 50, pp. 3–4; WD, 25th Inf Div, 1 Sep 50. For movement of the 1st Battalion, see Ltr, Waymon R. Ransom to John A. Cash, 22 Oct 88, CMH files; Intervs, MacGarrigle with Carter, 21 and 24 Jun 94; William T. Bowers with Edward H. Skiffington, 14 Apr 94. See also 25th Inf Div GO 178, 28 Mar 51, awarding Silver Star to Skiffington.

Engineer Road to a new position.[45] The situation might have disintegrated further, but for the good work of fighter bombers from the U.S. Fifth Air Force. Throughout the day on 1 September they laid bombs and napalm on enemy forces attacking American units from the flank and rear.[46]

The inclination of many of the men of the 2d Battalion to abandon their positions and their unwillingness to go back on line became the source of angry comment among whites at the scene but also among some blacks. "There were large numbers of the 2d [Battalion] milling around and running to the rear at Haman," the white executive officer of the 1st Battalion, Maj. Eugene J. Carson, declared. "The few officers left were attempting to gather the men up. When the area came under mortar fire, the entire group took off, except for the officers."[47]

Colonel Roberts was equally disturbed. Although careful to state that the men of Company G stayed in position until overrun, he also made it a point to remark on incidents of mass hysteria he had seen. When officers returned one group of stragglers to the front and placed the men in foxholes, the soldiers were so skittish that they headed for the rear at the least provocation. When American tanks came up, he said, the men heard the noise and immediately withdrew in disorder, "stomping and running over each other."[48] The executive officer of Company G, white 1st Lt. John L. Herren, remarked that even if a number of the men in his unit held out, forming scattered pockets of resistance, the conduct of others left much to be desired. After the enemy entered Haman, he said, he had been ordered to set up a blocking position south of the town: "I ordered quite a large group of G Company to join me, but finally wound up with approximately eight men." The others "would not

come." They "remained under cover of a concrete wall which surrounded the regimental CP compound."[49] Lieutenant Ellis, a black, was among the angriest of the officers who commented. After summarizing his experiences in the 1 September attack, he observed that commanders had become afraid to use the word *withdraw*. "You say that, and you get a mob on your hands."[50]

Colonel Champeny was incensed at the performance of his men. Observing in an interview that the 2d Battalion had discarded most of its weapons during its withdrawal, he told of Lieutenant Ellis' difficulties in holding Company E in place. When he asked the officer for a solution to the problem, he said the lieutenant had responded that "he did not believe any all-colored outfit would ever be reliable, that his solution would be to put a few colored troops with the whites." Champeny added that he considered Ellis "one of my good company commanders."[51]

Overall, Champeny's sense of disgust with his unit was readily apparent to other whites. When the 1st Battalion of the 27th Infantry joined Companies A and C of the 1st Battalion of the 24th on the afternoon of 1 September, in an attempt to restore the positions of the 2d Battalion, a first lieutenant in the all-white unit, Uzal Ent, recalled vividly how Champeny drove slowly through the chaos on the road leading out of Haman. He kept shaking his head and saying over and over to the deploying white troops, "I'm sorry boys. I'm sorry."[52]

Summarizing the opinions of officers who had served in or dealt with the 24th Infantry at Sangju and in the Pusan Perimeter, the Eighth Army's inspector general gave special prominence to "Negro characteristics" as a possible reason for the problems the unit had experienced. According to

[45] Intervs, MacGarrigle with Gustav H. Franke, 14 and 28 Jul 94; WD, 159th FA Bn, Sep 50, box 3756, RG 407, WNRC.

[46] Barth, Tropic Lightning and Taro Leaf in Korea, n.d., p. 28. See also Robert F. Futrell, *The United States Air Force in Korea, 1950–1953* (Washington, D.C.: Office of Air Force History, 1983), pp. 142–43.

[47] Interv, IG with Maj Eugene Carson, 6 Sep 50, exhibit 21, Kean Letter file.

[48] Interv, IG with Roberts, 13 Sep 50, exhibit B–1, Eighth Army Inspector General Investigation.

[49] Interv, IG with Herren, 16 Sep 50, exhibit B–8, Eighth Army Inspector General Investigation.

[50] Interv, IG with Ellis, 15 Sep 50, exhibit B–5, Eighth Army Inspector General Investigation.

[51] Interv, IG with Champeny, 28 Sep 50, exhibit B–22, Eighth Army Inspector General Investigation. See also Intervs, MacGarrigle with Sam J. Adams, Jr., 15 and 17 Jun 94; Preston Davis, 18 Apr 94.

[52] Memorandum for the Record (MFR), MacGarrigle and Bowers, 26 Oct 93, CMH files.

those witnesses, black soldiers as a group were hardly as alert as white soldiers and tended to sleep while on duty. In addition, they strayed from their positions more, lacked trust in one another, suffered from too much imagination at night, tended to panic under adversity, disliked digging foxholes or remaining in them, and seemed to have no sense of responsibility for equipment or supplies.[53]

In fact, if the 2d Battalion had failed, strictly military reasons were most often the cause, not some putative set of Negro characteristics. It is clear from the comments of observers, for example, that the unit was hardly as well positioned as it could have been. A platoon of poorly trained and unpredictable South Koreans separated each one of its elements, leaving them all vulnerable to attack from the flank. Colonel Fisher, to the north, was much more perceptive. He put all of his South Koreans in one place so that if they broke, the rest of his line would remain intact.

In the same way, while forward units of the 24th may have been dug in, the front they guarded was too extensive for the force available. Instead of organizing around several small, easily defended strongpoints, as Fisher had, Champeny and his officers attempted to use the 2d Battalion to guard a two-mile line.[54] That might have been feasible if a strong enough reserve had been available—guarding the more critical Masan road, Fisher had five companies on line and part of a battalion in reserve—but Champeny's 1st Battalion had already lost Company B to Corley on Battle Mountain, and Company C was virtually combat ineffective from the beating it had received during the previous week's fighting. That left Company A, fewer than one hundred and fifty men, to counterattack an invading force of possibly two thousand.

As if that were not enough, while the 24th's forward positions appear to have been well enough prepared, fall-back positions to the rear of at least some of Champeny's line units appear to have been inadequate, a possibly fatal weakness if the troops were forced into a retreat. In the case of Company F, for example, when the 27th Infantry's counterattack regained what had been the unit's former rear positions late on the afternoon of 1 September, a cursory inspection of the site revealed only a few foxholes. "There was nothing to indicate there was a company position here previously," Lieutenant Ent observed. "We remarked on it at the time."[55]

Tactical dispositions, however, were only the beginning of the problem. Because of the racial antipathies prevalent in the regiment, the practices they gave rise to and the suspicions they engendered, the men of the 24th Infantry mistrusted many of their officers. Although regimental and division war diaries often attempted to cover up failures, Cpl. Joel Ward, for example, was convinced that many of the white officers in the regiment wanted the unit to appear to fail. To that end, he said, they suppressed good news so that its men would receive no credit for anything they did well.[56]

The tensions that resulted often overlapped onto black officers who seemed too intent upon developing their careers. Lieutenant Ellis provides a case in point. Although he had performed about as well as any officer in the attack at Haman, some of his men clearly loathed him because they believed his attitudes were more white than black. He had a Creole wife and seemed to think he was superior, Ward believed. "We think he had an identity crisis. . . . I recall seeing him standing in a rice paddy mired up to his knees firing his .45's into the air. He allegedly was cracking up. Everyone had a distaste for him. He tried to show everyone up, even in Gifu."[57]

[53] IG, Eighth Army, Summary of Comments by Witnesses, n.d., exhibit D–20, Eighth Army Inspector General Investigation.

[54] Department of the Army (DA) Field Manual (FM) 7–50, *The Infantry Division*, 11 Jan 50, p. 237. When defending on a frontage of more than 10,000 yards, a regiment was to organize key terrain as "self-sustaining powerful fighting forces capable of continued resistance even when bypassed or surrounded." The rest of the main line of resistance was to be lightly held.

[55] Ibid. Quote from MFR, MacGarrigle and Bowers, 26 Oct 93. See also Interv, MacGarrigle with Preston Davis, 18 Apr 94.

[56] Interv, Cash with Ward, 21 Jul 88.

[57] Quote from ibid. For another view of Ellis, see Interv, MacGarrigle with Preston Davis, 18 Apr 94. For other comments on the lack of trust between enlisted men and officers, see Interv, Muehlbauer with Charles B. Gregg, 8 Sep 88.

The chaos always attendant upon war only compounded the problem. During the first sixty days in Korea, another corporal in Company E, Nathaniel Reed, observed in an interview that his own unit went through four platoon leaders who were either killed or wounded. There were also too many changes among lieutenants and company commanders, he continued. "What do you do when you lose your leadership and are disorganized and have no confidence in those who come in as replacements?" Reed answered his own question. Given the poor leadership and bad communications that seemed to dog the unit, he said, the men ran. "I know for a fact that I ran, too. . . . Everybody ran, but we were poorly led and equipped. I remember when we were out on listening posts without commo [communications equipment]. We would put these new replacements out there, and in the morning they would be gone."[58]

The arrival of the 1st Battalion of the 27th Infantry, commanded by Lt. Col. Gilbert Check, at 1000 on 1 September helped to stem the enemy advance. But before the unit could counterattack it had to push its way through the confused mass of vehicles and men clogging the roads around Haman. "During the period we were at the 24th's regimental CP," Check's executive officer, Capt. Don R. Hickman, recalled, "the regimental CO and his S–3 were out in the middle of the road personally stopping vehicles and taking stragglers off."[59] The sort of difficulties Check and his men encountered were described by a white military policeman, Sgt. Jack W. Riley. He, along with a chaplain, three officers, and another military policeman, had stopped all traffic on a section of Engineer Road. Taking stragglers off vehicles, they collected about two hundred and fifty soldiers, only a little more than half of whom had weapons. Suddenly Riley

heard a mortar shell hit and a short burst from a machine gun in the distance, then I looked up and heard the men shouting and then I saw men running down the

mountain. I would ask them, why don't you stay and fight, haven't you got a rifle? Most of them would not answer, but a few said they were out of ammo. I then went back and reported to the 24th regiment commanding officer and told him we would go through the artillery battery and pick up all the men we could. We rounded up about 50 stragglers the rest of the evening. Out of all the men we stopped, we asked for sergeants and officers, but none volunteered. You ask them why they wouldn't stay and fight and they would laugh at you and say, "We didn't see any M.P.s on the hill."[60]

From time to time mortar shells would land, targeted on Champeny's command post. When they did, they had the effect of rocks falling into a pond, setting off waves of confusion among the retreating troops as individuals and groups of men scampered for cover or hastened their way to the rear. No counterattack occurred until late in the afternoon, when General Kean finally ordered Check to restore the abandoned positions. By then most of the men of the 24th had passed, and the road west had cleared. Over the next three hours, assisted by Companies A and C of the 24th, which served as a reserve, Check's men advanced three miles, reaching the 24th's former fall-back positions but still some two hundred yards short of the unit's main line of resistance on 31 August. As the force neared its goal, it came upon a mass of abandoned arms, equipment, and vehicles. Reequipping itself with the discarded materiel, it dug in for the night. Resuming the attack the next morning, the battalion reached its goal at noon.[61]

During the day that followed, 2 September, Check's men beat off a strong enemy counterattack but also spent some time recovering machine guns, mortars, ammunition, and other equipment abandoned by the 24th. "It was reported to me," Hickman told investigators a week later, "that our men went right into prepared positions left by the 24th and took over the crew-served weapons and

---

[58]Interv, Cash with Nathaniel Reed, 6 Jan 90. Reed was court-martialed and convicted of straggling but was later exonerated.

[59]Interv, IG with Capt Don R. Hickman, Exec Ofcr, 1st Bn, 27th Inf Rgt, 8 Sep 50, exhibit 32, Kean Letter file.

[60]Interv, IG with Jack W. Riley, 3 Sep 50, exhibit 23, Kean Letter file.

[61]Interv, IG with Hickman, 8 Sep 50, exhibit 32, Kean Letter file. See also WD, 1st Bn, 27th Inf Rgt, 1 Sep 50, and 1st Bn, 27th Inf Rgt, Opns Rpt, 1–30 Sep 50, p. 1, both in box 3755, RG 407, WNRC; Intervs, IG with Lt Col Gilbert J. Check, 8 Sep 50, exhibit 31, Kean Letter file; MacGarrigle with Owen Carter, 21 and 24 Jun 94.

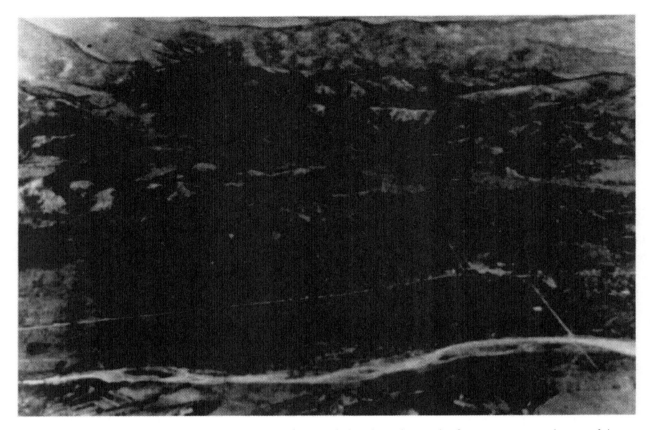

Mountain mass west of Haman: the town is in the center foreground; the 2d Battalion, 24th Infantry, position is on the crest of the second ridge above the town.

ammunition and used them on the spot." Over the next two days the 27th held the line against several strong, persistent enemy attacks.[62]

By the evening of 4 September the companies of the 2d Battalion of the 24th had been reorganized. At 1900 that day Miller's 1st Battalion, with Companies E and F attached but without Company B which remained on Battle Mountain, relieved Check's men in the positions that Roberts' 2d Battalion had held on 31 August. Check moved his battalion to a location east of Haman. At the same time, Champeny returned his regimental command post to Haman, stationing the 2d Battalion's Companies G and H along the high

ground to the west of Haman as security. The 24th's men arrived, according to Check, in "good shape and fashion."[63]

The enemy tried again just before dawn on 5 September, launching attacks against a number of points to the front of the 1st Battalion and its attached units as well as to the rear. Elements of Company H near Champeny's command post received one of the first assaults. In the face of at most a harassing attack, the force abandoned two machine guns and withdrew.[64] Shortly thereafter an attack of at best moderate size occurred against Company C, which likewise left its position. Whether Company E came under pressure at that

[62] Interv, IG with Hickman, 8 Sep 50, exhibit 32, Kean Letter file. For a list of weapons and equipment recovered in the 2d Battalion's area. see Encl 2. Kean Letter file.

[63] Interv, IG with Check, 8 Sep 50, exhibit 31, Kean Letter file. See also WD, 24th Inf Rgt, Sep 50, pp. 7–9.

[64] Interv, IG with Roberts, 6 Sep 50, exhibit 30, Kean Letter file.

time remains unclear, but the unit also relinquished its place in the line.[65]

Adding weight to an impression growing among the men that a major attack was in progress, infiltrators launched a grenade assault against the regimental command post in Haman. Several tanks and the regiment's intelligence and reconnaissance platoon drove them back, but not before they had blown up an ammunition truck located less than two hundred yards from the command post.[66] In a similar assault, a platoon of enemy infantrymen crept to within hand-grenade range of the 1st Battalion's command post to the south of Haman. The unit's executive officer, Maj. Eugene J. Carson, managed to beat back the attack, but by the time he did, his original complement of 45 Americans and 20 South Koreans had dwindled to no more than 30 men, 7 of whom were wounded. At dawn, Carson said, "I looked down the hill and saw approximately 40 men get up out of the rice paddies and go over to a tank. . . . This same group reported to regiment that they were driven off the hill."[67]

The situation remained confused for some time after the attacks. A white captain who said he was the commanding officer of Company E of the 24th led thirty to forty soldiers to the command post of the 1st Battalion of the 27th Infantry. He reported that a force of perhaps 2,000 North Koreans had overrun a blocking position his unit had assumed on a road outside of Haman. Meanwhile, he said, obviously referring to the incident in which the ammunition truck had exploded, it appeared that the regimental command post had been overrun and that the ammunition dump had blown up. Colonel Check immediately dispatched a rescue force consisting of a platoon of tanks, one platoon of infantry, and the

group from the 24th.[68] Entering Haman, Check's officers established that nothing of major importance had occurred, but during their trip into the town they encountered a number of fleeing men who reported that the 24th had again been overrun. "I got out on the road and started to turn some of these soldiers around," the 27th's operations officer, Capt. James Hunsaker, reported. "Some of them were very reluctant to go back and I took my carbine off my shoulder, pointed it at them and started them back up the hill. . . . I told them . . . that any man who turned around or turned back would be shot." No further incidents occurred. The men made it to Haman unopposed. Later that morning, Company C counterattacked and regained the ground it had lost.[69]

Colonel Corley Takes Command

The following day, 6 September, Colonel Champeny was inspecting the frontline positions of Roger Walden's Company F to the west of Haman. Despite warnings that enemy snipers were near, he went ahead with his inspection and soon fell wounded.[70] Shortly thereafter General Kean appointed the commander of the 3d Battalion, Colonel Corley, to lead the 24th, making him, for the moment, the youngest regimental commander in Korea. The executive officer of the 3d Battalion, newly promoted Lt. Col. Graydon A. Tunstall, took Corley's place in the unit.

The new regimental commander took stock of the 24th and did not like what he saw. All of the unit's battalions had been hard hit or overrun in either the 1 September attack or in earlier operations, Corley told investigators ten days after succeeding Champeny. Although the regiment had maintained its integrity as a fighting force, he believed it could never be depended upon in a major action and might not hold if another strong enemy assault occurred. Meanwhile, the 2d and 3d Battalions had become so intermingled that tactical unity was affected; training

[65] Statement of Lt Col Charles R. Herrmann, 17 Sep 50, exhibit D–20, Eighth Army Inspector General Investigation; Interv, IG with Check, 8 Sep 50, exhibit 31, Kean Letter file. See also Interv, IG with Maj Eugene Carson, 14 Sep 50, exhibit B–2, Eighth Army Inspector General Investigation; WD, 24th Inf Rgt, Sep 50, p. 11.

[66] WD, 24th Inf Rgt, 1–30 Sep 50, p. 10.

[67] Interv, IG with Carson, 14 Sep 50, exhibit B–2, Eighth Army Inspector General Investigation; Ltr, Ransom to Cash, 22 Oct 88, pp. 9–10.

[68] Interv, IG with Check, 8 Sep 50, exhibit 31, Kean Letter file.

[69] Quote from Interv, IG with Capt James D. Hunsaker, 6 Sep 50, exhibit 33, Kean Letter file. See also WD, 24th Inf Rgt, 1–30 Sep 50, p. 11.

[70] Walden comments to Carlisle, 25 Feb 87.

was so poor that the men tended to fire off all their ammunition at the beginning of an engagement without thinking about what would happen when it was gone; most key noncommissioned and staff officers had been killed or wounded; bickering between whites and blacks was on the rise; and morale within the unit seemed at low ebb.

Corley was particularly concerned about his noncommissioned officers, a number of whom he believed had failed to carry a fair share of the load. In order to compensate during the 1 September attack, all of the 3d Battalion's first sergeants had served on the battle line and none could be spared for important tasks that arose elsewhere. In the same way, staff officers had been forced to fill gaps at the front when they should have been at the rear headquarters in Masan seeing to their primary responsibilities. Most of all, straggling seemed epidemic within the regiment. During Corley's three weeks in command of the 3d Battalion, hundreds of men had abandoned their positions without leave or satisfactory cause.[71]

Corley was unwilling to blame continued straggling on the low quality of the replacements he was receiving. Those men were, he told investigators, about as good as could be expected. Neither was he certain that race was all that great a factor. He had the same problem with straggling among the South Korean troops assigned to the regiment, he said, yet North Korean troops attacked and fought "like demons." He suggested that blacks as a group might hold their ground better if they were integrated into white units. But even then, either out of prejudice or for practical reasons, he declined to suggest that whites, except in isolated cases, should ever be assigned to formerly all-black units.[72]

Paradoxically, the Army was having so much difficulty finding trained replacements that, at the very moment when he was stating his reservations, a number of white sergeants were serving in the 24th Infantry, and blacks were beginning to be assigned to all-white units in the 25th Division.[73]

In the days following his assignment as commander, Corley took steps to remedy many of the inadequacies he had seen. Rallying his sergeants and staff officers, he issued instructions that senior noncommissioned officers and personnel and logistical officers were to remain where their assignments placed them rather than attempt to remedy conditions in forward areas. He also took steps to reemphasize the necessity for improved fire discipline. Within a week, he said, he felt he could see results from the changes he had made. Efficiency within the unit had improved, and firing discipline was better. The men were also digging foxholes with more consistency. As one of Corley's sergeants observed in a 15 September interview with the inspector general, they no longer had any doubts. "You don't have to tell them [to dig] anymore."[74]

There was, however, no quick and easy solution to the straggling. Where Colonel White had hesitated to use courts-martial to enforce discipline, Champeny had been very aggressive in bringing charges against soldiers for misbehavior before the enemy. Yet except for 1st Lt. Leon A. Gilbert, who received a death sentence on 6 September, and another soldier in the service company convicted on 2 September, none of those cases had come to trial by the time Corley took command and none had made much impression upon the men. Straggling continued on such a large

[71] Interv, IG with Corley, 16 Sep 50, exhibit B–18, Eighth Army Inspector General Investigation; MFR, Lt Col John T. Corley, 22 Jan 51, sub: Background of Founding of *Eagle Forward*, CMH files. The bickering is described in Frank Whisonant, "Charge Discontent Riddling 'Fighting 24th,' GI's Gone Sour on White Officers Slandering Outfit," *Pittsburgh Courier*, 2 Sep 50. For other views of the regiment by new arrivals, see Intervs, MacGarrigle with Joseph Baranowski, 24 Aug 94; Roscius C. Newell, 10 Nov 94.

[72] Interv, IG with John T. Corley, 16 Sep 50, exhibit B–18, Eighth Army Inspector General Investigation. See also exhibit C, in General Headquarters, Far East Command, Report of Investigation Regarding Alleged Irregularities in the Administration of Military Justice in the 25th Infantry Division, 27 Mar 51, boxes 1013–1014 (hereafter cited as Far East Command Inspector General Investigation), RG 159, WNRC.

[73] The Eighth Army's adjutant general issued instructions to assign blacks to all-white units on 5 September 1950. See also WD, 25th Inf Div, 5 Sep 50, boxes 3752–3754, RG 407, WNRC; Interv, MacGarrigle with Gustav J. Gillert, 4 May 94.

[74] Interv, IG with M Sgt Wilbur Lawton, 15 Sep 50, exhibit B–12, Eighth Army Inspector General Investigation.

Commander	Number Charged	Charges Preferred by Blacks	Number Convicted	Number Acquitted	Number Withdrawn
White.......... 4	3	3		1
Champeny 38	16	17	3	18
Corley......... 13	9	12	1	
Total.......... 55	28	32	4	19

Table 7—24th Infantry General Courts-Martial July–October 1950

Source: Exhibits C, D–1, D–2, in General Headquarters, Far East Command, Report of Investigation Regarding Alleged Irregularities in the Administration of Military Justice in the 25th Infantry Division, 27 Mar 51, boxes 1013–1014, RG 159, WNRC.

scale that between 15 August and 15 September at least four hundred and sixty individuals had abandoned their posts. To make the troops more aware of what could happen to them if they were arrested and charged, Corley instituted a system of strict record keeping that kept track of first offenders. He warned the men that future violations would result in court-martial and that the maximum penalty could be death. Nevertheless, whether that policy or subsequent trials of offenders would have any effect on straggling would be a matter of conjecture until the 24th once more faced heavy combat.[75] (*Table 7*)

Concerned that punitive measures alone would never improve the fighting ability of the 24th and that morale would continue to decline within the regiment unless some way were found to build pride and self-respect among the men, Corley, with Roberts' assistance, decided to begin a unit newspaper. If properly handled, he reasoned, a publication of that sort would open communications within the command. Officers would be able to explain practices and procedures clearly and succinctly,

giving the men more familiarity than ever before with official policies and orders of the day. Meanwhile, company columns would go uncensored and company reporters would be allowed to write what they felt. In that way, by allowing the troops to sound off, commanders could not only defuse tensions within the regiment but also would gain a feel for the mood of the men.[76]

Named *Eagles' Flight* after the 24th's successful athletic teams in Japan, the "Eagles," the first edition appeared on 13 September. Begun on a hit-or-miss basis, the paper met with such great success among the men that it rapidly became a daily. The first edition, however, almost immediately became the brunt of wisecracks and jokes among white members of the Eighth Army, who paired the publication's title with the 24th's growing reputation as a "bug-out" unit. Recognizing the problem, Corley changed the name to *Eagle Forward*, an allusion to the code-word designation that General Omar N. Bradley had selected for the advance headquarters of his famed 12th Army Group in Europe during World War II. After that, the jokes ceased. First

[75] Interv, IG with Corley, 16 Sep 50, exhibit B–18, Eighth Army Inspector General Investigation. See also exhibit C, Far East Command Inspector General Investigation.

[76] MFR, Corley, 22 Jan 51, sub: Background of Founding of *Eagle Forward*.

Lieutenant John S. Komp became the paper's editor with a roving reporter and a clerk-typist working for him. Colonel Roberts had a separate column of his own, entitled "Advice from the Old Man."[77]

Corley was much concerned, as he told the inspector general a week after taking command of the regiment, that "the 24th, since its entry into combat, has never had a little victory." He continued that

This may be one of the . . . factors that contribute to this fading away attitude that prevails among a large portion of the men. The fighting ability of the men who stay and fight is all that could be expected, but for every man that pulls out, he takes at least 6 men with him. It is difficult for troops to hold position when they see so many others moving out to . . . the rear. It is felt that, in time, we may overcome this deficiency . . . after we have withstood an attack and gained a victory. To date this regiment has not had a clear cut victory over the enemy in some 60 days of intensive combat.[78]

In an obvious attempt to overcome that defect, Corley decided to build up what some considered the unit's proudest moment in Korea, the battle of Yech'on. Shortly after taking command, in an open letter to "The Fighting 24th Infantry regimental combat team," he affirmed, "In sixty days of continuous combat you have witnessed a roughness of battle which I have not seen in five campaigns in Africa, Sicily and Europe. You held ground against superior odds. You have lived up to the regimental motto, 'Semper Paratus' (Always Ready). The first United States victory in Korea was your action at Yechon. It has been noted in Congress. . . . Other units have been unable to accomplish what depleted companies of the fighting 24th have done. I am proud of the 'Blockhousers.'"[79] That Yech'on had involved little enemy opposition and had been among the least significant of all the 24th's engagements in Korea was

unimportant to Corley. Unlike Colonel Champeny, he believed he could achieve better results by praising his men than by tearing them down, even if exaggeration was sometimes necessary.

Privately, however, Corley's concerns about his unit continued. They came out briefly in instructions he delivered to white 2d Lt. Philip H. Harper shortly after that officer joined the regiment. "Remember, Harper," he said, repeating a rumor that had gained currency among the white officers of the unit, "you're not leading white troops. If you're ever wounded, you're dead. These men will never bring you down off the hill."[80]

Corley's first full day as regimental commander was challenging. On 7 September the enemy attacked all along the 25th Division's line, laying down heavy concentrations of fire and then punching forward with ground assaults. Both the 5th and 35th Infantry regiments succeeded in repelling the attacks, but the 24th once more experienced difficulties. On the unit's northern flank, following artillery and mortar attacks against the regimental command post and that of the 1st Battalion, the enemy swept into Company F's position astride the Haman–Chungam-ni road. Inexperienced replacements wavered and began to straggle, forcing the unit to pull back. Because of the terrain it occupied and its placement on the line, Company A was able to take the attacking force under fire, buying time for Company F to reorganize and rendering the North Korean position untenable. With that assistance, Company F counterattacked. By 1100 it was back in its old position, and the enemy was in retreat.[81]

Farther south on Battle Mountain, the 3d Battalion also came under attack. Although Company B repelled one assault, an estimated enemy battalion succeeded in penetrating South Korean positions on the mountain. It then drove a wedge through Company K, forcing most of that unit and Company B to pull back. A small remnant of Company K managed to hold in place without

77 Ibid. See also Intervs, MacGarrigle with John S. Komp, 5 May and 1 Jun 94; Ltr, Komp to MacGarrigle, 14 Apr 95.

78 Interv, IG with Corley, 16 Sep 50, exhibit B–18, Eighth Army Inspector General Investigation.

79 Memo, 11 Sep 50, sub: Col. John Corley to The Fighting 24th Inf Rgtal Combat Team, CMH files. It is significant that Corley made his comment to the inspector general five days after issuing this memorandum to his men. See also Intervs, MacGarrigle with Komp, 5 May and 1 Jun 94.

80 Ltr, Philip H. Harper to MacGarrigle, n.d. [Apr 95], CMH files.

81 WD, 25th Inf Div, 1–30 Sep 50, pp. 14–17, boxes 3752–3754, RG 407, WNRC; WD, 24th Inf Rgt, 1–30 Sep 50, pp. 12–15.

communications until forced to withdraw by friendly mortar fire.[82]

As the fighting continued, straggling once again became significant. The newly arrived commander of Company K, white Capt. Buckner M. Creel, who had led a rifle company in heavy combat during World War II, described the situation in his unit:

When I took over Company K [on 19 August], the unit had not achieved any successes. Nor did the men of Company K have a sense of belonging. Morale was not particularly good. During the two weeks I first commanded the company, some men fell back during attacks without orders, offering one excuse after another. I made a practice to keep my executive officer in the rear to turn people around. There were times that the stragglers had to be rounded up and led back to the company position. . . . When a man straggled, he traveled light—leaving much of his equipment behind, but often would take his weapon with him. At daybreak, most who left would be found at the bottom of the hill, waiting to be told to return. . . . When I first arrived, some troops left their position to go down from the hill . . . in ones and twos— no mass "bugout." One night I heard a whispered voice say "TT-TL." I was told by a soldier next to me that meant "'tam time,' travel light." He said that earlier the code for taking off was "get your hat." On the day I was wounded [7 September], about half the company left their positions without permission and went down Battle Mountain. Those around me, and which I could control, generally stayed. I was told that the partial unauthorized withdrawal actually was a big improvement. Before, almost all the men had taken off.[83]

With a large hole gaping in the 24th's line, Corley had no choice but to call in his reserve, the 3d Battalion, 27th Infantry. The unit spent the remainder of the day counterattacking, but the enemy mounted a dogged resistance. The 3d Battalion fought on until midnight and suffered heavy casualties but was unable to regain the lost ground.[84]

The attempt to reclaim the mountaintop continued for two more days, but despite all efforts the enemy held out. Late on the afternoon of 9 September, with the 3d Battalion of the 27th urgently needed to the south to assist in the relief of the departing 5th Infantry, Corley decided to abandon the attack. Leaving the enemy in place, he sought to contain the North Koreans through the skillful positioning of his troops and the application of artillery and air assaults.[85] To that end, doubting that many of his men would hold if hit in force, he attempted to situate his units so strategically and in depth that individuals would find it difficult to withdraw without unnecessarily exposing themselves.[86]

General Kean had had enough of the 24th. Following the breakthrough at Haman, on the same day that Corley began to reposition his forces, 9 September, Kean sent a letter to General Walker requesting that the Eighth Army inactivate the regiment and distribute its soldiers as replacements to other units. "It is my opinion," Kean explained, "that the 24th Infantry has demonstrated in combat that it is untrustworthy and incapable of carrying out missions expected of an infantry regiment." Kean added that if there "are a number of individuals in the 24th Infantry who have been and are performing their duties in a creditable manner," the efforts of that minority had been "completely nullified by the actions of the majority." According to Kean, many of his officers and noncommissioned officers, whether black or white, agreed. Walker took the request under advisement, but, beyond inaugurating his own investigation of the regiment, made no immediate decision.[87]

---

[82]WD, 24th Inf Rgt, Sep 50, pp. 12–15. See also Intervs, MacGarrigle with Charles E. Green, 16 Jun 94; William A. Hash, 18 and 22 Mar 94; Muehlbauer with Yadon, 22 May 89.

[83]Intervs, MacGarrigle with Buckner M. Creel, 3 Nov and 3 Dec 93; Muehlbauer with Yadon, 22 May 89.

[84]WD, 24th Inf Rgt, 1–30 Sep 50, pp. 12–15; WD, 3d Bn, 27th Inf Rgt, Sep 50, box 3755, RG 407, WNRC.

[85]WD, 25th Inf Div, 1–30 Sep 50, p. 17; WD, 24th Inf Rgt, 1–30 Sep 50, p. 15. Company C, 65th Engineer Battalion, replaced the 3d Battalion, 27th Infantry, as Corley's reserve on 10 September. See WD, 24th Inf Rgt, Sep 50, p. 16.

[86]Corley told the inspector general that he had made it a practice to position his men in this manner. The terrain to the south of the regimental sector, he said, favored such a defense. See Interv, IG with Corley, 16 Sep 50, exhibit B–18, Eighth Army Inspector General Investigation.

[87]Ltr, Maj Gen W. B. Kean, 25th Inf Div, to Commanding General, Eighth U.S. Army (Korea), 9 Sep 50, sub: Combat Effectiveness of the 24th Infantry Regiment, exhibit A, in Eighth Army Inspector General Investigation. The letter was

Over the next several days, Corley's 1st and 2d Battalions patrolled in the lowlands while the 3d remained in position on ridges approaching Battle Mountain. The enemy fired mortars and launched several minor probes, but little other action occurred. Overall, the entire period was marked by an unfamiliar calm.[88]

Circumstances changed early on the morning of 14 September. To the north, about 0330, Company C came under attack but repelled the enemy. Farther south on the high ground, Company L also came under assault. Holding until after sunrise, the unit received supplies and reinforcements at 0800 and then made a tactical withdrawal to regroup. Launching a counterattack at 1220, it then restored its position. Located somewhat to the north of Company L, Company I also came under attack but held firm. As firefights continued around the two units and evening neared, a reinforced platoon from Company K attempted to relieve Company L but met with stiff enemy resistance and had to fall back to a nearby ridge.[89] At 1500 elements of Company B, which had been in reserve near Haman, arrived. Around that time, Corley replaced Tunstall as 3d Battalion commander with Maj. Melvin R. Blair. An experienced combat veteran, Blair had fought in the China-Burma-India Theater during World War II, where he had received a Distinguished Service Cross as a member of the famed Merrill's Marauders.[90]

At some time during the early morning hours of 14 September, Company L's highly regarded commander, black 1st Lt. Randall P. Stephens, had fallen wounded. The officer available to take his place, a first lieutenant who had been with the unit for only two days, proved unable to instill confidence in the men. Stephens attempted to continue commanding from a stretcher, but the unit dwindled overnight from approximately a hundred men to perhaps forty. Realizing that Company L was short of officers, Blair moved forward to determine how it was doing. Arriving at 1400, he learned that one platoon had lost a vital defensive position. Rallying the men who remained, the major regained the position but was unable to hold against fierce enemy attacks that followed. At 0700 on the fifteenth, with most of his ammunition gone, Blair ordered the unit to disengage. After staying behind with six enlisted men to cover the withdrawal, he and his small group were ambushed while making their way to the rear and he was wounded.[91]

To the north, Company I also came under heavy attack. "We did not give an inch of ground all night," the unit's commander, black Capt. Vernon C. Dailey, avowed the next day.

Our ammunition started giving out. How they got under the barbed wire and through the mines, I do not know. They kept hitting us all night. We had 8 known casualties. We figured they would do the same thing tonight. We were completely out of ammunition, except for a few rounds of carbine ammunition. They were making it so hot on our position that we . . . decided to pull in with "L" company and bolster their right flank. We found nothing but dead soldiers and North Koreans. I gave the order to withdraw.[92]

Blair had little confidence in Dailey's account. In a telephone call recorded shortly after coming off the mountain, he told General Kean, "I am not sure 'I' Company was pushed off [of its position]. When I came down to the road, I found 'I' Company. I asked how many wounded they had, and they did not know." The conversation would have gone unnoticed, but investigators from the inspector general's office were present in the regimental command post at the time when Blair spoke with Kean.

---

accompanied by thirty-three statements, including two from black officers and one from a black noncommissioned officer. Not all were negative. See, for example, Statement 18, by white 1st Lt Clair L. Rishel.

[88] WD, 24th Inf Rgt, 1–30 Sep 50, pp. 17–18.

[89] WD, 3d Bn, 24th Inf Rgt, 1–30 Sep 50, p. 6, box 3755, RG 407, WNRC; WD, 24th Inf Rgt, 1–30 Sep 50, pp. 17–18.

[90] WD, 3d Bn, 24th Inf Rgt, 1–30 Sep 50, p. 6.

[91] EUSAK GO 31, 18 Jan 51, Distinguished Service Cross Citation (OLC) for Maj Melvin R. Blair; Interv, IG with Corley, 16 Sep 50, exhibit B–18, Eighth Army Inspector General Investigation; WD, 24th Inf Rgt, 1–30 Sep 50, p. 19. While Stephens was being carried down the hill on a stretcher during the evacuation, Corley pinned captain's bars on him. See Intervs, MacGarrigle with Randall P. Stephens, 18 and 27 Jul 94.

[92] Intervs, IG with Capt Vernon C. Dailey, 15 Sep 50, exhibit B–9, Eighth Army Inspector General Investigation; Cash with Charlie Lee Jones, 6 Sep 89.

One of them ordered his stenographer to transcribe Blair's half of the conversation without the major's knowledge.[93]

Corley was unhappy about the course of the entire affair. Reporting the straggling in Company L, Blair's role in saving the unit, and Company I's simultaneous withdrawal, he asserted that the two units had inflicted at least one hundred and twenty-five casualties on the enemy and would have won a victory if they had been determined to hold their position, whatever the seeming odds against them. "The casualties for 'L' Company were approximately 17, and 8 for 'I' Company," he told the inspector general on the day after the fight. "The losses, in proportion to the danger inflicted on the area, and for the type of fighting engaged in, were relatively few. Former units I commanded would have suffered heavier casualties and would have held their position in an organized manner, despite the hopelessness of the situation. Coordination of artillery and mortar support during this attack . . . was all that could be expected."[94]

The 3d Battalion attempted all the next day, 16 September, to recover its positions on Battle Mountain. Company K bogged down in the advance and gained only 300 yards. Company I reported heavy casualties and withdrew. A patrol from Company L reached its objective but failed to hold on and fell back. Because of the critical situation, General Kean organized a battalion-size task force out of units from the 65th Engineer Combat Battalion and the 27th and 35th Infantry regiments and assigned it to back up Corley's effort.

Under the command of Maj. Robert L. Woolfolk of the 35th Infantry, the force moved to the attack on 17 September, achieved a few small gains, and then began to slow. Suffering from adverse terrain and incurring heavy casualties, at one point during the day Woolfolk requested per-

mission to withdraw and reorganize. Instead, Corley himself arrived and ordered the unit to advance. In the end, Corley's determination notwithstanding, there was little anyone could do. Bowing to the inevitable, the colonel disbanded the force on 19 September and ordered the 3d Battalion off Battle Mountain. From then on, the 24th would have to attempt to contain the enemy with artillery fire and to thwart any attack that occurred by fighting in the foothills and valleys to the south of Haman.[95]

Corley's decision made little difference. By then, the war had entered a new phase. Early on the morning of 15 September the commander of United Nations forces in the Far East, General MacArthur, had launched an amphibious assault upon Inch'on, a transportation hub and seaport located on the coast of the Yellow Sea, some twenty-five miles west of South Korea's capital city, Seoul, and more than a hundred miles north of the Pusan Perimeter. With an American bridgehead firmly established by 17 September and Seoul in line for attack, the North Koreans had to fight in two directions at once, against MacArthur's landing force to the north and Walker's increasingly powerful Eighth Army in the south. Already bloodied by the severe fighting on the Pusan Perimeter and under the psychological burdens imposed by the presence of an aggressive enemy to their rear, the enemy held for a time but in the end began to pull back rather than face destruction in detail. Battle Mountain no longer mattered. The fight for Pusan had ended.[96]

In assessing the performance of his division in the fighting west of Masan, General Kean was well satisfied with most of his regiments but not with the 24th. Fisher's 35th Infantry, in defense of its sector, had done all that could have been asked of any unit. The 5th, under its new commander, John Throckmorton, had shown great improvement since Bloody Gulch and had held its positions

[93] Statement, Maj Melvin R. Blair, 15 Sep 50, exhibit D–4, Eighth Army Inspector General Investigation. The quote is from a telephone conversation between Blair and Kean on the morning of 15 September while Blair lay wounded at the regimental command post.

[94] Interv, IG with Corley, 16 Sep 50, exhibit B–18, Eighth Army Inspector General Investigation.

[95] WD, 24th Inf Rgt, 1–30 Sep 50, pp. 24–26. See also Appleman, *South to the Naktong, North to the Yalu*, pp. 569–70.

[96] Appleman, *South to the Naktong, North to the Yalu*, pp. 542–45, 568–72.

against strong enemy attacks. Meanwhile, Michaelis' 27th Infantry had maintained its reputation as the Eighth Army's "fire brigade" by clearing enemy breakthroughs in the 35th's and 24th's sectors. In contrast, the 24th's performance had been lackluster from start to finish. The collapse of the 2d Battalion on 1 September and the failure of the regiment's other units either to hold positions or to retake lost ones had provided all the evidence the general needed to demonstrate the regiment's unreliability.

Although Kean had already made his decision about what should become of the 24th, there seemed some reason for hope. The attempts of the 27th Infantry and Task Force Woolfolk to retake Battle Mountain had shown that combat in Korea was not easy, even for all-white units. Meanwhile, despite the 24th's poor performance, there was a base of good in the regiment. The heroic and capable efforts of numerous soldiers and leaders and the resourcefulness and combat effectiveness shown by some squads, platoons, and companies had kept the unit, even at its darkest moments, from collapsing as a whole. With that as a foundation, there seemed reason to believe that training and morale-building would have a positive effect. More important, for the first time in the war, the regiment not only had a commander who was tactically competent and experienced but also one who, in his search for the reasons behind the unit's failure, seemed to have an open mind about the abilities of the black soldier.

CHAPTER 8

To Kunu-ri and Back

In support of the landing at Inch'on, the Eighth Army's staff devised a plan to break out of the Pusan Perimeter. Of the more than 150,000 men General Walker had at his disposal, the six South Korean divisions holding the northeastern portions of the Perimeter were to attack northward, up the east-coast highway and into the Taebaek Mountains.[1] To the west, a newly formed I Corps—commanded after 11 September 1950 by Maj. Gen. Frank W. Milburn and composed of the U.S. 1st Cavalry and 24th Infantry Divisions, the 5th Regimental Combat Team, a British brigade, and a South Korean division—would cross the Naktong River at Waegwan and move west toward Taejon and beyond. To the south, the U.S. 2d and 25th Infantry Divisions—initially under the direct control of the Eighth Army but later as part of a new IX Corps commanded by Maj. Gen. John B. Coulter—would press forward in a northwesterly direction toward Kunsan, a seaport some one hundred miles distant on South Korea's west coast. The offensive would follow the same corridors that the North Koreans had used for their attack into the South. In the 25th Division's sector, it would employ in its early stages the same roads and lines of advance that Task Force Kean had used during the division's first week at Masan. In general, it would complement the Inch'on-Seoul attacks, keeping the North Koreans off balance and forcing them to dissipate their waning combat strength between two allied armies.[2]

The Eighth Army's planners expected the landing at Inch'on to demoralize the enemy forces facing them and waited a full day after the attack before launching their own offensive to leave time for the effect to sink in. Enemy commanders at first declined to inform their subordinates of what had happened to the north and retained the initiative for almost a week. On 19 September, however, following the 2d Division's successful crossing of the Naktong, they had no choice but to pull back. Enemy forces defending Waegwan broke into a panic-stricken retreat and those occupying P'il-bong, Sobuk-san, and the other heights west of Masan began to abandon their positions and to flee north. The 2d Battalion of the 24th Infantry came up against heavy enemy resistance and suffered fifty-five casualties taking Hill 212, three and one-half miles due west of Haman, but elements from the unit's 1st and 3d Battalions began to reoccupy the regiment's old positions on Sobuk-san and Battle Mountain, ultimately advancing across them into the valley beyond.[3]

---

[1] The strength figure is drawn from Appleman, *South to the Naktong, North to the Yalu*, p. 547.

[2] Appleman, *South to the Naktong, North to the Yalu*, pp. 542–45.

[3] War Diary (WD), 25th Inf Div, 19–22 Sep 50, boxes 3752–3754, Record Group (RG) 407, Washington National Records Center (WNRC), Suitland, Md.; 25th Inf Div

Members of the 24th Infantry march down a road behind Battle Mountain on 21 September 1950.

Breakout and Move North

During the days that followed, the enemy fought a series of sharp delaying actions against the 35th Infantry regiment at Chungam-ni and the 27th Infantry regiment to the south, but American forces sensed a kill and moved in. The 24th Infantry greeted the threat, as Colonel Corley put it, "in good formation and in good spirits." The 1st Battalion moved into Tundok with dispatch, taking the town and capturing the enemy supply depots hidden in the nearby mines. General Wilson was so elated by the swift and efficient manner in which the troops performed the task that he gave Corley a fine watch inscribed on its back with the date of the town's capture.[4]

The enemy nevertheless had his say. Early on the morning of 22 September, infiltrators stole into the bivouac area of Company A of the 1st Battalion, where they killed two sleeping men and wounded

several others. Shortly thereafter, enemy mortars inflicted nearly sixty more casualties on the unit, killing the commander of the battalion's headquarters company and wounding its intelligence, personnel, and executive officers. Later in the day, the men of the unit moved out to find and eliminate the mortars. They succeeded, sometimes with great bravery, but the effort brought down two more officers. By the end of the day, virtually the entire command structure of Company C had been eliminated, leaving only an inexperienced second lieutenant to take charge. Those losses were nonetheless only temporary. The enemy retreat was gathering momentum. U.S. forces were everywhere on the move.[5]

On 23 September operational control of the 25th Division passed to Coulter's IX Corps, freeing General Walker and his staff from tactical concerns and allowing them to concentrate on the larger issues which the developing American offensive

---

Narrative Rpt, Sep 50, bk. 1, pp. 33–39, boxes 3752–3754, RG 407, WNRC; Appleman, *South to the Naktong, North to the Yalu,* pp. 568–71. Casualties are from WD, 24th Inf Rgt, Sep 50, app. 5, box 3755, RG 407, WNRC.

[4] John T. Corley, "Policy Lifted Morale, Confidence: Colonel Corley's Story," *Pittsburgh Courier,* 7 Jul 51, p. 10.

[5] WD, 25th Inf Div, 22 Sep 50; 25th Inf Div Narrative Rpt, Sep 50, bk. 1, pp. 33–39; WD, 24th Inf Rgt, 1–30 Sep 50, p. 28, box 3755, RG 407, WNRC; Appleman, *South to the Naktong, North to the Yalu,* pp. 568–71. For the status of 1st Battalion officers, see Officer Roster, 24th Inf Rgt, Sep 50, dtd 1 Oct 50, p. 3, in WD, 24th Inf Rgt, Sep 50.

Colonel Corley

With the bridge gone and enemy resistance continuing, General Kean devised a two-pronged attack to capture the objective. While Torman's force, renamed Task Force Matthews after its new commander, Capt. Charles M. Matthews, persisted in its assault from the south, units from the 35th Infantry crossed the Nam downstream, two and one-half miles to the northeast, and attacked from that direction. The maneuver succeeded. On 25 September, despite the efforts of some three hundred enemy troops employing mortar and artillery fire, the town fell. Meanwhile, sixteen miles downstream from Chinju, engineers worked all day against sporadic enemy mortar fire to construct a sandbag ford across the Nam. Elements of the 27th Infantry then crossed the river and secured the town of Uiryong before fighting their way to Chinju against negligible enemy resistance. The fall of Chinju eliminated any threat to the port of Pusan from the west.[8]

Over the days that followed, General Kean pressed his advantage. In the north, two companies of armor from the 89th Medium Tank Battalion and two infantry companies from the 35th Infantry, forming a task force under Lt. Col. Welborn G. Dolvin, sought to cut the enemy's main line of retreat by attacking along a major road that ran to the north of the highest peak in South Korea, 7,000-foot Chiri-san. Meanwhile, to the south the 24th Infantry, spearheaded by Task Force Matthews, swung toward the town of Hadong and then northwest around the south side of Chiri-san to the town of Namwon, which fell on 28 September. More than eighty American prisoners of war were in the town. The men were in tatters and weak from lack of food, but all were soon crying and shouting in happiness and relief at their good fortune.[9]

entailed.[6] That same day, as the 24th Infantry advanced toward the road junction at Much'on-ni, General Kean established an armored task force to exploit the breakthrough fully and to keep the enemy off balance. Named for its commander, Capt. Charles J. Torman, and composed of the 25th Reconnaissance Company, Company A of the 79th Heavy Tank Battalion, and smaller medical, engineer, and tactical air control units, the force was to attack along the coastal road from Kosong through Sach'on to Chinju. The assault made good progress at first, but it ground to a halt temporarily when Torman was wounded and a bridge collapsed. Resuming the attack the next day, 24 September, the force fought several sharp engagements before finally stopping three miles short of Chinju. Over the night that followed, while the Americans drew breath, the enemy destroyed the one highway bridge across the Nam River that would have given Torman and his men easy access to their objective.[7] (*Map 10*)

[6] WD, 25th Inf Div, 23 Sep 50, boxes 3752–3754, RG 407, WNRC.

[7] WD, 25th Inf Div, 23–29 Sep 50, boxes 3752–3754, RG 407, WNRC; 25th Inf Div Narrative Rpt, Sep 50, bk. 1, pp. 33–39; WD, 24th Inf Rgt, Sep 50, pp. 29–30. See also

Appleman, *South to the Naktong, North to the Yalu,* pp. 574–75.

[8] 25th Inf Div Narrative Rpt, Sep 50, bk. 1, pp. 43–45; Appleman, *South to the Naktong, North to the Yalu,* pp. 574–75.

[9] Most sources give Task Force Dolvin the credit for liberating the prisoners. Appleman points out that Matthews and the 3d Battalion of the 24th Infantry were in fact responsible. See Appleman, *South to the Naktong, North to the Yalu,* pp. 576–77; WD, 3d Bn, 24th Inf Rgt, Sep 50, p. 17, box 3755, RG 407, WNRC.

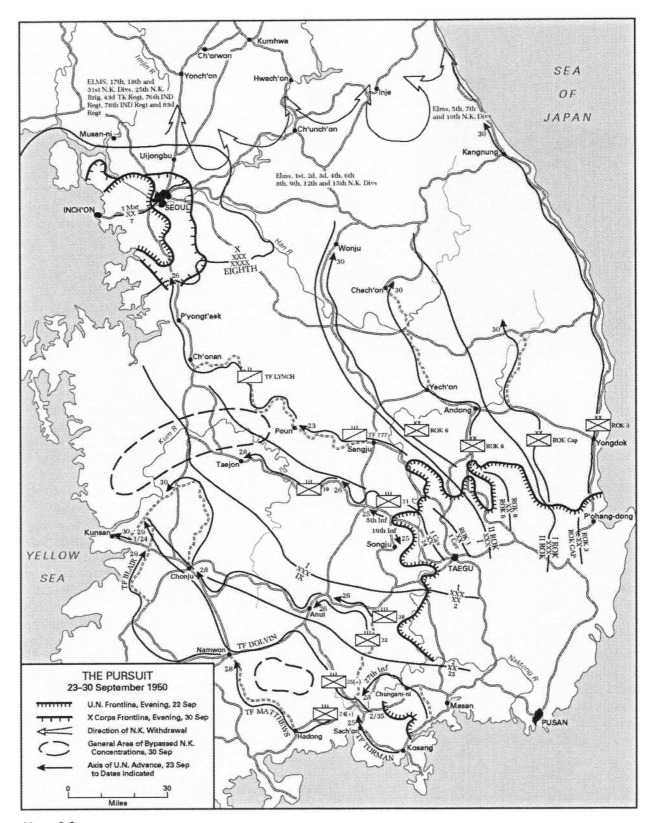

SEA
OF
JAPAN

ELMS. 17th, 18th and
31st N.K. Divs. 25th N.K.
Brig. 43d Tk Regt, 76th IND
Regt, 76th IND Regt and 83d
Regt

Elms. 5th, 7th
and 10th N.K. Divs

Kangnung

Elms. 1st, 2d. 3d, 4th, 6th
8th, 9th, 12th and 15th N.K. Divs

Kumhwa
Ch'orwon
Yonch'on
Imjin R
Musan-ni
Uijongbu
Hwach'on
Inje
Ch'unch'on
Wonju
Chech'on
INCH'ON
1 Mar
XX
7
SEOUL
X
XXX
XXXX
EIGHTH
Han R
26
P'yongt'aek
Ch'onan
Yech'on
Andong
TF LYNCH
Kum R
Poun
23
ROK 6
ROK 3
ROK Cap
Yongdok
Taejon
28
Sangju
TF 777
ROK 6
ROK 6
ROK 6
ROK 6
P'ohang-dong
19 26
25
Sth Inf
31
19th Inf
25
Songju
ROK 1
ROK 1
II ROK
I ROK
1 ROK
ROK 3
ROK CAP
II ROK
Kunsan
30 29
1/24
TAEGU
TF BI-AIR
29
Chonju
28
I
IX
I
XXX
XX
2
YELLOW
SEA
26
Anui
26
38
TF DOLVIN
Namwon
23
2
XX
23
28
35(+)
27th Inf
28
Chungam-ni
Masan
TF MATTHEWS
Hadong
24(+)
25
2/35
Sach'on
TF TORMAN
Kosang
Naktong R
PUSAN

THE PURSUIT
23–30 September 1950

⌁⌁⌁⌁⌁	U.N. Frontline, Evening, 22 Sep
⌁⌁⌁	X Corps Frontline, Evening, 30 Sep
⬅	Direction of N.K. Withdrawal
⬭	General Area of Bypassed N.K. Concentrations, 30 Sep
←	Axis of U.N. Advance, 23 Sep to Dates Indicated

0   30
Miles

Map 10

At Namwon, the two prongs of the 25th Division's attack temporarily converged, but Task Force Dolvin then broke off to the northwest toward I-ri, 45 miles distant from Namwon, while the 24th continued on toward Sunch'ang, 15 miles to the west. Taking the town, the 24th then curved to the northwest toward the coast and the seaport at Kunsan, 50 miles distant by air from Namwon and 110 miles to the south of Seoul. As the advance continued, Task Force Matthews ran out of fuel and had to be replaced by Task Force Blair, a motorized force composed of the 3d Battalion of the 24th Infantry, Company D of the 89th Medium Tank Battalion, and attached engineer and artillery elements.[10] The march meandered from Namwon, through Chongup, Kumje, and I-ri. Arriving at the objective on 30 September, the unit found that the enemy had abandoned the city but had left behind large stores of ammunition, gasoline, and weapons.[11]

During October, as the Eighth Army pressed its advance north, the 25th Division remained to the south, mopping up bypassed enemy forces and protecting lines of supply. By 16 October the unit had relocated its headquarters to Taejon, 40 miles northeast of Kunsan. The 24th Infantry had responsibility for securing an area stretching roughly from that city northward to Suwon, 20 miles south of Seoul. The 35th Infantry operated in the region directly to the regiment's south while the 27th Infantry occupied the area immediately to the east. Organized enemy resistance was negligible throughout the period, but there were a number of skirmishes with stragglers, guerrillas, and the remnants of defeated and bypassed enemy units.[12]

Besides eliminating the remnants of the North Korean Army—many of whose members were by then reduced to moving in groups at night and to raiding farms and villages for food and clothing—the men of the 24th Infantry had charge of finding and collecting the arms and ammunition that enemy forces had left behind. At Kunsan, they came across a supply dump that contained thousands of rounds of ammunition, hundreds of drums of gasoline and petroleum by-products, dynamite, blasting caps, and antitank mines. They also guarded highway and railway bridges and tunnels and maintained the principal supply route and communications lines for the 25th Division. All the while, they made certain that law and order prevailed within what was left of the local civilian population. Since many of the enemy soldiers they encountered were eager to surrender, they also accounted for a large number of enemy prisoners of war.[13]

Patrolling continued throughout October but the 24th was also heavily engaged in a program of instruction that stressed individual, squad, and platoon training, leadership development, and weapons familiarization. Colonel Corley hoped that by improving his command's efficiency in those areas he might be able to raise standards of discipline within his regiment. He also sought to correct deficiencies that had become all too apparent during the weeks of combat that had preceded the breakout from Pusan.[14]

Adding to Corley's concern, by the end of October more than two-thirds of the 3,663 enlisted men in the regiment were replacements. During August, 841 new men had arrived, followed in September by 756 more. By 1 November another 674 would arrive. Many were truck drivers, heavy equipment operators, communications specialists, engineers, or cooks rather than trained infantry-

[10] WD, 25th Inf Div, 24 Sep 50, boxes 3752–3754, RG 407, WNRC.

[11] WD, 1st Bn, 24th Inf Rgt, Sep 50, p. 12, box 3755, RG 407, WNRC. See also Interv, John A. Cash with Oliver Dillard, 3 Jun 89, CMH files. All interviews hereafter cited by John A. Cash, Bernard L. Muehlbauer, Timothy Rainey, William T. Bowers, Richard O. Perry, and George L. MacGarrigle are in CMH files.

[12] Overlay 4, 24th RCT Zone of Responsibility, 16 Oct 50, in WD, 24th Inf Rgt, Oct 50, box 3760, RG 407, WNRC.

[13] The condition of the North Koreans is mentioned in WD, 24th Inf Rgt, Oct 50, p. 7. The responsibilities of the regiment sometimes varied from day to day. They are spelled out in the regimental war diary, especially in Appendix 6, dealing with operations orders and directives. The most succinct account of what the unit did appears in HQ, 24th Inf Rgt, Office of Civil Affairs Officer, Rpt for Oct 50, in WD, 24th Inf Rgt, Oct 50, app. 7.

[14] The program and its rationale are outlined in HQ, 24th Inf Rgt, Training Directive 1, 2 Oct 50, in WD, 24th Inf Rgt, Oct 50, app. 6.

Members of a 24th Infantry communications element checking radios

men. They had to learn how to maintain and operate unfamiliar equipment, maneuver in combat formations, decipher arm and hand signals, fire their weapons, and conduct patrols. Corley did his best to see that they received what training they needed, but some still complained years afterward that they went directly into combat without a chance to perfect their skills.[15]

Many units in the Eighth Army were having problems finding suitable enlisted replacements. Of more concern were the 24th's officers. Because of heavy turnover during the first months of the fighting, a circumstance unique to the 24th, only 12 of the 43 officers assigned to the unit's nine rifle companies at the beginning of November had

served at Gifu. Eight had arrived during July and August, but the remaining 23 had come during September and October. Of the rifle company commanders, only 2 of the 9 had been with the unit in Japan. One of those had been wounded almost immediately at Sangju in July and returned to duty only in October. Two of the rest had come in September and 5 in October. The same was true of the regiment's battalion commanders. One, Colonel Miller, had arrived on 27 July, but the other two, Major Blair and the 2d Battalion's new commander, Maj. George A. Clayton, joined the regiment in September.[16]

The loss of so many seasoned officers had a number of effects. On one hand, the influx of new officers led to a breakdown in the unit's system of segregated command. As early as July, with casualties among officers mounting, experienced black

---

[15] The replacement numbers are in HQ, 24th Inf Rgt, Strength and Replacement Statistics, 1–30 Sep 50, in WD, 24th Inf Rgt, Sep 50, app. 4. The October figures are in WD, 24th Inf Rgt, Oct 50, app. 5. See also Intervs, Bernard L. Muehlbauer with Lindsey Bowers, 20 Apr 89; Albert Pough, 5 Aug 88; James C. Yadon, 22 May 89; Wallace C. Mims, 14 Oct 88. Alonzo Cooper complained about having to go into combat without a chance to perfect his skills. See Interv, Cash with Alonzo Cooper, 8 Sep 88.

[16] Problems with replacements for units of the Eighth Army in general are mentioned in Schnabel, *Policy and Direction*, pp. 132–34, 167, 239. The officer profile was compiled by comparing regimental staff rosters for July, August, September, and November. All are in CMH files.

officers began to receive assignments wherever the need arose, regardless of the race of the officers they would rate. After the breakout from Pusan, black Capt. Milford W. Stanley thus received command of Company C, a unit that contained a number of white lieutenants, even though white captains were available.

On the other hand, the presence of officers with combat experience is nonetheless of enormous value to a unit entering battle, and on that score the 24th's commanders were sometimes sorely lacking. Although a number of the new men were veterans of the fighting in World War II, others had been commissioned in 1950 directly from the Reserve Officer Training Corps and the U.S. Military Academy at West Point. They arrived in Korea without additional training, sometimes with specialties in branches of the service that had little to do with the infantry. In addition to being unfamiliar with the responsibilities that would pass to them once they entered combat, according to the motor officer for the 2d Battalion, 1st Lt. Lloyd Ott, a number were reserve officers involuntarily recalled to active duty who had little wish to be there. Others, according to 1st Lt. Charles E. Green, a company commander, were so out of shape physically in comparison with the battle-hardened veterans who had survived the fighting around Sangju and Masan that they seemed "fat and happy."[17]

Complicating matters further, by October the image of the 24th Infantry had sunk so low that rumors had begun to circulate among the troops in Korea about the unit's poor performance in combat.[18] When men were wounded and repatriated to the United States, the stories went with them. As a result, white 1st Lt. Adolf Voight for one began to receive warnings to avoid the 24th before he even departed for Korea, while waiting in San Francisco to board ship. "Man, you don't want to go with them nigger bastards," one officer told him. "You'll get yourself killed."[19] In the end, even officers who were well-intentioned toward blacks began to have second thoughts. Aware that African-Americans often possessed lower aptitude scores than whites, as white 2d Lt. James Yadon observed, they could hardly help wondering about the loyalties of the men they would command, "with their [inadequate] training and less education and so forth."[20]

Overall, a combination of time, training, and experience appears to have offered the best solution to the problem. Lieutenant Voight, for example, received an assignment to the 24th Infantry despite his reservations and joined the 3d Battalion in late September. The high morale of the troops when he arrived, he remarked years later, was immediately apparent. There was none of the malingering he had been told to expect. A second officer, a platoon leader in Company K who had accompanied the 24th to Korea, 1st Lt. Alfred Tittel, agreed. When he joined the regiment during July at Gifu, he said, his unit had an obvious drug problem and a number of his troops had appeared to be affected. The loss of those individuals in combat and the infusion of new blood, however, provided a tonic. As a group, the new men performed well and proved to be excellent soldiers. The commander of Battery C of the 159th Field Artillery Battalion was similarly impressed. Although he had little respect, he said, for some of the individuals who had accompanied the regiment to Korea because they had panicked far too often in the face of the enemy, the situation changed after the breakout from Pusan. The unit "firmed up" under Corley's hand and began to act the way it should have all along.[21]

Despite the new men and the new esprit evident in the 24th, the unit's old image died hard. On

[17] Intervs, Muehlbauer with Robert F. Fletcher, 5 Aug 88; William T. Gant, 15 Sep 88; Fred Sheffey, 27 Feb 89; George L. MacGarrigle with Gustav H. Franke, 14 and 28 Jul 94; Charles E. Green, 16 Jun 94; Lloyd V. Ott, 19 Jul 94. Joseph Baranowski agreed with Ott's comment. See Interv, MacGarrigle with Joseph Baranowski, 24 Aug 94.

[18] A member of the 23d Infantry, 2d Infantry Division, described the song. See Interv, Cash with Robert C. Bjorak, 1 May 89. Veterans of the 24th also mentioned it. See Intervs, William T. Bowers with Bradley Biggs, 23 Mar 94; Muehlbauer with Calvin Bryant, 1 Mar 89; MacGarrigle with Roscius C. Newell, 10 and 15 Nov 94.

[19] Interv, Cash with Adolf Voight, 21 Sep 88.
[20] Interv, Muehlbauer with Yadon, 22 May 89.
[21] Intervs, Cash with Voight, 21 Sep 88; MacGarrigle with Alfred F. Tittel, 20 Apr 94; Franke, 14 and 28 Jul 94.

6 September 1st Lt. Leon A. Gilbert was convicted and sentenced to death in one of the first in a series of courts-martial of black infantrymen for misbehavior before the enemy, a violation of the 75th Article of War. Many of the men involved alleged that they had been the victims of racial discrimination and that they had been railroaded to set an example for the rest of the regiment. Their complaint appears to have had at least some weight. According to white 1st Lt. John S. Komp, who edited the regiment's newspaper and knew what was going on within the command, "At the time, and I'm not sure of the name, there was a white officer in 1st [Battalion], who kept evading courts-martial because charges were never brought against him for one reason or another. I'm sure that this was general knowledge in the battalion." Whether a double standard existed in the regiment or not—officers within all-white regiments were court-martialed whenever the need arose—Gilbert's conviction and those of the others added weight to General Kean's contention that the regiment was a threat to the well-being of the entire 25th Division.[22]

A number of the convicted men requested that the NAACP represent them on appeal. The organization responded by sending its chief legal counsel, Thurgood Marshall, to Japan and Korea to investigate. Arriving in February 1951, Marshall visited General MacArthur and interviewed the imprisoned men. Although he remarked in an interview years later that he came to mistrust Gilbert's word because he caught the officer in two lies, he still concluded that the condemned men had been the victims of deep-seated racial prejudice. There was a deliberate pattern of drumhead courts-martial, he avowed.

Although Kean was responsible, MacArthur had backed everything that had happened.[23]

Marshall reported his conclusions in a 15 February memorandum to General MacArthur. The three regiments of the 25th Division, he said, had been on the front line for up to ninety-two days. The 24th Infantry in particular had received favorable press notices for its performance. Nevertheless, 60 blacks had been charged with cowardice before the enemy. If the charges against 24 blacks had been dismissed and 4 had been declared not guilty, 32 of the men were convicted, receiving sentences that ran from death to life imprisonment to terms in prison from five to fifty years. Despite the severe punishments, a check of trial records showed that many of the men had never received a full and vigorous defense. Some alleged that they had seen their defense counsels for the first time only on the mornings of their trials. Others asserted that even though some meetings with counsel had occurred, they had never had sufficient time to discuss their cases in detail or to call all the witnesses they believed they needed. The men failed to protest at the time, Marshall said, out of "a feeling of hopelessness" brought on by excessive time in the line. Sgt. Nathaniel Reed, for one, had a slip in his pocket signed by a captain in the Medical Corps stating, "If possible, this patient should be given duty away from the front lines for a few days, as he is bordering on combat fatigue." The soldier failed to tell even his defense counsel about it, Marshall said. The others who shared his plight were in a similar frame of mind.

Marshall continued that the trials themselves were conducted in groups, sometimes at what seemed breakneck speed. One lasted 42 minutes, another 44, and two took 50 minutes each. In all of those cases, the defendants received sentences of life imprisonment. Over the same period only eight whites from the 25th Division were charged with the same crime and only two appeared to

---

22 Ltr, Maj Gen W. B. Kean, 25th Inf Div, to Commanding General, Eighth U.S. Army (Korea), 9 Sep 50, sub: Combat Effectiveness of the 24th Infantry Regiment. Kean's letter and its attachments are contained in Far East Command Inspector General Investigation, sec. BX, boxes 1013–1014, RG 159, WNRC. Statements attached to General Kean's letter each have an exhibit number and are hereafter cited as in the Kean Letter file. See also Thurgood Marshall, "Summary Justice—The Negro GI in Korea," the Crisis (May 1951): 297–355. Komp's allegation is in Ltr, John S. Komp to George L. MacGarrigle, 14 Apr 95, CMH files. No reason exists to disbelieve it, but there is also no evidence to substantiate it.

---

23 Interv, Cash with Thurgood Marshall, 2 May 90. See also Marshall, "Summary Justice—The Negro GI in Korea," pp. 297–355.

have been convicted. Four whites were acquitted. A reading of investigation reports, Marshall continued, indicated that if all legal technicalities had been observed, the trials themselves, with a few exceptions, had been conducted in an atmosphere that "made it improbable, if not impossible, to mete out justice." As for the officers standing as defense counsel, all maintained that they had sufficient time to prepare their cases. Their assertions were understandable, Marshall said, "but I do not believe that any lawyer will deny that it is impossible to prepare for the trial of a capital offense in a period of a day or so. . . . There is no question in my mind that before a man is sentenced to life imprisonment at hard labor, counsel and the court should give the fullest time and effort to be as certain as possible that the man is guilty and deserves the stiff sentence."[24]

Marshall made no attempt to deal in detail with conditions in the 24th that might have contributed to the situation, but he did allude to them. "The men I talked to," he said,

all made it clear to me that several of the white officers assigned to the 24th Infantry [had] made it known that they would have preferred not to be commanding Negro troops. There is considerable lack of understanding and mutual respect in many of the companies. . . . If the 24th had been completely integrated, I am not sure that there would not have been this disproportionate number of charges and convictions of Negro troops under the 75th Article of War. . . . Although the morale of the 24th is better now . . ., I am convinced that . . . [the unit] will never reach its highest efficiency as long as . . . [it] remains a segregated outfit.[25]

The Far East Command investigated Marshall's allegations but concluded that many of them were groundless.[26] Although several of the convictions

had by then been set aside as unfounded and many of the sentences had been reduced upon review by higher authorities, the authors of the command's final report insisted that Marshall had based his conclusions upon the self-serving comments of convicted shirkers and malingerers who could hardly have been expected to say anything else. Overall, the men had been defended with as much vigor as possible under the circumstances. If their trials had seemed short, the charges in question had been relatively easy to prove, and the men themselves had failed in many cases either to take the stand or to call witnesses in their own defense. Anytime the presence of a witness had been requested, the individual had been called to appear. In each case the accused had a qualified attorney as part of his defense team. The attorneys involved, many of them black, insisted that they had worked hard and that they had even gone into frontline units to interrogate witnesses. "[The accused] did not have the witnesses [they needed] to cast a doubt [on the allegations]," one had remarked, "or at least we could not find anything from interrogating the accused that would have warranted spending days and days waiting."[27]

If the accused suffered from a sense of hopelessness, the officers who wrote the report continued, the evidence still indicated that the Army had exercised considerable restraint. Out of sixty initially charged for misbehavior before the enemy, a considerable number were never tried and four were acquitted. In that sense, if a feeling of hopelessness was present, it may have come from a recognition on the part of those who remained to be prosecuted that if they were guilty they would have little chance of escaping conviction and punishment. All concerned had been informed of the possible results of their refusal to return to the front and had been given an opportunity to comply with the orders they had initially chosen to disobey. All had refused in one manner or another.

[24] The two preceding paragraphs are extracted from Memo, Thurgood Marshall for General MacArthur, 15 Feb 51, exhibit A–10, in General Headquarters, Far East Command, Report of Investigation Regarding Alleged Irregularities in the Administration of Military Justice in the 25th Infantry Division, 27 Mar 51, boxes 1013–1014 (hereafter cited as Far East Command Inspector General Investigation), RG 159, WNRC.
[25] Ibid.
[26] General Headquarters, Far East Command, Office of the Inspector General, Report of Investigation Regarding Alleged Irregularities in the Administration of Military Justice

in the 25th Infantry Division, 27 Mar 51, Far East Command Inspector General Investigation.
[27] Ibid., p. 17.

The courts-martial in that sense were a last resort. As for Reed, the authors acknowledged in an appendix to their report that at the time of his trial the soldier had indeed carried a letter from a physician indicating that he might be suffering from combat fatigue and needed a rest. They noted, however, that Reed had earlier presented the slip to his captain, who had seen to it that he received a two-day rest. His offense had occurred after that, when he had returned to his unit on the line. Following the arrest, the black battalion adjutant, Capt. Gorham Black, Jr., had seen to it that Reed was examined by the battalion surgeon. The doctor reported back that the soldier had made a sound and considered decision and that no psychiatric disturbances were involved.[28]

The report's authors had strong grounds for some of their assertions, but their response to Marshall's claim that there was a considerable lack of understanding and mutual respect between whites and blacks in the 24th Infantry tended only to prove Marshall's assertion. Noting with some justice that even if racial prejudice was present in the unit it hardly constituted grounds for straggling, they dismissed the possibility that segregation itself might have had a powerful influence on what had happened. Instead, they quoted a number of comments by black officers to the effect that, as black Capt. Dan V. Snedecor observed, the relationship between white and black officers was "wonderful" and that racial prejudice, while perhaps always a danger, hardly mattered where the 24th Infantry was concerned. That some of the officers had made their comments only in the context of the trials also went unobserved, as did the possibility that few of those individuals would have said anything to an inspector general that might have harmed their careers in a segregated Army.

The investigators dismissed Marshall's charge that some of the regiment's white officers had made no secret of their preference for service in an all-white unit. The allegation, they said, was "so general and vague in its nature" that it was difficult to

determine, and it failed to recognize that "the shortcomings of the Negro soldiers" themselves might also have been to blame. "In view of the excessive number of stragglers and the numerous instances of misbehavior in the face of the enemy," they continued, "it is understandable that an officer would prefer to be with a unit where these faults were not so prevalent. . . . The percentage of officers killed in action is 10% of the total of the regiment, as compared with an average of 6% in the other two regiments of the division. In other words, an officer assigned to the 24th Infantry has only 60% of the chance of survival of an officer assigned to other regiments of the division." In making those arguments, the authors clearly put the effect in place of its cause and avoided addressing the real issue: that it was difficult to make a first-class soldier out of a second-class citizen.[29]

Appearing at almost the same time as the Far East Command's report, the summary of the Eighth Army's investigation into General Kean's recommendation to disband the 24th was far more circumspect. Recounting the regiment's problems at Sangju and Masan, the investigators noted that because of the dearth of qualified replacements within the command, many black soldiers had been assigned to all-white regiments within the 25th Division as well as to units in the 2d and 24th Divisions. Fighting in combat units, those individuals had caused no problems. Instead, all of the concerned commanders had insisted that the performance of the blacks was identical to that of the whites. The investigators then devoted an entire paragraph to the comments of three black war correspondents, L. Alex Wilson of the *Chicago Defender*, Frank Whisonant of the *Pittsburgh Courier*, and James L. Hicks of the *Baltimore Afro-American*. All had agreed that there were difficulties within the 24th Infantry, but they ascribed them "to lack of leadership, esprit-de-corps, and close relationship between officers and men; discrimination against negro officers; and poor quality of replacements. Their opinions were that complete integration was the solution, and

[28] Ibid., Encl 27, Rpt, sub: General Prisoner Nathaniel A. Reed.

[29] Ibid., pp. 21–24.

Mr. Hicks stated that 75 percent of the men in the regiment favored such action."[30]

The Eighth Army's investigators concluded that even though the facts clearly argued in favor of integration, with seventy-seven units of company size or larger in the Eighth Army, the administrative burdens involved in disbanding the 24th at that time were "practically insurmountable." In addition, there was the 24th's long heritage of service to consider. If the regiment was designated for inactivation, they said, the move would "place the Brand of Cain upon the present and former members of the regiment living, and also upon the memories of those who died while serving with the organization. This drastic course does not seem warranted." In the end, General Walker accepted his investigators' advice and retained the 24th in service.[31]

Whatever the conclusions of official investigators and despite the courts-martial, by the end of October morale within the 24th was at a peak. The breakout from the Pusan Perimeter and the northward pursuit of the enemy had been, as 1st Lt. Sandro A. Barone remarked, "a godsend, a confidence builder."[32] The feeling on the part of the men was that the war was over and that everyone would be going home, perhaps even before Christmas. When orders arrived to begin preparations to cross over into North Korea, they came as a shock to many.[33]

The plan General MacArthur had devised for the advance called for Walker's Eighth Army to pro-ceed up the Korean peninsula from the west, while X Corps, after conducting an amphibious landing at Wonson on North Korea's east coast, moved from the east. The Eighth Army would have three parts. The I Corps, composed of the 1st Cavalry Division, the 24th Infantry Division, and the 1st South Korean Division, would occupy the left flank and spearhead the attack. The South Korean II Corps, incorporating the 6th, 7th, and 8th South Korean Divisions, would hold the right and portions of the center. The IX Corps, with the 2d Infantry Division operating to the east and the 25th Infantry Division to the west, would follow. A newly formed organization whose untrained headquarters would arrive in Korea only on 10 October and whose communications battalion was slated to follow three weeks later, IX Corps would serve as a reserve, securing lines of communication and policing captured enemy areas. The initial objective of the Eighth Army would be the North Korean capital at P'yongyang, some one hundred and twenty miles north of Seoul.[34]

The first phase of the assault began on 9 October, when elements of the Eighth Army entered North Korea. Only I Corps moved forward at that time because U.S. logisticians were unable to support any more troops north of the Han River. Even then, since most of the rail lines in North Korea had been heavily damaged by American air attacks, supplies for the invading force had to be trucked more than a hundred miles along roads ill prepared for such heavy traffic. Nonetheless, by 19 October P'yongyang had fallen to allied forces. On 23 October General Walker informed General Coulter that the South Korean III Corps would relieve IX Corps as soon as practicable and that he should be prepared to move his force into North Korea no later than 10 November.[35]

By the end of October, the 24th Infantry was over strength in officers (105 percent) and enlisted men (103 percent) because a number of wounded

[30] Ltr, Headquarters, Eighth U.S. Army, Korea, Office of the Inspector General, to Commanding General, Eighth U.S. Army, Korea, 15 Mar 51, sub: Report of Investigation Concerning 24th Infantry Regiment and Negro Soldiers in Combat, p. 5, boxes 1013–1014 (hereafter cited as Eighth Army Inspector General Investigation), RG 159, WNRC.

[31] Quote from ibid., pp. 5, 6. Although the final report of the Eighth Army's investigation was not completed until March 1951, three months after Walker's death, Walker was briefed on the conclusions and approved the recommendation to retain the 24th. See MacGregor, *Integration of the Armed Forces*, p. 437.

[32] Interv, MacGarrigle with Sandro A. Barone, 14 Apr 94.

[33] Intervs, Bowers with Edward H. Skiffington, 14 Apr 94; Muehlbauer with Isaac Smith, 27 Sep 88; Charles Piedra, 3 Nov 88. The American objective in North Korea is dealt with in Appleman, *South to the Naktong, North to the Yalu*, p. 607.

[34] Appleman, *South to the Naktong, North to the Yalu*, pp. 610–11; Schnabel, *Policy and Direction*, pp. 135–36.

[35] Appleman, *South to the Naktong, North to the Yalu*, pp. 638–53.

soldiers had returned to duty after hospitalization in Japan. Even so, and despite Corley's program of training, the combat efficiency of the unit was off because of the loss of crew-served weapons in the engagements around Masan and a lack of trained personnel to man the remainder.[36]

As was the case in the rest of the Eighth Army, with winter coming and the evenings turning cold, a lack of warm winter clothing was also becoming a serious concern. An effort to remedy the problem was under way, bringing in enough woolens by November to provide for 90 percent of the regiment, but supplies of some winter gear were still short. At one point, according to the operations officer of the 3d Battalion, Capt. Roscius C. Newell, each man was limited to one fur- or pile-lined garment, be it a field jacket, cap, or gloves. Apparently, only drivers and soldiers habitually exposed to the elements received winter overcoats and parkas. Even then, proper sizes were often lacking, forcing the men to make do with whatever was issued, whether it fit or not. By then, instruction teams had begun to operate within the regiment to ensure that the troops understood how to avoid frostbite and other cold-weather ailments. Understanding that uniforms should hang loosely to insulate properly, the trainers regarded the ill-fitting clothing with some dismay.[37] Their concern was well placed. When the weather turned decidedly cold in mid-November, eighty-five of the men came down with frostbite.[38]

The order for the 25th Division to begin the move north arrived on 2 November. The next day the division's command post moved to Kaesong, thirty-eight miles northwest of Seoul and some one hundred and fifty miles from the unit's former base at Taejon. The 24th Infantry began its march north by rail and motor on 6 November, arriving at Musan-ni, some fifteen miles south of Kaesong at the mouth of the Imjin River, on the evening of 8 November and the morning of the ninth. The unit's battalions then moved by truck and foot to Chindong-myon, sixteen miles to the northeast, where they established a base. The regiment immediately sent out a reinforced patrol to reconnoiter the perimeter of the regimental area. The force made no contact with the enemy but came across caches of enemy mortar and artillery ammunition.[39]

By that time the 27th and 35th regiments had already arrived and portions of the 27th were engaged in a push toward the town of Ich'on, forty miles northeast of Kaesong. Since intelligence estimated that from seven to eight thousand enemy troops were present in the territory south and east of Ich'on, a region close to the supply routes feeding allied forces in P'yongyang, the Eighth Army decided to sweep the area with the 25th Division.[40] To that end, on the morning of 9 November, learning that an enemy force occupied the town of Yonch'on, just ten miles to the north of Chindong-myon above the 38th Parallel separating North from South Korea, the 24th Infantry dispatched a task force to clear the town. Composed of Company A, the intelligence and reconnaissance (I&R) platoon, a platoon from the heavy mortar company, and various recoilless rifle and light machine-gun elements, the unit came under fire from an estimated two hundred enemy but secured high ground south of the town before pulling in for the night. Seventy-five South Korean soldiers and eight hundred South Korean police reinforced the attack by holding the ridges above the town. The next morning, after a brief firefight, the enemy withdrew to the north, leaving Yonch'on in allied hands. A quick survey found that the town contained large stocks of enemy ammunition, clothing, and medical supplies.[41]

[36] WD, 24th Inf Rgt, 1–31 Oct 50, pp. 2–11, box 3760, RG 407, WNRC.

[37] Intervs, MacGarrigle with Roscius C. Newell, 10 and 15 Nov 94; WD, 25th Inf Div, 1–30 Nov 50, 1 Nov 50, 6 Nov 50, boxes 3761–3763, RG 407, WNRC; WD, 24th Inf Rgt, 1–30 Nov 50, p. 3, box 3764, RG 407, WNRC.

[38] Daily Journal, 24th Medical Co, Casualties for 14–17 Nov 50, in WD, 24th Inf Rgt, Nov 50, box 3764, RG 407, WNRC.

[39] WD, 24th Inf Rgt, Nov 50, pp. 3–4; 24th Inf Rgt Unit Rpt 39, 9 Nov 50, box 3764, RG 407, WNRC.

[40] WD, 25th Inf Div, 8 Nov 50, boxes 3761–3763, RG 407, WNRC.

[41] WD, 24th Inf Rgt, Nov 50, pp. 6–7; 24th Inf Rgt Unit Rpt 40, 10 Nov 50, box 3764, RG 407, WNRC; WD, 25th Inf Div, 10 Nov 50, boxes 3761–3763, RG 407, WNRC; WD, 1st Bn, 24th Inf Rgt, Nov 50, pp. 11–12, box 3764, RG 407, WNRC; Intervs, Cash with Waymon R. Ransom, 5 Aug 88; MacGarrigle with Baranowski, 24 Aug 94.

Spending the better part of the day destroying the enemy's stores, the task force received instructions that afternoon to leave Yonch'on under the control of the South Korean police and to return to base. It began the process immediately but lacked sufficient trucks to move as a body. As a result, half of the troops made the trip to Chindong-myon but the remainder, perhaps a hundred and twenty men, stayed behind to await the arrival of more trucks. Finally, toward dark the group reported that it was on the way.[42]

Two thousand yards south of the town, the convoy passed a large assemblage of men that many assumed to be South Korean police. A short distance farther, the lead truck hit a mine and the rest of the trucks came under heavy fire from portions of the group they had just passed. Some of the troops had apparently been told to unload their weapons because of an earlier accidental discharge and were unprepared to fire back. Those who could still walk or crawl piled out of their burning vehicles into a ditch beside the road where they took cover.[43]

Following toward the rear with the I&R platoon, M. Sgt. Waymon Ransom heard the explosion and the firing and rushed forward. He rallied the troops in the ditch, but when enemy mortars zeroed in on the position and further resistance appeared futile, he ordered them to withdraw. Cpl. John L. Hicks described what happened. "It looked like a million of them was coming after us," Hicks said.

Sergeant Ransom cried out to run for it, but he did not because there were many wounded men. He jumped from his position and walked into the enemy firing and swearing. . . . I called him but he didn't stop. It suddenly dawned on me what he had said some time ago, "Buster (that's my nickname), one of these days they are going to make me so mad with their 'banzai,' . . . [I'm] going to make one of my own.[44]

Ransom charged into the advancing enemy, firing until his weapon jammed. He kept fighting hand to hand, but finally went down with several wounds. "I rolled over and played dead," he recalled years later. "They stomped me around some and took my field jacket and my billfold and cap. Then they left me. . . . I think they shot anybody they saw was still moving."[45] Later, another group of the enemy stole Ransom's boots, discovered he was alive, beat him, and again left him for dead. Nearly frozen, he survived nonetheless until the next day, when a relief force from the 1st Battalion reached the scene. In all, 42 Americans were killed in the action, 8 were listed as missing, and 24 were wounded. Ransom received the Distinguished Service Cross for his heroism.[46]

The attack caused a number of difficulties for the 24th, which had lost two platoons of Company A and a significant portion of its I&R platoon. Colonel Corley began work to rebuild those units, but in the interim, the loss of Ransom, his men, and his trucks severely limited the regiment's intelligence-gathering abilities. Corley attempted to compensate by sending out patrols from his battalions, but the teams failed to operate aggressively and brought back little information of any consequence.[47] On top of those problems, a sudden freeze shortly after the ambush sidelined twelve more vehicles, causing shortages in some types of ammunition, signal supplies, and quartermaster items that normally moved by truck.[48]

Limping from its losses and increasingly wary, the 24th reoccupied Yonch'on on 13 November and pushed on to seize the city of Ch'orwon, thir-

---

[42] Ibid.

[43] Floyd Williams of Company A made the allegation. See Interv, Cash with Floyd B. Williams, 6 Aug 88. Waymon Ransom also remarked that the men did not have ammunition, but did not say why. See Interv, Cash with Ransom, 5 Aug 88.

[44] Statement by Cpl John L. Hicks, attachment to Recommendation for Distinguished Service Cross for M Sgt Waymon Ransom, 4 May 51, box 167, RG 338, WNRC.

[45] Interv, Cash with Ransom, 5 Aug 88. Ransom also spoke about the ambush in a follow-up interview with Cash on 22 August 1991.

[46] WD, 24th Inf Rgt, Casualty Statistics for 1–30 Nov 50, 25 Dec 50, box 3764, RG 407, WNRC. See also 24th Inf Rgt Unit Rpt 42, 12 Nov 50, box 3764, RG 407, WNRC; 25th Inf Div Periodic Intelligence Rpt 116, 12 Nov 50, boxes 3761–3763, RG 407, WNRC. For a published account of the action, see Rishell, With a Black Platoon in Combat, pp. 116–25. An outline of the action is in WD, 1st Bn, 24th Inf Rgt, Nov 50, p. 11. See also Intervs, Cash with Alonzo Cooper, 8 Sep 88; MacGarrigle with Baranowski, 24 Aug and 6 Sep 94; Muehlbauer with Ray Koenig, 20 Mar 89.

[47] WD, 24th Inf Rgt, S–2 Summary for Nov 50, 14 Jan 51, box 3764, RG 407, WNRC.

[48] WD, 24th Inf Rgt, S–4 Summary for Nov 50, n.d., box 3764, RG 407, WNRC.

teen miles to the north. Although the enemy resisted mainly with artillery and mortar fire, causing no casualties, a brief flurry of concern arose when Colonel Corley disappeared. He turned up, however, shortly thereafter. A fervent Catholic, he had stumbled across a church of his faith and had stepped inside to pray. No further incident occurred. The regiment occupied the town, uncovering in the process more enemy supplies, some artillery pieces, and a T34 tank.[49] As for the episode in the church, it became part of the legend that was beginning to surround the popular colonel.[50]

In the days that followed, the 1st Battalion held blocking positions three miles north of Ch'orwon. Meanwhile, the regiment's 2d Battalion patrolled the unit's main supply route through Yonch'on, which was constantly subject to sniper fire, while the 3d Battalion guarded crossing sites over the Imjin River.[51] There were some discipline problems among the men. After the regiment crossed the 38th Parallel, a former company commander, Capt. Buckner M. Creel, observed that some individuals in his unit took the attitude that the enemy's land was "fair game." Sneaking into nearby towns at night, they raped and pillaged. If a few offenders were apprehended, most went unpunished because local residents had difficulty recognizing their assailants.[52] Although Creel spoke only of his own soldiers, blacks were hardly the only guilty parties. Rapes were also occurring in areas under the sole

responsibility of all-white units.[53]

The Push Toward the Yalu

On 17 November, with the Eighth Army's preparations for its final offensive north to the Chinese border in full swing, the 24th turned the region around Ch'orwon over to the South Koreans and began the process of moving nearly a hundred miles north to Sunch'on, 30 miles above P'yongyang. The trip took more than two days. Shortly after arriving, Colonel Corley received instructions to move 30 miles farther to the town of Kunu-ri, located 70 miles southeast of the nearest point on the Yalu River, North Korea's border with China, and 15 miles east of Anju on the Ch'ongch'on River. (Map 11) There the regiment was to participate in the 25th Division's relief of the 1st Cavalry Division, which had seen heavy fighting during late October and early November in combat with Chinese forces that were already moving down into Korea. Because of a gasoline shortage, many of the troops covered the final leg of the journey on foot.[54] The troops observed Thanksgiving on 23 November, the day before the Eighth Army's attack was to begin. Although some of the men in the field had to make do with C-rations, most had turkey with all the trimmings. The weather was clear but cold.[55]

American commanders were optimistic that they had the war won, but rough estimates still indicated that the enemy retained substantial forces just to the north and east of Anju along the Ch'ongch'on River valley, the line of departure for

[49] WD, 1st Bn, 24th Inf Rgt, 15 and 16 Nov 50, pp. 15–16, box 3764, RG 407, WNRC.

[50] 25th Inf Div Periodic Opns Rpt 24, 12 Nov 50, boxes 3761–3763, RG 407, WNRC; WD, 24th Inf Rgt, Nov 50, p. 9. The story of the church was recalled by Chaplain Gray Johnson and Gustav Gillert. See Intervs, Cash with Gray Johnson, 23 Mar 89; Gillert, 25 Mar 89.

[51] 25th Inf Div Periodic Opns Rpt 28, 13 Nov 50, boxes 3761–3763, RG 407, WNRC; WD, 24th Inf Rgt, Nov 50, p. 9.

[52] Interv, MacGarrigle with Buckner M. Creel, 3 Dec 93. Edwin W. Robertson, a retired Air Force major general attached to the 24th as a liaison officer, also dealt with the subject. See Interv, Cash with Edwin W. Robertson, 29 Aug 89. Vernie Scott, the regimental headquarters sergeant, mentioned a rape after the breakout from Pusan but did not pursue the issue. See Interv, Cash with Vernie Scott, 7 Sep 88. Charles

Bussey describes an attempted rape by two sergeants from one of the 24th's heavy weapons companies north of Kunu-ri. See Bussey, *Firefight at Yechon*, pp. 237–38.

[53] See, for example, IX Corps Periodic Intelligence Rpt 62, 27 Nov 50, box 1769, RG 407, WNRC.

[54] WD, 24th Inf Rgt, Nov 50, p. 12. The presence of the Chinese is noted in WD, 25th Inf Div, Intelligence Annex to Opns Order 15, 21 Nov 50, boxes 3761–3763, RG 407, WNRC. For more on the Chinese and their presence in North Korea, see Billy C. Mossman, *Ebb and Flow, November 1950–July 1951*, United States Army in the Korean War (Washington, D.C.: U.S. Army Center of Military History, Government Printing Office, 1990), pp. 51–60.

[55] Intervs, Muehlbauer with Charles A. Hill, 28 Feb 89; MacGarrigle with Reginald J. Sapenter, 21 Mar 94.

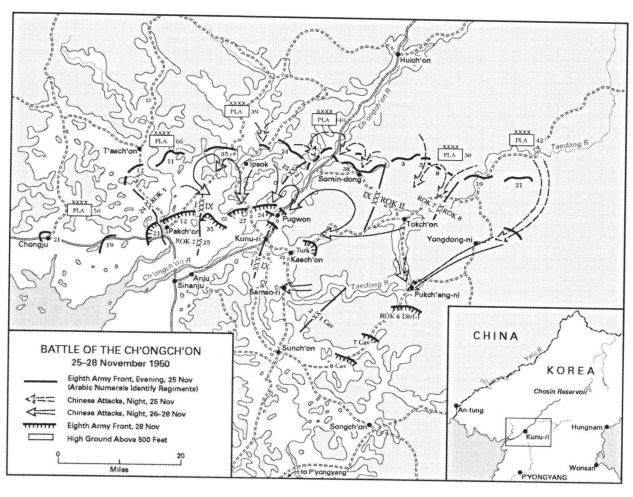

BATTLE OF THE CH'ONGCH'ON
25–28 November 1950

	Eighth Army Front, Evening, 25 Nov (Arabic Numerals Identify Regiments)
	Chinese Attacks, Night, 25 Nov
	Chinese Attacks, Night, 26–28 Nov
	Eighth Army Front, 28 Nov
	High Ground Above 500 Feet

0   20
Miles

Map 11

the 25th Division's push to the Yalu. To the immediate front of the division, according to intelligence analysts, stood at least two Chinese divisions and part of a North Korean division, a total of 14,600 men. Another 4,800 men waited in reserve just to the rear, and behind them 14,600 more. In all, the 25th Division's intelligence analysts estimated that the unit faced a combined enemy force of about thirty-four thousand men.[56]

The particular contribution the Chinese would make in contesting the attack remained unclear. Intelligence estimates indicated that between forty and seventy thousand Chinese soldiers had entered North Korea. Everyone expected them to be active. Portions of that force had already bloodied the U.S. 1st Cavalry Division and the 1st South Korean Division in an area to the north of Anju that the 25th Division would have to cross. It had also fought the South Korean II Corps farther to the east, crippling a South Korean division and a U.S. regiment. The Far East Command's analysts believed, however, that the Chinese were only bluffing. When the time came, so the reasoning went, they would conduct counterattacks in self-defense but would refrain from

---

[56] Enemy forces are covered in 24th Inf Rgt Opns Order 20. 22 Nov 50. annex 1. box 3764. RG 407. WNRC.

committing themselves to an all-out war with the United States.[57]

In fact, when the Eighth Army launched its attack on 24 November, it came up against six Chinese armies composed of nineteen divisions totaling some 150,000 men. The 25th Division itself confronted three of those divisions, close to its original estimate. Lightly armed and inadequately supplied, those forces would have little staying power in comparison with the heavily armed Americans, who had been joined by that time by Turkish and British allies. Since the Chinese units were composed almost entirely of fighting men, however, they would be able to deliver telling blows over the short term, especially against units that had no idea of their location or intentions.[58]

As the Eighth Army advanced toward the Yalu, it spread out along an eighty-mile front that stretched from Chonju on the left, some twenty miles to the north and west of Anju, to Yongdong-ni on the right, sixty miles to the east. The I Corps took the far left flank, IX Corps the center, and the South Korean II Corps the right. Advancing northward from the Chosin Reservoir, forty miles to the north of Hungnam on North Korea's east coast, X Corps would connect with II Corps' easternmost flank while moving toward the Chinese border, a distance of some seventy miles to the northwest of the unit's point of departure.[59]

Within IX Corps, General Kean's 25th Division took position to the left and Maj. Gen. Laurence B. Keiser's 2d Infantry Division to the right. Within the 25th's sector, the 35th Infantry moved on the west toward the town of Unsan, some eighteen miles north of Kunu-ri on the west side of the Kuryong River, a south-flowing tributary of the Ch'ongch'on. Corley's 24th Infantry advanced on the right, moving into mountains east of the river valley. Since the 25th Division's area of operations was too wide for a two-regiment front and Kean wanted to keep his third regiment, the 27th, in reserve, a task force under Colonel Dolvin held the center. Task Force Dolvin comprised elements from the 89th Medium Tank Battalion, the 25th Division's reconnaissance company, Company E of the 27th Infantry, Company B of the 35th Infantry, and the 8213th Ranger Company. The 27th Infantry stood in reserve behind Task Force Dolvin, prepared to move in any direction as the need arose.[60]

The plan of operations for the force was relatively simple. While Task Force Dolvin maneuvered up the east side of the Kuryong River valley between the 35th and 24th Infantry regiments, the 2d Division to the east was to move up the Ch'ongch'on River valley. The 9th Infantry regiment of the 2d Division, located at Won-ni, some five miles east of Kunu-ri, stood on the 24th Infantry's right flank. Its 3d Battalion was the only all-black infantry unit in the Eighth Army besides the 24th.[61]

In general, Kean expected Task Force Dolvin and the 35th Infantry to do the work. As a result, he placed them in low-lying areas on relatively good routes where Dolvin's armor in particular could advance with ease. The 24th Infantry was to keep pace, working its way through the mountainous region between the Kuryong and Ch'ongch'on River valleys and maintaining contact between Dolvin on the left and the 2d Division to the right.[62] (Map 12) According to Colonel Corley, Kean gave the regiment that task because he lacked confidence in its abilities and had long before developed a policy of placing the unit in areas where, if it performed poorly, it would not affect the outcome of a battle.[63]

---

[57] The figures are from Roy E. Appleman, *Disaster in Korea: The Chinese Confront MacArthur* (College Station: Texas A&M University Press, 1989), pp. 44–45. See also Mossman, *Ebb and Flow*, p. 65; 25th Inf Div Periodic Intelligence Rpt 125, 20 Nov 50, boxes 3761–3763, RG 407, WNRC. For the Chinese attacks, see Appleman, *South to the Naktong, North to the Yalu*, pp. 673–75, 689–708.

[58] Appleman, *Disaster in Korea*, pp. 44–45.

[59] Appleman, *Disaster in Korea*, p. 42; Mossman, *Ebb and Flow*, pp. 63–64.

[60] Ibid.; Historical Rpt, 25th Inf Div, 22–24 Nov 50, boxes 3761–3763, RG 407, WNRC; S–3 Journal, 27th Inf Rgt, Nov 50, pp. 14–15, boxes 3764–3765, RG 407, WNRC; Unit Journal, 89th Medium Tank Bn, Nov 50, Encl 3, WD, Task Force Dolvin, Nov 50, p. 1, box 3765, RG 407, WNRC. The composition of Dolvin is described in Unit Journal, 89th Medium Tank Bn, Nov 50, p. 3.

[61] Historical Rpt, 25th Inf Div, 22–24 Nov 50.

[62] 24th Inf Rgt Opns Order 20, 22 Nov 50.

[63] Interv, Roy E. Appleman with John T. Corley, 4 Jan 52, CMH files.

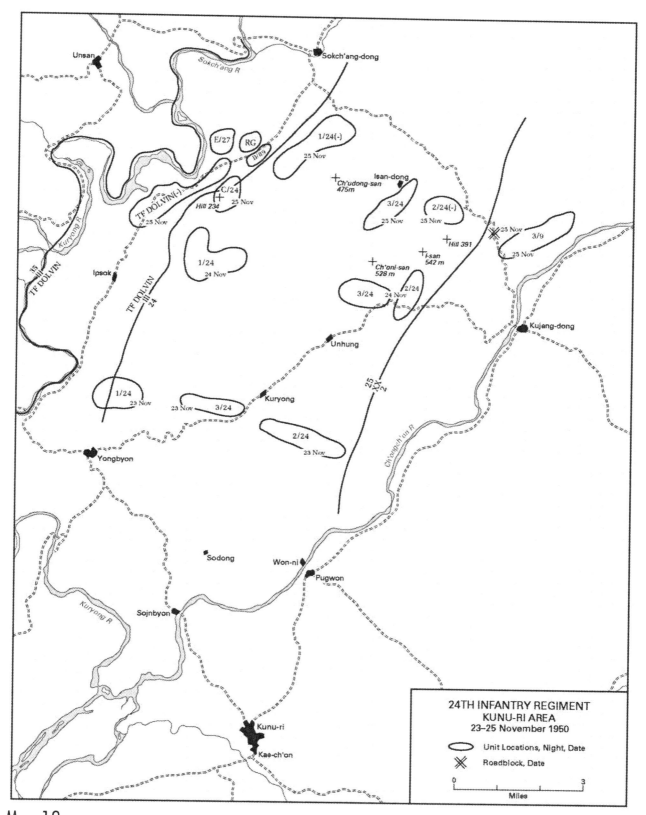

Unsan

Sokch'ang R

Sokch'ang-dong

E/27   RG
        B/89
1/24(-)
25 Nov

Ch'udong-san
475m   Isan-dong

C/24
25 Nov   3/24   2/24(-)
Hill 234   25 Nov   25 Nov
TF DOLVIN(-)   25 Nov   3/9
25 Nov   Hill 391
                          25 Nov
Kuryong R

.35
TF DOLVIN

TF DOLVIN   I-san
                         542 m
Ipsak
TF DOLVIN
24   Ch'oni-san
1/24   528 m
24 Nov   3/24   2/24
                  24 Nov

                            Kujang-dong
          Unhung
1/24
23 Nov   XX
        23 Nov   3/24   25
                 Kuryong   2

                 2/24
                 23 Nov
Yongbyon

Ch'ongch'on R

Sodong   Won-ni
              Pugwon

Kuryong R

Sojnbyon

Kunu-ri

Kae-ch'on

24TH INFANTRY REGIMENT
KUNU-RI AREA
23–25 November 1950

Unit Locations, Night, Date

Roadblock, Date

0   3

Miles

Map 12

Whatever General Kean's intentions, the region he assigned to the 24th was rugged and inaccessible. A single unpaved highway crossed it. Beginning at the ancient walled town of Yongbyon, ten miles northwest of Kunu-ri, that road described a rough triangle whose first leg ran some twenty miles to the north and northeast toward the town of Sokch'ang-dong on the Sokch'ang River, a tributary to the Kuryong. Turning southeast at that point, the highway entered its second leg, moving a distance of ten miles to Kujang-dong on the Ch'ongch'on River. Just before reaching that town, the route's third leg began with a swing generally to the west. Following a small valley some eight miles to the village of Unhung, it then beat twelve miles through another valley and the town of Kuryong to its starting point at Yongbyon. The region along the Yongbyon–Sokch'ang-dong road paralleled the right bank of the Kuryong River. Characterized by low-lying hills but otherwise relatively flat and accessible, it would be the area of operations for Task Force Dolvin. By contrast, the territory to the east under the charge of the 24th was a jumble of hills and rocky outcroppings. Corley's unit was to move northwest across that expanse and, as its initial objective, seize the Kujang-dong–Sokch'ang-dong road. After that it was to proceed to the Yalu with the rest of the Eighth Army.[64]

The 24th's sector had no north-south roads capable of assisting the unit's advance. The east-west portion of the highway between Yongbyon and Kujang-dong was helpful, becoming for lack of anything better an extension of the regiment's main supply route from Kunu-ri through Yongbyon, but that road's eastern end at Kujang-dong was in the hands of the 2d Division. Corley had to request permission before he could maneuver his forces and supply trains into the area. In the same way, the Kujang-dong–Sokch'ang-dong road was accessible only through the 2d Division.[65]

Within the 24th Infantry's area, which ran generally southwest to northeast, vehicular movement above the Yongbyon–Kujang-dong road was also problematic. Only rough tracks existed, and many of those routes died out before reaching a definable destination. In addition, three mountains blocked the regiment's advance. The 1st Battalion on the left faced 475-meter-high Ch'udong-san. The 3d Battalion in the center had to deal with 528-meter-high Ch'oni-san. And the 2d Battalion to the right had 542-meter-high I-san to consider. In the 2d Battalion's area, I-san completely blocked all progress north. Elsewhere, even where motorable tracks existed, the heights tended to bar the way to all but the smallest and lightest trucks. In the end, in order to resupply units operating in the region, Colonel Corley had to depend upon Korean porters and parachute drops, neither of which posed an attractive alternative. Although fifty porters were assigned to most of the companies operating in the area, there was no guarantee that they would do their jobs when fighting began. As for the drops, efforts of that sort succeeded when danger was remote but were not reliable when enemy forces threatened.[66]

On the morning of 24 November the three battalions of the 24th Infantry moved out abreast from positions on the north side of the Ch'ongch'on River. Since the Chinese had pulled back their main forces in order to gather breath for their own offensive, leaving only observation teams and small screening forces on ridge lines to face the American advance, the regiment encountered little enemy opposition during the first day of the attack. Proceeding rapidly through the mountain valleys, the 1st Battalion managed to keep pace with Task Force Dolvin.[67] Accompanied by General Kean for

[64] 24th Inf Rgt Opns Order 20, 22 Nov 50. See also Appleman, *Disaster in Korea*, p. 137.

[65] Map, Korea, 1:50,000, series L751, Army Map Service (AMS) 1950, sheets 6333 I and 6433 IV, National Archives and Records Administration (NARA), College Park, Md.

[66] Ibid. See also Intervs, MacGarrigle with George A. Clayton, 10 and 11 Aug 94. The 2d Battalion's war diary shows the problems with porters and airdrops. See WD, 2d Bn, 24th Inf Rgt, Nov 50, p. 26, box 3764, RG 407, WNRC; Memo, 25th Inf Div G–3, 23 Nov 50, sub: Activities Report for 22 Nov, 25th Division Staff Records, Nov 50, in WD, 25th Inf Div, Nov 50. In all, the 24th Infantry had 300 Korean ammunition carriers.

[67] WD, 25th Inf Div, 24 Nov 50, boxes 3761–3763, RG 407, WNRC; WD, 24th Inf Rgt, Nov 50, p. 13; WD, 1st Bn,

several hours during the day, the 2d Battalion also made good progress, as did the 3d. By evening, Colonel Corley could report that his regiment's forward command post had reached Kuryong, five miles to the east of Yongbyon on the road to Kujang-dong, and that his unit as a whole had advanced nearly five miles.[68]

The rest of the Eighth Army moved apace. The 35th Infantry on the west of Task Force Dolvin covered three miles over the same period. The 9th Infantry on the east flank of the 24th was already several miles ahead of the other attacking units. It adjusted its position by moving forward some two miles, but then held in place with the rest of the 2d Division until the 25th Division's units could move up. The South Korean II Corps to the far right of the 2d Division was the only element of the force to meet significant enemy opposition. The South Koreans gained from one-quarter to a full mile in some areas but in others found themselves unable to advance. The weather was cold over the entire region. Despite warming temperatures during the day, temperatures fell to -15°F at night. There was snow on the ground in some places.[69]

That evening, elements of Task Force Dolvin began to report enemy patrols near their positions. Although the night passed largely without incident, the tempo of enemy activity increased the next day, 25 November, when Dolvin was able to advance only 2,000 yards against very heavy opposition. At that time, Companies A and B of

the 1st Battalion of the 24th, along with Colonel Miller's command group, moved off in a column to the northeast past Ch'udong-san toward their objective, the northernmost stretch of the Kujang-dong–Sokch'ang-dong road. Meeting increased enemy resistance, Company B ended the day a mile short of the road. Company A stopped about one and one-half miles farther to the rear. Since Dolvin's lead elements—Company E of the 27th Infantry, the 8213th Ranger Company, and Company B of the 89th Medium Tank Battalion—were about one mile west of Company A, the two units from the 24th were well positioned to protect the task force's eastern flank overnight and to continue their attack the following morning.[70]

Even closer to the task force, Company C of the 24th had by then reached Hill 234, located some two miles to the southwest of Company A above a choke point on the Kuryong where foothills dominated a bend in the river. Protecting the right flank of Dolvin's Company B of the 35th Infantry, which was attempting to advance up the lowlands near the river, the unit came under heavy enemy mortar fire, took seven casualties, but still held in place all day. Toward noon the 25th Division removed it from the control of the 24th Infantry and attached it temporarily to Dolvin.[71]

The forces operating farther to the east of Dolvin and the 1st Battalion were meanwhile experiencing mixed results. Attacking into the rugged high ground that separated the 1st from the 2d Battalion on the morning of the twenty-fifth, the forward units of Colonel Blair's 3d Battalion skirmished with the enemy but reported toward evening that they had still reached all their objec-

24th Inf Rgt, Nov 50, p. 24. The Chinese strategy is discussed in Mossman, *Ebb and Flow*, pp. 59–60. The reasons for the 1st Battalion's speed are mentioned in Interv, MacGarrigle with Baranowski, 24 Aug 94. Baranowski was the operations officer of the 1st Battalion.

[68] WD, 24th Inf Rgt, 1–30 Nov 50, p. 14; WD, 25th Inf Div, 24 Nov 50; WD, 2d Bn, 24th Inf Rgt, Nov 50, p. 6; WD, 3d Bn, 24th Inf Rgt, Nov 50, p. 10, box 3764, RG 407, WNRC. See also Interv, MacGarrigle with Sapenter, 21 Mar 94. Kean's presence was mentioned by the 2d Battalion commander. See Intervs, MacGarrigle with Clayton, 10 and 11 Aug 94.

[69] WD, 25th Inf Div, 24 Nov 50; 25th Inf Div Periodic Opns Rpt 60, 24 Nov 50, annex to WD, 25th Inf Div, Nov 50. South Korean gains are described in Mossman, *Ebb and Flow*, p. 63. The weather is mentioned in Intervs, Appleman with Corley, 4 Jan 52; MacGarrigle with Charles E. Green, 16 Jun 94; Sapenter, 21 Mar 94.

[70] WD, 1st Bn, 24th Inf Rgt, 25 Nov 50, box 3764, RG 407, WNRC; 25th Inf Div Periodic Opns Rpt 62, 25 Nov 50, annex to WD, 25th Inf Div, Nov 50; Map Overlay to 25th Inf Div Periodic Opns Rpt 63, 25 Nov 50, in WD, 25th Inf Div, Nov 50; Interv, MacGarrigle with Baranowski, 6 Sep 94.

[71] Ibid. The situation in Company C is mentioned in Ltr, Howard H. Eichelsdoerfer to John A. Cash, 23 Sep 90, CMH files. See also Narrative Account of Action, Task Force Wilson, 26–27 Nov 50, attachment to Medal of Honor Award file for Reginald Desiderio, box 159, RG 338, WNRC; 24th Inf Rgt Unit Rpt 55, 25 Nov 50, box 3764, RG 407, WNRC; Interv, Cash with Harry Cramer, 27–28 Aug 89.

Bivouac site of a headquarters unit

tives. They dug in for the night in the hills some four miles to the northeast of Unhung.[72]

To the east the 2d Battalion and the rear elements of the 3d had difficulties. Since the I-san blocked the way north, the 2d Battalion's commander, Lt. Col. George A. Clayton, with his three rifle companies, moved into the hills north of the Yongbyon–Kujang-dong road to skirt the mountain. Company F, under Capt. Roger Walden, struck out to the northwest while Clayton with Companies E and G moved northeast and then north around Hill 391.[73]

The rest of the 2d Battalion received leave from the 2d Division to move the unit's trains along with two tanks, engineers, and a 4.2-inch mortar platoon through that division's area of operations and up the Kujang-dong–Sokch'ang-dong road. They intended to link up with Clayton at the 2d Battalion's objective for the day, an area just off the road about halfway between the two towns. Combining with command and support elements from the 3d Battalion that were seeking an easy way to reach their own forward units, the convoy, composed of some fifty vehicles, moved nearly twelve miles toward its goal before a message arrived from the 2d Division canceling the move. An enemy force farther ahead had blocked the road.[74]

The command post for the 3d Battalion pulled back and bivouacked for the night, but part of the convoy attempted to reach the objective by a different route. Since Clayton and two of his three companies had struck off overland through the mountains, the column had no chance of following them. Walden's Company F, however, had taken a more easily traveled route through the 3d Battalion's area of operations to the west. The vehicles fell in behind it. Over the afternoon that followed, Clayton's force

---

[72] WD, 3d Bn, 24th Inf Rgt, Nov 50, p. 11; Map Overlay, attachment to 24th Inf Rgt Unit Rpt 55, 25 Nov 50; Interv, Appleman with Corley, 4 Jan 52.

[73] WD, 2d Bn, 24th Inf Rgt, Nov 50, p. 6; WD, 3d Bn, 24th Inf Rgt, Nov 50, p. 11. See also Intervs, MacGarrigle with Clayton, 10 and 11 Aug 94, 5 Oct 94; Ralph J. Davis, 31 Oct 94, with review comments. A first lieutenant, Davis was the assistant operations officer of the 2d Battalion.

[74] Ibid.

skirted the northeastern edge of the I-san and reached the high ground south of its objective.[75]

The units that had followed Company F were less fortunate. Encountering strong enemy opposition some three and a half miles above Unhung, they had no choice but to pull to the rear. Out of touch with Clayton because of a breakdown in communications, Walden and his men likewise withdrew. They held for a time on a large hill to the northeast of Unhung but then received instructions to move up the Yongbyon–Kujang-dong road to the boundary between the 25th and 2d Divisions. There they would guard the 25th Division's right flank and maintain contact with the 9th Infantry to the east.[76]

By the evening of 25 November, two days into the operation, difficulties were beginning to mount for the 24th. Although the weather was often below freezing, some of the men had yet to receive all of their cold-weather gear. Insulated footwear was in particularly short supply. Meanwhile, as had been the case with the 2d Battalion's convoy, motorized supply trains were finding it difficult if not impossible to make their way into the mountains. The porters called in to substitute succeeded in resupplying some of the troops on the evening of the twenty-fifth, but after that, as enemy attacks increased, they tended to melt away.[77]

Compounding those problems, with the high peaks in the area impeding electronic transmissions and the cold weather reducing the efficiency of radio batteries, communications between regimental and battalion commanders and their units in the field were beginning to break down. Although supply officers sent fresh batteries forward whenever possible and radio relays through Task Force Dolvin, the 159th Field Artillery Battalion's liaison officers, and other nearby units compensated to a degree, there was never any certainty as to when contact with a company or battalion in the field would begin or end. Connections with Company C, for example, were often tenuous, and the whereabouts of the unit, according to the 1st Battalion's operations officer, Capt. Joseph Baranowski, were vague from the start. The same was true for the rest of the 1st Battalion, which was operating well to the fore of the regiment. As for the 2d Battalion, reports from the unit all but ceased. The headquarters of the 3d Battalion was similarly out of touch. After its units had penetrated deep into the mountains, their radios failed and it lost contact with its company commanders.[78]

The Chinese Attack

The enemy's counterattack began in earnest on the night of 25–26 November. To the west of the 25th Division, Chinese forces struck the 1st South Korean Division, pushing it back on its right flank with heavy casualties. Meanwhile, to the east of the 25th, the U.S. 2d Division fought desperately to prevent encirclement. The largest threat, however, came on the Eighth Army's easternmost flank, where massive enemy forces penetrated the South Korean II Corps, allowing up to six Chinese divisions to begin moving into the Eighth Army's rear.[79]

The situation was little better in the 25th Division's zone. In the center, the 8213th Ranger Company and Company E of the 27th Infantry, located about one and one-half miles to the front of Company C on Hill 205 and a north-south ridge line to its left, came under heavy attack along with other portions of Task Force Dolvin. Although Company E held its ground, the Rangers suffered forty-one casualties out of a strength of sixty-six men and had to withdraw. A battery from a field artillery battalion

---

[75] Ibid. See also Roger Walden comments to David Carlisle, 25 Feb 87, CMH files.

[76] The position of Company F between 25 and 27 November is unclear because of errors in map coordinates for the unit recorded by the 24th Infantry. Walden, however, says his unit was probably on I-san mountain. Whatever the case, by the morning of 27 November, the company was stationed on the Yongbyon–Kujang-dong road where the 2d and 25th Division boundaries met. See Roger Walden Reply to George L. MacGarrigle interviews on 28 and 29 June 1995, 7 Sep 95, CMH files; 24th Inf Rgt Unit Rpts 55, 56, and 57, 25–27 Nov 50, box 3764, RG 407, WNRC. See also Interv, MacGarrigle with Ralph Davis, 31 Oct 94, with review comments.

[77] Intervs, MacGarrigle with Baranowski, 24 Aug 94, 13–14 Oct 94; Clayton, 10 and 11 Aug 94; Owen H. Carter, 21 and 24 Jun 94; Appleman with Corley, 4 Jan 52; Ltr, Eichelsdoerfer to Cash, 23 Sep 90.

[78] Ibid.

[79] Appleman, *Disaster in Korea*, pp. 79–87, 150–53, 175–202; Mossman, *Ebb and Flow*, pp. 68–76.

was also overrun and one gun captured. According to a platoon leader in Company C, 1st Lt. Howard H. Eichelsdoerfer, Company C was ordered to go forward at that time, possibly to assist in repelling the attack. After it had advanced a few hundred yards, however, it received instructions to pull back into its original position on Hill 234. Shortly after finishing that move, the unit came under what Eichelsdoerfer considered friendly artillery fire and suffered several casualties. About that time, the 2d Battalion of the 27th Infantry, minus Company E which was already present, arrived in the area to serve as a reserve for the task force.[80]

On 26 November at about 0745, Colonel Dolvin was preparing to counterattack when General Kean ordered him to hold up. Overnight, the Chinese had attacked the units on the immediate flanks of the 25th Division. The 1st South Korean Division to the west had been pushed back on its right flank with heavy casualties, and a gap between that unit and the 35th Infantry to the east was opening. To the east of the 25th, the 9th Infantry had been hard hit, losing two companies and a battalion command post. Farther east, in the South Korean II Corps sector, large enemy forces had not only penetrated between units to move into rear areas, where they were posing a major threat, but they were also threatening to overwhelm the South Koreans, who were on the verge of collapse. Kean and his staff needed time to assess the situation.[81]

Over the next two hours the task force directed heavy artillery and tank fire into enemy positions in an effort to discourage further enemy assaults. Then at 0945 Kean instructed Dolvin to "get word to Miller" to move Company B of the 24th Infantry, which had advanced the farthest into enemy territory, back to a position west of Company A, where it could assist in forming a line against advancing Chinese forces. The message made it clear that counterattack was out of the question and that defense was the order of the day. "You will not resume attack until further instructions," Kean said. "You are authorized to adjust your lines in order to put your troops on better defensive positions. I want Miller to coordinate his disposition with Dolvin's." Miller relayed the order to Company B, which began moving to its new position.[82]

From that point on, the sequence of events involving the 1st Battalion and its units is difficult to determine. At 1045 General Kean informed Colonel Dolvin that he was sending his deputy, Brig. Gen. Vennard Wilson, forward to take command of the task force, which was then to be renamed Task Force Wilson. At that time, the entire 1st Battalion of the 24th was to come under General Wilson's control.[83] When Wilson arrived and assessed the situation, he ordered the forward elements of Dolvin to fall back to better defensive positions to the west of Company C of the 24th Infantry.[84] (Map 13)

[80] WD, Task Force Dolvin, n.d., p. 4, attachment to WD, 89th Medium Tank Bn, Nov 50, box 3765, RG 407, WNRC; WD, Task Force Wilson, 26–27 Nov 50, p. 1, attachment to Medal of Honor Award file for Reginald Desiderio, box 159, RG 338, WNRC; Ltr, Eichelsdoerfer to Cash, 23 Sep 90. Whether friendly fire was actually involved is unknown. According to Harry Cramer, Jr., the son of an officer in the 24th who was killed in Korea, the incident involved enemy fire. Cramer has kept all of his father's letters and many more from other individuals involved with the 24th. According to a letter in his possession from the first sergeant of the 1st Battalion's weapons company, Sergeant McLeod, as soon as the attack occurred, Company C called to request that Company D halt its firing. The unit's mortars, however, were not in service at that time. According to McLeod, who has since died, Company C was under enemy attack.

[81] WD, Task Force Dolvin, n.d., p. 4, attachment to WD,

89th Medium Tank Bn, Nov 50; WD, 3d Bn, 9th Inf Rgt, Nov 50, p. 2, box 2471, RG 407, WNRC; Appleman, *Disaster in Korea*, pp. 155–86; Mossman, *Ebb and Flow*, pp. 65–68.

[82] WD, Task Force Dolvin, n.d., p. 4, attachment to WD, 89th Medium Tank Bn, Nov 50; WD, Task Force Wilson, 26–27 Nov 50, p. 1, attachment to Medal of Honor Award file for Reginald Desiderio. Quotes from Unit Journal, 89th Medium Tank Bn, 26 Nov 50, item 11, in WD, 89th Medium Tank Bn, Nov 50, box 3765, RG 407, WNRC. Intervs, MacGarrigle with Baranowski, 13 and 14 Oct 94.

[83] The war diaries for the 1st Battalion, the 24th Infantry, and the 25th Division all say that the entire 1st Battalion was attached to Task Force Wilson. The war diary for Wilson says "the 1st Battalion, 24th Infantry Regiment (less Companies 'A' and 'B')." See WD, 1st Bn, 24th Inf Rgt, 26 Nov 50, p. 26, box 3764, RG 407, WNRC; WD, 24th Inf Rgt, Nov 50, p. 15; WD, 25th Inf Div, 26 Nov 50, boxes 3761–3763, RG 407, WNRC; WD, Task Force Wilson, 26–27 Nov 50, p. 1, attachment to Medal of Honor Award file for Reginald Desiderio.

[84] Unit Journal, 89th Medium Tank Bn, Nov 50, box 3765, RG 407, WNRC; WD, Task Force Dolvin, p. 5, in WD, 89th Medium Tank Bn, Nov 50.

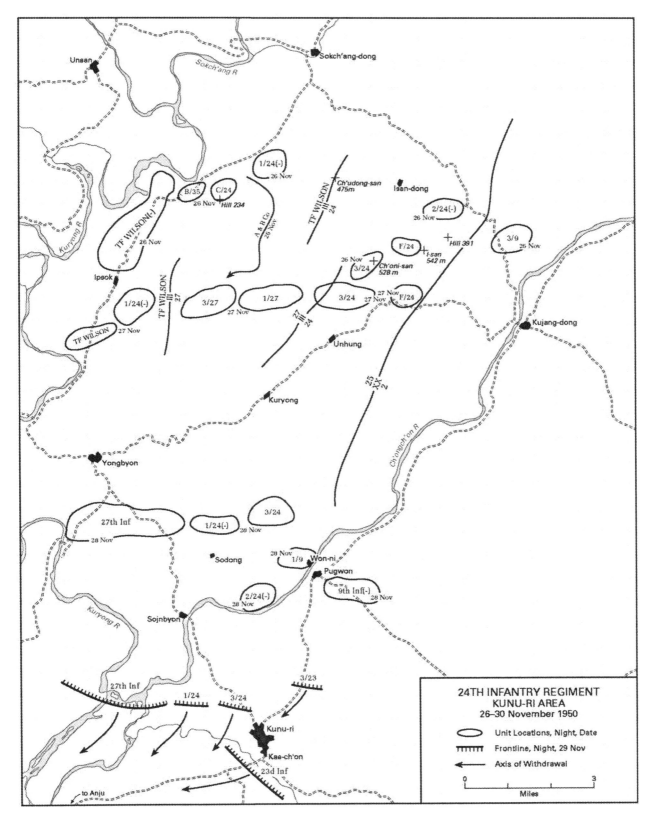

Unsan

Sokch'ang-dong

Sokch'ang R

1/24(-)
26 Nov

TF WILSON
24

Ch'udong-san
475m

Isan-dong

B/35
26 Nov

C/24
26 Nov

Hill 234

TF WILSON(-)
26 Nov

A & B Co
26 Nov

26 Nov

3/24

Ch'oni-san
528 m

2/24(-)
26 Nov

Hill 391

F/24

3/9
26 Nov

I-san
542 m

Kuryong R

Ipsok

1/24(-)
27 Nov

TF WILSON
27

TF WILSON III
27

3/27
27 Nov

1/27

III
27
24

3/24

27 Nov

27 Nov

F/24

Kujang-dong

TF WILSON
27 Nov

Unhung

25
IX
2

Kuryong

Ch'ongch'on R

Yongbyon

27th Inf
28 Nov

1/24(-)
28 Nov

3/24

Sodong

28 Nov
1/9

Won-ni

Pugwon

9th Inf(-)
28 Nov

Kuryong R

2/24(-)
28 Nov

Sojnbyon

3/23

27th Inf

1/24

3/24

Kunu-ri

Kae-ch'on

23d Inf

to Anju

24TH INFANTRY REGIMENT
KUNU-RI AREA
26–30 November 1950

⬭ Unit Locations, Night, Date

ᅲᅲᅲ Frontline, Night, 29 Nov

⬅ Axis of Withdrawal

0   3

Miles

Map 13

Colonel Corley visited the 1st Battalion's command post, located near Task Force Wilson's headquarters, a short while later. Learning for the first time of the attacks on Dolvin's lead elements and of the readjustments Wilson had ordered, he instructed Miller to leave his forward units and to return to his command post, where he would be in the best position to make decisions as the quickly changing situation evolved. Miller complied, leaving his operations officer, Captain Baranowski, in charge of the two companies.[85]

At 1600 that afternoon, Baranowski and his men received an air drop of supplies. Shortly thereafter Wilson ordered them to pull back. Whether the general recognized the perilous position of the force, which was at that time all but naked to enemy attack because it jutted precariously to the northeast of Company C, is unknown. He may only have been seeking to increase his available reserves to repel further enemy attacks or to improve his position before continuing his own assault north the next day. Whatever the reason, Companies A and B struck camp after dark and continued their move south throughout the night.[86]

While they did so, Wilson received word that enemy patrols were operating throughout the area and that the Chinese were about to launch a full-scale attack against the entire task force. Late on the night of 26 November and early on the morning of the twenty-seventh, indeed, Company B of the 35th Infantry, to the left of Company C, came under a strong enemy frontal assault and began to receive fire from the rear. Meanwhile, other units also came under attack, particularly the command post for Task Force Wilson, which was located to the rear and somewhat to the west of Company B of the 35th. With two defending tanks knocked out by enemy rocket fire, the commander of Company B decided he could not hold his position and received permission to withdraw to the next ridge line to his rear in coordination with Company C of the 24th. By that time the situation was becoming critical. Enemy roadblocks were operating to the rear of portions of the task force and it had become impossible to evacuate the wounded. The rest of Task Force Wilson thus held its ground until daybreak, when the 25th Infantry ordered a general withdrawal to a new line of defense about two miles to the south.[87]

Although Company B of the 35th Infantry made its withdrawal during the night, Company C of the 24th immediately to its east apparently failed to receive word that it was to pull out as well. When the commander of the 1st Battalion's weapons unit, Company D, Capt. Charles Piedra, passed through the unit that night, Company C's commander, Capt. Milford W. Stanley, showed no sign of preparing to withdraw and even invited Piedra to spend the night with his unit. Piedra declined, wishing to rejoin his men.[88]

Why Stanley never received the order to move out that night is unclear. His radios may have failed, but he was close enough to Company B of the 35th to have learned from them. Confused lines of com-

85 Appleman, *Disaster in Korea*, p. 138; S. L. A. Marshall, *The River and the Gauntlet: Defeat of the Eighth Army by the Chinese Communist Forces, November 1950, in the Battle of the Chongchon River, Korea* (New York: William Morrow, 1953), p. 190; Intervs, MacGarrigle with Baranowski, 13 and 14 Oct 94; Stuart Force, 17 Oct 94; Curtis H. Alloway, 20 Oct 94. Alloway, who was the battalion executive officer, states that he was told by Wilson to have Miller return to the command post. He does not recall seeing Corley in the 1st Battalion's area at that time.

86 See Intervs, MacGarrigle with Baranowski, 13 and 14 Oct 94; Force, 17 Oct 94. Baranowski stated that after the airdrop, an order was received to withdraw to the south. There was no mention of taking position to the immediate east of Company C. Force had accompanied Miller to the command post and had stated that the withdrawal applied also to Company C, but that the unit did not acknowledge that it had received the message. Wilson's withdrawal order, issued soon after the general took command, applied only to Task Force Dolvin, not to the 1st Battalion of the 24th. Documents originated by Task Force Wilson and Task Force Dolvin mention that Companies A and B were not in position, but the meaning of those references is unclear. Messages and reports generated by the 25th Division between 2030 and 2300 are also unclear. One document puts the units in the positions they occupied at the time of the 1600 airdrop. The other has them moving into those positions. See Task Force Dolvin Narrative, pp. 5–6, in WD, 89th Medium

Tank Bn, Nov 50; WD, 1st Bn, 24th Inf Rgt, 26 Nov 50; Msgs, IX Corps G–4 to IX Corps G–3, 261215 Nov 50 and 262030 Nov 50, both in box 1767, RG 407, WNRC; 25th Inf Div Periodic Opns Rpt 66, 26 Nov 50, in WD, 25th Inf Div, Nov 50.

87 WD, Task Force Wilson, 26–27 Nov 50, p. 1, attachment to Medal of Honor Award file for Reginald Desiderio.

88 Interv, Muehlbauer with Charles Piedra, 3 Nov 88.

mand may have been part of the reason. Map over-lays prepared by Task Force Wilson indicate that General Wilson expected Company C to move off to the south with its sister units, Companies A and B of the 24th. The 1st Battalion's commander, Colonel Miller, appears to have assumed that the company would take its orders directly from Task Force Wilson. It had after all been a part of that force since noon of the twenty-fifth and was tied in with Company B in Wilson's forward defensive line. Rather than leave anything to chance, howev-er, when Stanley failed to acknowledge Wilson's instructions, Miller set out on his own to deliver the message himself. He failed in the attempt because it was dark, he was on foot, and combat in the area was too heavy. In the end, all that can be said is that Stanley and his men, through no fault of their own, fell through a hole in the 25th Division's communications. The 24th Infantry's war diary reported that when the enemy attack developed, "all units of the regiment fought desperately to maintain contact and tactical unity. There was much confusion in all sectors and the location of battalions was constantly in doubt."[89]

According to a platoon leader in the unit, Lieutenant Eichelsdoerfer, Company C stayed in position without communications until dawn, when radio links were reestablished. "Based on our queries by radio," the officer continued, the unit finally learned of the order to withdraw. Stanley pulled his men from the hill they had covered into the valley floor. Receiving instructions to move south—"the last communication we had," accord-ing to Eichelsdoerfer—the company headed in that direction but encountered heavy enemy fire. Backing up, it then swung to the west toward the road Task Force Dolvin had first followed. "Enemy were clearly visible to both east and west moving parallel to us," Eichelsdoerfer recalled, "many

appeared to be carrying supplies. We received harassing fire. . . . A few casualties occurred. . . . At this point, some few of our company had become separated and were missing."[90]

After a time, the main body of the company hit an enemy roadblock. Pulling back once more, it retired to the north, where it began to receive enemy small-arms and mortar fire from high ground to its north, east, and south. Proceeding in the only direction that remained, west, it crossed the Kuryong River and then attempted to regroup. There were "substantially fewer troops" compared to the number who had started the trek, Eichelsdoerfer said. Ammunition was short. Most of the unit's heavy weapons were gone. There were neither radios nor radio communications:

A liaison aircraft appeared and circled our position. No contact was possible. Increasingly heavy and somewhat effective fire caused us to move west away from the river, only to be confronted by heavy MG [machine gun] fire. It gave the impression of what might have been [an] MG company. Attempts to bypass proved to be impossible, the enemy just increased their fire. It was at this point the company surrendered. There was no vote and little discussion. In view of the then existing situation, it appeared to be the prudent thing to do. Weapons were destroyed and what little ammo remained was buried.

The enemy—Chinese—separated the wounded and the remainder were moved northwest as soon as darkness fell. . . . As we moved out, it became apparent that when we crossed the river, we had stumbled into a major [headquarters] with attachments. In retrospect, my impression is that throughout the day, we were directed, herded in the direction they wanted us to move by using the amount of fire required to accomplish their objective.

---

[89] Ibid. See also WD, 25th Inf Div, 27 Nov 50. Quotes from WD, 1st Bn, 24th Inf Rgt, 27 Nov 50, p. 27, boxes 3761–3763, RG 407, WNRC; and WD, 24th Inf Rgt, 1–30 Nov 50, p. 16. Baranowski talks about support for Company C. See Interv, MacGarrigle with Baranowski, 24 Aug 94. Stuart Force tells of Miller's attempt to reach Company C. See Interv, MacGarrigle with Force, 17 Oct 94.

[90] First Lieutenant Howard Eichelsdoerfer gave the most coherent account of what happened. His letter even included a detailed map, drawn from memory, of the company's journey. Since the landmarks he gave correspond closely with the known topography of the area and his memories seemed clear and unjumbled, his account is the one generally followed here. See Ltr, Eichelsdoerfer to Cash, 23 Sep 90. Eichelsdoefer's account differs in some details from those of other veterans of the event. See Intervs, Cash with Walter Chambers, 3 Aug and 5 Sep 90; Muehlbauer with Fletcher, 5 Aug 88. First Lieutenant Charles Winn, who changed his name from Wysoczynski, along with Eichelsdoerfer, is a source for the assertion that portions of the company became separated from the main body and were lost. This may be one reason why the accounts of some veterans dif-fer. See Interv, Cash with Charles Winn, 6 Jul 90.

Eichelsdoerfer concluded that the surrender was a command decision based on a review of the facts confronting the unit and that there was no dissent at the time. Other veterans of the event disagree. Enlisted man Robert Fletcher asserts that Stanley gave the men a choice and they voted. Enlisted man Walter Chambers maintains that one lieutenant wanted to hold out but that a Chinese negotiator arrived while he was making the plea and shot him dead on the spot. However the decision was made, 4 officers and 136 enlisted men fell into enemy hands. A single lieutenant and 6 enlisted men who had been separated earlier from the main body of men made it back to American lines.[91]

As the fate of Company C unfolded, the rest of the 1st Battalion was also under stress. Located near the headquarters for Task Force Wilson, the battalion's command post and part of its weapons unit, Company D, fought off continual enemy attacks overnight. During the day on 27 November the two withdrew to the south, fighting their way through enemy roadblocks along the way. Meanwhile, Companies A and B began moving south to a point about five miles north of Yongbyon, where they were to form a line with the remnants of Task Force Wilson and the 27th Infantry, which had been assigned from reserve to cover the withdrawal.[92]

At one point in the journey, after dark, as the 1st Battalion's intelligence officer, Capt. Gustav Gillert, related, the two companies stumbled upon a Chinese detachment cooking food over campfires. Advancing in column, they stopped just short of the encampment, doubled back for a short distance, shifted their line of march somewhat to the west, and then kept moving south as though nothing had happened. The Chinese for their part failed to react. "The only thing we could figure out later," Gillert observed, "is they just assumed that since we were coming from the north that we were Chinese. They didn't say 'stop,' 'hello,' or anything." After walking six or seven more miles and engaging in a firefight with an enemy force that had infiltrated to the rear of American positions, the companies reached their destination. Falling in between units of Task Force Wilson to the west and portions of the 3d Battalion of the 27th Infantry to the east, they held that position until late on 28 November, when they again began moving south. It was so cold at the time, Gillert recalled, that a radio operator froze to death. "To get that radio off that kid's back," he said, "we had to cut it off."[93]

While the 1st Battalion was undergoing its ordeal, the 2d Battalion, Companies G and E, located on the seam separating the 25th Division from the 2d Division and under Colonel Clayton's direct command, were also in trouble. About 2100 on the evening of 25 November an enemy attack had split Company G into two parts, one falling back southeast into the 9th Infantry's lines and the other joining Company E.[94] (See Map 12.) The next morning, after holding overnight, Company E and the remnant of G continued their move north. Toward noon, an observation aircraft had dropped a message to inform Clayton that a large enemy force was to his front and that allied fighter-bombers would shortly arrive to take it under fire. The message instructed Clayton to hold nearby and to wait for an airdrop of food. The air strike occurred, but it had little effect on the enemy, who continued to press forward. As for the airdrop, the situation on the ground was so fluid that the enemy took pos-

[91] Ltr, Eichelsdoerfer to Cash, 23 Sep 90. The numbers are from Morning Rpt with attachments, Co C, 24th Inf Rgt, 28 Dec 50, CMH files. For the views of one who escaped, see Interv, Cash with Robert H. Yancy, 21 Jan 89.

[92] WD, 25th Inf Div, 28 Nov 50, boxes 3761–3763, RG 407, WNRC; WD, 1st Bn, 24th Inf Rgt, 27 Nov 50, p. 27, boxes 3764–3765, RG 407, WNRC; Interv, MacGarrigle with Force, 17 Oct 94.

[93] WD, 1st Bn, 24th Inf Rgt, 28 Nov 50, p. 28, box 3764, RG 407, WNRC; 27th Inf Rgt S–2 Periodic Rpt for 16–27 Nov 50, boxes 3764–3765, RG 407, WNRC; Msg, 25th Inf Div to IX Corps, 271305 Nov 50, box 1769, RG 407, WNRC; IX Corps Periodic Opns Rpt 189, 27 Nov 50, box 1769, RG 407, WNRC; 25th Inf Div Periodic Opns Rpts 70, 28 Nov 50, 71, 28 Nov 50, and 73, 29 Nov 50, all in boxes 3761–3763, RG 407, WNRC; Interv, Cash with Gillert, 25 Mar 89. Baranowski also told the story of the meeting with the Chinese detachment but did not recall that Gillert was present. See Interv, MacGarrigle with Baranowski, 24 Aug 94. Stuart Force, however, put Gillert with the column. See Interv, MacGarrigle with Force, 17 Oct 94.

[94] Intervs, Bowers with George M. Shuffer, 5 and 6 Dec 94.

session of the target area before the aircraft arrived. Higher authorities had no choice but to cancel it.[95]

Shortly after the air strike, the enemy surrounded Clayton's force and attacked in regimental strength from all sides. Clayton's men staggered under the onslaught, and the battalion command post itself was almost overrun. Only quick action by Sfc. Nicholas Smith saved it. Moving forward on his own, his rifle leveled, Smith distracted the enemy just long enough to allow the command group to escape. He kept firing as the enemy converged on his position, bringing down seventeen of the attackers and forcing the remainder to seek cover. Thanks to Smith and timely action by Company E's commander, white Capt. Frank Knoeller, who seemed to be everywhere on the battlefield and who even manned a machine gun when the gunner went down, the force soon regrouped. Company E held position on a hill just to the west of the Kujang-dong–Sokch'ang-dong road, and part of Company G clustered nearby to the southwest. Surrounded, both units fought for their lives, inflicting heavy casualties on the enemy but incurring many losses of their own.[96]

Earlier, Clayton had lost communication with the regimental command post and the elements of the 24th to his west. Because of the topography of the area, however, he was able to maintain radio contact with the 3d Battalion of the 9th Infantry's command post to his southeast. Toward dark, he availed himself of that connection and informed the unit's commander that he intended to break out after dark and to lead his men into the 3d Battalion's positions. Stationed on one of the enemy's main lines of attack and sorely pressed himself, the commander of the 3d of the 9th, Lt. Col. D. M. McMains, welcomed the news that an infusion of new troops would be arriving.[97]

After dark on 26 November, with Company E in the lead and Company G in trail, Clayton and his men slipped away from the enemy, carrying their wounded with them. Most of Company E made it through without any problem but Company G was less fortunate. Enemy forces stationed on the shoulders of the pass belatedly discovered the move and fired on the retreating unit. There were some losses, but between 300 and 350 men from the 2d Battalion still managed to join the 9th Infantry. The unit fed them, resupplied them with weapons and ammunition, and evacuated some 150 casualties, many suffering from frostbite, to the rear.[98]

[95] IX Corps Periodic Opns Rpt 184, 26 Nov 50, and Msgs, 25th Inf Div to IX Corps, 1700 and 1730, 26 Nov 50, all in box 1769, RG 407, WNRC; WD, 2d Bn, 24th Inf Rgt, Nov 50, p. 7; 24th Inf Rgt Unit Rpts 56, 26 Nov 50, and 57, 27 Nov 50; Msg, IX Corps G–4 to IX Corps G–3, 260915 Nov 50, box 1769, RG 407, WNRC. The exact location of the two units is in doubt. Unit Report 56 puts Company E to the east of the road, but Clayton himself is unsure about whether his force reached that point. Since the road was a main avenue of attack for enemy units pressing southward and the enemy already had struck the 9th Infantry regiment of the U.S. 2d Division, this treatment places Clayton's two companies in positions laid out in an overlay that accompanied a Distinguished Service Cross recommendation for Sfc. Nicholas Smith. Whether the units crossed the road or not, they clearly pulled back to the more defensible positions shown on the overlay. See Interv, MacGarrigle with Clayton, 5 Oct 94; Overlay accompanying DSC Award Recommendation for Sfc Nicholas Smith, 17 Feb 51, with affidavits, Awards Branch files, U.S. Army Total Personnel Command (PERSCOM), Alexandria, Va. See also Intervs, MacGarrigle with Clayton, 10 and 11 Aug 94. Corley sent a radio vehicle into the 9th Infantry's area to maintain contact with Clayton and to coordinate the air strikes and the airdrop. See Interv, MacGarrigle with Ralph Davis, 31 Oct 94.

[96] 24th Inf Rgt Unit Rpt 56, 26 Nov 50; Intervs, MacGarrigle with Clayton, 10 and 11 Aug 94. The Smith story is taken from Affidavit, M Sgt Raymond I. Coleman, 25 Dec 50,

attachment to DSC Award Recommendation for Sfc Nicholas Smith, 17 Feb 51. For an act of heroism by a white officer, see Award Recommendation for Capt Frank O. Knoeller, 8 Feb 51, with affidavits, box 163, RG 338, WNRC.

[97] Intervs, MacGarrigle with Clayton, 10 and 11 Aug 94; Ralph Davis, 31 Oct 94; Memo, Col C. C. Sloane, Jr., Cdr, 9th Inf Rgt, 2d Inf Div, for Commanding Ofcr, 24th Inf Rgt, 11 Dec 50, sub: Action Elements, E and G Companies, 24th Inf Rgt, 9th Inf Rgt folder, CMH files. Sloane's memo is courtesy of Clay Blair and David Carlisle. It is mentioned in Brig Gen G. B. Barth, Tropic Lightning and Taro Leaf in Korea, n.d., CMH files, and Blair, The Forgotten War, p. 1032, n32. Corley had sent a radio vehicle with Lieutenant Davis, Clayton's intelligence officer, into the 9th Infantry's area to maintain contact with Clayton's group. Davis was the one Clayton contacted by radio. See also 24th Inf Rgt Unit Rpt 57, 27 Nov 50; WD, 3d Bn, 9th Inf Rgt, Nov 50, p. 2; 9th Inf Rgt Combat Narrative, Nov 50; 9th Inf Rgt S–3 Narrative Diary, 26–27 Nov 50, attachment to 9th Inf Rgt Combat Narrative, Nov 50. Last three in box 2471, RG 407, WNRC.

[98] Ibid.

The next morning, 27 November, in position on the Kujang-dong–Yongbyon road, Walden's Company F dispatched three ¼-ton trucks and twelve men to contact the companies with the 9th Infantry and to lead them back to their own regiment. The detachment came under heavy enemy fire, however, and had to return before reaching its goal. Five men were wounded, and two of the trucks were lost. Unable to retrieve the two companies, Corley filled the gap their loss created in his line by employing Company F and the 77th Engineer Combat Company to man what would have been the 2d Battalion's sector.[99] (*See Map 13.*)

The men of Companies E and G remained with the 3d Battalion of the 9th Infantry for the next several days. There they excelled. "On the night of 28–29 November," the regiment's commander, Col. C. C. Sloane, Jr., told Corley in a subsequent letter of commendation,

after the 9th Infantry had been ordered to withdraw from the vicinity of Kujang-dong to Pugwan, the two companies . . . were placed in a new defense line in depth. After the Chinese had over-run the forward elements of my 3d Battalion, they were surprised upon running into and coming under fire of your E and G Companies. As a result of their action, the Chinese onslaught for the time was halted. It was by this action that my 3d Battalion was able to hold this temporary defense line for a sufficient period of time to permit the 23d Infantry to occupy a new defense line further to the rear.[100]

Except for some moderate contact, Blair's 3d Battalion of the 24th went relatively unscathed during the first hours of the enemy attack. The unit had advanced well into the mountains during the day on 25 November, pulling up at dark toward the small village of Isan-dong, four and one-half miles to the north of Unhung and no more than two miles to the northwest of

Companies E and G. That night the battalion fought off three enemy probes.[101] (*See Map 12.*)

The fighting continued into the next day, 26 November. Toward noon, with the 9th Infantry to the east under heavy attack and Companies E and G of the 2d Battalion under increasing threat on the Kujang-dong–Sokch'ang-dong road, Corley ordered Blair's force to pull back several thousand yards toward the town of Sa-dong on the southern slope of Ch'oni-san mountain. It was resupplied at 1615 by air, but the drop fell near enemy-held territory. As a result, the unit had to fight the Chinese for its food and ammunition. The next day, 27 November, the battalion readjusted its position again, falling back into an area about one and one-half miles north of Unhung. At some time during the period, Colonel Corley appears to have lost all contact with the unit. Its position was so unclear that when the battalion finally reported in, the colonel concluded it had become disoriented and was nowhere near where its commanders said it was.[102] (*See Map 13.*)

According to the battalion's executive officer, Maj. Owen Carter, Colonel Blair was with his forward units only part of the time. Although he accompanied them into the field on the first few days of the attack and came up again on 27 November to inspect his companies' positions, he rarely if ever came forward after that. His conduct was in marked contrast with that of Colonel Miller of the 1st Battalion and Colonel Clayton of the 2d, both of whom remained with their troops in the field until either ordered to leave, or, in the case of Clayton, when their men came under the control of a different unit. Indeed, when it became necessary to move the 3d Battalion's command post after the unit received orders to withdraw, Blair supervised

[99] 24th Inf Rgt Unit Rpt 57, 27 Nov 50; Barth, *Tropic Lightning and Taro Leaf in Korea*, n.d., p. 44.

[100] Memo, Sloane for Commanding Ofcr, 24th Inf Rgt, 11 Dec 50, sub: Action Elements, E and G Companies, 24th Inf Rgt. For more information on the fighting, see 9th Inf Rgt Combat Narrative, Nov 50; WD, 23d Inf Rgt, Nov 50, p. 14, box 2472. RG 407. WNRC.

[101] 24th Inf Rgt Unit Rpt 56, 26 Nov 50; WD, 3d Bn, 24th Inf Rgt, 25–26 Nov 50, pp. 11–12, box 3764, RG 407, WNRC. See also Intervs, MacGarrigle with Newell, 10 and 15 Nov 94.

[102] WD, 24th Inf Rgt, Nov 50, pp. 15–16; 24th Inf Rgt Unit Rpts 56, 26 Nov 50, and 57, 27 Nov 50; WD, 3d Bn, 24th Inf Rgt, Nov 50, p. 11; Intervs, Appleman with Corley, 4 Jan 52; MacGarrigle with Sapenter, 21 Mar 94; Cash with Wilfred Matthews, 23 Sep 88. For the airdrop, see Msg, 25th Inf Div G–3 to IX Corps G–3, 262030 Nov 50, box 1767, RG 407. WNRC.

the task himself, leaving Carter to deal with his forward units, the exact reverse of normal procedures. Carter found Blair's conduct "somewhat puzzling" because the officer had won two Distinguished Service Crosses, one during World War II and one during the fighting at Haman.[103]

By 27 November the situation was becoming ominous throughout the 24th Infantry's zone, where enemy units had begun to penetrate to the rear of American positions. Enemy infiltrators ambushed a mess truck from the 3d Battalion moving up the 24th Infantry's main supply route, the road from Yongbyon to Unhung. Troops from Company M of the 24th, the 3d Battalion's headquarters company, and two tanks rushed to the scene to retrieve the truck and rescue the wounded, but even with the arrival of reinforcements later that afternoon they were unable to dislodge the enemy. During the fighting, Cpl. Earl Phoenix, although badly wounded twice, stayed at his machine gun until his ammunition was gone to keep his squad from being cut off and overrun. He later received the Distinguished Service Cross. Capt. George Anderson received a Silver Star for his conduct during the same action. Taking up a weapon dropped by an injured American after his own rifle had been shot from his hands, he covered the withdrawal of wounded personnel.[104]

That night at 2330, the 25th Division's medical clearing station two miles to the east of Yongbyon on the road to Unhung was also attacked and burned. The enemy then set up a roadblock just to the east of the facility in hopes of taking any relief force that arrived under fire. Elements from Captain Bussey's 77th Engineer Combat Company broke the roadblock and restored the site, but shortly after midnight on the morning of 28 November, the enemy attacked positions manned by Company M just four miles to the northeast. The fighting at that site continued until 0400, when the enemy withdrew. Shortly thereafter, at 0605, in a shuffling of command responsibilities designed to compensate for the deteriorating situation, the Eighth Army shifted the IX Corps boundary to the east. At that time, it transferred control of the 25th Division to I Corps.[105]

During the night of 27–28 November, the 27th Infantry moved from reserve to take a position in the line between Task Force Wilson and the 24th Infantry. Enemy attacks continued throughout the following day, forcing the Americans back. By dark on 28 November, the 25th Division was occupying a line two miles to the south of Yongbyon across the road that led from that city south to Kunu-ri. That evening General Kean began the process of dissolving Task Force Wilson, shifting the 1st Battalion of the 24th east through the lines of the 27th Infantry to rejoin its regiment.[106]

Fighting was particularly heavy on the flanks of the 24th Infantry. To the left, the 3d Battalion, 27th Infantry, astride the Yongbyon–Kunu-ri road, sustained a strong enemy attack. One company was overrun and another suffered a severe penetration. To the right, the 9th Infantry remained under stress, with combat so fierce that the sound of firing was clearly audible to men of the 24th Infantry

103 WD, 3d Bn, 24th Inf Rgt, Nov 50, p. 12; Intervs, MacGarrigle with Owen Carter, 21 and 24 Jun 94. The battalion's intelligence officer, Oliver Dillard, likewise asserted that Blair was almost always with him and that he was rarely with the troops. See Intervs, Bowers with Dillard, 8 and 9 Mar 95. The operations officer of the 3d Battalion, Roscius Newell, considered Blair a fine officer but noted that Blair, at the time, seemed exhausted. See Intervs, MacGarrigle with Newell, 10 and 15 Nov 94. Clayton's radio man, who accompanied him, was sometimes frightened by his commander's determination to be close to the action. "Clayton went further forward than he should have gone," he said, "but he felt that it was his position to be there for that encouraged the men to fight better." See Interv, Muehlbauer with Arthur Thompson, 14 Sep 88.

104 WD, 3d Bn, 24th Inf Rgt, Nov 50, p. 12; 24th Inf Rgt Unit Rpt 57, 27 Nov 50; Intervs, MacGarrigle with Sapenter, 21 Mar 94; Cash with Voight, 21 Sep 88; Award file for Capt George Anderson, box 156, RG 338, WNRC; Award file for Cpl Earl C. Phoenix, Jr., box 167, RG 338, WNRC. Phoenix was nominated for the Medal of Honor. The award was reduced to the Distinguished Service Cross. Anderson was nominated for a Distinguished Service Cross, but his award was reduced to a Silver Star.

105 The loss of the medical clearing station is mentioned in Bussey, Firefight at Yechon, pp. 237–38. See also IX Corps Periodic Intelligence Rpt 63, 27 Nov 50, and Periodic Opns Rpt 190, 27 Nov 50, both in box 1769, RG 407, WNRC; Interv, Cash with Voight, 21 Sep 88.

106 27th Inf Rgt Historical Narrative, Nov 50, pp. 10–11, boxes 3764–3765, RG 407, WNRC; WD, 25th Inf Div, Nov 50; 25th Inf Div Periodic Opns Rpt 72, 29 Nov 50, in WD 25th Inf Div, Nov 50.

located several miles to the west across the Ch'ongch'on River.[107]

Problems continued on 29 November. Moving into the 25th Division's new defensive line, the 3d Battalion of the 24th once more lost contact with supporting units and for a time came under the fire of friendly mortars and artillery. That afternoon, with the enemy pressing and the 3d Battalion reportedly involved in a heavy firefight near the town of So-dong, four miles to the southeast of Yongbyon, Corley began to reconnoiter a way across the Ch'ongch'on and new positions near Kunu-ri on the river's opposite side. When Kean ordered all 25th Division units to move south of the river, Corley was ready. Moving his troops to a site on the river four miles to the northwest of Kunu-ri, he began the crossing at 1600 that afternoon. The 1st Battalion of the 9th Infantry, newly arrived from the fighting at Kujang-dong, came up from the east to assist the 27th Infantry in covering the redeployment.[108]

Even as the 25th Division began to pull back, enemy units, moving through the collapsed lines of the South Korean II Corps to the east, were threatening to cut off the Eighth Army's lines of supply to the south. Although the 1st Cavalry Division and the 24th Infantry Division both shifted to the east to block the Chinese advance, their presence at best slowed the assault. When it became clear during the afternoon of the twenty-ninth that the Eighth Army would have to fall back, General Walker ordered his forces to withdraw to a new line south of the Ch'ongch'on that ran almost to Kunu-ri but curved to the southeast toward Sunch'on before reaching the town. Later that afternoon, as circumstances continued to deteriorate, Walker ordered a deeper withdrawal to a line some twenty miles to the south of Kunu-ri. The IX Corps received the two orders and during the early evening instructed the 2d Division to retreat to a point well below Kunu-ri. The I Corps held the line of the Ch'ongch'on for the time being, leaving the 25th Division in place north of the town, but the commanders involved appear to have understood that their forces would withdraw in due course. None, however, realized how precipitate the process would be.[109] (*Map 14*)

Fresh from the fighting at Pugwon, four miles north of Kunu-ri on the road from Kujang-dong, elements from Companies E and G were the first portions of the 24th to depart the battlefield. Leaving the 9th Infantry on the morning of the twenty-ninth, the companies had congregated initially near Kunu-ri. That evening, as soon as Walden's Company F arrived along with the remainder of the 2d Battalion's headquarters and weapons companies, the entire force moved off in no particular order toward the town of Anju, about fifteen miles west of Kunu-ri. At that point, the battalion turned south, proceeding some twenty-five miles by road to an area west of Sunch'on, where it regrouped.[110]

---

[107] Unit History, 3d Bn, 27th Inf Rgt, Nov 50, boxes 3764–3765, RG 407, WNRC; WD, 3d Bn, 24th Inf Rgt, Nov 50, p. 13; WD, 9th Inf Rgt, Nov 50; WD, 23d Inf Rgt, Nov 50, p. 14.

[108] WD, 24th Inf Rgt, Nov 50, p. 18; WD, 3d Bn, 24th Inf Rgt, Nov 50, p. 13; 25th Inf Div Periodic Opns Rpt 71, 28 Nov 50, in 25th Inf Div Staff Records; Msg, I Corps G–3 to IX Corps G–3, 291130 Nov 50, box 1769, RG 407, WNRC; WD, 1st Bn, 9th Inf Rgt, Nov 50, p. 2, box 2471, RG 407, WNRC; WD, 9th Inf Rgt, Nov 50, S–3 Narrative, 29 Nov 50, p. 5, box 2471, RG 407, WNRC; Unit History, 3d Bn, 27th Inf Rgt, Nov 50; Historical Narrative, 27th Inf Rgt, Nov 50, boxes 3764–3765, RG 407, WNRC. The 3d Battalion war diary reports heavy contact, but the unit's operations officer, Roscius Newell, asserted in an interview that the battalion's withdrawal was orderly and without enemy opposition. See Intervs, MacGarrigle with Newell, 10 and 15 Nov 94. The battalion's executive officer, Owen Carter, says the same. See Intervs, MacGarrigle with Carter, 21 and 24 Jun 94. The situation was so fast moving that the actual timing of Kean's order to the 24th is in doubt, but the 27th Infantry received the order to move south of the river at 1304. See WD, 27th Inf Rgt, Nov 50, S–3 Journal, boxes 3764–3765, RG 407, WNRC. No written order was issued.

[109] Mossman, *Ebb and Flow*, pp. 108–17; 25th Inf Div Periodic Opns Rpt 75, 29 Nov 50; 25th Inf Div Opns Instructions 23, 28 Nov 50, and 24, 30 Nov 50, boxes 3761–3763, RG 407, WNRC. It appears that the I Corps staff did not realize that IX Corps had ordered the 2d Division to withdraw from Kunu-ri. The I Corps Opns Directive 28, 291600 Nov 50, ordered the 25th Division to occupy and defend the south bank of the Ch'ongch'on River. It was not until 2355 on 30 November that the 25th Division was ordered to move at dawn to the new line south of Anju. See WD, I Corps, Nov 50, journals and records for 29 and 30 Nov 50, box 1496, RG 407, WNRC.

[110] WD, 2d Bn, 24th Inf Rgt, Nov 50, p. 8; Intervs, MacGarrigle with Clayton, 10 and 11 Aug 94; Joseph C.

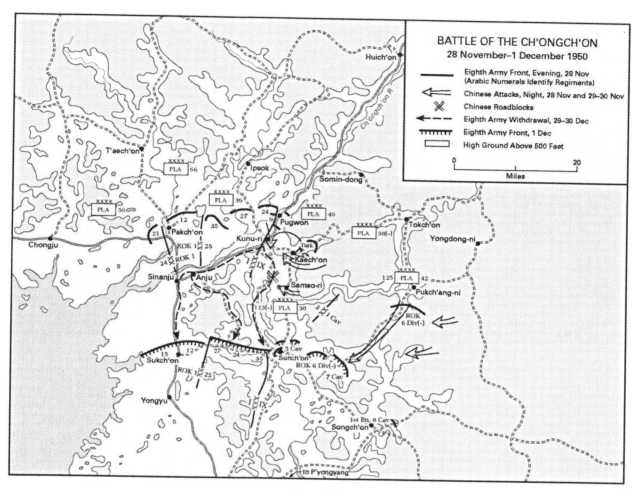

Map 14

The unit was sorely depleted and heavily worn. During the trip south, however, it coalesced, with parties of individuals from the same platoons and companies linking up with one another. By the time it reached its destination, most of its components had reassembled and Clayton was able to establish that between 400 and 450 "effectives" remained out of the 900 men who had first accompanied him on the attack toward the Yalu. There had been equipment losses, he later remarked, but

most of his men had retained their personal weapons. In the same way, since many of the battalion's vehicles had also made it out, Company H had been able to save most of the unit's heavy mortars and machine guns. Arriving at their objective in relatively good order, the troops of Clayton's battalion soon went into the line to provide cover for other portions of the 25th Division that were also beginning to congregate in the area.[111]

Moving across the Ch'ongch'on, Colonel Miller's 1st Battalion, minus all but a few men from

Muzyka, 25 Oct 94. See also 25th Inf Div Periodic Opns Rpts 73 and 75, both 29 Nov 50, for locations of the 2d Battalion of the 24th.

[111] Ibid. Lloyd Ott spoke about the withdrawal of the 2d Battalion's vehicles. See Interv, MacGarrigle with Ott, 19 Jul 94.

Men of the 24th Infantry and 159th Field Artillery Battalion prepare to leave an assembly area.

Company C, took up a blocking position to the west of Kunu-ri. The last unit of the 24th to cross the river, Blair's 3d Battalion also moved into the area. For a time, there appears to have been some confusion in Blair's headquarters about the location of Companies I and L. They had been involved in fighting earlier in the day and were thought to be still on the road. Later in the evening, however, they and the rest of the battalion were located. Tying in with Miller's unit, they had dug in on huge dikes bordering a large rice paddy just northwest of Kunu-ri. Colonel Blair had already situated his command post in a large building in the center of the town, and Corley had sited the regiment's forward command post in the same area, about a quarter of a mile to the southwest.[112]

As the evening of 29 November lengthened, heavy fighting continued to the east and southeast of the 24th Infantry, where the Chinese were pressing to dislodge the 2d Infantry Division. The enemy also began to push into Kunu-ri. At 2030 mess personnel from the 3d Battalion reported that an enemy roadblock in the northern sector of the town had prevented them from reaching their unit.[113]

The 3d Battalion's Ordeal

At 2300 the sound of combat ceased. Soon thereafter, the main road through Kunu-ri became clogged with vehicles as the 23d Infantry regiment of the 2d Division, which had been stationed to the east of the 3d Battalion, withdrew to the south. The executive officer of the 3d Battalion, Maj. Owen Carter, was in

---

[112] WD, 24th Inf Rgt, Nov 50, pp. 18–19. The location of the 3d Battalion is mentioned in Interv, Appleman with Francis G. Nordstrom, 31 Aug 51, CMH files. Nordstrom was the commanding officer of Company D, 89th Medium Tank Battalion. A platoon leader in Company K, James Yadon, spoke about the dikes. See also Intervs, Muehlbauer with Yadon, 22 May 89; MacGarrigle with Baranowski, 24 Aug 94; Force, 8 Aug 94.

[113] WD, 24th Inf Rgt, Nov 50, p. 19; WD, 3d Bn, 24th Inf Rgt, Nov 50, p. 13; WD, 89th Medium Tank Bn, Nov 50, box 3765, RG 407, WNRC. For more on the fighting in the 2d Division area, see WD, 23d Inf Rgt, Nov 50, pp. 14–15; S–3 Journal, 3d Bn, 23d Inf Rgt, Nov 50, box 2472, RG 407, WNRC. The enemy force was probably the *120th Chinese Communist Forces (CCF) Division.* See IX Corps Periodic Intelligence Rpt 64, 29 Nov 50, box 1769, RG 407, WNRC.

Men from a 24th Infantry company await instructions.

the area delivering supplies and checking on his unit's positions. Going out to the road to investigate, he encountered the commanding officer of the 23d's rear guard, who informed him that his regiment was pulling back. Before the conversation ended, the last segments of the convoy on the road passed. Commenting in a matter-of-fact manner that to the best of his knowledge there were no longer any "friendly" troops to the east, the officer stepped into his jeep and drove off to the south after his men.[114]

There were in fact other units to the east and north of the 24th. Company L of the 23d Infantry, for example, had remained north of Kunu-ri to cover the withdrawal of the 38th Infantry, which was moving down from the east.[115] Carter, however, had no

way of knowing that. Concluding that the right flank of the 24th Infantry was open and unprotected, he returned to the 3d Battalion's command post in Kunu-ri to inform Blair of the development. The colonel immediately called Corley, who in turn contacted General Kean's headquarters, which confirmed that the 2d Division was indeed withdrawing. A short while later, at 0100 on 30 November, Corley decided to move the 3d Battalion to a new position southwest of Kunu-ri on the road to Anju. The unit would again tie in with the 1st Battalion, which would have to bend its line somewhat to the south to accommodate the change.[116]

Corley telephoned Blair to pass along those instructions, but while the two were talking a burst of machine-gun fire through Blair's window cut the conversation short. Blair, who had been resting,

---

[114] WD, 24th Inf Rgt, Nov 50, p. 19; WD, 3d Bn, 24th Inf Rgt, Nov 50, p. 13; Intervs, MacGarrigle with Owen Carter, 21 and 24 Jun 94; Ltr, Owen H. Carter to MacGarrigle, 30 Jul 94; CMH files.

[115] WD, 23d Inf Rgt, Nov 50, pp. 14–15; S–3 Journal, 3d Bn, 23d Inf Rgt, Nov 50; Interv, Appleman with Major Radow, 16 Aug 51, CMH files. Radow was the commander of the 1st Battalion, 23d Infantry. About the same time that Carter reached the 3d Battalion's command post, the 23d

---

Infantry's commander, Col. Paul Freeman, also arrived. Freeman informed the 3d Battalion that his regiment was withdrawing through the town. See Intervs, MacGarrigle with Newell, 10 and 15 Nov 94.

[116] Ibid.; Intervs, MacGarrigle with Owen Carter, 21 and 24 Jun 94; Cash with Dillard, 3 Jun 89.

dove under a table. Soldiers reached for their weapons and scrambled outside to return fire. The clothing of the battalion's intelligence officer, 1st Lt. Oliver Dillard, was peppered with enemy burp-gun fire but the officer himself was unscathed. Carter was less fortunate. A grenade exploded near him, knocking him unconscious and killing the battalion's sergeant major.[117]

From that moment, chaos reigned in the command post. Blair decided to abandon the site and departed for Corley's headquarters with part of his staff, without apparently much attempt to contact any of his units stationed nearby. As a result, bits and pieces of the battalion headquarters made their way out as best they could, and a portion of Lieutenant Voight's platoon from Company M was cut off and overrun in Kunu-ri. Only seventeen out of thirty-eight of Voight's men escaped. As for Blair and his party, they took some time to reach their destination because Corley's headquarters itself had come under fire and had moved to a point near where the 3d Battalion was to have relocated. When they finally arrived, they had traveled through several streams. Their feet were wet, making frostbite an imminent threat.[118]

As the full dimensions of what had happened began to emerge, Corley himself became incensed. According to mortarman James Miller, an eyewitness, he turned on a group of officers from the 3d Battalion and rebuked them. "You had the best battalion in the regiment," he said, "and you went off and left them." As for Blair, Corley tore into the officer, ordering him to get control of his unit and to establish a defensive line. "Tempers were flying and Blair was crying," the commander of the 3d Battalion's headquarters company, Capt. Noah Armstrong, recalled. "I witnessed this."[119]

Dillard, who said he had driven a jeep "right down the main drag" of Kunu-ri, "getting shot at all the time," had just arrived at Corley's command post. Lacking any means to reach the three companies because the 3d Battalion's communications were down, Corley turned to him and remarked, "You're going to have to go out and make contact." Seeing the bullet holes in the officer's clothing and

[117] Newell claimed that the soldiers guarding the command post froze when the enemy attacked and that only officers were returning fire. See Intervs, MacGarrigle with Newell, 10 and 15 Nov 94. The 3d Battalion's abbreviated account of what happened at Kunu-ri is carried in the unit's war diary for December, where it is mistakenly dated for 1 December. See WD, 3d Bn, 24th Inf Rgt, Dec 50, p. 1, box 3770, RG 407, WNRC.

[118] Ibid. Corley spoke of Blair's wet feet. See Interv, Appleman with Corley, 4 Jan 52. Severely critical of Blair and Carter, a former warrant officer with the 3d Battalion, Thomas H. Pettigrew, describes the scene in the command post in Thomas H. Pettigrew, Jr., *The Kunu-ri (Kumori) Incident* (New York: Vantage Press, 1963), pp. 18–22. Pettigrew implies that Carter deserted the command post before Blair gave the order and that Carter was at best lightly wounded. Carter tells a different story. Bleeding from a score of fragmentation wounds, he said, he picked up his rifle, collected about thirty stragglers and walking wounded, and made his own way to Corley's command post on foot. There, Corley ordered him to seek medical attention. See Intervs, MacGarrigle with Owen Carter, 21 and 24 Jun 94. Although silent on the episode in the command post, unit war diaries generally substantiate much of Carter's account of what happened on 29 and 30 November. Indeed, unit records indicate that Carter was wounded seriously enough to spend two

months recuperating from his injuries. See 24th Inf Rgt Command Rpt, Sep 51, box 3848, RG 407, WNRC; HQ, 25th Inf Div, Reported Casualties of the 24th Infantry Regiment, n.d. [Jul 50–Sep 51], box 3848, RG 407, WNRC. Corley also talks about what happened in an interview with the *Pittsburgh Courier*. See Frank Whisonant, "True Story of the 24th: Colonel Corley Gives Facts to Courier War Reporter," *Pittsburgh Courier*, 23 Jun 51, p. 1. Voight tells his story in Interv, Cash with Voight, 21 Sep 88. James Yadon confirms that a part of Company M was in Kunu-ri at the time of the attack. See Interv, Muehlbauer with Yadon, 22 May 89.

[119] Intervs, Muehlbauer with James Miller, 1 Nov 88; Noah Armstrong, 22 Oct 88. An account by Edwin W. Robertson, a forward air controller attached to Corley's command post, generally parallel's Armstrong's story. Robertson, who retired a major general in the Air Force, was also present when Blair arrived. See Interv, MacGarrigle with Edwin W. Robertson, 24 Feb 95. The regimental S–2, Maj. Walter Simonovich, told his friends that when Blair arrived at Corley's command post, he was hysterical and screamed, "We can't win, we better give up." He said that Corley tried to settle him down. See Intervs, MacGarrigle with Baranowski, 13 and 14 Oct 94. Blair, in an interview forty-five years later, denied going to Corley's command post. He said he hitched rides in vehicles moving to the rear and walked what seemed long distances until finding his battalion late the next day, several miles south of Anju. See Interv, MacGarrigle with Melvin Blair, 15 Feb 95. This account accepts the word of the officers who said they saw Blair at the command post. Robertson's account, in particular, was extremely detailed, and the officer had no reason to dissemble.

apparently taking pity on him, he then withdrew those instructions and instead turned the mission over to Blair and 2d Lt. Levi Hollis. At that time he instructed the regiment's forward air controller, Capt. Edwin W. Robertson, a white Air Force officer, to accompany the group and call in air strikes to cover the 3d Battalion's withdrawal. Later in the evening, Lieutenants Tittel and Voight also apparently received instructions to attempt to make contact with the lost battalion.[120]

Having delivered his instructions, Corley departed to relocate his command post to the rear near a hill in the possession of the 23d Infantry. It was "black dark," Robertson recalled, and still several hours until daylight. "Corley had not been gone more than ten minutes," Robertson continued, "when Blair turned . . . and said that he was going to the rear to establish his CP and that Robertson and Hollis should get word to the 3d Battalion . . . to withdraw. Blair added that his company commanders were experienced officers and could handle the withdrawal without him." The two lieutenants did as they were told, departing on their mission at first light. Shortly thereafter, they determined that Blair's battalion had been cut off and was exposed to the enemy.[121]

Meanwhile, at the regimental command post, Corley was becoming increasingly anxious. When it became clear that the three companies had not moved and that the effort to reach them had been unproductive, he turned to Colonel Miller, the commander of the 1st Battalion, whose unit remained on the left flank of the 3d Battalion's companies. Under instructions from the 25th Division by then to withdraw entirely from the Kunu-ri area at daybreak and to relocate to Sukch'on, fifteen

miles due south from Anju, he told Miller to have his patrols pass the word along to Blair's units. Miller agreed, but again in the confusion the message never made it through. After daybreak, with the 1st Battalion withdrawing but the three companies of the 3d nowhere in sight, apparently at Robertson's request, an artillery liaison aircraft went up to look. It spied the better part of a Chinese division massing to the north of Kunu-ri and brought artillery and air strikes down upon it. It also discovered the 3d Battalion's lost companies and dropped a message to them in a can.[122]

A platoon leader in Company K, Lieutenant Yadon, recalled seeing the airplane. Observing that the 23d Infantry had been heavily engaged with the enemy just to the east of the 24th, he remarked:

Well, . . . that night was when the 23d left. They had a hell of a fire-fight over on our east, it simmered down, they had withdrawn. The next morning, . . . we were roaming around behind the great big dikes, the rice paddies there. We could see movement back on these ridges, and later on we had an attack air fly over. . . . We . . . needed ammunition [but] . . . the thought of withdrawing hadn't entered our minds. We were still a viable unit. We had the battalion for the most part, a little bit of our heavy weapons company was back in town. I remember this airplane threw a note out on a stringer. Told us that we were in a precarious position. The Chinese were massing. It said it would be well if we made plans to depart. They even told us to head . . . southwest. . . . So we began to make some plans. I remember the company that was to the southwest, which was L Company, [was] to start first, and then K Company, which was facing the Chinese on the south was to withdraw, peel off, and I Company was to start back from the rear. The plane flew over again and threw another note in an empty grenade can and said "Imperative you start now." So we started.[123]

Toward midday, Company L appears to have moved out as planned, pulling back to a point where it could cover the withdrawal of Companies

[120] Intervs, Cash with Oliver Dillard, 3 Jun 89; MacGarrigle with Robertson, 24 Feb 95. Dillard does not mention that Blair received the mission; otherwise his account is close to Robertson's. He says that one of the two officers was a sergeant, a natural mistake since Hollis had just received a battlefield commission to the rank of lieutenant. The roles of Voight and Tittel remain unclear but both also apparently received instructions to assist in leading the 3d Battalion to safety. See Interv, MacGarrigle with Tittel, 23 May 94.

[121] Handwritten Ltr, Edwin W. Robertson to George L. MacGarrigle, 7 Mar 95, CMH files.

[122] WD, 24th Inf Rgt, Nov 50, p. 20; 25th Inf Div Opns Instruction 24, 30 Nov 50; Intervs, Appleman with Corley, 4 Jan 52; MacGarrigle with Sapenter, 21 Mar 94; Robertson, 24 Feb 95; Muehlbauer with Yadon, 22 May 89. The timing of Corley's instructions to Miller is in doubt, but the colonel obviously made several attempts to contact the 3d Battalion.

[123] Interv, Muehlbauer with Yadon, 22 May 89.

I and K. The other two companies then began their moves, but the Chinese were upon them almost immediately. Bursting over the dike, they caught the men unprepared and began to mingle in among them in an attempt to escape the air strikes that had to that point taken a great toll on their number. The nature of the terrain and the naivete of some of the troops aided them. A large irrigation ditch stretched across the position. Some of the retreating men attempted to seek cover there because the trench was low and seemed safe. "I can remember cussing and yelling and kicking and scratching and telling them to get up out of there, get up over that hill," Yadon recalled. "Some of them thought they were safe there hidden, but they weren't." A squad leader in Company M, Sgt. Richard Sanders, told a similar story. He ordered his men to move out two at a time across a field and take cover behind several tanks some three hundred yards away on the other side. The men refused. Sanders ordered them to follow him and took off by himself. He tripped. As he fell, enemy tracers went over his head, but he finally made it to safety. His men were not so lucky. Most were captured after they refused to cross the field.[124]

Standing on a hill about two miles to the rear of the 3d Battalion, the commander of the 23d Infantry's Company B, Capt. Sherman Pratt, watched the scene unfold through his binoculars:

I could see troops moving in the valley below us. But they were still too distant to make out. It was clear though that they weren't organized. They were moving around in bunches, this way and that, like chickens in a barnyard, with no clearly discernible direction.

We watched them for a while through our binoculars, and as they got closer one of my lieutenants said, "My God, Captain, I think they're GIs!"

Black GIs, I might add. We could recognize their American uniforms, but most had no helmets, and few had any weapons. Even at that distance they looked thoroughly disorganized and terrorized. From up on our hill we could see them running and stumbling over the frozen ground. Some would fall and not get back up. Here and there we could see one of them stop, look back and fire. Although there wasn't much of that, because so few still had their rifles.

Then we noticed that mixed among these black GIs were Chinese. They were running in among the Americans, grabbing them and trying to pull them to the ground. We could see fistfights as the GIs tried to throw off the Chinese. We saw other GIs hitting the Chinese with what appeared to be clubs or sticks. The wild melee continued, off and on, for two or three hours. Watching it, we felt helpless and frustrated. It was too far below us to go out and help, and we couldn't fire on the Chinese without the risk of hitting the GIs.[125]

In their arrogance, according to rifleman Wilfred Matthews, some of the Chinese would run alongside fleeing American soldiers, shove them from the rear, and say, "Run Joe."[126]

As chaos spread, one platoon of Company L under the command of 1st Lt. Alonzo O. Sargent functioned as a rear guard. Wielding two pistols, sometimes in hand-to-hand combat but always in a hail of gunfire, Sargent jumped from position to position, administering first aid to those who were wounded and shifting the aim of his men to meet each new enemy threat. Whenever the Chinese temporarily lost momentum or paused to take stock, he moved the wounded first and then directed his men into new firing positions to the rear. In that way, he and his troops finally reached a sunken railroad track on the edge of the field. There he and another officer, 1st Lt. Sandro Barone, rallied frightened soldiers who had congregated in the draw and succeeded in leading them off. For his bravery, Sargent later received the Silver Star, as did Barone.[127]

A number of other officers were similarly bold. Collecting anyone who would respond, they fought their way out, sometimes against great

---

[124] Ibid.; Intervs, Muehlbauer with Richard Sanders, 16 Dec 88; Appleman with Corley, 4 Jan 52; MacGarrigle with Sapenter, 21 Mar 94.

[125] Pratt is quoted in Rudy Tomedi, *No Bugles, No Drums, An Oral History of the Korean War* (New York: John Wiley & Sons, 1993), pp. 66–67. The commander of the 1st Battalion, 23d Infantry, Maj. Sam Radow, gave a similar description. See Interv, Appleman with Sam Radow, 16 Aug 51.

[126] Interv, Cash with Matthews, 23 Sep 88.

[127] Affidavits of Sfc George M. Bussey, Sfc Olin Dorsey, Jr., and Cpl Donald Daniels, attachments to Award Recommendation for 1st Lt Alonzo O. Sargent, 21 Dec 50, box 168, RG 338, WNRC; Interv, MacGarrigle with Barone, 14 Apr 94.

odds. As for the enlisted men, although some gave in to their fears, many others held firm. Responding to a call for volunteers to man automatic weapons, a group of between twenty and thirty, for example, stayed behind at a critical moment to cover the withdrawal.[128]

Air strikes assisted. Coordinated by Robertson on the ground, some thirty-five fighter-bombers were stacked up over the battlefield. They fired their machine guns and dropped bombs and napalm on the advancing Chinese throughout the day, killing many of the enemy while separating them from the retreating troops. Unavoidably, they also injured and killed some of their own men.[129]

In the confusion, the lieutenants who had been ordered to find the battalion did their job. There was no real organization as the troops left the field, according to Tittel, a member of the group. Everyone remained close to the ground until they were out of small-arms range. Then they stood up and moved away from the noise of the battle. In all that day, the 3d Battalion appears to have lost 1 killed, 30 wounded, and 109 missing in action.[130]

That evening the 24th Infantry began to fall back toward Anju, the first leg in the 25th Division's withdrawal to the south. Except for the 1st Battalion, which had gone ahead on foot, most of the troops moved in trucks supplied by the artillery and the 35th Infantry. Somewhere to the south, the convoy halted briefly in a location that was near the regimental command post. At that time, a freezing platoon leader in Company I, 2d

Lt. Reginald Sapenter, caught sight of his battalion commander, Blair, warming himself by a bonfire on the side of the road. The image stayed with him over the next forty years.[131]

When the 25th Division was finally able to take stock later in December, it found that the 24th Infantry had suffered grievous damage in the retreat. From the standpoint of materiel, the unit had lost most of its radios and a large quantity of its equipment. On the human level, however, the harm had been even worse. The regiment had suffered the loss of 20 percent of its officers and 33 percent of its enlisted personnel. Company C of the 1st Battalion was gone and would have to be rebuilt from scratch, and both the 2d and 3d Battalions were sorely depleted. The men who remained were often in pain. Many suffered from exhaustion. Frostbite and trench foot seemed epidemic.[132]

Within the 24th Infantry, morale was low and tempers continued to be short. Some of the officers blamed Blair for the disaster at Kunu-ri, and Corley himself had become concerned that the 3d Battalion's commander was "out on his feet." The problem came to a head several days after the retreat from Kunu-ri, when Robertson finally rejoined the regiment. Learning from the officer that Blair had declined to follow his instructions and had gone to the rear rather than to find his companies, Corley ordered the colonel to report to him immediately. When Blair arrived Corley listened to his story and then relieved him, according to Robertson, "on the spot." At that time, he told Blair he could say it was because of combat fatigue.[133]

[128]Intervs, MacGarrigle with Barone, 14 Apr 94; Cash with George Bussey, 13 Nov 88; Matthews, 23 Sep 88; Bowers with Roscoe E. Dann, Jr., 23 Mar 94.

[129]Intervs, Cash with Robertson, 29 Aug 89; MacGarrigle with Robertson, 24 Feb 95.

[130]WD, 24th Inf Rgt, Nov 50, pp. 20–21; WD, 3d Bn, 24th Inf Rgt, Nov 50, pp. 14–15; WD, 3d Bn, 24th Inf Rgt, Dec 50, p. 1; Intervs, Appleman with Corley, 4 Jan 52; Muehlbauer with Yadon, 22 May 89; MacGarrigle with Sapenter, 21 Mar 94; Tittel, 23 May 94. The statistics are from 24th Inf Rgt S–1 Rpt of Casualty Statistics, attachment to WD, 24th Inf Rgt, Dec 50, box 3770, RG 407, WNRC. According to the S–3 journals of the 1st and 3d Battalions, 23d Infantry, most of the men of the 24th were off the battlefield by 1630 that evening. See S–3 Journals, 1st and 3d Bns, 23d Inf Rgt, 30 Nov 50, box 2472, RG 407, WNRC.

[131]WD, 24th Inf Rgt, Dec 50, pp. 20–21; Intervs, MacGarrigle with Sapenter, 21 Mar 94; Tittel, 23 May 94.

[132]24th Inf Rgt Narrative History, Dec 50, p. 4, box 3770, RG 407, WNRC; WD, 3d Bn, 24th Inf Rgt, Nov 50, pp. 14–15.

[133]Corley's forward air controller, Robertson, was emphatic when giving his eyewitness account of what happened. See Interv, MacGarrigle with Robertson, 24 Feb 95; Handwritten Ltr, Robertson to MacGarrigle, 7 Mar 95. Blair said he was transferred to division because General Kean needed an interim chief of intelligence. See Interv, MacGarrigle with Blair, 15 Feb 95. WO Thomas Pettigrew, who claimed also to have been present at Blair's relief, told a different story but his version remains unsubstantiated. By his account, Corley and Blair argued, and Corley relieved the officer. See Pettigrew, The Kunu-ri (Kumori) Incident, pp. 27–28; Interv, Cash with

Several months after the episode, Blair gave an interview to Harold H. Martin of the *Saturday Evening Post*. According to Martin, Blair alleged that the enemy had put his command-post security guard to flight at Kunu-ri without a shot in return and that he had watched from a distance the next day as the enemy had cut his battalion to pieces. "All three companies broke at once," Martin wrote. "The men fled like rabbits across the great open field, and the commander could see them fall." Later that afternoon, Martin continued, Blair had encountered a group of black soldiers huddled around a campfire singing. Questioning the men about their song, he learned that it was what they called "the official song of the 24th Infantry," the "Bugout Boogie." Set to a tune with an easy swing, Hank Snow's "Movin' On," the lyrics went: "When them Chinese mortars begins to thud, the old Deuce-four begin to bug."[134]

Martin went on to observe that the attitude the song betrayed was at the heart of the Army's problem with the black soldier. Going back as far as 1867, when the first black regiments had been formed, the service had never succeeded in determining how best to employ all-black forces. During World Wars I and II, as a result, those units had performed poorly, and according to Blair's story they continued to do so. Martin concluded that black soldiers fighting as part of all-white units did about as well or as poorly

as their white counterparts and that integration of the armed forces was the obvious solution to the problems of all-black units.[135]

Blair asserted in an interview forty-four years later that the reporter had distorted his comments. He had never watched the enemy cut his battalion to pieces, he said, and the "Bugout Boogie" episode had taken place much earlier, shortly after he had assumed command of the battalion at Battle Mountain. Indeed, as other veterans of the war have noted, the "Bugout Boogie" was sung by many units in Korea, usually about themselves as a joke or about rival units. "The 2d Division is second to none," one variation went. "The 1st Cav is the first to run. A rumble of thunder, [a] stomp of feet, the 1st Cav (or Deuce Four or 2d Division) is in full retreat."[136]

Whatever the case, the African-American press took umbrage at the article. If Martin had presented a strong argument in favor of integration, *Pittsburgh Courier* correspondent Frank Whisonant avowed, "he had bloodied the nose of the Negro in doing so" by implying that the 24th's problems were related to the race of the troops rather than to the influence of segregation and the reduced expectations it instilled. When the black soldier faltered he got all the blame, the reporter charged, but when he did well his officers received the credit.[137]

Whisonant turned to Colonel Corley for a rebuttal, authoring a series of three articles based on interviews. Without alluding to the fact that Blair appeared to have been nowhere near his three companies at the time when they came to grief at Kunu-ri and that he was never the eyewitness Martin had made him out to be, Corley denied that the men of the 3d Battalion had been at fault. "As for the attack on our positions which caused Major Blair to flee," he said,

he and I and the regiment are responsible. . . . It was also just plain luck of battle, as the regiment was caught in an awkward position. . . . [The men] were dead tired on

Thomas H. Pettigrew, 21 Dec 89. The two stories are not necessarily incompatible. Pettigrew may have seen one set of actions, Robertson another. Both may have contributed to Corley's decision to remove Blair. Describing an argument with Blair and other bizarre behavior on the part of the colonel, Corley himself remarked in an interview that he had concluded Blair was suffering from combat fatigue and had recommended a staff job for the officer until he could recover and return to the line with another combat command. See Interv, Appleman with Corley, 4 Jan 52. The 3d Battalion's operations officer, Maj. Roscius Newell, also recalled that Blair was suffering from pronounced fatigue. See Intervs, MacGarrigle with Newell, 10 and 15 Nov 94. Blair could not recall ever seeing either Corley or Robertson in the retreat from Kunu-ri. His version does not square with the written record or with eyewitness accounts provided by Corley, Robertson, and Armstrong. See Ltr, Melvin Blair to George L. MacGarrigle, 24 Sep 95, CMH files.

134 Harold H. Martin, "How Do Our Negro Troops Measure Up?" *Saturday Evening Post*, 16 Jun 51, p. 32.

135 Ibid.

136 Interv, MacGarrigle with Blair, 15 Feb 95. Quote from Interv, Bowers with Bernard L. Muehlbauer, a veteran of the Korean War with contacts in many units, 8 May 95.

137 Frank Whisonant, "Whisonant's Reply," *Pittsburgh Courier*, 30 Jun 51, p. 1.

their feet. And, . . . Blair's battalion had just fought for three days breaking out of an enemy trap. . . . In August and September, the regiment might have been unpredictable like Martin said, but that is not true now. Today, the regiment is a fine regiment and quite predictable. It is a much more seasoned outfit.[138]

By assuming the blame for the 24th's problems, Corley was charitable in the extreme. Confusion and uncertainty at all levels had in fact dogged the regiment from the first moment of the Chinese attack, leaving the unit with at best a mixed record. Although the 1st Battalion had performed well, coming close to its objectives despite the rugged country and extreme cold, the disorder that followed the Chinese attack and that accompanied Task Force Wilson's efforts to contain the assault had left the unit's Company C exposed. Surrounded, the force had ultimately surrendered. The 2d Battalion had done well, withstanding a major Chinese onslaught. But if the unit maintained its cohesion and continued to fight, Companies E and G found that they had no way to return to their regiment. Sorely depleted, they joined the 3d Battalion of the 9th Infantry instead, where they fought on with distinction. As for the 3d Battalion, Blair's apparent exhaustion and the lack of leadership that resulted from his absence, along with confusion at the division and corps levels, led to the progressive isolation of the unit and calamitous losses.

Problems of that sort, however, were hardly unique to the 24th Infantry. In the 2d Division, Company K of the highly regarded all-black 3d Battalion of the 9th Infantry, lacking communications and occupying an insecure position, was all but destroyed in the enemy attack. The men of Company L of the same unit, poorly supervised and suffering from the cold because of a lack of overcoats, had meanwhile lit bonfires to keep warm. Short of ammunition when the enemy attacked their well-lit position, they too were destroyed as a fighting force. While those incidents were occurring, to the east of the 9th Infantry the headquarters and the 3d Platoon of Company G of the all-white 38th Infantry, occupying a poorly selected site and out of touch with neighboring units, were annihilated with only one survivor. The rest of the company was devastated. Out of 4 officers, 115 enlisted men, and 44 South Koreans present at the start of the attack, only 1 officer and 60 enlisted men survived. Similar stories could be told of other American units, and of the troops of the South Korean II Corps farther to the east, which bore the brunt of the enemy attack. Combat units were stretched to their limits everywhere above Kunu-ri as the momentum of the enemy's attack built in strength. If many units survived because of good luck or superior leadership, many others suffered grievous losses.[139]

The difficulties those units experienced were not blamed on race but on tangible military considerations—poor supply, improper training, ineffective leadership, or merely the fortunes of war. A case in point was the segregated 3d Battalion of the 9th Infantry. Although the unit had suffered some setbacks during the fighting, the causes of the problems it encountered were attributed to military considerations, rather than race, as were the unit's successes. The atmosphere prevalent within the 9th Infantry itself was the reason. Because of casualties, replacements had been assigned where needed within the unit, whatever their race. In that way, a black officer had taken command of an all-white company and about two hundred and twenty black soldiers had joined formerly all-white platoons. Meanwhile, several white enlisted men had joined the 3d Battalion.[140]

[138] Quote from Whisonant, "True Story of the 24th: Colonel Corley Gives Facts to Courier War Reporter," p. 1. See also John T. Corley, "I Was Proud of My Men: Colonel Corley's Story," *Pittsburgh Courier*, 30 Jun 51, p. 1; Corley, "Policy Lifted Morale, Confidence: Colonel Corley's Story," p. 10; Frank Whisonant, "Whisonant's Answer," *Pittsburgh Courier*, 7 Jul 51, p. 10.

[139] These and many other stories can be found in Appleman, *Disaster in Korea*, pp. 154–92.

[140] Interv, Inspector General with Maj Gen Laurence B. Keiser, 14 Nov 50, exhibit B–24; Memo, Lt Col D. M. McMains for Col Perry, 31 Oct 50, exhibit D–7; and Memo, Col C. C. Sloane, Jr., for General Craig, 29 Oct 50, exhibit D–6. All in Eighth Army Inspector General Investigation.

The end result was a natural process in which mutual confidence and respect had grown under the strains of combat. As a white squad leader in the black 3d Battalion, Sgt. Lyman D. Heacock, remarked when offered a transfer to a white unit:

Right now I would prefer to go back to the colored unit. When I first went into the company, I had a sort of a funny feeling, kind of out of place. I just took it easy. Now I don't even look at the color anymore. It can be done, it is up to the individual himself. I don't think there is any difference between white and colored in combat.[141]

_____

[141] Interv, IG with Lyman D. Heacock, 15 Nov 50, exhibit B–30, Eighth Army Inspector General Investigation. For additional comments about the attitudes in the regiment, see Intervs, IG with Cauthion T. Boyd, 15 Nov 50, exhibit B–29, and Freeman R. Tiffany, 15 Nov 50, exhibit B–26, both in Eighth Army Inspector General Investigation.

Overall, building on a host of similar experiences, commanders had come to judge units and individuals within the regiment on performance and nothing more. The 3d of the 9th benefited.

The same was not true in the case of the 24th Infantry. If the regiment, as Corley had observed, was stronger and more self-reliant than earlier in the war and had conducted itself as well as any other in the attack toward the Yalu, any credit it might have received for its overall performance disappeared with the loss of Company C and the debacle involving the 3d Battalion. Although Companies E and G had won commendation from the 9th Infantry and most of the other companies in the regiment had fulfilled their roles before pulling back, accomplishments of that sort hardly mattered. Martin's charges in the *Saturday Evening Post* prevailed. The already battered reputation of the 24th fell to the lowest point it would ever reach in the Korean War.

CHAPTER 9

Across the Rivers

The retreat from the Ch'ungch'on proved disastrous for the 2d Division. When the unit withdrew along a route that ran directly from Kunuri to the town of Sunch'on, some twenty miles to the south, the enemy set up a roadblock at a pass eight miles along the way and managed to stop almost the entire force. In the agony that followed, the Chinese destroyed a column of trucks and other vehicles many miles long and inflicted a multitude of casualties. Air strikes saved the day, with pilots sometimes flying so low against enemy positions that the men on the ground thought the planes would crash. By the time the 2d Division reassembled at Sunch'on on 1 December 1950, it had shrunk by nearly half. Of the 18,931 men who had marched north toward the Yalu on 25 November, only 10,269 remained.[1] (*See Map 14.*)

The 24th Infantry regiment had few difficulties by comparison, but none of the soldiers present would have said so at the time. The unit's path of withdrawal fell farther to the west than that of the 2d Division, through the town of Sinanju, where few enemy were present. Even so, to avoid Chinese ambushes on the road south the 77th Engineer Combat Company had to cut a steep bypass through the mountains. Since many of the regiment's trucks were unable to climb the trail, they were burned along with surplus supplies. Already suffering from the effects of previous marches, various injuries from the cold, and exhaustion, the men of the regiment took only what they could carry on their backs. There was little food, and the cold was so intense that temperatures sometimes fell to as low as -6°F at night.[2]

The Eighth Army Withdraws

The retreat continued in the days that followed. General Walker saw no alternative. He estimated that the Chinese force opposing him numbered a full six armies with eighteen divisions and 165,000 men. Against it he could mount only the 1st South Korean Division; the U.S. 1st Cavalry and 24th and 25th Infantry Divisions; and two British brigades. Much of the rest of his force—the U.S. 2d Infantry

---

[1] The withdrawal of the 2d Division is detailed in Mossman, *Ebb and Flow*, pp. 117–27. The book also contains the strength statistics. See also Appleman, *Disaster in Korea*, pp. 226–93; Marshall, *The River and the Gauntlet: Defeat of the Eighth Army by the Chinese Communist Forces, November 1950, in the Battle of the Ch'ongch'on River, Korea*, pp. 280–361.

[2] 24th Inf Rgt Exec Ofcr's Daily Journal, 2 Dec 50; 24th Inf Rgt Unit Rpt 62, 2 Dec 50; War Diary (WD), 1st Bn, 24th Inf Rgt, Dec 50, p. 1; Morning Rpt, 1st Bn, 24th Inf Rgt, 24 Dec 50. All in box 3770, Record Group (RG) 407, Washington National Records Center (WNRC), Suitland, Md.; Brig Gen G. B. Barth, Tropic Lightning and Taro Leaf in Korea, n.d., pp. 47–48, CMH files; Intervs, John A. Cash with Robert H. Yancy, 21 Jan 89; George L. MacGarrigle with Buckner M. Creel, 3 Nov and 3 Dec 93. All interviews hereafter cited by John A. Cash, Bernard L. Muehlbauer, Timothy Rainey, William T. Bowers, Richard O. Perry, and George L. MacGarrigle are in CMH files.

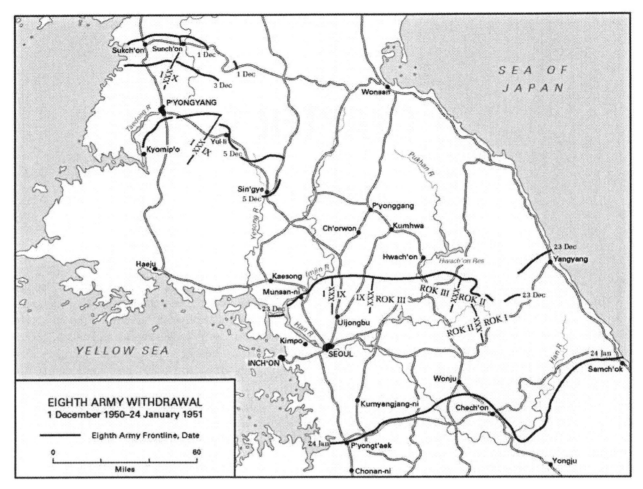

Map 15

Division; the Turkish Brigade; and the 6th, 7th, and 8th South Korean Divisions—was heavily worn and in grievous need of repair. As for reserves, he had a number of disparate allied units from the Netherlands, France, Thailand, and the Philippines; a U.S. airborne regimental combat team; and four South Korean divisions. Most of those units were either very new to the war or relatively untrained.[3] (*Map 15*)

Given the available resources, when a threat arose that the enemy might cut the American line of withdrawal by launching a drive into P'yongyang

from the east, Walker decided that he had no choice but to abandon the city. Pulling his forces farther south, he opened Army storehouses and depots in the area to his retreating troops and then ordered his men to burn everything that remained. Eight to ten thousand tons of supplies went up in flames, including fifteen operable M46 tanks that had to be destroyed with air strikes when they were mistakenly abandoned on a railroad siding. Many of the men in the 24th took advantage of the situation to reequip themselves with clothing and arms, but the unit itself appears to have received little benefit from Walker's order. On 4 December regimental supply officers took stock of their inventories and decided

---

[3] Mossman, *Ebb and Flow*, p. 149.

to replenish critically needed supplies by returning to P'yongyang to retrieve what they needed. By the time they arrived the city was in flames and its ammunition dumps were exploding.[4]

From there the Eighth Army pulled progressively to the rear, occupying a series of positions farther and farther south. It came to rest toward mid-December on a line twenty miles above Seoul that ran across the Korean peninsula from the mouth of the Imjin River on the west to the seacoast town of Yangyang on the east. The 24th set up its headquarters at Karhyon-ni, northwest of Seoul and just to the east of the confluence of the Han and Imjin Rivers. In a touch of absurdity, the mail arrived just as the retreat was ending, bearing with it not only letters from home but also recently ordered gear for the regiment's football team. Seizing on any chance for levity, as soon as it seemed safe some of the men made light of their misery by donning helmets and numbered jerseys.[5]

The weather was so cold during the period that it became a constant threat to the well-being of the regiment. Soldiers selected to hold flanking positions out of reach of their buddies had to guard against freezing to death in their foxholes overnight, and carbon monoxide poisoning became a problem because cold infantrymen declined to keep truck windows and hut doors ajar to circulate the air. The worst afflictions dogging the 24th, however, were frostbite and other cold-weather injuries. Although the men's clothing appears to have been no better or worse than that of the members of all-white regiments, the rate of cold-wet injury in the unit far exceeded that of either the 27th or the 35th Infantry regiments. Indeed, between 15 November and 31 December

1950, the 24th suffered 469 cases of frostbite while the 27th incurred 77 and the 35th 112.[6]

A number of causes have been suggested for the high incidence of cold-weather injuries in the 24th. Since the unit may have had more men than either of the other two regiments in the 25th Division, its size may have accounted for part of the disparity. Poor morale may also have had an influence. The white operations officer of the 3d Battalion, Maj. Roscius C. Newell, observed that some of the men in his unit were so disheartened and naive that a few intentionally attempted to freeze their feet by pouring water into their boots to gain a trip to the rear for treatment.[7]

That a large number of soldiers would have injured themselves in order to win reprieve from the war is not as improbable as it seems. Armies in every conflict have experienced the phenomenon, sometimes on a large scale. Yet officers within the 25th Division were on the watch for the problem and deterred those who might have sought to maim themselves by taking immediate action against violators. During December 1950, as a result, despite an inspector general investigation into the high incidence of cold-weather injuries in the 24th, the regiment's medical officers could identify only six instances in which they suspected that soldiers had done violence to themselves. Overall, according to a report by the 25th Division's inspector general during March, self-inflicted wounds within the division were few in number, and when they occurred they were seldom intentional.[8]

[4] WD, 24th Inf Rgt, S–4 Summary for 7 Dec 50, box 3770, RG 407, WNRC; Intervs, MacGarrigle with Curtis H. Alloway, 20 Oct 94; George A. Clayton, 10 and 11 Aug 94; Mossman, *Ebb and Flow*, pp. 149–51; Barth, Tropic Lightning and Taro Leaf in Korea, n.d., p. 48.

[5] WD, 24th Inf Rgt, Dec 50, box 3770, RG 407, WNRC; Mossman, *Ebb and Flow*, pp. 149–51; Barth, Tropic Lightning and Taro Leaf in Korea, n.d., p. 48. John Komp recalled seeing the football gear as did Roscius Newell. See Ltr, John S. Komp to George L. MacGarrigle, 15 Jun 94, CMH files; Intervs, MacGarrigle with Roscius C. Newell, 10 and 15 Nov 94.

[6] 24th Inf Rgt Regimental Narrative Summary for Dec 50, box 3770, RG 407, WNRC; Intervs, MacGarrigle with Creel, 3 Nov and 3 Dec 93; Ltr, Komp to MacGarrigle, 15 Jun 94. The frostbite statistics are from WD, 25th Inf Div, Jan 51, p. 21, box 3766, RG 407, WNRC.

[7] 24th Inf Rgt Regimental Narrative Summary for Dec 50; WD, 24th Inf Rgt, S–4 Summary for Dec 50, box 3770, RG 407, WNRC. The demoralization of the men was mentioned both by Newell and by Curtis Alloway. See Intervs, MacGarrigle with Newell, 10 and 15 Nov 94; Alloway, 20 Oct 94. The understrength condition of all-white units at this time is described in Eliot A. Cohen and John Gooch, *Military Misfortunes, The Anatomy of Failure in War* (New York: Free Press, 1990), pp. 182–84.

[8] The 25th Infantry Division's inspector general observed in March 1951 that self-inflicted wounds within the division had declined sharply by February because of prompt investi-

A more important consideration may have been the physical makeup of the men themselves. Army studies later in the war determined that blacks as a group were more susceptible to cold injury than whites. During the winter of 1951–1952, when integration was a fact in the Eighth Army, investigators determined that while whites constituted 91.1 percent of the strength in U.S. regiments in Korea, blacks were only 9.9 percent. Even so, whites experienced a rate of only 5.8 cases of cold-weather injury per 1,000 men while blacks suffered 35.86. Although clothed and fed in the same manner as their white counterparts and subject to the same discipline, the blacks came down with frostbite after somewhat shorter periods of exposure and began to experience injury at temperatures somewhat higher than their white counterparts.[9]

Whatever the reason, once the leaders of the 24th became conscious of the extent of the problem and took action to impose remedies, the situation readily yielded to good management. As soon as officers began daily inspections, insisted on regular foot massages, and inaugurated a program that distributed up to 2,300 pairs of dry socks per day to the men, the number of injuries declined. During January 1951, as a result, frostbite cases reported by the regiment numbered only 68 for the month, as compared with 72 cases in the 27th and 91 in the 35th.[10]

While the officers of the 24th were pushing to control frostbite, they were also working to restore the fighting efficiency of the regiment. The task was enormous. By 2 December more than one-third of the unit's men had fallen in battle or become the victims of frostbite and other ailments. In addition, the regiment had lost most of its signal equipment and much of its ordnance. Antifreeze was in such short supply that the unit's vehicles had to be left running overnight, a severe waste of gasoline, or to be drained of fluids every evening and refilled the next morning.[11]

The problem of supply gave way so quickly to the efforts of logisticians that by Christmas most of the regiment's lost equipment had been replaced. Personnel shortages, however, proved more difficult to correct because replacements were scarce. Even when an influx of new men occurred toward the end of the month, unit efficiency rose only slightly. Lacking money, facilities, and experienced trainers to handle a large infusion of draftees, the Army had reduced basic training from fourteen weeks to six. Most of the new arrivals, as a result, still required considerable supervision. As for officer replacements, they were usually better trained, but some nevertheless arrived after only the most basic orientation. One lieutenant, a World War II

gation and disciplinary action. See 25th Inf Div Inspector General Command Rpt for Feb 51, 7 Mar 51, p. 2, box 3777, RG 407, WNRC. The inspector general investigation of cold-weather injuries is mentioned in 25th Inf Div Inspector General Command Rpt for Dec 50, 12 Jan 51, box 3768, RG 407, WNRC. The statistics on the 24th Infantry are from 24th Inf Rgt Medical Co Journal, Dec 50, box 3770, RG 407, WNRC.

[9] The susceptibility of blacks to cold-weather injury is detailed in Kenneth D. Orr and D. C. Fainer, Cold Injury—Korea, 1951–52, Rpt 113 (Fort Knox, Ky.: Army Medical Research Laboratory, 1953), pp. 372–88. Orr and Fainer noted (pp. 387–88) that a study of Norwegian ski troops had found that dark-complected Norwegians tended to develop frostbite of the ears and face more often than blond individuals when exposed to virtually identical circumstances. They cautioned, however, that until psychosocial factors are more nearly adequately appraised the validity of their hypothesis had to be held in abeyance. They added, nonetheless, that as a practical measure, "recognizing the Negro as being at greater risk, unit commanders responsible for cold weather orientation and training must emphasize . . . hygiene, mobility, and proper wearing of gear to the Negro to a greater degree to overcome this disparity in vulnerability." Orr and Fainer published a digest of their findings in "Cold Injuries in Korea During the Winter 1950–1951," Medicine 31 (1952): 177f. Later studies have confirmed many of the Orr and Fainer study's findings. See, for example, Lt. Col. Mark S. Taylor, "Cold Weather Injuries During Peacetime Military Training," Military Medicine 157 (November 1992): 602. The Army's principal textbook on military dermatology notes that "Race is an important risk factor" in cold-weather injury, "with blacks being 2- to 6-fold more vulnerable to frostbite than whites." See Col. William D. James, MC, U.S. Army, Military Dermatology (Falls Church, Va.: Department of the Army, Office of the Surgeon General, 1994), p. 26.

[10] Intervs, MacGarrigle with Clayton, 10 and 11 Aug 94. Instructions for remedying the problem are detailed in 25th Inf Div Command Rpt for Dec 50, p. 23, box 3761, RG 407, WNRC. The frostbite statistics for January are in 25th Inf Div Narrative Rpt for Jan 51, p. 21, box 3773, RG 407, WNRC.

[11]WD, 24th Inf Rgt, S–4 Summary for Dec 50. Strength figures are from 24th Inf Rgt Unit Rpt 62, 2 Dec 50.

veteran, according to the commander of Company C, Capt. Joseph Kahoe, had been processed so quickly that he had eaten Thanksgiving dinner at home the month before as a civilian. In general, officer replacements went into the line where need- ed. There were no illusions left in the 24th about maintaining companies with all-black or all-white officer groupings.[12]

Fortunately for all concerned, the Chinese lacked the means to sustain the intense pressure they had exerted during their initial attack in November. By failing to follow up on their victory at the Ch'ongch'on, they gave the Eighth Army time to heal. Occupying its position on the Imjin line, the 24th Infantry, for one, had the latitude to keep only one-third of its men in position at any time and to allow the rest to train, repair equip- ment, lay mines and wire, fill sandbags, participate in foot-care programs, and just keep warm.[13]

Those efforts, along with warm food and the arrival of additional winter clothing, had their effect on morale within the regiment. By mid-month, con- fidence was growing among the men and patrolling had once more begun. On the night of 18–19 December, for example, the regimental intelligence officer conducted a foray across the frozen Imjin River to determine the enemy's whereabouts. Penetrating six miles into the no-man's-land that separated the armies, the force encountered and drove off a band of North Korean or Chinese sol- diers guarding eight civilian youths. The youths later explained that they were about to be executed for having aided United Nations forces. After an early holiday dinner on 23 December the unit set- tled down to prepare for an enemy offensive that

intelligence officers had predicted would occur sometime near Christmas Day.[14]

As combat eased, a series of changes occurred within the 25th Division and the Eighth Army. On 9 December the commander of the 35th Infantry, Colonel Fisher, was hospitalized for pneumonia and a well-experienced combat commander, Lt. Col. Gerald C. Kelleher, took his place. About that time, Col. John H. Michaelis left the 27th Infantry to be succeeded by another well-regarded officer, Lt. Col. Gilbert Check. On 22 December, Brig. Gen. Vennard Wilson broke his back in an airplane crash and had to be evacuated. He was replaced during February by the former assistant division commander of the 2d Division, Brig. Gen. J. Sladen Bradley, but when General Kean left Korea during February to take a routine reassignment, Bradley moved up to become the commander of the 25th Division. At that time, Colonel Michaelis, a brigadier general designee, took his place as assistant division commander.[15]

With the war lengthening, changes of that sort were to be expected. More telling was the loss of Lt. Gen. Walton H. Walker on 23 December in an automobile crash and his replacement within the week by Lt. Gen. Matthew B. Ridgway, a highly regarded combat commander who had led the 82d Airborne Division during the invasions of Sicily and Italy during World War II and had jumped into Normandy on D-day. The personal choice of General MacArthur, who placed complete confi- dence in him, Ridgway was deeply concerned about a defeatist mentality he believed had begun to fester within the Eighth Army. He was resolved to lead his forces back onto the offensive.[16]

Ridgway's intentions notwithstanding, the Chinese once more stole the initiative, launching their long-awaited attack on New Year's Eve, just four days after the new commander took charge. Their assault came all along the Imjin line, but it

---

[12] Strength figures are from 24th Inf Rgt Unit Rpt 91, 31 Dec 50, box 3770, RG 407, WNRC. Problems with supplying replacements are detailed in George Q. Flynn, *The Draft, 1940–1973* (Lawrence: University of Kansas Press, 1993), p. 115. See also Interv, Bernard L. Muehlbauer with Joseph Kahoe, 5 Dec 88.

[13] WD, 3d Bn, 24th Inf Rgt, Dec 50, p. 5, box 3770, RG 407, WNRC; Intervs, MacGarrigle with Alloway, 20 Oct 94; Muehlbauer with Kahoe, 5 Dec 88. See also Barth, Tropic Lightning and Taro Leaf in Korea, n.d., pp. 48–50. Mossman notes that some fighting did occur in areas to the east in the IX Corps zone. See Mossman, *Ebb and Flow*, p. 161.

[14] 24th Inf Rgt Regimental Narrative Summary for Dec 50, p. 3.

[15] Barth, Tropic Lightning and Taro Leaf in Korea, n.d., pp. 48–50.

[16] Mossman, *Ebb and Flow*, pp. 177–91; Bart Barnes, "Gen Matthew B. Ridgway Dies," *Washington Post*, 27 Jul 93.

struck the hardest against South Korean units located well to the east of the 25th Division. When those forces began to buckle and the Chinese gave evidence that they might be moving to encircle Seoul, Ridgway decided he had no choice but to withdraw. In an attempt to retain possession of Seoul, he pulled the Eighth Army into a line of prepared positions twenty miles to the south that maintained a bridgehead north of the city.[17]

On the evening of 3 January 1951, however, as the enemy continued to press and the whole allied front wavered and began to develop holes, he withdrew again and abandoned both the bridgehead and the city. Falling back in stages with the British 29th Brigade, which took heavy casualties, the 24th and 35th Infantry regiments made the trip in good shape. Serving as the 25th Division's covering force, the 27th Infantry did the same. On 7 January, while the rest of the Eighth Army consolidated on a new line some forty miles to the south of Seoul that ran through the town of P'yongt'aek and the 35th pulled into place just to the rear to reinforce forward units, the 24th and the rest of the 25th Division went into reserve at Ch'onan, some thirteen miles farther south.[18]

Time To Mend, January–March 1951

Over the next several weeks Ridgway pushed strong infantry and tank reconnaissance forces north to keep the Chinese off balance and to determine their positions and intentions. While those operations proceeded the 24th Infantry formulated counterattack plans in support of any contingency that might arise but otherwise spent much of its time repairing equipment and conducting a cleanup campaign to emphasize personal hygiene and the replacement of clothing and gear. Post exchange sales of beer, cookies, and other delicacies resumed after a long absence. Mail deliveries increased; new movie projectors

arrived along with a variety of feature films; and the regiment's chaplains began to hold regular services and counseling sessions.[19]

As morale improved, on 13 January the 1st Battalion received orders to secure the main supply route from Ch'onan to Taejon, a town some forty miles to the south by road. Guarding bridges, manning outposts at critical points, and searching for guerrilla hideouts, the unit was particularly successful at finding enemy infiltrators and South Korean draft dodgers hiding in the countryside.[20]

In the interim, on 11 January the battalion's commander, Colonel Miller, fell sick and had to be evacuated. He was replaced by the regiment's operations officer, Lt. Col. Joseph Missal, a close friend to Colonel Corley. A good staff officer but "unhappy being a battalion commander," according to his operations officer, Captain Baranowski, Missal found a new job and left after a bit more than two weeks. On 1 February the battalion's executive officer, Maj. Martin L. Davis, took his place, but he proved incapable of handling the assignment and was removed from command. On 14 February the executive officer of the 3d Battalion, Major Newell, took command.[21]

The 2d and 3d Battalions fulfilled roles similar to those of the 1st Battalion but experienced less turmoil within their commands. Initially, the 2d Battalion patrolled vigorously in areas adjacent to its position and conducted practice alerts to gauge the readiness of its companies and platoons. After 15 January, when the 27th and 35th regiments began probing north toward the town of Suwon in prepa-

[17] Mossman, *Ebb and Flow*, pp. 187–227. See also Barth, Tropic Lightning and Taro Leaf in Korea, n.d., pp. 51–53; 25th Inf Div Narrative Rpt for Jan 51, pp. 3–4.

[18] 24th Inf Rgt Regimental Narrative Summary for Jan 51, pp. 1–2, box 3841, RG 407, WNRC; 25th Inf Div Command Rpt for Jan 51, pp. 2–4, box 3773, RG 407, WNRC.

[19] 24th Inf Rgt Regimental Narrative Summary for Jan 51, pp. 2–4; 3d Bn, 24th Inf Rgt, Battalion Narrative Summary for the Month of Feb 51, box 3841, RG 407, WNRC.

[20] 24th Inf Rgt Regimental Narrative Summary for Jan 51, pp. 1–2; 1st Bn, 24th Inf Rgt, Evaluation To Accompany Battalion Narrative for Month of Jan 51, 1 Feb 51, attachment IX to Regimental Narrative Summary for Jan 51, box 3841, RG 407, WNRC.

[21] Ibid.; 1st Bn, 24th Inf Rgt, Periodic Opns Rpt 83, 11 Jan 51, S–3 Operations Instructions file, box 3841, RG 407, WNRC; Intervs, MacGarrigle with Joseph Baranowski, 24 Aug and 6 Sep 94. The commander of the 3d Battalion's headquarters company, Capt. Noah Armstrong, also mentioned that Davis had been unable to handle the job. See Interv, Muehlbauer with Noah Armstrong, 22 Oct 88.

A soldier relays a message to the S–3 of the 24th Infantry.

On 23 January the 25th Division began preparations to participate in Operation THUNDERBOLT, an attack north designed both to retake Seoul and to inflict, as Ridgway desired, as much damage upon the enemy as possible. When H-hour came on the morning of 25 January, the 35th Infantry and the Turkish Brigade, which had been attached to the 25th Division, spearheaded the attack in the 25th Division's sector, sometimes with fixed bayonets. The 27th Infantry fell into reserve, and the 24th continued its mission of securing supply routes and blocking to the rear of attacking forces. For a time the 3d Battalion of the 24th came under the operational control of the British 29th Brigade, but little else changed for the unit. Although hampered by extreme cold and icy roads, it experienced little contact with the enemy and concentrated on training, vehicle maintenance, and activities designed to build morale. Returning to the 24th Infantry's control on 30 January, the battalion assumed responsibility for the security of a newly recaptured airstrip at Suwon.[23]

Overall, during January, while the other regiments of the 25th Division had been sometimes heavily engaged, the 24th Infantry had had time to mend. On 1 February, as a result, having experienced no killed and at best fifteen wounded in action during the preceding month, the unit was once more at nearly full strength. At the beginning of January it had possessed a relatively full complement of officers but only 75 percent of its enlisted men. By the end of the month it could rate its enlisted ranks at a substantial 95 percent.[24]

During the first two weeks of February, the 25th Division advanced steadily north toward Seoul with Corley's 24th Infantry holding its left flank. On 5 February the 1st Battalion accompanied Turkish forces into the Inch'on peninsula.

ration for a new allied offensive slated for the end of the month, it also began conducting patrols, occupying blocking positions, guarding bridges, and securing lines of communications just to the rear of the advancing units. Although it took a number of enemy prisoners, it experienced little combat itself. The 3d Battalion did much the same in its own area of operations, to about the same effect.[22]

22 25th Inf Div Command Rpt for Jan 51, pp. 4–7; 24th Inf Rgt Regimental Narrative Summary for Jan 51, pp. 2–3. 24th Inf Rgt Exec Ofcr's Daily Journal, 24 Jan 51; 2d Bn, 24th Inf Rgt, Evaluation To Accompany Battalion Narrative for Month of Jan 51, 1 Feb 51, attachment X to Regimental Narrative Summary for Jan 51; and 3d Bn, 24th Inf Rgt, Evaluation To Accompany Battalion Narrative for Month of Jan 51, 1 Feb 51, attachment XI to Regimental Narrative Summary for Jan 51. All in box 3841, RG 407, WNRC.

23 I Corps, U.S. Eighth Army, Opns Directive 40, 23 Jan 51, in 25th Inf Div Command Rpt for Jan 51, p. 7, box 3773, RG 407, WNRC; see also pp. 39–63.

24 Memo, Capt Paul A. Carson, Medical Co, 24th Inf Rgt, for Commanding Ofcr (CO), 24th Inf Rgt, 1 Feb 51, sub: Historical Data of Medical Company, 24th Infantry, Period 1–31 January 51, box 3841, RG 407, WNRC. Strengths are contained in 24th Inf Rgt Unit Rpt 32, 1 Feb 51, box 3841, RG 407, WNRC.

General MacArthur salutes the men of the 24th Infantry at Kimpo Air Base and (*right*) presents the Distinguished Service Cross to Sergeant Pugh.

They made slow progress at first, taking some casualties, but on 9 February elements from the regiment probing to the east of the town discovered that the enemy was pulling back to prepare for an all-out defense of Seoul. Moving into the vacuum left by the departing Chinese and largely unopposed, the regiment moved past Inch'on to the northeast to secure the town of Kimpo with its strategic airfield. At that point it stood on the banks of the Han River, just five miles west of Seoul. Shortly thereafter, on 13 February, the 2d Battalion served as an honor guard for a visit by General MacArthur to Kimpo Airfield. During the day MacArthur singled out the unit by awarding a Distinguished Service Cross to Sgt. Curtis Pugh and by presenting Silver Stars to a number of the other men. While those ceremonies were taking place, the rest of the regiment was pulling back to the town of Kumyangjang-ni, thirty miles southeast of Seoul, where it relieved frontline units

from the 1st Cavalry Division and began preparations to recapture the last enemy bridgehead south of the Han River.[25]

The regiment began the attack on 15 February. Encountering high, rugged terrain, it came up against portions of two Chinese regiments backed by strong artillery, mortar, and machine-gun fire. There were no casualties at first, but enemy resistance consolidated the next day, when Chinese counterattacks forced Company G off of one of its objectives and the regiment incurred three killed and fifty-two wounded. Assisted by heavy tank and artillery fire, Company F soon regained the lost position, but not before a stream of visitors had begun to arrive at Corley's command post to check

---

[25] 24th Inf Rgt Regimental Narrative Summary for Feb 51, pp. 1–3, box 3841, RG 407, WNRC; Intervs, MacGarrigle with Clayton, 10 and 11 Aug 94. See also Mossman, *Ebb and Flow*, pp. 253, 256–57.

General Bradley meets troops of the 3d Battalion, 24th Infantry.

on the regiment and how it was doing in its first significant fight in months. Shortly after the start of the operation, at 0930, General Bradley arrived. Acting as the assistant division commander, he would take over as commander of the 25th Division within the next three days, as soon as General Kean departed for a new assignment. The 25th Division's operations officer, Lt. Col. George DeChow, followed an hour later to check, he said, on unit positions. The division's artillery commander, Brig. Gen. George B. Barth, appeared at 1100, and General Kean himself arrived at 1117. At 1405 the I Corps commander, Maj. Gen. Frank W. Milburn, arrived—again, so it was said, to check on the location of the troops. By then, all units were on their objectives and buttoning in for the night, and the 24th itself had advanced some sixteen miles. Its new command post was located at P'abalmak, about twelve miles southwest of Seoul. By 19

February patrols from the regiment had reached the Han, and surveys had begun to determine the best ground near the river for defenses and to lay out possible crossing sites.[26] (*Map 16*)

On that day Bradley succeeded Kean as commander of the 25th Infantry Division. A combat-experienced officer who had led the 126th Infantry regiment during the New Guinea Campaign in World War II, he had won the Distinguished Service Cross and two Silver Stars for heroism during that conflict. Following the war he had served for a time as the assistant commandant of the

---

[26] 2d Bn, 24th Inf Rgt, Command Rpt for Feb 51, 12 Mar 51, box 3841, RG 407, WNRC; 24th Inf Rgt Unit Rpts 46, 15 Feb 51, and 47, 16 Feb 51, both in box 3841, RG 407, WNRC. Enemy dispositions are mentioned in 24th Inf Rgt Opns Order 26, 14 Feb 51, box 3841, RG 407, WNRC. The stream of visitors is noted in 24th Inf Rgt Exec Ofcr's Daily Journal, 16 Feb 51, box 3841, RG 407, WNRC.

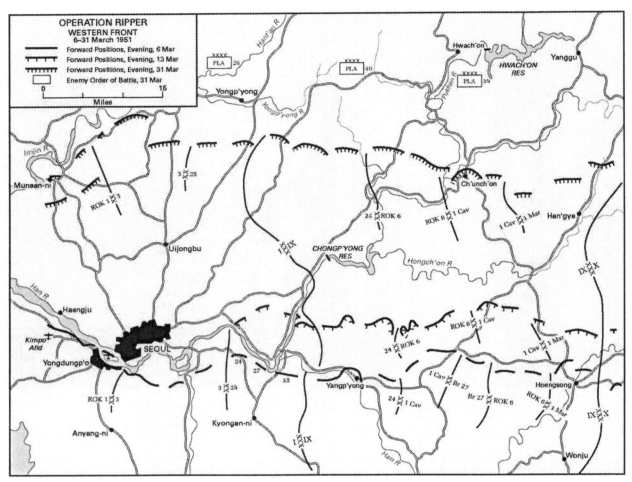

Map 16

Infantry School, but shortly after North Korea invaded South Korea, he had been appointed the assistant commander of the 2d Infantry Division. Evacuated shortly after that unit's disastrous retreat from the Ch'ongch'on, he had spent much of December and January in the hospital and had just returned to the field. According to Michaelis, Bradley was somewhat high strung with a nervous stomach. "Any time before any major engagement, he'd get violently ill. . . . He was a good division commander other than that. He ran it well, delegated."[27]

Arriving at P'abalmak on 20 February, the day after taking command, Bradley came into immediate conflict with Colonel Corley, who apparently disagreed with him on what dispositions were best for the 24th Infantry. According to a staff member present at the time, the regiment's assistant operations officer, white 1st Lt. John S. Komp, Corley had set elements of the unit in a defensive position on the back side of a slope, the sort of location that keeps troops safe from enemy artillery but is otherwise dif-

---

[27] Office of the Secretary of Defense for Public Affairs (OSDPA) Press Release, sub: Major General Joseph Sladen

Bradley, n.d., CMH files; Interv, Clay Blair with John H. Michaelis, n.d., U.S. Army Military History Institute (MHI) Senior Officer Oral History Program, Combat Leadership in Korea series, MHI, p. XXII-81, Carlisle Barracks, Pa.

ficult to defend unless the men are well disciplined and experienced. The reason why Corley made the decision to adopt that posture is unknown, but he clearly believed his troops could do the job. While he was never sure of the regiment, he told an inspector general on 14 February, he believed the unit was up to any task it received. Casualty rates would be high, "but we get better every day."[28]

Bradley, according to Komp, was of a different mind. The ensuing argument became so loud, according to Komp, that everyone present could hear it. In an attempt to create privacy, Bradley took Corley aside, but the effort had little effect. Finally, Komp said, the general told Corley in tones audible well outside the headquarters, "Perhaps you'd understand me better if you stood at attention!" What Bradley said next was inaudible, but shortly thereafter Corley left the regiment and the unit's executive officer, Lt. Col. Paul F. Roberts, took temporary charge.[29]

If Corley had been relieved of command, it was hardly to the advantage of either Bradley or his superiors that the fact should become general knowledge. The officer was revered by the men of the 24th, almost all of whom stood in awe of him.[30] That he should have been disciplined could only have harmed their confidence in the division's command. At the same time the black newspaper reporters who covered the 24th Infantry also thought highly of the colonel. They would have inevitably scrutinized the reasons for his relief and might well have sided with him in print. Although it is difficult to say how the black community would have responded, some sort of outcry might have developed. The effect would inevitably highlight the Army's policy of segregation and the service's continued intolerance for the black soldier.[31] Whatever the reason, the regimental executive officer's journal for the day said nothing about Corley's relief. Instead, it noted blandly that the officer had left for the 25th Division's clearing station at 1320 for ten days and that Bradley had arrived at 1645, more than three hours later.[32]

As for Corley himself, he never said anything about the episode, stating in his interview with the *Pittsburgh Courier* that he had been evacuated because of a bad back. In the end he was promoted to brigadier general, but unlike Michaelis, who was already on the list for promotion and would ultimately achieve four stars, it took him twelve more years to reach the rank. During that time, his wife noted in an interview years later, because of his defense of the 24th in his interview with the *Pittsburgh Courier*, he was under orders at least

28 Ltr, Komp to MacGarrigle, 15 Jun 94. Quote from Interv, Inspector General (IG) with Col John T. Corley, 14 Feb 51, exhibit B–134, in General Headquarters, Far East Command, Report of Investigation Regarding Alleged Irregularities in the Administration of Military Justice in the 25th Infantry Division, 27 Mar 51, boxes 1013–1014 (hereafter cited as Far East Command Inspector General Investigation), RG 159, WNRC.

29 Ltr, Komp to MacGarrigle, 15 Jun 94. Gustav Gillert also witnessed the argument. He remembers Bradley telling Corley, "You can blame it on your back," but he adds that "[Corley] made the mistake of taking on the CG [Bradley] and thinking they needed him to 'handle' the 24th." See Interv, MacGarrigle with Gustav J. Gillert, 4 May 94. Baranowski says much the same thing, observing that while he was not a witness to the argument, he had heard the story afterward from an officer who had been present. He mentions that Corley may have forced Bradley's hand during the argument by committing an act of insubordination. The colonel avowed, he said, that he believed he could "get along quite well without [Bradley's] . . . guidance," or words to that effect. See Intervs, MacGarrigle with Joseph Baranowski, 24 Aug and 6 Sep 94. Baranowski's version is hearsay. Except for the comment about possible insubordination, however, it is a virtual duplicate of Komp's and Gillert's eyewitness reports. Clay Blair questions whether Corley was relieved of command, quoting Michaelis to the effect that Corley knew he could never get along with Bradley and therefore chose to depart. See Blair, *The Forgotten War*, p. 684. The daily journal of the regimental executive officer supports that view by giving a different sequence of events. It puts Corley's departure more than three hours before Bradley's arrival. See 24th Inf Rgt Exec Ofcr's Daily Journal, 20 Feb 51, box 3770, RG 407, WNRC. In

light of Komp's and Gillert's recollection and the reminiscences of Baranowski, those versions seem suspect. Indeed, Michaelis was no more present at the event than Baranowski, and Komp and Gillert had no reason to lie. As for the regiment and Corley, however, both had every reason to cover up what happened.

30 Interv, MacGarrigle with Baranowski, 24 Aug 94. Out of all of the interviews conducted in the research for this study, there were only two individuals who did not have a high opinion of Corley. See Bussey, *Firefight at Yechon*, pp. 212–15; Interv, Timothy Rainey with Conway Jones, 26 Mar 90.

31 See Whisonant, "True Story of the 24th: Colonel Corley Gives Facts to Courier War Reporter," p. 1, and "Whisonant's Answer," p. 10.

32 24th Inf Rgt Exec Ofcr's Daily Journal, 20 Feb 51.

part of the time to stay away from the press. "[General] Mark Clark got on my husband in September [1951] when we first arrived," she said. "At that time he was getting a lot of inquiries about the 24th, when they were getting ready to break it up. . . . John talked to reporters and mentioned individual cases of heroism." Corley retired from the Army in 1966.[33]

The Han River Crossing

In the days that followed Corley's departure, Roberts moved the 24th up to the Han River. There the unit conducted patrols and improved its defenses by preparing alternate positions, laying mines, and stringing thousands of yards of barbed wire. By 1 March the regiment was firmly entrenched and speculation was beginning to rise about when the Eighth Army would attempt a crossing and the possible role of the 24th.[34] (Map 17)

On 3 March the 25th Division answered those questions. Roberts received word that the main attack would come to the right of his unit in sectors controlled by the 27th and 35th Infantries and farther east in the IX Corps zone. The 24th would use its 2d Battalion to conduct a diversionary attack on the left flank designed to broaden the 25th Division's front and to prevent the enemy from rushing troops to the main crossing points when their locations became clear. The 3d Battalion was to prepare to reinforce the 2d's attack. The 1st, assisted by the 2d Battalion of the 27th Infantry, was to support the crossing by firing into enemy positions from hills to the rear of the bridgehead overlooking the Han. If all went well and the 25th Division's attack succeeded, General Barth told commanders during a visit to the regiment, the terrain gained might well become the hinge upon which the Eighth Army would swing back north to the 38th Parallel.[35]

In preparation for the assault, code-named RIPPER, tanks began patrolling along the bank of the Han in the 24th's sector to determine enemy positions and by their presence to draw the defenders' attention away from areas to the east where the main attack would occur. On 4 March the 1st Battalion of the 7th Infantry regiment (3d Infantry Division) moved up to assume the positions of the 2d Battalion of the 24th, allowing that unit to begin a program of vigorous training for the crossing. Meanwhile, the 77th Engineer Combat Battalion and Company A of the 65th Engineer Combat Battalion began preparations to construct a footbridge on the day of the attack. The units would also build two motor rafts, one of eight tons capable of carrying three jeeps or their equivalent, the other of fifty tons and large enough for tanks.[36]

Information on the enemy was scarce, but extensive photographic coverage from observation planes revealed that both the far bank of the Han and the mountains beyond were heavily fortified. Forays by tanks toward the river also attracted heavy artillery and antitank fire, making it clear that the enemy intended to mount a determined defense. Under the circumstances, since only overwhelming firepower stood any chance of preventing heavy casualties within the attacking force, the 25th Division's artillery planned to conduct one of the heaviest artillery preparations of the war, firing 5,000 rounds over a mere twenty minutes from the more than 150 howitzers available near the 25th Division's zone. In addition, some sixty-three tanks and thirty-six 4.2-inch mortars would combine their fire with that of every other heavy weapon in the division, from antitank guns to quadruple-mounted 50-caliber machine guns normally employed in antiaircraft batteries. In all, excluding munitions to be expended in air strikes against targets of opportunity after the sun came up and air controllers could begin to operate, planners intended to fire off close to nineteen thousand artillery, tank, and mortar rounds prior to the assault.[37]

33 Corley, "I Was Proud of My Men: Colonel Corley's Story," p. 1; Interv, Cash with Mrs. John T. Corley, 2 Nov 89.
34 24th Inf Rgt Narrative Summary for Feb 51, p. 5; 24th Inf Rgt Command Rpt for Mar 51, 14 Apr 51, p. 1, box 3842, RG 407, WNRC.
35 24th Inf Rgt Command Rpt for Mar 51, 14 Apr 51, pp. 1–4; Barth, Tropic Lightning and Taro Leaf in Korea, n.d., p. 67.
36 24th Inf Rgt Command Rpt for Mar 51, 14 Apr 51, p. 2.
37 Ibid., pp. 3–5; Barth, Tropic Lightning and Taro Leaf in Korea, n.d., pp. 67–69. Artillery statistics and ammunition expenditures are from a condensation of the commander's

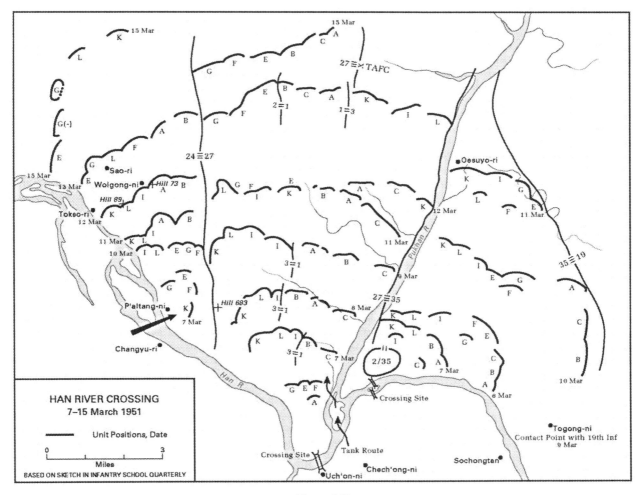

Map 17

Since any forward movement by artillery or engineering units would alert the enemy to an impending attack, commanders went to extremes to hide bridging equipment in nearby streambeds and to disguise newly prepared artillery positions by moving tanks into them as soon as possible. Tanks also made continual sorties toward the river during the nights prior to the crossing. The hope was that the enemy would become so used to their noise that he would disregard the clamor that would inevitably arise when the time for the final attack came and tanks

moved forward pulling trailers loaded with assault boats. Apparently the ruse worked. On the night of 6 March, when the tanks delivered their cargo and assumed firing positions along the river's bank, the enemy failed to respond with a single shot.[38]

The attack began before first light on 7 March, at 0545 precisely. For twenty minutes, General Barth recalled, the guns of the 25th Division

kept up an almost continuous roar as 5,000 shells arched across the river, making bright bursts of light as they exploded. We could see the flashes as forty-five

---

report on the operation. See "Operation RIPPER," *Infantry School Quarterly* 39 (October 1951): 13–16.

[38] Barth, Tropic Lightning and Taro Leaf in Korea, n.d., p. 69.

tanks and forty anti-aircraft guns fired over the heads of the men on the river bank waiting to launch their boats for the assault. Far to the left but out of sight, the fire of the guns and tanks in support of the 24th Infantry . . . lit up the river. The spectacle was one I'll never forget. It resembled a Fourth of July celebration, but one designed for death and not amusement. I watched anxiously and breathed a sigh of relief when the cannonade ended without a single round falling short on our infantry. . . . At 6:15 the artillery fire lifted to targets well back from the river bank, and in the dim light of dawn the assault boats of the infantry crossed.[39]

All three regiments of the 25th Division launched their attacks at the same moment. In the center Companies I and L of Colonel Check's 27th Infantry made the principal crossing, using a landing site with a firm and trafficable beach, well serviced by all-weather roads, that the North Koreans had employed as a point of debarkation for ferries transporting vehicles across the Han. By 0742 the two units had their initial objectives in hand, and by midmorning, with a footbridge in place, the rest of the regiment was streaming across the river.[40]

The enemy's response was halfhearted and hardly more than a harassment to the men, in part because of the furious barrage that had preceded the assault and in part because Company C of the 89th Medium Tank Battalion had managed to ford the river some eight hundred yards east of the regiment's main bridgehead. Its appearance in that area outflanked enemy positions opposing the 27th's crossing and, in combination with an assault by the 1st Battalion of the 27th about the same time, so surprised an enemy artillery battery that its men abandoned their guns and fled in terror. The 24th Infantry also contributed. Firing from the west across the river, which made a wide curve at that point, a 75-mm. recoilless rifle platoon from the unit's 1st Battalion delivered at least one hundred and seventy rounds into the back side of a hill

the 27th had been assigned to assault. The fire caught the enemy off guard and saved many lives in the attacking force. By 1700 the 27th had advanced between four and five thousand yards inland and was digging in for the night. It had suffered six killed and thirty-six wounded.[41]

To the right of the 27th, the 35th Infantry had a more difficult time. Taking advantage of the shock delivered by the artillery, the unit's 3d Battalion made the crossing with ease and rapidly moved into the lee of a railway embankment intersecting its area of operations. By that time, however, the enemy was recovering and a series of mishaps had begun to occur. Although a footbridge that was supposed to speed the unit's crossing was constructed on time, the structure's moorings were too weak to hold against the river's current, which was running at least five miles per hour faster than planners had anticipated. As a result, one end of the bridge broke loose and swung back against the opposite shore. With daylight advancing and enemy fire increasing, all attempts to rebuild the footway in time to assist the attack proved unsuccessful. In the same way, a fifty-ton floating bridge for vehicles was under construction, but enemy fire was so heavy that the engineers were unable to complete it until the following morning. When the men of the 35th began to cross in assault boats, an enemy gun concealed at the mouth of a railway tunnel added to the havoc. Although Barth's artillery found and destroyed the weapon, before that happened it succeeded in sinking two of the regiment's assault boats, causing many casualties.[42]

In the end the 35th still managed to make its way, using the assault boats, two amphibious trucks, and a small ferry. Four out of its five tanks also got across, despite considerable doubt at first that the ford they had found was shallow enough to use. By 1415 the regiment was on its objectives. By 1600 Colonel Kelleher had ordered all battalions to emplace their tanks, register their artillery, and dig

39 Ibid., pp. 69–70.

40 Unit History, 27th Inf Rgt, Mar 51, n.d., pp. 2–5, box 3851, RG 407, WNRC. The story of the recoilless rifle platoon is told in 1st Bn, 24th Inf Rgt, Periodic Opns Rpt 139, 8 Mar 51, box 3842, RG 407, WNRC. Casualty statistics are from 27th Inf Rgt Command Rpt for Mar 51, S–1 Summary, Casualty List, box 3851, RG 407, WNRC.

41 Ibid.

42 35th Inf Rgt Command Rpt for Mar 51, 14 Apr 51, pp. 11–16, box 3861, RG 407, WNRC; Barth, Tropic Lightning and Taro Leaf in Korea, n.d., p. 70.

in for the night. In all, the regiment had lost seven killed and thirty-three wounded in the attack.[43]

To the left of the 27th, the 24th Infantry had its share of problems, but they seemed minor during the first day of the attack. Company F, commanded by black 1st Lt. George M. Shuffer, took the lead, with the mission of establishing and securing a beachhead. The unit made its way to the target without undue opposition, but during the crossing the swift current disorganized some elements of the force. Seeing the problem and exercising good leadership, Shuffer stepped in immediately, corrected the situation, and pressed on with the mission. By 0800 he and his men were on their objective, the western edge of Hill 688, near the seam between their regiment and the 27th Infantry.[44]

By then, the enemy had recovered from the shock of the artillery barrage and had begun to concentrate heavy small-arms and automatic-weapons fire on a footbridge and landing rafts the engineers had begun to build. The engineers finished the footbridge in short order, but enemy artillery in the hills beyond the landing site scored a direct hit on a heavy barge they were assembling. A number of men were either killed or wounded. By midmorning, nonetheless, at least the footbridge was in place and in full use.[45]

Company E, which crossed the Han shortly after Shuffer's unit, had slightly harder going than Company F, but by 0945 it too was on its objective, a few hundred feet to the northwest of Company F. Company G crossed later in the morning. By 1600 it was in place just to the southwest of Company E,

where it guarded the stretch between that unit and the river. Company K of the 3d Battalion crossed the Han at 1300. Under the operational control of the 2d Battalion, it fell into position just above the river to the south of Company F to protect that unit's flank. By 1730 all of the 24th's forward units were in place and buttoned up for the night. The remainder of the regiment remained south of the Han, where it could be available to react immediately if an emergency arose either in its own sector or that of the 27th Infantry to the east. It had lost two killed and thirty-four wounded.[46]

All remained quiet overnight in the 27th's and 35th's sectors. Shortly after first light the next morning, both regiments moved out in good order. Enemy resistance was so light that each secured its objectives by early afternoon.[47]

The 24th Infantry found the going more difficult. At 0315 on 8 March Company F came under heavy attack by an estimated reinforced battalion. Within five minutes the unit's commander reported that the enemy had penetrated his company's position. Shortly thereafter, the commander of Company E also called to report that his unit was under attack and that grenades were coming into his position from the rear. About that time several squads of men in forward platoons were overrun, and Company G began to receive fire. At 0530, with Company G holding, the two forward units pulled back to form a perimeter while still clinging to the ridge overlooking the river. There they held, taking a heavy toll of the enemy.[48]

[43] 35th Inf Rgt Command Rpt for Mar 51, 14 Apr 51, pp. 11–16. Casualty statistics are from ibid., S–1 Summary, Casualty List.

[44] 2d Bn, 24th Inf Rgt, Command Rpt for Mar 51, 4 Apr 51, p. 1, box 3842, RG 407, WNRC. Recommendation for Silver Star Award, with attachments, 1st Lt George M. Shuffer, 18 Apr 51, box 168, RG 338, WNRC, hereafter cited as Shuffer Award Recommendation; 24th Inf Rgt Unit Rpt 66, 7 Mar 51, box 3842, RG 407, WNRC. See also "Operation RIPPER," pp. 24–25. Shuffer retired from the Army as a brigadier general. He states that the current did not affect the early crossings but did have some effect on those that came later. See Intervs, William T. Bowers with George M. Shuffer, 5 and 6 Dec 94.

[45] 2d Bn, 24th Inf Rgt, Command Rpt for Mar 51, 4 Apr 51, p. 1. The hit on the barge is mentioned by Barth, Tropic Lightning and Taro Leaf in Korea, n.d., p. 70.

[46] 2d Bn, 24th Inf Rgt, Command Rpt for Mar 51, 4 Apr 51; Shuffer Award Recommendation; 24th Inf Rgt Unit Rpt 66, 7 Mar 51; 24th Inf Rgt Command Rpt for Mar 51, 14 Apr 51, S–1 Rpt Casualty Statistics (1–31 Mar 51), box 3842, RG 407, WNRC; "Operation RIPPER," pp. 24–25. See also Intervs, MacGarrigle with Clayton, 10 and 11 Aug 94; Baranowski, 24 Aug 94; Creel, 3 Nov and 3 Dec 93; Bowers with Shuffer, 5 and 6 Dec 94; Muehlbauer with Lindsey Bowers, 20 Apr 89; George W. Brown, 28 Feb 89; Kahoe, 5 Dec 88; Arthur Thompson, 14 Sep 88; Levine White, n.d.; Cash with William M. Dandridge, 7 Aug 88; Carey A. Harris, 8 Sep 89; Oscar Robinson, 18 Aug 88; Robert H. Yancy, 21 Jan 89.

[47] Unit History, 27th Inf Rgt, Mar 51, pp. 2–5; 35th Inf Rgt Command Rpt for Mar 51, pp. 11–16.

[48] The best description of what happened appears in Colonel Clayton's award recommendation for Lieutenant Shuffer. See Shuffer Award Recommendation. See also Intervs,

Although it seemed for a time that the 2d Battalion might lose the bridgehead and the unit's command post took the precaution of withdrawing back across the Han, Colonel Clayton stayed forward with his men. Meanwhile, within an increasingly pressed Company F, Lieutenant Shuffer moved through intense small-arms and mortar fire to reassure his troops and to see to the care of the wounded. At one point, Company E lost contact with Shuffer and his men but reported that it could hear considerable small-arms fire coming from their direction. With the dawn, enemy fire from higher on the hill concentrated with great accuracy upon individual foxholes, but commanders once more prevailed upon their men to hold their ground. There was no panic. At 0700 the hard-pressed battalion counterattacked but made only marginal gains. As a result, at 1105 Clayton ordered Company K into the line to the right of Company F. Even with the extra weight, however, the 2d Battalion was unable to regain the ground it had lost. At nightfall, despite inflicting severe casualties on the enemy, it was still 300 yards short of its position on the previous day.[49]

The battalion resumed the attack at 0655 the next day, following a five-minute artillery and mortar barrage. Although Company G was pinned by enemy fire for a time, the men of Company K moved up the hill against only light resistance. Entering the enemy's former position, they found that the Chinese had pulled back in such haste that they had discarded enough equipment to supply the better part of a company—15 Japanese 25-caliber rifles; up to 150 U.S., Japanese, and Russian rifles; 6 machine guns; 3 Johnson automatic rifles; 5 Bren guns; 3 pole charges; and 4 boxes of 60-mm. mortar ammunition. In all, over the two-day fight the enemy had suffered 446 killed and 72 captured. As for Companies E and F of the 24th,

Men of the 24th Regimental Combat Team shield themselves from exploding mortar shells.

they had incurred a total of 17 killed and 85 wounded out of a line strength of no more than two hundred and forty men. Significantly, despite those losses, which approached 50 percent, both units were so solid that each remained an effective fighting force. Indeed, the next day, despite their losses, the men of the 2d Battalion secured the slopes of Hill 688 and tied in with the 27th Infantry to their east. They then joined with the 3d Battalion in launching tank-infantry patrols to the north to feel out enemy positions for the following day's attack. In the process, they assisted in routing two enemy companies, inflicting 75 killed and capturing 17 prisoners of war.[50]

With that the enemy began a phased withdrawal, moving to the rear in stages behind screening forces that kept his opponents at bay at little

---

Bowers with Shuffer, 5 and 6 Dec 94. For additional accounts, see 2d Bn, 24th Inf Rgt, Command Rpt for Mar 51, 4 Apr 51, p. 1; 2d Bn, 24th Inf Rgt, Periodic Opns Rpt 147, 8 Mar 51, box 3842, RG 407, WNRC; "Operation RIPPER," pp. 24–25. The timing of events and summaries of radio calls can be found in 2d Bn, 24th Inf Rgt, S–3 Journal, 8 Mar 51, box 3842, RG 407, WNRC.

[49] Ibid.

[50] 2d Bn, 24th Inf Rgt, Periodic Opns Rpt 148, 9 Mar 51, box 3842, RG 407, WNRC. The equipment is tallied in 2d Bn, 24th Inf Rgt, Periodic Opns Rpt 150, 11 Mar 51, box 3842, RG 407, WNRC. See also 2d Bn, 24th Inf Rgt, G–3 Journal, 8 Mar 51, box 3842, RG 407, WNRC. The fighting on 9 March 1951 is mentioned in 2d Bn, 24th Inf Rgt, Periodic Opns Rpt 149, 10 Mar 51, box 3842, RG 407, WNRC; U.S. I Corps Command Rpt for Mar 51, p. 62, box 1517, RG 407, WNRC.

long-term cost. On 10 March the 2d and 3d Battalions of the 24th launched a coordinated assault that covered up to twelve hundred yards in just a few hours. By 1100 that morning, the two units had reached their objectives and had launched patrols to the next ridge line. Those probes came up against the enemy's well-entrenched screening force, experienced heavy mortar and small-arms fire, and made no further headway. Even so, the next day, when the 1st Battalion of the 24th relieved the 2d on the line and moved forward with the 3d, the two units met with only slight opposition and forward patrols reported no enemy resistance. The same pattern occurred over the days that followed throughout the 25th Division. Wherever roads were lacking, slopes were steep, and natural approaches were few, the enemy took his toll but then fell back. Overall, attacking units encountered tank obstacles and some small-arms and automatic weapons fire but had little difficulty keeping to their schedules. Between 7 and 14 March, as a result, the 25th Division advanced eight miles with relative ease. On 14 March word arrived that the enemy was abandoning Seoul. The next day, I Corps moved to secure Line Golden, a stretch of high ground that extended to the north and east of the city.[51]

During the advance, on 11 March, Col. Henry C. Britt had taken charge as commander of the 24th Infantry regiment, replacing the acting commander, Roberts, who returned to the United States. One week later, Lt. Col. Hugh D. Coleman took over as the regiment's executive officer. A graduate of the West Point class of 1932, Britt had nowhere near the pedigree of the much decorated Corley, but he was on the spot and available since he was already serving as the assistant intelligence officer of General Milburn's I Corps. In addition, he had experience in dealing with black troops. He won two Bronze Stars and two Commendation Ribbons during the Italian campaign of World War II while serving as a battalion commander and regimental executive officer in the all-black 92d Infantry Division.[52]

Whatever Britt's qualifications, the colonel failed to make much of an impression on the men he had come to command. During more than two hundred interviews, not one enlisted veteran of the 24th mentioned him. The officers were more familiar with him, but even they had little to say, and those who did tended to give lukewarm appraisals. The regiment's white assistant operations officer, Lieutenant Komp, thought well enough of him. Having endured enemy attacks with White, Champeny, and Britt in Korea, he said, he had come to the conclusion that all three officers were "cool under fire and quite capable of making decisions."[53] One of the regiment's most experienced white combat commanders, Colonel Clayton, was less positive. Remarking that he saw Britt in a forward position only once between March and May 1951—in sharp contrast to Corley, who was often up front with the troops—he implied that the commander was much more detached from the fighting than he should have been. Since Britt relieved Clayton of command in May, Clayton's opinion may be suspect, but the white executive officer of the 3d Battalion, Capt. Buckner Creel, agreed with him, remarking that Britt rarely came forward and hardly seemed as dedicated to his job as Corley. The 1st Battalion's commander at the time, white Maj. Roscius Newell, made much the same observation. Britt never came up to visit units in the field, he said. Instead, after dark, battalion commanders, "myself, Clayton, and [Lt. Col. William D.] Mouchet, would have to travel three to five miles to reach Britt's CP. Normally we were tired and dirty, while he was well rested and wore starched fatigues." Black Chaplain Gray Johnson compared Britt to Corley, remarking that Corley's accommodations were always austere but that Britt

[51] U.S. I Corps Command Rpt for Mar 51, pp. 62–85; "Operation RIPPER," pp. 27–30; U.S. Eighth Army Command Rpt for Mar 51, sec. 1, Narrative, and U.S. I Corps Opns Directive 48, 15 Mar 50, both in box 1517, RG 407, WNRC. The men of the 24th called the line Lincoln, but most histories refer to it as Line Golden.

[52] *Register of Graduates and Former Cadets of the United States Military Academy* (West Point, N.Y.: Association of Graduates, USMA, 1993), p. 231.

[53] Ltr, Komp to MacGarrigle, 15 Jun 94. Komp made the point that he never came under attack when Corley was regimental commander.

Colonel Britt after receiving the Silver Star for gallantry in action

set up his command post like a fortress, a source of much amusement to the men. Britt for his part appears to have felt little affinity for his regiment. According to the white former commander of Company B at Sangju and Masan, Capt. William A. Hash, who served with the officer in an assignment following the Korean War, Britt never had anything good to say about the 24th.[54]

For all of the hard fighting between 1 and 15 March, Operation RIPPER failed to have much effect upon the enemy's overall combat capabilities. As United Nations forces poured across the Han, their Chinese and North Korean opponents managed to keep the bulk of their forces and supplies just out of reach by fighting a delaying action on the high, rugged ground to the front of the advancing force.

Laying mines in likely bivouac areas and along roads and trails, they sometimes put up a fierce resistance, but more often they took what toll they could and then pulled back before becoming heavily engaged.[55] (Map 18)

On 21 March, in an attempt to destroy the enemy forces and materiel that remained to his immediate front, General Ridgway began moving I Corps in stages toward Line Kansas, some thirty miles above Seoul and extending in a northeasterly direction along high ground just to the south of the 38th Parallel. While the 1st South Korean Division held the left flank of the attack, the U.S. 3d Infantry Division took to the center, and Bradley's 25th Division swung from the right. Within the 25th Division, the 24th and 27th Infantry regiments would make assaults, but the 24th would be the spearhead. In a special briefing, General Bradley informed the officers of the regiment that he knew they would appreciate the honor and that he believed the unit was ready to do the job. The instructions under which they were to operate were simple. The attacking force was to take on any enemy within its reach that was strong enough to jeopardize friendly units.[56]

The attack began on the morning of 22 March with the 24th Infantry encountering minefields and sporadic enemy resistance. The 1st Battalion in particular came up against enemy groups concealed in caves and had to root them out one by one with flamethrowers and grenades. Meanwhile, two communications jeeps hit mines with a loss of three killed and five wounded. By day's end, despite long gains, the regiment was short of its objectives, but when the assault continued the next morning, the fighting went well. Although the regiment continued to be annoyed by mines, the enemy lacked the resources and materiel to put up a concerted resis-

[54] Intervs, MacGarrigle with Creel, 3 Nov and 3 Dec 93; William A. Hash, 9 Jun 94; Clayton, 10 and 11 Aug 94; Newell, 10 and 15 Nov 94; Cash with Gray Johnson, 23 Mar 89; Ltr, George A. Clayton to George L. MacGarrigle, 9 Sep 94. CMH files.

[55] 25th Inf Div Command Rpt for Mar 51, 15 Apr 51, pp. 9–15, box 3779, RG 407, WNRC; 24th Inf Rgt Opns Order 42, 15 Mar 51, box 3842, RG 407, WNRC; Mossman, Ebb and Flow, p. 334.

[56] 25th Inf Div Command Rpt for Mar 51, 15 Apr 51, p. 8; 24th Inf Rgt Opns Order 29, 21 Mar 51, box 3842, RG 407, WNRC; Mossman, Ebb and Flow, p. 335. Bradley's talk is mentioned in 24th Inf Rgt Exec Ofcr's Daily Journal, 21 Mar 51, box 3842. RG 407. WNRC.

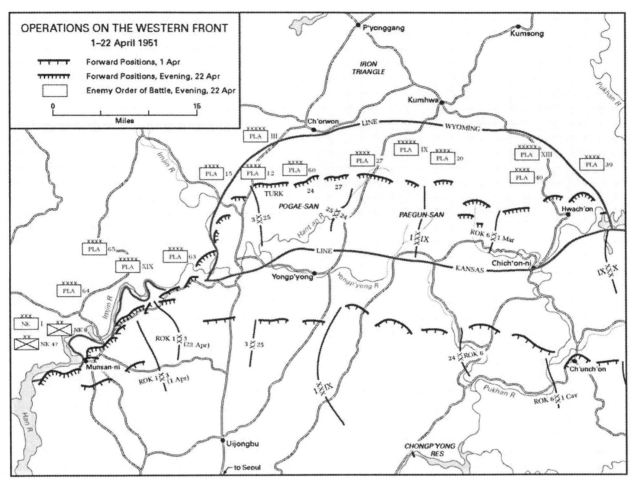

Map 18

tance and backed off to bide his time. So it went over the next several days. The enemy fell back after making some initial resistance while the 24th Infantry along with the rest of the 25th Division made considerable gains at moderate cost. The 24th, for one, except for its losses on 22 March, suffered no killed and fewer than fifty wounded during the period.[57]

Although the assault was progressing in good order, General Ridgway had no doubt that the enemy retained the ability to mount a counterattack employing tens of thousands of troops. In that case, even if United Nations forces inflicted heavy casualties, they were so thinly spread that they would inevitably have to give way. Rather than see another disaster of the sort that had occurred at Kunu-ri, followed by another retreat from Seoul, the general ordered the construction of strong fallback positions just to the north of Seoul along Line Golden.

The regiments and artillery batteries of the Eighth Army would provide supervisory personnel for the effort, but most of the construction was to be performed by some two thousand South Korean

---

[57] 1st Bn, 24th Inf Rgt, Periodic Opns Rpt 155, 23 Mar 51, box 3842, RG 407, WNRC; Mossman, *Ebb and Flow*, pp. 337–44. Casualties are taken from 24th Inf Rgt Command Rpt for Mar 51, 14 Apr 51, S–1 Rpt Casualty Statistics (1–31 Mar 51).

Men of the 24th Infantry adjust cases of ammo on "A" frames of Korean porters.

laborers. Stringing wire, surveying fields of fire, rigging trip flares, and laying mines, crews were to build enough gun emplacements and camouflaged bunkers to protect both the city and the Han River crossings from an all-out enemy attack. In locations where stony ground prevented digging, they were even to blast foxholes so that everything would be in readiness for a strong defense if a pullback to the position became necessary. By 23 April, just in the sector assigned to the 25th Division, workers had completed 786 crew-served weapons positions, installed 74,000 yards of double-apron fence, strung 5,400 rolls of barbed wire, put down 510,000 sandbags, and laid out 30,000 pounds of demolitions.[58]

As the 25th Division's advance neared Line Kansas, enemy resistance increased. On 28 March the 24th Infantry came up against an estimated reinforced regiment well entrenched in difficult terrain. Despite artillery support and repeated attacks, it proved unable to break through and had to pull back with heavy casualties in some units. The 1st Battalion alone incurred some five killed and sixty wounded. True to form, however, the enemy backed off the next morning, allowing the 24th, with the assistance of the 27th Infantry regiment on its right

flank and the 187th Infantry regiment on its left, to sweep the position with little difficulty. The force then began to advance swiftly. On 30 March the 27th took the 24th's place in the line, allowing the regiment to pull back into reserve.[59]

Crossing the Hant'an

By 5 April the 25th Division had advanced to Line Kansas and the heights overlooking the Hant'an River, a narrow and relatively shallow but rapidly flowing tributary to the Imjin. The next day, orders arrived for the 25th to cross the river and to continue in stages to a line named Wyoming, which looped about twenty miles farther north toward what was known as the Iron Triangle. This strategic rail and communications nexus was marked to the north by the town of P'yonggang and to the south by the towns of Ch'orwon on the west and Kumhwa on the east. If United Nations forces invested the region, so the reasoning went, they would cause many enemy casualties and impede the enemy's ability to move troops and supplies into forward areas.[60] (Map 19)

In preparation for the attack, on the night of 9–10 April the 5th Ranger Company crossed the Hant'an near Hill 383, some four miles to the northeast of the bridgehead selected for the main attack. The unit secured the hill but had to pull back after a short time because of a strong enemy counterattack backed by mortars and automatic weapons.[61]

Undeterred by the enemy's vehement response, General Ridgway announced that day that the Eighth Army's attack would begin before dawn on the following morning, 11 April. To the west the 65th Infantry of the 3d Division reinforced by Philippine units and two companies from the 64th Tank Battalion would push north along Route 33, the main north-south road to

[58] 25th Inf Div Command Rpt for Mar 51, 15 Apr 51, p. 9; 25th Inf Div Command Rpt for Apr 51, 26 Jun 51, p. 1, box 3783, RG 407, WNRC; Barth, Tropic Lightning and Taro Leaf in Korea, n.d., p. 74; Mossman, Ebb and Flow, p. 366.

[59] 24th Inf Rgt Command Rpt for Mar 51, 14 Apr 51, pp. 15–16; 1st Bn, 24th Inf Rgt, Periodic Opns Rpts 160, 28 Mar 51, and 162, 30 Mar 51, both in box 3842, RG 407, WNRC; Barth, Tropic Lightning and Taro Leaf in Korea, n.d., p. 75.

[60] 25th Inf Div Command Rpt 5, 1–30 Apr 51, 8 Jul 51, p. 2, box 3779, RG 407, WNRC; Mossman, Ebb and Flow, pp. 348–49; Barth, Tropic Lightning and Taro Leaf in Korea, n.d., p. 75.

[61] 24th Inf Rgt Regimental Narrative Summary for Apr 51, p. 3, box 3843, RG 407, WNRC.

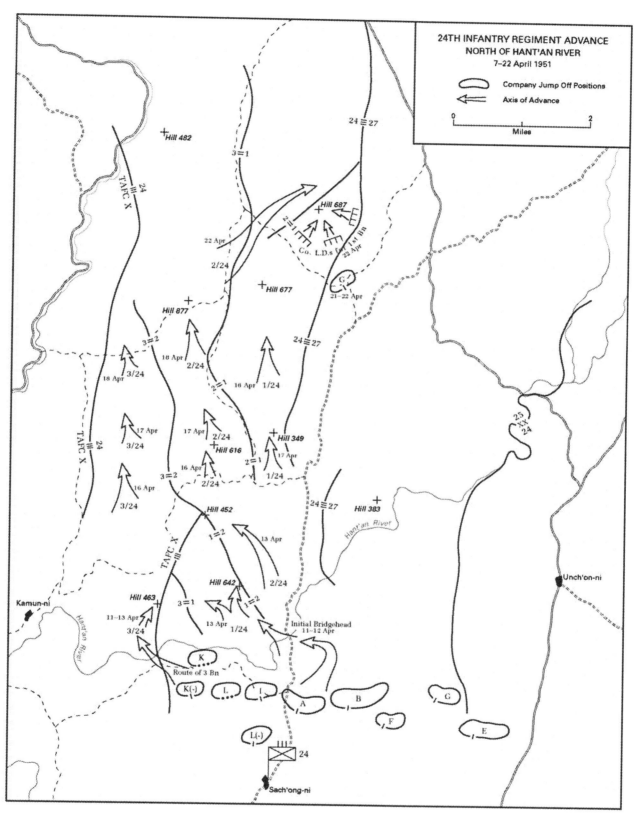

24TH INFANTRY REGIMENT ADVANCE
NORTH OF HANT'AN RIVER
7–22 April 1951

Company Jump Off Positions

Axis of Advance

0   1   2

Miles

+ Hill 482

+ Hill 687

24 ≡ 27

3 ≡ 1

TAFC X
24

2 ≡ 1
22 Apr

Co. L.D.s
Bn 1st Bn
22 Apr

2/24

+ Hill 677

G
21–22 Apr

+ Hill 877

24 ≡ 27

3 ≡ 2
18 Apr

18 Apr 2/24

18 Apr 3/24

2 ≡ 1
16 Apr 1/24

TAFC X
24

17 Apr
3/24

17 Apr 2/24

+ Hill 616

+ Hill 349
17 Apr

25
XX
24

16 Apr
3/24

3 ≡ 2
16 Apr

2/24

2 ≡ 1
1/24

+ Hill 452

1 ≡ 2

24 ≡ 27

+ Hill 383

13 Apr
2/24

Hant'an River

TAFC X
24

Hill 642

1 ≡ 2

Hill 463

3 ≡ 1

13 Apr 1/24

Initial Bridgehead
11–12 Apr

Unch'on-ni

Kamun-ni

Hant'an River

11–13 Apr
3/24

Route of 3 Bn

K

K(-)   L   I

A

B

G

F

E

L(-)

III 24

Sach'ong-ni

Map 19

Ch'orwon. The 25th Division would take the center, pressing toward the same objective through the rugged Pogae-san mountains. Advancing on the division's western and eastern flanks respectively, the Turkish Brigade and the 24th Infantry would spearhead the 25th's assault while the 27th and 35th Infantry regiments remained south of the Hant'an in reserve. Next in line to the right came the 24th Infantry Division, which would attack north along the Yongp'yong River valley. To its east in the IX Corps zone, the British 27th Brigade would clear enemy forces from the Paegun-san mountains.[62]

Facing his first major operation as a commander, Colonel Britt selected the 1st and 3d Battalions to make the crossing while putting the 2d Battalion in reserve. The commanders of the two assault battalions, experienced infantrymen from World War II, were well suited to the task. The 1st Battalion's commander, Major Baranowski, who had served as a company commander and battalion operations officer before taking command in April, had fought with his unit at Kunu-ri and knew it well. The 3d Battalion's commander, Colonel Mouchet, had replaced Blair in early December. Although the battalion's intelligence officer at the time, black Capt. Oliver Dillard, found him paternalistic, the officer had gone on to win the respect of his unit by attempting to be fair, maintaining a professional attitude, and demonstrating that he knew the business of commanding troops.[63]

Britt's original plan on 6 April called for the 1st Battalion to make a daylight crossing to secure a bridgehead while the 3d followed to add momentum to the attack. Based upon reconnaissance indicating that the heights across the river were held by strongly entrenched enemy forces, Britt decided to launch the assault at night to limit enemy observation as much as possible. On the day before the operation was to begin, however, he had second thoughts. Although patrols had confirmed that the site he had selected was the best available, he struck new orders on 10 April, the day before the attack was to begin. Under his new plan, so hastily devised it was apparently never written down, the 3d Battalion was to shift to the west and to cross in the sector controlled by the Turkish Brigade. The change in plans left little time for reconnaissance. Furthermore, the new location was not well suited either for a crossing or for the attack that was to follow into the hills above the river. According to Captain Dillard, it was a "terrible crossing site," and Mouchet was "outraged that we were trying to . . . attack here." The 3d Battalion executive officer, Captain Creel, agreed. Mouchet "was not pleased—perhaps a better word would be disgusted—with the regimental plan," he remarked in an interview, "but [he] saluted and set out to implement his portion of it."[64]

About twelve miles south of Ch'orwon, the location selected for the attack would have been difficult under any circumstances. Two hills dominated it, Hill 463 in the 3d Battalion's sector to the west, and Hill 642 in the 1st Battalion's zone to the east. Both were screened by trees and underbrush and dotted with well-concealed bunkers and hiding places from which the enemy could fire, and the draws that led toward the heights often con-

---

[62] Mossman, *Ebb and Flow*, pp. 371–72.
[63] Intervs, MacGarrigle with Creel, 3 Nov and 3 Dec 93; Yadon, 9 Dec 94; Stuart Force, 8 Aug 94; Baranowski, 24 Aug 94; Bowers with Oliver Dillard, 8 and 9 Mar 95. See also Rishell, *With a Black Platoon in Combat*, pp. 137–38; *Army Register*, 1951 and 1964 (Washington, D.C.: Government Printing Office, 1951 and 1964).

[64] 24th Inf Rgt Opns Instruction 53, 6 Apr 51, and Opns Order 32, 9 Apr 51, both in 24th Inf Rgt Command Rpt for Apr 51, box 3843, RG 407, WNRC. Quotes from Intervs, MacGarrigle with Creel, 20 Dec 94; Bowers with Dillard, 8 and 9 Mar 95. There is no written record of a new order being issued. Unit reports on 10 April make no mention of any change in plan and all patrolling was directed toward the regiment's front and not into the Turkish Brigade sector. See 24th Inf Rgt Unit Rpt 99, 10 Apr 51, and 3d Bn, 24th Inf Rgt, Unit Rpt 41, 10 Apr 51, both in 24th Inf Rgt Command Rpt for Apr 51, box 3843, RG 407, WNRC. The only explanation for the change in plan is provided by the regiment's executive officer and is unsatisfactory in several respects. See Interv, Edward C. Williamson with Hugh D. Coleman, Exec Ofcr, 24th Inf Rgt, 13 Jun 51, attachment to Eighth U.S. Army, Korea (EUSAK), Command Rpt, Hant'an River Crossing, May 51, CMH files, hereafter cited as Hant'an River Crossing Intervs. See also Intervs, MacGarrigle with Baranowski, 24 Aug 94; Creel, 3 Nov and 3 Dec 93.

Captain Dillard receives the Silver Star from General Bradley.

tained blind approaches that became virtual death traps by ending in sheer cliffs. Complicating matters even more, there was no bridge in the 3d Battalion's zone or in that of the Turkish Brigade just to the west. The men of both units would have to wade a sometimes shoulder-high stream in the dark using only ropes strung from bank to bank to steady themselves. An ungraded dirt trail led to the 1st Battalion's crossing. The Chinese had constructed a rude mud and stick bridge at the site but had carefully destroyed the structure's center span after retreating to the river's north bank. A patrol from the 24th had surveyed the break, however, and had assured the engineers that they would be able to span the gap with a mere twenty feet of planking.[65]

Despite the benefits that the trail and the bridge offered, the spot assigned to the men of the 1st Battalion was particularly dangerous. Not only was the river waist deep, 125 feet wide, and fast flowing, it also bent sharply to the south no more than a quarter of a mile to the west of the point where they were to cross. Flowing for almost a half-mile in that direction before looping north again through a deep gorge toward the 3d Battalion's crossing, it formed a finger of land surmounted by an eighty-meter-high knoll. Once the sun arose, enemy observers would have a clear view of the battalion's crossing site from that slope and would be able to dominate the area with machine guns and mortars.

The 24th began its attack at about 0430 on 11 April. There was virtually no enemy opposition at first because the unit achieved surprise by avoiding the sort of preparatory artillery barrage that would have signaled an imminent assault. Even so, problems began almost immediately, particularly in the 1st Battalion's zone. The patrol that had surveyed the bridge across the Hant'an had apparently made its measurements by eye rather than by tape. When the engineers arrived with precut timbers, they found that the gap they had to span was at least fifteen feet longer than they had planned. Because of the delay in construction that followed, Companies A and B had no choice but to wade across the river. As they did, several of the men slipped and were swept away, causing enough of a commotion to alert the enemy. As a result, when the first platoon to enter the river reached the far shore and proceeded up the bank, it was met with a challenge in the Chinese language and then a hail of grenades and machine-gun fire. One American was killed. In the fighting that followed, the wind and rain made it easy to conceal movement, but they impaired artillery and air support by limiting visibility throughout the area.[66]

[65] Hant'an River Crossing Intervs; 24th Inf Rgt Regimental Narrative Summary for Apr 51, p. 6; Intervs, Williamson with Coleman, 13 Jun 51, attachment to Hant'an River Crossing Intervs; MacGarrigle with Alfred F. Tittel, 23 May 94.

[66] 25th Inf Div Periodic Opns Rpt 21, 11 Apr 51, box 3784, RG 407, WNRC; 24th Inf Rgt Regimental Narrative Summary for Apr 51, pp. 5–6; Ltr, Joseph Baranowski to George L. MacGarrigle, n.d., CMH files; Intervs, MacGarrigle with Baranowski, 24 Aug 94; Williamson with 1st Lt Gordon J. Lippman, Cdr, Co A, 16 Jun 51; Sfc Willie Robinson, platoon sergeant, 1st Platoon, Co A, 16 Jun 51; 1st Lt Edward Greer, artillery liaison ofcr, 13 Jun 51. Last three attachments to Hant'an River Crossing Intervs.

Men of the 1st Battalion, 24th Infantry, fight with Chinese Communists north of the Hant'an River.

Those problems notwithstanding, the 1st Battalion began crossing the river and moved to the attack. Companies A and B took the lead but came under heavy fire and were almost immediately pinned down. That discouraged Company C from crossing, but strong leadership quickly asserted itself. The commander of the unit, who had crossed before his men, went back and rallied them. By then the engineers had repaired the bridge. Dodging machine-gun fire that continued to rake the structure, the men crossed and began their assault. The knoll that commanded the area and the machine guns that had tormented them became their first objectives, with the company's 1st Platoon taking responsibility. The attackers were driven back several times by grenades and automatic weapons, but they kept trying, and after three attempts, at about 0715, they captured the position.[67]

Meanwhile, the 2d Platoon of Company A formed a line of skirmishers and attacked across

an open field toward the 1st Battalion's main objective, Hill 642. While patrols reconnoitered the hill in search of a route to the top, other members of the 1st Battalion crawled forward to secure a firm foothold at the base of the mountain. In the fighting that followed, they knocked out a series of strongly fortified enemy positions with flamethrowers and hand grenades. The fighting was often vicious and sometimes touch and go. By 1835 on 11 April the men of the battalion were, as the unit's commander, Major Baranowski, reported, "pretty well beat up." Even so, the unit itself was well positioned in a crescent of companies along the south and southeastern approaches to the mountain. Although enemy dugouts were present and might have provided convenient overnight protection for the men, most of the troopers, despite their fatigue, preferred to dig their own foxholes. The enemy's positions were full of dead and infested with fleas.[68]

---

[67] 25th Inf Div Periodic Opns Rpt 21, 11 Apr 51; 24th Inf Rgt Regimental Narrative Summary for Apr 51, pp. 5–6.

[68] Ibid. Quote from Interv, Williamson with Baranowski, 12 Jun 51, attachment to Hant'an River Crossing Intervs. Ltr,

The 3d Battalion also experienced a hard crossing. There was no bridge in the unit's area, so its men had to wade the river with the assistance of ropes strung from shore to shore. According to the operations officer of the 3d Battalion, Maj. Stanley P. Swartz, the "water was swifter than hell, chest deep." About halfway across, a soldier stepped into a hole and fell. As the river carried him away, he screamed for help. Another did the same. The noise alerted the enemy, who began firing blindly into the dark toward the noise. In the confusion that followed, two men drowned and one platoon of Company K became partly disorganized. Nonetheless, as with the 1st Battalion, the unit reached shore, collected itself, and began to attack its objective, Hill 463. Company L followed shortly thereafter while Company I held to the rear in reserve.[69]

At dawn, around 0600, the enemy began firing his mortars. The troops at first moved well under the assault. By 0755 Company K reported that it was approaching its first objective, a ridge line that connected Hill 463 with Hill 642, but that it was receiving heavy fire from enemy bunkers along the side of the hill. At that time the unit began to run short of rifle ammunition and grenades and requested resupply by air. Visibility was too poor for an immediate air drop, but portions of the 1st Battalion, located to the east, began attacking toward the ridge line in hopes of relieving some of the pressure on the 3d Battalion.[70]

Over the next hour the situation in the 3d Battalion began to spin rapidly out of control. Waving flags, firing burp guns, and throwing grenades, the enemy launched a fierce counterattack into Company K's position. A machine gunner went down in the 2d Platoon. The unit began to waver and then to pull to the rear. From a forward observation post, the battalion's commander, Colonel Mouchet, radioed for the 1st Platoon to hold firm. It did, for a time, but then, under increasing pressure and taking casualties, it also began to pull back. In the confusion, disorder began to spread to Company L, which had also come under fire and was beginning to withdraw. When the men of the two units learned that Company I was still to the south of the river but under machine-gun fire from the opposite bank, they pushed westward into the Turkish zone. At that point, according to white 1st Lt. Alfred Tittel, a platoon leader in Company K, the withdrawal turned into a rout. If the Turks had not covered for the fleeing men, the commander of Company K, white 1st Lt. John L. Herren, said, the battalion would have incurred far greater losses than it did. As it was, the executive officer of the 24th Infantry, Colonel Coleman, would report that some two hundred and forty men from the 3d Battalion were missing from the unit when it finally made its way south of the Hant'an.[71]

The full extent of what was happening dawned only gradually on General Bradley at 25th Division headquarters. Regular reports had come in from the 24th Infantry throughout the morning of 11 April but no word that anything was amiss. At 1000, however, Bradley received an alarming message from the Turkish Brigade requesting permission to fire artillery on Hill 463 since Company K had withdrawn. Five minutes later a second message arrived with word that the 3d Battalion's commander had gone to the crossing site, "to personally sense the 3d Battalion sit-

Baranowski to MacGarrigle, n.d.; Intervs, MacGarrigle with Baranowski, 24 Aug 94; Williamson with Lippman, 16 Jun 51; Sfc Willie Robinson, 16 Jun 51; 1st Lt Edward Greer, 13 Jun 51. Last three attachments to Hant'an River Crossing Intervs.

[69] 25th Inf Div G–3 Journal, 11 Apr 51, box 3784, RG 407, WNRC; 24th Inf Rgt Regimental Narrative Summary for Apr 51, pp. 5–7; Hant'an River Crossing Intervs, pp. 2–3; Intervs, Williamson with Maj Stanley P. Swartz, 13 Jun 51, attachment to Hant'an River Crossing Intervs; MacGarrigle with Tittel, 23 May 94.

[70] Hant'an River Crossing Intervs, pp. 6–7; 25th Inf Div G–3 Journal, 11 Apr 51.

[71] What happened to the 3d Battalion remains unclear because the records chronicling the event are uncommunicative and many of the officers involved, both at the time and later, had little they wanted to add. This account is drawn from Hant'an River Crossing Intervs, pp. 6–7; 25th Inf Div G–3 Journal, 11 Apr 51. See also Intervs, Williamson with 1st Lt Scott K. Cleage, artillery liaison ofcr, 20 Jun 51; Swartz, 13 Jun 51; 1st Lt John L. Herren, 13 Jun 51; Coleman, 13 Jun 51. All are attachments to Hant'an River Crossing Intervs. Intervs, MacGarrigle with Tittel, 23 May 94; Creel, 3 Nov and 3 Dec 93.

uation." Thoroughly alarmed, Bradley notified Colonel Britt that "I am placing no restrictions on your reserve battalion, but at such time as you wish to move it, please notify me immediately."[72]

At 1050 the operations officer of the 24th Infantry notified Bradley's headquarters that the 3d Battalion was reorganizing but would jump off in a new attack about 1200. "Earlier this morning," he explained, "3d Battalion got right into the enemy positions and then was split up." At 1155, Bradley called the 24th to ask how preparations for the attack were coming: "Where are Companies L and K?" He received more assurances that although the two had fallen back "along the north bank of the river," they were reorganizing and resupplying and would attack as soon as artillery fire lifted, "which should be soon." When no attack occurred, at 1230 Bradley instructed the commander of the 27th Infantry, Colonel Check, to be prepared to move a battalion to the north to back up the 24th Infantry, or to the west to assist the Turks.[73]

An hour later, Bradley arrived at the 24th Infantry's command post to see for himself. Ten minutes after that, furious at the dissembling of the regiment's officers, he notified his command post that "3d Battalion, 24th Infantry is disorganized and south of the river. I have directed Col. Britt to reform the battalion on I Company which had not crossed river. I have also directed that the battalion recross the river prior to dark if that can be done in an organized fashion. If this cannot be done, the battalion will cross at daylight tomorrow." In a comment that could only have sent chills through officers within earshot, Bradley ended his transmission by ordering his division's operations section to "make this conversation a matter of record."[74]

The 3d Battalion never made it back across the river that day. At 2130 Company K was still fifty-four

men short and Company L fifty-eight. Indeed, toward night the Turkish Brigade, which had made good progress all day and was on or near most of its objectives, had to pull one of its companies to the south of the Hant'an because the absence of the 3d Battalion from the line had left the unit's flank exposed. The 1st Battalion of the 24th was also affected. The men of that force had performed admirably throughout the day and were well positioned to continue their attack when they dug in for the night of 11 April, but their accomplishment received little notice. Instead, at 1555 Bradley instructed Baranowski to have an officer in the field verify that the companies of his unit had indeed achieved the advances they claimed. The next day the assistant division commander, Colonel Michaelis, arrived at the battalion's command post and demanded to see "all those dead people" whom the unit's officers had reported killed. In both cases, Major Baranowski was only too happy to comply.[75]

Throughout the day on 11 April the engineers worked to construct a bridge across the Hant'an. A masterpiece of improvisation resting on prefabricated log cribs that should have taken up to three days to build, it was passable to wheeled vehicles within just seven hours. When the attack jumped off the next morning, as a result, tanks were able to cross the river in support of the 1st and 3d Battalions. From then on, they placed direct fire in front of the advancing troops and made periodic dashes up a valley to the east of the attackers to lay fire on the Chinese from that direction.[76]

Following a fifteen-minute artillery barrage, the 1st and 3d Battalions kicked off the attack at 0700 on 12 April. By 1025 the leading elements of the 1st

the division, it is clear that the regiment, in its reports to division, was trying to present a more optimistic picture of the situation than the one reported by the 3d Battalion.

[75] 25th Inf Div G–3 Journal, 11 Apr 51. Quote from Interv, MacGarrigle with Baranowski, 6 Sep 94.

[76] 24th Inf Rgt Regimental Narrative Summary for Apr 51, p. 8; Hant'an River Crossing Intervs, p. 7; Intervs, Williamson with 1st Lt David K. Carlisle, asst S–3, 65th Engr Combat Bn, 20 Jun 51, and 1st Lt Orval Belcher, CO, Co B, 89th Medium Tank Bn, 16 Jun 51, attachments to Hant'an River Crossing Intervs; 24th Inf Rgt Unit Rpt 101, 12 Apr 51, box 3843, RG 407, WNRC; Ltr, Baranowski to MacGarrigle, n.d.; Interv, MacGarrigle with Baranowski, 6 Sep 94.

[72] Quotes from 25th Inf Div G–3 Journal, 11 Apr 51. For clarity, we have spelled out abbreviations within quotations from the journal. See also S–3 Journal, 24th Inf Rgt, 11 Apr 51, box 3843, RG 407, WNRC; 25th Inf Div Periodic Opns Rpt 22, 11 Apr 51, box 3784, RG 407, WNRC.

[73] Ibid. Quotes from 25th Inf Div G–3 Journal, 11 Apr 51.

[74] Ibid. Quotes from 25th Inf Div G–3 Journal, 11 Apr 51. By a comparison of the operations journals of the regiment and

Battalion had begun to climb Hill 642 and were receiving small-arms, automatic-weapons, and mortar fire from a well-dug-in enemy. They responded with flamethrowers. As they climbed the mountain, the trail became steeper. Sometimes the men had no choice but to advance hand over hand. By 1200, according to Michaelis, lead elements of Company A were within fifty yards of the top but were unable to make further progress against the stream of hand grenades and automatic-weapons fire that seemed to pour from the crest.[77]

Late in the afternoon, aware that Company A was down to about half strength and hoping that a less battered unit would be able to make some headway, Baranowski passed Company B through A to lead the attack. The unit's men ran bravely, one at a time, across a precarious dip and up the ridge, but were again unable to make much headway. Seeking to apply even more pressure, General Bradley removed Clayton's 2d Battalion from reserve and placed it at Britt's disposal. By the time the unit arrived, however, evening was deepening and it seemed best to hold up for the night. It pulled in to the right of the 1st Battalion, where it held until morning. Fire from tanks at the bottom of the hill kept the enemy at bay for the two battalions until first light the next day.[78]

As the 1st Battalion continued its progress up Hill 642, the 3d Battalion recrossed the Hant'an and renewed its attack on Hill 463. Although officers at the scene reported that the river was higher than the day before, complaints from the field continued throughout the morning that the unit's men "aren't moving too aggressively." The enemy offered little opposition at first, but by 1045 the battalion was receiving mortar fire from the hill. By 1200 all of the unit's companies were pinned down. At 1500 an intense artillery assault against the hill broke the impasse. According to a forward observer, 1st Lt.

Scott K. Cleage, the men "advanced beautifully in close coordination with the artillery." By 1600 they were within seventy-five yards of their objective, but despite heavy fire, the Chinese continued to fight, replacing their losses again and again.[79]

At 1930 Colonel Mouchet reported that two of his men had made it to the top of the hill but that the enemy retained possession of the north slope of the mountain. Because of that, he would be unable to hold the steep south slope in case of a counterattack. When the executive officer of the 24th, Colonel Coleman, who was with Mouchet, backed the colonel's recommendation, Colonel Britt ordered the 3d Battalion to break off the attack for the night and to withdraw once more across the Hant'an. Ten minutes after Britt gave the order, an exasperated Bradley radioed him to issue a direct order. "Your 3d Battalion," he told the colonel, "will cross the river again tomorrow and will remain across the river."[80]

At 2050 on 12 April Colonel Britt requested permission to pull officers back from Line Golden, where they, along with representatives from other regiments, were supervising construction of the Eighth Army's fall-back position. Forward, in the 1st Battalion, Company A had only one officer remaining, a brand-new second lieutenant. Company C had two officers and Company B only one. General Bradley accepted the request but imposed a condition. Concerned that a major enemy attack was in the offing and that Line Golden would be of critical importance if it occurred, he allowed Britt to pull officers back to staff his companies, but only if individuals from other portions of the regiment took their places. The number of transfers that followed remains unclear, but some definitely occurred.[81]

On the night of 12–13 April a tank platoon moved through the Turkish area to support the 3d Battalion in the next morning's attack. By the time

[77] 25th Inf Div G–3 Journal, 12 Apr 51, and 25th Inf Div Periodic Opns Rpt 24, 12 Apr 51, both in box 3784, RG 407, WNRC; Hant'an River Crossing Intervs, pp. 9–10.

[78] Ibid. See also Intervs, Williamson with Baranowski, 12 Jun 51; 1st Lt David A. Freas, Cdr, Co A, 16 Jun 51; and Capt Morgan D. Griffiths, 12 Apr 51. All attachments to Hant'an River Crossing Intervs.

[79] Quote from 25th Inf Div G–3 Journal, 12 Apr 51. Interv, Williamson with Cleage, 20 Jun 51, attachment to Hant'an River Crossing Intervs.

[80] Ibid. Quote from 25th Inf Div G–3 Journal, 12 Apr 51.

[81] 25th Inf Div G–3 Journal, 13 Apr 51, box 3784, RG 407, WNRC.

the assault occurred, however, the bulk of the enemy's forces had pulled off of Hill 463. When the 3d Battalion moved out at 0700 on 13 April it encountered no resistance and made good progress. By 0950 it had secured the hill and was preparing to move up the ridge line to join the 1st Battalion on Hill 642.[82]

The 1st and 2d Battalions found the going more difficult. The 1st Battalion secured Hill 642 by 1055, but only at a cost of many casualties. The unit then began dispatching patrols to the northeast to protect the left flank of the 2d Battalion, which was moving up to its right. That afternoon it cleared two enemy bunkers defended by an estimated platoon. Meanwhile, to the east, operating on a ridge line that ended in a sheer cliff, the 2d Battalion came up against stiff resistance. Encountering Chinese at the top of the cliff who yelled, waved flags from long poles, and threw hand grenades, it came within no more than a hundred and fifty yards of its objective before having to stop for the night. By then, nonetheless, the contest for the hill was over. The enemy had begun pulling back, and General Bradley was already making plans for the next day's operations to the north. In all, between 10 and 13 April the 1st Battalion incurred 48 killed and wounded, the 2d Battalion had 12, and the 3d Battalion had 52.[83]

Although the enemy had withdrawn, the ground still favored him. In the days that followed, the wooded, rocky hills north of the Hant'an

increased steadily in height, forcing the men of the 24th to make major exertions while providing their opponents with ample cover. Gullies and narrow defiles that rose precipitously provided the only avenues of approach to many of the hills. The crests of those ridges were easily defended by relatively few troops wielding hand grenades, which were particularly effective in that terrain.[84]

On 14 April the 24th made steady advances against light small-arms and mortar fire. One of its attached units, Company B of the 89th Medium Tank Battalion, achieved a particular success. Patrolling to the north, it brought two enemy platoons under fire and drove them off. In the process it destroyed the ammunition dump of the *76th Chinese Division*. Late in the day the 24th shifted its boundaries to the left to make room for the arrival of the 27th Infantry, which was pulling into position to its right. It then held in place for a day while the Turkish Brigade moved up on the left and the 27th relieved the 1st Battalion, which went into reserve for a much-needed rest. Despite the relative calm, during the day reconnaissance patrols to the front reported back that the enemy was building and improving bunkers all along possible lines of advance into the mountains, a sure sign that he was determined to resist further inroads by the 25th Division at all costs.[85]

Problems with the 3d Battalion occurred again early on the morning of 16 April, when the 11th Company of the Turkish Brigade, alarmed by some sound or movement to its front, began to fire into the dark. Surprised, some fifty men of Company I abandoned their positions and ran. Within the hour between twenty and thirty of them turned up in the Turkish sector, fifteen of them without arms. Initial reports alleged that all of Company I had fled, but a later investigation by the executive officer of the 3d Battalion, Maj. James W. Boring, indicated that no more than fifty

---

[82] 24th Inf Rgt Unit Rpt 102, 13 Apr 51, and 24th Inf Rgt S–3 Journal, 13 Apr 51, both in box 3844, RG 407, WNRC; Hant'an River Crossing Intervs, p. 11; 25th Inf Div Periodic Opns Rpt 25, 13 Apr 51, box 3784, RG 407, WNRC.

[83] Ibid. Casualty statistics used here are from HQ, 25th Inf Div, Reported Casualties of the 24th Infantry Regiment, n.d. [Jul 50–Sep 51], box 3848, RG 407, WNRC. Reports from the time noted higher numbers but seem extreme and cannot be verified. For example, the Eighth Army's after-action report for the Hant'an River crossing indicates that in taking the crest of Hill 642 on 13 April, Company B incurred three killed and forty-four wounded. It cites a forward observer and the commander of Company B. Those numbers do not jibe with the official total listed by name and unit for that date. They may have included men who were only slightly wounded and returned to duty, but, if such was so, casualties of that sort would have had little significant impact upon the unit's strength. See Hant'an River Crossing Intervs, pp. 10–11.

[84] 24th Inf Rgt Intelligence Summary for Apr 51, attachment to 24th Inf Rgt Regimental Narrative Summary for Apr 51, box 3843, RG 407, WNRC.

[85] 24th Inf Rgt Regimental Narrative Summary for Apr 51, pp. 8–9; 24th Inf Rgt Exec Ofcr's Daily Journal, 15 and 16 Apr 51, box 3843, RG 407, WNRC.

men had been involved. Since the unit had suffered at least fifty-two casualties during the fighting to that point, however, that number still represented a significant portion of its fighting strength. Companies K and L for their part were uninvolved in the episode.[86]

Although some ground was initially lost in the confusion, by 0530 many of the stragglers had been collected and the company was moving back into position. That day's attack stepped off shortly thereafter, at 0720, with Companies K and L taking the lead. By evening the 24th had advanced another 1,500 yards against continuous enemy fire. Although the 2d Battalion was unable to achieve its goal for the day and pulled back at dark, the 3d Battalion attained its objective. Even so, Colonel Britt was furious at the unit's performance to that point. At 1905 he radioed the commander of the 3d Battalion, Colonel Mouchet, to provide instructions for the following morning's attack and to issue a stern warning: "Mission tomorrow, seize and secure Phase Line Daisy in Zone. . . . Your personal future dependent upon your efforts to accomplish assigned mission."[87]

The 25th Division's advance continued over the next four days. On 17 April the enemy withdrew to the north, allowing the division to move with relative impunity against scattered, light resistance. There was no change on 18 and 19 April. The 24th

Infantry gained about a mile each day while incurring at most minor casualties. The Turkish Brigade to the regiment's left moved forward apace, as did the 27th Infantry to its right. By 20 April the 27th was well ahead of the 24th, with its forward elements occupying the northernmost limit of the Eighth Army's advance during that phase of the war. In the 24th's zone the 3d Battalion took the left while the 1st Battalion occupied the right. The 2d Battalion was in reserve.[88]

Enemy resistance began to stiffen on 20 April. The 25th Division's attack continued with little letup during the day, but problems soon occurred. The 3d Battalion met with heavy resistance as it approached Hill 482, some eight miles north of where it had crossed the Hant'an, and had to pull back overnight to a more tenable position. Meanwhile, in the 1st Battalion's area, after making progress all day, Company B began to receive mortar and small-arms fire. At 2140 between fifty and seventy-five enemy attacked through heavy fog, forcing elements of the unit off of a ridge.[89]

The company counterattacked and restored the position, but indications continued that the enemy had no intention of retreating further. On 21 April the 1st Battalion made slow gains on three sides of Hill 687, located some nine miles to the north of the Hant'an, but in the end proved unable to seize the objective and had to withdraw. Much the same thing happened to the 3d Battalion, which made slow gains all day in the hills to the west of the 1st Battalion but also never gained its objective and withdrew to the positions it had occupied the previous night. (*Map 20*) Either that evening or the next day, weary with the continuing slow progress of the 3d Battalion, Colonel Britt replaced Mouchet with the unit's executive officer, Major Boring.[90]

---

[86] 25th Inf Div G–3 Journal, 16 Apr 51, box 3785, RG 407, WNRC. It was later alleged that the company was attacked by an estimated enemy platoon. See 25th Inf Div Periodic Opns Rpt 31, 16 Apr 51, box 3785, RG 407, WNRC. As reported by the very candid 25th Division G–3 Journal, however, officers at the scene who investigated were of the opinion that no contact with the enemy occurred. That version is the one followed here. The assistant S–3 of the 3d Battalion, 1st Lt. James Yadon, noted in an interview that the episode occurred at a time when Colonel Mouchet was out of his command post and somewhere forward with Companies K and L. See Intervs, MacGarrigle with Yadon, 9 Dec 94.

[87] 25th Inf Div G–3 Journal, 16 Apr 51; 25th Inf Div Periodic Opns Rpt 32, 16 Apr 51, box 3785, RG 407, WNRC; 24th Inf Rgt Unit Rpt 105, 16 Apr 51, box 3843, RG 407, WNRC. Quote from 24th Inf Rgt Exec Ofcr's Daily Journal, 16 Apr 51. The 2d Battalion's commander, George Clayton, noted that Mouchet had experienced a personality conflict with Britt and had already asked to be relieved. Britt, he said, had refused. See Intervs, MacGarrigle with Clayton, 10 and 11 Aug 94.

[88] 25th Inf Div Command Rpt 5, 1–30 Apr 51, 8 Jul 51, pp. 37–40, box 3779, RG 407, WNRC; 24th Inf Rgt Regimental Narrative Summary for Apr 51, pp. 10–12.

[89] Ibid. See also 25th Inf Div G–3 Journal, 20 Apr 51, box 3785, RG 407, WNRC.

[90] 24th Inf Rgt Regimental Narrative Summary for Apr 51, pp. 12–13; 25th Inf Div Periodic Opns Rpt 42, 21 Apr 51, box 3785, RG 407, WNRC; 25th Inf Div Command Rpt 5, 1–30

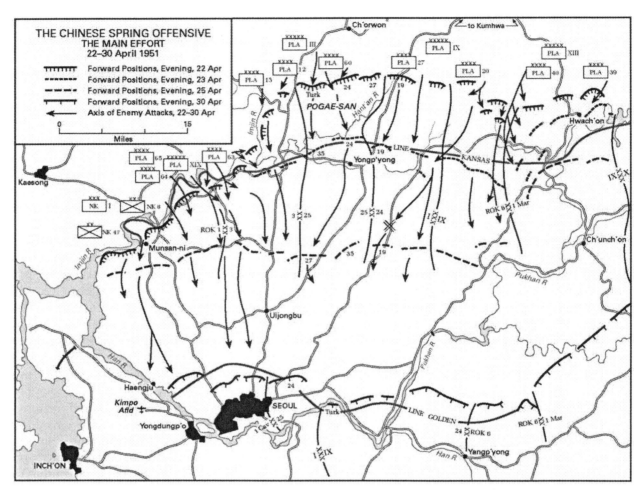

Map 20

The Chinese Spring Offensive

The next morning, 22 April, while the 3d Battalion rested and reorganized, the 1st and 2d Battalions continued the attack on Hill 687. The fighting was difficult all day with the troops sometimes eye-to-eye with the enemy, but by evening the force had seized its objective. Even so, as the light faded forward observers began to report that the Chinese were massing just to the north. Units all along the Eighth Army's line also began to report incoming artillery fire.[91]

The Chinese launched their long-awaited Spring Offensive shortly after midnight the next day, 23 April. Three field armies, a total of 270,000 men, were involved. To the west, the *Chinese First Field Army* moved on a twelve-mile front against the 1st South Korean Division, the British 29th Brigade, and other allied units located near the Imjin River. To the east, the *Third Field Army* moved against the 5th and 19th regiments of the U.S. 24th

---

Apr 51, 8 Jul 51, box 3783, RG 407, WNRC. The position of the 3d Battalion is mentioned in 24th Inf Rgt Exec Ofcr's Daily Journal, 21 Apr 51, box 3843, RG 407, WNRC.

[91] 24th Inf Rgt Regimental Narrative Summary for Apr 51, pp. 14–15; 25th Inf Div Periodic Opns Rpt 43, 22 Apr 51, and 25th Inf Div G–3 Journal, 22 Apr 51, both in box 3785, RG 407, WNRC; 25th Inf Div Command Rpt 5, 1–30 Apr 51, 8 Jul 51.

Infantry Division and the 27th Infantry regiment of Bradley's 25th Division, all of which were blocking the route to Seoul along the Kumhwa-Uijongbu road. The main attack, however, came between those two assaults in the region below Ch'orwon, where the *60th Army* of the *Chinese Second Field Army*, moving in a column of divisions, attacked toward Seoul down the seam between the U.S. 3d and 25th Divisions. It brushed up against the 24th Infantry regiment, holding the relatively well-protected ridges of the Pogae-san mountains, but threw much of its weight against the Turkish Brigade, which held a long valley leading through the mountains toward Seoul.[92]

As the attack developed, the enemy encountered little difficulty in penetrating the valley that separated the 24th Infantry from the Turkish Brigade, apparently because neither of the two units had positioned blocking forces along the valley's floor. In the fighting that followed, Britt received permission from Bradley to pull his exposed 3d Battalion onto the slopes of Hill 877, one and a half miles to the south. If the 24th's line bent, however, it did not break. Even in withdrawing, the regiment fought hard, inflicting many casualties on the enemy. To the east, the 27th Infantry also stood up well, stopping the enemy in his tracks.[93]

The Turks were a different matter. Heavily engaged at almost every point and so intermingled with the enemy that artillery fire proved useless, their units lost communication with one another. One company was annihilated. Several more were surrounded but managed to fight their way to safety as units. A few collapsed. Toward dawn on the morning of 23 April, with nearly a thousand disor-

Companies B and C, 24th Infantry, battle Communist counterattacks on rocky mountain slopes on the western central front.

ganized Turkish stragglers congregating to the rear, General Bradley instructed what was left of the brigade to reorganize south of the Hant'an and moved the 35th Infantry forward to take its place.[94]

If most of the 25th Division had held its ground or had withdrawn in good order, Hill 877 still proved impossible to hold against the enemy's onslaught. Indeed, as the men of the 3d Battalion of the 24th went up one side, mortarman Levine White recalled, the enemy went up the other. For a time the fighting was intense, but the contest soon ended. By 0730 enemy troops were swarming on the hill and Colonel Britt had pulled the 3d Battalion another one and a half miles to the south under the covering fire of the 159th Field Artillery Battalion.[95]

[92] Mossman, *Ebb and Flow*, pp. 379–84; Roy E. Appleman, *Ridgway Duels for Korea* (College Station: Texas A&M University Press, 1990), pp. 454–55.

[93] The failure to set up blocking positions is mentioned in Interv, MacGarrigle with Creel, 20 Dec 94. Creel was the commander of Company L, which had responsibility for maintaining contact with the Turkish force. This account of the action is drawn from 25th Inf Div G–3 Journal, 23 Apr 51, box 3785, RG 407, WNRC. The journal gives an almost moment-by-moment account of what was happening. See also 24th Inf Rgt Exec Ofcr's Daily Journal, 23 Apr 51, box 3843, RG 407, WNRC; Interv, MacGarrigle with Baranowski, 24 Aug 94.

[94] 25th Inf Div G–3 Journal, 23 Apr 51; Mossman, *Ebb and Flow*, pp. 384–85.

[95] Interv, Muehlbauer with Levine White, n.d.; 25th Inf Div G–3 Journal, 23 Apr 51.

Members of the 24th Infantry fighting south of Ch'orwon, Korea

Little more than an hour later, the I Corps command instructed all of its units to withdraw across the Hant'an to Line Kansas, which at that point ran just north of the Yongp'yong River, a tributary of the Hant'an, flowing some three miles to the south. In the move that followed the 24th was, for a time, strung out in a column of companies almost nine miles long. The enemy, however, took little advantage of the circumstance. He had by then suffered grievous losses of his own and needed time to gather breath. By 1540, as a result, the entire regiment was across the Hant'an, and engineers had begun the process of dismantling the bridge over the river. They completed the task at 1900 in such good order that they managed to recover up to 75 percent of the valuable metal decking that had paved the structure.

On Line Kansas the 35th Infantry held the western flank of the 25th Division, the position formerly occupied by the Turkish Brigade. To its east came the 24th Infantry, with the 3d Battalion taking the sector to the left, the 1st Battalion the center, and the 2d Battalion the right. The 27th Infantry stood in reserve to the rear. The regiments of the 24th Division took position to the east of the 24th Infantry.[96]

Although the 24th escaped, it was hardly done fighting. The enemy wasted little time crossing the Hant'an and was soon pressing the regiment hard. At 0100 on 24 April Company A came under attack and all three battalions of the regiment began to

---

[96] 25th Inf Div G–3 Journal, 23 Apr 51.

Battling a Chinese counterattack south of Ch'orwon

receive fire. By 0230 commanders in the field reported that the enemy had overrun Company A and that the entire 1st Battalion was "pretty badly shot up." The fighting seesawed back and forth all the rest of the day. The 1st Battalion relinquished its position early in the morning, but it counterattacked successfully later that afternoon with the assistance of units from the 27th Infantry. In the interim, however, the 2d Battalion came under such a heavy assault that no one could estimate the number of the enemy involved. Forced off of its position, that unit also counterattacked, but to no avail.[97]

The situation degenerated further as night fell. With the 1st Battalion of the 24th under continuing heavy pressure and members of a Turkish blocking force behind the regiment straggling individually and in groups to the rear, both the regiment and the 25th Division had no choice but to withdraw to new positions. Shortly thereafter, following five days of heavy, bitter fighting, the 25th Division withdrew the sorely battered 24th from the line and placed it in reserve. In all, during April the regiment had lost 381 killed and

[97] Quote from 25th Inf Div G–3 Journal, 24 Apr 51. 25th Inf Div Periodic Opns Rpt 47, 24 Apr 51; 25th Inf Div Periodic Opns Rpts 48, 25 Apr 51, and 49, 25 Apr 51; Msg, Commanding General (CG), 25th Inf Div, to CO, 24th Inf Rgt; CO, 25th Reconnaissance Co; and CG, Turkish Army Forces Command (TAFC), 240630 Apr 51. All in box 3785, RG 407, WNRC. 24th Inf Rgt Exec Ofcr's Daily Journal, 24 and 25 Apr 51, box 3843, RG 407, WNRC.

Men of the 3d Battalion withdraw near Ch'orwon after heavy counterattacks by Communist forces.

wounded. One hundred and ninety-three of them fell in just the five days between the twenty-first and twenty-fifth of the month.[98]

Overall, throughout the first four months of 1951 the regiment's performance had been generally solid. After the retreat from Kunu-ri and a long period of training and rebuilding, the unit had participated energetically in the 25th Division's advance on Seoul. In the crossing of the Han River, the 2d Battalion performed as well as any other unit. Suffering the only enemy counterattack the night after the crossing, the battalion gave ground but did not break, a significant improvement over its performance at Haman on 1 September of the year before. In the same way, the 1st Battalion was outstanding in the discharge of its duties during the crossing of the Hant'an River. The unit secured its bridgehead and advanced steadily toward its objectives against a determined, well-dug-in enemy. At the Hant'an, however, and during the days following the attack the 1st Battalion's success was overshadowed by the failure of the 3d Battalion.

In that case, given the achievements of the rest of the regiment, it might be tempting to blame Mouchet for what happened, much as Britt did. When the officer was relieved of command, however, he immediately transferred to the 27th Infantry, where he performed ably enough to preserve his future in the Army. He retired a few years later as a full colonel.

In that light, Britt's change of plan takes on great weight in explaining what happened. The 3d Battalion was thrown, almost at the last moment, with only the barest of plans, into a dangerous night river-crossing on difficult terrain in the face of strong enemy opposition. It is conceivable that any combat-experienced, cohesive unit would have had problems, but the 3d Battalion, still recovering from its experience at the Ch'ongch'on, floundered. By contrast, the men of the 1st and 2d Battalions had the benefit of a known situation for which there was time both to plan and to prepare physically and mentally. Indeed, under more stable circumstances and despite grave danger, in the retreat to Line Golden during the Chinese Spring Offensive, the 3d Battalion fought ably along with the rest of the regiment, incurring a host of casualties in some of the most vicious fighting of the war.

Even so, time was growing short for the 24th. Whatever the good performance of the regiment, the 3d Battalion's experience had again left higher commanders with doubts. Already convinced that segregated units were unreliable and possessing the time and resources at last to do something about it, they were resolved to end forced separation of the races in Korea and to move ahead on Kean's recommendation to disband the unit. Although the 24th would see further fighting in the weeks that followed, its days were numbered.

---

[98] 25th Inf Div G–3 Journal, 24 Apr 51. Casualties are from HQ, 25th Inf Div, Reported Casualties of the 24th Infantry Regiment, n.d. [Jul 50–Sep 51].

CHAPTER 10

Last Days

Over the days that followed the pullback from the Hant'an, enemy pressure forced the 25th Division into a series of withdrawals. By the morning of 28 April 1951, the unit had fallen back as far as Line Lincoln, the series of strong fortifications that General Ridgway had constructed just north of Seoul. At that time, following several days of rest, the 24th Infantry returned to the front, where it began the process of strengthening its position with mines and wire. The area the regiment had to defend, the unit's executive officer, Lt. Col. Hugh D. Coleman, noticed, was far smaller than in the past, making it "the best defensive line . . . we've . . . occupied in Korea." At least a few of the unit's enlisted men had a different opinion. Viewing the fortifications and realizing that a major fight was at hand, some of the soldiers began to circulate rumors that commanders expected the regiment to hold to the last man and that everyone would soon be dead. Morale was good up until that point, a medic in Company E, Lawrence Holmes, declared. Then it began to fall.[1]

The concerns of the men proved groundless. Although the enemy began a large buildup in the 25th Division's zone, powerful air attacks and artillery barrages removed any possibility of a major attack in that area. Instead, toward the end of the month newly captured Chinese and North Korean prisoners began to reveal that the enemy's organization and system of supply was collapsing and that motivation was lagging among the troops because of the pounding they had received and heavy casualties among the political officers who maintained discipline within the force. By the first week in May patrols were penetrating up to six miles into enemy territory without major opposition and combat consisted mainly of quick skirmishes and chance encounters.[2]

On 14 April, following a major controversy in which President Truman replaced General MacArthur with General Ridgway as U.S. commander in the Far East, Lt. Gen. James A. Van Fleet took charge of the Eighth Army. A proven combat commander who had led the 8th Infantry of the U.S. 4th Infantry Division on Utah Beach during the Normandy invasion and had won three Distinguished Service Crosses during the fighting at Cherbourg, on the Siegfried Line, and in the Battle of the Bulge, Van Fleet began immediate

---

[1] Quote from 24th Inf Rgt Exec Ofcr's Daily Journal, 28 and 29 Apr 51, box 3843, Record Group (RG) 407, Washington National Records Center (WNRC), Suitland, Md. Interv, John A. Cash with Lawrence Holmes, 18 Aug 89. All interviews hereafter cited by John A. Cash, Bernard L. Muehlbauer, Timothy Rainey, William T. Bowers, Richard O. Perry, and George L. MacGarrigle are in CMH files.

[2] 25th Inf Div Command Rpt for 1–31 May 51, box 3787, RG 407, WNRC; Mossman, *Ebb and Flow*, pp. 435–36.

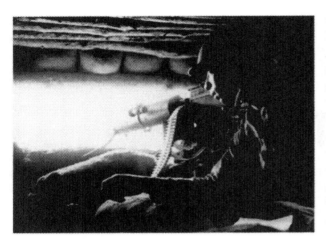

Ready and waiting in a bunker for the Chinese advance along the front near Seoul

plans for a counterattack to regain the territory United Nations forces had lost in the enemy's Spring Offensive. On 16 May, however, the Chinese and North Koreans preempted that plan with a major attack of their own, centering it some seventy-five miles east of Seoul in the rugged Taebaek Mountains. The fighting was touch and go for a time, but United Nations forces soon slowed the enemy enough to permit Van Fleet to proceed.[3]

On 20 May, as a result, Operation PILEDRIVER began. Involving a general attack along the Eighth Army's entire line, the assault laid heavy emphasis upon the I Corps zone, where the U.S. 1st Cavalry Division and the 3d and 25th Infantry Divisions were to press north toward the mouth of the Imjin River and the towns of Ch'orwon and Kumhwa to its east. When the attackers reached their goals and began to penetrate the Iron Triangle above Ch'orwon and Kumhwa, so the reasoning went, they would block the enemy's main routes of access to the fighting on the eastern front and would relieve much of the pressure on allied forces in that area.[4] (*Map 21*)

Earlier in the war U.S. commanders would have expected to drive past the Iron Triangle

toward North Korea's border with China. During May, however, President Truman had redefined American ends in the conflict by promising to stop the fighting just as soon as he could conclude a suitable armistice with the enemy. Because of that, toward the middle of the month the Joint Chiefs of Staff instructed Ridgway to keep the enemy off balance with limited operations, but to make no major moves north of the area above Ch'orwon without permission from higher authority. From then on, military actions in Korea were to concentrate less on seizing territory than on causing the sort of damage to the enemy's forces that would preserve South Korea while speeding a negotiated settlement to the war.[5]

During the assault north, the 24th Infantry occupied the eastern flank of the 25th Division's attack, moving up Route 3 toward Kumhwa. Enemy opposition was light at first, leading intelligence officers to conclude that the Chinese and North Koreans had shifted their main forces to the east for their attack in that area. Temperatures were relatively cold at night throughout the period but warm during the day, and rain was frequent.[6]

Enemy resistance stiffened on 21 May. Advancing up a hill at 1045, a platoon from Company E in Colonel Clayton's 2d Battalion encountered heavy enemy machine-gun and mortar fire and withdrew. As it pulled back, the two platoons nearest to it did the same. The officers of the units involved reorganized their men and returned them to the attack. Supported by a platoon of tanks from the 89th Medium Tank Battalion, the troops advanced well enough after that. Despite sometimes telling enemy artillery fire, they reached their objective by 1230. Even so, the episode aggravated officers at the 25th Division. One of them, the division's operations officer, noted in his journal for the day that Company E broke under pressure.[7]

[3] Mossman, *Ebb and Flow*, pp. 444–65, 485.
[4] Ibid.

[5] Ibid., pp. 488–90.
[6] Weather mentioned in 3d Bn, 24th Inf Rgt, Unit Monthly Summary, 1–31 May 51, box 3844, RG 407, WNRC. Stiffening combat and intelligence analyses are mentioned in 25th Inf Div Command Rpt for May 51, p. 7, box 3787, RG 407, WNRC.
[7] 25th Inf Div G–3 Journal, 21 May 51, box 3788, RG 407, WNRC. See also 2d Bn, 24th Inf Rgt, Periodic Opns Rpt

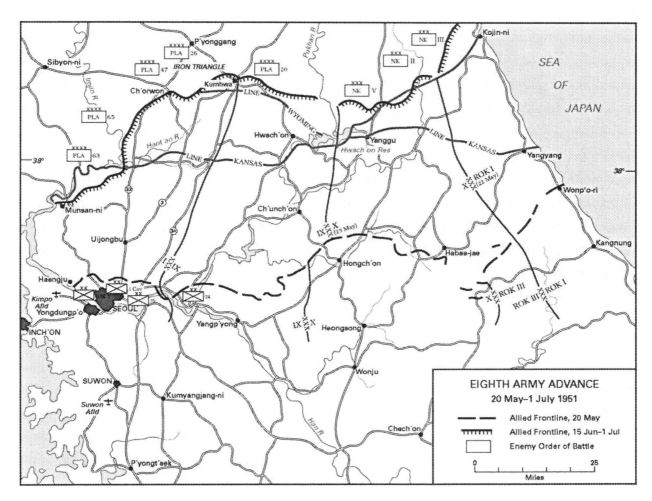

Map 21

The next day Clayton's Company F took its objective but then encountered similar problems and withdrew a thousand yards to the south. Clayton went forward to see what was wrong and soon had the situation in hand, but the regimental commander, Colonel Britt, apparently held him responsible for what had happened and shortly thereafter relieved him of command. By then the officer had been a battalion commander in the line for seven full months. His weight had dropped from 180 to 135 pounds and he was approaching exhaustion. The 2d Battalion's popular executive officer, Maj. Franklin W. McVay, took charge of the unit, remaining in command for the next several months until killed by a mine.[8]

The 2d Battalion went into reserve to give McVay time to organize, but the 1st and 3d Battalions continued the attack north. In the days that followed, the Chinese and North Koreans pulled back and then broke contact completely. Only on 1 June, when the 25th Division

221, 21 May 51, box 3844, RG 407, WNRC; 25th Inf Div Periodic Opns Rpt 41, 21 May 51, box 3788, RG 407, WNRC.

[8] 25th Inf Div G–3 Journal, 22 May 51, box 3788, RG 407, WNRC; 2d Bn, 24th Inf Rgt, Command Rpt for May 51, 10 Jun 51, box 3844, RG 407, WNRC; Intervs, George L. MacGarrigle with George A. Clayton, 10 and 11 Aug 94.

Sergeant Charlton

approached Kumhwa and the Iron Triangle and began to threaten important supply lines to the west and east, did the enemy begin to mount any sort of determined resistance. That night they launched a ferocious artillery and mortar attack against the 24th, sending more than a hundred rounds into the vicinity of the regimental command post. Several hundred more rounds fell on artillery positions and other nearby installations. Heavy casualties resulted.[9]

The next day Company L of the 3d Battalion attacked a heavily fortified enemy hilltop but fell back with five killed and thirty wounded. Company C of the 1st Battalion then entered the fray, but because of heavy automatic weapons fire it also made little progress. At that time the platoon sergeant of the 3d Platoon in Company C, Sgt. Cornelius H. Charlton, began an advance of his own against heavy fire. He reached the enemy's main position and held in place for a time, but then fell back in a hail of bullets and grenades. Learning that his lieutenant had fallen wounded,

he then took command of the platoon to lead it in another attack. An enlisted man in the company, Pfc. Ronald Holmes, recalled what happened. Charlton was wounded in the chest, Holmes said, but he refused to be evacuated. "He got the rest of the men together, and we started for the top. The enemy had some good emplacements . . . we couldn't get to him. Grenades kept coming at us and we were chased back down. Again we tried, but no luck. Sgt. Charlton said he was going to make it this time and he yelled, 'Let's go,' and we started up again. We reached the top this time. I saw the Sergeant go over the top and charge a bunker on the other side. He got the gun but was killed by a grenade." Charlton caused heavy casualties among the enemy and saved many lives among his own men. He posthumously received the Medal of Honor.[10]

The 24th continued its assault north the next day, but the going proved difficult because the enemy was well entrenched along a rocky ridge line that commanded the valley below. Launching frequent counterattacks, he leveled heavy fire against the advancing Americans, who could make little use of their tanks and machine guns on account of the terrain but still managed to make their way by lashing the hillsides with great waves of artillery and mortar fire. The artillerymen appear to have resented the extra work. The white commander of the 159th Field Artillery Battalion, for one, belittled the 24th, observing in a letter to his wife during the early part of the operation,

[9] 25th Inf Div Command Rpt for May 51; 24th Inf Rgt Regimental Narrative Summary for Jun 51, box 3845, RG 407, WNRC.

[10] The quote, with punctuation added for clarity, is from Statement, Pfc Ronald Holmes, 9 Sep 51, attachment to Medal of Honor Recommendation for Sgt Cornelius H. Charlton, 28 Nov 51, box 173, RG 338, WNRC. See also Statement, 2d Lt Moir E. Eanes, 13 Nov 51, attachment to Medal of Honor Recommendation for Sgt Cornelius H. Charlton, 28 Nov 51; Department of the Army (DA) GO 30, Award of the Medal of Honor, 19 Mar 52. Both in box 173, RG 338, WNRC. In 1951, after Charlton had already been buried, the Army failed to offer him a final resting place in Arlington National Cemetery due to what it said was an administrative error. Whether that was so or not, his family never doubted that the lapse was racially motivated. In March 1990 he was re-buried with full honors in the American Legion Cemetery in Beckley, West Virginia. The controversy surrounding Charlton's burial is outlined in Shawn Pogatchnik, "After 39 Years, a Town Honors Its Black Hero," *Los Angeles Times*, 28 May 90.

"This regiment we support is averse to shooting their rifles so the artillery has to do it all." Whatever the case, on 4 June the men of the 24th withdrew. The 35th Infantry regiment took their place in the line, allowing them to pull twenty miles to the rear to the town of Uijongbu to become the I Corps reserve.[11]

From that moment on, discipline within the regiment began to lag. On 10 June, nearly a week after the regiment withdrew from combat, a regimental inspection team reported that some units had decided that their status as corps reserve constituted a rest period. Soldiers were taking showers during working hours, indulging in athletic activities, and cleaning equipment and gear that should have undergone maintenance one or two days after the unit pulled back. Meanwhile, officers had been caught sleeping during the middle of the day, soldiers attending training classes were paying little attention to the instructors, and the instructors themselves seemed unprepared. The situation appeared serious to the inspectors. Units in reserve were expected not only to work on correcting faults and deficiencies that had arisen during their time in combat but also to be prepared to move back into combat on a moment's notice if an emergency arose.[12]

Part of the problem appears to have arisen with the leadership of the regiment, which at that time seemed to be suffering from a malaise of the spirit closely related to how some officers viewed their service in the 24th. As with the soldiers who had complained that they would all surely die on Line Lincoln, those individuals appear to have believed that they were doomed. "Our officer personnel . . . [are] pretty low at this time," the executive officer of the 24th thus told the chief of personnel for the 25th Division on 17 June. "You see, we have some intelligent people here and they are wondering just how they'll get out of here. They are well aware of the fact that the casualty rate among officers is far

Men from Company D, 24th Infantry, clean their weapons after spending thirty-eight days on the front lines.

greater in this regiment than [in] any other unit in the Eighth Army."[13]

An enemy air attack on 20 June did nothing to remedy morale problems in the regiment, but it may have put the unit back on alert. Flying in at dusk, a lone raider who usually appeared at that time of the day killed 8, wounded 8, and damaged 14 vehicles in Company M. He also caused 5 wounded in Company I. From then on, according to the intelligence officer of the 2d Battalion, 1st Lt. Ralph J. Davis, who recalled the incident, the regiment took its antiaircraft defenses more seriously.[14]

On 8 July Colonel Britt returned to the United States. A battalion and regimental commander in Europe toward the end of World War II who would later rise to the rank of major general, Lt. Col. Richard W. Whitney, took his place. General Bradley also departed during July, relinquishing

[11] 24th Inf Rgt Regimental Narrative Summary for Jun 51. Quote from Ltr, T. E. Watson to his wife, 23 May 51, CMH files.

[12] Memo, Maj Walter D. Stevens, Jr., Adjutant, 24th Inf Rgt, 10 Jun 51, in 24th Inf Rgt Command Rpt for Jun 51, box 3845, RG 407, WNRC.

[13] The quotation, edited slightly for clarity, is from 24th Inf Rgt Exec Ofcr's Daily Journal, 17 Jun 51, box 3845, RG 407, WNRC. That the unit's executive officer had his clerk record his remarks verbatim in his journal is an indication of how concerned he was about morale among his officers at the time. For other comments along the same line, see Interv, MacGarrigle with Buckner M. Creel, 20 Dec 94.

[14] The air attack is mentioned in 24th Inf Rgt Exec Ofcr's Daily Journal, 20 Jun 51, box 3845, RG 407, WNRC. See also Ltr, Ralph J. Davis to George L. MacGarrigle, 12 Dec 94, CMH files.

charge of the 25th Division to Maj. Gen. Ira P. Swift, an officer of long experience who had served as the assistant commander of the 82d Airborne Division in Europe during World War II.[15]

The 24th stayed in reserve until 15 July, when it relieved the 7th Cavalry regiment on Line Wyoming, six miles southwest of Ch'orwon. The 2d Battalion patrolled aggressively, meeting stiff enemy resistance at first, but as the probes continued the enemy faded away. The weather was poor. It rained heavily throughout the final two weeks of the month.[16]

On 31 July the 24th moved three miles northwest of Kumhwa, where it established a company-size patrol base in the vicinity of Hill 400, a height that stood just north of an abandoned railroad embankment running east-west between Ch'orwon and Kumhwa. Securing the right flank of the 35th Infantry, the rest of the regiment took position near the town of Ugu-dong, some four miles west of Kumhwa, in hills just south of the rail line.[17] (Map 22)

Antipathy toward the 24th on the part of whites remained heavy during those days, as a description provided by an artillery forward observer assigned to Company B, white 2d Lt. Gaston Bergeron, indicates. When the regiment moved up to Kumhwa to replace an all-white unit in the line, Bergeron, recalled, its men made the final leg of the journey on foot, walking up one side of a narrow dirt road while the soldiers they were relieving walked down the other. During that time, the officer said, the whites hurled terrible insults and racial slurs at the blacks without any interference from their officers, who were present. In the end, Bergeron said, the only thing a man could do was tuck his chin down into

the collar of his coat and keep on walking. It was "ten hours of crap." The lieutenant added that the experience was hardly unique. The same thing had happened to him before during his tour of duty with the regiment. How, he asked, could any soldier, subjected to such abuse time after time, develop a good opinion of himself or summon up a resolve to fight for the country that permitted it to occur?[18]

The men of the 24th nonetheless went about their duties. The unit spent the first two weeks of the month improving its position, training, and patrolling in force. The enemy was active in the area but engaged mainly in laying mines on the roads. On 7 August the 3d Battalion, less its heavy weapons unit, Company M, came under the operational control of the Eighth Army and moved 100 miles to the rear to the area around Chech'on, where it would spend the next several months guarding strategically important tungsten mines from possible guerrilla attack. Ten days later, after only five weeks in command, Colonel Whitney departed the regiment to become the chief of staff of the 25th Division. An armor officer who had served on the I Corps staff from the early days of the war, Col. Thomas D. Gillis, took his place.[19]

By that time, according to Lieutenant Bergeron, morale had fallen within the regiment. No longer on the offensive, the unit's men participated in patrols and blocking operations but otherwise had considerable time on their hands. The Army's rotation program was in full stride. Old soldiers were departing, and those who would leave shortly were increasingly concerned with the possibility that they might be killed or dismembered. As for the officers and the sergeants, Bergeron said, some were outstanding but

[15] U.S. Army, Office of Public Affairs, Biography of Maj Gen Richard W. Whitney, USA, Jun 70, and U.S. Army, Office of Public Affairs, Biography of Maj Gen Ira Platt Swift, USA, Nov 53, both in CMH files.

[16] 25th Inf Div Command Rpt for Jul 51, box 3794, RG 407, WNRC; 24th Inf Rgt Command Rpt for Jul 51, box 3845, RG 407, WNRC. See also 159th Field Artillery (FA) Bn Command Rpt for Jul 51, 15 Aug 51, box 5185, RG 407, WNRC. Most of the 24th Infantry was in reserve from 24–30 July 1951.

[17] 24th Inf Rgt Command Rpt 10, 1–31 Aug 51, 15 Sep 51, box 3846, RG 407, WNRC.

[18] Interv, Bernard L. Muehlbauer with Gaston P. Bergeron, 1 Mar 89.

[19] Thomas D. Gillis Diary for 1951, attachment to Ltr, Thomas D. Gillis to Clay Blair, 13 Nov 84, Clay Blair file, U.S. Army Military History Institute (MHI), Carlisle Barracks, Pa. When the 24th Infantry disbanded in October, the 3d Battalion was redesignated the Eighth Army Special Provisional Battalion. The unit remained all black and was inactivated 27 December 1951. See DA GO 80, 22 Nov 54, CMH Unit Data files. See also Interv, MacGarrigle with Creel, 20 Dec 94. A forward observer with the regiment located the position of the unit. See Interv, Muehlbauer with Bergeron, 1 Mar 89.

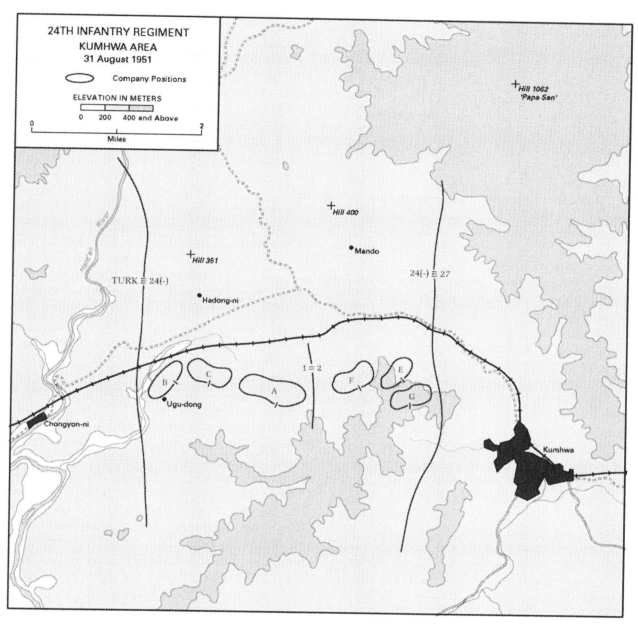

Map 22

many others seemed inept. Company B, as a result, did little more than required.[20]

The status of the 24th Infantry only added to the unit's problems. Toward the end of the month, the men learned from press and radio announce-

[20] Interv, Muehlbauer with Bergeron, 1 Mar 89. Creel also mentioned the personnel turbulence in the regiment at this time, noting that many old timers were departing and new men arriving, a fact that forced regimental officers to begin a program of training and review for everyone. See Interv,

MacGarrigle with Creel, 20 Dec 94. The executive officer of the 2d Battalion, Maj. Curtis H. Alloway, also remarked on the problem. See 2d Bn, 24th Inf Rgt, Exec Summary, 1–31 Aug 51, box 3847, RG 407, WNRC.

ments that the Army planned to inactivate their unit. No date was given, but the individual soldier began to feel that his job was over and that he was, as the executive officer of the 2d Battalion, Maj. Curtis H. Alloway, remarked in a report, "just wasting time waiting for the event." Alloway was convinced that morale would have been much higher if the pending dissolution of the regiment had not become public.[21]

Under the circumstances, it was probably inevitable that discipline problems would increase in the regiment. According to Alloway, while on patrol or in combat the men performed in a satisfactory manner. When located in static positions, however, they tended to wander to the rear. Straggler lines were in place, so most failed to get far, but some of the men were gone for weeks at a time. When finally apprehended, those individuals were usually arrested. During the first part of the year, while heavy combat continued, the 24th thus experienced only a small number of court-martial cases, no more than in any of the other regiments in the 25th Division. As the summer lengthened, however, and the period of static warfare began, the situation changed. By September the 24th had 14 general court-martial cases, versus 2 for the 27th Infantry regiment and 1 for the 35th. And in October 1951 the regiment had 11 cases to only 1 for the 27th and none at all for the 35th.[22]

Overall, in the context of the thousands of men present in the three regiments, the number of judicial proceedings was small, and few of the cases in any of the regiments had to do with the sort of straggling in combat that had afflicted the 24th during the early months of the war. Indeed, the 25th Division's staff judge advocate made it a point to investigate the 24th's problems to see whether its difficulties were having any impact on unit effectiveness. He concluded, as he told General Swift,

that "the character of service of the offenders . . . had been [in the main] 'poor' and 'unsatisfactory' prior to their being assigned to the regiment, and thus their actions could not truly reflect the efficiency of the regiment as a combat unit."[23]

Colonel Gillis had been warned of the regiment's problems prior to taking command. General Swift had pulled him aside to inform him of the unit's poor condition and that he believed the 24th had "the weakest line in all of the Eighth Army." Arriving at the regiment's headquarters, Gillis found himself, despite some preconceived notions, "neither favorably nor unfavorably impressed," but he quickly decided that much still needed to be done. The unit's former commanders, he noted, had failed to develop a proper line of outposts and had located the troops on the forward slopes of a heavily wooded hill among trees and underbrush that obstructed fields of fire. Setting out to improve the situation, he relieved a battalion commander, a battalion executive officer, several company commanders, and a number of platoon leaders for dereliction of duty and other infractions. Rather than attempt to rebuild the poorly sited positions the men occupied, and possibly because many of the troops had too much time on their hands and could use the activity, he requested permission to move his lines forward and began the work of tunneling the regiment into the railroad embankment that ran through the unit's sector. Building two-man emplacements with firing ports facing the enemy and railroad ties piled on top for protection, he reinforced everything with sandbags and strung barbed wire everywhere it was needed. When he was done, he reported years later, many of the men detested him because of the work he had forced them to do, but General Swift was well impressed.[24]

As work proceeded on the regiment's new position, Gillis continued a program of ambushes and

[21] 2d Bn, 24th Inf Rgt, Exec Summary, 1–31 Aug 51.

[22] The September statistics are from 25th Inf Div Judge Advocate General Rpt for Sep 51, box 3804, bk. 2, RG 407, WNRC. The October statistics are from 25th Inf Div Judge Advocate General Rpt for Oct 51, box 3807, bk. 2, RG 407, WNRC. Alloway's remarks are in Interv, MacGarrigle with Curtis H. Alloway, 20 Oct 94.

[23] Memo, Lt Col Edgar R. Minnich, Div Staff Judge Advocate, for Commanding General (CG), 25th Inf Div, 11 Oct 51, sub: Staff Section Report for September 1951, box 3804, RG 407, WNRC.

[24] Quotes from Ltr, Thomas D. Gillis to David K. Carlisle, 12 Sep 86, copy in CMH files. See also 24th Inf Rgt Command Rpt for Aug 51, p. 5, box 3846, RG 407, WNRC; Gillis Diary, 28 Sep 51.

tank-infantry patrols begun earlier in the month. The success of the ambushes, as Gillis observed in his diary, was "not apparent." As for the patrols, the Chinese and North Koreans responded vigorously but mainly in a defensive manner. A large number of tanks was lost to mines, but there were no major enemy attacks. On 8 September Company B launched a heavy assault on Hill 351, slightly more than a mile north of the regiment's main line on the embankment. The force in possession of the hill resisted vigorously, withdrew to regroup, and then counterattacked, but the Americans prevailed. In the process, however, Company B suffered two killed and twenty-five wounded.[25]

The most significant combat of the month occurred on 15 September, when Company F of the 2d Battalion mounted an attack on Hill 400, two miles northeast of Hill 351, in an attempt to prevent the enemy from using the height to fire on the 24th's positions, some two miles to the south in the valley below. The attackers came within twenty feet of the top of the hill, but at 0845 that morning, in the face of a furious enemy assault with grenades and mortars, they pulled back with nine casualties. The unit went back up the hill at 1215, but again withdrew in the face of heavy enemy fire. Recognizing that the company had been slow in mounting its attacks and had committed squads and platoons piecemeal, Gillis and the 2d Battalion's commander, Maj. Joseph Baranowski, arrived at the scene to take personal charge of the attack. Following a ferocious mortar barrage, the men of the company charged the hill once more, this time with fixed bayonets. Within moments, the men of one squad reached the top and began what Gillis described as "the damndest hand-to-hand grenade fight I've ever seen." By 1435 the hill was secure. In all, the 24th suffered forty-four wounded.[26]

Patrolling continued throughout the remainder of the month and other hills were taken, but the incident on 15 September marked the last significant attack conducted by the 24th Infantry. On 22 September the regiment received formal notice that on 1 October the 14th Infantry regiment would replace it on the line and that it would cease to exist as a unit. In the days that followed, commanders arranged for final disposition of their equipment, the return home of those of their men who qualified, and the assignment of the rest to racially integrated units. At that time General Swift agreed that since the men of the 24th had been on duty for seventy-two days without relief, those moving to new units would be able to remain in rear areas for a few days to rest before having to go back into combat.[27]

For a time, some thought had been given to the possibility that the 24th might remain in Korea as an integrated force. In that case, since many of the unit's men were eligible for rotation, the regiment would merely have exchanged groups of personnel with the 34th Infantry regiment, then training in Japan. In the end, however, the Far East Command rejected the plan. The reason sometimes given was that integration would have violated the 1866 act of Congress that had designated the 24th as an all-black unit, but that law had in fact been repealed during the early months of 1950. Whatever the reason, when integration came the all-black 3d Battalion of the 9th Infantry regiment remained in existence, dropping the asterisk from its name that designated it as a segregated unit and exchanging personnel with other regiments in the 2d Division. The 64th Tank Battalion did the same, trading its people with other tank units in the Eighth Army. Only

[25] 24th Inf Rgt S–2 Rpt, 1–31 Aug 51, box 3846, RG 407, WNRC; Gillis Diary, 21 Aug 51, 23 Aug 51. Company B's attack is described in 25th Inf Div Periodic Opns Rpts 16, 8 Sep 51, and 17, 9 Sep 51, both in box 3802, RG 407, WNRC. See also 24th Inf Rgt Command Rpt for Sep 51, p. 5, box 3848, RG 407, WNRC.

[26] 24th Inf Rgt Command Rpt for Sep 51, p. 2; S–3 Journal, 24th Inf Rgt, 15 Sep 51, box 3848, RG 407, WNRC. Quote from Gillis Diary, 15 Sep 51. See also Ltr, Thomas D.

Gillis to John A. Cash, 31 Oct 89, CMH files. The bayonet attack was described in *Stars and Stripes*. See Sgt. James Gilbert, "Heroic Eagle Men Rack Up Red Hill," *Stars and Stripes*, undated clipping attached to Ltr, Gillis to Cash. Baranowski had given up command of the 1st Battalion in May when a lieutenant colonel had arrived. He took over the 2d Battalion on 3 September when the commander was relieved by Gillis.

[27] Eighth U.S. Army, Korea, GO 717, Inactivation of Unit, 22 Sep 51, box 3848, RG 407, WNRC; Gillis Diary, 30 Sep 51.

Members of the mortar platoon of Company M, 24th Infantry, prior to inactivation of the regiment, 1 October 1951

the 24th Infantry, because of its peculiar legal status, ceased to exist.[28]

The loss prompted little concern in the United States. The editors of the *Pittsburgh Courier* met the dissolution of the unit with what they called a "twinge of regret," but said they preferred to concentrate on the "new deal" a completely integrated Army would bring to the African-American soldier. There were some objections from interested members of Congress, according to Col. Steve G.

Davis, who had served in the Pentagon at the time as a member of the Army's Plans Division, but the Army itself argued that inactivation would preserve the regiment's well-founded reputation as an all-black unit. Since the same reasoning had been given to justify the inactivation of all-white units, all concerned dropped the matter. On 1 October, as a result, the 24th Infantry passed into history to only the briefest notice in the United States. Its men departed Kumhwa for their final destinations just as they had arrived, the way infantrymen often do, on foot.[29]

[28] MS, 1st Lt Charles G. Cleaver, History of the Korean War, vol. 3, pt. 2, Personnel Problems, Jun 50–Jul 51 [Military History Section, Far East Command, 1952], pp. 150–58, copy in CMH files. The 1866 law was repealed in Public Law 581, Army Organization Act of 1950, Section 401 (81st Cong.), published in *DA Bulletin* 9, 6 Jul 50. See also MacGregor, *Integration of the Armed Forces*, p. 443.

[29] *Pittsburgh Courier*, 4 Aug 51, quoted by Dalfiume, *Desegregation of the U.S. Armed Forces*, p. 212; Intervs, Cash with Steve G. Davis, 2 Sep 88; Muehlbauer with Bergeron, 1 Mar 89.

CHAPTER 11

Conclusion

What happened to the 24th Infantry in Korea? The regiment's experiences were similar in many respects to those of all-white units. It had its heroes and its cowards, its successes and its failures, its good times and its painful memories just as any other military force in the war. Yet it was stigmatized for its deficiencies while its accomplishments passed largely into oblivion. In the end it became the only regiment in Korea recommended for dissolution. It was unreliable, Maj. Gen. William B. Kean told his superiors, and a hindrance to the well-being and good performance of the rest of the 25th Division.

Were Kean's charges accurate, or were they the products of racial prejudice? If they were false, were there nonetheless some grains of truth at the base of the regiment's poor reputation? If they were true, what were their immediate causes, and were there underlying considerations that might elude the passing observer? In the final analysis, where does the truth end and bias begin?

The 24th's record in Korea reveals an undue number of military failures, particularly during the early months of the war. White leaders blamed the problem on the supposed racial characteristics of their African-American subordinates, but a lack of unit cohesion brought on by racial prejudice and the poor leadership it engendered at all levels was mainly at fault. Some units within the regiment performed well, and many black soldiers laid down their lives willingly and heroically for their comrades in arms. Segregation and the racial prejudices behind it—the entire system of beliefs and practices that assigned blacks to an inferior position within society and the Army—nonetheless hindered the emergence of effective leadership within the regiment and destroyed the bonds of mutual trust and reliance that were necessary if the unit was to hold together in combat. With military commanders at all levels prone to expect less from the black soldier than the white and inclined to discount the mistakes of white commanders leading black units, misfortune became virtually inevitable.

The problems the regiment experienced grew out of a history extending back over a hundred years to the abolition of slavery that had marred the American experience from its beginning and the attempts of the nation and its people to come to terms with the dilemmas that resulted. For once the African-American had been freed of his bondage and had gained some rights of citizenship, it made sense that he should serve in the nation's armed forces. Yet vast hostility to blacks remained in the very fabric of the society, so much so that the integration of whites and blacks within the armed forces seemed out of the question. As a result, although black units were often brigaded with white regiments or incorporated into white divisions, black soldiers were never included in all-white units. They served their time in the Army apart, segregated into battalions, regiments, and divisions reserved exclusively for them.

Despite the affliction of racial prejudice, African-American soldiers fought dependably and creditably in the Civil War, on the Western frontier, in the Spanish-American War, and during the Philippine Insurrection. Even so, they never seemed able to overcome the misgivings of the predominately white nation that employed them. Instead, the white world pulled back into itself and enacted "separate but equal" laws that had the effect of rendering African-Americans and their accomplishments invisible. When segregated soldiers rebelled against that system in Houston and elsewhere, attacking civilian communities that had oppressed them, the mistrust they engendered among whites erased whatever credit blacks had received in earlier wars and influenced how white commanders viewed them in World Wars I and II.

In both conflicts the African-American soldier seemed destined for failure from the beginning. Accepting assertions that blacks were lazy, shuffling, and of low intellect, the Army's commanders would have been happy to have them out of the service completely and used them mainly to perform menial tasks such as unloading ships and digging ditches. Even when finally compelled by political pressure from the black community and white liberals to form all-black regiments and divisions and to allow them to enter combat, the Army employed them with reluctance. Then, when African-Americans performed well, as when they fought under French command in World War I, white America made little of their successes, but when they failed the news was well circulated. Overall, few in positions of authority were willing to admit that their own attitudes might be at fault or that a lack of mutual confidence and respect between the black soldier and his white commanders might have destroyed the sense of oneness, mutual dependency, and self-worth in black units that is at the core of every successful military force.

At the end of World War II, the Army's commanders began to seek ways to use the black soldier more effectively. Falling back on the successful example which black platoons integrated into all-white units had set in the European theater, they began to advocate the dissolution of all-black regiments and divisions and the inclusion of their platoons and battalions into white units. The nub of the problem remained, however. Although panels such as the Gillem Board endorsed equality in the work place, they put off dealing with segregation and left important issues unresolved, such as whether blacks could ever command whites. Indeed, even when President Truman issued Executive Order 9981, which stipulated equality of treatment and opportunity for all within the armed services without regard to race, the Army temporized, well aware of the racism prevalent in the community it served and unwilling to do anything that might harm its ability to gather funds and recruits.

The 24th Infantry in Japan was a model not only of the tensions that dogged all-black units in that day but also of the subtle interplay those problems could have in combination with the many challenges the Army faced in the postwar period. On the surface, conditions within the unit seemed favorable. The regiment was well situated at Camp Gifu, and life seemed good for its troops. Down below, however, there was much that was wrong.

To begin with, the Army itself was undergoing extreme turbulence. Personnel strengths declined rapidly following World War II and then swung drastically up and down in both white and black units as budgets and manpower policies shifted with the political winds. Training declined, equipment shortages grew, and officers who might have sought to make the military a career found themselves without employment. Training improved in 1949, but if Lt. Gen. Walton H. Walker's Eighth Army is any criterion, it remained incomplete. Complicating matters, soldier and officer alike were unprepared mentally for war. Many had joined the Army to get an education, to improve their economic prospects, or because there was nothing better for them in the civilian world. War was the last thing on their minds.

The Eighth Army again provides a case in point. Many of the unit's soldiers were civilians at heart, intent upon enjoying the pleasures of life in occupied Japan, where a G.I.'s salary could pay for an abundance of readily available pleasures. Black-market activities thrived among the troops, alcoholism flourished, and venereal disease was rampant. But the number-one transgression in the Eighth Army in the spring of 1950 was drug abuse, which spread with apparent abandon in some units, particularly those such as the 24th Infantry regiment which operated in or near large port cities.

The 24th Infantry experienced the same difficulties as the rest of the Eighth Army, but if the unit's duties at Kobe increased the incidence of venereal disease and drug-related problems within its ranks, the regiment appears to have managed the situation relatively well once deployments to the port ceased in September 1949. Maintaining generally high esprit de corps, the unit gained a deserved reputation for its prowess at sports and its fine marching. Its training was on a par with that of most other regiments in the Eighth Army, and at the beginning of the Korean War it was one of only a few that had undergone some form of regimental maneuvers. While the Army General Classification Test scores for the 24th Infantry's men were significantly lower than for the whites in its sister regiments, those figures were inadequate as measures of innate intelligence. Indeed, many white officers assigned to the regiment would later insist that the enlisted men and noncommissioned officers of the unit, whatever their schooling, often knew their jobs and did them well.

All that said, the 24th nevertheless suffered from a virulent racial prejudice that ate incessantly at the bonds uniting its men. Its effects were often hidden at Camp Gifu, which had become an artificial island for blacks—"our own little world," as some of the men described it—but even there, discontent festered just beneath the surface calm. Unwritten but firmly held assignment policies, for example, ensured that black officers, whatever their competence, would rarely if ever command whites. Except for Lt. Col. Forest Lofton, as a result, the senior commanders of the regiment were all white. As for the field-grade officers, only the chaplains and a few majors in staff assignments were black.

The mistrust that smoldered on both sides at Camp Gifu was largely hidden behind a screen of military conventions and good manners, but it was still there. Aware that most promotions and career-enhancing assignments went to white officers, some of whom were clearly inferior in education and military competence to their black colleagues, many black officers were frustrated and resentful. Since few if any of them would ever rise to a rank above captain, they could only conclude that the Army considered them second class. They retaliated by developing a view that the 24th was a "penal" regiment for white officers who had "screwed up." The whites, for their part, although a number got along well with their black counterparts, mainly kept to themselves.

The tensions that existed among the regiment's officers had parallels in enlisted ranks. Although black soldiers worked well with their white superiors at times and relations between the races were open, honest, and mutually fulfilling, those cases involved situations in which white officers recognized the worth of their subordinates and afforded them the impartiality and dignity they deserved. Many whites nevertheless shared the racially prejudiced attitudes and beliefs common to white civilian society, and the labored paternalism and condescension they practiced were readily apparent to any soldier with a mind to see them.

Although it would be a mistake to conclude that every black soldier disliked his white superior, the enmity that resulted ran deep enough in some cases to overlap onto the black officers of the regiment. Although Capt. Richard W. Williams, Jr., was well admired because he stood up to the white power structure, those officers who gave evidence, whether true or not, of attempting to play along with the whites were sometimes vilified for abandoning their race. "He had a Creole wife and seemed to think he was superior," one soldier thus said of 1st Lt. Charles Ellis. "We think he had an identity crisis."

As the regiment's stay lengthened in Japan, an unevenness came into being that subtly affected military readiness. In companies commanded by white officers who treated their men with respect but refused to accept low standards of discipline and performance, racial prejudice tended to be insignificant. A bond of sorts developed between those who were leaders and those who were led. In other companies, often commanded by officers who failed to enforce high standards because they wished to avoid charges of racial prejudice or because they were simply poor leaders, mutual respect and reliance were weak. On the surface, all seemed to run well. Underneath, however, hostility and frustration lingered, to break forth only when those units faced combat and their soldiers realized their lives depended on officers they did not trust.

The problem might have had little effect on readiness if commanders had received the time to work out their relationships with their men, but the competition among some of the unit's officers for Regular Army commissions, the Competitive Tour program, produced a constant churning within the regiment as officers arrived at units, spent three months in a position, and then departed for new assignments. In addition, the officer complements of entire companies might change to maintain segregation or to ensure that a black would never command whites. Under the circumstances, officers often had little time to think through what they were doing. A confluence of good men might produce a cohesive, effective, high-performing company or platoon, but everything might dissolve overnight with a change of leaders.

Given the situation, the personality of the regimental commander was vital, and for much of the time in Japan the unit was endowed with an officer who seemed ideally suited for the job. Strong, aggressive, and experienced, Col. Michael E. Halloran held the respect and support of most of his subordinates, whether commissioned or enlisted. Although a few claimed that his policies undermined the chain of command and contributed to an atmosphere of condescension and low standards, the performance of the regiment while he was in charge was all that anyone could have expected at that time and in that place. The effectiveness of Halloran's successor is more in question. Col. Horton V. White was intelligent and well intentioned, but his low-key, hands-off style of command did little to fill the void when Halloran departed.

It would be interesting to know what the results would have been if the 24th had gone to war under Halloran rather than White, but the efficiency of a unit in combat is rarely determined by the presence of a single individual, however competent, experienced, or inspiring. What is clear is that if the 24th went into battle much as the other regiments in the Eighth Army did, incompletely trained, badly equipped, and short on experience, it carried baggage none of the others possessed—all the problems of trust and self-confidence that racial prejudice had imposed.

The mistrust endemic to the regiment began to appear just as soon as word arrived that it was to depart for Korea. Almost immediately rumors began to circulate among both whites and blacks that the unit would never go into combat because of the supposed poor performance of all-black units in earlier wars. Then, as the date of departure approached, white officers began to hear reports that a black chaplain had undermined the chain of command by suggesting during a sermon that it was inappropriate for men of color to fight one another on behalf of whites. Black officers received unsubstantiated word that the black commander of the 1st Battalion, Colonel Lofton, had been reassigned to prevent him from commanding whites in combat. Even as the unit moved from Pusan to Sangju, a purely speculative story made the rounds to the effect that the regimental executive officer had pretended to have a heart attack rather than go into combat with an all-black unit. None of those stories were ever substantiated and the one about Lofton may have been wrong, but they were still indicative of the deep divisions that existed within the regiment.

Although symptomatic of poor discipline in portions of the 24th and a source of doubts on the part of some whites about the advisability of committing the regiment to war, the disturbances at Camp Gifu and at Moji on the first leg of the trip to Korea involved only a small minority of the unit's men and said little about its readiness. In fact, on paper the 24th was probably more prepared for combat than most of the other regiments that accompanied it. It had three full battalions instead of two, and if its equipment was old and worn and its men nervous and unseasoned, it had at least exercised at the regimental level in field maneuvers. Unlike General Dean's 24th Division, the unit also had the opportunity to introduce itself gradually to combat rather than having to face enemy fire from almost the moment it arrived. Indeed, the 3d Battalion was fortunate enough to achieve a success at Yech'on, one of the first accomplishments of the war for United Nations forces.

While hardly significant to the overall course of the war, Yech'on could have had important benefits for both the 3d Battalion and the rest of the 24th. Once the soldier has tasted victory, so the reasoning goes, his self-confidence rises and combat becomes easier for him to face. In the case of the 24th, however, there was no time for Yech'on to take root. Almost immediately the unit began to encounter misfortunes that shattered the faith of its men in their officers and the trust of its officers in their men.

There was no single reason for what happened. An aggressive enemy, inadequate equipment, inexperience at all levels, leadership failures high and low, casualties among key personnel, and a lack of bonding and cohesion in some units all played their part. There was no lack of courage among the regiment's officers and men. A number of well-trained squads, platoons, and companies performed ably. Nevertheless, all military units undergo a weeding-out process when they first enter combat. Inept officers and NCOs die or move aside to make room for the more competent.

Much the same thing happened in the other American regiments fighting in Korea at that time. The same reasons for failure were present and the same process of winnowing occurred. But within the 24th, when disturbing trends emerged, no one took action. Although straggling increased to sometimes epidemic proportions, the leadership of the regiment did little more to stop it than to return offenders to their units. Every occurrence made the next one easier. Some squads and platoons became so accustomed to withdrawals that their men began to abandon their positions after only the sound of firing in the distance or minor enemy sniper or mortar fire. As the trend continued, the trust of one soldier on the line for the man next to him deteriorated and each became more inclined than ever to flee.

Other regiments experienced the same phenomenon, but what happened to the 24th was complicated by mistrust and the expectations it fostered. In an attempt to lead by example, commissioned and noncommissioned officers stayed at their posts with those of their men who were willing to hold and suffered inordinately high casualties as a result. As they did, suspicions took root among them and rumors began to rise about how black soldiers would sometimes abandon wounded white officers. Feeding the process, failures in the 24th tended to be attributed less to their military causes than to the race of the unit's soldiers. Blacks were afraid of the dark, so the stories went. They would not dig foxholes, and they lacked the innate intelligence to keep their equipment in good repair.

The problems confronting the regiment deepened when the fighting shifted south from Sangju to the area west of Masan. Casualties among officers reached critical levels, with some companies going through five commanders in less than a month. The replacements were often inexperienced and untrained in infantry skills. The situation was little better among the sergeants. As for the enlisted men, replacements arrived who were unable even to load and fire their rifles without first receiving instruction. Although a number of soldiers continued to perform capably, the self-confidence of the unit as a whole and the trust of its members in one another continued to decline, and as they did more failures occurred.

Despite the pattern, when the 24th pulled into the Pusan Perimeter, it managed to hold the line. In the fight for Battle Mountain, Company C was reduced to a shell and other portions of the regiment suffered greatly. Focused on the mountains south of Haman rather than on the low hills just west of the town, the regiment was nevertheless unprepared on 1 September when the enemy attacked through the center of its position and the 2d Battalion collapsed. Poorly trained South Korean troops manning portions of the line were partially to blame. So was a weak regimental reserve and poorly fortified positions. A key ingredient in the collapse, however, was the large number of stragglers who left their positions without permission during the early portions of the attack. Remnants of Companies E and G held on. Much of Company F escaped to the north, and the battalion command post conducted a brief but spirited defense, but the 2d Battalion ceased to exist as a combat organization. Only the fortuitous presence of the 27th Infantry regiment saved the day.

The white leadership of the regiment and the division blamed the soldiers of the 24th for what had happened, but they themselves were at least as much at fault. The new regimental commander, Col. Arthur J. Champeny, and his staff had not only approved the weak tactical dispositions of the 2d Battalion, Champeny himself had done much to destroy whatever trust was left in the regiment with ill-advised, public remarks about the conduct of blacks in World War II.

At that point General Kean recommended that the Eighth Army dissolve the regiment. The evidence submitted—a whole series of interviews with black and white officers—gave overwhelming testimony to the presence of heavy straggling within the unit but said little about the tactical incompetence and the accumulating failures of leadership at the root of what had happened. Perhaps, given the climate of the time, there was little possibility for any other conclusion. Whites expected blacks to fail. When they did, few looked beyond race to find a cause.

Kean's recommendation led to further investigations and to a determination by the Far East Command that the 24th should be disbanded, but the Eighth Army's inability to organize a new regiment to take the 24th's place on short notice put the decision on hold for a time. In the interim Champeny and his successor, Lt. Col. John T. Corley, moved at last to punish chronic stragglers. That long overdue effort, combined with reforms which Corley instituted, put an effective end to the problem. The courts-martial that followed did nothing to rehabilitate the 24th Infantry's reputation. Indeed, the sentence of death handed down against

1st Lt. Leon A. Gilbert only added to the aura of shame surrounding the regiment.

The 24th itself soldiered on despite those difficulties. Over the preceding months, casualties had taken a heavy toll on the unit's problem soldiers, but a core of brave, capable enlisted men had remained. Those individuals had performed numerous acts of heroism, sometimes standing their ground when all had seemed lost and earning many medals for bravery under fire. To their number was added a whole new shift of soldiers, untrained and inexperienced but also lacking the feelings of mistrust, racial alienation, and drug dependency that had afflicted a number of their predecessors. Those men learned their jobs and drew together under the strain of combat. A new group of white officer replacements also arrived. Some were also inexperienced, but many were capable, combat-seasoned veterans of World War II. If they had their prejudices, they kept them enough to themselves to gain the confidence of their men.

The regiment took long strides toward recovery during the attack north that followed the Inch'on landing and the break out from Pusan. The men had time to train, and in the process of fighting their way back to Seoul they grew in confidence. The order to attack north across the 38th Parallel came as a shock to some because they were looking forward to a return to Camp Gifu, but all concerned made the best of a difficult moment and performed their mission.

The test for the regiment came shortly after United Nations forces crossed the Ch'ongch'on River and neared North Korea's border with China. Advancing through rugged terrain while flanking units moved to either side along valley floors, the body of the regiment played only a minor role in meeting the Chinese counterattack. Portions of the regiment, however, incurred heavy damage. Located on a ridge overlooking a valley where part of the enemy's main assault occurred, Companies E and G held off strong attacks for most of the day before escaping overnight into the lines of the 9th Infantry regiment. There they fought on with distinction. To the west, most of the 1st Battalion was able to pull back with only minor difficulty, but Company C, fighting with Task Force Wilson, was less fortunate. Because of communications failures and confused command arrangements, the unit found itself abandoned and eventually surrendered. Occupying the center, the 3d Battalion withdrew without major difficulty and in relatively good order, but breakdowns in control at the battalion's command post as well as at the corps and division levels led to another tragedy. Holding in an exposed position at Kunu-ri while the rest of the regiment received orders to pull back, the unit collapsed in an enemy attack and was all but overwhelmed in the debacle that followed. In that case, as with Company C, what happened was the product not only of the confusion of war but also of a failure of command. It received heavy play in the press, however, as an example of black ineptitude and the inability of all-black units to carry their load in combat. After that, visitors to the regiment from higher commands became frequent, always inspecting to see whether the old problems would reappear.

The regiment once more recovered. When it reentered combat in late February it demonstrated its ability both in the attack and on the defense, but it was hardly immune to the misfortunes of war. The unit's performance at the Han River crossing, for example, was all that anyone could have hoped for. The assault across the Hant'an, however, only added to the mistrust encircling the regiment. In that operation, the 1st Battalion performed well, securing a crossing and then advancing through difficult terrain against a strongly emplaced enemy. Setbacks in another area nonetheless diminished that accomplishment. The 3d Battalion also crossed the river, but only after a last-minute change of plans that put it well downstream from the 1st Battalion in difficult terrain heavily defended by a well-entrenched enemy force. The unit did as it was ordered, made the crossing, and pressed forward up a steep mountainside, but then it collapsed under enemy fire and fell back in disorder. Either inadvertently or on purpose, officers passed information to the rear depicting a far more favorable situation than the one that prevailed. When the division commander found out, he lost all confidence in the regiment forever.

From that day on, the division followed the unit's operations even more closely. Although the regiment delivered a generally solid performance in the attack north of the Hant'an and then conducted a withdrawal to Line Golden after the Chinese Spring Offensive, the suspicion never departed. The unit participated in the Eighth Army's drive back to the north in May and June 1951 and again performed well.

When the last commander of the regiment, Col. Thomas D. Gillis, took charge in August 1951, Maj. Gen. Ira P. Swift warned him that the 24th held the weakest line in all of the Eighth Army. Gillis was not convinced. Surveying the regiment, he concluded that leadership was the problem and proceeded to relieve a number of officers. His efforts were rewarded on 15 September, when Company F conducted a heroic bayonet and grenade assault, but the accomplishment, like so much that had happened to the 24th, went largely unnoticed. Although it received minor mention in a small article in *Stars and Stripes*, it went unrecognized by higher commanders in the crush that accompanied the dissolution of the regiment.

What, in the end, can be said about the 24th? All told, it seems clear that if the unit failed at times, the race of its people was not the reason. Instead, in addition to the lapses of command and the deficiencies in training and supply that burdened any military unit at the time, whether black or white, the regiment labored under a special burden, unique to itself, that seemed to doom it to misfortune. Afflicted by a stereotype that African-Americans were innately inferior, the finest black officers were unable to rise to positions of responsibility within the organization. Meanwhile, if some highly talented whites were present, they were too few to have the sort of effect that might have made a difference. Most whites of high potential had little incentive to seek duty with the regiment and actively avoided it when they could.

With leadership deficient, particularly at the beginning of the war, failures large and small proliferated. As they did, the self-confidence and motivation of the common soldier declined, and he began to lose any sense that he was part of something worthwhile, larger than himself. In the end every man stood alone, unsure not only of his own abilities but also of those of the soldier next to him. Many fought well but others fled. In that light, the regiment's achievements—during the first weeks of the war, in the breakout from the Pusan Perimeter, at the Han and Hant'an River crossings, and elsewhere—bear a special mark. They underscore the courage, resilience, and determination of those among the unit's members who chose to do their duty, to fight in the face of adversity, and to prevail.

Appendix A—Infantry Regiment Organization

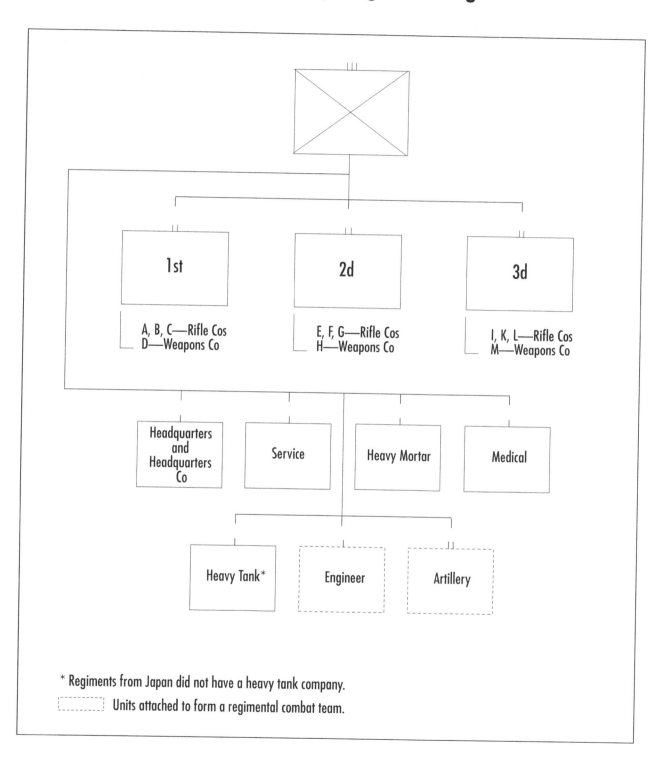

1st — A, B, C—Rifle Cos; D—Weapons Co

2d — E, F, G—Rifle Cos; H—Weapons Co

3d — I, K, L—Rifle Cos; M—Weapons Co

Headquarters and Headquarters Co

Service

Heavy Mortar

Medical

Heavy Tank*

Engineer

Artillery

* Regiments from Japan did not have a heavy tank company.

Units attached to form a regimental combat team.

Appendix B—Black Units Serving in the Korean War September 1950–September 1951

2d Ranger Infantry Company
2d Rocket Field Artillery Battery
24th Infantry regiment
25th Chemical Decontamination Company
28th Transportation Truck Company
42d Transportation Truck Company
46th Transportation Truck Company
47th Transportation Heavy Truck Company
48th Transportation Heavy Truck Company
49th Transportation Truck Company
51st Military Police Criminal Investigation
    Detachment
54th Transportation Heavy Truck Company
55th Engineer Treadway Bridge Company
55th Ordnance Ammunition Company
56th Army Band
57th Ordnance Recovery Company
58th Armored Field Artillery Battalion
58th Quartermaster Salvage Company
60th Transportation Truck Company
64th Tank Battalion
65th Ordnance Ammunition Company
69th Ordnance Ammunition Company
69th Transportation Truck Battalion
70th Transportation Truck Battalion
71st Chemical Smoke Generator Company
73d Engineer Combat Battalion
73d Transportation Truck Company
74th Engineer Combat Battalion
74th Transportation Truck Company
76th Antiaircraft Artillery Automatic Weapons
    Battalion
76th Engineer Dump Truck Company
77th Engineer Combat Company
78th Antiaircraft Artillery Automatic Weapons
    Battalion
78th Antiaircraft Artillery Gun Battalion
91st Ordnance Medium Automotive Maintenance
    Company

93d Engineer Construction Battalion
95th Transportation Car Company
96th Field Artillery Battalion
112th Army Postal Unit
130th Quartermaster Bakery Company
159th Field Artillery Battalion
167th Transportation Truck Battalion
212th Military Police Company
231st Transportation Truck Battalion
250th Quartermaster Laundry Detachment
375th Chemical Smoke Generator Company
376th Engineer Construction Battalion
396th Transportation Truck Company
402d Engineer Panel Bridge Company
403d Signal Construction Company
503d Field Artillery Battalion
505th Quartermaster Reclamation and
    Maintenance Company
506th Quartermaster Petroleum Supply Company
512th Engineer Dump Truck Company
512th Military Police Company
513th Transportation Truck Company
514th Transportation Truck Company
515th Transportation Truck Company
529th Quartermaster Petroleum Supply Company
539th Transportation Truck Company
540th Transportation Truck Company
541st Transportation Truck Company
546th Engineer Fire Fighting Company
548th Engineer Service Battalion
549th Quartermaster Laundry Company
551st Transportation Truck Company
553d Transportation Heavy Truck Company
556th Transportation Heavy Truck Company
558th Medical Collecting Separate Company
558th Transportation Amphibious Truck
    Company
559th Medical Ambulance Company
560th Medical Ambulance Company

563d Military Police Service Company
567th Medical Ambulance Company
568th Medical Ambulance Company
570th Engineer Water Supply Company
571st Engineer Dump Truck Company
573d Engineer Pontoon Bridge Company
584th Transportation Truck Company
595th Engineer Dump Truck Company
619th Ordnance Ammunition Company
630th Ordnance Ammunition Company
636th Ordnance Ammunition Company
665th Transportation Truck Company
696th Ordnance Ammunition Company
715th Transportation Truck Company
726th Transportation Truck Company
811th Engineer Aviation Battalion
821st Quartermaster Bath Company
822d Engineer Aviation Battalion

839th Engineer Aviation Battalion
849th Quartermaster Petroleum Supply Company
863d Transportation Port Company
866th Transportation Port Company
933d Antiaircraft Artillery Automatic Weapons
    Battalion, Battery A
945th Quartermaster Service Company
999th Armored Field Artillery Battalion

Source: Army Directory and Station List, published bimonthly during the Korean War. In this directory, black units were designated by an asterisk ("*") before the unit name through September 1951. After that date black units are not separately designated, so it is impossible to state which black units served in Korea from November 1951 through the end of the conflict.

Bibliographical Note

Primary Sources

For the most part, except in the early chapters, we based this book on records, reports, and documents generated in the course of the operations it describes. With a few exceptions, most are housed in the National Archives Center in College Park, Maryland. The collection is uneven because some items have been lost, but much that is pertinent to the story of 25th Infantry Division and the 24th Infantry regiment still remains on file.

The records of U.S. Army commands, including correspondence and histories pertaining to the units themselves, are contained in Record Group (RG) 338 at College Park. This record group also contains documents relating to the I Corps command in Japan. The box numbers prefaced with a "P" are particularly important. Although not completely cataloged, they contain much of value for the history of the Eighth Army in Japan and Korea, especially the Kobe base files. The Awards files in RG 338 are incomplete, but the general orders for awards are located at the Awards Branch of the U.S. Total Army Personnel Command, Alexandria, Virginia. Some of the materials in RG 338 are duplicated in files of the adjutant general's office, RG 407, which contains war diaries and other official reports submitted by units. There, most of the reports, journals, and registers of the 25th Division and the various regiments included in this study

are found. The provost marshal records are in RG 331. The Okinawa records are in RG 200, and the Far East Command Observer Team reports are in RG 337. The inspector general interviews and reports are housed in RG 159. Box numbers have been cited in the footnotes, but they may be different now because the National Archives sometimes rearranges its material.

Some annual reports from individual commands are on file in the collections of the U.S. Army Center of Military History (CMH) in Washington, D.C., especially those for 1946, 1947, 1948, and 1949. Copies of the Eighth Army's command histories for those years are also there. Documents and interviews compiled by journalist Clay Blair for his book *The Forgotten War* were of great use. All are now housed in the collections of the U.S. Army Military History Institute at Carlisle Barracks, Pennsylvania. The Army's view of the Houston affair is in Headquarters, Southern Department, Office of the Department Inspector, Report on the Houston Riot, 13 September 1917, file 370.61 (Riots), 11 October 1917, RG 393, National Archives and Records Administration (NARA) Washington, D.C. Backup papers and documents pertaining to Billy Mossman's *Ebb and Flow* and Roy Appleman's *South to the Naktong, North to the Yalu* are on file at NARA. Records and notes that deal with Appleman's commercial works are housed at the U.S. Army Military History Institute.

The maps used in this study are all available in the Cartography Division at the National Archives Center in College Park, Maryland.

Oral History Interviews and Manuscript Sources

We also based this book heavily on oral history interviews conducted over a space of several years by John A. Cash, Bernard L. Muehlbauer, Timothy Rainey, Mary L. Haynes, William T. Bowers, Richard O. Perry, and George L. MacGarrigle. The transcripts of those sessions are in CMH files, but they will ultimately go either to the National Archives or to the U.S. Army Military History Institute.

A number of sources that are either in manuscript or limited-distribution form were also of value. Francis E. Lewis' "Negro Army Regulars in the Spanish-American War: Smoked Yankees at Santiago De Cuba" (M.A. diss., University of Texas at Austin, 1969) was useful for the Spanish-American War period. The opinions of white officers on the performance of African-American units during World War I are set down in MS, Historical Section, Army War College, The Colored Soldier in the U.S. Army [May 1942], CMH files. For a brief history of the 92d Division in World War I, see MS, Jehu C. Hunter and Major Clark, The Buffalo Division in World War II [copyright Jehu C. Hunter, 1985], CMH files.

Two particular works were of special importance. Brig. Gen. George B. Barth's Tropic Lightning and Taro Leaf in Korea, an undated, limited-issue publication in CMH's collection, was composed as a history of the 25th Division's artillery force. Candid and forthright, if overly observant of the artillery's point of view, the work tracks the 24th through most of its first year in combat. It is an important source for aspects of the regiment's story that have gone unnoticed until now. Also of value was Col. Thomas D. Gillis' handwritten diary for the few weeks he commanded the 24th. An invaluable picture of the regiment during its last days, the work is on file with the transcript of Gillis' interview at CMH. Other diaries and several collections of letters home to wives were available to the

authors, but only as background. Their owners declined to have them cited or used in any form. Although they were of no value as sources for this study, their descriptions of some units of the 24th at Gifu and during training exercises at Fuji were telling. We hope those collections will become available to researchers at some future date.

Secondary Sources

A number of printed works detail the role of blacks in the U.S. armed forces during the early years of American history. Among the most comprehensive are Bernard C. Nalty, Strength for the Fight: A History of Black Americans in the Military (New York: Free Press, 1986), and Morris MacGregor and Bernard C. Nalty, Blacks in the United States Armed Forces, Basic Documents (Wilmington, Del.: Scholarly Resources, 1977).

John Hope Franklin's From Slavery to Freedom: A History of Negro Americans (New York: Vintage Books, 1969) provides a general history of the African-American in American life. More specific works dealing with the early years include Benjamin Quarles, The Negro in the American Revolution (Chapel Hill: University of North Carolina Press, 1961); Lorenzo Johnston Green, "The Negro in the War of 1812 and the Civil War," Negro History Bulletin (March 1951); and Roland MacConnell, Negro Troops in Antebellum Louisiana: A History of the Battalion of Free Men of Color (Baton Rouge: Louisiana University Press, 1968).

African-Americans came into their own as soldiers during the American Civil War. Good general histories are Dudley T. Cornish, The Sable Arm: Negro Troops in the Union Army, 1861–1865 (New York: Longmans, Green, 1956), and Benjamin Quarles, The Negro in the Civil War (New York: Da Capo Press, 1989). Joseph T. Glatthaar, Forged in Battle: The Civil War Alliance of Black Soldiers and White Officers (New York: Free Press, 1990), is a more recent study that deals with officer-enlisted relations during the period.

The black soldier during the Indian Wars has been the subject of many studies. Among the more important are the following: William H.

Leckie, *The Buffalo Soldiers* (Norman: University of Oklahoma Press, 1967); Monroe Lee Billington, *New Mexico's Buffalo Soldiers, 1866–1900* (Niwot: University of Colorado Press, 1991); Arlen Fowler, *The Black Infantry in the West, 1869–1891* (Westport, Conn.: Greenwood Press, 1971); and Preston Amos, *Above and Beyond in the West: Negro Medal of Honor Winners, 1870–1890* (Washington, D.C.: Potomac Corral of the Westerners, 1974). Frank Schubert has two recent studies of the subject: *Buffalo Soldiers, Braves and the Brass, The Story of Fort Robinson, Nebraska* (Shippensburg, Pa.: White Mane Publishing Co., 1993) and *On the Trail of the Buffalo Soldier: Biographies of African-Americans in the U.S. Army, 1866–1917* (Wilmington, Del.: Scholarly Resources, 1995). Paul H. Carlson's *Pecos Bill, A Military Biography of William R. Shafter* (College Station: Texas A&M University Press, 1989) contains considerable information on the 24th Infantry and its campaigns in Texas during the 1870s.

For background on the late nineteenth century and the repression of African-Americans during the period, see C. Vann Woodward, *The Strange Career of Jim Crow* (New York: Oxford University Press, 1966). Among the most prominent articles on blacks in the armed forces during the period are Frank N. Schubert, "Black Soldiers on the White Frontier: Some Factors Influencing Race Relations," *Phylon* 32 (Winter 1971); Schubert, "The Fort Robinson Y.M.C.A., 1902–1907," *Nebraska History* 55 (Summer 1974); Schubert, "The Suggs Affray: The Black Cavalry in the Johnson County War," *Western Historical Quarterly* 4 (January 1973); Schubert, "The Violent World of Emanuel Stance, Fort Robinson, 1887," *Nebraska History* 55 (Summer 1974); John H. Nankivell, ed., *The History of the Twenty-Fifty Regiment, United States Infantry, 1869–1926* (Fort Collins, Colo.: Old Army Press, 1972); and Marvin Fletcher, *The Black Soldier and Officer in the United States Army, 1891–1917* (Columbia: University of Missouri Press, 1974).

Graham A. Cosmas' *An Army for Empire: The United States Army in the Spanish-American War*, 2d ed. (Shippensburg, Pa.: White Mane Publishing Co., 1994) provides a general history of the Army's role in the Spanish-American War with special insights on the Battle of San Juan Hill and its environs. Cosmas also deals with the role of black regulars at San Juan in "San Juan Hill and El Caney, 1–2 July 1898," in Charles E. Heller and William A. Stofft, eds., *America's First Battles, 1776–1965* (Lawrence: University of Kansas Press, 1986), pp. 109–48. Willard B. Gatewood, Jr., "Negro Troops in Florida, 1898," *Florida Historical Quarterly* 49 (July 1970), is a good account of black-white relations in Florida just prior to the American force's departure for Cuba. Gatewood also has an excellent, full-length study on African-Americans in the age of empire. See Willard B. Gatewood, *Black Americans and the White Man's Burden, 1898–1903* (Urbana: University of Illinois Press, 1975). Initial reports of the 24th's role in combat during the war itself are contained in U.S. War Department, *Annual Report of the War Department for 1898* (Washington, D.C.: Government Printing Office, 1898).

Conditions during the effort to quell the Philippine Insurrection are described in Michael C. Robinson and Frank N. Schubert, "David Fagen: An Afro-American Rebel in the Philippines, 1899–1901," *Pacific Historical Review* 44 (February 1975), and Willard B. Gatewood, "Black Americans and the Quest for Empire," *Journal of Southern History*, vol. 37. For firsthand accounts of the conflict, see Sanford M. Thomas, *War in the Philippines* (Privately published, 1903), MacArthur Memorial, Norfolk, Va., and Willard B. Gatewood, *Smoked Yankees and the Struggle for Empire: Letters From Negro Soldiers, 1898–1902* (Fayetteville: University of Arkansas Press, 1987). Thomas was a black noncommissioned officer who served in Company H of the 24th.

An early examination of the Brownsville affair was conducted by the Constitution League of the United States. The league's preliminary report, along with basic documents relating to the episode, is in U.S. Congress, Senate, *Preliminary Report of the Commission of the Constitution League of the United States on Affray at Brownsville, Texas, August 13 and 14, 1906*, 59th Cong., 2d sess., 10 December 1906, doc. 107 (Washington, D.C.: Government Printing Office, 1906). For more modern treatments, see

John D. Weaver, *The Brownsville Raid* (New York: W. W. Norton, 1970), and Ann J. Lane, *The Brownsville Affair* (Port Washington, New York: National University, 1971).

The best examination of the Houston Riot and its aftermath is Robert V. Haynes' *A Night of Violence: The Houston Riot of 1917* (Baton Rouge: Louisiana State University Press, 1976). Shorter treatments include Rosalind Alexander, "Houston's Hidden History," *Texas Observer*, 7 April 1989, and "The Houston Riot and Courts-Martial of 1917," n.d., copy in CMH files. Garna L. Christian examines a little-known episode of the same sort involving the 1st Battalion of the 24th at Waco, Texas, in "The Ordeal and the Prize: The 24th Infantry and Camp MacArthur," *Military Affairs* 50 (April 1986).

Timothy K. Nenninger's "American Military Effectiveness in the First World War," in Allan R. Millet and Williamson Murray, eds., *Military Effectiveness: The First World War* (Boston: Unwin Hyman, 1990), vol. 1, provides an overall context for how well-prepared American forces were prior to and during World War I. William E. B. DuBois dealt with the problems of the black soldier in "The Negro and the War Department," the *Crisis* 16 (May 1918). DuBois' work is heavily summarized in Ulysses Lee, *The Employment of Negro Troops*, United States Army in World War II (Washington, D.C.: U.S. Army Center of Military History, Government Printing Office, 1990). For a first-person description of the 93d Infantry Division and its 371st regiment, see Chester D. Heywood, *Negro Combat Troops in the World War, The Story of the 371st Infantry* (Worcester, Mass.: Commonwealth Press, 1928). For more on the subject, see Arthur E. Barbeau and Florette Henri, *The Unknown Soldiers: Black American Troops in World War I* (Philadelphia: Temple University Press, 1974).

The most detailed study of the African-American in World War II is Lee's *The Employment of Negro Troops*. Sociological and anthropological dimensions of the subject are treated in Samuel A. Stouffer et al., *The American Soldier: Adjustment During Army Life* (Princeton: Princeton University Press, 1949). Excellent oral histories are Mary Penick Motley's *The Invisible Soldier: The Experience*

of the Black Soldier, World War II (Detroit: Wayne State University Press, 1975) and Phillip McGuire's *Taps for a Jim Crow Army: Letters From Black Soldiers in World War II* (Lexington: University of Kentucky Press, 1993). McGuire has also written a biography of Judge William H. Hastie. See Phillip McGuire, *He, Too, Spoke for Democracy: Judge Hastie, World War II, and the Black Soldier* (New York: Greenwood Press, 1988). Based on personal interviews with black and white officers in command of African-American troops during the war, Bell I. Wiley's monograph, *The Training of Negro Troops*, Study 36 (Washington, D.C.: Historical Section, Army Ground Forces, 1946), provides important background information on the problems the members of all-black units encountered during this era.

The period between World War II and the Korean War, the Korean War itself, and the effort to integrate the Army are dealt with in a number of important works, the most thorough being Morris J. MacGregor, Jr.'s *The Integration of the Armed Forces, 1940–1965*, Defense Studies series (Washington, D.C.: U.S. Army Center of Military History, Government Printing Office, 1989). Richard M. Dalfiume's *Desegregation of the U.S. Armed Forces: Fighting on Two Fronts, 1939–1953* (Columbia: University of Missouri Press, 1969) is very effective in describing the problem with racial quotas. Lee Nichols' *Breakthrough on the Color Front* (New York: Random House, 1954) is an unfootnoted, journalistic account that nonetheless provides important insights into the integration of the armed forces. For a report on the effectiveness of the black soldier in combat in Korea, apparently written specifically to justify integration, see Operations Research Organization, Johns Hopkins University, *Utilization of Negro Manpower in the Army: A 1951 Study* (Washington, D.C.: Research Analysis Corporation, 1951).

Among the most thorough works on President Truman and his views are Margaret Truman, *Harry S. Truman* (New York: William Morrow, 1972), and David McCullough, *Truman* (New York: Simon & Schuster, 1992). For a detailed history of the period, see Steven L. Reardon, *History of the Office of the Secretary of Defense, The Formative Years, 1947–1950*

(Washington, D.C.: Historical Office, Office of the Secretary of Defense, 1984).

Two works on homosexuality in the armed forces during this period were of interest and use: Allan Berube, *Coming Out Under Fire: The History of Gay Men and Women in World War Two* (New York: Free Press, 1990), and Colin J. Williams and Martin S. Weinberg, *Homosexuals and the Military* (New York: Harper & Row, 1971).

There are a number of general works on combat in Korea that proved of particular usefulness. Roy E. Appleman's *South to the Naktong, North to the Yalu (June–November 1950)*, United States Army in the Korean War (Washington, D.C.: U.S. Army Center of Military History, Government Printing Office, 1961), remains the most thorough and authoritative source for combat operations during the early period of the war. Appleman later produced two somewhat less well-organized but still detailed works: *Disaster in Korea: The Chinese Confront MacArthur* (College Station: Texas A&M University Press, 1989) and *Ridgway Duels for Korea* (College Station: Texas A&M University Press, 1990). James F. Schnabel, *Policy and Direction: The First Year*, United States Army in the Korean War (Washington, D.C.: U.S. Army Center of Military History, Government Printing Office, 1972), covers high-level concerns. Clay Blair's more popularly written *The Forgotten War: America in Korea, 1950–1953* (New York: Times Books, 1987), is particularly valuable for the insights it gains from interviews. Billy C. Mossman's *Ebb and Flow, November 1950–July 1951*, United States Army in the Korean War (Washington, D.C.: U.S. Army Center of Military History, Government Printing Office, 1990), describes the period following the breakout from Pusan. Walter G. Hermes' *Truce Tent and Fighting Front*, United States Army in the Korean War (Washington, D.C.: U.S. Army Center of Military History, Government Printing Office, 1992), covers the final three months of the 24th's existence. Rudy Tomedi's oral history, *No Bugles, No Drums, An Oral History of the Korean War* (New York: John Wiley & Sons, Inc., 1993), has interviews with soldiers from all-white units who witnessed the 3d Battalion's retreat at Kunu-ri. The

book is also valuable for the descriptions it contains of the fighting experienced by all-white units.

Among shorter works, studies of specific aspects of the fighting for the early days of the war include William Glenn Robertson, *Counterattack on the Naktong, 1950*, Leavenworth Papers 13 (Fort Leavenworth, Kans.: Combat Studies Institute, 1985), and Roy K. Flint, "Task Force Smith and the 24th Division," in Charles E. Heller and William A. Stofft, eds., *America's First Battles, 1776–1965* (Lawrence: University of Kansas Press, 1986). For a South Korean officer's view of the 24th and some of its officers, see General Paik Sun Yup, *From Pusan to Panmunjon* (Washington, D.C.: Brassey's [U.S.], 1992). Although sometimes too quick to judge, S. L. A. Marshall's *The River and the Gauntlet: Defeat of the Eighth Army by the Chinese Communist Forces, November 1950, in the Battle of the Chongchon River, Korea* (New York: William Morrow, 1953), re-creates the pain and confusion prevalent when the Chinese attack occurred. "Operation RIPPER," *Infantry School Quarterly* 39 (October 1951), is a good source for details of the 25th Division's counterattack.

Works on military cohesion in combat that proved particularly useful include William Darryl Henderson, *Cohesion: The Human Element in Combat* (Washington, D.C.: National Defense University Press, 1985); Nora Kinzer Stewart, *South Atlantic Conflict of 1982: A Case Study in Military Cohesion* (Alexandria, Va.: U.S. Army Research Institute for the Behavioral and Social Sciences, 1988); and Richard Holmes, *Acts of War: The Behavior of Men in Battle* (New York: Free Press, 1985).

There are a number of works on the 24th Infantry itself. Among the more important are William G. Muller, *The Twenty-Fourth Infantry Past and Present* (Fort Collins, Colo.: 1972; reprint, n.d.); L. Albert Scipio II, *Last of the Black Regulars: A History of the 24th Infantry Regiment (1869–1951)* (Silver Spring, Md.: Roman Publications, 1983); Michael J. T. Clark, "A History of the Twenty-Fourth United States Infantry Regiment in Utah, 1896–1900," (Ph.D. diss., University of Utah, 1979); and L. Albert Scipio II, *The 24th Infantry at Fort Benning* (Silver Spring, Md.: Roman Publications, 1986). Charles

Bussey's *Firefight at Yechon: Courage and Racism in the Korean War* (Washington, D.C.: Brassey's [U.S.], 1991) gives a veteran's view of the 24th's experience not only in Korea but also in prewar Japan. David Carlisle has two articles on the regiment: "Remember Yechon!" *Assembly*, March 1994, and "The Last of the Black Regulars," *Assembly*, November 1994. Lyle Rishell's *With a Black Platoon in Combat: A Year in Korea* (College Station: Texas A&M University Press, 1993) contains a very personal account of some of the fighting the 24th endured. A warrant officer with the 3d Battalion, Thomas H. Pettigrew, Jr., constructs an impressionistic picture of the fighting at Kunu-ri in *The Kunu-ri (Kumori) Incident* (New York: Vantage Press, 1963).

Index

Chinju: 125, 129, 134, 135, 136, 181
Ch'onan: 224
Ch'ongch'on River: 194, 196, 208, 209–10
Chongju: 95
Ch'oni-san: 196, 206
Ch'orwon: 191–92, 238–41, 250, 251, 254
Ch'udong-san: 196, 197
Ch'unch'on: 68
Civil War, American: 3, 4–5
Clark, General Mark: 230
Clayton, Lt. Col. George A.: 184, 198–99, 204–05, 206, 207n, 209, 234, 235, 245, 247n, 254, 255
Cleage, 1st Lt. Scott K.: 245
Climate. *See* Weather.
Coast artillery units: 12
Cobb, Cpl. William: 54, 55, 120, 139
Cohoon, Lt. Col. William M.: 73, 89, 97, 100, 101, 102, 103, 104, 105, 115
Cold-weather injuries: 190, 205, 212, 215, 219, 222–23
Cole, Lt. Col. George R.: 137, 145, 148–49, 153
Coleman, Lt. Col. Hugh D.: 235, 243, 245, 253
Columbus, Ga.: 18
Combat frontages
 north of 38th Parallel: 194
 on Pusan Perimeter: 129n, 145, 147, 153, 157, 168
Combat readiness
 of troops during period after World War II: 27, 40
 of troops in Japan: 61–62, 65, 77, 265–66
Command of Negro Troops, The: 55–56
Communications
 battlefield: 92, 100, 102, 115, 148, 163, 164, 166, 199, 202–03, 208, 249
 with Eighth Army headquarters: 87
 and messages dropped by aircraft: 204, 213
 problems with: 87, 100, 115, 148–49, 163, 164, 169, 199, 202–03, 208, 212–13, 268–69
 radio: 100, 102, 199, 205
 and runners: 100
Communications equipment
 abandonment of: 116, 130
 batteries for: 77, 199
 effects of cold on: 199
 losses: 215
 and radios: 77, 85–86, 100, 112, 130, 199, 203, 204, 215
 shortages: 77, 85
 spare parts for: 85
 and telephones: 112
 and wire: 77
Competitive Tour program: 47–48, 72, 75, 76, 266
Constitution League of the United States: 13n
Construction: 17, 237–38, 241, 244, 245, 260
Cook, Maj. Theodore J.: 86n–87n, 88n, 137
Cooper, Alonzo: 184n
Corcoran, Capt. Laurence: 84, 134n, 139, 148, 149, 150,

Corcoran, Capt. Laurence—Continued
 151–52, 153, 154
Corley, Col. John T.
 appointed regimental commander: 171
 assigned to 3d Battalion: 141–42
 at Battle Mountain: 151–52, 174–78
 and defense of Seoul: 224, 226–27, 228–29
 at Kunu-ri: 191–92
 leadership style of: 235–36
 and morale of troops: 174–75
 and operations north of the 38th Parallel: 191–92, 196–97, 202, 205n, 206, 208, 210–13, 215, 216–17, 218
 relief of: 229–30
 and straggling: 171–73, 268
 and training: 183–84, 185, 190
 at Tundok: 180
 and unit newspaper: 173–74
 and visit to church: 192
 at Wonsan: 141–43
Corps
 I: 179, 189, 194, 207, 208, 227, 235, 236, 250, 254, 256–57, 258
 IX: 179, 180–81, 189, 194, 207, 208, 223n, 230, 240
 X: 189, 194
Cory, Rennie M.: 104n
Coulter, Maj. Gen. John B.: 179, 189
Courts-martial
 of black soldiers: 29–30, 46, 78, 117, 185–88, 189
 for disobedience to a superior officer: 150
 in period after World War II: 29–30
 for racial incidents: 14–15
 for straggling: 141, 169n, 172–73, 185–88, 260, 268
 World War I: 16
Cramer, Harry, Jr.: 200n
Crawford, Neb.: 8
Creel, Capt. Buckner M.: 175, 192, 235, 240, 249n, 259n
Crisis: 13, 25
Cuba: 9–10, 12

Dailey, Capt. Vernon C.: 109, 142n, 176
Dann, 2d Lt. Roscoe E., Jr.: 74, 80, 120, 122
Davis, Brig. Gen. Benjamin O.: 19, 20, 26
Davis, 2d Lt. Benjamin O., Jr.: 18
Davis, Joseph: 80
Davis, Maj. Martin L.: 224
Davis, Preston: 164n
Davis, 1st Lt. Ralph J.: 198n, 205n, 257
Davis, Col. Steve G.: 262
Davis, Sylvester: 121, 141
Dean, Ellis: 76
Dean, Maj. Gen. William F.: 68n, 69, 82–83, 93, 95, 96
DeChow, Lt. Col. George: 227
Demarcation line (38th Parallel): 67
DeMarco, 2d Lt. Joseph W.: 51, 69–70

Homosexuals: 41, 59–60, 76
Hooks, Pfc. Jesse: 109n
Horne, Sgt. Edward L.: 45
Hospitals, military: 20–21
Hough, William: 79
Housing: 44, 48–49, 57, 63
Houston, Tex.: 14–15
Howitzers, 105-mm.: 68, 110
Hull, Lt. Gen. John E.: 33
Hunsaker, Capt. James: 171
Hunt, 2d Lt. Alexander: 150

Idang: 97, 100, 102, 103, 104
Ie Shima: 41, 44, 52, 60
Imjin River: 190, 192, 221, 223–24, 248–49
Inch'on: 177, 179
Inch'on peninsula: 225–26
Indian reservations: 6–7
Indian Territory: 6–7, 8
Infantry Battalions: 33
  1st, 9th Infantry: 208
  3d, 9th Infantry: 194, 205, 206, 217–18, 261
  1st, 24th Infantry: 14, 21, 22, 40, 47, 56, 58, 63–64, 70,
    71, 72, 76, 77, 83, 84, 95–96, 103, 105, 108, 110,
    111n, 112, 115–16, 117, 118, 119, 120, 121–22, 129,
    133–34, 136, 137–39, 141, 145, 147, 150, 153, 154,
    161, 166, 170, 171, 174, 176, 179, 180, 191, 192,
    196–98, 199, 200, 202–03, 204, 207, 209–10, 211, 213,
    215, 217, 224, 225–26, 230, 232, 235–36, 240–42, 243,
    244–45, 246, 247, 248, 250–52, 255–56, 261n, 268–69
    headquarters company: 40, 180
      Company A: 40, 56n, 73n, 75, 105, 108, 110, 111n,
        115–16, 119, 121, 147, 153, 160, 161, 166, 167,
        168, 169, 174, 180, 190, 191, 197, 200, 202–03,
        204, 241–42, 244–45, 250–51
      Company B: 22, 40, 54, 56, 57, 64, 75, 76, 77,
        110–11, 112, 116, 117, 147, 149, 150, 153,
        154–55, 161, 168, 170, 174–75, 197, 200,
        202–03, 204, 241–42, 245, 246, 247, 258–59, 261
      Company C: 40, 41, 56, 73n, 75, 84, 108, 116, 118,
        122, 134n, 137–39, 141, 147, 148, 149, 150, 151,
        152, 153–55, 161, 167, 168, 169, 170–71, 176,
        180, 185, 197, 199–200, 202–04, 209–10, 215,
        217, 218, 242, 245, 256, 267, 268–69
      Company D: 40, 56n, 57, 71, 72, 73n, 76, 115–16,
        122, 200n, 202, 204
  2d, 24th Infantry: 10, 47, 54n, 61, 63–64, 71, 72–73, 82,
    83, 84, 87–88, 89, 95, 96–97, 100–103, 104, 105, 108,
    110–11, 115, 118–19, 120, 121–22, 129, 136, 137,
    139–40, 141, 143, 145, 147, 148, 153, 161, 163, 164,
    166–67, 168, 170, 171–72, 176, 178, 179, 184, 192,
    196–98, 199, 204–05, 206, 208–09, 215, 217, 224–25,
    226, 230, 233–35, 240, 245, 246, 247, 248, 250–51,
    252. 254. 255–56. 257. 258. 261–62. 267–68

Infantry Battalions—Continued
  headquarters company: 100–103, 166, 208
    Company E: 44, 56, 72–73, 76, 77, 96–97, 100–102,
      103, 105, 115, 119, 120n, 122, 140n, 147,
      148–49, 150, 153–54, 160, 163, 165, 166, 167,
      169, 170–71, 198, 204–05, 206, 208, 217, 218,
      233, 234, 253, 254, 268–69
    Company F: 18, 40, 44, 63, 72, 73n, 77, 96,
      100–101, 103, 105n, 114–15, 118, 122, 139, 147,
      153, 163, 164, 165, 168, 170, 171, 174, 198–99,
      206, 208, 226–27, 233, 234, 255, 261, 268, 269
    Company G: 44, 56, 72, 73n, 77, 96, 100–101, 103,
      110–11, 115, 118–19, 120, 122, 139–41, 144,
      147, 148–49, 150, 163, 164, 165, 166, 167, 170,
      198, 204, 205, 206, 208, 217, 218, 226–27, 233,
      234, 268–69
    Company H: 72–73, 82, 96, 105, 140n, 165, 170, 209
  3d, 24th Infantry: 14, 21, 47, 54, 63–64, 69, 70, 71,
    72, 73, 77, 80, 81, 83, 84–87, 88, 89, 91–92, 93n,
    95, 96, 103, 108, 109–11, 112, 114, 118–19, 120,
    121–22, 129, 131n, 132–33, 136, 137, 141, 142,
    143, 145, 147, 150–51, 153, 161, 163, 171–72,
    174–75, 176, 177, 179, 181n, 183, 185, 190, 192,
    196–99, 206–07, 208, 210, 211–15, 216–17, 218,
    224–25, 230, 233, 234–35, 240–41, 243–47, 248,
    249, 250, 252, 255–56, 258, 267, 268–69
    headquarters company: 40, 110, 119, 199, 207, 211–12
    Company I: 55, 73n, 80, 86, 87, 88, 89, 91, 92, 105,
      109–11, 112, 113, 119, 122, 129, 131, 137, 142,
      143, 150, 151, 152–53, 154, 176, 177, 210,
      213–14, 243, 244, 246–47, 257
    Company K: 11–12, 54, 56, 57, 73, 76, 89, 91, 92,
      109–10, 112, 113, 119, 120, 122, 137, 142, 154,
      174–75, 177, 185, 210n, 213–14, 233, 234,
      243–44, 246–47
    Company L: 56, 77, 81, 89–90, 91, 92, 109, 110–11,
      112, 113, 119, 122, 129, 130, 132, 142, 144, 150,
      151, 152–53, 176, 177, 210, 213–14, 243, 244,
      246–47, 249n, 256
    Company M: 39, 40, 69–70, 90, 92, 110, 129, 131,
      207, 212, 214, 257, 258
  1st, 27th Infantry: 113–14, 167, 171, 232
  2d, 27th Infantry: 63–64, 169, 200, 230
  3d, 27th Infantry: 175, 204, 207–08
  1st, 29th Infantry: 128
  3d, 29th Infantry: 128
  1st, 35th Infantry: 148, 162
  2d, 35th Infantry: 89, 104, 114, 162–63
  3d, 35th Infantry: 232
  1st, 371st Infantry: 16–17
Infantry Division, 25th: 96n, 101n, 223–24, 227, 257–58
  area of responsibility: 82, 87, 95–96, 128–29, 134, 149,
    157, 161, 179, 189, 190, 192–94, 199, 207, 208,
    219–20. 236. 238–40. 248. 254

CPSIA information can be obtained at www.ICGtesting.com
Printed in the USA
BVOW10s1817291214

380996BV00010B/2/P